Big Business

Economic Power in a Free Society

Big Business

Economic Power in a Free Society

Advisory Editor
LEON STEIN

Editorial Board
Stuart Bruchey
Thomas C. Cochran

A NOTE ABOUT THIS BOOK

The Civic Federation of Chicago assembled bankers, businessmen, government officials, labor leaders, professors, preachers, politicians, economists, and farme to discuss combinations and trusts. John Bates Clark later noted that Americans would have to deal with the trust problem "on the basis of such arguments as thi (four day) conference has heard." Proposed solutions ranged from annihilation to worker takeover. Clark foresaw political solutions which would ensure the econon benefits of consolidation "without permitting the principle of competition to be suppressed and a true monopoly to be established."

CHICAGO CONFERENCE
ON TRUSTS

THE CIVIC FEDERATION OF CHICAGO

ARNO PRESS
A New York Times Company
New York / 1973

Reprint Edition 1973 by Arno Press Inc.

Reprinted from a copy in The Newark Public Library

BIG BUSINESS: Economic Power in a Free Society
ISBN for complete set: 0-405-05070-4
See last pages of this volume for titles.

Manufactured in the United States of America

———◆———

Library of Congress Cataloging in Publication Data

Chicago Conference on Trusts, 1899.
   · Chicago Conference on Trusts.

   (Big business: economic power in a free society)
   Reprint of the 1900 ed. published by the Civic
Federation of Chicago, under title: Speeches,
debates, resolutions, list of the delegates,
committees, etc.
   Conference sponsored by the Civic Federation of
Chicago, held Sept. 13-16, 1899.
    1. Trusts, Industrial--United States--Congresses.
I. Civic Federation of Chicago (1894-1932).
II. Series.
HD2783.A3 1899c   338.8'5'0973   73-1996
ISBN 0-405-05078-X

CHICAGO CONFERENCE
ON TRUSTS

GEORGE W. ATKINSON
Governor of West Virginia

W. A. POYNTER
Governor of Nebraska

HAZEN S. PINGREE
Governor of Michigan

W. E. STANLEY
Governor of Kansas

EDWARD SCOFIELD
Governor of Wisconsin

CHICAGO CONFERENCE ON TRUSTS

SPEECHES, DEBATES, RESOLUTIONS,
LIST OF THE DELEGATES,
COMMITTEES, ETC.

Held September 13th, 14th, 15th, 16th, 1899

CHICAGO
THE CIVIC FEDERATION OF CHICAGO
1900

The Lakeside Press
R. R. DONNELLEY & SONS COMPANY
CHICAGO

LOCAL COMMITTEE OF ARRANGEMENTS FOR CHICAGO CONFERENCE ON TRUSTS.

FRANKLIN H. HEAD, President Civic Federation of Chicago, Chairman.

RALPH M. EASLEY, Secretary Civic Federation of Chicago, Secretary.

HENRY S. TOWLE,
President Chicago Bar Association.

JOHN M. STAHL,
Sec'y Farmers' National Congress.

WILLIS YOUNG,
President Northwestern Traveling Men's Association.

WM. R. HARPER,
President University of Chicago.

D. K. CLINK,
Past Counselor United Commercial Travelers.

R. S. LYON,
President Board of Trade.

W. B. CONKEY,
President Illinois Manufacturers' Association.

M. W. PHALEN,
President Traveling Men's Protective Association.

EDWARD CARROLL,
President Building Trades Council.

JAMES O'CONNELL,
President International Association of Machinists.

CHARLES W. GINDELE,
President Builders' and Traders' Exchange.

HENRY WADE ROGERS,
President Northwestern University.

GEORGE A. SCHILLING,
Ex-State Labor Commissioner.

JAMES H. ECKELS,
Ex-Comptroller of the Currency.

HARRY P. ROBINSON,
Editor Railway Age.

GEO. R. PECK,
General Counsel C. M. & St. P. Ry. Co.

FRANKLIN MACVEAGH,
Wholesale Grocer.

LAWRENCE E. MCGANN,
Commissioner of Public Works.

WILLIAM C. HOLLISTER,
Hollister Brothers.

F. W. MORGAN,
Manufacturer of Rubber Goods.

E. S. LACEY,
Ex-Comptroller of the Currency.

A. C. BARTLETT,
President National Association of Merchants and Travelers.

E. G. KEITH,
Pres't Metropolitan National Bank.

A. M. COMPTON,
Credit Man, John V. Farwell Co.

JOHN W. ELA,
General Counsel National Business League.

ALEXANDER H. REVELL,
Wholesale Furniture Dealer.

W. D. KERFOOT,
City Comptroller.

GRAHAM TAYLOR,
Warden Chicago Commons Social Settlement.

LA VERNE W. NOYES,
Manufacturer.

PAUL J. MAAS,
Ex-Organizer American Federation of Labor.

JOSIAH L. LOMBARD,
Ex-President Civic Federation of Chicago.

ROBERT J. BENNETT,
Wholesale Grocer.

WILLIAM A. GILES,
Capitalist.

A. F. GARTZ,
Treasurer Crane Company, Machinery Manufacturers.

ALFRED L. BAKER,
President Chicago Stock Exchange.

CONTENTS.

iv

vi

PORTRAITS.

x

PREFACE.

The discussion of the general subject of trusts and trade combinations during the past summer occupied seemingly more than any other the public mind. The greatest need in such discussions seemed, to use the happy expression of Lyman Abbott, to be light and not heat. For the purpose of eliciting the fullest possible discussion of such subjects from all standpoints, the Civic Federation of Chicago invited the Governors of the various states and the leading commercial, industrial and labor organizations to send delegates to a conference to be held in Chicago from the 13th to the 16th of September. A considerable number also of students of economics from the various colleges and universities were invited to give expression to their views upon the same general topic. The response to this invitation was gratifying, and a most able and intelligent body of men from all parts of the country assembled for such conference.

The delegates appointed by the governors represented every interest in the respective states, including congressmen, ex-congressmen, ex-governors, ex-supreme court judges, attorneys-general, presidents of banks, presidents of railroads, manufacturing and commercial organizations, and representatives of labor, agricultural and educational interests.

In the arrangement of the program especial care was taken that every side of the general subject should be represented in the discussion by its ablest advocates.

At the opening of the conference there seemed among the delegates to be a widespread suspicion as to the fairness of the discussions, and a feeling that some political motive might be behind the call for its assembling. Before the close, however, of the first day's proceedings this feeling had entirely disappeared, and people who supposed themselves to be entirely antagonistic as to their aims and the methods of obtaining certain ends found that all shades of opinion had much ground in common. The discussion proceeded with an amount of good feeling and friendliness among the delegates scarcely to have been looked for among men of such diverse views. At the close of the conference the whole body of delegates seemed to recognize that the purpose of the Civic Federation to make the occasion an educational one by throwing the greatest possible light upon all phases of the general subject had been accomplished.

The interest on the part of the public grew day by day as the reports of the proceedings in the newspapers illustrated the breadth of view covered by the various speakers.

The desire seemed to be general that the proceedings be published in a permanent form which should make them accessible to the larger public which had not the opportunity of hearing the various speakers. The debate as set forth in the pages following gives the widest view yet presented of the important subjects discussed, and it is hoped that it may reach a wide audience.

FRANKLIN H. HEAD.

PROCEEDINGS

OF THE

CHICAGO CONFERENCE ON TRUSTS.

The conference on "Trusts," called by the Civic Federation, was called to order in Central Music Hall, Chicago, at 10:45 o'clock Wednesday morning, September 13, 1899, by President Franklin H. Head, who stated the objects of the conference as follows:

FRANKLIN H. HEAD.

President The Civic Federation of Chicago.

The Civic Federation of Chicago is a non-partisan organization, embracing in its membership, supporters and well wishers, a goodly proportion of the active business and professional men of our city; of the men who in their several ways have helped to win for our city its position as a metropolitan capital. Some months since it realized that no topic seemed so widely discussed as what was designated by the general title of "Trusts"—and that, too, upon no current topic was there so widespread and general an ignorance and confusion of ideas. There seemed to us a crying need for education upon the subject; of an education which would show the broad distinction between the various trade combinations and trusts, and to promote such education this conference is now in session.

It is not a trust or an anti-trust conference, but a conference in search of truth and light. With this end in view the attendance has been solicited of men of every shade of opinion upon the general subject; from the men who regard trusts and trade combinations as the standing menace to our national prosperity, and even to the perpetuity of our system of government, to those who feel that trade combinations and large aggregations of active capital are simply a natural evolution in the development of our industrial and commercial life, and that such aggregations are absolutely necessary to enable us to compete with the vast accumulations and experience of the older nations, and their almost total control outside of food products, of the markets of the world. We are also to hear from those holding views between either extreme; those who believe in the value of combinations properly organized, but who recognize in the reckless and excessive capitalization of many of such combinations a peril leading to widespread panic and distress from such inflated stocks being absorbed by the small investors, whose savings may be thus in great measure lost.

We hope to hear the general subject discussed from all possible standpoints—from the view not only of the organizers of the combinations, but also from the workmen and customers of the industrial corporations. We hope that light will be thrown upon the difference between the class of trusts which tend to monopolies and the industrial combinations which in many cases seem to be to the advantage of all.

We are now in a period of a large advance in the prices of most classes of manufactured goods, especially in iron and steel products, and we hope that some of our speakers will illustrate how much of this advance is due to combinations, and how much to the vastly increased demand, which in all lines has always in the past resulted in advanced prices under the immutable law of supply and demand. There has been no trust or combination, for instance, among our farmers, but we all recollect how two years ago the short wheat crop abroad caused such an increased demand as to legitimately advance the price of that staple over 50 per cent within a period of four months, and that later an enormous demand for wheat from one of our own citizens, Mr. Joseph Leiter, whose hunger for wheat gave him a world-wide reputation, caused an advance of another 50 per cent.

The very general response to our invitations to this conference, from the governors of nearly all the states, who have appointed as delegates their most eminent citizens—from the great commercial bodies, the universities and the labor, agricultural, and other organizations which have sent their ablest men and most profound students of economic problems—this response has been gratifying beyond measure, and illustrates the abiding interest everywhere felt in the general subject and its impartial discussion. This response also fills us with hope as to the great advantages which will result from the full discussion of all phases of the most vital topic of the day.

We trust that this discussion may be able, scholarly and dignified, as becomes the subjects and the occasion, and that when
these discussions reach their proper audience—the millions of
people in every town and hamlet who from the newspapers receive the reports of your deliberations, it may lead to such action
as may tend to preserve in our trade combinations all which is of
value, as well as to point out methods by which the evils of such
combinations may be avoided or done away.

The Civic Federation recognizes also that with the assembling
of the delegates to this conference and its brief preliminary exercises, its participation in your proceedings is at an end. You
will, gentlemen, make your own program and plans—at the same
time I wish to tender to you on the part of the Federation, with
its best wishes, the services of any of its committees, officers or
members, whenever such services can in any way facilitate your
work.

EDWARD C. AKIN.

Attorney-General of Illinois.

Representing Governor John R. Tanner, Attorney-General
Akin, on behalf of the State of Illinois, welcomed the delegates
to the convention. Mr. Akin said:

The pleasure of addressing you on this occasion is as gratifying as it is unexpected, and the fact that the substitutions were
announced long before either Governor Tanner or myself knew
of any such purpose, is but a deserved compliment to the energy
and prophetic power of the average Chicago newspaper reporter.

Owing to the serious illness of Governor Tanner, which alone
prevents his presence here to-day, the privilege of welcoming
you on this occasion has been generously accorded to me. The
casual stranger, who comes without evil intent, is entitled to
passive welcome as a matter of mere courtesy, but to you a most
generous welcome is due, because many of you occupy positions of
high trust and importance in the various states you represent, because among you are the leading minds of the great world of letters and of science. You are entitled to welcome, not alone because of these, but because of the objects and the purposes that
have brought you together. The chief end of government is
the accomplishment of the greatest good to the greatest number. Whether that great evolution of modern trade and commerce, commonly known as the trust, is to prove of benefit

or injury to the masses of our people, and if of benefit, how it may safely be promoted, and if of injury, what the remedy shall be, how and by what authority applied, are questions that lie close to the well-being and happiness of our people, and in which they are to-day above all other matters vitally interested.

The personnel of this conference is guarantee that these great questions will not only be ably discussed, but along educational, conservative lines, which are the underlying principles of this conference, and it is because of the courtesy ordinarily due to strangers within our gates, and is due also because of high considerations of personal regard; it is because of the prominence which you have attained in the public estimation; it is because of the purposes and objects that have brought you together; and it is because we believe that as a result of this conference our people will have a better and a wider knowledge of these great questions, and that here will be sown the seed which shall blossom into legislation, if legislation be needed, at once wise and conservative, having in view alike the interests of capital and of labor, of the consumer and the producer.

It is because of all these that on behalf of the great state of Illinois and on behalf of its governor, I extend to you a hearty and cordial welcome.

HOWARD S. TAYLOR.

Prosecuting Attorney, City of Chicago.

On behalf of the City of Chicago, and speaking for Mayor Carter H. Harrison, City Prosecutor Howard S. Taylor extended a welcome to the delegates to the city, saying:

I am requested by His Honor, the Mayor, now absent from the city, to be present on this occasion and in his name to bid you a most hearty welcome to Chicago, with the assurance that this great city, whose motto is "I Will," shrinks from no problem, but with the characteristic intelligence and liberality that from old Fort Dearborn till now has always distinguished her welcomes into her forum with perfect confidence every free utterance and inquiry that may give inspiration and wisdom to the great republic of which we are a constituent part. Chicago, through all her history, has believed that there is more danger in suppressing truth than in publishing falsehood; and, therefore, she clings to the old doctrine of free and full speech on every question of public interest.

The matter that has brought you together is of prime importance to Chicago and to the whole country. We are a nation of wealth producers and distributors. We can fight if need be—from Washington down to Miles, from John Paul Jones to Admiral Dewey, we have no apologies to make for our conduct on land or sea. We have also contributed our full quota to the world's treasury of literature and art; but, after all, Providence and the genius of our people have, in the main, led us in the ways of peace and production. To challenge nature, to wring from her strongholds the material gains that shall make us a people of happy homes and hopeful hearts, has been the history of our honorable past and the prophecy of our growing future. Whatever, therefore, touches the question of wealth production and distribution touches the center of our civilization and invites from all our people such counsel and action as shall secure for us and our posterity the greatest possible good—that benevolent reign of peaceful industry that shall

"—Scatter plenty o'er a smiling land
And read its history in a nation's eyes."

That the subject which you are to discuss is one both of eminence and imminence is proven not only by your presence here, but by the wide discussion which is now going on in the magazines and newspapers and in every other place where public opinion is created or expressed. Gentlemen may differ in their opinions concerning the nature of trusts, their cause and cure; but there is no questioning the fact that a new and portentous phenomenon has risen above the horizon of our national life, and one of such grave import as to justify the fullest, fairest study that this convention can command.

His Honor, Mayor Harrison, has his views upon this subject—clear and pronounced; but he entertains them as an American citizen, and will not take advantage of his official position to promulgate them. As chief magistrate of the city, he does not desire to bias nor anticipate your conclusions; but, confident always in truth as an end and free speech as a means, he approves your convention and bids you, through me, a most cordial welcome to Chicago.

Attorney-General T. S. Smith, of Texas, moved that Franklin H. Head and Ralph M. Easley, respectively president and secretary of the Civic Federation of Chicago, be made the temporary officers of the conference, and that the Civic Federation be requested to furnish the program for the first day, or pending the formation of the permanent organization. This was seconded by Congressman R. D. Sutherland, of Nebraska, and was unanimously carried.

Yellott, of Maryland, introduced the following resolution:

RESOLVED, That a committee on organization and program, composed of one delegate from each state and each organization represented by invitation of the Civic Federation, of Chicago, be appointed by such delegation to have charge of the proceedings of this conference, and report on the order of proceedings that shall govern the same. That the permanent chairman of this meeting shall act in concert with such committee, and he, together with the committee, shall determine what papers shall be read and what lines of discussion shall be allowed.

Rosewater, of Nebraska, raised a point of order, demanding that a list of delegates be read and credentials be in some manner passed upon. This was received with applause, but a general discussion of considerable warmth ensued. The point of order was sustained, and Secretary Easley read the list of delegates appointed, and after several minor corrections it was declared the official roll.

APPOINTED BY GOVERNOR JOHNSTON, OF ALABAMA.

Eyre Damar, Mobile.
Gordon McDonald, Montgomery.
Reed B. Barnes, Opelika.
W. W. Quarles, Selma.

Wallace Haralson, Ft. Payne.
E. M. Ragland, Tuscumbia.
B. B. Comer, Birmingham.

APPOINTED BY GOVERNOR MURPHY, OF ARIZONA.

M. J. Egan, Clifton.
C. W. Wright, Tucson.
W. H. Barnes, Tucson.

E. M. Does, Flagstaff.
J. C. Adams, Phœnix.
John M. Hamilton, Chicago.

APPOINTED BY GOVERNOR THOMAS, OF COLORADO.

Thos. M. Patterson, Denver.
T. S. McMurray, Denver.
H. V. Johnson, Denver.
Mrs. Sarah S. Platt, Denver.

Alva Adams, Pueblo.
H. H. Seldomridge, Colorado Springs.
Jas. W. Bucklin, Grand Junction.

APPOINTED BY J. H. HUGHES, SECRETARY OF STATE, DELAWARE.

John H. Rodney, Wilmington.
William S. Hilles, Wilmington.
John W. Causey, Milford.
Henry Allaway, Dover.
James L. Wolcott, Dover.

John H. Hoffecker, Smyrna.
Charles M. Cullen, Georgetown.
Chas. F. Richards, Georgetown.
James Ross, Seaford.

APPOINTED BY GOVERNOR TANNER, OF ILLINOIS.

Shelby M. Cullom, Springfield.
David Ross, Springfield.
Charles A. Hill, Springfield.
Lloyd F. Hamilton, Springfield.
Wm. E. Mason, Chicago.
Horatio W. Seymour, Chicago.
Geo. W. Hinman, Chicago.
R. W. Patterson, Chicago.
James H. Eckels, Chicago.
E. S. Lacey, Chicago.
George B. Swift, Chicago.
John A. Roche, Chicago.
John P. Hopkins, Chicago.
George A. Schilling, Chicago.
Clarence S. Darrow, Chicago.
Theodore Brentano, Chicago.
L. C. Collins, Chicago.
John M. Smyth, Chicago.
John W. Gates, Chicago.

George R. Peck, Chicago.
J. Ogden Armour, Chicago.
H. B. Wickersham, Chicago.
John F. Scanlan, Chicago.
Frank F. Holmes, Chicago.
John E. Enander, Chicago.
Joseph W. Fifer, Bloomington.
Adlai E. Stevenson, Bloomington.
Charles H. Deere, Rock Island.
W. F. Eastman, Moline.
W. R. Jewell, Danville.
John W. Fornof, Streator.
S. M. Dalzell, Spring Valley.
Perry C. Ellis, Quincy.
Charles Voris, Windsor.
William P. Halliday, Cairo. (Since deceased.)
Charles B. Cole, Chester.
Homer Tice, Greenview.

APPOINTED BY GOVERNOR MOUNT, OF INDIANA.

Solon L. Goode, Indianapolis.
Allen W. Clark, Greensburg.
E. B. Martindale, Indianapolis.
John B. Stoll, South Bend.
R. S. Taylor, Fort Wayne.
Josiah Gwin, New Albany.
Aaron Jones, South Bend.
John W. Spencer, Evansville.
Goodlet Morgan, Petersburg.
Jos. Swain, Bloomington.
Leonard J. Hackney, Shelbyville.
Wm. H. O'Brien, Lawrenceburg.
Isaac H. Strouse, Rockville.

William Dudley Foulke, Richmond.
Daniel P. Irwin, Indianapolis.
Wm. H. Eichhorn, Bluffton.
A. M. Scott, Ladoga.
A. L. Kumler, La Fayette.
M. Winfield, Logansport.
J. N. Babcock, Topeka.
A. P. Kent, Elkhart.
John B. Conner, Indianapolis.
Amos W. Reagan, Indianapolis.
George W. Geiger, Indianapolis.
Charles M. Walter, Rossville.

APPOINTED BY GOVERNOR MAYES, CHEROKEE NATION, INDIAN TERRITORY.

James S. Stapler, Tahlequah.
Joe M. Lahay, Claremore.
James S. Davenport, Vinita.
W. W. Hastings, Tahlequah.

Charles O. Frye, Sullisuw.
John C. Dannenburg, Tahlequah.
F. H. Nash, Ft. Gibson.

APPOINTED BY GOVERNOR SHAW, OF IOWA.

James G. Berryhill, Des Moines.
George E. Clarke, Algona.
Thomas Updegraff, McGregor.
W. R. Green, Audubon.
Robert H. Moore, Ottumwa.
John Story, Lake Mills.

Ambros P. McGuirk, Davenport.
Paul MacLean, Creston.
Edward H. Thayer, Clinton.
Cato Sells, Vinton.
John J. Hamilton, Des Moines.

APPOINTED BY GOVERNOR STANLEY, OF KANSAS.

W. J. Bailey, Baileyville.
George H. Buckman, Winfield.
W. A. White, Emporia.
John E. Hessin, Manhattan.

Harry L. Pestana, Russell.
Charles E. Elliott, Wellington.
C. Wood Davis, Peotone.
J. K. Cubbison, Kansas City, Mo.

APPOINTED BY GOVERNOR BRADLEY, OF KENTUCKY.

W. C. P. Breckenridge, Lexington.
P. W. Hardin, Harrodsburg.
John W. Lewis, Springfield.

William Lindsay, Frankfort.
W. H. Holt, Frankfort.
W. P. Kimball, Lexington.
John W. Yerkes, Danville.

APPOINTED BY GOVERNOR POWERS, OF MAINE.

Henry B. Cleaves, Portland.
A. H. Gardner, Rockland.
Nathaniel Butler, Waterville.
J. P. Bass, Bangor.
Chas. H. Prescott, Biddeford.

S. D. Leavitt, Eastport.
Henry C. Emery, Brunswick.
Wm. H. Newell, Lewiston.
Cyrus H. Blanchard, Wilton.
Victor W. McFarlane, Greenville.

APPOINTED BY GOVERNOR LOWNDES, OF MARYLAND.

Charles J. Bonaparte, Baltimore.
Wm. T. Dixon, Baltimore.
John K. Cowen, Baltimore.
Felix Agnus, Baltimore.

Benj. F. Newcomer, Baltimore.
Stevenson A. Williams, Bel Air.
Herbert B. Adams, Baltimore.
John I. Yellott, Towson.

APPOINTED BY GOVERNOR PINGREE, OF MICHIGAN.

Russell A. Alger, Detroit.
J. N. Klock, Benton Harbor.
J. W. Hannen, Traverse City.
George W. McBride, Grand Haven.
William H. Lockerby, Quincy.
Fred Stone, Hillsdale.
Cyrus G. Luce, Coldwater.
A. P. Greene, Eaton Rapids.

George B. Horton, Fruit Ridge.
L. D. Watkins, Manchester.
Fred A. Maynard, Grand Rapids.
Edwin Henderson, Detroit.
E. C. Davidson, Escanaba.
Phil B. Kirkwood, Negaunee.
Elliott G. Stevenson, Detroit.
Henry C. Adams, Ann Arbor.

APPOINTED BY GOVERNOR STEPHENS, OF MISSOURI.

F. M. Cockrell, Warrensburg.
E. C. Crow, Jefferson City.
Joseph A. Graham, St. Louis.
Alexander G. Cochran, St. Louis.
David R. Francis, St. Louis.
F. W. Lehmann, St. Louis.
Emil Pretorius, St. Louis.
John A. Hockaday, Fulton.

L. A. Vories, St. Joseph.
C. C. Fuller, Mound City.
Frank P. Sebree, Kansas City.
F. C. Farr, Kansas City.
John S. Haymes, Buffalo.
L. F. Cotty, Edina.
Marsh Arnold, Benton.
N. O. Nelson.

APPOINTED BY GOVERNOR McLAURIN, OF MISSISSIPPI.

J. W. Cutrer, Clarksdale.
John Sharpe Williams, Yazoo City.
Frank Burkitt, Okolona.

S. S. Calhoon, Jackson.
A. H. Whitfield, Jackson.
Henry Christmas, Tchula.
E. H. Moore, Rosedale.

APPOINTED BY GOVERNOR SMITH, OF MONTANA.

Martin Maginnis, Helena.
J. K. Toole, Helena.
Chas. S. Hartman, Bozeman.
A. J. Campbell, Butte.

J. E. Rickards, Butte.
H. H. Swain, Dillon.
W. F. Sanders, Helena.

APPOINTED BY GOVERNOR POYNTER, OF NEBRASKA.

Edward Rosewater, Omaha.
Lorenzo Crounse, Calhoun.
William V. Allen, Madison.
R. D. Sutherland, Nelson.

William Jennings Bryan, Lincoln.
A. H. Hipple, Omaha.
Frank T. Ransom, Omaha.

APPOINTED BY GOVERNOR ROLLINS, OF NEW HAMPSHIRE.

Henry W. Blair, Manchester.
John P. George, Concord.
H. B. Viall, Keene.
J. W. Remick, Littleton.

Chas. H. Sawyer, Dover.
Edward H. Wason, Nashua.
Dorrance B. Currier, Hanover.

APPOINTED BY GOVERNOR VOORHEES, OF NEW JERSEY.

S. H. Grey, Trenton.
Eugene Stevenson, Paterson.
Edward Q. Keasbey, Newark.

Henry H. Isham, Elizabeth.
Allan L. McDermott.

APPOINTED BY GOVERNOR OTERO, OF NEW MEXICO.

Frank Springer, East Las Vegas.
Frank A. Manzanares, East Las Vegas.
Thomas D. Burns, Parkview.
Anthony Joseph, Ojo Caliente.

A. R. Graham. Hudson.
J. W. Dwyer, Raton.
E. V. Chavez, Albuquerque.
C. J. Gavin, Raton.
Albert Lawrence, Catskill.

APPOINTED BY GOVERNOR ROOSEVELT, OF NEW YORK.

Chauncey M. Depew, New York City.
John G. Carlisle, New York City.
W. Bourke Cockran, New York City.
Albert Shaw, New York City.
George Gunton, New York City.
Francis B. Thurber, New York City.

Henry White, New York City.
Stephen P. Corliss, Albany.
John McMackin, Albany.
John B. Clark, New York City.
Jacob G. Schurman, Ithaca.
Robert B. Adam, Buffalo.
Thos. M. Osborne, Auburn.
George E. Green, Binghamton.

APPOINTED BY GOVERNOR FANCHER, OF NORTH DAKOTA.

David Morgan, Devils Lake.
James D. Benton, Fargo.
M. H. Jewell, Bismarck.
A. W. Edwards, Fargo.
Roderick Rose, Jamestown.

John M. Cochrane, Grand Forks.
David Bartlett, Cooperstown.
David Wellman, New Rockford.
Wm. T. Perkins.

APPOINTED BY GOVERNOR BUSHNELL, OF OHIO.

John Sherman, Mansfield.
J. B. Foraker, Cincinnati.
Charles Foster, Fostoria.
M. E. Ingalls, Cincinnati.
Asa W. Jones, Youngstown.
Washington Gladden, Columbus.
Paul J. Sorg, Middletown.

F. S. Monnett, Columbus.
Jas. E. Neal, Hamilton.
C. L. Kurtz, Columbus.
Selwyn N. Owen, Columbus.
I. F. Mack, Sandusky.
R. E. McKisson, Cleveland.
John P. Jones, Columbus.

APPOINTED BY GOVERNOR GEER, OF OREGON.

M. C. George, Portland.
Sylvester Pennoyer, Portland.
C. W. Fulton, Astoria.
M. A. Miller, Lebanon.

B. F. Alley, Baker City.
Walter L. Tooze, Woodburn.
Wm. Colvig, Jacksonville.

APPOINTED BY GOVERNOR STONE, OF PENNSYLVANIA.

M. M. Garland, Pittsburg.
W. P. Potter, Pittsburg.
Joseph N. Pew, Pittsburg.
Wm. C. Bullitt, Philadelphia.

Lyman D. Gilbert, Harrisburg.
A. Louden Snowden, Philadelphia.
H. W. Palmer, Wilkes Barre.
A. Leo Weil, Pittsburg.

APPOINTED BY GOVERNOR ELLERBEE, OF SOUTH CAROLINA.

J. H. Marshall, Charleston.
L. W. Youmans, Fairfax.
J. E. Boggs, Pickens.
T. L. Gantt, Spartanburg.

J. S. Brice, Yorkville.
A. H. Williams, Lake City.
S. H. Rodgers, Port Royal.
A. C. Kaufman, Charleston.

APPOINTED BY GOVERNOR LEE, OF SOUTH DAKOTA.

R. F. Pettigrew, Sioux Falls.
W. T. La Follette Chamberlain.
John E. Kelley, Flandreau.
S. H. Wright, Chamberlain.

Freeman Knowles, Deadwood.
M. S. Sheldon, Watertown.
W. E. Kidd, Aberdeen.
Chauncey L. Wood, Rapid City.

APPOINTED BY GOVERNOR McMILLEN, OF TENNESSEE.

C. E. Snodgrass, Crossville.
John W. Gaines, Nashville.
J. D. Richardson, Murfreesboro.
N. N. Cox, Franklin.

T. W. Sims, Linden.
Rice A. Pierce, Union City.
E. W. Carmack, Memphis.

16

APPOINTED BY GOVERNOR SAYERS, OF TEXAS.

T. S. Smith, Austin.
Cecil Smith, Sherman.
Dudley G. Wooten, Dallas.
L. J. Wortham, Austin.
R. E. Prince, Corsicana.
A. B. Davidson, Cuero.

W. T. Burns, Houston.
E. R. McLean, Austin.
Eugene Williams, Waco.
W. L. Grogan, Sweetwater.
E. B. Perkins, Dallas.
E. P. Curtis, Temple.

APPOINTED BY GOVERNOR WELLS, OF UTAH.

Geo. W. Bartch, Salt Lake City.
Jos. L. Rawlins, Salt Lake City.
Geo. C. Cannon, Salt Lake City.

C. C. Richards, Ogden.
Lafayette Holbrook, Provo.
D. O. Rideout, Draper.

APPOINTED BY GOVERNOR ATKINSON, OF WEST VIRGINIA.

Randolph Stalnaker, Wheeling.
W. B. McMechen, Wheeling.
Philip C. Adams, Sutton.
E. S. Hutchinson, Maybeury.
R. B. Cassiday, Charleston.
J. W. Roche, Charleston.
James R. Smoot, Newberg.
S. H. Gramm, Grafton.
Samuel Dixon, Macdonald.
Hullihen Quarrier, Wheeling.
Darwin E. Abbott, Huntington.

I. Schwabe, Charleston.
E. C. Gerwig, Parkersburg.
E. Tracey Tobin, Philadelphia, Pa.
W. A. McCorkle, Charleston.
John W. Harris, Lewisburg.
Daniel B. Lucas, Charles Town.
John W. Mason, Fairmount.
John Brannon, Weston.
F. J. Hearne, Wheeling.
Z. T. Vinson, Huntington.

APPOINTED BY GOVERNOR SCOFIELD, OF WISCONSIN.

John C. Spooner, Madison.
Wm. J. Anderson, West Superior.
John V. Quarles, Milwaukee.
Madison Halford Erickson, West Superior.
J. J. Jenkins, Chippewa Falls.
S. S. Barney, West Bend.
Wm. F. Vilas, Madison.
Edward S. Bragg, Fond du Lac.
John M. Whitehead, Janesville.

A. M. Jones, Waukesha.
Thomas M. Blackstock, Sheboygan.
George F. Merrill, Ashland.
John Hicks, Oshkosh.
John Nagle, Manitowoc.
E. T. Wheelock, Wausau.
J. G. Monahan, Darlington.
Ellis B. Usher, La Crosse.
Emil Baench, Manitowoc.

APPOINTED BY GOVERNOR RICHARDS, OF WYOMING.

F. W. Mondell, Newcastle.
B. B. Brooks, Casper.
C. P. Arnold, Laramie.
R. W. Breckens, Cheyenne.

Andrew McMicken, Rawlins.
J. Dana Adams, Sheridan.
Robert Hinton, Evanston.

GOVERNORS.

G. W. Atkinson, West Virginia.
W. E. Stanley, Kansas.
R. B. Smith, Montana.
Charles S. Thomas, Colorado.
W. A. Poynter, Nebraska.
F. B. Fancher, North Dakota.

L. M. Shaw, Iowa.
H. S. Pingree, Michigan.
J. R. Tanner, Illinois.
L. V. Stephens, Missouri.
Edward Scofield, Wisconsin.
J. A. Mount, Indiana.

ATTORNEYS-GENERAL.

Wm. L. Taylor, Indiana.
E. R. Hicks, Wisconsin.
G. R. Gaither, Jr., Maryland.
C. J. Smyth, Nebraska.
E. C. Crow, Missouri.
A. A. Godard, Kansas.
E. P. Rucker, West Virginia.
C. B. Nolan, Montana.
W. B. Douglas, Minnesota.

John C. Davies, New York.
J. A. Van Orsdel, Wyoming.
W. B. Lamar, Florida.
A. C. Bishop, Utah.
T. S. Smith, Texas.
Jefferson Davis, Arkansas.
Horace M. Oren, Michigan.
Milton Remley, Iowa.

CONGRESSMEN NOT ON DELEGATIONS.

D. B. Henderson, Dubuque, Ia.
Vespasian Warner, Clinton, Ia.
James H. Lewis, Seattle, Wash.
George W. Taylor, Demopolis, Ala.
H. A. Cooper, Racine, Wis.
Francis G. Newlands, Reno, Nev.
James S. Sherman, Utica, N. Y.
L. F. Livingstone, Atlanta, Ga.
S. W. Smith, Pontiac, Mich.
E. D. Crumpacker, Valparaiso, Ind.
George W. White, Tarboro, N. C.
D. S. Alexander, Buffalo, N. Y.

John A. T. Hull, Des Moines, Ia.
R. R. Hitt, Mount Morris, Ill.
J. A. Tawney, Winona, Minn.
J. H. Davidson, Oshkosh, Wis.
George W. Prince, Galesburg, Ill.
E. L. Hamilton, Niles, Mich.
Walter Reeves, Streator, Ill.
Theodore Otjen, Milwaukee, Wis.
Charles Dick, Columbus, O.
A. J. Hopkins, Aurora, Ill.
D. Meekison, Napoleon, O.
J. P. Dolliver, Fort Dodge, Ia.
James R. Mann, Chicago, Ill.

MILLERS' NATIONAL ASSOCIATION.

Frank Barry, Secretary, Milwaukee, Wis.

B. A. Eckhart, Chicago, Ill.

BRICKLAYERS' AND MASONS' INTERNATIONAL UNION OF AMERICA.

M. R. Grady, Chicago, Ill.

NATIONAL GRANGE PATRONS OF HUSBANDRY.

George B. Horton, Fruit Ridge, Mich.
Oliver Wilson, Magnolia, Ill.

H. E. Huxley, Neenah, Wis.
C. O. Ranie, Benjamin, Mo.
S. H. Ellis, Waynesville, O.

COMMERCIAL TRAVELERS' NATIONAL LEAGUE.

P. E. Dowe, President, Bedford Park, New York City.

NEW ENGLAND FREE TRADE LEAGUE.

Byron W. Holt, New York City.

COMMERCIAL CLUB OF TOPEKA.

George W. Crane, Topeka, Kan.

ORDER OF RAILROAD CONDUCTORS.

E. E. Clark, G. C. C., Cedar Rapids, Ia.

A. B. Garretson, Assistant Grand Chief Conductor, Cedar Rapids, Iowa.

W. D. Anderson, Associate Editor Official Organ, Order of R. R. Conductors, Cedar Rapids, Ia.

LITTLE ROCK BOARD OF TRADE.

LITTLE ROCK, ARK.

U. M. Rose.
S. R. Cockrill.
John F. Fletcher.
John M. Moore.
Edward Fitzgerald.
Charles F. Penzel.
T. H. Bunch.
Herman Hahn.

Chas. T. Ables.
W. S. Holt.
H. L. Remmel.
W. J. Thompson.
Morris M. Cohn.
George R. Brown.
B. J. Brown.

INTERNATIONAL ASSOCIATION OF MACHINISTS.

James O'Connell, Washington, D.C. George Preston, Washington, D.C.

THE NATIONAL ASSOCIATION OF AGRICULTURAL IMPLEMENT AND VEHICLE MANUFACTURERS.

H. C. Staver, Chicago, Ill.

COMMERCIAL CLUB OF TERRE HAUTE.

TERRE HAUTE, IND.

W. C. Ball.
Adolph Herz,
J. Smith Talley.

J. C. Kolsem.
Charles H. Ehrman.

ORDER KNIGHTS OF LABOR.

J. G. Schonfarber, Baltimore. Md.
I. D. Chamberlain, Pueblo, Col.
John W. Hayes, General Secretary, Washington, D. C.

August E. Gans, Chicago, Ill.
E. J. Lindholm, Chicago, Ill.

NEW YORK BOARD OF TRADE AND TRANSPORTATION.

W. H. Parsons, President, New York City.
G. Waldo Smith. New York City.
S. A. Robinson, West New Brighton, Staten Island, N. Y.

Charles A. Schieren, Brooklyn.
John H. Washburne, New York City.

NEW ORLEANS BOARD OF TRADE.

W. W. Howe, New Orleans, La.

ST. LOUIS TRAFFIC BUREAU.

A. J. Vandlandingham, Commissioner, St. Louis, Mo.

THE MERCHANTS' AND MANUFACTURERS' ASSOCIATION, MILWAUKEE, WIS.

A. K. Hamilton.
G. G. Pabst.
O. C. Fuller.

E. P. Hackett.
B. Leidersdorf.

WISCONSIN STATE GRANGE PATRONS OF HUSBANDRY.

S. C. Carr, Milton Junction, Wis.

AMERICAN FEDERATION OF LABOR.

Samuel Gompers, Washington, D. C.

CHAMBER OF COMMERCE, LOS ANGELES, CAL.

C. D. Willard.

INTERNATIONAL TYPOGRAPHICAL UNION.

Samuel B. Donnelly, President, Indianapolis, Ind.

CHAMBER OF COMMERCE, NEW HAVEN, CONN.

Max Adler, President.

COLLEGE REPRESENTATIVES.

J. W. Jenks, Cornell University, Ithaca, N. Y.

Wm. F. King, President Cornell College, Mt. Vernon, Ia.

R. I. Holaind, Georgetown College, Washington, D. C.

S. A. Martin, President Wilson College, Chambersburg, Pa.

Charles F. Thwing, President Western Reserve University, Adelbert College, Cleveland, O.

David Kinley, University of Illinois, Urbana, Ill.

Frank W. Taussig, Harvard University, Cambridge, Miss.

George A. Gates, President Iowa College, Grinnell, Ia.

Robt. B. Robinson, The John Hay Normal and Industrial School, Alexandria, Va.

J. H. Kirkland, Chancellor Vanderbilt University, Nashville, Tenn.

Isaac Althaus Loos, Prof. Political Science, University of Iowa, Iowa City, Ia.

Wm. J. Kerby, Catholic University, Washington, D. C.

Richard T. Ely, Professor Political Economy, University of Wisconsin, Madison, Wis.

Henry C. Adams, University of Michigan, Ann Arbor, Mich.

Edward C. Mitchell, President Leland University, Newton Center, Mass.

John F. Forbes, President John B. Stetson University, DeLand, Fla.

John Graham Brooks, Lecturer University of Chicago, Cambridge, Mass.

Henry Wade Rogers, President Northwestern University, Evanston, Ill.

James R. Weaver, Department Political Economy, De Pauw University, Greencastle, Ind.

A. E. Rogers, Professor Political Economy and History, University of Maine, Orono, Maine.

STATE RAILROAD COMMISSIONERS.

R. S. Kayler, Ohio.
Benjamin F. Chadbourne, Maine.
C. M. Runyan, Statistician Ohio Railroad Commission.
Union B. Hunt, Indiana.

D. N. Lewis, Secretary State Board of R. R. Commissioners, Iowa.
Edward A. Dawson, Iowa.
David J. Palmer, Iowa.
I. A. Macrum, Oregon.

STATE LABOR COMMISSIONERS.

H. U. Thomas, North Dakota.
I. V. Barton, West Virginia.

Thos. P. Rixey, Missouri.
W. L. A. Johnson, Kansas.

INTERSTATE COMMERCE COMMISSION.

Martin A. Knapp, Chairman, Syracuse, N. Y.

W. J. Calhoun, Danville, Ill.
Charles A. Prouty, Newport, Vt.

THE NATIONAL BOARD OF FIRE UNDERWRITERS.

E. C. Irwin, President, Philadelphia, Pa.
Thomas S. Chard, Chicago, Ill.
M. D. Driggs, New York City.

Charles S. Hollingshead, Philadelphia, Pa.
George W. Babb, New York City.
I. S. Blackwelder, Chicago, Ill.

THE COMMERCIAL CLUB OF BIRMINGHAM, ALA.

John W. Tomlinson.

INDIANA STATE BOARD OF COMMERCE.

Wm. Fortune, President, Indianapolis.
C. J. Murphy, Secretary, Evansville.
John H. Holliday, Commercial Club, Indianapolis.
A. M. Higgins, Commercial Club, Terre Haute.

J. R. Goodwin, Evansville.
Mortimer Levering, Commercial Club, Lafayette.
Chas. R. Lane, Commercial Club, Ft. Wayne.
D. M. Parry, Board of Trade, Indianapolis.
A. F. Potts, Indianapolis.

FARMERS' NATIONAL CONGRESS.

B. F. Clayton, Indianola, Ia.
H. E. Heath, Omaha, Neb.
Lafayette Funk, Shirley, Ill.

J. J. W. Billingsley, Indianapolis, Ind.
John M. Stahl, Secretary.

ASSOCIATION OF WESTERN MANUFACTURERS.

Edward P. McFetridge, President, Baraboo, Wis.
Walter Fieldhouse, Secretary and Treasurer, Chicago, Ill.
George Brickner, Sheboygan Falls, Wis.

H. G. Niles, Jr., South Bend, Ind.
E. C. McFetridge, Beaver Dam, Wis.
Richard Yates, Jacksonville, Ill.

BOARD OF TRADE, SPRINGFIELD, ILL.

F. W. Tracey.
S. P. Wheeler.
J. T. Peters.

L. E. Wheeler.
D. W. Smith.
J. F. Miller.

NORTHWESTERN TRAVELING MEN'S ASSOCIATION.

George J. Reed, Chicago, Ill.
John M. Levis, Chicago, Ill.
R. A. Scovel, Chicago, Ill.
W. H. Cribben, Chicago, Ill.

S. H. Crane, Chicago, Ill.
G. M. Pennoyer, Chicago, Ill.
Willis Young, Chicago, Ill.
George W. Bailey, Chicago, Ill.

BUSINESS MEN'S LEAGUE OF DUBUQUE, IA.

James McFadden.
A. F. Frudden.
John M. McDonald.
J. F. Merry.

John Mehlop.
Robert W. Stewart.
M. M. Walker.

IOWA STATE TRAVELING MEN'S ASSOCIATION.

DES MOINES, IOWA.

F. E. Haley, Secretary and Treasurer.

T. M. Langan, Chairman Board of Directors.

MILLERS' NATIONAL ASSOCIATION.

C. B. Cole, President, Chester, Ill.
B. A. Eckhart, Chicago, Ill.

F. H. Magdeburg, Milwaukee, Wis.
Frank Barry, Milwaukee, Wis.

BUSINESS MEN'S LEAGUE OF ST. LOUIS.

J. C. Birge.
S. M. Kennard.
Edward Devoy.

Leo Rassieur.
Corwin H. Spencer.
J. S. Finkenbiner.

BOARD OF TRADE, CHICAGO.

R. S. Lyon, President.
Wm. T. Baker.
F. G. Logan.

D. E. Richardson.
B. A. Eckhart.
George F. Stone.

CINCINNATI BOARD OF TRADE AND BUREAU OF TRANSPORTATION.

James J. Hooker, President.
J. Gordon Taylor.
J. M. Macdonald.

W. J. Breed.
E. P. Wilson.

COMMERCIAL CLUB OF OMAHA.

Euclid Martin.
H. W. Yates.
George W. Wright.

I. W. Carpenter.
W. D. McHugh.

NATIONAL GRAIN GROWERS' ASSOCIATION.

S. H. Greeley, Chicago, Ill.
M. P. Moran, Graceville, Minn.
J. C. Hanley, St. Paul, Minn.

M. S. Blair, Ojatta, N. D.
S. Lindsay, Irene, S. D.

TARIFF REFORM COMMITTEE, REFORM CLUB OF NEW YORK.

Lawson Purdy.

INDIANAPOLIS BOARD OF TRADE.

John S. Lazarus, President.
John L. Griffiths.

Samuel E. Morss.

DETROIT CHAMBER OF COMMERCE.

George H. Barbour.
Homer Warren.
W. A. C. Miller.

W. A. Pungs.
J. C. Hutchins.

ST. LOUIS MANUFACTURERS' ASSOCIATION.

J. W. Van Cleave.
W. E. Nolker.
Elias Michael.

R. L. Blackmer.
John C. Roberts.

NATIONAL FARMERS' ALLIANCE AND INDUSTRIAL UNION OF AMERICA.

John C. Hanley, St. Paul, Minn.
John Hill, Jr., Chicago, Ill.
P. H. Rahilly, Lake City, Minn.
J. B. Sossaman, Charlotte, N. C.

Miss Bessie Murray, Wintersette, Iowa.
Thomas Dodd, Hope, N. D.
A. S. Stephens, Beardsley, Minn.

PATENT LAW ASSOCIATION OF CHICAGO.

Taylor E. Brown.
L. L. Bond.
Lysander Hill.

James H. Raymond.
P. C. Dyrenforth.

MINNEAPOLIS BOARD OF TRADE.

Cyrus Northrop.
W. W. Folwell.
T. B. Walker.
W. S. Dwinnell.

J. S. McLain.
S. A. Harris.
Frederick W. Lyman.

UNIVERSITY OF CHICAGO.

Wm. R. Harper, President.
Harry Pratt Judson.
Frank Frost Abbott.
Adolph Caspar Miller.
Charles Herbert Thurber.
Francis Wayland Shepardson.
William Hill.

Oscar Lovell Triggs.
Shailer Mathews.
Charles Zeublin.
James Hayden Tufts.
William Isaac Thomas.
Ralph C. H. Catterall.
Albion W. Small.

ILLINOIS COMMERCIAL MEN'S ASSOCIATION.

James O'Donnell, Chicago, Ill.
L. A. Tyler, Chicago, Ill.
George H. Holden, Chairman
  Board of Directors.

George W. Smith.
R. A. Cavenaugh.

DETROIT MERCHANTS' AND MANUFACTURERS' EXCHANGE.

George H. Barbour.
Clarence A. Black.
Edwin Armstrong.
John B. Howarth.
James Inglis.

John S. Gray.
Fred F. Ingram.
Walter S. Campbell.
O. R. Baldwin.

MICHIGAN STATE MILLERS' ASSOCIATION.

J. J. Hanshue, Secretary and Treasurer, Lansing, Mich.

SINGLE TAX LEAGUE OF THE UNITED STATES.

Richard Dalton, Saverton, Mo.
F. H. Monroe, Chicago, Ill.
Louis F. Post, Chicago, Ill.

Millard F. Bingham, Chicago, Ill.
John Z. White, Chicago, Ill.

AMERICAN ANTI-TRUST LEAGUE.

M. L. Lockwood, Zelienople, Pennsylvania.

W. B. Fleming, Kentucky.

STATEN ISLAND CHAMBER OF COMMERCE.

Samuel Adams Robinson, West New Brighton, S. I.

COMMERCIAL TRAVELERS' AND HOTEL MEN'S LEAGUE.

E. M. Tierney, Binghamton, N. Y.

AMERICAN ACADEMY OF POLITICAL AND SOCIAL SCIENCE.

E. J. James, Chicago, Ill.
Stuart Wood, Philadelphia, Pa.
John H. Gray, Evanston, Ill.

Clinton Rogers Woodruff, Philadelphia, Pa.
Franklin MacVeagh, Chicago, Ill.

CINCINNATI CHAMBER OF COMMERCE.

Wm. M. Alms.
James N. Gamble.
C. H. Kellogg.

A. H. McLeod.
J. J. Hooker.

OSHKOSH BOARD OF TRADE.

J. W. Hollister.
M. H. Eaton.
W. J. Wagstaff.
F. H. Josslyn.
Geo. A. Buckstaff.
Charles Barber.

E. R. Hicks.
John Hicks.
B. J. Daly.
J. H. Davidson.
F. C. Stewart.
Leo Haben, Secretary.

CLEVELAND CHAMBER OF COMMERCE.

J. G. W. Cowles.

AMERICAN SOCIAL SCIENCE ASSOCIATION.

C. R. Henderson, Chicago, Ill.
Wm. A. Giles, Chicago, Ill.

W. H. Daly, Pittsburg, Pa.

BALTIMORE BOARD OF TRADE.

Blanchard Randall.

COMMERCIAL CLUB OF INDIANAPOLIS.

John L. Griffiths.
S. E. Morss.
W. L. Taylor.

Justus C. Adams.
Evans Woollen.

NATIONAL ALLIANCE OF THEATRICAL STAGE EMPLOYES.

Lee M. Hart, Chicago, Ill.

DAVENPORT BUSINESS MEN'S ASSOCIATION.

C. A. Ficke.
G. Watson French.
J. R. Nutting.

A. R. Judy.
M. J. Eagal.

ILLINOIS RETAIL HARDWARE DEALERS' ASSOCIATION.

Z. T. Miller, Bloomington, Ill.

CHAMBER OF COMMERCE.

ST. PAUL, MINN.

E. V. Smalley.
E. W. Peet.
W. L. Chapin.

Ambrose Tighe.
Ross Clarke.

CHAMBER OF COMMERCE.

MILWAUKEE, WIS.

C. A. Chapin.
E. P. Bacon.
John Johnston.

David Vance.
C. E. Lewis.

UNITED STATES INDUSTRIAL COMMISSION.

Jas. H. Kyle, South Dakota.
J. W. Jenks, New York.
J. M. Farquhar, New York.

Theo. Otjen, Wisconsin.
L. F. Livingstone, Georgia.
C. J. Harris, North Carolina.

CHAMBER OF COMMERCE.

QUINCY, ILL.

Charles H. Williamson.
Cicero F. Perry.

Edmund H. Botsford.
Perry C. Ellis.

AT LARGE.

Benjamin R. Tucker, Editor Liberty, New York City.
E. P. Ripley, President A., T. & S. F. Ry., Chicago.
James B. Dill, North American Trust Company, New York City.
Theodore C. Search, President National Manufacturers' Association, Philadelphia, Pa.
P. J. McGuire, General Secretary United Brotherhood of Carpenters and Joiners of America, Philadelphia, Pa.
Stuyvesant Fish, President Illinois Central Railroad, New York City.
P. H. Morrissey, Grand Master Brotherhood of Railroad Trainmen, Peoria, Ill.
James H. Eckels, ex-Comptroller of the Currency, Chicago.
D. K. Clink, Past Counselor United Commercial Travelers, Chicago.
M. W. Phalen, President Traveling Men's Protective Association, Chicago.
Paul J. Maas, ex-Organizer American Federation of Labor, Chicago.
Franklin H. Head, President The Civic Federation of Chicago.
Ralph M. Easley, Secretary The Civic Federation of Chicago.

25

Joseph Nimmo, Jr., President National Statistical Association, Washington, D. C.
Samuel M. Jones, Mayor, Toledo, O.
Geo. A. Schilling, ex-Secretary Illinois Bureau of Labor Statistics, Chicago.
Laurence Gronlund, Editorial Writer (since deceased), New York Journal, New York City.
Howard K. Wood, Corporation Trust Company of New York, Jersey City.
E. S. Lacey, ex-Comptroller of the Currency, Chicago.
Harry P. Robinson, Editor Railway Age, Chicago.
Graham Taylor, Warden, Chicago Commons, Chicago.
A. M. Compton, John V. Farwell Co., Chicago.
A. C. Bartlett, President National Association Merchants and Travelers, Chicago.
W. D. Hoard, President Farmers' National Congress, Ft. Atkinson, Wis.
James W. Ellsworth, New York City.
H. T. Newcomb, United States Census Office, Washington, D. C.
Edward W. Bemis, Bureau of Economic Research, New York City.
John R. Commons, Bureau of Economic Research, New York City.
Thomas J. Morgan, Chicago, Socialist.
A. M. Simons, Chicago, Socialist.

The roll was corrected and approved at 12:05 o'clock.

An amendment was offered by Raymond, of Illinois, to Yellott's resolution providing that the committee on organization and program be appointed by the chair. The amendment was accepted by mover, but after a hot debate, McGuirk, of Iowa, and Jones, of Wisconsin, leading the opposition, was lost.

An amendment was offered by Gans of Illinois, and seconded by Cockran of New York, providing that the committee include one delegate from the Knights of Labor and one from each organization of more than state scope represented in the conference. The amendment was accepted and adopted, after discussion, and the motion with the two amendments prevailed.

Pending the appointment and organization of the committee, unanimous consent of the conference was given to proceed with the program as originally planned.

J. W. JENKS.

Statistician United States Industrial Commission.

With the preface that the speaker represented the industrial commission as an expert in the investigation of "trusts," the chairman introduced Professor J. W. Jenks, head of department of Political Economy of Cornell University, who said:

With the preface that the speaker represented the Industrial Commission as an expert in the investigation of "trust," the answering them. It is certainly true that a long step has been taken toward the solution of any problem when the problem itself has been clearly stated. It was thought that it might be of service, therefore, if various questions which the present combinations of capital have raised (and toward the solution of which this conference may well contribute much), were to be brought together at the beginning of the deliberations. I cannot expect to state clearly all of those questions. I mention some of the most important ones as they have been called to my attention.

1. Competition versus combination.

It has often been assumed that industrial combinations are monopolies that have abolished competition. On the other hand, managers of the most important ones invariably assert that they have much competition, and that the principle of competition is still active as long as anyone is legally free to set up a rival establishment. Many students of the question have asserted that among great industrial organizations, competition is fiercer than among smaller establishments, and that combination does not abolish competition, but simply raises it to a higher plane. So long as there is not a state monopoly like that of the postoffice, or a legal monopoly, like that established by a patent, there is of course at least potential competition. The law permits a rival to enter the lists. But a question still remains: How far do large combinations of capital possess a monopoly in fact, if not in law? How far are these large industrial combinations able to fix prices on the monopolistic principle of securing the highest net returns with little reference to what others charge, even though there may exist in the business some few other, but relatively speaking unimportant establishments? How far can an establishment which sells a high percentage, from 75 to 90 per cent, of the total product, secure monopolistic gains? Is competition to be considered free when one establishment controls from 75 to 90

27.

per cent of the total product in market? Will not the fear of so powerful an organization deter rivals from entering the field?

2. Combinations of capital and combinations of labor.

Some most active opponents of organized capital have been found in the ranks of organized labor. Some managers of industrial combinations assert that they have been forced to combine on account of the power of organized labor. They assert that the principle of combination is the same in both cases, and that labor organizations are no less tyrannous than are organizations of capital. Before legislation regarding combinations is undertaken, the question should be clearly answered, whether the two classes of organizations are the same in principle, and whether a law which restrains one will be held by the courts to restrain the other also. The differences in principle, if they exist, should be made perfectly clear.

3. Combinations caused by special privileges.

(a) Mr. Havemeyer has lately asserted that the "mother of all trusts is the customs tariff law." Many industries, however, in which great combinations exist, have no protection of their products by the tariff. Managers of combinations which have been formed in protected industries assert often that it has been the fierceness of home competition that has driven them into combination, and that if the tariff has been in any sense the cause of the combination, it has been such only by developing the home industry to so great an extent that fierce competition was unavoidable. How large a proportion of the trusts does the protective tariff favor? Would a lowering of the tariff on protected industries in which industrial combinations have been formed destroy the combination, or would it merely lead to international combination such as already exists in at least one or two instances, or, without breaking the combination, would it have the effect of lowering prices through foreign competition?

(b) Other combinations of great power have been formed in industries protected by patents, and have secured monopolistic prices through the aid of the patent laws. Would it be in the interest of the public, and would it be practicable so to amend our patent laws as to remove from them the element of monopoly, while still securing to the inventor, by royalty or otherwise, a suitable reward for his inventive skill?

(c) It has been frequently asserted that the success of many of the leading combinations of capital has been due to special favors granted them by the railroads. On the other hand, some declare that the most successful combinations of the present day find it rather for their interest to observe strictly the interstate commerce law, and to insist upon it that the railroads shall make no discriminations for anyone, whereas it is for the interests of those small combinations that are still struggling for a firm foothold to secure such discriminations. It is believed by many people that railroad discriminations are very frequent. Most important questions to be solved are first, one of fact: To what extent, and to whom do the railroads grant discriminating rates? and do these discriminations build up trusts? And second: What further remedy can be found for such discrimination beyond that which now exists under the interstate commerce law and the laws of the several states? Shall the Interstate Commerce Commission prescribe for the railroads their methods of bookkeeping, and shall the commission be given the power officially to inspect and audit their books? Is the national ownership and management of the railroads a feasible proposition for the United States to-day?

4.· Other causes for the formation of combinations of capital.

Managers of the great capitalistic organizations usually assert that they have been driven into combination through the fierceness of competition; that without combination, fair earnings on capital could not be realized; and that the trust instead of being an aggressive combination, is really capital on the defensive. They also assert that it is only through the power that comes from a large aggregation of capital that they are able to meet foreign competition in foreign trade, and that without such combination our export trade could not well be developed. They declare that with the development of foreign trade brought about through the combination of capital, they are enabled so to increase their output that not only the profits of capital, but also the demand for home labor is greatly increased. How far is such a statement true? The president of one of the large combinations told me a few days ago that he expected during the coming year to bring in to the United States for investment here, half a million dollars in profits from their export trade in the far East. All of the raw material for this export trade was produced in the United States, and he asserted that the number of laborers set to work here in producing the raw material for this export trade far exceeded the number of those thrown out of employment by the combination. How far is this example a typical one, and how far are these arguments of the capitalists to be considered valid? In this connection it must not be forgotten that a clear distinction is to be drawn between a large and powerful organization and a monopoly. The fiercest competition is that among the giant corporations.

29

5. Over-capitalization.

Most of the newer combinations of capital have issued large amounts of stock, common and preferred, as well as of bonds. It is important, at least for the investor, to know the facts regarding it: How much of this capital is represented in plants at a fair valuation? How much in patents or brands? How much in good-will in the proper sense of that word? How much is "water"? It is asserted by some that no harm is done the public even though the capitalization be much beyond the value of the plants; that the amount of capitalization has no effect on prices. Others, who believe that in these combinations an element of monopoly is found, think that an attempt to pay dividends on a large capitalization does increase prices. One class of persons asserts that capital stock should be limited to the amount of capital actually paid in in cash, or in plants taken at a conservative valuation. Another class believes that capitalization should be fixed by the probable earning capacity of an establishment. It is urged as an example, that a newspaper with a plant valued at a hundred thousand dollars may well earn large dividends on a million owing to the genius of the editor. Why, it is asked, not capitalize at a million? But on the other hand it is asked, should we put into permanent securities to be bought by the investing public a value depending so largely upon the talents of one short-lived individual? Again, a street railway which costs $500,000, and whose franchise may have cost nothing, may well pay good profits on $1,000,000, or $2,000,000. Is it in the public interest that a public franchise be thus capitalized into permanent securities, so as to pay dividends on $1,000,000 or $2,000,000, especially if the people are prevented thereby from seeing the source of profits? Most persons would readily grant that genius, or even the nerve that is shown in investing capital in new enterprises should meet with a fitting reward. It is a question not yet practically settled, and one which most people have not yet even settled in principle in their own minds, whether it is in the interest of the public that by high charges dividends should be earned on capitalization which represents a public franchise, or on that which represents the monopolistic element created simply by the aggregation of capital, without the application of special talent or exceptional skill. Is it desirable to limit capitalization or to give to the public by taxation part of the profits or to make the nature of the capitalization of each organization public, so that any investor can readily learn how large a proportion in every case is represented by plant, how much by patents or special brands, how much by good-will, and how much is nothing but "water"? Would such knowledge adequately protect the investor? Would such knowledge, by inviting competition, if real profits were made public, sufficiently protect the consumer? Many of our best thinkers think no further remedy is needed. Are the interests of the stockholders in the stability of business and the interests of the consumers in steady and low prices, under present industrial conditions, the same?

6. Effects of the combinations.

(a) On prices. It remains still to be fully established what the effects of these combinations are upon the prices of raw material and of the finished products. Are prices of raw materials held lower than is normal by the combination? Are the prices of the finished product lowered or made higher by the combination? Is it possible that competition can force prices so low, that by driving into bankruptcy a large number of establishments the interests of the public will be seriously injured? Is it in the interests of the laborers and of the public at large, that the fiercest possible competition in prices be encouraged? One of the leading rivals of the sugar combination has lately asserted that he believed the formation of the sugar trust had the effect on the whole of lowering prices. Although the trust immediately put prices up, had competition continued longer so many more refiners would have failed, he thought, that the short supply on the market would have pushed prices far above the rate established by the trust.

(b) On wages. Despite the fact that the wage-earners themselves seem to be in good part opposed to the industrial combinations, it is often asserted by the managers of the trusts that combinations of capital have increased the wages of the laboring men. The laborers themselves assert often that these combinations throw many men out of employment. They believe also that combinations, by controlling practically all of the plants of any one industry, are in much better condition to resist the demands of labor, and to endure any pressure that can be brought upon them by threats of strikes. A strike in one or two, or several establishments, will not affect the combination materially, provided it can carry on production in its other establishments at the same time. The growth of great corporate organizations of capital, they think, therefore, will give the death blow to trade unions. But the question is not yet settled. May the laborers possibly, by making also a thorough combination covering the whole of any one industry, be as well able to deal with their employers as they are at the present time? If their organization covers only two or three plants, they appear to be at a disadvantage. If their organization covers the entire industry, can the laborers and capitalists then act together as a unit in fixing wages over the whole territory? Through their agreements on wages, can they more readily control the prices to consumers than has ever been the case heretofore? Would not the capitalists prefer to tax the consumer, rather than the workman if he has a choice, and if one must suffer, to give him his profit? If so complete a system of organization of labor is difficult to start and to manage, will it be in the interest of the employers to aid the laborers in making, and holding, this organization, in order more effectively to control prices? These questions are not yet settled; and a fertile subject, not for speculation merely, but for serious thought, remains in the possibility of such an extension of labor unions that the employers and employees throughout an entire industry, can, with little fear of successful opposition, practically fix prices arbitrarily by agreement. Another form of union to reach the same end, and one which has already a basis in successful experience, is for the workmen to become stockholders in the combination, and thus to divide with the capitalist the profits of monopoly. How generally can this plan be made practicable? The effects upon the consuming community at large of any such union of employer and workingman need also careful study.

(c) Upon middlemen. A third complaint against great capitalistic organizations comes from the middlemen, particularly from jobbers and wholesale dealers, who assert that the trusts are eliminating them. Is this elimination of the middlemen, as well as the saving of labor, to be considered on the whole a gain to the community or a loss? If the trust can deal directly with two or three large jobbers, can fix their prices, and guarantee their profits, will there be enough saving in energy to the community to make up for the loss to the others who are driven out of business temporarily? Will it also be possible within a comparatively short time for those persons whose business is thus ruined, as well as for the laborers who are driven out of employment by the combinations, to secure employment elsewhere through the added demand that may come from the saving of cost and of labor energy, and from the increase in the export trade?

It is asserted that the trust, by killing the small establishment, checks the growth of individuality in young business men, making of them mere hirelings. Others assert that no one is fit for command till he has first learned to obey; that in the great organizations there are many positions of responsibility, in which individual initiative can have full play; that the distribution of rewards to men of real merit is much more certain and just when

82

business is well organized; and that the places at the top are much more worthy the ambition of the man of great individual power. An example has been lately suggested: If a dozen small railroads unite into one great system, few men lose positions. The general superintendents of the small roads become division superintendents of the large system, with no decrease in pay, with substantially the same duties and responsibilities, although frequent reports are required from a general superintendent. Before the consolidation, reports went to the president and directors. The best men have better opportunities for higher position; the average men do not lose; the poor men are more surely thrust down to pure routine labor. Will not the same effect be generally found in all consolidations?

The question is perhaps the most vital one of the whole discussion. Only experience can give the final answer.

On the whole, then, are we to consider the new form of organization a means of saving energy comparable with a new invention like the steam engine or the railroad, so that we may be fairly sure that, although temporary suffering occurs, there will be enough saving to lower prices and to increase the demand for goods to so great an extent that the total demand for labor will in the long run be increased and the public benefited? Or, on the other hand, is the new form of organization a conspiracy of the few rich and powerful to oppress the many? Each view is taken by thousands.

7. Legislation.

If the state needs to interfere in this modern industrial movement, what form of legislation is wisest? Should it be destructive, attempting to prevent combination, or should it be regulative, permitting combination freely, but attempting so to control that evils to the public may be avoided? Of legislation aiming at destruction we have had many examples. The question still remains unsettled as to how far this legislation will prove effective. Some points have been given interpretation by the courts; some have yet to be tested; experience only will show the outcome.

So far as legislation is to be regulative, will it be sufficient to secure publicity, or can something be done to prevent undue raising or lowering of prices and wages?

A second question of not less import is this,—How far can such legislation be national under the general provisions of our constitution regarding interstate commerce, and how far must the legislation be state?

To be more specific as we summarize: Can there be, if it seems desirable, within a reasonable time, a national incorporation of great industries, over which the federal government shall have sole control? Can organizations then, which place themselves under federal supervision and control, be exempt from a variety of legislation, either friendly or hostile, of the several states?

Can Congress now, under our present constitution, providing for the regulation of commerce between the states, secure by new legislation full information regarding the nature of the property and business of great corporations, railroad and others, and frequent reports regarding the condition of the business with power of inspection of records, so that confidence may be assured? If such publicity is sought, must a special commission or bureau be created for the administrative work?

If such inspection shows very high profits, will the fear and possibility of competition so lower prices as to distribute these profits among the public, or would it be wise to attempt, without destroying the spirit of enterprise, to give part of the profits to the public through taxation?

Can the separate states, by any of the measures suggested, or by others, effectively promote the interests of their citizens by legislation without substantial uniformity of legislation among them all? Can such uniformity be secured, or even hoped for?

There are other problems created by the industrial combinations. I have mentioned the most important ones to which my attention has been called. It is hoped that wise counsel and conservative though bold action, may, in no long time, solve some of them.

If it will not be considered out of place, may I venture to suggest that the security of the state, and the welfare of the people, is always best attained, not through suspicion and denunciation, but through confidence in an opponent's honesty of purpose, and through an earnest endeavor to get the other man's point of view. I have known many of the trust leaders and advocates, and many of their chief opponents. In uprightness, sincerity, public spirt, patriotism, there is little difference among them. Likewise in earnest determination to look out for themselves and to protect what they consider their own, there is little difference. We all have our weaknesses: few of us are all bad. The chief endeavor of men in legislatures or elsewhere should be not as opponents, for each to hold his own regardless of right, as is only too natural, but as students, for each to be sure that he understands the other

34

and respects the other's sincerity. Lincoln's dictum of "charity for all" was not only Christlike, it was also statesmanlike. The true statesman seeks the truth and through candor and fair dealing and mutual respect can one best attain the truth.

At 1:10 o'clock the conference took a recess until 3 o'clock.

AFTERNOON SESSION, SEPTEMBER 13.

The caucuses of the delegations in selecting the members of the committee on organization and program prevented a full attendance of delegates until some time after the afternoon session was called to order by Chairman Head at 3 o'clock. The galleries were filled, however, and an ovation was given Professor Henry C. Adams, head of department of Political Economy of the University of Michigan, when he was introduced.

HENRY C. ADAMS.

Statistician Interstate Commerce Commission.

I have been requested to undertake a statement of the questions that arise in the consideration of the trust problem. In doing this I shall say nothing that is new, nor shall it be my aim to be exhaustive. It is possible, however, that questions which are familiar may present themselves in a new light when brought together in a single statement.

Whatever the trust problem may be, it has to do with business organization, and on this account the first question that suggests itself is one that pertains to the science of economics. We observe in almost every form of business that industrial power is concentrating itself, that organizations are growing in size, that individual industry and small enterprises are being crowded to the wall, and that the sphere of competition is constantly being narrowed. This tendency is opposed to the theory upon which our system of jurisprudence rests, and it is pertinent to inquire whether it is inherent in the nature of the industries that are thus tending toward consolidation, or whether its explanation is to be found in the peculiar conditions under which industry at the present time is carried on. This is a most important question; for if the tendency toward consolidation be natural, remedial legislation should address itself to the control

35

of the industrial forces thus brought together. If, on the other hand, this tendency be artificial, the legislature in dealing with the situation must seek to restore those conditions under which individual enterprise may be able to maintain itself. Without undertaking the analysis of industrial conditions and motives which a consideration of this question involves, I shall state at once what seems to be the correct opinion upon this subject. Industries are not all of the same kind. They do not all possess the same character. Some tend toward consolidation and combination, while others are well fitted by their character to continue a separate and a competitive existence. The transportation industries are of the former class. The manufacturing industries are, speaking generally, of the latter class. Railways by their very nature tend toward combinations and consolidations. The biscuit industry, the manufacture of nails, the refining of oil, on the other hand, are well fitted for individual management and administration. If these latter, like the former, show a tendency toward consolidation, the explanation will be found in the peculiar conditions under which they are carried on. Thus again, upon the threshold of this discussion, do we discover the imperative necessity of industrial analysis, as a guide to right policy and sound legislation.

Before coming to questions of general policy, there is another question which will undoubtedly be made the subject of warm discussion by this convention. Are the combinations commonly called trusts advantageous or disadvantageous? Is the tendency toward consolidation one to be approved or disapproved? It is likely that this discussion will turn upon three points: First, does consolidation of manufacturing industries tend toward the reduction of cost? Second, will manufacturing under trusts, by measuring the output to the current demand, tend to guard society from the evils of commercial panics and commercial depressions? And lastly, is this new organization of industry in harmony with a democratic organization of society? Here again I must ask the privilege of expressing an opinion, as the time allotted this paper does not permit a full statement of the reasons upon which my opinion rests.

It is common to say that increase in the size of a manufacturing plant permits the production of commodities at less cost than would otherwise be the case. There is undoubtedly some truth in this statement. The development of machinery has gone hand in hand with the growth of factories, and as a result the product is furnished at a cheapened rate. But there is a limit to the application of this rule. Every manufacturing industry, considered from the point of view of production, has at any particular time a size which may be regarded as its normal size of maximum efficiency. This normal size of maximum efficiency is determined by the extent to which division of labor and the use of machinery can be applied. To increase such an industry by one-half would not result in a decrease of the cost of manufacture, for it would occasion a less effective application of the principle of division of labor. While, therefore, it is true that the concentration of capital and labor under a single direction is followed by economy up to a certain point, it is not true that combination and concentration beyond that point tends to reduce the cost of production. He who accepts this statement of the case must conclude that manufacturing combinations (I say nothing of other forms) contribute nothing to the reduction of the cost of manufacture beyond what would be contributed should each of the industries continue its independent competitive existence. This is a curt answer to a profound question, but it is believed to rest upon sound analysis and to lead to the conclusion that the motive for a trust organization of manufacturing industries is not found in a desire to benefit the public by the reduction of cost.

It is not so difficult to suggest the line of reasoning upon the second question submitted. The chief argument in favor of combinations among producers is that by this means product will be measured to demand, and consequently there will be no overstocking of the market, no commercial depression, and no commercial panic. I shall not undertake to argue this proposition, but content myself with a single comment. Opposed to this theory of commercial depressions stands the well-wrought theory of socialistic writers which rests upon the claim that a stocked market is due to an uneconomic distribution of values, and not to an overproduction of goods. It certainly is true that goods cannot be sold when the property in the goods, as also the money with which to purchase them is in the same hands. A steady market implies an equation between goods on the one hand and purchasing power in the hands of those for whom the goods are made on the other. You perceive at once the bearing of this line of reasoning upon the claim that combinations tend to steadiness of trade. For if the trusts which tend to concentrate industrial control, concentrates also industrial values, it is evident upon the theory of industrial crises just related that such organizations intensify the conditions that lead to commercial crises. An adjustment of the output to the current effective demand is of the utmost importance. It may be questioned, however, whether

37

a yet further concentration of industrial power than that which now exists is the best means of attaining this result.

In addition to these purely industrial considerations it is necessary to inquire respecting the general social and political results of trust organizations before one can accept them as a healthful tendency in modern life. It must be remembered that our industrial society rests upon English jurisprudence, that English jurisprudence acknowledges the individual as the center of all industrial activity, that it provides for him the institution of private property, holds him to strict accountability, and assumes that competition between producers, on the one hand, and purchasers, on the other hand, is a guarantee of justice and equity in all industrial conduct. Do trusts fit naturally into this theory of society? For the preservation of democracy there must be maintained a fair degree of equality in the social standing of citizens; do trusts tend to such equality? For the normal workings of that industrial society which is the product of six centuries of history the door of opportunity must not be closed; do trusts tend to close the door of opportunity? For the realization of the American idea of government there must be a balance of power, not only between the several departments of government, but between the government on the one hand, and the interests that lie outside the government, on the other hand; do trusts tend to destroy this balance of power? I would not claim, without discussion, that the trust organization of society destroys reasonable equality, closes the door of industrial opportunity, or tends to disarrange that fine balance essential to the successful workings of an automatic society; but I do assert that the questions here presented are debatable questions, and that the burden of proof lies with the advocates of this new form of business organization.

If the current tendency toward consolidation in manufacturing industries does not spring from the nature of the industry, and if the benefits accruing to the public from these consolidations are at least questionable, it is incumbent upon us next to inquire out of what conditions these modern industrial organizations have sprung. I shall venture but three suggestions in this connection. Doubtless many more will be presented as this convention proceeds in its deliberations.

The inequalities which exist in established schedules of railway rates, as also the proneness of railways to depart from published schedules in order to secure the business of large shippers, works toward the consolidation of manufacturing industries and commercial enterprises. It is not intended to say that mal-administration on the part of railways is of itself responsible for

38

present industrial tendencies. It is, however, true that in so far as railways discriminate in favor of large shippers, they present a motive to shippers to become as large as possible. This is too familiar a fact to call for discussion. The truth is that the business of transportation underlies all other businesses, it determines the conditions upon which other forms of industry are carried on, and by the manipulation of rate schedules tone, color and character can be given to industrial society at large. While the solution of the railway problem would not necessarily cause all trusts and combinations to disappear, its solution is essential for dealing wisely with the trust problem. No one can deny that inequitable railway charges and discriminations in railway rates are important elements in the conditions that foster commercial combinations.

In further explanation of the current tendency toward business combination on the part of industries that by their nature are not monopolistic, reference may be made to the fact that the commercial jurisdiction of modern business is much broader than the political jurisdiction of the governments whose protection they seek and by whom they should in theory be controlled. The federal government has no authority over many of the questions raised by a study of trusts, while the state governments are confined in the exercise of their authority to their local jurisdictions. Such a condition must result in confusion of laws, in uncertainty of procedure, and in enabling the interstate enterprises which rest upon state foundations to become a law unto themselves, so far as the conduct of their affairs is concerned. Competition cannot work inequitably under such conditions. Justice attends competition only when competitors stand on an equal footing. It is, therefore, no occasion for surprise to one who is familiar with the present condition of state laws upon industrial affairs that small and localized industries should find themselves at a disadvantage in their struggle for existence with the great combinations. A national market has taken the place of the local market, but we still rely upon local law for its regulation and control. Uniformity of law and harmony of procedure is as essential as uniform railway rates and absence of discrimination, to restore those conditions in which competition can effect its normal and beneficent results.

We are thus carried by our analysis from the consideration of economic relations to the stupendous question of political organization and legislative procedure. He who believes in local government will not readily consent to the proposition that the federal Congress should assert exclusive authority over commercial and industrial conditions. Nor, on the other hand, will he who appreciates the significance and the beneficent results of a world's market consent to the suggestion that the business transactions of a state concern should not extend beyond the borders of a state. Here is a problem for statesmen to contemplate, and it is possible before arriving at its solution that the constitutional relations between the local and the federal government will be subjected to modification. Without entering upon this phase of the subject, may I submit for consideration the following proposition: The true function of a central government in dealing with problems of internal economy is to determine the fundamental principles of legislation, while the true function of local government is to express those principles in the terms of local conditions and to administer the laws thus expressed. By this means harmony of action at least would be secured and one of the conditions out of which industrial combinations spring will have been set aside.

My third suggestion in explanation of the persistence of combinations in industries which from their nature are subject to competition is found in the unsatisfactory condition of state laws of incorporation. This is a question that should be considered by a lawyer, but by the lawyer who is familiar with the industrial history of the English speaking people. Originally a corporation created by the state was regarded as an arm of the state. Individuals were clothed with some degree of public authority because they undertook to perform what were regarded as public duties. The East India Company, which planted an empire, is an illustration of such a corporation. The modern idea of a corporation is entirely different. It is regarded merely as a business organization. I have not time to discuss this abstruse question, even had I the ability, but of one thing I am confident: The theory of law which now prevails respecting industrial corporations should be so changed that the public element is again brought into prominence. Industries should be classified, and the right of incorporation granted to one class and denied to another, and special restrictions, if not constant supervision, should be exercised over such industries as are incorporated before we can again reintroduce into this modern, complex machine-organized industrial society the conditions favorable to the normal working of the beneficent principle of competition.

Whatever may be said upon the questions thus far submitted, there is one point respecting which all should agree. Industrial combinations, whatever their form, whatever their purpose, whatever their explanation, are matters of public concern. It is said,

OFFICERS OF THE CONFERENCE

DUDLEY G. WOOTEN
First Vice-Chairman

HENRY V. JOHNSON
Second Vice-Chairman

FRANKLIN H. HEAD
Temporary Chairman

WILLIAM WIRT HOWE
Permanent Chairman

STEPHEN P. CORLISS
Third Vice-Chairman

RALPH M. EASLEY
Secretary

we do not know enough of this new form of industrial organization to judge properly respecting it. If this be true, and if on this account trusts are to be allowed a probationary existence, it is the plain duty of government to hold them meantime to strict account. The statistician should be pressed into service, the keeping of books should be regarded as of paramount importance, and the rule according to which accounts are kept and reports made should be formulated in the interest of investigation. The propriety of this suggestion can be questioned by no one. If trusts are what they claim, that is to say, the vanguards of a new industrial organization which holds within itself great industrial benefits, the sooner this fact is recognized by the public, the better for all concerned. If, on the other hand, there is danger in the extreme application of this form of organization, the government certainly has a right to possess itself of all facts necessary for a judicious opinion and for effective legislation. It would be a step in the right direction should the states make provision for an interstate organization of statistical inquiry and confer upon such an organization adequate authority for the uniform prosecution of its investigation. Where competition controls, the government may safely refrain from interference, but where competition is excluded, or where the conditions for its exercise are such as to give one competitor an advantage over another, nothing remains but public supervision; and, I repeat, the most important, indeed the essential agency for legislation or for administrative supervision is a thoroughly organized bureau of statistics and accounts clothed with authority over the auditing departments of these industrial associations.

Permit me in closing to pass in rapid review the questions, so far as they have been presented, which underlie the problem now claiming your attention. It was first suggested that industries differ in their fundamental character and that no wise policy can be adopted until those which are naturally monopolistic are separated from those which by nature are subject to competitive control. It was, in the second place, suggested that before a reasonable opinion could be entertained respecting trusts their relation to prices, to commercial depressions, as also their influence upon democracy, should be clearly grasped. Turning, then, in the third place, to a consideration of the current tendency toward monopoly in industries which naturally are subject to competitive control, it was stated that the explanation of this tendency is found in the conditions under which manufacturing and commercial enterprises are carried on. Three of these conditions were mentioned: First, the fact that railways do discriminate in favor of large shippers; second, that the extension of commercial relations beyond the jurisdiction of the states has resulted in confusion of law and uncertainty of procedure—a condition especially favorable to the encouragement of great interstate industries; third, attention was called to the unsatisfactory condition of the laws of incorporation as one of the elements in the conditions by which trusts are fostered. And finally, your attention was called to the fact that whatever else may be determined upon, provision should be made by the states for an efficient, comprehensive and harmonious control over the auditing departments of such industries as choose the trust organization for the prosecution of business.

The question before this convention is indeed a great question. It moves in many directions and embraces many considerations. It is at bottom a question of social theories and social ideas. Its vastness will be appreciated when it is observed that its judicious treatment will result in securing for the people the advantages of the industrial development of the past century, while to ignore it or to fail in its solution would result in prostituting the wealth created by an hundred years of phenomenal development to the service of a class.

DUDLEY G. WOOTEN.

Member Texas Legislature.

At the conclusion of Professor Adams' remarks, the chairman introduced Hon. Dudley Goodall Wooten, of the Texas Legislature. Mr. Wooten was the first speaker on the uncompromising anti-trust side of the debate. The gallery audience was in sympathy with his views, and, carried away by the eloquence of the gifted orator, punctuated his address with salvo after salvo of applause. Mr. Wooten said:

The delegates from Texas are highly sensible of the honor of having one of their number called upon to address this learned and representative body upon the first day of its assembling. It is I believe understood that this day's session shall be devoted to a general discussion of the problems under consideration, leaving to the subsequent proceedings of the Conference the detailed and special examination of the various phases of the subject. I therefore feel less hesitation in responding to the call made upon me at this time, and in the remarks that I shall endeavor to submit I shall attempt to merely present in outline and in general terms the views entertained by my people. In what I shall say I make no pretense of discussing Trusts and Monopolies from the standpoint of an economic expert, but prefer rather to address myself to the broad features of these combinations and the principles that seem to me to underlie their causes, promote their consequences, and must accomplish their reformation or removal.

We come from a state whose location, area, resources and population, in our judgment, entitle us to entertain very positive and pertinent convictions upon the great problems that have called this assembly together, and which will hereafter provoke the learned discussions of the distinguished gentlemen here present. First of all, we are mainly producers of raw materials and consumers of manufactured products, and whatever tends to arbitrarily control the prices of the one or to monopolize the output of the other is a direct injury to our people and their industrial pursuits. In the next place, aside from the material aspects of the subject as affecting the markets in which we buy and sell, we believe that there is a fundamental principle of political ethics and governmental science involved in the problems under discussion. We believe that there are some things more valuable, more to be desired and more worthy to be contended for by a free people than mere industrial activity, commercial progress or the accumulation of worldly wealth. We do not believe in that school of political philosophy that despises the wisdom and experience of the fathers of English and American liberty and law, that rejects as antiquated and inadequate the great precepts and principles of a venerable jurisprudence at the behest of modern monopoly, that salves the wounds of freedom with the oil of avarice, and condones a constitutional crime with the argument of pelf and greed.

In the Constitution under which we in Texas live—handed down to us by the heroes of the Alamo and San Jacinto—we are taught that "monopolies are contrary to the genius of a free government, and shall never be allowed"; and we adhere with unhesitating loyalty to both the letter and the spirit of that declaration. In the Federal Constitution under which we all live—handed down to us all by the heroes of Lexington and Saratoga and Yorktown—we have been taught that "all rights not delegated to the United States nor prohibited to the States, are reserved to the people"; and among the most valuable of those reserved rights we esteem the traditional freedom of trade, contract and labor that has been cherished and defended by Anglo-Saxon yeomen in every age since their history began. Nay, more than that, Mr. Chairman, accepting in good faith that Amendment to the Federal Constitution which the heroic legions of the South resisted unto death on a thousand battlefields, we believe that "neither slavery nor involuntary servitude, except as punishment for crime, shall exist in the United States or any place subject to their jurisdiction"; and we confidently assert that the commercial and industrial bondage being rapidly imposed upon the toil and talents of seventy millions of American citizens by the syndicated wealth of a few great corporate monopolies, is more dire and dangerous than the slavery that once bowed the heads and burdened the backs of four millions of Southern black men.

And above and beyond these great written guarantees of equality and justice, we look to the lessons of history and appeal to the authority of experience. When we are told that the spirit of commercial combination promises golden rewards to the present tendencies of our economic system, we remember that no republic has ever survived the mercenary despotism of merchants and money-changers. We recall the fate of that little group of Italian states whose political institutions were wrecked by the touch of commercial greed and whose republican freedom vanished before the breath of commercial ambition. Their glittering fragments strewed the shores of the Mediterranean like shattered baubles as soon as their commerce became mightier than their constitutions, and their shipping more potent than their statesmanship. We recollect that from the day the Saxon set his sway on British shores, through all his successive conquests and assimilations of Celtic, Danish and Norman invaders, the one virtue that made him strong and kept him free and proved him triumphant was his invincible loyalty to the genius of that liberty that springs from the soil and that civilization that centers in the rights and aspirations of the individual man. And we reflect today that, although the sails of imperial Britain whiten every sea, while her commercial activity stirs every port and dominates half the globe, yet she has preserved the immemorial virtues of her Saxon lineage. The source of all her strength and the citadel of all her civilization are still housed beneath the roofs of her sturdy yeomanry, proud of their natural rights and tenacious of their inherited freedom. The commerce of the world has made her glorious and rich, but the independent citizenship of her personal subjects sustains the fabric of her national power,—

"Broad bas'd upon her people's will,
And compass'd by the inviolate sea."

Coming to this Western World, we remember the fortitude and sagacity that founded this republic upon the same great traditions of civil and political rights that had glorified the centuries of English constitutional growth, but framed its institutions along yet broader and freer lines. We love to recall that Washington warned his countrymen against the dangerous seductions of commercial power and the corrupting influence of consuming wealth; that he commended to them the frugal methods and easy paths of individual enterprise, and, with his last breath, bade them beware the encroaching tyranny of ambitious greed. We admire the intrepid radicalism and daring democracy of Jefferson when he proclaimed that he "would rather see the whole earth reduced to a single pair and them free, than to behold a populous world groaning beneath the exactions of privileged monopoly." We recollect that the elder Adams said that "the highest ideals of political perfection are not compatible with the selfish standards of material prosperity," and that Webster declared that "the deadliest canker that can attack the heart of the nation is the corroding disease of commercial avarice."

Line upon line and precept upon precept this cumulative creed of political philosophy comes down to us from the lips and lives of all our sages, heroes and statesmen, and is verified in every step and stage of our national career.

In the face of such lessons and such authority we must be permitted to dissent from the academic arguments that seek to reason away our faith and history, and to repudiate utterly the scholastic speculation that would silence the voices of our wisest patriots and reverse the judgments of our soundest jurists. The academic element has never been friendly to practical freedom nor contributed sensibly to the solution of any great social or political problem, and its attitude in this discussion is in line with its historic assumption of authority without wisdom and counsel without sympathy.

Remembering and revering these ancient and approved principles and precepts, we must be allowed to believe that the modern trust and its more modern successor—the consolidated corporate monopoly—are the practical realization of the commercial spirit in its most despotic form; that they represent in crystallized and perfected triumph the concentrated evils that have been resisted by our ancestors and denounced by our laws and traditions since Anglican freedom had its birth and American institutions began their growth.

Developing under the frown of judicial disfavor, the modern trust has passed from the loose and imperfect combination of affiliated corporations until it issues in the condensed and consolidated union of huge capitalized monopolies under one charter

45

and a centralized control. Their fundamental purposes are to reduce expenses by lowering the prices of raw materials, minimizing the cost of labor, and concentrating the expenditure of energy into the smallest possible compass; to destroy competition by absorbing all rival industries, squeezing out the small, coercing the weak and amalgamating the strong; to monopolize and control trade and industry by absolutely dominating the market and subsidizing or terrorizing the free and normal course of commerce, transportation and labor. These are the avowed and undisguised objects of every great manufacturing and commercial syndicate of the age. They seek to justify their operations on the plausible ground that they improve the quality and increase the quantity of manufactured products, reduce the prices to the consumer, save money, time and labor to the customer, and add to the aggregate wealth and prosperity of the country. It might be admitted for the sake of argument that some of these contentions are true, while the monopoly is perfecting the machinery of its despotism, but ultimately none of them is true or possible in the nature of things. But suppose some of these things to be correctly stated; are there no other factors to be considered in the problem? At what and whose expense are these much praised results attained? At the expense of the producer of the raw materials, whose products are forced upon the market at ruinous prices; at the expense of discharged employees and laborers, whose places are filled by fewer hands or improved machinery, whose wages cease, whose families must starve or steal or join the great army of tramps and paupers, whose crimes and penury are the shame and the menace of the republic; at the expense of the toil and enterprise of every honest competitor, who is driven out of business by the combination or closed up by forcible absorption; at the expense of every customer who is compelled to handle the trust goods upon arbitrary terms and at such profits as the syndicate may prescribe; at the expense of the entire public, which is sooner or later left no choice but to submit to such exactions as the triumphant monopoly may dictate. And who is benefited thereby? The few fortunate employees who are able to retain their employment under the new system; the speculators in the watered stock that was floated at the inception of the enterprise and which has become valuable by the manipulations of the monopoly; and the limited number of promoters who have amassed millions of money by the scheme that defrauded, impoverished and enslaved millions of men. Wealth and prosperity and a limited degree of happiness have perhaps blessed a few selfish incorporators and their more selfish families, while poverty, discontent, despair and the bitterness of ruined hopes and homes have darkened the minds and desolated the hearts of countless thousands of honest, industrious, aspiring citizens of a free republic.

This is merely the material side of the picture, but to describe it is to announce it as a drama of wrong and woe. I say nothing of the grievous injustice and inequality of any political system that permits such a monstrous perversion of all the traditions of our liberties and laws. To recite the outlines of English and American constitutional history is to denounce in every line and landmark the whole origin, operation and consequences of the modern commercial and industrial trust.

Entertaining as we do these deliberate and decided convictions, there is in our view of the matter but one phase of the problem left open for discussion, and that is how best to remedy the evil and remove its causes. Upon this branch of the subject there may well be differences of opinion among those otherwise agreed upon the propositions just advanced. When we come to devise and to enforce remedies against these disastrous agencies, we confront a difficult and delicate question of both law and fact. It involves vested rights, the obligations of contract, the immunities and privileges of citizenship, and the intricate mechanism of trade and economics. But these are mere details of method and reform. We prefer at this time to brush them aside and go direct to the heart of the subject. If we may find the germs that give vitality to the whole system of syndicated monopoly and combined capital, it ought to be possible to contrive means for their extermination or control.

The courts of the country have uniformly and correctly held that, but for the existence and methods of private corporations, trusts and monopolies in their present form could not exist for an hour. The loose and risky methods of personal enterprise, the legal limitations and vicissitudes of individual investments, and the motives of selfish caution that control the actions of men or firms engaged in business on their own responsibility, all render it impossible for great industrial and commercial monopolies to be built up in that way. It is only by the corporation, with its peculiar and artificial attributes, that trusts and trade combinations can be successfully carried out. Here, then, we have the root of the evil, and here, too, we are again confronted with a profound question of political and governmental science. It has been said that this question of trusts is not a political question. We beg to say that it is, of all other questions of the age, fundamentally and essentially a political one. Its discussion and

47

solution involve the vitals of our whole political system and institutions. They are inseparably connected with the first principles and practical philosophy of republican government.

The trust and its parent, the private corporation, are radically opposed to that individualism whose full and free exercise is the basis of all democratic forms of government. The predicate upon which are laid the whole theory and argument of the Declaration of Independence and the provisions of our Constitutions, state and federal, is the inalienable and indestructible sovereignty of individual manhood and natural citizenship. When it is declared that "All men are created free and equal, and endowed with certain inalienable rights," we are to understand natural men, with the sentiments, sympathies, aspirations, hopes and limitations of human nature. When it is said that all rights not otherwise disposed of in the Constitution are "reserved to the people," we must believe that the fathers of the Union meant a real people, created by Divine power, embodying the instincts, attributes and capabilities breathed into man by his Maker—loving freedom, despising despotism, responsive to the impulses of patriotism, bound by the ties of gratitude and the motives of generosity, dutiful to the obligations of humanity here and conscious of an everlasting responsibility hereafter. Upon no other kind of foundation can a free and stable government stand; of no other kind of citizenship can a prosperous republic be composed.

And yet, within the past fifty years, there has grown up under the sanction of the Constitution and with the approval of the courts, congresses and legislatures, a new and dangerous innovation upon the original conceptions of the framers of our institutions. Side by side with the natural man created by God, there has arisen an artificial person, conceived by the mischievous ingenuity of mercantile greed, created by the capricious legislation of human assemblies, protected by the fictions of fallible tribunals, vested with practical immortality, endowed with every attribute, power and function that may belong to the natural person, and exempt from every limitation, influence and restraint that render human nature honest, charitable, generous and conscientious. And, worst of all, by the very nature of their constitutions and the opportunities of their artificial methods, and the capacity which they enjoy for indefinite combinations of power and illimitable acquisitions of wealth, these cold and calculating creatures of the law, though few in numbers as compared with the mighty mass of the true citizenship of the country, have been enabled to engross the bulk of the national resources, to dominate

48

the popular will, and to dwarf and paralyze the sovereignty of the individual manhood of the republic.

Forty years ago Abraham Lincoln declared that this republic could not exist "half slave and half free," and the titanic struggle of a four years' war vindicated the prophetic wisdom of his declaration.

Would that some second Lincoln could arise, with the sublime courage and majestic patriotism of that splendid seer, to tell this generation of Americans that the Union cannot endure nor its freedom be insured half composed of natural citizenship and half of artificial citizenship. Nay, the condition is even worse than that. Under the sinister conditions brought about by the inordinate growth and overshadowing power of private corporations, the division is not even in equal portions, for the government-created citizens completely dominate their natural rivals and crush out the divinity and the manhood of the individual sovereigns of the nation. Not satisfied with the inequality that arises from the very nature of these artificial creatures of law and license, the government itself has established and maintained a system of tariff laws avowedly framed for the especial benefit of these unnatural giants of commerce and industry. The artificial immunities and franchises conferred upon corporate citizenship by legislation and judicial favor have been supplemented by the protective duties levied and enforced for the purpose of enriching incorporated monopoly at the expense of the independent and unprotected industries of personal enterprise. The tariff has enabled the corporations to establish and solidify their despotism by forty years of legalized plunder of the people, and to-day it hides behind them as behind the breastworks its own iniquities have erected.

It is along these lines that all efforts to curtail and control trusts and monopolies must be directed in our judgment. The germ of the syndicated system is the private corporation and its favored privileges, and these must be shorn of their hurtful power. Legislation of a radical kind is necessary, and the nature of our governmental institutions points the way for proper and effective laws on this subject. Our government is a dual system, partly federal and partly state, and all action, to be practical and successful, must comprehend a harmonious co-operation of both the federal and the state authorities. In the economy contemplated by the founders of the republic it was intended that where the states failed by reason of local restrictions, the federal power should supplement their sovereignty over all matters of universal concern, and this problem calls for the highest and widest exercise of all the jurisdiction of the states and the Union.

The great bulk of the commercial traffic and industrial trade of the union is interstate commerce, subject to the jurisdiction of the federal government alone, and subject also to the jurisdiction of the federal courts by reason of the diverse citizenship of the parties engaged. Properly speaking the whole subject of corporations engaged in interstate business ought to be under the control of the federal authority for that reason, but in order to accomplish that end there must first be concert of action and harmony of policy and sentiment on the subject. For the several states to do anything effective and valuable they must co-operate. If there be need for uniform statutes on marriage and divorce, wills, insolvency and other similar interests in which the entire country has a common and identical share, then certainly there is need for it on this the most vital question that affects the prosperity, happiness and freedom of the republic at large. It was this consideration that induced the governor of Texas to call the meeting of governors and attorney-generals which will convene in St. Louis next week, and it is to be hoped that some harmonious and united plan of legislation will be agreed upon by them. If we are asked along what lines this universal and uniform legislation shall be framed, then we unhesitatingly answer that it should be in the direction of limiting the purposes for which private corporations shall be chartered, so as to reduce their number, and by limiting also the amount of capital stock for which a company may be incorporated so as to curtail their enormous power to amass undue wealth and exercise despotic control over the commerce, industry and policies of the nation.

It is one of the most alarming symptoms of the age that no sort of private enterprise can be inaugurated without the artificial aids of incorporation. The original and normal purpose for which corporations were intended was to enable those things to be done that were of such magnitude that individual effort and capital could not successfully manage them, and yet were of such utility and public importance as to be proper and desirable to exist. In other words, they were only meant for enterprises of a quasi-public character. Corporations for private profit are in themselves essentially vicious and inconsistent with that equality of right and absence of special privilege guaranteed by the institutions of a free republic, but if they must exist then they should be limited to as few purposes as possible, and their capital stock should never be beyond that which a fair and reasonable conduct of private business requires. It is folly to complain of trusts and suppress pools and combinations between several corporations, and at the same time permit the formation of single corporations with larger capital than any syndicate yet known. The fact is all such consolidated corporate enterprises are simply trusts in disguise, they are so declared by the recent Texas statute, and they ought to be rendered impossible by allowing no company to be chartered for any other than a quasi-public purpose with a capital authorized beyond a reasonable amount commensurate with the equality between natural and artificial citizenship and industry. These are the lines along which we believe that the remedy lies, so far as the states can furnish and apply that remedy.

But the burden of this great work can not and ought not to be thrown entirely upon the states. Notwithstanding the high authority of the attorney-general of the United States and his presumable familiarity with trusts in their natural habitat, we believe that the federal government both can and should assume the initiative in the movement to suppress and restrain these great corporate monopolies. First of all, it can and should dissolve the iniquitous partnership that exists between trusts and syndicated wealth, by abolishing the tariff system that has been the most prolific and profitable adjunct the trusts and monopolies have had for the past thirty-five years. It is useless and dishonest to denounce these oppressive and unjust combinations and aggressions on the part of commercial and industrial capital, while the government itself is promoting and sustaining them by its revenue system and adding to their strength by the legalized plunder of the people. The day that witnesses the withdrawal of the sustaining arm of the federal tariff from the unlawful combines and trusts of the country, will witness the most signal and significant movement possible toward their extinction. In the next place, Congress can prevent all corporations connected with monopolies and trusts from engaging in interstate commerce. Of this power and duty on the part of our federal legislature there can be no question, and the moment it is exercised the main support and means of despotism over the trade of the union by these combinations will have been destroyed. And finally, if it shall become necessary and the states can arrive at a harmonious and united line of policy on the subject, the federal authority can assume entire control of corporations engaged in interstate business, issuing them their charters, limiting their capital stock, curtailing the purposes for which they may exist and enforcing upon them the most rigid and exact compliance with the rights of the public and the freedom of the citizen. This no doubt might require an amendment to the Constitution, but if that is the only way the desired end can be attained the people will eventually indorse it.

By these two means—state and federal legislation combining to reduce the number, power and privileges of private corporations—the rapid growth and menacing tyranny of the corporate monopolies can be controlled and restrained, but in no other that we can perceive. The methods suggested may appear radical and revolutionary to some, but the time has come when the country must face the crisis and solve it conscientiously, courageously and completely, unless we are to surrender those principles for which the union was formed and without which it is not worth preserving. The qualities of all others required in this conflict between the just and equal rights of the masses against the classes, between the independent freedom of individual enterprise and corporate monopoly, between republican institutions of liberty and law and syndicated combinations of mercenary power, are the qualities for which our ancestors, English and American, have always vindicated their characteristic loyalty. Devotion to manhood rather than money, to the principles of freedom and free institutions rather than a servile worship of mere material ideals, to the fundamental rights of the citizen in his personal relations rather than the grandeur and power of collective might. If government of the people, by the people and for the people is to continue in this republic, then we must place national righteousness above national wealth, ethics above economics, political principles above pecuniary profit, the Constitution above the commerce of the country. To do these things at this time and under the overshadowing menace of established industrial and commercial conditions will require a degree of courage and constancy never before demanded by any crisis that has arisen in the history of the nation.

The glory and fascination of war and strenuous struggle for the life of the government as our people understood it have made heroic the annals of the past and shed luster upon the fortitude, loyalty and self-sacrifice of every section of the union. But in this struggle the cold and calculating spirit of avarice and artificial ambitions will combat the patriotism and fidelity of the people, the seductions of wealth, the corruptions of mercenary greed, the pampered power of government-created and government-protected monopolies, the plausible arguments of scholastic speculation and the sordid schemes of venal statesmanship will all be arrayed against the plain and practical traditions and principles of our institutions and our inherited love of freedom and justice. So far as the men of my state are concerned they are ready for the

Conflict and will not be found to falter in its prosecution. We have not forgotten the heroic periods of our own history. We remember now as did the soldiers of San Jacinto the splendid tragedy of the Alamo and Goliad. We recall the names of our earlier worthies, and as we recollect how they faced the physical despotism of an empire in arms against a handful of hardy pioneers, we are not afraid that our citizenship of this age will be less sturdy and valiant in the great moral, social and political battle that now confronts the whole Union. Texas will make good her right to wear the heritage of her illustrious past, and will be found standing by the side of all the states in the endeavor to rescue the labor and enterprise and freedom of our whole country from the paralytic grasp of monopoly and greed.

At the conclusion of his remarks, Mr. Wooten was given an ovation, and it was some moments before the chairman was able to introduce William Fortune, President of the Indiana State Board of Commerce, who made an earnest plea for conservative procedure as a more hopeful course than the application of revolutionary or too radical measures to an evolutionary problem. He suggested the danger capital may bring to itself by heedless abuse of its power, and indicated the importance to it of seeking proper regulations which will make trust methods acceptable rather than obnoxious to the people by whose permission and toleration only can their existence continue. His speech was a plea for the practicable rather than theoretical approach to the subject, which, in its present stage, the speaker believed to be too immature to give basis for conclusive judgment as to the extent of either its harmful or beneficial effects. He said in the course of his remarks:

WILLIAM FORTUNE.
President Indiana State Board of Commerce.

In the progress of civilization we have advanced step by step in methods of co-operation. In various ways the great institutions of the world have been wrought by union of effort. The instinct of association has made society, the sympathy of aspiration has made the church, appreciation of preparation of the individual for the duties of life has brought to us our educational system, men have been rallied into armies to fight for common cause, and on the demand for equal rights of all in the pursuit of happiness is based the greatest government of the world. These, our cherished institutions, have been made possible by methods of co-operation, and patriots do not cry out against them, but well we know that they would not be held as cherished institutions if there was aught but common good in their aims.

Step by step, the tendency for ages has been toward increase of organized forces. In some of its differentiations this tendency was first resisted, then encouraged and fostered as a rightful means of advancing human welfare where the individual suffered from single-handed strife against the competitive system. The evolution of organization has carried us rapidly through different forms of progress and co-operative beneficence, all of which we have regarded with more of approbation than apprehension, but now when we are confronted with vast developments, which have come by natural processes from social, industrial and economic tendencies, we awaken to the discovery that we have been running with our eyes shut. A startled cry of danger ahead echoes over the land, and in the first flush of excited feeling there is a general demand from the people for protective measures. This demand comes too late to check the tendencies which have gathered irresistible force from the sources of their rise and too early for the formation of unerring judgment as to what may best be done. For the instant we stand as helpless before the vast problem as the spectator of a passing cyclone. We regard it with alarm, we expect to find destruction and wreckage in the path it sweeps, but we know that all will not fall victims to the mighty power of its passing.

A pause for investigation will afford the best preparation for averting whatever may be the dangers of the future. If there is good cause for the present alarm it is well to know as definitely as possible the extent of the harm and how it is wrought. When this is clearly determined we will know better what to do to eradicate the evils and break the power that now terrifies ere it touches people. The clamor raised by politicians may carry them into office, but too often it has no other result to warrant faith in it as a means of solving a great problem. A rush of legislation is apt to be as ineffectual as the premature and misdirected fire of troops who indiscreetly attack before they discover the position and force of the enemy. Much of truth may be revealed or indicated in the discussions at this convention, and there will be much of helpful thought advanced to lead the way to sound conclusions, but there is risk of falling into serious error if we assume that at this stage of approach to the evolutionary problem before us, it is possible to know all that should be known, as the basis of an adequately comprehensive doctrine applicable to commercial combinations.

It is clear that there is both good and evil in the present operations of the trust scheme. In the good features there is enduring vitality; it is the evil that the people will seek to eliminate, and there is nothing surer than that in this they will ultimately succeed. Methods of co-operation which will inure fairly to the benefit of any set of men will not, when understood, be obnoxious to the public; but when, through selfishness and greed, there is a perversion of these methods that results in fraud, in oppression of or exactions from one class for the illegitimate advantage of another class, there is manifestly need for the exercise of the restraining power of government in the maintenance of equitable relations between the people. Common justice and morality demand this. A government by the people will not fail to protect the people in their rights. Dishonesty in capitalization and practices which violate good morals, must, like other criminal acts, be brought under governmental restraint. It will be folly to undertake reckless warfare for the annihilation of trusts, but the claws of the monster, if that it be, can be cut, and, under the restraining influences of good regulations, this Behemoth, biggest born of commerce, may become a docile, harmless and really amiable family pet. It is not to be expected that regulations can be reasonably established which will eliminate individual hardships. We know that economic progress has ever been pitiless in its sacrifices, and that in its conflict with human industry its advance cannot long be hindered. This humanitarian cry against the individual hardships of trusts, however distressing it may be and however much it may appeal to sympathy, will not be more effectual than has been the outcry for the same reason against labor-saving machinery and methods. It is not clear that the power of regulation can be effectively exercised in any other way than by the application of fundamental moral principles for the protection of rights of men and in the interest of public policy. Economic operation is in itself an inexorable law. Theories of revolutionary effect may be helpful indications of what may ultimately come, but, in wise procedure, the first steps should be in the direction of experimental test of powers that have served us well in the past. More radical measures will come if necessary, but, in the light of present knowledge, can any careful thinker say that this problem, now in its evolutionary stages, can best be solved by revolutionary measures? Is it not better to patiently seek to apply practicable thought to the correction of natural tendencies? If radical measures should become necessary their success will be hastened by preceding failure in reasonable efforts, as history proves in the instances of great changes brought about in the past. A wise radical is first a patient conservative.

The danger now most gravely apprehended is not that labor will suffer from combinations of capital, but that aggregated capital will drive out of competitive channels the weaker capital, and that commercial monopoly will result in oppression of multitudes of consumers who have no share in the benefits of combinations. The defensive power of labor, wisely directed through organization, is strong enough to compel capital to accord to it the share due it. There is a nearer approach to identity of interest between the two, which tends to bring them into closer relationship as allies, than ever before. In some instances a primary factor in combinations of capital has been to compel higher prices from the consumer to enable the employers to pay increased wages to employees. The unorganized classes who are consumers and who are accorded no direct benefits from the allied interests of combinations, are the unprotected, but there is ultimate safety for them in their numbers, for they constitute a majority of the people, and if they move in alarm to demand a broader application of the benefits of unity it must be perceived that there are possibilities ahead which have, from the present point of view, chaotic aspects. Labor can well afford to view the situation more complacently than might reasonably be expected from capital, but the pig in the trough is always unmindful of his surroundings while the swill holds out.

While it seems that manipulators and beneficiaries of trusts are heedlessly making the most of their opportunities, it must be recognized that these opportunities exist by permission of the people, and abuses can continue only so long as there is toleration of them. In their quick development they have grown beyond established restrictions. It must be recognized that they spring from ineradicable conditions, and that as larger developments of economic progress they have the elements of vitality from which civilization has derived its greatest strength. Shall they be brought under the regulations which we have sought to establish for the protection of society? Shall they be brought under the light of publicity and examination so that the good and bad in their tendencies can be better determined, so that dishonesty and unfairness in their methods may be discovered, so that the inequitable effects of their operations may be judged? It is the right of society to know if this new-born creature of conditions is humanity's offspring or is a coiled serpent. If it is of us and for us it will have our care, but it should be brought up as a member

56

of the family in the way it should go. More should be known about it than is known now; it should be studied as it grows, but at all times it should be required to conform strictly to the regulations which preserve good morals and protect the rights of the majority. It seems clear enough that it can be regulated; it is doubtful if it can be deprived of existence; we do not know that it is desirable that it should be destroyed; on the contrary, the conditions from which it has grown have brought us our best realizations and it may be, when perfected, our greatest boon. The darkness of ignorance must first be dispelled. Only those who are gifted with the ready assumption of prophecy can tell us all that we want to know, and however interesting this may be, it is not competent evidence. We know enough now to make it clear that the first steps should be in the direction of regulation, and as we proceed with regulation, study the development of the problem. These are practicable gradations of progress, and though the promise be less the results will be quicker than the uncertain realization of Utopian hopes or radical demands."

JOHN GRAHAM BROOKS.

Lecturer University of Chicago.

Mr. Fortune was loudly applauded, as was also Professor John Graham Brooks, who followed, speaking on the subject: "Are the New Combinations Socially Dangerous?" He said:

It is our misfortune that no opinion upon the so-called trust has at present much value. The movement is too new—it is too vast, it is, above all, too undeveloped. People are frightened by the new phenomenon, as many were alarmed a century ago by a quickened tendency of business to pass into corporations. The man of most insight at that time, Adam Smith, thought to quiet the unrest by saying in effect, "Corporations can't do much harm because only a few simple routine branches of business can possibly be carried on by corporations. People won't work for corporations as they will work for themselves."

His ideal was the old common partnership. This partnership was, at a still earlier stage, thought to be very dangerous. Men had hitherto carried on business alone by themselves. The partnership brought them into a common organization. People then considered this a "restraint on trade." What was to become forsooth of manly independence, if several men were to combine their business interests? As the market extended and finer division of labor became possible, the partnership approved itself as the necessary agency of doing business under the new conditions. But the partnership finally reached its limits and a still wider market compelled new and further organization. The utter unfitness of the old partnership has now grown clear to the slowest man upon the street. The corporation slowly took the place of the partnership for an enormous part of the world's business. We have lived to see a large part of the world's work done under corporate form. We have also learned that for nothing will men toil harder than for a corporation. At the close of this century, the instinct toward still vaster and more compact organization is everywhere asserting itself, and again men are frightened. Are there signs that the monster is dangerous to the common weal? It would be very simple-minded to answer by an unqualified yes, or no. We do not say a corporation is good or bad until we know what the corporation is, or does. If the business is properly safeguarded, the corporation renders a social service as essential as the college, the library, or the church. If the larger combinations, now under discussion, can be so far controlled, even as well as a large part of Massachusetts corporations are controlled, I should say " The trust is not to be feared, but to be welcomed." The supreme question that confronts us, is that of possible regulation.

This discussion, if it is to help us, has to assume one momentous fact, viz., the pitiful lack of anything like adequate organization over large areas of industrial life. Several great primary industries are in a state so chaotic as to affront our intelligence. The extreme clumsiness of organization, both in production and distribution, has thus far had no searching investigation. One gets a hint of it when he sees at a single hotel in a small city five drummers competing against each other in selling the same product. I have heard one of the most successful business men in the East say, " If people generally knew how stupidly and wastefully much of the large business is carried on, we should become objects of ridicule." Has not the chairman of the Interstate Commerce Commission himself used the following words about railway management?

"I undertake to say that if the worst enemy of the railroads whom you can name were elected President of the United States, and if he should pack the Interstate Commerce Commission with the worst Populists of the land, those men would never dare to do the reckless and indecent things which the managers of railroads themselves have done. Can you name any five men so ignorant, so prejudiced, so inimical to the common interests of the country that they would upset the commerce of the country and demoralize rates and business in the way the railroad men have done by putting in force the rates that now prevail to the seaboard by way of Galveston from the Missouri River? Would they let the Missouri River rate be as low as the Chicago rate? Would they allow flour to be carried from Minneapolis to the Atlantic cheaper than from Chicago? In such things the railroads are making a fearful misuse of their power."

This puts no slander on the intelligence of the managers; it shows the pass to which an unregulated competition has brought things. What boasting there has been about the marvels of organization in insurance. Yet, I have heard from one of the foremost men in that business this criticism: "It would not be safe to have it known how badly and how extravagantly things are managed, or to what sorry shifts we are driven." I asked in this city a very prominent insurance man if this were fair criticism, and he replied, "Oh, competition has got us now where the only dress we ought to wear is the cap and bells."

It would be silly for an outside observer to offer opinions like these. I am therefore careful to go to competent and unbiased authority. On the avenue in which I live in Cambridge there have come, at the same time, as many different milk concerns as there are houses. This has long been the stock illustration of crude and preposterous lack of method, but the slightest study in detail shows that scores of our great industries have crudities almost as grotesque. To the extent, then, that these charges are true, I submit that the time is at hand for some *kind* of wide, thorough and effective organization. Nor do I believe it open to doubt, that the immense pressure of this necessity is producing the so-called trust. It makes itself far more than it is made. Men will fight it as they fought machinery, and with precisely the same results. From the United States law of 1890 to the various attempts in different states there is thus far no hint that these colossal forces toward new organic forms can be hindered. They can be made worse, as in the anti-pooling legislation. They cannot be stopped. I believe it to be the beginning of practical sense to understand that the new combinations can in no sense be permanently smashed. The party which proposes to do this, in the sense of absolutely checking them, will have plenty of leisure to regret it. The real problem, immediate and imperious, is, how to regulate and guide the new force that stands merely for the latest stage of industrial growth. If the combinations are to work for public as well as for private good, three things, two of them now largely under the voters' control, must be brought

59

about: (1) As absolute a publicity of methods and accounts; (2) Every artificial advantage given by the tariff must be removed. Not to do this, is to allow the trust to play against the community with loaded dice. It is of extreme interest that already Canada has deliberately deprived monopolies of tariff protection. One of the chief practical dangers at the present moment is that the public will be drawn away from the possible *uses* of the trust, to consider far too exclusively the *abuses*. The tariff directly and powerfully aggravates those abuses and thus adds to the general bewilderment. Nor do I mean by this that the tariff, as is often said, causes trusts. The proof that it does not is that free-trade England shows, though on a far more modest scale, all that is essential to these combinations. They spring straight from the new conditions of an intense competition widening into a world market. But no disinterested person will deny that a high tariff strengthens a trust, giving it a power that is purely artificial and one not depending on its own business merits. This difficulty will prove less formidable, as there are plenty of signs already that if trusts show rapid growth they will themselves develop the most powerful antagonism that the tariff ever has met. (3) A third requisite, just as vital, is that railroad discriminations shall not be allowed to these combinations. There is probably no difficulty more desperate than this. No one but a socialist can solve it with gay and final confidence. But whatever the future may have in store, we are not yet ready for state control of railways. For the immediate future (a decade or two) the best intelligence must go to this special evil of railroad discrimination. The trust *plus* special railroad favors can never be other than a danger because it makes directly for an economic inequality that is based on secret privileges that are impudently unfair. What is even more serious, it opens the door to those forms of political corruption that have become the gravest peril to the commonwealth.

I therefore assume that no answer is possible to my subject, "Are the new combinations dangerous?" Unless that measure of control is secured which is represented by (a) complete publicity; (b) removal of tariff privileges; (c) the ending of special railway favors, I should defend this opinion not upon theoretical grounds, but upon such practical experience as one may observe already on the field.

Of these restraints upon abuses, I believe an absolute above-board method of doing business (as complete as that to which the national banks must now submit) to be by far the most important. This remedy lies, moreover, along the line of practical and possible achievement. No one in the community knows better the necessity of such publicity than the very men who make the trusts. Nor have I even heard this necessity stated so strongly and so convincingly as by some of these gentlemen. I say that this remedy is practical because there is now a wide and various experience for our guidance. Germany has plenty of these larger corporations—that we are now discussing under the antiquated name of trusts—but the rights of the stockholders, to every whit of information necessary to their security, are assured in that country. A competent writer upon trusts, like Dr. von Halle, is astounded in his investigations in the United States that a people famous for practical business shrewdness should suffer the gross abuses which this secrecy involves. England has also her powerful "alliances." A good authority has estimated that capital has been shifted from the smaller to the larger corporations to the extent of two billions of dollars within the last dozen years. But the law gives to the stockholder very definite rights of publicity, and the Lord Chief Justice, since the Hooley scandals, says that these rights must be made more exacting still. The forced publicity for private as well as for public corporations in Massachusetts makes any dangerous degree of stock-watering extremely difficult. Evasion in the case of private corporations is still to some degree possible; but it is certain that the law has proved so far successful that it may be made the basis of further legislation of a most hopeful character.

Give us, then, an absolute publicity of methods and special dangers like "over-capitalization" are practically met. If the trust movement spreads, as now seems likely, by far the larger part will go to the wall from sheer speculative bravado. The people meanwhile will be rapidly educated, and above all, the banks will be swift to learn the lesson, and refuse to underwrite if the venture is too daring in its risks. Only those trusts will survive that are prudently organized, and deal with a product which lends itself to the conditions imposed by the new combination. Economic discussion is at last so far popularized that the people will take a passionate interest in the coming debate. Popular economic training always tells if it turn upon vivid concrete events that stir great waves of interest. No industrial event ever gave a more magnificent occasion for education upon what is deepest in the so-called social question. The essence of the new combination is that it is a more cunning, and more powerful machine applied to industry. That means that it carries in it the very heart of the social question. The pithiest formula I could give of the social question (on its material side) is this: It is the struggle for the advantages of applied science and invention to industry. At bottom, this is the fight in our great strikes. The coming contest in our municipalities is accurately this: Who is to control the vast machinery such as lighting and transportation? Socialism itself cannot be better defined than by its attitude toward machinery. Industrial organization on a great scale did not begin until after the Civil War, say 1867. Then, beginning with the railroad, we had an outburst of vast organization of business. At this point trade unions begin an entirely new epoch in their history. They, too, strike for organization on a far wider plan. More significant still: here, too, are the beginnings of large farmers' alliances. Whether as Grangers or as Populists, no one will explain the farmers' movement without constant and closest reference to the angry feeling that the great machine that touched them (the railroad) was somehow used unfairly against the farm interests. Now another period for necessary reorganization is upon us. The mechanism for this is the yet more stupendous combination we are considering. It will do precisely what the great machinery has always done: create temporary disturbance. It will shut hundreds of offices, and drop thousands who were working on the displaced machines. But meantime the new work has to be done under new forms, and when the readjustment comes, more men and not fewer will be required to do it. What right has one to say that? There is now the most absolute proof that the growth of industrial machines is putting to work a larger and larger proportion of the people of the United States. The new combinations that survive are not likely to act differently in this respect from the weaker corporations which preceded them. But the alarm is raised about "absolute monopoly." "The trusts are to corner the very necessities of life." How much evidence do we need to show that this cannot be done? Attempts have been made by the thousand, but almost without exception, it is a history of dismal failure. Certain "practical monopolies" may be formed, and have been formed, but they cannot endure unless they put some kind of economic superiority upon the market. They must serve the consumer better, or they will be crowded from the field. The Standard Oil is too exceptional in its nature to furnish a safe analogy. The sharp geographical limits that shut in our anthracite coal would seem to offer a rare chance for autocratic monopolizing of prices, but a dozen states, filled with soft coal that cannot be monopolized, constitute a powerful and permanent check. Is there a sign that sugar—powerfully organized as it is—can be absolutely monopolized? Or can we imagine bread, shoes, bricks, clothing, lumber to be brought under complete and permanent monopoly? The simple fact that capital is increasing so much faster than population, and is pressing at every point for profitable investment, goes far to prove this fear groundless. This is "the ever possible competition" of which economists have made so much. It acts with increasing and with relentless power to put the monopolist upon his good behavior. Nor does any day pass that does not make the complete monopoly of wide necessities over long periods of time less and less possible. A great deal of money will be made, especially by the earlier successes. But the very nature of the risks makes this inevitable. A bit of history is very wholesome for us on this point.

Whenever a great change has come in economic evolution, there is naturally extreme danger connected with the new undertaking, because traditional methods can not be depended upon. The dangers of disaster are extreme, and only men of great boldness, willing to take larger risks, come to the front. It is this type of man that has caught the wave as it rose, and made, if he succeeded, enormous profits. Human wit has never yet prevented this, and it is more than doubtful if it would be well to do it, if we could. A single illustration is worth giving: When the new organization of the factory began there was such extreme uncertainty, the dangers of disaster were so great, that only the more far-sighted and courageous were willing to take the risks. Those who took them and succeeded, made enormous profits. Profits of 200 per cent, 300 per cent, and 400 per cent were not uncommon in England during the formative period. Does anyone believe that, in the state of knowledge then existing, this rich tribute of the successful could have been stopped? Two things steadily lowered these extraordinary returns to capital: competition, and the control of factory legislation. Very few trusts will make 200 to 300 per cent profits. But nothing under heaven will prevent the daring and successful from reaping for a time unusual rewards from the new ventures. If competition plus legal regulation work now as they have worked, however bunglingly in the past, nothing will long prevent the consuming public from sharing the advantages of the coming organizations. Note further that when the house and village industries were crowded out by the factory, there was extreme and widespread alarm. "What is to become of the independent worker?" it was said; "the factory destroys independence and makes an army of dependents." But after legislation had done its proper work it became clear and indisputable that the dependence of the village and house industry was in every essential point greater than in the factory. The new organization in the long run made for a more complete independence. When competition has reached such terrible limits as it now has in many phases of making and distributing wealth, it is, according to our mood, the climax of humor or pathos to talk too loudly of universal economic independence. As all may observe, it is for a large percentage of small business men a most haphazard and tottering independence.

It is this helter-skelter condition that we have to compare with what the new combinations will eventually bring about.

Once more, it is said of the trusts, "they will raise havoc with our politics." That this is a far graver peril than any economic one is too clear. Recognizing the magnitude of this danger and with no desire to minimize it, I express this hope. The trust that *stays* will bring the very ablest men to the front. They will very soon have to carry on business in an atmosphere of public opinion thoroughly alert and aroused upon these issues. It appears to me very unlikely that men of first ability will so fail in tact as to disregard and affront an alarmed, suspicious and powerful public opinion.

Nor have I the slightest question that if it become plain to the people that the combinations manipulate politics to their own private ends and persist in this, they will have themselves to thank for driving the country further and faster into socialism than any and all forces that have ever shown themselves in our public life.

No disinterested student of this new period of organization that has come upon us will fail to look with alarm at the signs of risk and danger it may bring to organization among the wage-earners. If organization is so all-important, as the capitalist employer claims, the importance cannot be good and necessary at the top alone. It should be good and necessary at the bottom also. Nowhere does competition work more powerfully and more pitilessly than among the laborers. In this desire to see fair play, will not the public insist that if organization be indeed so essential for the employer, it is just as essential for the employed? It is also to be hoped that the exigencies of organization among the laborers will tend (as it does among employers) to bring the really strong and able men to the front in the trade unions?

AZEL F. HATCH.

Member Illinois Bar.

The general movement toward industrial consolidation, which
is recognized and assumed by the call for this conference, did
not come into being without causes, and cannot be explained as a
popular delusion.

Nothing is more conservative than capital. It always clings
to the established order until something better has been demonstrated. When, therefore, we observe great industries forming
into national organizations, changing the form of investment of
hundreds of millions of dollars; when transportation companies
become continental in their spheres of influence; and when this
drift includes within its scope almost everything in manufactures,
transportation and commerce, and almost every form of labor,
we intuitively search for adequate causes.

The rush and roar of the torrent of combinations now attract
the attention of all, and create the impression that the movement
is of present origin simply because we have not observed nor
recognized as capable of their present development the causes
which have for a considerable period been shaping, accumulating
and accelerating the industrial development of the country. For
more than twenty-five years there have been constant efforts, in
the formation of pools, "gentlemen's agreements," trusts and
traffic agreements, to avoid the intolerable conditions which unrestrained competition have produced, and to find a way to make
secure a fair compensation for invested capital. These efforts
have generally failed after short periods of existence, because they
could not be enforced. It was only when some of the states had
passed liberal and comprehensive laws authorizing the formation
of corporations, with powers commensurate with the necessities
of modern methods of business, that an effectual way to combine
and consolidate great industries was found.

Among the causes which have tended to inaugurate the present movement toward consolidation of industries, are to be
found the following:

First—The modern multiplication and perfection of the
means of communication and transmission of intelligence have
rendered possible a vastly enlarged supervision and control by
the individual manager. The telegraph, the telephone, the fast
mail, and the limited express have nearly eliminated time and
distance in his transactions, and the stenographer and typewriter have multiplied his capacity to dispatch business. The

intelligent use of modern facilities for the transaction of business has rendered possible and practical the concentration and consolidation under single management of a magnitude and multiplicity of business interests which a generation ago would have been physically impossible.

Second—The great increase in this country of unemployed capital and the steady decrease of interest rates have made it possible to secure the necessary capital for large enterprises. When, therefore, liberal corporation laws made investments in industrial enterprises secure, a new and attractive field for investment was opened up, and corresponding opportunity and impetus were given to industrial expansion and development.

Third—The enactment of liberal laws authorizing the organization of corporations, with unlimited capital and for the transaction of all kinds of lawful business, has opened up many avenues heretofore closed. The progress toward greater liberality has been general, and in some of the states has been very marked, and during the last twenty years has been more rapid than ever before. This has been a positive and direct stimulus to organization and co-operative investments, and has done much to familiarize the people with investments in corporations.

Fourth—Probably the most potent cause is to be found in the folly and wastefulness of unrestrained competition. Several salesmen striving to secure a single order; making sales without profit or at a loss, to prevent a competitor from selling; the useless multiplication of selling agencies and selling expenses; the necessity of meeting the prices of rivals or necessitous competitors who are selling at less than cost; these practices, and many others almost too foolish and suicidal for credence have converted competition in many industries into a ruinous warfare, destructive to all engaged in the industry. Combination in such cases becomes a means of self-preservation. The simple fact is that the wonderful developments of manufacture in this country, through improved machinery and division of labor and other causes, have reached a stage where the present domestic market is inadequate to keep the wheels in motion. We must restrict production, find new markets, or go into bankruptcy.

Fifth—The enumeration of some of the economies of consolidation is another way of pointing out the loss and wastefulness of the present methods. A consolidation of a large percentage of an industry is able to buy in large quantities and at original sources, and upon correspondingly advantageous terms.

It also sells in large quantities. It can do the business with fewer salesmen and with a smaller number of branches or places of business and at a smaller percentage of expense. By reason of its extent, and because it handles a large percentage of the product of the entire industry, its managers can obtain a better knowledge of the market, and avoid the necessity of carrying large stocks. By diminishing the aggregate of stocks it makes a saving in interest, insurance, storage, and shop wear. By the greater specialization of manufacture, it is enabled to employ the several plants upon those lines of manufacture for which they are best adapted. Those plants which are best equipped can be run full capacity and to the best advantage. The advantages of patents and of special machinery can be more fully utilized. The best quality of goods can be produced, the number of styles diminished, and the best and most profitable kinds of manufacture prosecuted to the full capacity of the plants. Experience and skill and improved methods of manufacture have larger fields for their employment and usefulness, and the grade of goods can be improved by comparative administration of the several plants. The plants situated in various parts of the country can supply the demand in their several neighborhoods, thus saving a large amount of cross-shipments and freights. The ability to reach out for foreign trade and to prepare for and meet every demand is very greatly enlarged. In the case of fire, flood, or local strikes, the work goes on elsewhere, and prevents loss upon contracts or loss in trade. The terms of sale are more uniform and the credits safer.

I think the foregoing causes explain to some extent why the proprietors of industrial enterprises have recently received suggestions of combination with so much favor. They show how and why such combinations can be accomplished now more readily than formerly.

It does not follow, however, because economies and advantages in consolidation are found in one industry, that they are to be found to the same degree or at all in every other industry. While it is undoubtedly true that some of the advantages above mentioned will generally apply to combinations, the degree of benefit must be largely determined by the nature, extent, and situation of the industry.

If it be admitted or stands proven that combinations in an industry, when properly managed, are economical; that they prevent waste and more fully utilize the fruits of industry, the conclusion follows that they are a natural evolution in industrial progress and are analogous to all other improvements in business, like improved machinery, department stores, and improved facilities in transportation.

If the foregoing conclusions are sound then industrial combinations have come to stay. The world of industry is not marching backward. Nor is it an evidence to the contrary that some are injured by combinations. Every advance leaves somebody behind. All improvements which work economies result in displacing certain elements of labor. Consolidations will displace salesmen, will close stores, and in some cases manufactories, and will dispense with the services of middlemen, just as the reaper and mower displaced the scythe and the cradle, and the threshing machine the flail and the threshing floor. The railroad rendered the stage antiquated and displaced thousands engaged in the old methods of transportation. The sewing machine threw thousands of needle workers out of employment, but the ultimate result of all these changes in industry was for the advantage of the whole community, notwithstanding the hardship to some individuals.

That criticism which calls every corporation or consolidation a trust, and which condemns every aggregation of capital as a public danger, is both ignorant and vicious. Corporations are no better nor worse than the individuals who manage them. Some are law-abiding and are entitled to the same protection of the laws and the same support and encouragement in developing the resources of the country and in affording employment to its inhabitants, that are given to the public-spirited individual. The powerful always need restraint. Great corporations are no exception to this rule. They should be compelled to observe the same methods of business, to obey the same laws, and to confine their operations to the same limits to which individuals are confined. They must be compelled to pay their share of taxes and to bear their portions of public burdens. They must be fair in their methods of competition. They must be held to terms of equality in freights and in all other semi-public dealings. No public favors, by tariffs or otherwise, should be extended to them.

Some of the dangers to the public from these organizations are to be found in the great power placed in the hands of single individuals, and in their ability to influence legislation and to become factors in political management and manipulation. This danger emphasizes the necessity of removing every temptation to influence legislation on the part of the man in business. Aside from tariff legislation, there is little which can affect the interest

68

of manufacturers or those engaged in general commerce, but this is a danger which has long been in existence, and the evils of which are not confined to present or future combinations. All of the methods of unfair competition which have been employed, may, in the hands of a great organization, become greatly intensified and aggravated. The public should be protected against all such aggressions and all of the evil-doers, whether great corporations or powerful individuals, should be punished alike.

It is not to be gainsaid that these organizations are beset by numerous dangers. The loss of the good-will of the business of the constituent members of the consolidation is one of its greatest dangers. There is always the possible danger that managers of sufficient ability to control, direct, and successfully manage a great corporation cannot be found. It is one thing to manage a small business under the immediate observation of its owner, and another to successfully manage a large number of plants scattered all over the United States, and aggregating, in the volume of trade and business, many times any one of its constituent parts. There is always the danger that the individual interest of the local managers will not be aroused and their best efforts will not be secured in the same sense that they are in the case of private ownership. These are matters to be determined by experience, and if these combinations are to succeed, methods must be found to enlist the thorough and consistent efforts of all of the employes of these great organizations.

Some of the changes which are brought about by the great consolidations in progress are factors of business safety. In every consolidation there is a great liquidation of the indebtedness of the several concerns entering into the consolidation. The lines of credit theretofore extended to the several constituent concerns are extinguished. The new company generally begins business with a large cash working capital. If it has debts, they are in the form of long-term bonds, instead of demand accounts and short-time notes, which in times of contraction and financial distress become an element of danger. The movement to that extent becomes a contraction of credit, and is an element of conservatism and safety. The large organizations are generally doing business upon a cash basis, or upon a more conservative basis than the constituent members of which the organization was composed. This is true to such an extent that there has been a noticeable decrease in the amount of commercial paper offered at financial centers during the last few months.

Another element of safety is found in the ability to oversee the field of industry and prevent unnecessary and ruinous gluts in the market. A man who manufactures and sells but two or three per cent of the products in an industry never can be sure that his business indicates the general condition of the trade, but the manager who handles sixty or seventy per cent of the products of that industry can much more safely gauge the extent of the market and the future demand. This tends to prevent an unnecessary extension of credit and an overproduction in manufacture.

Another factor of safety is to be found in the ability to enlarge the market by the extension of foreign trade and by the steadier and safer market due to the extent of the domestic sales. The larger and broader the market, the steadier and safer it is.

Again, by means of the great extent of the corporation and the placing of its securities upon the general exchanges of the country, its stock becomes distributed among a large number of holders, and has a known value and a ready market. The organization thereby becomes a distributer rather than a concentrator of wealth. Where the original owners were numbered by hundreds, the ultimate stockholders are numbered by thousands.

The control of prices, which is often apprehended, can be brought about permanently only by such a superiority in the methods of manufacture as will successfully defy competition. Any price established by a combination which enables competitors to make a reasonable profit will soon encourage such competition as will reduce the price. No permanent monopoly, not founded upon some governmental privilege in the nature of a patent or a public license or a tariff protection, can long exist, unless founded upon the superior excellence and economy in manufacture. The present combinations do not destroy competition. They, on the contrary, are themselves the creatures of competition. The fundamental cause of these combinations has been an effort for self-preservation against the evils of unrestrained competition. The wise manager of a combination, even if he has it within his power temporarily to control the prices in any industry, will not raise those prices to a point which encourages the establishment of competing plants. The economies of consolidation and a fair return upon capital invested afford a sufficient protection and encouragement to every consolidation without an attempt to control prices.

While a corporation engaged in a private business, and holding no rights or privileges by public grants, is under no obligation to disclose its business to the public generally, any more than an individual in the same business, the managers, officers, and directors of every corporation are trustees for its stockholders, and are bound to exercise perfect good faith toward them. Any concealment from such stockholders which operates to their injury, and every advantage gained by the trustee which he appropriates to his personal gain, is a plain dereliction of duty, and should be punished by law. Stockholders should have access to the books and records of the corporation at all reasonable times, and should have the power to compel disclosure of all information necessary for the protection of their interests. All corporations which appeal to public support by placing their stocks upon the public exchanges, thus inviting investment by the public in their securities, should give the greatest degree of publicity to their affairs. If the public are invited generally to invest in the securities of a corporation, the truthfulness of all representations made should be enforced, and the same degree of publicity to which the stockholder is entitled should be extended to the public. This is founded not on any supposed right of the public to pry into the private business of people associated in the form of a corporation, but to prevent fraud and imposition upon the public in selling the stocks of corporations. This publicity should be enforced not only by the stock exchanges where these stocks are dealt in, but by public statute. If I am invited to buy the stock of a corporation, I have a right to know what assets it represents, and what its earnings and expenses are, and all the details which give light upon the value of the stock, and, having bought the stock, I have a right to know how my interest in the company is being administered by its officers and directors.

This publicity would make overcapitalization comparatively harmless. The facts which go to the question of success of the business of a corporation are those which determine whether or not it is doing its business at a profit, and whether or not it is indebted. If it is free from debt and doing business at a profit, it is immaterial, so far as the business success of the corporation is concerned, whether its stock be worth ten or a hundred, or whether it be one million or ten millions in amount. Multiplying the number of shares of a corporation does not affect its assets nor its earning power. It is difficult to understand how an attempt to pay dividends on a large capitalization increases prices, as some claim, unless we assume that the managers of corporations with small capitalizations do not try to make as large profits as they can, and voluntarily depress prices to their own disadvantage. We have never discovered such a charitable disposition in business, even among managers of corporations organized on a cash basis. It is safe to assume that everyone in business will make his profits as large as he can. Overcapitalization is a danger to the investor, rather than to the corporation or to the public dealing with the corporation. It is a kind of inflation. It amounts to a creation of fictitious stock, which affords an opportunity to impose upon the unwary investor. This is an evil wherever there is any concealment of the affairs of the corporation. Issuing a false prospectus or a false statement of a corporation ought to be punishable here, as it is in England.

R. S. TAYLOR.

Member Indiana Bar.

At the beginning of the recent remarkable movement toward large combinations in business, the organizations were in the form of trusts, properly so called. The associated corporations put their stock, with its voting power, into the hands of a trustee or trustees; and so, while the different corporations retained their separate legal existence, they became subject to a single, central control. Such arrangements are very vulnerable. They are so plainly combinations in restraint of trade that they are easily reached under the law. Hence they have been, for the most part, abandoned and replaced by great, single corporations; and these, for want of a better name, we continue, quite inappropriately, to call trusts. But it is material to note that the things with which we have to deal are corporations, lawful and regular in form and ostensible objects, and differing from the ordinary corporation only in the scale of their operations.

Legal remedies are directed against legal wrongs. The ascertainment of the wrong logically precedes the study of the remedy. What real harm, therefore, do these great corporations do or threaten to society which calls for intervention by the law?

It is manifest that we are just now in the midst of a trust craze. But that will have its day, and end probably in a crash. Many persons who are investing in the inflated stocks and bonds of these "industrials" will suffer heavily. That the law should lay some restraining hand on the formation of such organizations for the protection of investors is very obvious and very easy to say.

But the interest of investors in the shares of such enterprises is a small consideration beside the interest of the general mass of the people whose food, clothing, and transportation are controlled by them. Nothing can be more certain than that the

WILLIAM JENNINGS BRYAN   W. BOURKE COCKRAN
CHARLES FOSTER   HENRY W. BLAIR

day of small, divided, competing industrial organizations has gone by. The growth of corporations is one feature of the universal evolution. The big ones we have are here to stay in some form, and grow larger, rather than smaller. They will survive the collapse of their inflated capitalization just as the railroads have survived a like experience. What harm will they do to society as permanent institutions?

There is one result attending them which it is impossible to contemplate without a feeling of regret, whether the feeling be entirely justifiable or not. It is the limitation of individual opportunity and the diminution of individual independence which the new order involves. But these are inseparable concomitants of the system. They can be prevented by law only by forcibly breaking up the large organizations and compelling men to go back to the old business methods. That, I assume, is not regarded as possible by any intelligent man.

The other most important result of the aggregation of business in few hands, and the one which we think and talk about most, is the control which it places in the hands of the great organizations over production, supply and prices. Does this menace the welfare of society, and is there any legal remedy for that wrong?

Such a situation contains within itself some elements of self-regulation against extremes. The putting of a very extravagant price on a commodity defeats its own purpose by breeding insuppressible competition, or, if the price be maintained, by restricting the market. But within these limitations there is a margin of overcharge which will yield a maximum of profit and may be permanently maintainable. One mill per pound on sugar would mean about half a cent a month per capita for the people of the United States—not much of a burden, even if it were an unjust one, but amounting in the aggregate to $4,500,000 per annum. If the sugar trust is doing 75 per cent of the business of the country, as is said to be the case, and receiving one-tenth of a cent a pound more than a just price, it is taking from the people more than three and a third million dollars a year to which it is not in justice entitled. And with its terrible power to punish competition, it might be able to maintain that unjust imposition permanently. That may be, and probably is, in some measure, what the Standard Oil Company has been doing for years past— enforcing prices so little too high that they do not invite dangerous competition, nor provoke violent resistance from consumers, but enough too high to constitute a wrong toward the public of great magnitude in the aggregate. If all commodities should be brought under similar control by like organizations and treated in the same way, the immensity of the robbery of the public would be enormous, and none the less robbery because perpetrated by means of infinitesimally small extortions. It is to some such complexion as this that the present development seems to me to point as its ultimate result.

Here we have elements of permanent and serious evil. The levying of unjust prices, or the exercise of unjust, arbitrary control over production or exchange is a wrong, simple, primary and direct, which is not mitigated by its skillful distribution among its subjects in such manner that they can bear it, and live to bear it to the natural end of life. The building up of vast fortunes in few hands by means known to be iniquitous but nevertheless tolerated by law, and the discontent and disloyalty to government and law which such things are bound to produce, are evils even greater in magnitude.

Here we have, to my mind, the main problem. How shall we distinguish among corporations? Shall we put arbitrary limitations upon their capital or the amount of business they may do, or the territory they may occupy with their trade? Shall we attempt to exercise a control by law over the great ones which we do not exercise over the small ones? In the exercise of that control, shall we prescribe prices by law, and undertake to say beforehand how much the sugar trust and the Standard Oil Company shall charge the people for sugar and oil? Is the legislature wise enough to exercise such a power safely? If it were, could it do it without impairing the principle of free competition?

In nearly all our legislation, so far, we have followed the theory of the common law that the power to control the production and prices of commodities is one so sure to be abused that it is too dangerous to be entrusted to anyone, and that the remedy against such wrongs is to forbid outright all organizations and combinations of men the effect or operation of which will be to put that power in their hands. But nothing can be clearer than the ineffectualness of such laws to meet present conditions. For years past, the states have been enacting them in terms of increasing severity, while the trusts and combines have been thriving as though anti-monopoly statutes were only food for their growth. We shall gain nothing by persevering in that direction. The law must change its methods. It must direct its prohibitions and penalties against the real wrongs. It is impossible to meet the conditions of 1900 with the laws of 1700. We must recognize and deal with the situation as it is.

It does not hurt us to get our sugar from one trust and our oil from another, if we get them at fair prices. It does not hurt us that railroads agree on rates, if they are fair ones. If the courts of the United States had been at liberty in dealing with the Trans-Missouri Freight Association to inquire into the justness and fairness of the rates fixed by it, the merits of the question could have been considered and the real wrong, if there was any, would have been reached. But the Sherman bill, as the Supreme Court decided, gave the court no such power. It was compelled to declare the association illegal because it was forbidden; and it was forbidden because there was, in the judgment of the law, danger that it would use its power to injure the public. If the Constitution would give Congress power over the whole subject of railroad transportation, state as well as interstate, and Congress would give the courts the power to investigate rates, charges, rules, and regulations which it has given to the Inter-State Commerce Commission, and render judgments accordingly, or would give the Inter-State Commerce Commission the powers of a court, little more would be required to put that great department of public concern under the complete control of the law.

I think the time is ripe for this step forward. The Inter-State Commerce Commission has done an invaluable work, one beneficial in its immediate results, but still more valuable in leading the way toward a more perfect system. The people are quite prepared in their minds now for governmental supervision of railway rates; not the fixing of rates in advance, but the declaration by law of principles upon which rates shall be established and a compulsion by law of the observance of those principles. We have come to this frame of mind with regard to railroads because the combinations and consolidations which they have made among themselves have placed the public at their mercy. Nothing but the strong hand of the government can protect the people from extortion by the railroads if they choose to practice it.

We have not quite reached the same attitude of mind with regard to commodities. But when we come to the point at which all commodities will be supplied to us as sugar and oil are now, each by a single concern powerful enough to control the trade of the country in its line, and the fact becomes apparent that that vast centralization of control is to be a permanent condition, we shall be as ready for governmental interference in those fields as we are now with regard to railroads. If we are to have such interference, it is none too soon to begin to feel our way toward it now.

He would be one of those who "rush in where angels fear to tread" who would undertake to formulate offhand a plan for dealing with so great and difficult a problem. But a man would confess his disbelief in the capacity of the race for self-government who should give it up as unsolvable. It is the glory of the common law that it grows with the needs of society, and, either by its own processes, or by pointing the way to the necessary legislation, finds an adequate remedy for every new wrong. The wrong to be remedied in the case of oppressive dealing with the public by the trusts is the abuse of a power over production and trade secured by great aggregation of capital and working instrumentalities in the imposition of unjust prices. Where a wrong of that kind has been perpetrated, it ought to be possible to allege and prove the fact and punish the perpetrator. While the law is not wise enough to say what the price of sugar ought to be next year, it ought to be able to find out with reasonable certainty whether or no a given price was a fair one last year.

A bit of useful side-light is thrown upon the trust problem by its analogy with the labor problem. The labor union is only another form of trust and combination. Every organized strike, the object of which is to compel an employer by some kind of punishment to do something that he is unwilling to do is as distinctly unlawful by all the law in the books as the combination of employers to control prices or production. And yet we cannot abolish labor unions by law. No one is proposing to do it. The people will not permit it. It would be ruinous to the best interests of society to do it. If workingmen were forbidden to organize—if each one of them were required to make his own terms with the great employers and hold his place at his employer's mere option—they would speedily become slaves, eating their bread by the grace of their masters. Having permitted and recognized the unions, we must allow them to make their organization effective, if it is to mean anything; and this, not by mere argument, or persuasion, or entreaty, which would avail nothing with certainty, if it were certain that nothing more could follow; but by meeting threat with threat and compulsion with compulsion. When the employer says, "Come to my terms, or go without your dinner," the union must be permitted to answer, "Come to our terms, or shut up your shop."

Combinations of capital and combinations of labor are alike inevitable concomitants of social growth, steps in the evolution of the race. The forces which impel them are stronger than the law. It seems sad that it should be so; that just as the white banner of international peace is lifted at the Hague, the grim spectre of industrial war should confront us at home. But so it is.

The unions are here, and here to stay. Society approves them. The great tribunal of public opinion, the final supreme court, has decided that they and their proceedings, even to punishment and compulsion of employers, are lawful and necessary. It is for the law to admit that fact, put the unions into the category of institutions to be recognized, controlled, and governed, and provide suitable proceedings for that purpose.

Exactly the same thing is true of the great corporations. It is useless to persevere in the course we have been following, to make our laws more and more drastic, to try in that way to break up the great combinations now existing, and prevent others, and so bring business back to the conditions of forty years ago. We must face the situation as it is; recognize the great corporations as institutions to be dealt with according to their greatness, their power of evil, and the danger of their abuse of their powers. We must define the wrongs which are to be feared from them, and provide means for the adequate investigation and punishment of those wrongs.

This will tax the wisdom of the legislature to its utmost and put on the courts burdens which they have never borne before. It will require judicial investigations into wages, prices, profits, risks, and all the elements that enter into the conduct of business. It will incorporate into the law and its administration much that now belongs to the domain of economics. It will compel disclosures by the corporations which they will be very unwilling to make. It will make it necessary for them to do business in daylight and have no secrets from the state. It will make an end of fictitious stocks and bonds. While giving full play to invention, enterprise, organization, and every form of human effort, it will impose on all the one condition of universal fair dealing.

A. LEO WEIL.

Member Pennsylvania Bar.

Parallels to the apprehended evils from the present era of concentration may be found in the evils once predicted from all forms of association—evils long since proved to have existed in imagination only, and finally so recognized by solemn legislative enactment or formal judicial decision.

At first the Roman law required no special state authorization to form a corporation. Under the empire special permission from the state became necessary, which the pagan emperors granted reluctantly.

Thus we find Pliny the Younger suggesting to the Emperor Trajan the advisability of forming a company of firemen, adding: "I will take care none but those of that business shall be admitted into it, and that the privileges granted them shall not be applied to any other purpose. As this corporated body will be restricted to so small a number of members, it will be easy to keep them under regulations."

To this reasonable request the Emperor replied, declining to grant the necessary permission, adding, "Whatever name we give to them, and for whatever purposes they may be founded, they will not fail to form themselves into factious assemblies, however short their meetings may be."—(Pliny's Epist., B. 10, Lets. 42 and 43.)

The English statute of 6 Geo. I. Cap. 18, declared that where there was no act of incorporation, the practice of making subscriptions for commercial undertakings, with the certificates of subscribers transferable, was a common nuisance.

In a case in which an indictment was found under this statute against a number of parties who had agreed to raise two hundred shares of £210 each, by paying in monthly installments, in order to build houses for one another, it was said that such clubbing together for the purpose of carrying on trade was calculated to put down individual industry and competition, which are most advantageous to the public.—(Pratt vs. Hutchinson, 15 East, pp. 516-517.)

Many similar decisions were rendered. Without reference to the statute, but at common law, beginning with Lord Eldon, the courts of England held that companies with large capital, arising from numerous small contributions, were injurious to the public and illegal; though at a later period, Lord Brougham decided this question the other way. For a considerable period, the formation of partnership associations for purposes of trade was prohibited under severe fines and penalties. Compare the state of the public mind of that era with the notion to-day, which favors the partnership association as against the corporation.

Were it not for its quaint and now obsolete terms, this old English statute of 6 Geo. I, so commemorative of popular error, might be mistaken for a *resume* of the speeches of some of our modern prophets, who pretend to foresee the evils of industrial consolidations.

"Whereas, it is notorious that several undertakings or projects of different kinds have, at some time or times been publickly contrived and practised, or attempted to be practised, which manifestly tend to the common grievance, prejudice and inconvenience of great numbers of your Majesty's subjects in their trade and commerce, and other their affairs; and the persons who contrive or attempt such dangerous and mischievous undertakings or projects, under false pretences of publick good, do presume, according to their own devices and schemes, to open books for publick subscriptions, and draw in many unwary persons to subscribe therein towards raising great sums of money whereupon the subscribers or claimants under them do pay small proportions thereof, and such proportions in the whole do amount to very large sums, * * * * And whereas in many cases the said undertakers or subscribers have * * * presumed to act as if they were corporate bodies, and have pretended to make their shares of stocks transferable or assignable, without any legal authority, either by act of parliament, or by any charter from the crown for so doing; * * * and many other unwarrantable practices (too many to enumerate) have been and daily are and may hereafter be contrived, set on foot, or proceeded upon, to the ruin and destruction of many of your Majesty's good subjects, if a timely remedy be not provided; and whereas it is become absolutely necessary that all publick undertakings and attempts, tending to the common grievance, prejudice and inconvenience of your Majesty's subjects in general, or great numbers of them, in their trade, commerce or other lawful affairs, being effectually suppressed and restrained for the future, by suitable and adequate punishments for that purpose to be ascertained and established."

This statute, with its solemn enumeration of grievances, which the logic of time and events clearly demonstrated were not the essentials of such associations, was expurgated from the English system of laws, and in its place were substituted enactments giving the utmost freedom of organization, without limitation as to capital or purpose. Modern jurists, political economists and students of public affairs entertain very different views of the utility of associated capital:

Judge Caton: "Corporations have become among the greatest means of state and national prosperity." 19 Ill., 353.

Judge Gibson: "The combination of capital for purposes of commerce, or to carry on any other branch of industry, although it may in its consequences indirectly operate on third persons * * * is a common means of the ordinary course of human affairs which stimulates to competition and enables men to engage in undertakings too weighty for one individual." Commonwealth vs. Carlisle, 1 Brightly.

Another Court said: "Associations are so common an element, not only to commerce, but to all affairs of life, that it would be rather perilous on the part of the court to assert that they impair competition, destroy emulation and diminish exertion. There is scarcely an occupation in life, scarcely a branch of trade from the very largest to the smallest, that does not feel the exciting and invigorating influence of this wonderful instrumentality." Jones vs. Fell, 5 Fla. 510.

Judge Field: "As a matter of fact, nearly all enterprises in this state, requiring for their execution the expenditure of large capital, are undertaken by corporations. They engage in commerce; they build and sail ships; they cover our navigable streams with steamers; they construct houses; they bring the products of earth and sea to market; they light our streets and buildings; they open and work mines; they carry water into our cities; they build railroads and cross mountains and deserts with them; they erect churches, colleges, lyceums, and theaters; they set up manufactories, and keep the spindle and shuttle in motion; they establish banks for savings; they insure against accidents on land and sea; they give policies on life; they make money exchanges with all parts of the world; they publish newspapers and books, and send news by lightning across the continent and under the ocean. Indeed, there is nothing that is lawful to be done to feed and clothe our people, to beautify and adorn their dwellings, to relieve the sick, to help the needy, to enrich and ennoble humanity, which is not to a great extent done through the instrumentality of corporations." Railroad Tax Cases, 13 Fed. Rep. 743.

John Stuart Mill (Political Economy, Vol. 1, p. 189,) says: "When markets are large and a large opening for exportation, large systems of business are effective. Large establishments are substituted for small ones. This change from small to large is wholly beneficial. It may have some drawbacks, but when once the system of large establishments is established, the change from large to larger systems is an unqualified benefit."

Again, (p. 510):

"The progress of productive arts requiring that many sorts of industrial occupations should be carried on by large and larger capitals, the productive power of industry must suffer by whatever impedes the formation of large capitals through the aggregation of smaller ones."

Henry G. Carey says:

"That the more perfect the power of association the greater

the power of production, and the larger the proportion of the product which falls to the laborer's share."

Professor Sumner says:

"There is every indication that we are to see new developments of the power of aggregated capital to serve civilization and that the new developments will be made right here in America. Joint stock companies are yet in their infancy; and incorporated capital, instead of being a thing which can be overturned, is a thing which is becoming more and more indispensable. * * Aggregated capital will be more and more essential to the performance of our social tasks. * * * This tendency is in the public interest. * * * We are to see the development of the country pushed forward at an unprecedented rate by an aggregation of capital, and a systematic application of it under the direction of competent men. This development will be for the benefit of all."

While it is now generally conceded that corporations or associated capital are a necessary part of our trade and industrial system, yet it is sometimes said that these large corporations, formed by the consolidation of a number of industrial enterprises, with their great capitalization and their solidarity of management, will prevent competition, create monopoly, be hurtful to labor, and thereby prove injurious to the public. Again, it may be observed, these prophets of evil are forgetting the lessons of history, are ignoring the changed conditions under which we now live, and have misused terms.

Replying to those who would prevent consolidations, commonly called "trusts," I maintain:

Legislative restrictions upon trade have always proved baneful, and, in most cases, have only aggravated the evils they sought to prevent.

Consolidations, understood as the amalgamation of a number of industrial plants, do not prevent that kind of competition which is beneficial to the public, and do not create monopolies.

Consolidation, instead of being an injury, is a benefit to labor.

Large capitalization is a relative term, and considered with reference to the present trade conditions, the capital employed is not larger than is necessary successfully to carry on such enterprises.

Consolidations are the outgrowth and the symptom of the advancing civilization of to-day, and the inevitable tendency of its complex trade conditions.

Reverting again to English history, we find the ancient prototype of the modern statute which proposes restraint upon trade.

In 1552 the statute of 5 and 6 Ed. VI, Cap. 14, enumerates certain offenses against trade, under the titles of regrating, forestalling and ingrossing, and shows that even prior to that time such laws had existed, but were not enforced. Thus it begins:

"Albeit divers good statutes heretofore have been made against forestallers of merchandises and victuals, yet for that good laws and statutes against regrators and ingrossers of the same things have not been heretofore sufficiently made and provided, and also for that it hath not been perfectly known what person should be taken for a forestaller, regrator or ingrosser, the said statutes have not taken good effect, according to the minds of the makers thereof, etc."

Briefly stated, a forestaller was defined as a person who bought goods when they were on their way to market; a regrator was one who bought in any market certain food products and victuals that had been brought to market to sell, and sold the same again in the same market or any other market within four miles therefrom; an ingrosser was one who obtained "by buying, contracting or promise taking" any "grain, butter, cheese, fish or other dead victuals whatsoever," with intent to sell again.

This act visited severe penalties for any of these offenses, the offender on a third conviction being set on the pillory, forfeiting all his goods and remaining in prison during the king's pleasure. These laws were thought necessary in the infancy of trade to preserve competition. The statutes of that age abound in the most minute regulations of trade, as, for example, "An act for stuffing of feather beds, bolsters, mattresses and cushions," (5 and 6 Edw. VI, Cap. 23), which begins, "For the avoiding of the great deceit used and practiced in stuffing of feather beds, bolsters, pillows, mattresses, cushions and quilts," etc.

Under the statute against forestalling, regrating and ingrossing, many prosecutions were had. The arguments of counsel and the opinions of the courts cover almost the same ground now gone over in the attacks upon consolidation. We have such judges as Lord Eldon and Lord Kenyon pronouncing tirades from the bench against these crimes—crimes forsooth—to buy goods on the way to market; to buy goods in market to sell again; to buy any grain or food stuffs to sell again. Thus in Rex vs. Rusby, (Peake's Nisi Prius Cases, 189), decided in 1800, Lord Kenyon aired his views, and in a scathing charge to the jury secured the conviction of Rusby, who was guilty of the heinous crime of buying 250 bushels of oats, and selling the same at a profit of six cents a bushel. This in part is what he charged the jury:

"This case presents itself to your notice on behalf of all ranks, rich and poor, but more especially the latter. Though in a state of society some must have greater comforts and luxuries than others, yet all should have the necessaries of life; and if the poor cannot exist, in vain may the rich look for happiness and prosperity. * * *

"The law has not been disputed; for though in an evil hour all the statutes which had been existing above a century were at one blow repealed, yet, thank God, the provisions of the common law were not destroyed. * * *

"Even amongst the laws of the Saxons are to be found many wise provisions against forestalling and offenses of this kind, and those laws laid the foundation of our common law. That it remains an offense nobody has controverted. * * * Speculation has said that the fear of such an offense is ridiculous, and a very learned man, a good writer, has said you might as well fear witchcraft. I wish Dr. Adam Smith had lived to hear the evidence of to-day, and then he would have seen whether such an offense exists, and whether it is to be dreaded. If he had been told that cattle and corn were brought to market, and then bought by a man whose purse happened to be longer than his neighbor's, so that the poor man who walks the streets and earns his daily bread by his daily labor could get none but through his hands, and at the price he chose to demand; that it had been raised three pence, six pence, nine pence and more per quarter, on the same day, would he have said there was no danger from such an offense?"

Just think of it. This crime was nothing more than what is now the occupation of every jobber, broker, and wholesaler. He bought 250 bushels of oats, which he afterwards sold at a profit of 6 cents a bushel. This charge was given after the passage of the Act of 12 Geo. III., c. 71, repealing the laws against regrating, ingrossing, forestalling, etc., but Lord Kenyon decided that these acts were common law offenses, and the courts generally of that date, urged thereto by the clamor of the masses, still continued to entertain charges of this character. Men who were engaged in buying grain to sell again, who bought in market to sell again, who bought goods on their way to market to sell again, were prosecuted, and sometimes convicted and punished. It was the same cry, the demand for free competition, the protection of the weak against the strong, the prevention of monopoly, that we now hear. At last Parliament, by 7 & 8 Vict. cap. 29, in response to the demand of a more enlightened public sentiment, struck down at one blow about forty of these so-called regulations, after reciting that they had proved an injury to trade, and especially to those for whose protection they were designed, thus:

"Whereas, divers statutes have been from time to time made in the Parliaments of England, Scotland, Great Britain and Ireland, respectively, prohibiting certain dealings in wares, victuals, merchandise and various commodities, by the names of badgering, forestalling, regrating and ingrossing, and subjecting to divers punishments, penalties and forfeitures persons so dealing: And whereas, it is expedient that such statutes, as well as certain other statutes made in hindrance and in restraint of trade, be repealed: And whereas, an act of the Parliament of Great Britain was passed in the twelfth year of the reign of King George the Third, entitled an Act for repealing several laws therein mentioned against badgers, ingrossers, forestallers and regrators, and for indemnifying persons against prosecutions for offenses committed against the said acts, whereby, after reciting that it had been found by experience that the restraint laid by several statutes upon the dealing in corn, meal, flour, cattle, and sundry other sorts of victuals, by preventing a free trade in the said commodities, have a tendency to discourage the growth and to enhance the price of the same, which statutes, if put in execution, would bring great distress upon the inhabitants of many parts of this kingdom, and in particular upon those of the cities of London and Westminster," * * *

After this preamble follows the most sweeping repeal of some forty or more statutes and the formal declaration that badgering, ingrossing, forestalling, and regrating were not offenses, and no prosecutions could be had therefor.

This is what Buckle (Vol. I., p. 277) says of the laws repealed by the above statute, and of like amendments:

"Every European Government which has legislated respecting trade has acted as if its main object were to suppress the trade and ruin the traders. Instead of leaving the national industry to take its own course, it has been troubled by an interminable series of regulations, all intended for its good, and all inflicting serious harm. To such a height has this been carried that the commercial reforms which have distinguished England during the last twenty years have solely consisted in undoing this mischievous and intrusive legislation. It is no exaggeration to say that the history of the commercial legislation of Europe presents every possible contrivance for hampering the energies of commerce. In every quarter and at every moment the hand of Government was felt. Bounties to raise up a losing trade and taxes to pull down a remunerative one, this branch of industry forbidden and that branch of industry encouraged. Laws to regulate wages, laws to regulate prices, laws to regulate profits, interference with markets, interference with manufactories, interference with machinery, interference even with shops."

There were those, and they were in the majority, who looked to these regulations as their only protection, and who thought that society would be overwhelmed if they were removed. As has been shown, learned judges shared these views; yet experience demonstrated that the progress of trade and the good of society were hampered, not helped, by these attempts at regulation. These laws and decisions were made at the time when trade was primitive, when there was no middleman, when the producer sold to the consumer direct. They were intended to prevent the entree of the jobber, the wholesaler and the broker upon the stage of commerce, for whose entree the evolution of trade had given the cue. They were futile. They could not prevent that trade progression which the march of civilization demanded. They could not understand that nature's law of competition would assert its supremacy in the more complex conditions of trade that accompanied the advent of the middleman. This confounding of the prevalent form of competition with the principle itself has been and is at the root of all the reactionary attempts to restrict trade by law from that day to this.

It may with propriety be assumed that at some future date the student of events will clearly see that the attempts of to-day at the restriction of industrial combinations, which are also steps in the evolution of trade, were as unnecessary and as ridiculous as appear to us those laws against regrating, forestalling, and ingrossing, those laws which sought to punish the middleman as a criminal. Macaulay was truly prophetic when, writing of the opposition once made to the introduction of fast stage coaches in England, he said: "We smile at these things. It is not impossible that our descendants when they read the opposition offered by cupidity and prejudice to the improvements of the nineteenth century, may smile in their turn." We have already had our laugh, we are now furnishing means for the amusement of our own descendants.

If consolidation of industrial plants prevented competition and created monopolies, all thinking men would condemn them; but if, as some believe, they only prevent that competition which is injurious and stimulate that competition which is beneficial to the public, then instead of curses they are blessings.

It is never justifiable to appeal to deep-seated prejudices by simply using terms and phrases when the circumstances do not warrant the application of such terms. Monopoly is offensive to every liberty-loving people. Even the word arouses antagonism from every fiber of a freeman's nature. Why is this so? Monopoly is a relic of tyranny, and was one of the most odious exercises of tyranny. Monopoly was thus defined by Lord Coke:

"An institution or allowance by the King, by his grant, commission or otherwise, to person or persons, bodies political or corporate, of or for the sole buying, selling, making, working or using of anything whereby any person or persons, bodies politic or corporate, are sought to be restrained of any freedom of liberty they had before, or hindered in their lawful trade" (7 Bacon's Abridgement, 22).

The Supreme Court of the United States defines monopoly with reference to present conditions thus:

"The withdrawing of that which is a common right from the community and vesting it in one or more individuals, to the exclusion of all others" (Charles River Bridge Case, 11 Peters, 567).

These definitions and the history of monopolies in England show how the antipathy to monopoly became so deep-seated in the Anglo-Saxon mind; and how and why the mere application of the term creates an aversion to whatsoever it is applied.

Prior to 1601, when they were successfully assailed in the courts, and to 1624, when Parliament declared them void, there were grants of monopoly by letters patent from the Crown, whereby, for favoritism or valuable consideration, certain persons were granted the exclusive right to buy and sell specified articles of trade, or the exclusive right to perform certain classes of labor. As may be inferred, the power to confer these valuable rights was greatly abused, and those who received such grants were not slow to misuse their privilege by extortionate demands.

Sir John Culpepper thus refers to the English monopolies:

"Like the frogs of Egypt they have gotten possession of our dwellings, and we have scarce a room free from them. They sup in our cup; they dip in our dish; they sit by our fires. We find them in the dye fat, wash bowl and powdering tub. They share with the butler in his box; they will not bait us a pin. We may not buy our clothes without their brokerage. These are the leeches that have sucked the Commonwealth so hard that it is almost hectical."

Monopolies cannot be created by association or agreement. We now have no letters patent giving exclusive right except under our patent laws for new inventions and discoveries. The letters patent of old creating monopolies were of the same character as those now granted to the discoverer of some new and useful invention. It is therefore wholly unjustifiable to use the term monopoly as applied to the effects of industrial consolidation.

"Competition is the life of trade," is a saw of the counting house which, like many others, contains a minimum of truth with a maximum of error. It would be more truthful to say "Competition, as generally practiced, if the life of trade, is the death of the trader." True competition does not mean the cut-throat methods of overreaching that once prevailed, where rival tradesmen were mortal enemies; nor does it mean that the better equipped and better managed establishment, with its increasing trade and business, must sleep by the roadside of commerce until the slow-going and non-progressive competitor catches up. Competition may be constructive or destructive. The true and only kind of competition that is desirable is the constructive, which wins by decreasing cost or improving product.

It was of the destructive kind of competition that the court spoke in Kellogg vs. Larkin, 3 Pinney, 150:

"If it be true, also, that competition is the life of trade, it may follow such premises that he who relaxes competition commits an act injurious to trade; and not only so, but he commits an overt act of treason against the commonwealth. But I apprehend that it is not true that competition is the life of trade. On the contrary, that maxim is one of the least reliable of the host we may pick up in every market place. It is in fact the shibboleth of mere gambling speculation, and is hardly entitled to take rank as an axiom in the jurisprudence of this country. I believe universal observation will attest that in the last quarter of a century competition in trade has caused more individual distress than the want of competition.

"Indeed, by reducing prices below or raising them above value (as the nature of the trade permitted) competition had done more to monopolize trade, or to secure exclusive advantages in it, than has been done by contract. Rivalry in trade will destroy itself, and rival tradesmen seek to remove each other, rarely resorting to contract unless they find it the cheapest mode of putting an end to the strife."

In the case of Mogul Steamship Co. vs. McGreggor (57 L. R. Ex. Cases, 541), Lord Coleridge, upon August 11, 1888, delivering an opinion, said: "It must be remembered that all trade is, and must be, in a sense, selfish. Trade not being infinite, nay, the trade of a particular place or district being possibly very limited, what one man gains another man loses. In the hand-to-hand war of commerce, as in the conflicts of public life, whether at the bar, in Parliament, in medicine, in engineering, men fight on without much thought of others, except a desire to excel or defeat them. Very lofty minds, like Sir Philip Sydney, with his cup of water will not stoop to take an advantage if they think another wants it more. Our age, in spite of high authority to the contrary, is not without its Sir Philip Sydney, but these are counsels of perfection which it would be silly indeed to make the measure of the rough business of the world, as pursued by ordinary men of business."

Justice Gray, in Leslie vs. Lorrillard (110 N. Y. 519), says: "I do not think that competition is invariably a public benefaction; for it may be carried on to such a degree as to become a general evil."

That competition only is desirable which stimulates to cheap producing, and selling at a reasonable profit, supplying the most for the money. This competition need not be direct, it may be indirect; nay, the fear of competition may be as efficacious, if not more so, than the competition itself. To-day the whole world is one market place; space has been annihilated, and distance destroyed. Communication throughout the world is practically instantaneous. The manufacturer of one place or country is a competitor of every other manufacturer of the same goods in every other place or country. The capital of America competes with the capital of every country on the globe, and so the capital of every country on the globe competes with the capital of America.

No consolidation, however large the proportion of any particular industry it may have absorbed, dares to raise prices beyond the point where an inducement is made to other capital to engage in the same business—nay, more than this, I maintain that no consolidation can continue its control of any line of industry unless it can produce and supply the trade with its product at a price less than that of the individual competitor; this because of the smaller area of business of the individual competitor, and the element of personal equation. Direct competition from those engaged in the same industry not only can, but does, confront every large aggregation of capital in every line of business in which consolidations have been formed. And experience has shown that the formation of consolidations has been followed in every instance by new capital embarking in the same line of industry in competition with the consolidation. Large numbers engaged in the same industry, some competent, some otherwise, have invariably produced seasons of very high and very low prices, because reasonable regulation of such trade was impracticable, and capital, even when necessary, was deterred from embarking in enterprises subject to such hazards. The organization of a consolidation is the signal that wiser counsels will prevail, and forthwith capital seeks the opportunity for profitable investment.

The evil, therefore, of high prices, or rather unreasonable profits, is reduced to a minimum, because the direct competition of those in the business exists, and judging from experience always will exist, while capital, ever eager for profitable investment, stands like a watchdog, guarding the public against excessive profits by other capitalists.

Every well-managed consolidation, by the natural laws of trade, must result in reducing the cost of production and distribution. With the improperly managed consolidation we have nothing to do. No argument for or against consolidation can be predicated thereon. You cannot make men wise or competent by legislation. You cannot expect counsels of perfection from imperfect mortals. We can only reason from essential features of consolidation, not from incidental mistakes made by incompetent management. That such large enterprises reduce the cost of production, is an economic fact too well established now to need further authentication. The saving, incident to the handling by one company of ore, in and from the mine to the finished steel structure on its site, as compared with a dozen intermediaries, each applying more or less of skill, and each claiming more or less of profit, is so patent as to require statement only. Improvements in processes, there being no obstacle to the adoption of the latest and best; the economies from standardization of wares; continuous operation on certain goods, and the consequent opportunity for introducing special machinery; savings in freight; and facilities and capital for purchasing in any quantity to provide for any contingency, are advantages only available to large enterprises with abundant capital and competent management. The cost of production being reduced, the cost to consumer is reduced, if actual competition, or the fear of competition, commonly called "potential competition," prevents the consolidation from demanding unreasonable returns. This proposition must be conceded, unless the laws of trade are to be reversed, experience is to go for naught, and history is to be denied.

It will be urged, however, that the cheapening of cost will be at the expense of the laborer, the salesman and the small manufacturer. As to the salesman and the small manufacturer, it may be said no great economic change can take place without some temporary hardship, and the benefit of the public is a higher consideration than the temporary inconvenience of a comparative few. But there is another answer which involves no concession. The statistics show that of those engaged in business or trade, a large percentage fail—about ninety per cent. This goes to prove that a large number of those who are thus supplanted by the consolidation are incompetent to engage in business, and if they were left alone would fail. Many such, under the protecting wings of the consolidation, with the benefit of the better brains at the helm, earn in the aggregate much more than they would have accumulated, if they had continued as sole proprietors, without the benefit of the better brain and management of the experienced and selected few.

The laborer and salesman are placed in a more favorable position by the consolidation. Under the system of individual competition, with its eras of depression and overproduction, its shutdowns and its curtailment of output, there was no continuity of employment. At one time every available man was engaged, capacities of plants enlarged, and production increased until beyond the demand; then came the fall in prices, the bankruptcy of plants, the shut-downs; and laborers, salesmen, clerks and other employes were thrown out of employment, sometimes dependent upon charity, as in our large cities a few years since. These eras of overproduction were not infrequent. This is changed by consolidation. The supply and demand are kept approximate, overproduction is jealously avoided, and there results continuous employment.

Another consideration for the laboring man, is the fact that in the mad race of competition, where individual seeks to overreach individual, each striving to reduce his cost below that of his competitor, many find it necessary to begin their reductions with labor, because of their inability to take advantage of other economies, such as improved machinery large purchases of material, etc., which have been introduced by their more fortunate competitors, and thus begins the reduction of wages which spreads from factory to factory. There is generally abundance of labor in the different industries, frequently a surplus, so that laborers compete with each other in seeking employment, and among so many employers some are not loath to take advantage of this; and this is the bane of labor organizations or unions. But with the well-regulated consolidation, earning a reasonable profit, the laborer will be safe, he will be organized for self-protection, and will have fewer and better men with whom to deal. He will, therefore, by reason of the better regulation of supply and demand, be continuously employed, and his greatest curse, intermittent employment, with seasons of idleness, will be removed. Thus, while a fewer number of men may be employed, the aggregate days of employment, or the aggregate amount of labor employed, will be greater. There are those, however, who contend and not without good authority, that the consolidation, by reducing the price, will ultimately increase the consumption, and thereby in time will actually employ an even greater number of men.

On the whole, with or without consolidation, no more labor will be employed than is necessary to supply the goods for which there is demand. Under the one system, the supply is not so well regulated to the demand, as under the other; hence recur seasons of shut-down and idleness. The consolidation prevents this; hence it must be of advantage to the laborer. The history of the Standard Oil Company is an excellent illustration of this principle. In no other industry employing so large a number of men has the working man had so continuous employment or better wages for the kind of work performed.

The officers of the great labor organizations of this country, in their papers read before this convention, have almost to a unit borne witness to the truth of the above assertions, and they all speak from experience when they favor industrial combinations.

These views are entertained by some of the best thinkers and writers on political economy. Gunton says:

"If it is true that the concentration of capital tends to diminish the cost of production and intensify competition, it follows that prices will fall or wages will rise, or both, in proportion as large enterprises supplant small ones. And this is what all industrial history shows has taken place. Take for example the cotton industry in this country. In 1831 there were 801 cotton manufacturing establishments with an average capital of $50,702 each. * * * The ratio of consumption of cotton cloth to population was 5.90 pounds to 1, and the price of cotton cloth 17 cents per yard. In 1880 the number of establishments had fallen to 756. The average amount of capital invested in establishments had risen from $50,702 to $275,403; * * * the ratio of consumption of cotton cloth to the population was 13.90 pounds to 1; and the price of cotton cloth was 7 cents per yard, and wages were 80 per cent higher. It will thus be seen that, comparing 1880 with 1831, the capital invested per spindle was over one-third less, the number of spindles operated by each laborer nearly three times as large, the product per spindle one-fourth greater, the product per dollar invested twice as large, the product per laborer employed nearly four times as great, the price of cotton cloth 60 per cent less, wages 80 per cent higher, and the consumption of cotton cloth per capita of the population over 100 per cent greater. These are the results of the process of consolidation into large capitals, extending over half a century. What is true of this industry is equally true of all industries in proportion as the concentration of capital has increased."

Those who cry loudest for legislation point to certain evils, charged as incident to consolidations, and demand prevention by law. For example, the watering of stock, the practice of reducing prices for the express purpose of crushing a rival, and then raising prices to an unreasonable amount, the circulation of false or misleading reports by the officers of such associations, for the purpose of stock speculations, and the corrupting of legislatures and municipal bodies.

These evils are not essential incidents to consolidations, they apply equally to all corporations. If it be thought that these practices can be stopped by legislation, then such wise and temperate legislation as will best prevent such practices might well be passed; but will legislation accomplish this? I am not one of those who think that you can legislate morality into a community. Laws receive their impulses from the people. The impulses move upward from the people to the law, and not downward from the law to the people. Like a pyramid, the people are the base, the law the apex; the pyramid will not stand inverted, nor will the apex stand without its base. For these immoral and dishonest practices we must look behind the statute books, behind the courts, behind the doors of the counting-house—we must look into the consciences of men. The corporation is only a cloak covering the men on whom it rests. But in these times, concealed by this covering, sometimes called a legal entity, corporate officers, as well as the community, have established a code of morals different from that by which individuals are governed in their personal transactions. Men will do through the corporation, or against the corporation, what they would shrink from doing in a personal transaction. This false moral idea is not limited to the man in the corporation; the man outside of the corporation is equally guilty. Claims against corporations, or demands upon them, are made that would never be made upon an individual. This is due to a depraved and diseased moral sentiment of the community. It is a false standard of morality. The corporation is no thing apart from the stockholders. It is a society of men. An aggregation of men. The officers who manage its affairs, the shareholders who own its stock, are the same men who sit by you at the club or in the church. Why shall they be held to one code of moral responsibility in their personal conduct and to another code in their conduct as officers or shareholders of a corporation? We see the same men, and the same acts, but when done by the corporation, through its officer, there seems to be a kind of moral strabismus in the eye of the community, which looks over the evil doer to the thing done, and sees only the impersonal agent, the corporation, through which the evil was done. We are confronted by the same conditions in politics. It is the men of the community who are the corporation, the men of the community who manage the corporation. But because of the diseased moral sense of the community, those guilty of wrong doing as officers, or as stockholders of corporations, are not visited with the condemnation of their associates. The moralist and the ethical teacher must deal with this problem. Visit upon the offender the reprobation of the community for misdeeds against a corporation, as against an individual; for misdeeds as the officer or director of a corporation, just as for his acts as an individual, and if the moral sense of the community is high, just so high and no higher will rise the conduct of those dealing with or for corporations.

These same suggestions apply with even greater force to the charge that these large aggregations of capital tend to debauch politics by bribing legislatures and municipal governments. This charge presupposes for each corporation that succeeds in bribing, a large number of persons so corrupt that they will accept bribes. It assumes that legislatures and municipal bodies can be bribed. If this be true, and alas, there is not wanting much evidence that gives credibility to the imputation, the remedy surely would not be to suppress the corporation, any more than to suppress the legislature. The true remedy is to suppress the bribe taker, as well as the bribe giver. This can only be done by improving the moral tone of the community, because, after all, the legislatures, the municipal councils, aye, the corporations of a community, rise no higher and sink no lower in their moral tone than the general moral tone of their respective communities. This may seem an unsavory truth in this day of recriminations, but it is still a truth.

The capital employed in the enterprises of to-day may seem large when compared with the amount thus employed at one time, but it is no larger in proportion than are the transactions of this age compared with those of former ages. Once all trade was circumscribed, confined within small territorial areas, due to lack of facilities for transportation and communication. The market places of cities and towns in the past were the sole marts sometimes of whole counties, or even larger districts. To-day what is the situation? The price of a loaf of bread in Chicago is affected by a rumor of war in Asia, and the world's exchange goes up or down in accordance with the result of negotiations for a loan in Japan. Everything of importance occurring in the most remote portions of the world affects trade for good or evil in every other portion. Rumors of war or peace, the discovery of mineral deposits, a new and useful invention in any part of the world, reacts upon every other part. The whole world is every man's market. Transactions involving sums equal to a king's ransom are now of almost daily occurrence, and millions are now exchanged where hundreds once sufficed. Contracts for the supply of material involving tens of millions of dollars are not infrequent. The amount of capital employed in any enterprise signifies nothing except the magnitude of our dealings. These enormous amounts are not limited to companies formed by consolidation; they are likewise employed in business enterprise increased from small beginnings, by natural accretions, to keep step with the industrial progress and demands of the time.

The unification of the world into a single market place has come to pass through no human design, but as the natural result of improved facilities in transportation and communication. A man to-day in any part of the world may be in daily touch with his business, however remote; and with the markets in every other portion of the globe. These changed conditions have caused like changes in methods of business. Trade and commerce never lag behind the train of progress and improvement; they keep apace, sometimes they are in the van. Those who would prevent these vast aggregations of capital, would turn back the hands on the dial of civilization. They would seek to prevent the natural, inevitable tendency which has been superinduced by the exigencies of trade, and made imperative by the complex and complicated commerce of the world. Consolidations in industrial enterprises, large aggregations of capital, are not sudden creations, they are growths, forced upon the world by the law of progress. They are here by no man's fiat; they can be driven away by no human agency. They are natural—inevitable—necessary.

Consolidation is the protest of capital against extinction. Consolidations were formed in self-defense. They grew up by force of competition, to avoid destruction by competition. If the smaller and weaker had not combined to battle with the larger and stronger, they were doomed to annihilation. As the individual enterprise, whether partnership or corporate, grew and prospered, and added to its strength and power, appropriating more and more of a given trade, the trade of smaller concerns was thereby contracted, and if consolidation or combination had been denied, they would have been eliminated by the more powerful rival. By combination they at one step placed themselves in position to compete and to hold their own. To many concerns it was a choice between consolidation and insolvency. To many a proprietor it was a choice between losing all, going out of business, or remaining in business as a stockholder in the larger company, and saving his accumulations. Through consolidations and the consequent large stock issues, the public are given opportunity to become stockholders, and thus share in the profits and industries which formerly were closed to general investment. The successful manufacturer enlarged and increased his plant, but the ownership generally remained a family affair. Many of the multimillionaires of this country thus accumulated their wealth. There is no reason why skilled laborers receiving good wages, as well as others connected with the business, should not become sharers in the profits they help to earn, by acquiring an interest in the business in this way.

I come from Pittsburgh, a city where sit enthroned old King Coal and new King Steel. Consolidations have been effected in that section in almost every line of industry. Smoke is issuing from every stack, fires are burning in every furnace. Labor was never so well paid nor so much employed. Trade was never so good, times so prosperous, nor the outlook so favorable. Have not consolidations and these vast aggregations of capital something to do with this? How otherwise could we have taken such stupendous contracts for the supply of iron and steel in Europe, Russia, China, Japan, Australia, Africa—in fact all over the world? What could the ordinary industrial concern do with a six million dollar order for a railway in Russia? The public never was so well served as now, never supplied with better goods nor a greater variety, never supplied so promptly and so efficiently.

Would those who decry consolidation have this growing, prosperous, industrial nation, with an inventive genius the greatest in the world, and an adaptability never before approached, lie down in the ruin of its industries and hand over its trade to other nations—nations that are now madly striving for the same? Herr Krupp is not so far behind, nor other German manufacturers. England, with her gigantic industries (many the fruits of combination and consolidation, which she has never discouraged since she learned the errors of her ways), has not yet surrendered the marts of the world to her American competitor.

America has only recently been taught the lesson of the power for good of these great industrial plants. She is making good use of this knowledge now in securing her portion of the world's trade. These great aggregations of capital, created by combination and consolidation, have grown up among us, not without cause; they are the effect of the natural evolution of trade and commerce. They are steps, steps only, in the industrial progress of the present civilization. To what they will ultimately lead, we may speculate, but we cannot know. Natural laws—stronger, greater, higher than those of man's creation—will control them for good or ill. We touch them at our peril. We may help, we may hinder, the working of these higher influences. He would indeed be a wise prophet who could now foretell whither we are tending. No mortal eye can at one glance foresee the complex markets of the world. No human mind can at any instant comprehend the trade conditions of the globe. Such sight and such comprehension are imperative if legislation touching the mainsprings of trade is to be intelligently framed. We are in the presence of stupendous forces, set in motion by unseen power. As in the past, so in the future, the operation of natural laws will lead to that result which is best. I am one of those who have not lost confidence in natural law, and am content to let the God of evolution work out this great problem of the age. But in the light of history we may enquire, "Will trade, like man, play his part upon the world's stage, 'his acts being seven ages'?" Or has he more? There was an infancy of trade we know, a time when exchange was made in kind. So, too, we may recall another time, still an infancy, though then 'twas thought that trade had grown mature—when to buy, to sell again, was deemed a crime. How now we laugh at those toys of laws. Yet then, men were imprisoned for their infraction. Since then, how great has grown this child of trade, how strong, how large! And yet who knows but 'tis a "whining school-boy" still, and the generations yet to come will have their laugh on us, if we, too, err by assuming trade to be mature. Trade mature? Who dares assert civilization has passed the zenith, and that the shadows now point from west to east? Concurrent and co-extensive with the growth of civilization will be the growth of trade. When you can say civilization grows no more, then, too, you may say the same of trade, but not till then.

The Committee on Organization and Program was named as follows:

ALABAMA.—Eyre Damar.
ARIZONA.—J. C. Adams.
ARKANSAS.—Jefferson Davis.
CALIFORNIA.—Charles D. Willard.
COLORADO.—Henry V. Johnson.

DELAWARE.—Charles F. Richard.
DISTRICT OF COLUMBIA.—Joseph Nimmo, Jr.
FLORIDA.—John Franklin Forbes.
IDAHO.—Judge Claggett.

ILLINOIS.—Lorin C. Collins.
INDIANA.—John L. Griffiths.
IOWA.—T. D. Healy.
KANSAS.—John E. Hessin.
KENTUCKY.—W. B. Fleming.
LOUISIANA.—William Wirt Howe.
MAINE.—A. E. Rogers.
MARYLAND.—Maj. John I. Yellott.
MASSACHUSETTS.—John S. Clark.
MICHIGAN.—George W. McBride.
MINNESOTA.—W. W. Folwell.
MISSISSIPPI.—J. W. Cutrer.
MISSOURI.—F. C. Farr.
MONTANA.—H. H. Swain.
NEBRASKA.—R. D. Sutherland.
NEVADA.—Francis G. Newlands.
NEW HAMPSHIRE. — Henry W. Blair.

NEW JERSEY.—Edward Quinton Keasbey.
NEW MEXICO.—Frank Springer.
NEW YORK.—Stephen P. Corliss.
NORTH DAKOTA.—A. W. Edwards.
OHIO.—Charles Foster.
OREGON.—E. Hofer.
PENNSYLVANIA.—H. W. Palmer.
SOUTH CAROLINA.—A. C. Kaufman.
SOUTH DAKOTA. — Freeman Knowles.
TENNESSEE.—John W. Gaines.
TEXAS.—A. B. Davidson.
UTAH.—George W. Bartch.
WEST VIRGINIA.—John W. Harris.
WISCONSIN.—A. M. Jones.
WYOMING.—C. P. Arnold.

NATIONAL ASSOCIATION OF MANUFACTURERS.—Theodore C. Search, President.
NORTHWESTERN TRAVELING MEN'S ASSOCIATION.—George J. Reed.
AMERICAN FEDERATION OF LABOR.—Samuel Gompers, President.
BROTHERHOOD OF RAILROAD TRAINMEN.—P. H. Morrissey, Grand Master.
UNITED GARMENT WORKERS OF AMERICA.—Henry White, General Sec.
SINGLE TAX LEAGUE OF THE UNITED STATES.—F. M. Monroe.
ORDER OF RAILWAY CONDUCTORS.—E. E. Clark, Grand Chief Conductor.
BROTHERHOOD OF LOCOMOTIVE FIREMEN.—W. S. Carter.
NATIONAL GRANGE PATRONS OF HUSBANDRY.—H. E. Huxley.
ILLINOIS COMMERCIAL MEN'S ASSOCIATION.—George H. Holden.
NEW ENGLAND FREE TRADE LEAGUE.—Byron W. Holt.
AMERICAN ACADEMY OF POLITICAL AND SOCIAL SCIENCE.—Edmund J. James.
NATIONAL ALLIANCE THEATRICAL STAGE EMPLOYES.—Lee M. Hart, General Secretary and Treasurer.
NATIONAL BUSINESS MEN'S LEAGUE.—John W. Ela.
AMERICAN ANTI-TRUST LEAGUE.—M. L. Lockwood, President.
KNIGHTS OF LABOR.—I. D. Chamberlain.
UNITED STATES EXPORT ASSOCIATION.—Francis B. Thurber, President.
COMMERCIAL TRAVELERS' NATIONAL LEAGUE.—P. E. Dowe, President.
NATIONAL GRAIN GROWERS' ASSOCIATION.—S. H. Greeley.
NATIONAL FARMERS' ALLIANCE AND INDUSTRIAL UNION OF AMERICA.—J. C. Hanley.
NATIONAL TAX LEAGUE.—Lawson Purdy.
NATIONAL SOCIALISTS' LEAGUE.—A. M. Simons.
BRICKLAYERS' AND MASONS' UNION OF AMERICA.—M. R. Grady.
MILLERS' NATIONAL ASSOCIATION.—F. H. Magdeburg.
ASSOCIATION OF WESTERN MANUFACTURERS.—George Brickner.
AMERICAN SOCIAL SCIENCE ASSOCIATION.—Wm. A. Giles.
FARMERS' NATIONAL CONGRESS.—John M. Stahl, Secretary.
INTERNATIONAL TYPOGRAPHICAL UNION.—Samuel B. Donnelly, President.
TRAVELING MEN'S PROTECTIVE ASSOCIATION.—M. W. Phalen, President.
EX-OFFICIO.—Franklin H. Head, President Civic Federation of Chicago.
Ralph M. Easley, Secretary, Civic Federation of Chicago.

The conference took a recess until 8 o'clock.

EVENING SESSION, SEPTEMBER 13.

Chairman Head called the session to order promptly at 8 o'clock, and introduced Governor George W. Atkinson of West Virginia, who said:

G. W. ATKINSON.

Governor of West Virginia.

This gathering, as I understand it, is to consider the relations of our citizens to one another as citizens, and to consider also the best methods to be used to protect the masses from the encroachments of combines and trusts, for it seems that this is a period favorable to the organization of such combines all over the civilized world.

I believe in progression. In this respect I am an evolutionist. I believe that the world ought to grow, and that men ought to grow with it. Some sorts of combines are, I think, economic necessities which grow out of our complex civilization as a nation. The great manufacturing establishments of the world, covering all branches of industry, had very small beginnings; and we, in a large measure, owe the progress we have made to men of means who combined or united into what we call "corporations" to make this advancement possible. But there is a vast difference between an ordinary corporation and a trust. It seems to me that every citizen who possesses any sort of common sense will favor corporations, because individual citizens, as a rule, cannot in and of themselves alone furnish sufficient capital to develop the resources of any of the states of our republic. It requires vast sums of money to handle great undertakings. One man alone cannot supply the necessary capital to build up great industries, which have for their object the development of a state or a nation; but several men of means, by combining, can raise the necessary amount of capital to accomplish the desired purpose. This necessity brought corporations into existence. What one man cannot do, for lack of means, several men can accomplish by uniting the capital which all of them can command. In this way corporations are formed. In this manner railroads are constructed, mines are opened, mills and factories are built, industries are established, men are employed, and the natural resources of a country are developed, which necessarily employ labor and thus bring wealth into a country. Hence I say that every citizen of a country who possesses ordinary common sense should be favorable to corporations. Nevertheless, we have in our midst thousands and tens of thousands of our people who seem to hate them and fight them on every hand, notwithstanding the fact that they secure from such concerns reasonable compensation for their toil, and by means of which they obtain a proper support for themselves and those dependent upon them. With this class of people, my fellow citizens, I have no sort of sympathy. I assert here to-day that a corporation properly conducted is entitled to as much sympathy, support and respect as an individual, because a corporation in law is an individual. I wish therefore to be written down, my countrymen, as a friend and backer of corporations, because no state can be developed without them, and there can be no growth and development if they are inhibited by law or are not supported properly by the people. Without corporations to-day we would be without railroads, coal and coke operations, silver and gold producers, banks and other acknowledged necessities for the public weal. Therefore, Mr. Chairman, when I hear men in politics and elsewhere whining the demagogue cry, "Down with corporations," I am ready to join the crowd of enterprising people who will cry from the hustings and the housetops, "Down with that class of malcontents and demagogues!" I am not an optimist *per se,* nor am I a pessimist. I have no sympathy for any one who puts in his time whining against capital. We unfortunately have, however, too many of this class of croakers in our midst. What we need is more capital in legitimate business undertakings. We must have men everywhere who will invest their money in building up and opening up the industries of all of our states. We have in West Virginia more coal and coke and oil and gas and timber than the United States can consume in hundreds of years. What we now most need is capital to help us on in our work of development. We are ready and willing to welcome to our domain men of enterprise and means from all sections of the Union, and from abroad as well, to come among us and aid us in developing the resources which a wise and beneficent Providence has bestowed upon us, and which are open to all comers.

West Virginia, my friends, is the first oil and gas and timber state in the Union. She is second in coke, and third in coal. She has more coal area than any other state, and it is only a matter of limited time for her to be first in coal and coke production, as she is now first in oil and gas and timber, because the coal and coke business is after all only a question of the survival of the fittest. With more veins of coal than any other state, and all or mostly all of a better quality than any of our competitors, especially for gas and steam and heat and coke, we are bound to hold our own, and in the end come out on top of any and all competitors. Hence I again say, Mr. President, that West Virginians generally are friendly to corporations, and we will and do welcome men of means to come among us, and thus help them and us not only "to keep the wolf from the door," but at the same time to aid us to lay up a surplus for "rainy days" which will sooner or later come to one and all. We welcome, therefore, corporations and capital, because they help us as West Virginians to build for both the present and the future.

Now, I take it, Mr. President, that all present understand how I feel toward capitalists and toward corporations which always represent capital and capitalists. The next point to which I desire briefly to allude is the "labor problem." I am now and always have been a stanch friend of the toiling masses. I stand for the workingman because he alone produces wealth. He takes the iron ore, the coal, the oil, the gas, the precious metals, the lead, the zinc, etc., out of the bowels of the earth, and by his skill transforms them from the natural to the finished product. In this way he produces wealth. In the same manner he brings out of mother earth the necessary articles for the sustenance of mankind. He alone, therefore, is a wealth producer. Why, then, should he not have our honest, earnest support? I say unhesitatingly that he has my best wishes.

Labor and capital are interdependent. One cannot get on without the other. The laboring men have the same right to organize for their advancement and protection as have the capitalists. The same privileges must be extended to one class as to the other. So long as the laboring man does his duty and keeps within the limits of the law, he will have my sympathy and support. But I have never yet favored a strike or a lockout so long as it was possible to prevent it by just and friendly arbitration; and I have never yet known, and I say it boldly, a strike or a lockout, in all my experience and observations, that did not result in injury to both labor and capital. Therefore, Mr. Chairman, I favor arbitration to settle all disputed problems between capital on the one hand and labor on the other.

While I stand here as a representative of the common people, and insist that they should be properly treated, yet I confess that there are other trusts in this country than money trusts. Laboring men have their organizations, as I have hitherto stated they ought to have, and are entitled to have. But somehow, however, a portion of these organizations have not taken properly into account the strife and loss of time to themselves and their employers occasioned by strikes which they have seen fit to bring upon themselves. There are, therefore, not only capital trusts but there are sometimes labor trusts also. I wish to place myself on record against both, and especially so when the demands of either or both are not in accord with the well established rules of political economy and common sense and common honesty between man and man, whether rich or poor, black or white. Laboring men have no more right to combine for the purpose of sustaining that which is unjust and unreasonable than capitalists. Hence I wish to declare here and now that arbitration alone can properly adjust controversies of this sort, and the man who opposes this kind of adjustment is wholly out of joint with the spirit of the times in which he lives. Capital and labor should deal fairly with each other, and if they cannot at all times agree, let the controversy be arbitrated by a just, fair, unbiased and honorable tribunal. No conservative, honest man, in my judgment, can or will oppose such adjustment.

This brings me, Mr. President, to a brief consideration of trusts, which is the main question before this Federation. In all of my private and public acts in the past, my "musket" has always been pointed against trusts, and if I know myself to-day, it is still pointing the same way. It seems that our country has, within the past few years, gone trust crazy. I cannot understand why, but it appears to be a fact. Nevertheless, this lunacy fad, if I may call it such, is not confined to this country alone. It is just now reaping a harvest everywhere and in all lands. Nor is it confined to any one political party. I find about as many Democrats in trusts in the United States as Republicans, and I find at least two of the mammoth trusts of this country are, in a sense, Democratic trusts. Therefore, I conclude, Mr. Chairman, that we cannot choke them out by drawing political lines upon them. They have grown up as the result of existing conditions, and they cannot be stamped out by any and all political parties simply resolving against them. To sweep the trust issue into politics, and resolve one way or the other, as is the custom now-a-days in political conventions so to do, it seems to me, is "wasting fragrance on the desert air." We must come nearer home for a remedy than that. We must hit at its taproot by national and state legislation, by making it a penal offense against good government for men of great wealth to combine for the sole purpose of stifling and choking middle-men and small dealers, as trusts have generally done in the past.

Or, better still, if the trusts would take their employees into their combines and their confidence, and will, after paying a reasonable dividend on the actual amount of capital stock invested, and then agree to distribute a reasonable share of the profits among the skilled artisans whom they employ as a per cent or profit upon their wages, the trusts would then be placed upon an honest, popular and reasonable foundation, and no one could complain or justly oppose them. I can see no reason why such an experiment may not be made by employers, nor can I see why it would not succeed. To do this would bring about harmony to a large degree between labor and capital, and would measurably—though not entirely—take the fangs out of the trust and the combine. This is one of the ways, and it seems to me to be the logical way, to settle this ever-existing controversy, and settle it right, because it would then be a just, and, I may say, enlightened co-operation, and you all know that co-operation is the fundamental principle of a trust. It is, in short, the very heart of it. The trouble, however, with the most of the trusts as they are now conducted is that the "co-operation" is all one-sided—all in favor of the stockholders, while the skilled laborers and the consumers are wholly ignored. This seems to be the fundamental principle—the foundation, so to speak, on which the entire trust movement rests. Why, then, cannot its scope be widened so as to take in or embrace all the classes whose interests are involved? So long as the trust now stands, and so long as it is thus conducted, that long it will be antagonized by the masses, and it therefore cannot be enduring, nor can it result as a permanent, profitable investment for the stockholders, or can it in any way benefit the mechanics or the people in general.

Mr. President, I do not wish to be understood as opposing modern methods of progress. I believe in conserving in every possible manner the waste of time and energy of the great mass of our people. The day of wooden plows and stage coaches and horseback mails have gone by forever. To keep abreast of the times in which we live, we must use all modern discoveries and appliances. We must of necessity "keep in the push" or otherwise perish. All wise people will strive to reduce every possible waste of energy. The blacksmith shop and the wooden plow were good enough in their day. They answered the purpose then, but they are out of date now. Old methods have been steadily discarded, and economical appliances, operated by steam and electricity, have been substituted therefor. The same is true in almost every business avocation peculiar to our people. The trust seems, on its face, to be a step forward in the ever-shifting drama of growth and progress. It claims as its main purpose to save waste in production and distribution. Every student of political economy will admit, in a measure, the force of this particular claim, because the greatest enemy to human progress is waste. While it may be true that a number of factories in a particular industry, which have been competing with one another in a particular line of production, agree to unite for a common purpose, consenting to not fight one another, and purposing to furnish a particular article of manufacture to the consumer at a specific price, of itself is not necessarily wrong. Indeed, on its face it appears to be right; but it may be wrong—forever wrong —and usually is wrong, as I see it, for two especial reasons: First: This combine can and will (if they are looking out for their own interests alone) increase the price of their product to the consumer, and at the same time cut the wages of their employees; and, second, every small manufacturer engaged in that particular industry will either have to quit business or join "the combine." But the combine will doubtless say in reply that the small manufacturer can himself join the trust, or keep on as he is then doing, if he likes. How, I ask, can he continue his business successfully, if all of his competitors in the same line of production have combined against him? They can and will for the purpose of "freezing him out" cut prices until he has "to squeal and throw up the sponge," and then the combine has its own way and can fix its own prices, and it usually does so, and all of you who hear me know it and know it well. In cases of this sort, the small dealer succumbs, and the combine or trust fixes its own prices and the people are compelled to submit.

Nevertheless, Mr. Chairman and gentlemen, I confess I am one of the common people of this country who is not hysterical over this trust controversy. I am inclined to the opinion that it can and will be regulated by wise and proper legislation, and by public sentiment, which in the end always settles matters of this sort. All political economists agree that the prevention of waste (unnecessary waste) by all nations is the secret of their growth and success. This proposition is unquestionably true, and I will not therefore undertake to controvert it. A wise man will save every cent, every dime, every lump of coal, every particle of manure, everything that can be utilized to better his condition and help him on in life. But it seems to me that no intelligent man will favor any measure which will place him at the mercy of a few of his fellow-citizens who will have it in their power to say what he shall do, or what he shall pay for that which necessity requires him to purchase.

I am aware of the fact, Mr. President, that the backers of trusts set up three distinct claims or arguments in their defense, viz: First, that they pay the highest rates of wages to their employees; second, that they furnish the best articles to the consumer; and, third, that they furnish them lower or cheaper than they can otherwise be produced. While I admit that there is something in these claims, yet they are true only in a restricted sense. The first of these claims is, I think, absolutely true. Trusts pay big wages because they employ none but high grade men and women, which they can afford to do. The second proposition is perhaps true in most cases, but by no means in all. The third claim is only true in a few instances. If I had the time to-day I could definitely mention them to this Federation. But in the generality of cases, prices to consumers increase instead of diminish where trusts are enforced. Therefore the few, and not the many, are the direct beneficiaries of these trust combines. Consequently, my countrymen, when one pauses and carefully considers all the facts involved; when he thoughtfully weighs both sides of the issue before him; when he seriously reflects, as it is the duty of every good citizen so to do; when he sees the vast multitude of his fellow countrymen who have fitted themselves by education and experience as "middle-men" in the various avocations of life, necessarily thrown out of employment because of trusts; and when he goes farther and thinks of the thousands and tens of thousands of his fellow-countrymen of limited means, yet at the same time industrious, sober and enterprising, who cannot, because of their limited resources, cope with the trusts and the combines, and are necessarily forced to quit business, then the enormity of the wrong (not to say crime) of choking them out of an honest effort to support themselves and families, can be fully understood and fully appreciated.

If the advocates of and participants in the trusts could satisfy the masses upon the following propositions, they would then have but limited opposition in the years to come, viz.: First, Will you and can you, in all cases, as you claim, agree to furnish a better and cheaper article to consumers of all the necessaries of life covered by your trusts and combines? Second, What do you propose to do with the tens of thousands of middle-men now employed, who of necessity must lose their present positions? And, third, what will become of the "small dealers" scattered over our country from Maine to Florida, and from the surges of the Atlantic to the Sunset Sea whose waves make music in the golden sands of California? What are you going to do with this large class of our fellow citizens who are now prosperous and happy in their present occupations? These are momentous problems, and involve momentous results.

I may be wrong, Mr. President, in my conclusions; but it

104

HORATIO W. SEYMOUR   J. STERLING MORTON
FRANCIS G. NEWLANDS   MARTIN A. KNAPP
CYRUS G. LUCE   ROBERT S. TAYLOR

seems to me, as an unprejudiced, unbiased American citizen, whose only purpose is to do what he can to advance the interests of the great majority of all our people, that if the trust idea is to be carried out in this country, there will be no use for middle-men among us; and the small dealers and small manufacturers and small operators in any and all lines of business, who are now earning honest livings and supports for themselves and those dependent upon them, will be things absolutely of the past. Like Othello, their "occupations will be gone." And what of the other and the greatest of all the considerations before us as non-partisan American citizens, viz.: Will the trusts, can the trusts, dare the trusts here agree to furnish to the great living, helpless, and in many instances hapless mass of our people, a better and a cheaper article which all of them must of necessity use, than they are now required to pay for the same? If the trust can do this, I will call off my opposition, feeble as it is, and will join them and bid them Godspeed in their work. Otherwise, I am against them, and I desire that they will here and now class me as an enemy. It is not my purpose or desire, my fellow citizens, to block any avenue to the progress and development of my country; but it is my purpose and desire to do anything and everything that I can to prevent capital from overslaughing labor, and to do my utmost at all times and under all circumstances to aid the workingman to earn an honest livelihood for himself and those dependent upon him in the ever-existing scuffle between man and man to live and let live, which has been going on from Adam down to McKinley.

John W. Gaines of Tennessee announced that the committee on organization and program nominated as permanent officers of the conference:

Chairman, William Wirt Howe of Louisiana; First Vice-Chairman, Dudley G. Wooten of Texas; Second Vice-Chairman, H. V. Johnson of Colorado; Third Vice-Chairman, S. P. Corliss of New York; Secretary, Ralph M. Easley of Chicago.

The committee recommended the adoption of the following rules:

The conference shall hold three daily sessions, from 10 a. m. to 1 p. m., from 3 p. m. to 5 p. m., from 8 p. m. until such time as adjournment may be had. That all papers or addresses shall be limited to twenty minutes; that Jefferson's Manual and

Robert's Rules of Order and general parliamentary law shall be the rules of this body. That no proxies be allowed.

It was recommended that the vice-chairmen preside over the conference on the succeeding days in their regular order.

The committee further recommended the appointment of a committee whose duty should be to prepare a program for each session and provide rules governing special conditions, and recommended as such committee:

Henry W. Blair, New Hampshire; L. D. Sutherland, Nebraska; J. W. Gaines, Tennessee; J. C. Hanley, Minnesota; A. B. Davidson, Texas, and Chairman Howe and Secretary Easley, ex-officio.

On motion of Cockran, New York, seconded by Garland, Pennsylvania, the committee report was adopted without a dissenting vote.

Temporary Chairman Head introduced William Wirt Howe as his successor, and in accepting the gavel Mr. Howe briefly thanked the delegates for the honor conferred upon him, and promised to preside with impartiality. He introduced Attorney-General E. C. Crow of Missouri:

E. C. CROW.
Attorney-General of Missouri.

All now admit that trusts must, if they exist, be regulated in order to protect the individual interests from the combined interest of the trusts; but will regulations successfully protect the public from the evil influence of the trust organization?

That trusts when operating illegally can be restrained and dissolved by the process of the state courts, has been demonstrated in Missouri by the decision of the highest court in the state. But the loose and easy process of creating a legal corporate entity renders it practicable to form trust corporations by the score daily, while to demolish or restrain a trust often requires from one to three years of an expensive and hard fought legal battle by the state. These reasons urge us to look for a remedy that will prevent the formation of trusts, on the principle that it is more practicable to prevent an evil than to remedy it after it exists.

The individual was the primary basis of all business. It early became evident, however, that associations of individuals, combin-

106

ing their capital and efforts, would be advantageous in a business way, and this gave rise to partnerships. Copartnerships thus took the place of individual effort and capital, and made possible larger enterprises. Under the laws of this country the individual members of a partnership are compelled to respond with their individual fortunes for any liability of the partnership incurred in the prosecution of the partnership after the assets of the firm have been exhausted. This financial responsibility is a natural limitation on partnership enterprises, because of the desire of every man to limit his liabilities and protect himself from bankruptcy. An instrument of business that would enable men more widely to extend their business enterprises, with larger opportunities for profit, and less personal liability, was something eagerly sought, and it has been found in the modern private business corporation. In the private trading corporation, with fullpaid capital stock, no individual liability of shareholder exists for liabilities of the corporation, and no matter how great the loss a corporation sustains, or how entirely bankrupt it becomes, the individual fortune of the fullpaid stockholder is fully protected. Thus it will be seen at once the modern private business corporation makes possible the wildest of speculations by the corporate entity, with the absolute guarantee to the shareholders of non-liability beyond the amount of the full paid stock.

In a partnership enterprise the business may employ only a small portion of the capital of the individual, and but little of his personal time or effort, yet he stakes his financial all in the business—his good name, his possessions, his prospective acquirements, all stand sponsor for every liability of the partnership. On the other hand, a corporation risks nothing but the capital which it employs. Its field is as wide as civilization, and while it is not exactly immortal, yet death coming to its members does not dissolve the corporation. It is an intangible and an impalpable creation of the law, with unlimited powers and limited liabilities. It may have conveyed to it all the property, plants, business and rights of several corporations for the purpose of uniting all the different competing concerns under one management and thereby reduce expenses. This legal status which marks the broad distinction between partnerships and the liabilities thereof, and corporations and the liabilities thereof, should be clearly borne in mind in dealing with the modern monopoly or trust. For the financial reasons above set out, the most perfect and complete modern trust takes the shape of a corporation, to which is conveyed the property and the business of the various individuals and corporations that are to form the trust. A majority of stock in the corporation is most frequently controlled by two or three persons, thus giving the vast powers and business interests of perhaps an hundred firms and corporations in a single line of business into the complete control of two or three individuals, who by directing the destiny of the corporate entity whose stock they own absolutely dominate the single line of business.

The chief reason why the modern trust takes the corporate form is the financial one, to-wit: Relief from individual liability of the stock owners of the trust beyond the value of the stock owned by them. A corporate trust monopoly stands to win all the profits that may result from combined capital, crushing and destroying competition, while each stockholder is free from the chance of sharing with his personal fortune any of the loss that may come by business failure of the trust. On the other hand, each member of a partnership or association of persons not incorporated who organize or attempt to organize a trust, stands with his personal fortune to share individually the losses of the combine if losses exist.

In dealing with the question of private business corporations it should be clearly borne in mind that a private corporation is purely a creature of law. It is supposed to be created because of a public policy that demands combinations of citizens and capital to be clothed with corporate form to subserve the public good, and in the subservance of the public good can be found the only justification for the creation of private corporations. The usual argument put forward to justify the organization of private corporations is that in this way may be combined the efforts and capital of many individuals who carry forward enterprises of public utility which are beyond the ability of natural persons, whether acting as individuals or as a partnership. If this institution were strictly applied it would abolish the private business trading corporation, and would restrict corporate organizations to those of a public or quasi public nature only. But the laws of all the states have, as I believe, unwisely encouraged the formation or organization of corporations to invade every field of business enterprise, thus placing the individual at a disadvantage in his single efforts to carry on any line of business as against the combination of individuals in the guise of a corporation, which has special powers, privileges and advantages given it by law which the natural citizen can not have, and instead of the public necessity being applied as the true test for the right of corporate organization, we have now substituted simply the desire for private gain and the elusion of personal responsibility, and these are the sole motives that actuate in the organization of the business corporation of to-day. To these loose incorporation laws and the irresponsibility connected with the owning of shares of stock in private business corporations I attribute the great growth of the modern corporate trust. The struggle in all the commercial world has ever been, and ever will be, to secure the greatest opportunity for profit with the least amount of liability to loss. The legal status of the owner of the stock in a private business corporation presents exactly this opportunity. The present public policy of the states is against the organization and existence of trusts, as shown by the anti-trust laws enacted recently; but the policy of the corporate laws of the various states has been to allow loose control of corporations. The result is that when the people start to control trust corporations they are met with a system of loose corporation laws, builded up by years of legislation when little was thought of the effect of the corporate power on the business and property of citizens, and hence it is discovered that our corporate laws must be remodeled.

The corporation being the creature of the state and possessing only the power given it by the state, it should never be allowed to so act or conduct its business as to interfere with the interests of the public. There should be no particular inducement for the people, through their state government, to give men a portion of the power of the state through a corporate charter if the public interest is not to be subserved. On the other hand, if the public interest is to be injured there exists the strongest of reasons for the withholding of a corporate charter surrendering to the corporators a part of the sovereignty of the people. Formerly the interests of common carriers and other similar public and quasi public employments were not nearly so important as now. To-day the railroad employees of America number upward of a million of men. Those employed in other business of the same or similar public character aggregate a very large number. These public or quasi public employments touch and directly affect and shape to a greater or less extent the daily and hourly life and interests of the entire population of our country.

How directly do the steam and street railways, the telegraph and the telephone, the express and steamship companies, the waterworks, gas, light, turnpike, bridge, elevator, pipe line, bank and trust companies affect the interest, prosperity and property of every citizen? A clear and full appreciation of the complete protection of the right to contract, and of the vested rights of property is absolutely essential to be kept in mind in order to have a fair view of the trust question and its effect on our people and the remedies that may be proposed for any evil that may result from monopolies. The courts and the legislatures assert the right to regulate, restrain and dissolve trusts and monopolies to control trade, because trusts and monopolies are injurious to the public interests. The opponents of the anti-trust laws argue that such control and restraint interferes with the right of freedom to contract and the perfect right one should possess to dispose of his own property and manage his own business as he pleases. The argument is also advanced by opponents of anti-trust legislation that the logical and natural result of the interference of the state with the full freedom of the right to contract and the right of disposition of property will be the sure and speedy enactment of laws to correct the inequality of wealth which exists among men, and to legally establish the balance by taking, through legal processes, from those who have too much in order to give to those who have not enough, and that this course of legislation will soon be followed by laws making land and capital, which are the requisites of labor and the source of all wealth and culture, the common property of society upon the principle that the public welfare demands that land and capital be so managed as to confer the greatest benefit on the greatest number.

In this way the opponents of anti-trust legislation say we will be led speedily into socialism. The argument is made that the right to sell at the seller's own price only involves the right to contract, and is as much property as land or money. But this argument overlooks the fact that while the seller may have a right to freely dispose of his property, yet the buyer has a right, or should have, to buy in an open market. It overlooks the further fact that no man has a natural right or title to the possession of land or property, but that the right is given him by law. It also overlooks the fact that in all ages of the world and under all forms of government the will of the individual has been subordinated to the will of society. This argument loses sight of the fact that the right to contract is a relative, and not an absolute right.

Thus looking at the condition of affairs on this question we see presented on one side the spectacle of the masses of the people demanding that legal control of monopolies be immediate and drastic, and that special privileges be taken from combined wealth, clothed with corporate form, and equal opportunities in the business world be everywhere substituted; while on the other side the organized capital of the country stands seeking shelter and protection under the sacred constitutional rights of property and freedom in making contracts and carrying on business, and loudly proclaiming that interference by legislation with their private business, rights and privileges means the opening of the door to the abolition of the private ownership of property and the entrance upon an era of socialism which must soon wreck our government. There is a genuine note of warning on either side in this controversy. That the monopoly corporation, which is but a creature of the state, must yield to whatever extent the public demands is evident, because corporations can never be above the law, and as creatures of it must always be subject to the law. But, as has been well said, in our regard for private right we must not perpetuate public wrongs. "The commonwealth is greater than the corporation it creates. The Constitution has made trade free in the United States. It must not be so interpreted as to make monopoly supreme throughout a land dedicated to freedom." The mere fact of the combination is not itself so objectionable in public opinion, but the fact that under our law the few and not all have been enabled to enjoy the benefits of combination makes combines especially obnoxious. The benefits of combination must be secured for all or removed from all. Equality before the law, equal privileges for all and special benefits to none, are cardinal principles of American liberty that will never be surrendered. As someone puts it, "The struggle now on in the business world is one between equal opportunity and special privilege." The people stand for equal opportunity. Trusts and monopolies and their defenders stand for special privileges to the few, and unequal opportunities to the many. If a free vote and a fair count are given the majority will win, and equal opportunity for all and special privileges to none will exist.

It has been sought to establish the fact that the tariff is the cause of the trust, and that the removal of the tariff will remove the trust. This is not exactly correct. The tariff tends to make more easy combinations to create monopolies in highly protected articles, virtually closing out foreign competition, by reason of the excessive import duties imposed, thus leaving to a combine of American dealers in highly protected articles the sole control of the American market. The tariff, when sufficiently high, simply tends to remove foreign competition. As has been well said, "The tariff is but a wet nurse for certain kinds of trusts and monopolies"; but monopolies and trusts to control trade are of ancient origin, those of Queen Elizabeth's time being very similar in their character and operation to our own corporation trusts. Queen Elizabeth's monopolies held crown patents or licenses to control certain lines of trade. The modern corporation monopoly holds charter contract of the state creating it. The monopolies created by kings and queens were granted a portion of the royal right to rob the public in the guise of a legal grant. The combined corporate trust of to-day has given it by the loose corporation laws, a portion of the sovereignty of the state, to enable it to legally destroy competition and control trade. The abolition of the tariff would not affect a world-wide trust, one embracing all lands and all nations, and with capital sufficient to control the product in any particular line of business. I am forced to conclude, therefore, that the only effect of the tariff on the trust question is to make more easy the formation of a trust in America on highly protected articles, because it bars world-wide competition, and restricts business rivalry to American producers.

Of course, as to articles of commerce that are not on the tariff list, it could not be pretended that the tariff affects a combination or assists it. The state can control and restrain trusts in existence, but it involves a constant legal battle to do so. I do not believe you could induce men worth $1,000,000 or $2,000,000 to embark in great industrial enterprises where the liabilities assumed in carrying on the business would amount to a hundred or more million of dollars if the failure of the enterprise would subject their personal fortunes to liability for the payment of debts incurred in the prosecution of the business. We all know how carefully the very rich as a rule guard against personal liability. But if the trust organizers could only carry on their business through a co-partnership, the members of the trust would have the same liabilities and only equal opportunities with the individual competitor. Equality of opportunity in business instead of special privilege would exist. The action of the trust and its extension of business could only be carried on then by consent of all the members of the trust, if it was a co-partnership. Trusts either buy a rival or crush him, thus entailing, in the latter instance, great financial loss and frequently ruin. State statutes give a right of action for damages against trusts injuring competitors in efforts to control markets. If the trust is a corporation the action can only be against the corporate entity for damages; while if the trust was a partnership, then the right of action would be against not only the partnership, but also against each individual member thereof. That many such suits would be brought against partnerships and the members thereof operating a trust, goes without saying, and this fact would deter millionaires from becoming members of trade combinations. Trading corporations place partnerships and individual merchants and business men at a disadvantage in many ways. The co-partnership method, with its liabilities and responsibilities, collectively and individually, makes men cautious, and keeps down inflation of values and wild speculation. Mercantile partnerships develop individuality integrity and character in the commercial world. Commercial or trading corporations destroy individuality in business affairs, and by reason of non-liability, generate fictitious values and create a false condition of financial affairs.

In the old days, when great mercantile and manufacturing enterprises were carried on by partnerships, a young man was taken in as a clerk, and by industry, honesty and ability, could work his way up until gradually, as the heads of the firm retired, the younger man who had been growing up with the business was taken into the firm as a junior partner and eventually was given to him the entire charge of the business. But how is it now? What chance is there for a young man, by his individual worth, to rise from a clerkship in one of the great commercial trading corporations? If the head of the firm dies, the stock in the firm simply passes to his heirs and executors, and the business is carried on just as before, but no head clerks are promoted by reason of the death of the head of the firm. The impalpable, bloodless, intangible corporation is not affected by the physical disability or death of its shareholders. The incentive for the young man to develop individuality and character in mercantile life is largely removed. The young man, under the corporate *régime*, is simply a part of a great machine, and he is used until he is no longer valuable, and then replaced by some one of younger years. The corporation in ordinary business dwarfs individuality and creates inequality and lessens competition. The partnership in business develops individuality and creates equality and competition. I, therefore, am firmly of the opinion that the state should enact laws providing that no corporation should be organized for any but public and quasi public purposes, and name distinctly what shall be considered public and quasi public purposes. Of course, in the great commercial centers, strong opposition will exist to this. The argument will be made that corporate control of business is so absolute and easy that trading corporations are a necessity. It is true that the control of a trading corporation is easy, because it depends on the mere matter of dollars to buy a majority of the stock, and not on the will or the brains of the individual shareholder. One man may buy enough of the shares of stock to control a corporation, although there may be a hundred stockholders. If the transition back to co-partnerships be simply an inconvenience, and business corporations be desirable only for convenience, then let us have at once laws enacted that declare the members of a corporation responsible to the same extent as the members of a co-partnership for the debts, acts and liabilities of a corporation. This will leave the corporation existing. It will meet the argument that corporations are so convenient, because of being so readily controlled, and that therefore they are a necessity of modern commercial life. These laws will tend to equalize opportunities in the business world, and where opportunity is equal the natural law of supply and demand, guided by the ever-present power of competition, will regulate in a healthful and steady manner the business interests of the country.

I believe either of these remedies will solve the trust question by preventing to a great extent the organization of private trading corporations. Monopolies and trusts can only exist where consolidation and combination are easy and possible. As long as a mere matter of dollars sufficient to purchase a majority of shares of a corporation renders it possible to form a combine, thus long combines and trusts will exist. But partnerships are based on consent of the members, and the purchase of the interests of one member of a firm, or of all but one, will, unless all consent to the change, dissolve the co-partnership. Under the corporate system the investment of money alone will create a combination by the purchase of the shares of stock of the corporation desired to be absorbed, regardless of the will of the objecting members. Under the partnership system, mutual assent of all partners, those who buy and those who sell, as well as all interested, must be obtained before a combine is possible. Protection, equality, and justice reign in business transactions under the *régime* of partnerships; but under corporate control, inequality, tyranny, injustice, and above all, the mere power of the dollar, reign supreme.

The mere caution of men risking their all in one business venture will prevent the formation of great trusts where individual liability exists. If the trading private corporation is allowed to continue as it now exists, trusts will continue to be formed, and the protest of the people over their oppressive operation will take the form of laws that will necessarily, under the guise of regulating, at last go to the extreme of attempting to fix prices by law, and when this fails, then the natural recourse of the people will be the abolition of private ownership of property, which will usher in an era of socialistic governmental experiments, in the end bringing disaster to our people and republic.

I recognize that large masses of capital can be had and used to best effect only when capital is secure. Capital should be given the fullest opportunity possible consistent with the public good, but capital can usually take care of itself. It must be employed or it is useless. Capital and labor must use each other. The trust is a profitable field for capital, and hence capital seeks the trust. The trust is becoming the dictator of trade. Its powers are not limited by charter or public opinion. It enters all branches of industry. It reduces the price of raw material it buys, and raises the price of the product it sells. Its movements are secret, silent, unerring and all-powerful. Its vast profits will ever tempt wealth and enterprise, and the aim of capital to constantly seek profits will be ever a menace to the security of the trust investor. The struggle to obtain the special benefits for the few by the trust managers and the battle for equal opportunity for all in business is the point of interest the state should bend its energies to adjust at once, for herein lies the danger to our land.

I believe, therefore, that the coming assembly of governors and attorney-generals of the various states should take steps looking to the calling together of the legislatures of the various states, if necessary, for the purpose of enacting legislation along the lines I have suggested herein. If practicable, I believe that these various states should at once enact laws.

Following Mr. Crow's remarks, papers were presented by P. E. Dowe, president of Commercial Travelers' National League, New York; F. B. Thurber, of New York, president U. S. Export Association; Joseph Nimmo, Jr., of Washington, D. C., president National Society of Statisticians, and Stephen P. Corliss, representing the traveling men.

P. E. Dowe addressed the conference on the subject of "The Trusts and the Commercial Travelers":

P. E. DOWE.

President Commercial Travelers' National League.   Statistician of the American Anti-
Trust League.

I have listened time and again to my fellows, in discussion as to the definition of the word "trusts," and there appears to be a varied opinion as to its significance. The unabridged Webster's dictionary I make use of at my home fails to define the word, in the sense of commercial combinations, so a short discussion of the accepted meaning of the word does not seem out of place at this time.

I found the following definition in Maitland's Dictionary of English Slang and Americanisms: "Trust, a combination of manufacturers or dealers for the purpose of limiting production and advancing prices, or one of railroads, gas companies and other corporations for their own benefit and to the detriment of the public. See Combine."

"Combine (American), a word coined to express the same meaning as 'trust' and supposed not to be quite so distasteful to the opponents of monopolies."

The following I copy from the *New York Journal of Commerce, Commercial Year-Book:* Mr. Byron Holt's definition of the word "Trust":

"As popularly used the word 'Trust' is now applied to any consolidation, combine, pool, or agreement of two or more naturally competing concerns, which establishes a partial or complete monopoly, in certain territory, with power to fix prices or rates in any industry. Viewed from the standpoint of the consumer, the informal agreement and the iron-clad combine look alike if the one has the same effect as the other upon prices."

Trusts are organized for speculative reasons, primarily, in spite of the contentions of some unpractical writers upon social and economic conditions, who, good souls they are, dwell upon ethics or argue for the brotherhood condition of mankind, in anticipation of an approaching millennium.

If these men, inexperienced in the ways of the world, could be brought to a realization of the fact that their arguments are misapplied by promoters and officials of the commercial conspiracies known as trusts, are offered by Shylocks, with knife and scales clamoring for the pound of flesh, to excuse the attacks upon the commercial integrity and equality of this country, and to cover their hatred of the citizens who seek by the enterprise characteristic of American individualism, to throw off the galling yokes of serfdom to the monopolistic class, they would wish that the ink had dried upon their pens before the production of such dangerous weapons in the hands of unscrupulous speculators.

While trusts are for speculative purposes principally, they have other sinister designs; organized first for the money in the deals, secondly for a more marked line of differentiation between the few very rich and the many very poor, and thirdly for the virtual enslavement of labor; not for industrial economies and to reduce the prices of the commodities to the consumer; not for the good of the people, but against their welfare; and all claims by those interested in trusts or by their subservient tools to the contrary are veritable lies.

Another unpractical class who knowingly or unwittingly assist in the gigantic swindle of the age, surrounding with alluring and delicately worded fallacies, the miscalled scientific economies; clothed, so to speak, with the covering of the gentle sheep, but containing the ravenous wolf. I mean that proportion of the college professors who give in their lectures upon political economy the kind of arguments they are expected to propound, and for which they are paid. The sons of some wealthy fathers must be educated to enable them to take their places as the coming plutocrats, and must be taught the most approved methods for the subjugation of the common people. The majority of these sires sprung from lowly origin, but now aspire to an exclusive set, and are more than willing to enter into any movement, conspiracy or otherwise, to prevent other American citizens (neither better nor worse off than were once these so-called self-made men) from attaining the same degree of success—or a partial attainment. These men, most of whom are composed of the coarser kind of human clay, will open their hearts and purses to assist into political power the creatures who can be molded as easily as a handful of putty, to the wishes of snobs, who aspire to be of the upper class, the codfish aristocrats, by the grace of a rapid accumulation of wealth.

Still another class, that must bear a share of the responsibility for aiming to create a misconception of the trust question, is that proportion of the newspaper writers, managers, and proprietors, who have allowed themselves from political connections or from subsidizing processes applied by the direct or indirect influence of trust magnates, or for both reasons, to become the catspaws of the "inflationists for revenue only." The press owes some duty to the public, to the people, the plain people, who constitute the bone and sinew of the nation. Upon the press a great responsibility rests. The people desire from it the truth, the whole truth, and nothing but the truth.

There are many reliable news sheets and honest newspaper men, for which thank God; but the man who aims to purposely deceive the readers of the paper with which he is connected, by offering unhealthy doctrines and false argument, may not receive a just punishment for the crime (for so it is in a sense) while on this mundane sphere; but when he appears before the final tribunal will obtain the condemnation so richly deserved for betraying another kind of "trust" than those being considered here, i. e., the people's trust.

I have been told by a number of newspaper men that my previous public utterances respecting trusts and their effects were of especial interest, owing to the incidental statistics submitted, and as I shall make use of some figures to-day, it is but fair that an explanation be offered as to where and how they were obtained. I first became interested in the subject of trusts after reading Mr.

Lloyd's book, "Wealth Against the Commonwealth," a few years since, and began immediately thereafter the collection of newspaper clippings and books bearing upon the subject. It was not until I had been elected the president of the Commercial Travelers' National League in 1897, however, that it dawned upon my faculties that the commercial men were to be made the first victims of the situation; yet at that time I had but an imperfect conception of the great magnitude of the trust movement, and must confess that it was not until the last half of the year 1898 that I fully realized the danger and extent of the centralization of capital, and the monopolizing of commodities.

Reports began to reach me of first-class salesmen being dispensed with for no reason other than the fact that trusts, "Conceived of greed, born of dishonesty, and cradled in the lap of injustice," had assumed the octopus form, and taken within far-reaching tentacles, all or nearly all the concerns in specific lines of trade, and were sucking the life from fair and honest competition. Trust manipulation for the purpose of controlling a particular line, and fixing the prices and quality of its commodities, meant that the traveling salesmen must go, aye "go"—anywhere, to Heaven or the other place, for aught the trust magnates care.

Entering upon a systematic research and a close study of the situation, during which time I heard from more than six thousand commercial travelers, either in writing or verbally, or through reports of friends who were assisting in the work, I was enabled to submit in evidence before the industrial commission in Washington in June last, important data as to the number of traveling salesmen dispensed with directly or indirectly through the organization of trusts, and to-day I have no reason for changing my figures. I also stated the number of salesmen reduced in salary, from the effect of trusts; and gave figures furnished me by traveling men, either formerly, or at the time of giving information, employed in the lines of their greatest experience, as to the advances in the prices of trust commodities. I have with me a few copies of my testimony before the industrial commission and having new material to offer to-day, will not rehash that evidence, but will be glad to furnish the pamphlets containing the old material to the delegates to the Civic Federation desiring a copy.

There have been thirty-five thousand commercial travelers thrown out of employment; mostly traveling salesmen, but in part city salesmen who come under the title of commercial travelers; for the man who picks up his gripsack and drums city trade, or invites customers to his headquarters to inspect his samples, is a commercial salesman, or a commercial traveler, by a slight elasticity in the use of the name. A city salesman is eligible to membership in any of the commercial travelers' associations. The majority of city commercial salesmen make out-of-town trips occasionally, sometimes short distance, sometimes long distance journeys. I neglected to note in previous arguments this sub-classification; it is unimportant, however, as the city men are but a small proportion of the whole number affected.

I stated in Washington in June last that twenty-five thousand were reduced in salaries. Could add to-day a thousand to these figures. I was in error when I anticipated, on the 16th of June, that thousands more of the commercial travelers would be dispensed with on July 1st; for, from reasons best known to the trust officials, expected wholesale discharges did not take place. I have heard from less than one hundred discharged on that date, but have been notified of many cases of reduced salary. Reduction in salaries was not exclusively with trusts; many of the "outsiders," owing to the pressure of unfair competition and loss of trade, were obliged to make reductions.

The salesmen who lost positions, owing to the trusts, were all good men; being of energetic and progressive character, proverbial of the American, could not be discovered as tramping the streets wearing signs of distress. Nearly every one of them had some money saved; some found positions as travelers for other houses; some went into other pursuits; some had farms, and I know of more than forty instances where former drummers are doing farm work; and some are still looking for positions.

Commercial travelers are opposed to trusts, both from policy and principle, and consider them detrimental and demoralizing—detrimental as menacing the possession and enjoyment by the people of those rights to life, liberty, and the pursuit of happiness, and equal privileges and possibilities in the application of individual enterprise and experience; demoralizing as presenting un-American conditions; imitation of English business methods, as offering evidences of rascality and corruption. In this connection I will assert that if the statements in Lloyd's "Wealth Against the Commonwealth" will cause the blood of honest men to boil within their veins with indignation that such conditions could exist in this so-called free and enlightened republic, with a full appreciation by the people of the rottenness of the latter-day growth of trusts, a thousand times more corrupt and grasping than the *régime* of which Mr. Lloyd writes, they would sweep from political life the subservient tools of the trust power. The people ask to be shown the way to peacefully crush the growing monopolistic power or to cut its claws; and they will surely apply the one moving force greater than the power of money—the ballot—in a "landslide" for the candidates in whom they have confidence.

Improvement, progression, inventive genius, single enterprise, American manhood and vim are conspired against by the trust magnates.

I had prepared another paper to present to-day, but upon receipt of the question blanks issued by the Civic Federation to the secretaries of commercial travelers' organizations, labor bodies, trusts, wholesale merchants, and others, I decided to substitute this paper.

There are thirty-two leading associations for commercial travelers in the United States, two of which have local posts, about two hundred and fifty all told; there are also a few commercial men's social clubs, scattered throughout the country; in even numbers three hundred and twenty-five associations, great and small, of commercial travelers.

I could have written the secretaries of these three hundred and twenty-five associations at a great saving of expense in the investigation of the subject of "Trusts and Their Effects Upon Commercial Travelers"; the secretary of each organization could have given me some personal information, and acquainted me with some points obtained from friends, but unless he had communicated with the members of his association, his replies to a series of relevant questions would of necessity be more or less guesswork.

At my suggestion the American Anti-Trust League has begun a work of statistical investigation; they propose to show by authentic data that while the cost of living has increased within the last two years at an average of between 12 and 16 per cent, wages have been advanced less than 3 per cent; and that wages are lower to-day than in 1895. The statements regarding wages are upon information supplied by some well-known officials of labor organizations, who are thoroughly posted about the union scale.

The American Anti-Trust League will publish some new figures regarding trade balances, and comparisons of previous years, showing the proportion of export and domestic business, and demonstrating the effect the trust prices have had in swelling the figures.

I have here a list showing advances in the prices, due to the direct or indirect influence of trusts, of about 150 commodities; the advances ranging from 5 to 500 per cent. The list was obtained by representatives of the Anti-Trust League applying to manufacturers and dealers for information, and making daily reports. Nearly 500 establishments were visited. The list is sworn to. (See appendix.)

As I have been limited to a twenty minutes' discussion, I cannot run over the list, but have had it printed in sufficient quantity to supply one copy for each of the gentlemen of this conference. Will call attention to a few items: Ordinary shovels doubled in wholesale price, and snow shovels advanced 145 per cent; iron, 85 to 130 per cent; coal, 50 cents a ton wholesale; gasoline, 4 cents a gallon; shoes for the workingmen, 15 to 50 cents per pair, etc.

I submit the following letter:

"Lansing, Mich., July 8, 1899.

"P. E. Dowe, Esq., President Commercial Travelers' National League, New York.

"Dear Sir: In reply to yours of the 5th, will say, that a detailed report of the investigation of hotels will not be published for some time.

"The facts are, however, that over 90 per cent of 100 hotels interviewed claim a falling off of traveling men of 10 to 50 per cent during the past year, which in most instances they attribute to the effects of trusts and combinations.

"The reports otherwise show their business to be on the increase, and satisfactory, only complaining of the falling off of commercial men, which in most instances is made up by an increase of tourists and the traveling public.

"Yours most respectfully,

"(Signed.)   J. L. Cox,

"Commissioner of Labor."

The amount of the common and preferred stocks, of all the listed trusts and inclusive of their bonded indebtedness, is the vast total of $8,000,000,000 in round figures. This statement is made upon most reliable authorities.

Upon information furnished by a well-known newspaper statistician, have stated upon previous occasions that the intrinsic valuation in the aggregate of all the trusts is about $2,000,000,000, a four-to-one ratio for stock-jobbing manipulation; but, now think that this is an overestimate.

Previous to 1895 nearly 600 trusts were projected, and to include a great variety of commodities; several of these trade combinations failed to materialize, some disintegrated; but the processes for the centralization of capital and power continued, combination and recombination going on until in March last there were between 350 and 360 combines, yet their capitalization was billions more than the capitalization of the 600 trusts of 1894 and before. To-day my list shows 425 trusts.

The number of business concerns absorbed by the gradual and systematic efforts to obtain control of the markets and highways; 5,565, say 5,600 in round numbers; exclusive of the grape growers, lake vessels and dredges, milk dealers, and farmers' milk combines; also insurance, telephone and telegraph, railroads and street railways, electric light, gas, ice, water and steamship trusts.

I have no means at my command of ascertaining with certainty the amount of capital of each concern absorbed in the processes of combination and recombination. Dun's and Bradstreet's Commercial Agencies could secure this information by setting investigating forces at work. I will assume, for argument, that the capital will average for each concern not more than $200,000, or for 5,565 concerns, $1,113,000,000, about an eight-to-one ratio of valuation for speculative purposes.

The letter from Mr. Cox suggested the idea of similar lines of investigation in other states, and I communicated with several hundred hotels scattered over the country. The replies demonstrated a falling off of commercial trade, of an average of 18 per cent; and this did not tally with my figures; showing either an underestimate of the number of traveling salesmen affected by the trusts, or the accepted figures as to the total number of commercial travelers to be an over-approximation; I requested the Anti-Trust League to seek information from every hotel in the United States, to which they agreed.

I have received the statement of the printer that communications were addressed to 5,000 hotels last week; more will go out this week.

What if the trusts win? "The whole machinery of independence, as we have known it heretofore in this country, is entirely gone, and man, whatever his prospects might have been, is absolutely at the mercy of the trust. It must feed him, clothe him, shelter him, and educate him, as will serve its interests." The foregoing is quoted from a letter of an attorney-general.

I will now read a letter from a United States senator, one of the brilliant men of the day, and noted the world over for his sterling honesty and utter fearlessness:

"My Dear Mr. Dowe: The cause at stake—the restriction of trust combinations—I have very much at heart. We ought to urge it calmly and reasonably.

"Extreme demands and vituperate advocacy are what the monopolists desire to have us resort to. There is no need of this. We may freely admit the benefits from large capital and extensive plants engaged in productive industries; and we do not object to them up to a reasonable point.

"But we are sure that beyond such a point, when combinations become so large that competition ceases, low prices to the consumer also end; economies are no longer practiced; it is easier to pay huge salaries and raise the prices of the product than it is to adopt economies and reduce prices; and so up go the prices, and the people suffer. Individual enterprise is destroyed; energy and ambition on the part of the 'firms of small means,' as Mr. Depew describes them, die out; the struggling young men of small capital become merely the low-salaried employees of millionaires; and the nation becomes divided into two classes only, the few very rich and the many very poor. It will be a great misfortune to our free America if our present high rising prosperity is to be signalized by the inauguration of a system of great trusts in all production and the helpless subjugation of all the business men, the manufacturers and other producers, and the wage-earners, by the rich capitalists and speculators who organize and control the trusts.

"If the people are sufficiently determined, the march of trust organization can be arrested at a safe stage. By state and national legislation all evils can be prevented. I have not had time to examine the Texas anti-trust law as expounded in the *North American Review* by Governor Sayers, who is one of the ablest, most upright, and most courageous of our public men of to-day; but I am sure that suitable laws to be passed by the state legislatures and by Congress can be framed. Such laws are what we want, not mere resolutions of political conventions, to be abandoned and the cause destroyed by unfaithful legislators. Elect true men, and the work is done. Unfortunately, the selection and election of such men are difficult labors. The worst feature of the trust organizations is their interference with political government. Their managers care not for the declaratory resolutions if they can select the candidates for office. So they appear everywhere in politics. No young man can rise in his political party, become a local party leader, or aspire to public office until he has given the trusts to understand that he will not seriously exert himself to harm them.

"The resolutions of political conventions, therefore, should not be the whole subject of your efforts to limit trusts. The reso-

lutions you will easily secure. It is the members of the legislature and the Congressional nominees you need to look after.
    "(Signed.)   Wm. E. Chandler."

The remedy for the plague of trusts, now epidemic, I have
not discussed, excepting as contained in the suggestions of Senator Chandler; the purpose of my paper being to demonstrate
that trusts are considered as an abominable curse by the people.
I speak for the commercial travelers especially, but for the people
generally in opposition to trade combines; for the commercial
men have felt the pulse of the people, as could no other class.

Remedy for the evil is expected by the people from national
and state lawmakers; discussion as to the best medicine, so to
speak, is left to others, better qualified from professional training,
to prescribe.

As plain, every-day business men, the commercial travelers
submit the facts as they find them; and that class specifically I
have the honor to serve as a spokesman here.

Mr. F. B. Thurber addressed the conference on the subject of
"The Right to Combine":

F. B. THURBER.

President United States Export Association.

If this conference does nothing else than what it has done
in giving wide publicity to the brief utterances of two representative men, in their letters acknowledging the invitation to this conference, it has justified its being held.

The Rev. Lyman Abbott, of New York, said: "I think what
we most need on the subject of industrial, commercial labor and
transportation combinations is just what your letter indicates
this meeting will endeavor to secure—light, not heat. What we
need to understand, and what only experience can teach us, is
the relation between competition and combination—the one the
centrifugal, the other the centripetal force of society. He who
believes only in combination will logically be led to socialism;
he who believes only in competition will logically be led to nihil-
ism. Neither of these results can possibly furnish the solution
of the problems which now confront us. We must learn how to
secure the advantages of combination without destroying the
individual; to maintain brotherhood in practical forms without
sinking, obscuring or belittling personality."

Henry White, of the United Garment Workers of America,

said: "Your conference is called at an opportune time. The reorganization of industry, which is so rapidly taking place in many of the important industrial pursuits, presents a problem which cannot be given too much attention by the friends of industrial reform. It is of more consequence just now to understand the nature of this development than to declaim against it. That is the reason why I sympathize so strongly with the calling of this conference."

The right to combine has been recognized from time immemorial, subject to a due regard to the rights of others. The progress of the world has for centuries been largely promoted by combinations of labor, skill and capital, but it remained for the nineteenth century under the influence of steam, electricity and machinery to become, *par excellence,* the era of combinations. These forces could only be utilized to their fullest extent through combining the capital of individuals, and the advantages of such combinations are so numerous that they have revolutionized the industrial, commercial and political worlds. Bovee said: "In former times, war was a business, but in modern times business is war." It is certain that these forces enormously enhanced the force or war of competition, and this in turn has led to attempts through further combinations to regulate and control competition. The editor of *U. S. Consular Reports* for August, 1897, in discussing industrial centralization in Europe, said:

"Our period is distinguished by its tendency to centralization, not only in the state, but likewise in industry and commerce. Large firms are competing with small shops to such an extent that the latter are disappearing one after another. The factory has displaced the workshops. Everything is being done on a large scale; everything is becoming colossal.

"That is not all. We see now even the great factories, not finding themselves sufficiently strong alone, and fearing their reciprocal competition, renouncing their own autonomy and combining among themselves; and this tendency is everywhere manifest. The French *charge d'affaires* at Berlin calls attention to this centralization in Germany; the French consul at Glasgow mentions the same phenomenon at Glasgow.

"These facts are significant. They certainly indicate one of the tendencies—perhaps, it might be said, one of the necessities—of our epoch. It is certain that production is passing through a serious crisis. Competition has occasioned a considerable decline in prices, and in order to retain markets, certain industries have been obliged to work under unprofitable conditions. To avoid final ruin, they have agreed either to limit the production to maintain prices, or to conclude complete consolidation. Hence the cartels, the syndicates for production, the associations.

"We neither approve nor blame this new procedure; we simply record it, remarking that sometimes certain laws are developed, whatever may be their consequences."

The economic results have been so sudden and startling that it has occasioned alarm in the public mind, and this has been seized upon by sensational journals and political parties competing for public favor, to unduly exaggerate the evils attending the evolution, while the good has been overlooked. The best horse will shy at an umbrella if it is opened in his face too suddenly, but if allowed to smell of it and see that it is not dangerous, his alarm subsides; and I prophesy that when all sides of this question have been carefully studied, popular alarm at the organization of industry, commonly known under the misnomer of "trusts" will subside, but in a country with universal suffrage the only way to put down error is to argue it down. Sensational misrepresentations must be met with facts or grave injuries to our industries and institutions will result.

The state of alarm in the public mind is indicated by the following resolutions recently adopted by the Wholesale Grocers' Association of New Orleans regarding "Trusts":

"Whereas, it is the sense of this association that trusts and combinations controlling the output and prices on commodities are a menace to our national safety and existence. We assert as a fact that it is the intention and purpose of such combinations and aggregations of capital under the name of trusts, by capital and concentration to control and manipulate alike the values of raw material and manufactured products, thereby enabling themselves to dictate to the producer, the wholesale and retail dealers as well as the consumer, the prices they shall pay for all manufactured commodities. We further assert that the unopposed continuance and enlargement of trusts in our midst means, as certainly as any mathematical fact, the absolute destruction of our commercial existence. Be it therefore

"Resolved, By the Wholesale Grocers' Association of New Orleans, that viewed from a political standpoint, we believe it is to the best interests of all true American citizens to use every endeavor to cause the most extreme legislation against the operation of trusts that can be had consistent with our state and national constitutions."

And further illustrations are found in the action of our national and state legislatures in enacting special statutes to limit this supposed evil. Congress prohibited pooling agreements between railroads, and passed the Sherman anti-trust law, which declares every contract in restraint of trade illegal, and under this act the Supreme Court of the United States in the Trans-Missouri Freight Association case took the extreme view (by the narrow majority of five to four judges, however) that even a necessary agreement between carriers for establishing and maintaining reasonable and uniform rates of freight was a contract in restraint of trade. The legislature of the great commercial state of New York in 1896 enacted a law which provides:

"No stock corporation shall combine with any other corporation or person for the creation of a monopoly or the unlawful restraint of trade or the prevention of competition in any necessary of life. No foreign stock corporation formed by the consolidation of two or more corporations or by the combination of the business of two or more persons, firms or corporations for the purpose of restricting or preventing competition in the supply or price of any article or commodity of common use, or for the purpose of establishing, regulating, or controlling the supply or price thereof shall be authorized to do business in this state."

This law was the outcome of an investigation by the judiciary committee of the New York senate, which was remarkable for the bias shown against incorporated capital and the disregard of economic facts developed by the evidence. The report, among other things, denied the right of a manufacturing corporation to choose agents for the sale of its goods and fix the prices and terms upon which they should be sold.

From time immemorial it has been a common custom in trade for manufacturers to select agents to sell their goods and to fix the price and terms on which they shall be sold; also for agents to agree that in consideration of these and a certain commission or rebate they will only sell the goods of one manufacturer.

The legislature of the state of Texas at its last session enacted an anti-trust law which prohibits any person, partnership, firm, or incorporated body from entering into any agreement to regulate or fix the price of any article or thing whatsoever, or the premium to be paid for insuring property, or to fix or limit the amount or quality of any commodity. The act pronounces the refusal or failure to put on the market for sale by any corporation, firm or individual the product of any party a conspiracy to defraud, so as the refusal of any corporation, copartnership, firm, individual or association which may gather items of news or press dispatches for sale to newspapers to sell the same to more than one newspaper within a certain radius of territory. This act prohibits any person from selling at less than the cost of manufacture, or giving away manufactured products for the purpose of driving out competition. The act provides that if two or more persons or corporations who are engaged in buying or selling any article of commerce, manufacture, merchandise, mechanism, commodity, or any article or thing whatever shall enter into any pool, trust, agreement, combination, confederation, association or understanding to control or limit trade in any such article or thing or to limit competition in such trade by refusing to buy from or sell to any other person or corporation any such article or thing for the reason that such other person or corporation is not a member of or a party to such pool, trust, agreement, combination, confederation, association or understanding, or shall boycott or threaten any person or corporation for buying from or selling to any other person or corporation who is not a member of or party to such agreement shall be deemed guilty of committing a violation of the act and of a conspiracy to defraud, the penalty for which is a forfeiture by the offender of not less than $200 or more than $5,000 for every offense, and each day of such violation is made a separate offense.

The governor of Texas, Hon. Jos. D. Sayers, in commenting upon this law recently said:

"It has been asserted by some, who claim themselves qualified to speak upon the subject, that trusts, as operated in the United States, are not harmful, and that they are but the outgrowth of an evolution in industrial life that is natural, healthful and necessary. On the other hand it is insisted, and I think rightfully, that they are, in a great measure, if not entirely, due to vicious legislation, to the policy of the Federal Government in the matter of currency and taxation, and to that of the states in the creation of corporations. A high protective tariff, which excludes foreign competition, and a single gold standard which limits the volume of currency and enhances the value of that in circulation, supplemented by the easy formation of corporations under state authority, are the potent instrumentalities upon which the trust depends for its existence. If, under the trust-reign, the industries of the country be passing into the hands of the few, if the products of other lands be so heavily taxed as to be, in a great measure, denied entrance into our ports, and our people be thereby compelled to buy and use only those manufactured at home, if the cost of production and distribution is being reduced to the minimum, if the output is being so regulated as not to exceed a given quantity, and its selling price determined by the trust exclusively, if the small dealers are being put under duress as to those from whom and as to what they may buy, and as to how they may sell, if individual effort be no longer able to compete successfully with corporate power and corporate advantage, if young and weak industries are being strangled to death and the establishment of new and independent enterprises prevented, it cannot be doubted that for this untoward and unhealthy condition of industrial and commercial life legislation is, in a large degree, responsible. If the trusts shall be permitted to organize and to operate as for the last several years, the result is certain that a more disastrous panic than has ever been known will sooner or later occur. Much of the stock issued by these organizations is entirely fictitious, and does not represent real capital. Moneylenders will some day refuse to recognize it as safe security, and then the storm will burst forth in all its fury. Under such circumstances, what is the duty of the government? To it do trusts and corporations, either directly or indirectly, owe their being, and upon it therefore rests the obligation to see to it that they, its creatures, shall not harm the people.

"It is reported that the attorney-general of the United States has said that the Federal Government is helpless to wage a successful warfare against the gigantic evils which proceed from the trust-power, and that relief can only be had through the state governments. Congress can, if it but will, render the most effective and substantial assistance. Let it reverse the present policy as to the currency and the tariff, putting the two metals upon entire equality, and providing for a fairer and more general distribution of the currency, and lowering the duties on imports so that the productions of other countries may compete with those controlled by the trusts. This much Congress can and should do. In the meantime let the states perform their duty.

"I have lately assumed to suggest a conference of the governors and attorney-generals of all the states and territories, without exception, to consider the subject, and, if possible, to devise and unite upon such legislation as would overthrow the trust-power and prevent its revival. In this matter, I have acted upon my own responsibility, and with the sole view to correct, if possible, a great and growing evil—one that threatens much harm to the country. I have had, and I will have, no purpose in view other than that distinctly specified, and I trust that, should the conference be held, no other question will be considered except that of trusts, and the best method to be adopted by the states to insure their complete destruction within the shortest period possible.

"The trust should be regarded as a public enemy and should

be treated as such. Arrogant, unscrupulous and merciless in the exercise of its power, it should be fought unto the very death."

These quotations illustrate the state of mind that a considerable body of well-meaning citizens is in at the present time, and although such utterances appear somewhat hysterical to the student of this question and opposed to the facts, it is both a condition and a theory which should meet careful consideration by thoughtful men. The "ifs" mentioned by the governor of Texas are assumed to be facts, but they do not exist.

I have been a careful student of these organizations of industry from the beginning. I may say that when I began it was with a strong prejudice against them. I believed that they would tend to oppress the public with high prices, and also that their political influence was to be feared, but a careful study of their effect ranging over a period of years has materially modified my opinion. The first prominent illustration of the so-called "trust" principle was the consolidation of lines of railroad into vast·systems, with the result of better service, and, as a whole, lower rates. The people of the United States now get their transportation at about one-half those of other principal countries. The next was the Standard Oil Company, under whose operations the price of oil has declined more than other commodities not under trust control. Another is the American Sugar Refining Company, under whose operation prices have averaged 50 per cent lower in ten years succeeding its formation than they did during the preceding ten years. I used to think that combinations of capital would abrogate competition, but experience has shown that, instead of abrogating competition, it has elevated that force to a higher plane. If a combination of capital in any line temporarily exacts a liberal profit, immediately capital flows into that channel, another combination is formed, and competition ensues on a scale and operates with an intensity far beyond anything that is possible on a smaller scale, resulting in breaking down of the combination and the decline of profits to a minimum. A striking illustration of this is found in the sugar and coffee industries to-day. Arbuckle Bros. had attained a commanding position as roasters and sellers of coffee, and they also sold, but did not refine, sugars. Because the American Sugar Refining Company would not sell them cheaper than other buyers of sugar, they decided to go into the sugar-refining business, whereupon leading spirits in the American Sugar Refining Company, seeing that the margin in the coffee business was good, decided to go into the roasting and selling of coffee. The result has been that this contest of giants has reduced the profits in both industries to a minimum if not to a positive loss, making it hard for smaller manufacturers and dealers to live, but saving millions of dollars for consumers that would have otherwise inured to manufacturers and dealers.

The only trusts which have succeeded for any length of time have been those which have been conducted on a far-sighted basis of moderate margins of profit, relying upon a large turn-over and the economies resulting from the command of large capital intelligently administered. The truth of this is illustrated by innumerable failures in trust organizations to control prices, recent illustrations of which are the strawboard trust, the starch trust, the first wire nail trust, and the old steel trust. There are trusts, so called, in nearly every branch of business, and there is good and bad in all, but the good so far predominates that such aggregations of capital should be encouraged, accompanied by safeguards against abuses. The only additional safeguards needed are for stockholders and investors, whose interests are often sacrificed through lack of publicity. The average investor is the chief sufferer. So far as the interest of consumers is concerned, it is amply protected now; first by competition, as I have shown, and second by the common law which, if invoked, will nullify any contract in unreasonable restraint of trade, and any unreasonable combination is subject to indictment for conspiracy. Special "trust" statutes are not necessary, although many have been enacted.

As to the right to combine, it is so closely related to the right to contract that it affords a most interesting question. Commerce is nothing but a body of contracts. Every purchase and sale, from a peanut to a gold mine, and every transaction in the movement of merchandise; every agreement between employer and employee involves a contract either verbal, written or implied. No right is more sacred, and none has been more carefully guarded in our fundamental law. The Constitution of the United States, Art. 1, Sec. 10, says: "No state shall pass any law impairing the obligation of contracts." Art. 14, Sec. 1, says: "No state shall make or enforce any law which shall abridge the privileges or immunities of citizens of the United States, nor shall any state deprive any person of life, liberty or property without due process of law, nor deny to any person within its jurisdiction the equal protection of the law."

It seems to me that the tendency of legislative and judicial bodies in this country just now to sweepingly condemn contracts which in any manner restrict or regulate trade is unwise and against public policy. If capital is denied the right to combine, labor must be put under the same disability. Such statutes as those I have quoted are really statutes in restraint of trade rather than in the interest of the freedom of trade, and are opposed to the greatest good for the greatest number.

The opinion of the minority (four against five) of the Supreme Court of the United States in the Trans-Missouri Traffic Agreement case, as expressed by Judge Brewer, says:

"If there is one thing which more than another public policy requires it is that men of full age and competent understanding shall have the utmost liberty of contracting, and their contracts, when entered into freely and voluntarily, shall be held sacred and shall be enforced by courts of justice.

"The remedy intended to be accomplished by the act of Congress was to shield against the danger of contract or combination by the few against the interest of the many and to the detriment of freedom. The construction now given, I think, strikes down the interest of the many to the advantage and benefit of the few. It has been held in a case involving a combination among workmen, that such combinations are embraced in the act of Congress in question, and this view was not doubted by this Court (In re Debs, 64 Fed. Rep., 724, 745-755; 158 U. S. 564.) The interpretation of the statute, therefore, which holds that reasonable agreements are within its purview, makes it embrace every peaceable organization or combination of the laborer to benefit his condition either by obtaining an increase of wages or diminution of the hours of labor. Combinations among labor for this purpose were treated as illegal under the construction of the law which included reasonable contracts within the doctrine of the invalidity of contracts or combinations in restraint of trade, and they were only held not to be embraced within that doctrine either by statutory exemption therefrom or by the progress which made reason the controlling factor on the subject. It follows that the construction which reads the rule of reason out of the statute embraces within its inhibition every contract or combination by which workingmen seek to peaceably better their condition. It is, therefore, as I see it, absolutely true to say that the construction now adopted which works out such results not only frustrates the plain purpose intended to be accomplished by Congress, but also makes the statute tend to an end never contemplated, and against the accomplishment of which its provisions were enacted."

To the average mind it looks as if the opinion of the minority was right and that our American courts and legislatures have been "leaning over backward in their efforts to walk straight."

In Europe the rule seems to be different, as is evidenced by the celebrated Mogul Steamship case decided by the highest court in England, a clear statement of which is given in a recent pamphlet by William L. Royal, Esq., of the Virginia bar:

"Several lines of steamships traded to China all the year. The trade was unprofitable except in what is called 'tea season,' when it was very profitable. The losses of the year were made up and a profit gained by the freights on tea in 'tea season.' Another line of steamers traded to Australia all the year until 'tea season' came on, when its steamers were diverted to Hankow to get a part of the profitable tea trade. The lines which traded to China all the year entered, thereupon, into an agreement, called here 'trusts' or 'pools' or 'monopolies' or 'boycotts' or 'contracts in restraint of trade,' or whatever else of the same sort can be suggested. They agreed together to divide out freights amongst themselves, and they published a notice to all merchants in China that if they would ship everything all the year by one of the conference lines they would be allowed a rebate upon all freights at the end of the year of 5 per cent, and whenever one of the steamers of the Australian line came to Hankow the conference had a steamer there to underbid it on freights; so that whatever the Australian got caused a loss. Thereupon the Australian line applied to the English courts for protection, upon the ground that this combination of many against one was contrary to the principles of our law. It is plain that the case brought up for discussion all the questions relating to pools and trusts now agitating the American mind, and these questions received a treatment in England worthy of their magnitude and scope.

"The case was tried first by Lord Chief Justice Coleridge and Lord Justice Fry. It was then tried by Lord Coleridge alone, and upon appeal from his decision, by Lord Justices Bowen and Fry, and Esher, master of the rolls, and upon appeal from them to the House of Lords, it was heard before the Lord Chancellor, Halsbury, Lord Watson, Lord Macnaughten, Lord Bramwell, Lord Morris, Lord Field, and Lord Hannen. Each decision was in favor of the conference, and every one of these twelve eminent judges except Esher, M.R., held that the agreement was a perfectly good and valid one, according to the principle of our common law.

"The guiding principle in the case was held to be the one stated. If the parties contemplated their own improvement only, it was immaterial that they contemplated injury to the Australian, or that injury to him would be the result of their acts; but if they were actuated by malice toward the Australian, then the agreement would have been a vicious one, condemned by the principles of our law. This was held to be the test in all such cases."

The idea is very admirably brought out in the opinion that was delivered in the House of Lords by Lord Field, who said:

"It follows, therefore, from this authority, and is undoubted law, not only that it is not every act causing damage to another in his trade, nor even every intentional act of such damage, which is actionable, but also that acts done by a trader, in the lawful way of his business, although by the necessary results of effective competition interfering injuriously with the trade of another, are not the subject of any action.

"Of course it is otherwise, as pointed out by Lord Holt, if the acts complained of, although done in the way and under the guise of competition or other lawful right, are in themselves violent or purely malicious, or have for their ultimate object injury to another from illwill to him, and not the pursuit of lawful rights."

The Mogul steamship case finds a parallel in a recent case described in the Berlin *Tageblatt*, as follows:

"The highest court of the German Empire sitting at Leipsic, has rendered an important decision, which we summarize below, concerning combines or trusts. The decision will be of great interest to the other nations, and particularly to the United States, where trusts have come to exercise such a prominent part in commercial and industrial affairs. The court mentioned has declared emphatically that trusts and similar combines are entirely legal. The grounds upon which this decision was based were as follows: When in certain industrial pursuits the prices of products are sinking so low as to make business impossible or as to endanger the successful carrying on thereof, the crisis which necessarily follows is not only disastrous to the individual concern, but also to internal affairs generally. For this reason it is for the interest of the entire state that inadequate low prices shall not prevail too long in any industrial branch. Realizing this principle, the legislative bodies have repeatedly, and only recently, undertaken to bring about an increase in the prices of certain products by the establishment of protective duties. For this reason it cannot be deemed certainly, or generally speaking obnoxious to the interests of the community when the manufacturers of certain articles form what is called a 'trust' with the object in view of preventing ruinous competition, and for the purpose of mitigating the downward tendency in the prices of their particular manufactures. On the contrary, such combinations can be looked upon, not only as warranted by the instinct of self-preservation, but as a measure for the interest of the whole community as well. Especially is this true in cases where prices are so low that the manufacturers of the articles are on the verge of financial disaster. For this reason the building of syndicates or trusts has been designated by a number of authorities as a means which, when properly managed, would prove extremely expedient to prevent detrimental and unwarranted over-production."

Many good people have imagined a bogey monster that doesn't exist. They have accepted as facts the fancies of sensational journalism. The natural advances in price when demand exceeds supply have been debited, and the declines when supply exceeds demand have not been credited, to say nothing of economies in production and distribution which have made the present age the consumers' millennium.

Never before would a day's labor buy so much of the comforts and luxuries of life, but education of the masses to the wants of intelligence has progressed even faster and the rewards to the inventors and the captains of industry and finance, who have made this evolution possible, are envied. It is overlooked that corporations are really co-operations; that the number of partners as stockholders in any industry is increased, that anyone can become a partner, and that instead of being concentrators of wealth, they are distributers of wealth. It has been assumed that labor would be oppressed by the organization of capital, but experience has shown that organized labor has met organized capital, and that the largest organizations of capital have furnished the steadiest employment and have paid larger wages than individual employers. The grievances of individuals injured in this evolution of industries have been magnified and the general good minimized. The lesson of the stage driver thrown out of work by the locomotive, or the workman by the machine, is forgotten when the traveling salesman who loses his job through the economies of industrial organization appeals to public sympathy. That wider markets are necessary and that large capital intelligently administered is necessary to find them is not appreciated. That "the rule of reason," as expressed by the minority of the Supreme Court of the United States in the Trans-Missouri case, is in danger of being expunged from our statutes.

Within the limits of a paper like this it is of course impossible to do more than speak suggestively and touch upon but few of the many points involved, but I have faith that with further study of this subject by the American people that the facts will become plainer and they will appreciate that

"Through the ages one increasing purpose runs,
And the thoughts of men are widened by the process of the suns."

STEPHEN P. CORLISS.

New York Traveling Men's Association.

The gathering in Chicago under the auspices of the Civic Federation to discuss the all-absorbing subject of "Trusts" will doubtless present nearly as many different opinions as there are delegates assembled. And while it will not be possible to formulate any controlling decision upon the subject, there will be ideas, opinions and suggestions presented which will prove to be of value in determining, per chance, a solution of the trust problem, through regulation, rather than at an attempt of absolute prohibition. The evolution in business life that has led to a legitimate combination of a number of concerns in the same industry cannot be considered as the growth of a day nor the reasons leading to its fulfillment ignored. The possibility of their creation is attributed to various causes. A number of students of the question declare that the tariff, prohibitory in many of its classifications, is the foundation upon which the so-called trusts are enabled to successfully build.

Others contend that competition is the chief factor, the primary reason for the formation of so many industries under one general head. The former methods of conducting business made necessary large expenditures of money in administration and distribution—by the smaller corporations, firms and individuals seeking a market for their productions. In the new order of affairs there is a large saving of these expenses. It is undoubtedly true that this transition will cause a number of persons to lose their positions, yet the proposition or movement must be considered from the standpoint of its effect upon the community rather than the individual. The legitimate results that should accrue from the federation of a number of manufacturers for instance, under a general management, are an improvement in their methods of business in every way, reducing waste to a minimum, producing a better article than before for the same or less money, no attempt being made to control production or output, not capitalizing in excess of their business needs. If this plan is followed, it cannot prove much of a menace to our business econ-

THOMAS J. MORGAN   JAMES R. WEAVER
H. W. PALMER   CHAS. D. WILLARD
JOHN B. CONNER   MORRIS M. COHN

omy. A large part of the friction that has existed between capital and labor, causing strikes, lockouts and riots, was the result, in part, of overproduction. The product was unloaded at a loss, the owners tried to recompense themselves by cutting the wages of their workmen. This evil ought now to be remedied. While it is unquestionably true that capital is more strongly entrenched than ever before, the same can be said of the labor unions, these are having greater influence than heretofore, because they are choosing more intelligent and conservative leaders, who with advanced ideas recognize the law of mutual responsibility. The new combines, honestly capitalized and honestly conducted, ought to be in a great degree fruitful of peace and harmony in the industrial life of our country.

A recent writer has stated: "That the conquests of the future are to be won by the industrial armies." It is a fact that we lead the world in labor-saving machinery and in intelligent workmen to operate it. The swift evolution in our manner of doing things in the manufacturing and mercantile economy of our land will place us far ahead of the rest of the world in this direction, as the wildest imagination can dream of. In these advanced movements it is not fair to impugn the motives of those engaged nor to declare everything as evil because it upsets or changes former methods or old directing forces. It is a matter to be closely studied, for the true thing in the new era has come to stay, and the question of the hour is, how shall the changes necessarily a result of the new environment best be made that they conserve and harmonize conflicting interests? Undoubtedly these at first will loom up mountain-like in their proportions, but will silently disappear with experience in the new life and its practical demonstration of the undeniable fact that if it shall endure the employer, employee, and consumer must be harmonious elements of its existence.

Opponents of this transformation in our industrial life naturally say that the large body of consumers will be the sufferers, that as the combinations will control products they will raise prices, and that wages will be at their mercy; facts at present and probabilities of the future, however, do not indicate this line of conduct. Those favoring industrial concentration argue that it ought to strengthen our industries and be a safeguard against financial difficulties, when compactly organized, properly conducted and honestly financed; that holding in check reckless competition will curtail unwise credits and overproduction, that it will be easier to regulate the supply to the demand, that self-interest will best be subserved by disposing of products at fair prices, that when this consolidating of our producing and distributing forces becomes an economic fact, instead of dwarfing individuality, it should present greater incentives and rewards for the exercise of intelligence, energy and enterprise of the individual.

So far we have been considering the phase of combinations, corporations, etc., based upon principles of integrity in conception and honesty of purpose in administration. But, there are aspects and conditions prevailing in other corporations, large and small, diametrically the opposite to the line of conduct set forth by those that may be considered in any way a benefit to our people as a whole. These so-called trusts are of every conceivable kind, capitalized at large sums far beyond any possible demands of production, issue great blocks of preferred and common stock, knowing that a dividend can never be paid upon it, but with tempting promises and smooth persuasion availing themselves of the speculative craze so rampant, to dispose of the stocks to a gullible people. Promoters and schemers are in the main responsible for this sort of a combine, relying upon the sale of stock for their pay for creating the concerns. Several of the states of our union issue charters to all corporations applying for them, without discrimination, accept the fees, require no guarantee of good faith to the public; so many gigantic unscrupulous corporations are started upon a career that can have but one ending, and that is failure. Along its track are the wrecks financially of ignorant, innocent investors, who were led to believe in the soundness of the corporation because the state sanctioned its birth, and its directors, men of reputation. Of course the illegitimate trust, corporation, combination or whatever it may be called, ought to be an exceptional thing, still there should be such safeguards thrown about and such guarantees exacted, that the creation of any will be a misdemeanor. So many industrial combinations are so largely capitalized and present such a bonded indebtedness that they will no doubt create suspicion in the minds of the employed as to the possibility of their becoming paying institutions; the sequel to suspicion is unrest, dissatisfaction, revolt; this must be avoided by regulation if possible, by control if necessary.

So much regarding the abuse of trusts. As to the remedies: First of all the subject should be kept divorced from politics. It is not at all necessary that there shall be a plank in the platforms of both parties declaiming against trusts, for the party holding the last convention will simply exceed the force of language used by the other in denunciation of them. It seems to me that the state, issuing a charter to a corporation authorizing directly or indirectly the sale of bonds and stocks, should have a commission or the secretary of state, in his capacity as such, should have charge of corporate affairs, and determine upon a thorough examination, those worthy of charters, as well as a surveillance over combinations, corporations, etc., organized in any other state that seek a market for their bonds and stocks within the limits of the state of which said commission is a part. That all combinations, corporations or trusts shall pay to the state of which they are a part, a tax upon their plant or franchise, the value of which shall be determined by its earning power. As to national supervision of the question, there may be laws now upon the statute books giving Congress all necessary control, if not, I suggest that a commission shall be created by Congress who shall protect investors from the evils sure to accrue from over-capitalization, they also to have power to pass upon the quality of the securities behind any issue of bonds and stocks thrown upon the market by said combinations, corporations and trusts. Publicity is a safeguard that will in no way injure the concentration of capital and effort honestly directed. A paper published in New York recently said:

"There is a bill now before Congress intended to cover the whole subject of trusts; it is very simple and quickly read. It does not say one word about the tariff, the labor question, silver, railroads, or anything else which is commonly supposed to be the cause of trusts. It does not even say that corporations must organize under this national law. In fact it is admitted that many corporations will continue to exist under state laws. But this much is said: Where a corporation starts out to do a large business, control a large industry, and drive a large number of people out of their accustomed avocations, something must be returned to the community in lieu of it, and this something is absolutely safe securities. These securities, moreover, must be so safeguarded that the great mass of the community can take hold of them. When this is accomplished the trust question is settled."

The great interest excited in this country through the report of the American consul at Limoges, Mr. Walter T. Griffin, on what is known in England as the Smith Combination Scheme, caused the Civic Federation's Conference Committee on Arrangements to invite, through Consul Marshal Halstead, of Birmingham, Mr. E. J. Smith, of that city, the acknowledged father of the plan, to address the conference. Mr. Smith could not attend but sent the following paper which thoroughly describes his system. Also, through Mr. Halstead, Mr. A. W. Still, editor of the Birmingham *Gazette*, who opposes Mr. Smith's plan, was invited to attend. He sent the paper which follows that of Mr. Smith.

E. J. SMITH.

Birmingham, England.

I have received through Mr. Halstead, our American Consul in Birmingham, your kind invitation to address the conference of your Federation in September. I have delayed my reply because, had I replied at once, I could only have declined, and I have waited to discover if it were possible. I find it impossible, and now hasten to express my thanks and to say that nothing would have given me greater pleasure than to meet you, had I been able to do so, but the press of business in England forbids that I should leave it for so long just now. I can only hope that a visit to your country is a pleasure simply deferred.

I have been given to understand that you would like to discuss at your conference the trade movement with which my name is identified, and that you would like something from me to help you. If you care to read to your members this letter, it may provide some apology for my absence.

I gather from the list of questions you have sent me that your attention is fixed upon the "Trade Trusts" formed so naturally in your country, and sometimes in mine. I hesitate to express any opinion concerning things with which I am not fully conversant, and can therefore say nothing about your "Trusts." They may be formed upon principles which avoid the evils generally belonging to the "trust" system. Those evils are over-capitalization, which must be a curse wherever it exists; the desire to establish monopolies, which must help to destroy, not build up, the commerce of any country and the happiness of its people; and selfishness, which leaves out of consideration the element of labor, which has its rights as well as capital. If you have any trusts which do not contain these evils, you have some "better way" which I do not understand.

I must take it for granted that all these attempts to improve the position of certain people in business have been made because there was some evil to cure. I know what it is in my own country. It is the desire to make haste to be rich. It is a desire which destroys the best impulses of humanity; it leads to overproduction, insane competition, the lowering of wages, and bankruptcy. So far as I have been able to study the "trust" system, it makes greater haste to be rich, and it does not provide the remedy for the evils I have just mentioned.

I believe in trying to find a remedy for the sin of undue competition. I believe in putting every trade in a position which will enable it to demand and obtain from the consumer a fair price which carries with it a fair profit, and which enables it to pay a fair wage to the real producer. Having done this, I would make it compulsory that the fair profit should be obtained and the fair wages paid.

And I would do all this without strife. I believe in trade unionism, but if it is good for one side it is good for the other. The judgment of workmen is no more to be trusted than is that of employers. But there is no division of interest between them. In each case it is a matter of money, because with money you can buy the necessities or the luxuries of life. Neither side can make money without the help of the other. Anything which goes against the interest of the employer is fatal to the interest of the employed. I believe, therefore, in so binding them together that their interests must always be treated as one.

But this interest can only be made secure by honest dealing. Therefore the consumer, upon whom everything depends, can be charged only a fair price.

These are the objects aimed at in what is called "The New Trades Combination Movement." Whether or not the methods adopted are calculated to secure them is, I presume, the question you wish to discuss.

I do not intend to weary you with details which you can read for yourselves in the printed matter which has been before the public for years, and which you can now obtain in book form. These details are so far important that without them the scheme cannot be successfully carried out, but they are too elaborate to describe here. I will content myself with giving you the main principles of the plan whereby it has been found possible to obtain fair profits and pay fair wages, prevent strikes and lockouts from happening, and to do all this by charging only a fair price to the consumer, and all without any attempt to establish a monopoly.

I have not had the advantage of studying your system of trading, and therefore cannot speak with authority upon some points which are of great importance in England. It is, however, exceedingly likely that one evil which the system is intended to cure is as real with you as with us. I allude to the pernicious practice of selling manufactured articles without first ascertaining the real cost of production. After years of examination I have come to the conclusion that not more than one-third of our manufacturers carefully and properly take out their costs. From this arises the foolish and unnecessary, and even morally criminal, underselling, which has made some remedy a great necessity. The first part of the plan is, therefore, to insist upon the cost of production being ascertained by the joint wisdom and practical knowledge of the whole of the members of any trade sitting in conference. Should anyone suppose that this is impossible or even difficult, I can only reply that, notwithstanding the greatest prejudice, suspicion, and rivalry, it has been done successfully over and over again, and that it forms the very foundation of the system under which many trades here both make and sell. The removal of ignorance, the restraint of recklessness, and the mutual help which can only come from mutual confidence, in no way interferes with the proper and lawful competition and enterprise of individuals without which manufacturing would become stereotyped and stagnant. Of this we have had ample evidence.

Of course it is supposed that an association has been formed, and that rules and regulations providing for every necessity have been drawn up and adopted. These include provisions for the detection of underselling, or the violation of the conditions under which the association works, the imposing of penalties when such breaches of trust are proved, and the establishment of a monetary guarantee which can be called upon if found necessary. This latter is accomplished by a somewhat original method which avoids the inconvenience of having to take necessary capital out of a business to lie idle in a bank. The regulations also provide for the fair claims of each class of customer, the fixing of cash discounts, and the charges for carriage.

So far it can be truthfully said that there is very little in the system which could be called new, excepting the joint cost-taking. The arrangements are probably more complete than will be found in other associations, because so many trades have assisted in making them so, but they are not original.

The feature of the plan which is probably new is that which follows all I have mentioned, namely, a thorough arrangement and alliance between employers and employed. This neither stereotypes wages nor restricts the higher claims of those who by force of superior ability of any kind ought to be able to command better positions than others. It does not interfere with the wages already paid in the separate factories, and it does not attempt to bring about uniformity of wages. It does not hand over employers to the mercy of a trades union, or take away from them in any way the right and the power to manage their business in their own way. It does not aim at the 'destruction of trades unionism—it enunciates the principle in the surest way by making employers trades unionists themselves. Having formed a union on the one hand and an association on the other, it brings both together for one practical purpose and one common good. It prevents disputes from becoming quarrels, puts an end to strikes by removing the causes of them, compels the obtaining of fair profits, and secures to the workmen payment for their services which insures their good-will and hearty cooperation. This is done by the carrying out of the following agreement between the two forces, whose interests are presumably one:

1. No employer to engage a workman who is not a member of the workmen's union.

2. No workman to accept a situation with any employer who does not sell at such prices as include the minimum profit fixed during the cost taking process, or which may be fixed from time to time by the employers' association and approved by the joint board.

3. No workman to be permitted to leave his situation and no employer to be permitted to discharge a workman on account of any dispute as to wages, or the hours and conditions of labor.

4. A wages and conciliation board to be formed of half from each side, to whom all such disputes may be referred, and whose decision, or the decision of its arbitrator, must be accepted on both sides or the alliance ended.

5. The regulations as to the supply of work people of a satisfactory kind to be a mutual matter, with a view of making it neither superfluous nor inadequate.

6. Defaulting members, or outside competitors, if any, to be fought, if fighting is considered necessary, by both sides unitedly, and the cost evenly divided.

7. A guarantee to be given by the employers that the wages paid in each factory at the time of the signing of the alliance shall never be reduced while the alliance continues, unless it may be considered necessary by the whole of the board.

8. A bonus on existing wages to be paid by each employer from the date when the board has decided that it is sufficiently strong to enforce the selling prices upon which the minimum profit has been fixed—that is, when a sufficient number of employers and employed have been brought into the bargain; the

employers' association to be the first to bring a recommendation to the board to this effect. The percentage of the bonus to depend upon the proportion of the wages to the proportion of the cost of material which make up the selling prices.

10. No further bonus to be paid on any advance in selling prices which only covers any advance in the cost of materials, but this to be proved to the satisfaction of the board, which may appoint some independent person to investigate.

11. The first bonus paid to work people to be a fixture, but all other bonuses to be subject to a sliding scale depending upon the increase or decrease of *real profit obtained*. Should selling prices be lowered simply in proportion to the lower cost of materials, the bonus shall not be affected.

12. Any increase or decrease in selling prices to be approved by the board, or its arbitrator, before being put into operation.

These are the conditions upon which the two parties to the agreement consent to bury the hatchet and work together for mutual good. There is no necessity to point out how strong such amalgamation must be. It can accomplish all that it is intended to do. The principal charge against it is that it may do too much. The power so obtained, it is urged, may be abused, and so the consumer may have to pay an unfair price for the goods he has to buy.

This is a large question, and one which it is impossible to reply to thoroughly here. I have tried to do it elsewhere, and I start with saying that it is absolutely impossible that such a thing should happen. It may happen with trusts, syndicates, monopolies of every kind, but this system is neither. The safeguards against monopoly, and therefore against unjust charges, are:

1. There is no restriction attempted against newcomers into any trade; therefore if large profits are obtained, overproduction will make smaller profits absolutely essential.

2. The work people have to consent before any advance can be declared. They will consent readily enough while they are fully employed, but as the bonus does not compensate them for short time, they will not consent if there is danger of driving away any trade. This is not theory only. From every wages board—and I am chairman of many—the desire to keep selling prices, and therefore wages, at a reasonable level, is most strongly expressed by the work people. In one alliance the work people refused to receive any further bonus or to consent to any higher profits.

But the test of any theory must be its experiences. I challenge anyone to show that in any trade whatever, working under the alliance methods, any attempt even to make unjust profits has been made, yet the principles have been in operation for eight years.

It is right that the consumer should be protected against unjust charges, but does anyone in his senses believe that these charges can ever last for long? Even successful monopolies are generally short-lived. There is no method yet discovered by which a few people can for long absolutely control the manufacture of any necessary article. They may do so for a time, and even make wealth, but the end must come—generally speaking, it comes even before the wealth is made. In the combination system I advocate, it must be remembered that the profits are carefully ascertained, printed, and circulated amongst the members. They cannot be concealed, and the temptation to overproduction cannot be restrained should these profits be too high. And if they are not too high, the consumer has no case. He has never troubled himself when profits have been too low; he has no sympathy with the bankrupt whose goods he has been able to buy below cost, nor with his creditors; he may have called the manufacturer a fool—with good reason—but he has had no pity. So long as only just profits are imposed upon him, I have no pity for the consumer.

But the consumer benefits very naturally—indirectly—by a fair profit being obtained. It comes back to him in many ways, which I have tried to prove in an article on this subject. He suffers in the same proportion from bankruptcies and starvation wages. But if he does not care to pay a fair price for his goods, he can make for himself. He has no right to expect other people to work for his benefit without sufficient compensation.

I do not think I need say more to help you in the discussion of this question. It would take many articles to describe the method fully. I have given you its main principles. I wish only to add one more suggestion: America, by its tariffs, does much to keep its trade, and to keep out other people, but it does not prevent them from paying the tariff and selling in America very often without profit. Whenever this is done your profits must also suffer, and when we compete with you outside your country and ours, the competition is abused. I am looking forward to the day when the two countries will be drawn together by a bond stronger than that of sentiment only. If we are a nation of shopkeepers, you must be very near to it. Combination means unity of purpose and a desire and determination to get what belongs to us. I advocate nothing beyond this, but I think I can see a chance of combination between the respective trades in the two countries, securing to each advantages which would be impossible to either without it.

A. W. STILL.

Editor *Gazette*, Birmingham, England.

Even if I did not most highly esteem the honor of being permitted to contribute to the deliberations of this great representative conference, I should have deemed it my duty to promptly accept your invitation to submit a critical comment upon what has been known in Birmingham as the "Smithsonian System" of Trades Combination. It has been my lot to watch the evolution of this system and its author from the outset, and, in the course of professional duty, I have had to study its effects upon the commercial and industrial welfare of the Midland counties of England, and to express adverse opinion freely—no doubt, at times, in language more vigorous than polite. You may be told that this antagonism is captious, ignorant and personal; but I will content myself with assuring you that it is, and always has been, wholly disinterested and sincere. Let me dismiss all personal aspects of the question as promptly as possible by pointing out that they cannot affect your consideration of the "Smithsonian System" except to this extent: that you must bear in mind when listening to the eloquence of my friend Mr. E. J. Smith, that he is not the disinterested advocate of a novel principle in the science of political economy, but the defender of a plan which he charges large fees for adapting to the particular conditions of any trade that may invite his assistance. He draws £1,350 per annum as chairman of the Bedstead Association, £500 per annum from each of one or two other associations over which he presides, and, less than twelve months ago, he demanded £3,500 for establishing an association in the Staffordshire pottery trade. I am credited with having materially assisted in preventing the success of the last-named enterprise, and, considering the large fee involved, no one need blame Mr. Smith for treating me as a most irritating and vexatious person.

But the laborer is worthy of his hire, and the fact that Mr. Smith charges for his services is not, *per se*, a discredit to him or an argument against his system. If the system is good, no payment he has ever received can be regarded as excessive. If, as I believe, the system is bad, it is perfectly in accordance with one's experience of human nature to find that the person least ready to acknowledge its defects is the man whose pocket is most favorably affected by its propagation.

To one other point which is slightly off the main line of criticism, I must request your attention at the outset of my remarks. Every department of British commerce and industry is subject, more or less, to the influences of our free trade policy. As mere purchasers all our people have the advantage of abnormally low prices, and our working classes can live in comparative comfort upon wages which would scarcely ward off starvation if high protective tariffs barred the admission of plentiful supplies of cheap food, cheap clothing, and all other necessaries and luxuries. But, on the other hand, as producers and sellers, our people, under this system of free trade, are compelled to accept, even in our home markets, the prices fixed in open competition with rivals in every quarter of the world. Our farmers have to fight against the most favored wheat growers in the old world and the new; and their tiny stockyards are pitted against the huge cattle runs of the "Far West," and the virgin grazing lands of Australasia. Our manufacturers and artisans must adapt profits and wages to the prices at which the underpaid workers of Germany and Belgium can flood our shops with their wares; and the surplus output of highly specialized and perfectly equipped American factories may be dumped upon our shores to cut out or cut down the home producer who pays high taxes because the state has little or no income from customs duties.

I do not speak either as a protectionist or as a free trader. What I have said is merely a colorless description of the *status quo*. But it will be perfectly clear to you that a country which "buys in the cheapest markets" must produce at the lowest possible cost if it is to hold its own against external rivalry. It must take the fullest possible advantage of the cheap labor which cheap living creates, and it cannot afford the luxury of sentimental theories. The protective policy of other nations gives their capital and labor a solid advantage in home markets. British capital and labor have to compete as keenly in London, Edinburgh and Dublin, as in New York, Paris and Berlin. The Smithsonian system of trades combination is doomed to failure as a British institution, because it eliminates the free competition which results in "bottom prices," and substitutes inflated and wholly artificial rates of profit and of wages. In a protectionist country the system might flourish in any trade which relied wholly or mainly upon the home markets, but even under such specially favorable conditions it would develop peculiarities against which it is necessary that both capital and labor should be carefully forewarned.

The Bedstead Trade Alliance presents the best illustration of Mr. E. J. Smith's System. Probably most of you are familiar with Consular Report No. 444, issued by the Bureau of Foreign Commerce, Department of State, Washington, dated June 6, 1899, and signed by Mr. Walter T. Griffin. On reading this report I was somewhat surprised to find that it consisted in the main of extracts from the voluminous writings of Mr. Smith, and that Mr. Griffin had adopted the rosiest views of the system, and endowed them with all the weight of his authority, without giving to American readers the slightest hint that there is another side to the picture. For example, I notice that he quotes a speech made by the Right Hon. Joseph Chamberlain, five years ago, when the whole thing was in an experimental stage. Mr. E. J. Smith was, and is, one of Mr. Chamberlain's most ardent political supporters, and it was a graceful and costless recompense for his services when the Right Hon. gentleman advertised him as the founder of "a great social experiment." But I should have expected Mr. Griffin to point out that the results have not been so truly marvelous as Mr. Chamberlain anticipated. The Right Hon. gentleman mentioned a great trade in Bradford which had adopted Mr. Smith's principles. About the date when Mr. Griffin was making his inquiries for Consular Report No. 444, Smith's system was being ingloriously discarded by the wool dyers of Bradford, after having caused unlimited friction and vexation among all sections of the woolen trade. I am somewhat reluctant to characterize as nonsense the statement on page 3 of Mr. Griffin's report, that at the time the Bedstead Association was formed, "No manufacturer was making any money, wages were at the starvation point," etc., etc. But really no milder term than "nonsense" can be applied to a sweeping and wholly inaccurate statement which seems to be founded entirely upon the irresponsible chatter in which my good friend Mr. Smith occasionally indulges when he beams behind the smoke wreaths of a fragrant Havana.

I will endeavor to give you a somewhat more candid history of the formation of the Bedstead Association. In the early '90s, British trade was passing through a period of extreme depression. The causes were no doubt numerous, but low prices, which many eminent authorities traced to the appreciation of gold, and the fall in silver values, was doubtless the main factor in cramping commercial and industrial enterprise. The bedstead trade had its full share in the depression, and while the old established and wealthy firms were doing fairly well, taking full advantage of the plentiful supply of cheap labor and material, men with little or no capital behind them were hard pressed, and were recklessly underselling each other in the desperate competition for business. As in every other trade during the same period, the weakest went under, while the stronger survived. Mr. E. J. Smith is a self-made man, and it is certainly with no disrespectful thought that I mention the fact, well known to me, that he and his partners were very hard pressed during that crisis in their trade. He set himself the task of forming an association to prevent ruinous underselling, and soon induced a few of the smaller firms to join him in the movement. But as his plans developed, he was fortunate in gaining the support of Mr. W. J. Davis, a very able labor leader in whom the workpeople placed absolute confidence. At this early stage the Bedstead Association consisted of a comparatively weak minority of the manufacturers, but Messrs. Smith and Davis were able to form a workman's association, which included in its membership practically the whole of the operatives in the trade. The inducement held out to these workmen was an immediate advance of wages in the form of a 10 per cent bonus, and the assurance of further increases, in the form of additional bonuses upon each advance made in selling prices by the manufacturers. No great expenditure of eloquence was necessary to secure the cheerful support of the workpeople to such a policy as this. They were hearty and unanimous, and when they agreed to work only for firms which were members of Mr. Smith's manufacturers' association, the founder of the movement was in the happy position of being able to compel the outstanding firms to join him. The alternative to doing so was the withdrawal of their work people, the stoppage of their business, and the transfer of prosperity to their associated rivals.

In point of fact, the bedstead manufacturers, who desired to retain liberty of action, treated Mr. Smith as a person of no consequence, until they suddenly discovered that he had woven a net which they could neither break nor crawl through, and they had to submit to being caught in it with the best grace possible. In order to understand the undoubtedly remarkable success which attended his efforts, it is necessary to bear in mind that Birmingham was the home of the bedstead trade, that ten years ago it had practically no foreign rivalry to contend against, and that even in America it did a huge trade, and was able, owing to the low cost of production, to compete pretty fairly with the home makers, in spite of protective duties. Conditions such as these gave wholly exceptional advantages to Mr. Smith's movement. Broadly speaking, he was organizing a monopoly, and had little or nothing to fear until his operations created the inevitable competition. During the first year or two of its existence every member of the association was delighted. Large profits were made, high wages were drawn, and though the drastic espionage organized by Mr. Smith might provoke an occasional adjective, there was no serious disposition to fight against the master and guiding hand of the skillful originator of the scheme.

There was a rift within the lute when Mr. Smith, now the handsomely salaried chairman of the Bedstead Association, began to sell his advice to the manufacturers of bedstead components. Tube and mount manufacturers and workpeople were organized on the "Smithsonian" principle, and of course raised their prices to the bedstead makers, who soon found that the profits Smith gave with one hand were being taken away by Smith with the other. He comforted them with further advances, but the process has been continuous, and at the present time selling prices and wages in the bedstead trade are nearly double what they were when the association was formed seven years ago. Outside competition has been the inevitable consequence, and for several years past the Bedstead Association has had to expend enormous sums in fighting this kind of rivalry. But still more enervating is the constantly increasing tendency to hoodwink the association by granting secret rebates on association prices. This has been a thorny subject of debate and recrimination, the more so as it is practically impossible to prove the extent to which the system prevails; but experienced business men will form a pretty shrewd estimate of the "palm oil" possibilities in a business where freedom of competition is barred. I need only mention that a few months before Mr. Griffin presented his report, Mr. John Port, of Manchester, who owns, I believe, the largest bedstead works out of Birmingham, resigned his membership of the association because he found it impossible to book orders at list prices, owing to the extent to which other and less scrupulously honest firms were giving secret rebates. It surprises me that Mr. Griffin makes no allusion to a circumstance of so much importance.

The principle of a Smithsonian alliance is that members of the manufacturers' association shall employ none but members of the workmen's association, and that workmen shall only serve association firms. Mr. E. J. Smith has frankly admitted that the cornerstone of his system is coercion, and he maintains that without coercion it would be futile and inoperative. His candor on this important point is exceedingly helpful. It enables me to go direct to the all-important question of whether the advantages gained, either by employers or workmen, compensate for the loss of freedom which both classes suffer when they adopt his system. I will take as illustration the case of Mr. John Port, of Manchester, who, as I have already said, withdrew from the association early this year. Like every other member of the association, Mr. Port was one of the fighting fund guarantors, that is to say, he had made himself responsible to the association bankers for a certain amount, which, on his resignation, was used for coercing him. This coercion took the form of calling out all his workmen, the strike pay and allowance to pickets being drawn from the fighting fund. At the same time the association made every possible effort to prevent firms which have dealings with the bedstead trade supplying Mr. Port with materials, and powerful influences were brought to bear to prevent him selling any of his goods to the wholesale or retail houses. Practically the strike is still going on, but the coercive tactics of the association failed. Several independent firms of bedstead makers supplied Mr. Port with goods to meet the requirements of his customers, the customers stood by him, and in the course of a few weeks he was able to fill up most of the vacant places in his factory with free workmen drawn from other trades. When the success of Mr. Port's revolt was assured, Mr. William Robinson, of Northbrook street, Birmingham, retired, and again the policy of calling out all the alliance workmen was adopted, but this rebel has also succeeded in defying Mr. E. J. Smith and his system. An even more important defection was that of Messrs. Perry and Sons, of Bilston, near Birmingham. The Right Hon. Sir Henry Fowler, M.P., is a director of this firm, which withdrew because its heads were convinced that the coercive policy practiced under Mr. Smith's direction amounts to illegal conspiracy at common law. Sir Henry Fowler is a distinguished lawyer, and no doubt his fellow directors had the benefit of his advice. Messrs. Perry's workpeople signed an agreement and severed their connection with the workmen's section of the alliance.

The condition of several other combinations with which Mr. Smith is connected, such as the coffin furniture, the fender and fire brasses, and the jet and rockingham, is far from flourishing, and defections are frequent. I have already alluded to the collapse of the Bradford Wool Dyers' Association, to Mr. Smith's failure in the pottery trade, and may add that the Welsh tinplate trade, after listening to his eloquence, declined to adopt his plans. The blue brick manufacturers, and the bar iron makers, who have had ample opportunities of seeing his system in operation, have also refused to have anything to do with it. Last year the ordinary working expenses of the Bedstead Association exceeded £7,-000. This year special fighting levies amounting to over £12,000 have been made in addition to the ordinary expense levies. A great many of the members are in arrears with these levies, and the number of outside firms has increased, while the authority of the association officials is fatally injured by their failure to successfully coerce Messrs. John Port, Wm. Robinson, Perry and Sons, and some London and Glasgow outside firms, against whom a policy of selling at less than cost price was adopted a year ago.

You will see from this hurried summary of the present position of Smithsonian combinations that Mr. Walter T. Griffin has not said all that may be necessary to an intelligent appreciation of the position in Consular Report No. 444. I do not suppose that Mr. Smith will supplement the deficiencies, and I have no right to ask that you should place implicit faith in the statements I have made, though they are a mere summary of unchallenged news items which have appeared in the British press during the past twelve months. But you will permit me to suggest that before accepting Mr. E. J. Smith's system as a solution of the complex problem of how best to reconcile the interests of capital and labor, your great conference should direct a careful and independent inquiry to be made by capable and independent industrial experts, to whom I shall be most willing to give all the assistance that lies in my power.

In addressing an audience of employers on this subject, I should have to point out that those capitalists who adopt the "Smithsonian" system, imperil not only their freedom, but their trade. They lose their freedom and independence, because what Mr. Smith is pleased to call "scientific cost taking" compels a manufacturer to disclose every detail of his business to trade rivals, and the system of espionage, which Mr. Smith draws a salary of £1,350 a year for supervising in the bedstead trade, is so close that the most private papers and books relating to one's business must be opened to the association agent on demand. For every fault of omission or commission, a fine may be imposed, and woe to the man who happens to be out of favor with the governing and favored clique which invariably grows up under such an organization. The records of the limited companies engaged in the bedstead trade show that the profits do not exceed on the average 7 per cent. And the volume of trade, even at this small profit, is restricted, because the high prices created by pampering the workmen have encouraged the establishment of bedstead manufactories in Germany, in France, in Belgium, in Holland, and even in decadent and degenerate Spain, while on the Ameri-

152

can continent they have placed the British trader at a hopeless disadvantage. If any member of a Smithsonian combination finds that its control does not favor his welfare, he can only gain his liberty by making a large pecuniary sacrifice, with the galling certainty that his own money as well as that of fellow traders will be freely spent in a resolute endeavor to ruin him; and ruined he certainly will be if his purse is not abnormally long, his perseverance great, and his enemies comparatively weak. The successful revolt of Messrs. Port, Robinson, and Perry & Sons, marks the decay of the Bedstead Alliance, but in its palmy days it ruined several men who fought for liberty and gloried in sending one, at least, to a premature grave. I do not hesitate to say that, though the system may be a crutch to limping incapacity, it is a fetter to any man of vigor, enterprise, and ability. But even the ablest may be drawn into a sacrifice of their freedom without fully realizing what they do, and when the chains are welded a Hercules may be required to break them.

Those who noted carefully the description I have given of Mr. Smith's first essay in combination forming may have remarked that he triumphed rather as an organizer of labor than of capital. He paid well for the support of the workingmen, and having induced them to act as his coercionists, "the persuasion" of the employers followed in due course. It would be wholly unreasonable to blame the workmen for taking the course they did. Most of them live from hand to mouth, and trouble very little about principles of political economy. Besides, it has always been quite clear that next to the founder himself, they gained the lion's share of advantage from Mr. Smith's system. Their wages were raised at once, and have been rising steadily ever since, though frequently the gain has been rather nominal than real, in consequence of the scarcity of employment. It is perfectly true that since the alliance was formed, workingmen have experienced far greater difficulty in becoming employers, but this is not a consideration that carries much weight with the majority, who are apt to say, and not, I think, without some reason, that the worst masters are the smallest. On the other hand, the alliance rules provided that the bulk of strike pay should be found by the employers, a novel and agreeable experience to trade unionists; and when called out for coercive purposes the men were assured of an allowance equal to their wages, and had merely to do a little picket duty in return. Seven years' experience has somewhat dimmed the brightness of the prospect held out, yet I think the fact is undeniable that a majority of the workmen consider that they acted wisely in giving their support to Mr. Smith.

But in spite of this I would venture to appeal to the intelligence of any well organized body of workingmen, either in my own country or in America, for a vote against the principle of alliance with which Mr. E. J. Smith's name is associated. Seven years' experience has not been without its lessons to those who are willing to learn. It is now the opinion of a good many workmen that they degrade themselves by consenting to act as mere tools of coercion for an employers' organization against masters with whom, personally, they have no quarrel. Some of Mr. John Port's workpeople had been in his service for thirty years, and when he retired from the Bedstead Association it was a pathetic thing to see these old hands parting with a kindly employer who was quite willing to continue paying the association rate of wages, though he could no longer submit to the association rules and restraints. But the more serious aspect of the matter from a trade union point of view is that the slightest failure of the coercive system is quite as fatal to the Workman's Union as to the Employers' Association. Take the case of the three firms which have recently broken away from the Bedstead Association. Every trade unionist has been drawn away from these firms by order of Mr. E. J. Smith and his committee. But the firms have not closed their doors. They have simply drawn in skilled workmen thrown idle through depression in the cycle trade and similar industries, and are rapidly converting them into efficient bedstead hands. The men these firms formerly employed are thrown upon the alliance, which must either pay them for doing nothing or give them a share of the work available in alliance factories. Every outsider who starts a bedstead business (and the number is already considerable), and every defaulter from the association must train men to the business, and in due course these men become the rivals of union workmen. To admit them to the union would be fatal weakness; to leave them outside makes opposition to the alliance more easy. The tendency, therefore, is to develop two rival sections of workpeople, alliance and non-alliance, between whom, I suspect, there will be hatred, malice, and all uncharitableness, even when Mr. E. J. Smith has ceased to be a force in the industrial affairs of Mid-England. I doubt very much whether it will be possible to make workpeople risk these schisms in the ranks of labor, or sacrifice their independence for such advantages as the Smithsonian system has to offer. They will prefer to rely upon independent organizations, capable of dictating their own terms, and free to accept service under any employer by whom these terms are granted. The very limited success of this combination system is due far more to peculiar and strictly local conditions than to any special virtues of its own.

It seems hardly necessary to point out, after what has already been said, that as a means of preventing trade disputes the Smithsonian system is a dismal failure. Strikes are as frequent as before, and capital not only pays excessive wages to prevent them, but has to support the workpeople while they are in progress. If one grants that "ruinous underselling" has been checked, it is at once possible to retort that this is only done while outside competition and rivalry are undeveloped, and that within the last twelve months the Bedstead Association has sacrificed thousands of pounds in an attempt to crush opposition by selling under cost price. Though fashion on the continent of Europe has set strongly in favor of metallic bedsteads since the alliance was formed, there is no responsive increase in this branch of Birmingham trade, and within the year it was officially reported that half the workpeople were on short time. These are hard facts, which no amount of grandiloquent palaver can dissipate, and they are not what one would look for in the records of a "triumphant solution" of the industrial problem. It is also a hard fact that one Birmingham firm has transferred a considerable section of its plant to Spain, and that another is building a factory at Antwerp—in both cases with the object of escaping from alliance discipline.

The cardinal defect of Mr. Smith's system is that, unlike a trust, or an actual combination of works and capital, it effects no saving in any direction whatever. Not one solitary feature of it is economic. There is no saving in designing, in advertising, in order collecting, or in transport. No inducements whatever are offered to the workpeople to cheapen the cost of production by exceptional skill or industry. The employers are simply bound to pay workpeople 50 per cent more than they would be content with if no alliance existed; they have to subscribe to the salary of a chairman who does not allow them to call their souls their own; they have to give bank guarantees which will be drawn upon for their destruction if they claim liberty of action; they are fined like naughty boys if they make a mistake, or happen to be caught in giving a rebate which they know perfectly well is allowed *sub-rosa* by nine-tenths of their rivals in trade. They may at any time be called upon to subscribe their quota to the coercion of an honorable fellow trader. They may see splendid openings for enterprise, but if they move a hair's breadth from the beaten track, the lynx-eyed scientific cost-taker and his emergency committee of rival traders will be smelling round in a most inquiring frame of mind. The whole system savors of the ridiculous, and

I have marveled many times that my fellow-townsmen could tolerate the irksome espionage, or submit to the dictation of its designer, but they know how assiduously and how skillfully he has purchased the favor of the operatives section, and only the wealthiest and the most resolute will try a fall with him. In a word, the Alpha and Omega of the Smithsonian system is Mr. E. J. Smith, and I am one of his most dispassionate admirers. Remove him, and the system would collapse like a castle of cards.

I cannot hope to have carried conviction to all your minds by the somewhat disjointed comments in this brief and hastily prepared paper, and must be content if it has given pause to some who were carried away by the curiously one-sided and inadequate view of Mr. E. J. Smith's system, which has obtained official currency in the United States. The subject is worthy of far more careful and exhaustive examination than I have been able to prepare in the time at my disposal, but I may, at least, take comfort in the thought that you cannot scorn this criticism without conferring a benefit upon the commerce of my country!

Joseph Nimmo, Jr.—"The Limitation of Competition and Combination as Illustrated in the Regulation of Railroads":

JOSEPH NIMMO, JR.

President National Statistical Association.

In its essential features the important question of public policy which we are here to discuss is almost as old as the history of human government. It is the ever recurring question as to the manner in which and the extent to which combination and aggregated capital may beneficially and without detriment to the public interests, operate in restraint of competition. The discussion of a question so comprehensive and so radical inevitably touches upon the elementary.

The only universal laws of which we have knowledge are the laws of the Creator. No statute of His conflicts with another. Divine law is, in and of itself, the manifestation of an omniscient, omnipotent, and omnipresent Ruler. Absolute perfection characterizes His law. The laws of human society, on the other hand, are marked by the infirmities which attach to a world ruled by man and his passions. *Humanum est errare*. Human laws conflict with each other in innumerable ways, and hence are subject to restraints and limitations. The science of government and of human law is essentially a science of limitations. Every fundamental principle of government, every established rule of public policy and every wholesome statutory enactment must in practical administration be taken in connection with its qualifying conditions and limitations. Besides, inventions, newly discovered forces, and ever changing conditions necessitate changes in those rules of action which preserve the harmonious course of human interaction. This status of unstable equilibrium and of limitation and restraint is inevitable from the fact that in all our social and industrial pursuits we are actuated by two opposing motives. Individuality leads men to struggle with their fellows for the acquisition of everything worth having and holding, for we live in a world in which we are all debating. On the other hand, an equally virile human trait,—the social instinct,—leads men to associate themselves together in co-operative enterprise. Since the world began man's faith in his fellow-man was never before so pronounced as it is to-day. This is manifested in innumerable forms of social and industrial association. Out of these opposing forces has sprung the habit of competition and the habit of combination. The struggle between these conflicting dispositions has begotten two maxims, namely, "Competition is the life of trade," and "In union there is strength." Neither of these maxims affords a safe guide in the affairs of life. In many instances competition kills trade by constriction. There are also combinations for good and combinations for evil. Many combinations perish of their own weight and lack of vitality. Besides, the life of trade is a subjective element. It has its origin and force in human intelligence, ambition and acquisitiveness. Combination and competition are only modes of interaction. They are mutually regulative of each other. Together they operate as the balance wheel of self-government. The question before us is, therefore, one of differentiation, selection, and adaptation.

If, then, governmental institutions, laws, and rules of public policy, and even shrewdly devised maxims conflict and are all subject to limitations and restraints, is humanity adrift in its social, commercial, and industrial interaction? The answer is clear and sufficient to every reflecting mind. The peace and well being of human society proceed from laws, policies and institutions which experience has proved to be for the common good of all. Out of the lessons taught by centuries and even millenniums of experiment and struggle, there have been evolved those customs and usages, those beneficent principles of government, those rules of public policy, those wholesome systems of law, those wise judicial discriminations and those habits to which in their entirety we apply the generic term *civilization*. The world bows to the edicts of its own experiential knowledge. Said Patrick Henry in his immortal oration for liberty: "I have but one lamp by which my feet are guided, and that is the lamp of experience. I know of no way of judging the future but by the past." Theories built upon accepted laws of human experience are to a degree useful, but the idea of natural or universal law, other than moral law, is a solecism in the affairs of men.

In the excitement attending every epochal period and every popular movement for the correction of real or fancied evils remedies essentially revolutionary and destructive in character are apt to be proposed. Such will inevitably be the case now as attempts are being made to settle that great question the consideration of which has called together from all parts of the United States this convocation of men of learning and of large practical experience.

The fundamental error which usually confronts such efforts arises from the propensity toward doctrinarianism. It is one of Renan's profound sayings that the nation which devotes itself to social problems is a lost nation. That is undoubtedly true in so far as relates to attempts to formulate universal law. The science of law as evolved by the lessons of experience is the finest sociology.

The specific question presented for our consideration is that of "Trusts," as the word by a process of misuse has come to have significance in the public mind. The real issue relates to the manner in which and the extent to which the recent movement toward the restraint of competition through combination or through the power of aggregated capital should be limited or controlled by governmental authority. This question presents itself in innumerable forms, for there are many kinds of combinations, agreements and co-operative arrangements differing widely in character and in their constraining influence upon competition.

Again, it is a matter of vital importance to determine the question as to the nature and extent of proper governmental interference in the social, commercial, and industrial operations of the people. The love of liberty begotten of the circumstances attending the immigration of our forefathers to these shores, their colonial experiences, and the struggles which terminated in national existence led them to establish upon this Continent a system of government based upon the idea of the smallest possible interference with the commercial and industrial affairs of the people. Our whole theory of government is founded upon faith in the conservatism which inheres in the untrammeled interaction of forces, a faith expressed in the motto "In God we trust." This faith was the guiding star of all their conceptions of self-government. Thomas Jefferson was the most conspicuous apostle of that faith. In his first annual message to Congress as President he said, "Agriculture, manufactures, commerce and navigation, the four pillars of our national prosperity, are the most thriving when left most free to individual enterprise." The policy thus commended has with few departures been the guide of our national legislation and it may be regarded as the settled policy of the country.

New forces now assert themselves and new conditions confront us. Hence the old problems concerning the regulation of competition through combination and of governmental restraints upon combination present themselves under new conditions. The task which devolves upon the man of the present generation is to solve those problems, at least for our own time, upon approved principles of justice and of sound public policy, and in such manner as not to disturb the sure foundations upon which our civilization and our governmental system rests. The whole question, as I view it, relates to the limitations which should be imposed upon both competition and combination by the people themselves in the course of their own interaction and through beneficent governmental regulation justified by the lessons of experience. The subject runs into almost illimitable detail. The question as it touches each industry and occupation must be judged upon its particular governing facts and conditions. It appears to me that the proper way to conduct the inquiry is for each debater to consider and discuss the merits of the particular phase of the question to which he has devoted his best efforts as student, or in the course of his business experiences. In view of the fact that my business life began as civil engineer in the construction of railroads, was continued as officer of the national government charged with the duty of investigating and reporting upon matters relating to commerce and transportation, and latterly has related to my professional work as statistician and economist, it appears proper that on this occasion I should invite your attention to the American Railway System,—its evolution, the stages of its development, its efficiency, and the evolved law of its being.

The manner in which, and the extent to which, competition has been operative in the course of the development of railroad transportation in this country, are indicated by leading facts in the history of the evolution of the American railroad system. Such facts also indicate the manner in which and the extent to which railroad combination has been created by the interaction of commercial and industrial forces and by the exigencies of railroad management.

The year 1830 very nearly marks the genesis of railroad transportation in the United States and England. It was evident at the very beginning that in so far as relates to carriers it is impossible to apply the time-honored rules of the free highway to an avenue of commerce whose pathway is no wider than the wheel of the vehicle which moves upon it. It also became apparent that considerations of economy, of safety, and of commercial efficiency require that the entire railroad establishment, including roadway and equipment, must be placed under one central ownership and control, and that the management of the traffic interests of each railroad must be subjected to the same central authority. This gave to railroads at the very beginning a decided but absolutely unavoidable aspect of monopoly. Preconceived ideas in regard to the freedom of the highway at first caused the civilized world to be amazed at this conclusion. In order to meet public prejudices it was proposed that railroad transportation should be made a public function. The experiment of state ownership and management was tried in this country under conditions much simpler and much more favorable to success than those which exist to-day. Six states of the Union attempted the experiment, namely, the states of Massachusetts, Michigan, Pennsylvania, Illinois, Indiana and Georgia. Each one of these experiments resulted in absolute failure, and for a period of about sixty years the people of this country have acquiesced in railroad corporate management and control. The results of this system have been grand beyond the dreams of even the most sanguine railroad projector. There have been constructed in this country 247,532 miles of railroad track. More than half a continent has been reclaimed from a wilderness, the habitation of wild beasts and of savages and converted into homes of an enlightened and progressive people mainly through the facilities of transportation afforded by railroads. An internal commerce has been built up, the value of which is twenty times that of our foreign commerce. The facilities of direct trade to the remotest parts of this country have been provided for. Constant improvements in the mechanical features of roadway and equipment, increased facilities, advanced methods of administration and innumerable and ingeniously devised economies have so reduced the cost of transportation in this country that the average rate by rail is to-day only about one-third what it was even thirty years ago.

This enormous accretion to the world's commerce and this wonderful reduction in the cost of internal transportation have resulted in an ever tightening grasp of competition in all the productive industries. Besides there has been an uncontrollable and ever-quickening tendency toward a parity of values in all parts of the country. This in turn has become the most coercive cause of the reduction in transportation charges. Instead therefore of restricting competition, as at the beginning was feared might be the result of a railroad system of transportation under corporate ownership and control, the actual result has been a fiercer and a vastly more extended and potential competition than the world had ever before seen. The competition thus created is between rival towns and cities between different sections of the country, and between mines and manufactures and markets. Such competition for its intensity and the extent of its potentialities is unprecedented in history. Ever improving facilities, economies and administrative measures have so reduced the time and charges of transportation by rail as largely to divert commerce from competing water lines.

From the year 1830, until about the year 1850 each railroad in the United States was, as a rule, operated independently of all other railroads. Different track gauges were adopted in many instances for the express purpose of preventing "the carriage of freights from being, and being treated as one continuous carriage from the place of shipment to the place of destination," a practice now interdicted by the interstate commerce act as a public offense. (See Act to Regulate Commerce, Section 7.)

But a great change came. The social, commercial and postal necessities of the age, and the military exigencies of the late Civil War rapidly brushed aside all obstacles to the formation of that great American railroad system which is to-day unto the traveler and the shipper as one instrumentality of transportation, embracing 247,532 miles of track, administered and operated as though by one central authority. This wonderful organic unity embraces connected rails, a common track gauge, union depots, joint rates, the uniform classification of commodities, rate agreements of various sorts, through tickets, related time schedules, the unimpeded passage of freight, passenger, express and postal cars and locomotives over the tracks of different companies, and to a considerable extent the employment of operatives in the pay of one company, upon the lines of other companies. Each company has thus become, in many ways, the agent of other companies.

This practical unification of the great work of transportation by rail came about not as the result of design or forecast on the part of the companies, but as the outcome of an evolution responsive to the demands of the public interests. Objections to the juncture of lines and the combination of traffic interests which at first appeared insuperable were swept aside by an imperious force of circumstance. At last a consensus of the social, political and commercial forces of the country led to a statutory enactment by the national government which 'ratified the combination of railroad interests just described. I refer to the act of Congress approved June 15, 1866.

In view of the foregoing the historic fact stands out indisputably that the firmly united and deftly articulated American railroad system had its origin in acknowledged public needs and in a coercive public sentiment which remains unchanged to this day. It is a form of combination which subserves the interests of every person on this continent and it is prejudicial to the interests of none.

In the course of time, this extension of the facilities of joint railroad traffic placed the companies under a stress of competition and begat administrative difficulties which for years threatened the financial existence of every railroad corporation in the country. It also demoralized commerce. This was the inevitable outcome of a great organic unity lacking the means of administrative control. The situation, for years, was described by the late Albert Fink as follows:

"The stockholders, in the first place, surrender their control to a board of directors, the board of directors surrender it to the president, the president surrenders it to a general manager, who in turn surrenders it to the general freight agents of his own and a great number of other roads, who again surrender it to a large number of soliciting agents, and finally these soliciting agents surrender it to the shippers. The shippers practically make their own rates. The result is confusion and demoralization of traffic, and no end to unjust discriminations between shippers and localities."

In a word, the railroad system of the country fell into disorder. In the fierce struggle for traffic which ensued the executive officers of the railroads lost the power of maintaining rates, and the transportation and commercial interests of the country fell into confusion. Outrageous and absurd discriminations prevailed. The situation became intolerable.

The presidents of certain of the great trunk roads hit upon the expedient of so extending their lines as to gain control over the commerce of defined areas and in this way to maintain just rates and to preserve order. But after enormous railroad systems under single corporate management had been established it was found that the control over rates was farther from realization than before. The tendency of rates was constantly downward and discriminations continued. At last the companies which had indulged in the policy of expansion, to their astonishment, discovered that they had created new elements of competition more powerful and destructive than those which they had hoped to eliminate. Thus they were brought to realize the fact that elements other than the way of carriage control both rates and the course of traffic. At last it was realized by every intelligent student of the transportation problem that the whole trouble arose from a lack of administrative control; for no great organization can long exist without some sort of central directory. The world's history is replete with illustrations of this fact. The plan of railroad federations as a means of self-government and of protecting the public interests against the evils of an uncontrolled and demoralized transportation system was therefore devised. The late Albert Fink, a man of surpassing genius as an organizer and administrator of complex and involved commercial interests, was the author of this system.

The plan adopted had for its object the maintenance of order and the maintenance of rates. Boards of trade, chambers of commerce and representatives of trade interests of the country heartily concurred in this conclusion; for the demoralization of rates before alluded to had set the commerce of the country in confusion.

The railroad companies clearly perceived that in order to prevent unjust discriminations, the most important duty devolving upon them was to agree as to the relative rates which should prevail between competing points, as for example the relative rates which should prevail between Chicago and Boston, Chicago and New York, Chicago and Philadelphia, and Chicago and Baltimore. This was necessary in order to compose the competitive struggle between those four seaboard cities. The merchants of the cities mentioned also perceived the absolute necessity for agreement between the companies as to relative rates. In the absence of such agreements their trade with the great West had fallen into confusion; financial ruin confronted the merchants as well as the railroad companies. This in brief is the historic origin of agreements both as to absolute rates and as to the relative rates which shall prevail as between competing sections, cities, markets, and centers of production and distribution.

For years it was difficult, and finally it became impossible to maintain such rate agreements, none of which were enforceable at law. It became evident, therefore, that the companies must devise some remedial measure, suggested by the incidents of their own interaction, and by the commercial needs of the country with respect to transportation. Evidently such rule must also be sustained by that enlightened sense of self-interest which Blackstone has declared to be the substantial foundation of beneficent law. The expedient finally adopted was that of agreements as to the share of the competitive traffic which should be awarded to each competitor; as the first object in all competitive traffic struggles is to secure the largest possible amount of traffic, and the second to secure on it the best possible paying rates.

I think I mistake not in saying that in the minds of thoughtful men engaged in transportation, in commerce, in manufactures and in the great productive industries of the country the expedient thus adopted constituted the logical and beneficent adjustment of struggles which had run to demoralization and ruin. I think I am also justified in saying that the majority of the reflecting men who have been appointed to positions as state and national railroad commissioners are in favor of the maintenance of rates through agreements as to the division of competitive traffic.

From the foregoing the following conclusions appear to be justified:

First. While the railroads cannot, for the reason before stated, be free to all carriers, they can and must be free and impartial to all shippers.

Second. Experience, the only safe guide, has proved beyond all doubt that unrestrained competition in railroad transportation invariably runs to unjust discrimination and to disorder.

Third. Restraints of competition through combination in railroad transportation have been beneficial toward the public interests.

Fourth. Combination in railroad transportation under the limitations and restraints upon it which prevail in this country, has been beneficial toward the public interests.

When Mr. Nimmo concluded, the conference adjourned until 10:30 o'clock, September 14.

The Committee on Organization and Program held a protracted session before the conference assembled for the second day's work. The business before the committee was the question of the appointment of a committee on resolutions. This action was opposed in committee, but it was decided, after long debate, in the affirmative.

MORNING SESSION, SEPTEMBER 14.

The conference was called to order at 11 o'clock by Chairman Howe. The Committee on Organization and Program presented a report recommending the appointment of a committee on resolutions, said committee to be composed of fifteen delegates to be appointed by the chair, the committee to have authority to pass upon all resolutions presented, which should be sent directly to the committee without being presented to the conference.

Claggett of Idaho moved the adoption of the report, and was seconded by a number of delegates simultaneously.

An amendment was offered by McQuirk of Iowa that the committee be enlarged to include one from each state and national organization, and the members be selected by the state delegations.

Weil of Pennsylvania opposed the passage of any resolutions on the ground that the conference was for educational purposes and under the call could not adopt a policy.

Jones of Indiana and Rosewater of Nebraska led the debate in favor of a committee on resolutions. The opposition was led by Prince of Texas and Atkinson of West Virginia, who moved to lay the report on the table. A substitute was offered that all resolutions be referred to the Committee on Organization and Program.

The debate was exceedingly warm, but no party or sectional lines were drawn. A dozen delegates clamored for recognition. Cockran of New York secured the floor and moved the previous question, that of adopting the committee report. In doing so the speaker pointed out that the debate was doubtless the result of a misconception of the duties of the committee. He was desirous of careful action by which alone a harmonious conference could be completed, but was satisfied with the resolution, adding, however:

"I presume, with the consent of the mover, that on the last day of the conference motions shall be in order to discharge that committee from the consideration of any resolution which may have been committed to it and on which it has not been able to report."

The amendatory clause was accepted. The substitute sending the resolutions to the general committee was lost.

The report was then adopted with the amendments offered by Messrs. McQuirk and Cockran.

The chairman introduced the morning speakers in turn as named by Program Committee.

LAWSON PURDY.

New York Reform Club.

Lawson Purdy, of the New York Tariff Reform League, was then presented to the conference, and said:

The Commercial Year Book for 1899 defines the popular meaning of the word "trust" as "any consolidation, combine, pool, or agreement of two or more naturally competing concerns, which establishes a partial or complete monopoly, in certain territory, with power to fix prices or rates in any industry."

This definition may seem to include some concerns which it is not my purpose to discuss, and in order that they may be excluded, I wish to call attention to the words of the definition, "naturally competing concerns." I believe it is now generally conceded that there are certain kinds of business in which competition is not natural, and consequently any attempt to introduce competition in such businesses is certain to fail. Moreover, so long as competition continues, the public suffers by reason of the unnecessary expense of conducting the business. A broad distinction between naturally competitive concerns, and those which are not naturally competitive, lies in this, that any business which can be prosecuted by an individual or corporation without assistance from the state, and is, therefore, open to all, is naturally competitive business, and any business which can only be prosecuted if some state power is delegated to the individual or corporation which desires to engage in it, is naturally noncompetitive.

Examples of naturally noncompetitive businesses will occur to everyone. To supply a city with gas requires an exercise of governmental power, and it is at once seen that competition is extremely wasteful because of the necessity of the duplication of the plant.   In the same way it is impracticable to have true competition in the carriage of passengers through the streets of a city on a street railway, and no one can build such a railway without the delegation of state power.

Everyone is familiar with the attempt to foster and maintain competition in the supplying of gas and electricity and in the carriage of passengers and goods on railways, and the result has been the merging of competing lines, or some combination between them to maintain prices and divide the business.

The difference of opinion which now exists as to the manner in which natural monopolies such as these should be treated, is a difference of degree rather than a difference of kind.   The opinion is practically unanimous that there must be some governmental regulations and supervision, and more and more are coming to the conclusion that governmental regulation should extend to the point of absolute ownership and operation.

It is the combination of concerns which are naturally competitive, and such combination as establishes a partial or complete monopoly, which I wish to discuss.

Mr. Charles F. Beach, Jr., in an address on "The Trust an Economic Evolution," delivered before the Union League Club, Chicago, in 1894, says: "Nothing is so certain as that the profit of any sort of business can never be raised by increase of price to the consumer, beyond a normal amount for any length of time, without tempting the cupidity of men in other lines, and creating at once an outside competition.   No combination of manufacturers, not protected by government patents, by an iniquitous tariff, or by unholy alliances with railways, can, by never so stringent a compact between themselves, prevent any other set of men from going into their business, whenever the condition of the trade promises more than an average profit."   The important part of this statement by Mr. Beach is the exception, for the combinations not protected by an iniquitous tariff are few in number.   Of some four hundred trusts enumerated in the Commercial Year Book, more than two-thirds are direcly affected by the tariff, and there are very few which do not get some tariff assistance, directly or indirectly.

It is loudly asserted by some that England is a free trade country and that there are as many trusts in England as in the United States.   In the first place, England has not pushed the doctrine of free trade to its logical conclusion by any means, and still suffers from tax restrictions upon production and trade.   In the second place, those who assert that England is plastered with trusts have so far failed to name any which compare with hundreds in the United States in their power to raise prices and practice extortion upon the public.

In an article in the *Forum* of May, 1899, on "Trusts in Europe," Wilhelm Berdrow says that trusts have extended rapidly in Germany and France, but that "as far as England is concerned it must be admitted that, notwithstanding her great industrial activity and a competitive warfare not less pronounced than that of other states, the trust system has as yet found but tardy acceptance in that country. This is doubtless due in some degree to the thorough application of the principles of free trade, for it is well known that the largest trusts are powerless unless their interests are secured by a protective tariff excluding from the home market the products of foreign countries."

It is so obvious to the most ordinary intelligence that it is more difficult to make a combination of the producers in many countries than in one, that it hardly needs proof.

In 1889 the Hon. John Sherman said: "The primary object of a protective tariff is to divide the fullest competition by individuals and corporations in domestic production. If such individuals or corporations combine to advance the price of the domestic product and to prevent the free result of open and fair competition, I would without a moment's hesitation reduce the duties of foreign goods competing with them, in order to break down the combination. Whenever this free competition is evaded or avoided by combination of individuals or corporations, the duty should be reduced and foreign competition promptly invited."

I do not contend that the only cause for combination which restrains trade is the tariff, but the tariff does foster and assist in maintaining such combinations. The tariff is under the control of the federal government; the abolition of duties upon articles produced by trusts is easy, immediate, and effective. When this special privilege is withdrawn we will then be in a better position to do what further may be necessary.

Many manufacturers are selling goods for export at prices much lower than at home, and a condition which permits and induces manufacturers to do this is indefensible.

For many years manufactured goods have been sold cheaper for export than at home. In 1890 the *Australasian and South American*, a paper devoted to the export trade, made the following admission: "By comparing the prices at which goods are sold to the export merchant and the catalogue rates which the ordinary purchaser pays, it is possible to show a very striking discrepancy in favor of the exporter." The paper claimed that

PAUL MORTON
SAMUEL ADAMS ROBINSON
JAMES H. RAYMOND

BENJAMIN R. TUCKER
LAURENCE GRONLUND
H. T. NEWCOMB

these lower prices were for the wholesale trade alone, whereupon the New York *World* published a letter from the *Engineering and Mining Journal*, a paper which also paid special attention to the export trade. An extract from the letter, dated August 26, 1890, is as follows: "Your statement that the foreigner can buy at retail in this market cheaper than the domestic consumer is as indisputable as the daily revolution of the earth. We can enumerate any number of instances where houses have written us, 'Prices furnished are for export only, and it would be most injurious to us if these figures were circulated in the home market.'"

In a speech delivered a few months ago before the Foundrymen's Association of Philadelphia, Mr. A. B. Farquhar, a large manufacturer of agricultural tools, testified to the conditions which exist to-day. He says: "We must see at a glance that there are a great many products of manufacturing industries in this country which, whatever may have been their need of protection heretofore, most certainly do not need it to-day. In the ten months ending with April last, the country exported $276,-000,000 worth of manufactures, nearly 18 per cent more than the corresponding ten months of 1897 and 1898. This amount considerably exceeding that of our import of manufactured goods for the same period, covering a wide range of products, conclusively proves that we have nothing to fear from foreign manufactures. Yet a duty is still demanded on these very products, and why? Not for revenue, because the government gets no revenue from such duties, but to enable the combinations that monopolize their production to exact higher prices in this country than they can obtain abroad, and for no other reason. The Sugar Trust, with its rebates to encourage exportation and its high protective duty to keep up the price of its products within the country, thus favored by the law in two directions; the steel rail combine, which sends its product to all quarters of the globe (one mill recently shipping 70,000 tons of rails for the North China Railway), and put them down at the very doors of the British shops, while at the same time a Boston Company finds it cheaper to get rails from England and pay the duty than to buy at the terms allowed at home. . . . These and many other associations, all profiting handsomely by legislative favoritism, tempt us to appeal to the law not to lay its hand upon them in any way directly, but only to lift from us the hand with which it holds us down in order to give the monopolies advantage."

I believe we have passed the point where any objection can be raised to the abolition of protective duties on the ground that

they sustain or raise wages.   Years ago we had the testimony of
Mr. Evarts and Mr. Blaine that American labor was the cheapest
in the world, and received the smallest share of its own product.
We have grown great in manufacturing because we have the most
skilled labor and the best material with which to work.   The
truth is that the tariff, by shutting out foreign competition, enables the trusts to shut down domestic factories, employ less labor,
and thereby reduce wages.   Mills make money by shutting down
instead of by the production of goods.

Of course consumers suffer.   That is why this conference was
called.   Professor Maas, formerly chemical expert of the Glucose
Sugar Refining Company, testified before the Industrial Commission that the price of Glucose was doubled as soon as the trust
was formed and the glucose plant worth $6,000,000 was capital-
ized at forty.

The *National Glass Budget* on July 22d said editorially:
"Manufacturers have, through the strength of their combination,
succeeded in raising and maintaining prices to an extent that
would have been considered dangerous and ruinous to the industry if it had resulted directly from an advance of wages enforced
by the workers' organization, but having been the result of a
closer union among manufacturers, the thing is very different,
and the increased influx of foreign glass, stimulated by high
prices of domestic, with which conference committee men have
for decades threatened the workers, has, strangely, not material-
ized, but in spite of all that the workers are economically in a
worse position to enforce an advance than they have been for
many years."

The *Independent*, of Forest City, Iowa, reports that, "The
Indiana Wire Fence Company of Crawfordsville has been absorbed by the American Steel and Wire Company, and its buildings now stand deserted.   The fence factory was Crawfordsville's
chief industry.   The product became known all over the country,
and the demand increased so that the factory was enlarged almost
weekly.   There were regularly employed about seventy-five men,
sometimes more than that number, nearly all of whom have families.   The pay-rolls for labor alone amounted to nearly $52,000
a year, about every dollar of which was spent in Crawfordsville."
The company did not wish to sell out to the trust, but was threatened that the trust would cut prices so low that they would be
forced out of business, and the sale was made on January 23,
1899.   The account continues: "Then the blow fell upon Crawfordsville.   The men were thrown out of employment.   Most
of them had gone into building and loan associations, had bor-

rowed money, and were building themselves homes. They could not meet their payments. Their homes were taken away from them and they left the city. There was no work for them here. Clerks and salesmen lost their positions and every branch of business felt this blow."

It is sometimes said: "Law made trusts, and law can unmake them." I believe this is absolutely true, but I think it commonly conveys a wrong impression. Law has made trusts by conferring special privileges, and those privileges can be abolished. The chief privilege, and the one most easily reached, is the tariff. Let no one imagine that corporations, which are creatures of law, are the only trusts, for secret agreements between individuals have been effective to control supply and raise prices without a single corporation being involved.

The doctrine of *laissez faire* has been much abused, and it is common to hear that it has failed. It has never yet been tried. It does not mean, "Let things alone as they are," but "Clear the road and let them alone." Clear away every special privilege. Then, and not till then, can we know whether any restriction is necessary. While special privileges remain, attempts to restrain combination will be futile.

Trusts have little dread of statute law which the courts will take years to interpret. They fear the repeal of privilege, and "Repeal" should be the battle cry of those who believe in equal rights before the law.

BYRON W. HOLT.

New England Free Trade League.

Byron W. Holt spoke on "Tariff, the Mother of Trusts":

When H. O. Havemeyer last June startled the country with the declaration before the Industrial Commission that "The Mother of All Trusts is the Customs Tariff Bill," he came so near to telling the truth that the protectionist organs of the country immediately began calling him names and saying "sour grapes," and the organ of the Protective Tariff League is still devoting a large portion of its space to the wicked, traitorous Havemeyer. If he had said special privileges, of which the tariff is foremost, are the mother of trusts, he would have been still nearer to the truth.

That the tariff, by shielding our manufacturers from foreign competition, makes it easy for them to combine, to restrict production, and to fix prices—up to the tariff limit—ought to be evident to every intelligent man. It ought also to be evident to all here that the greatest objection to trusts is due to their ability to raise prices above a normal, profit-producing point. That the trusts raise prices whenever possible to what they consider the maximum profit point is certain. It is asserted by the trusts' advocates that trusts can produce more cheaply than individual firms, and that they have lowered prices. It may be, and probably is, true that trusts usually produce cheaper, but it is certainly not true that they have lowered prices.

Out of four hundred trusts which I have enumerated, I do not believe that ten have lowered prices. In fact, I know of none, except one or two, and these have depreciated the quality of their product. In one such case the prices are held so high that there are heavy imports of competing goods, although there is a duty on them of nearly 100 per cent. In nine cases out of ten trusts have raised prices—often more than 50 per cent. That much of the present rise in prices is due to general economic conditions is probably true. On the other hand, it is just as true that, had there been no tariff duties, the rise in prices would neither have been so general nor so great. The trusts have taken full advantage of the powers and special privileges derived from their tariff partner—the government. Congress should speedily dissolve this iniquitous partnership.

If time permitted, I should be glad to take up the trusts in detail and show how each is fostered and protected by the tariff. Some of these are the various glass, furniture, leather, iron and steel, paper, coal, woolen goods, and silk goods trusts. The sugar trust is still a tariff trust. The protection on refined sugar—on the cost of refining—is, as Henry T. Oxnard, of the beet sugar industry, says, fully 50 per cent, instead of only 3½ per cent, as Mr. Havemeyer told the Industrial Commission. It is, however, probably true that Havemeyer would be glad to see free trade in raw sugars and little or no duty on refined. He is anxious not only to compel his present cane sugar refining competitors to sell out to him at reasonable figures, but he wishes to prevent the further growth of the beet sugar industry.

If there is one industry more than any other to which the protectionists have always "pointed with pride," it is the American tin plate industry. "Just look at this great industry if you want to see an object lesson in protection!" There are two points of view—that of the manufacturer and that of the consumer.

To the manufacturer everything looks lovely. He asked to

have 2 1-5 cents per pound duty added to the price of imported tin plate until he could experiment to see if he could make it at a profit at about double the price of foreign tin plate. McKinley granted the request and the experiment began. It was rendered successful largely through the aid of cheap iron and steel from 1893 to 1898. So great was the reduction in the cost of steel bars and sheets that the 1 1-5 cents per pound duty of the Wilson bill, from 1894 to 1897, afforded about the same protection as did the McKinley duty of 1891. The profits of tin plate manufacturers were great, and by 1897 we were making half of the plates consumed in this country. In 1897 the duty was gratuitously raised to 1½ cents per pound.

By 1898 the great profits of the business had increased the number of tin plate plants to about forty and the number of mills to about 280. For the first time in our history internal competition had so lowered prices that but few plates were imported—except for re-export by large manufacturers who could avail themselves of the benefits of drawback duties—and our manufacturers were not reaping the full benefit of the duties levied especially for their benefit. This situation worried the manufacturers. A part of the duty was being wasted and lost by their foolish policy of competing with each other. They got together and formed a compact, air-tight monopoly, which is a credit to its mother—the tariff. To make certain that they would be able to put and hold prices up to the Dingley duty limit, they clinched their trust, it is said, by making a five-year contract with the producers of tin plate mills, which practically prevents others from starting in business during this period. They also, through their relations with the chief steel-bar producing companies, obtained such control of this principal raw material that even if an outsider could obtain a mill he would still be unable to produce tin plates for lack of raw materials. Hence, while there is some talk of outside competition, there is virtually no competition at present, nor is there likely to be any while the present duty is in force. The mills and plants of this trust are worth about $10,000,000. It is capitalized at $50,000,000—$20,000,000 preferred and $30,000,000 common stock. Big dividends will probably be paid on both kinds of stock, the total market value of which is now about $30,000,000.

Thus, from the standpoint of the manufacturers, all is rosy, and is likely to remain so if the wicked free traders will only let the tariff alone.

The consumer, if he has his eyes wide open, sees a different picture. He saw prices held up by duties until the tin plate infant was full grown and capable of giving him cheap tin plate, and now he sees them held up by means of a monopoly trust supported by what he considers an iniquitous tariff. He figures up what this duty has cost him. He finds that from the time the McKinley act took effect in 1891 to the Wilson law of 1894, there were 1,783,000,000 pounds of tin plate imported, on which he paid a duty of 2 1-5 cents per pound—amounting to $39,226,000. During this period our home manufacturers made 242,700,000 pounds, on which they virtually collected a duty of $5,339,400. From 1894 to 1897, 1,123,000,000 pounds were imported, on which a duty of $13,442,000 was paid. During this period the American manufacturers produced 948,000,000 pounds, on which about the full duty, or $11,376,000 was collected. The consumer therefore finds that when this infant was five years old it had cost him $69,383,400, or about $14,000,000 a year. During 1898 materials were cheap, and the infant cost only $5,000,000 or $6,000,000 to keep. The consumer hoped that by 1899 the infant would be able and willing to support itself. The price at which our manufacturers laid down tin plate in New York in 1898 ($2.75) was only 20 cents above the price of English tin plates in bond. Surely this slight difference could be overcome in 1899, and the consumer would no longer have to pay millions of dollars each year to support this costly infant. But the infant had been spoiled by too much protection and refused to give up its luxurious living and to support itself. It returned to its tariff nourishment, and is now eating it as greedily as ever. It has put up the price of tin plate from $2.75 per box of 100 pounds, in October, 1898, to $4.80, the price to-day—an advance of $2.05 per box, or over 70 per cent. During the same time the price of imported plates has risen from $2.50 to $3.60, or $1.10 per box in bond, or from $4 to $5.10 out of bond—a rise of only 27½ per cent. The consumer estimates that the tariff food for this greedy infant will cost him not less than $10,000,000 in 1899, and, at the present rate, will exceed $12,000,000 in 1900. He is getting out of patience with the youngster, and threatens to cut off his supply of tariff food and to let him shift for himself.

The protectionist gravely tells us that the tin plate tax is paid by the foreigner; that a combination of Welsh manufacturers kept up prices before the McKinley bill existed and extorted from the American consumers all the tariffs would bear; that they afterwards lowered their prices because they could not live without the American market, and that if we were not now producing our own tin plate the Welsh trust would be charging us just as much as are our own manufacturers. The fact that prices went up under the McKinley duty, down under the Wilson duty, and up again under the Dingley duty, upsets the plausibility of this theory, which, at best, is based upon unsubstantiated assertions.

It would be interesting to discuss the effect of the tariff upon wages, through the trusts. The only way in which tariff duties can benefit labor is through a double trust composed of both manufacturers and their employes. This can occur only when the employees are well organized and have iron-clad apprenticeship rules. It has occurred only temporarily, and in a few industries—notably in that of window glass. But even in this industry it is doubtful if the employees as a whole got much of the tariff benefits, for what they apparently gained in higher wages was lost through lack of employment when the mills were closed for the purpose of restricting production and raising prices.

It would also be interesting to discuss the relation between the tariff and the lower prices at which foreigners can obtain our trust products than are charged to American consumers. Nearly all kinds of manufactured goods are sold at considerably reduced prices when for export. An acquaintance of mine about to sail for India has just purchased a bicycle for $25 which agents are not allowed to sell for use in this country for less than $40. The Remington typewriter has for years been sold for export at 25 per cent below home market prices. The foreigner buys Disston's saws at a discount of 45 per cent, while our own dealers can get a discount of only 25 per cent, or, if they are wholesalers, 25 per cent and 10 per cent—an advance of 22 per cent on the prices to foreigners. Our sewing machines cost South Americans much less than North Americans. To fully appreciate the beneficent effects of American tariffs and trusts you must be a foreigner.

We are told, about once a week, by the New York *Tribune* and other high tariff organs, that the tariff cannot be the mother of trusts, because there are trusts in free trade England. It is true that there are occasional trusts in England. But it is not true that they have generally raised prices as have our own tariff-protected trusts. The British consumer has the whole world for his market, and, if some home trust attempts to raise prices, he can supply his wants from abroad. England has comparatively few trusts, and they are far less obnoxious than are the numerous trusts in protected Germany and America.

The heart of the trust problem is in our tariff system of plunder. The quickest and most certain way of reaching the evils of trusts is not by direct legislation against them, or by constitutional amendment, but by the abolition of tariff duties. Let

Congress take up the Dockery amendment to the Dingley bill, and, if there be any likelihood that it will pass, the lobbies at Washington will be filled with trust directors and agents. Let a constitutional amendment be proposed, and the trusts will take only a passing interest in the discussion. They care but little for legislation or constitutions, but they have a mortal fear of free trade.

The tariff-trust situation may be illustrated in this way:

A great city is on the banks of a river, the water of which is contaminated by the refuse of other cities further up the stream. The city gets its entire supply of water from this river, not because there is not an ample supply of pure water near at hand, but because the fathers of the city, in their wisdom, have passed prohibitive laws which practically prevent the people from obtaining the pure water. The city is stricken with disease, and the death rate has reached an alarming height. The city has twice as many doctors, druggists, and undertakers as other cities of similar size. The doctors have combined to obtain the highest possible rates for their services. The druggists, undertakers, coffin-makers, pill-makers, distilled water manufacturers, hearse-drivers and flower-growers and wreath-makers all have compact organizations, to make it as expensive as possible to die. All of these "protected" industries are in politics to see that the city council remain true to "home industries."

Money is spent freely to prevent the re-election of any councilman who is such a traitor to his own city as to advocate free and pure water. The citizens becoming rebellious at the high prices charged for doctors, medicine. coffins, hearses, and flowers, a trust conference has been called to discuss what evils, if any, grow out of these various death-dealing trusts, and what laws, if any, are necessary to do away with these evils or with the trusts themselves. Some assert that the present anti-trust laws are sufficient if only there were courageous attorneys-general and honest judges to enforce them. Others believe in more drastic anti-trust legislation and in constitutional amendments. Some of the learned doctors in the council attempt to quiet the alarm by asserting that the trusts have really lowered instead of raised the cost of dying, and that anyway people sometimes die in other cities. Some plain, ordinary citizens who have not much standing or power in the community suggest that the way to get rid of the trusts and to lower the death rate is to remove the restrictions and to give the people pure and cheap water. But little attention is paid to the suggestions of these "theorists," though some of the other delegates agree that pure water might be a partial remedy. When the conference adjourned it declared that trusts were both good and bad and recommended that a constitutional amendment be submitted to the people which would make it possible to annul the certificates and licenses of doctors and druggists found guilty of belonging to bad trusts.

What should have been the principal question discussed at that conference? More trust legislation or simply free water?

What is the vital question before this conference? More complicated and dangerous restrictive legislation or simply free trade?

JOHN F. SCANLAN.

Western Industrial League.

John F. Scanlan, of Illinois, spoke on "Trusts and Free Trade," and said:

After the object-lesson of the last panic it requires, shall I call it courage, for any person to come before the American people and ask them to adopt free trade as a system of political economy for this nation. For seventy years the industries of this country have been bombarded from within and without, with an energy born of the most vicious and destructive spirit, and the leading hosts in that bombardment have been and are enemies of our welfare, aided by a few theoretical professors, free trade dreamers and political free lances. Experience has pushed aside the free trade shibboleths of "the tariff is a tax," "robber barons," "the duty is added to the cost," "the farmer is robbed," etc., all these falsehoods have now been boiled down to a legitimate successor, "The tariff is the mother of trusts."

To charge the existence of trusts to protective tariff is as unfair, if not as ridiculous, as to charge them to the Declaration of Independence, which gave the opportunity, or to human life that gives us the energy. Were it not for protective tariffs, we now would be, not the leading farming, manufacturing and consuming nation, with the best credit and most gold of any in the world, on the contrary we would be down among the poor nations and would not be troubled with the problem of how to chain down to the best interest of the majority, this new development of American energy, the trusts.

The collecting of revenue is not the sole object of protection, That is secondary. The most important is the creating centers of industrial activity within our country; bringing the consumers and producers close together; adding the labor profit of both to the nation's wealth, which gives the people an opportunity to develop their natural genius, sure to produce more freedom and a better civilization; increase wages, lower the price of commodities and increase the consuming powers of the home market. Experience proves we cannot have these conditions under free trade.

All down through the ages man has lived under liberty or in slavery. There are two kinds of slavery, the slavery of purchase and the slavery of conditions. Man is a slave of conditions when he cannot use the forces of nature to help him to better results and higher civilization. The latter state is brought about by the absence of national industry or its destruction.

We have been victims of the latter system of slavery six times since the Republic was established, resulting from the six free trade panics, each of which was but a repetition of the losses and suffering, in proportion to the inhabitants, which we experienced in the recent panic of 1893 to 1897.

The dates of these panics are 1784, 1820, 1837, 1857, 1873, 1893. During those panics a great proportion of the wealth of the nation passed away from us. During the intervening protection eras all the wealth and progress we made was achieved, and if free trade will be adopted it will turn our home market again over to the tender mercies of foreign trusts. If we must have trusts let them be American with a well employed and a well paid labor, a prosperous free citizen to bring the trusts within the law. I wish to call your attention to the remarkable fact that every one of those free trade panics brought the same character of commercial losses and physical suffering to the people, namely:

1st. Low duties brought larger importations, loss of confidence and suspension of industries.

2nd. Labor idle, moody and rebellious, reduction of wages, workingmen fed at public soup houses.

3rd. Great increase of commercial bankruptcy.

4th. Gold leaves the country in vast quantities.

5th. Government revenues less than expenditures.

6th. Consuming powers of the home market greatly reduced.

Increase in the price of foreign goods, decrease in the price of home products, with a landslide progress of all the people towards the slavery of conditions, which always brought forth an agitation for the American system of tariff; when enacted it invariably stopped the panic and as regularly brought about the reverse of the above conditions, namely:

1st.   American industry fully and profitably employed and increased.

2nd.   Labor employed, good wage, progressive, saving money.

3rd.   Great stability in commercial circles, decrease in bankruptcy.

4th.   Government revenues more than expenditures.

5th.   Gold flows into the country in vast quantities.

6th.   Consuming powers of the people vastly increased, with great expansion of liberty, by reason of the wealth created through diversified industry, bringing prosperity and happy Saturday nights to the fireside of all the people.

Permit me to mention a few incidents brought about by those panics to illustrate the condition of a people and government suffering from the slavery of conditions.

During the panic of 1784 the woes of the people were so deplorable and our young government was in such danger that Washington, writing to Col. Humphrey on the calamity of that day, cried out: "For God's sake tell me what is the cause of these commotions?   *   *   *. It is but the other day that we were shedding our blood to obtain the constitution under which we now live—a constitution of our own choice and making—and now we are unsheathing the sword to overturn it." Of the panic of 1820 Benton wrote it was "a period of gloom and agony."

During the panic of 1837 labor was a lost art, corn was burned for fuel, the people were fed at public soup houses, the states could not pay interest on the public debt, and this now mighty nation could not then borrow $10,000,000 at any interest at home or abroad. During the panic of 1857 the people were idle, wages dropped down to the European standard, government revenues fell short $90,000,000, and the government paid as high as 36 per cent for the use of money to keep the machinery in motion.

You can place your ears to the ground and yet hear the dying wail of the groans and agony of the people's suffering from the panic of 1893. During each of those panics, as in the last one, it was utterly impossible to keep gold within the control of the nation. Between the dates of those free trade periods in the history of our country, protection controlled the destinies of our industries, during which years all was joy, ease and contentment; it may be said, in the Scripture phrase, of those protection periods, "The hills and the valleys sang with joy." During free trade we were the slaves of conditions, during protection we were the freemen of liberty.

I ask as a pertinent question, if we are to fight the evils of trusts, whatever they may be, which of the above conditions

179

shall govern our welfare while the fight is going on? That of the slavery of conditions, or that of well paid freemen, working beneath the canopy of universal national prosperity?

The free traders are now attacking, with all their forces, the tin industry, that being the last industry, which in a most wonderful manner, through protection, was lifted bodily over into our country from England. The true inwardness of those attacks may be gleaned from the statement of Mr. Holt, of the New England Free Trade League. He said "that the tariff, by shielding our manufacturers *from foreign competition* makes it easy for them to combine." The fact that the foreigners have lost their hold on our market is where the shoe pinches, and explains why free traders have so suddenly become such violent opponents of trusts.

Mr. Holt speaks correctly when he says that the protectionists point with pride to the victory of the American tin plate industry. Never in the history of nations was there such a peaceful industrial victory achieved as that of the transfer of the tin industry from England to the United States in the last nine years, and upon that victory and the reduction of the price of tin to the consumer the protectionists might, if needs be, rest all their laurels. The assertions of those modern Don Quixote tariff fighters that the tariff is the mother of trusts becomes a doubtful statement in the presence of the fact that the Standard Oil and sewing machine combinations, the two most powerful trusts in the country, have no interest in the tariff, and those industries are not in existence by reason of the influence of the tariff.

The perpetual cry of the free traders, and repeated in all its moods and tenses on this platform by Mr. Holt, that the tariff is added to price paid by the consumer, that the tariff is a tax, that the tariff does not raise wages, and that the tariff is a mother of trusts, is answered fully by the results of protection upon the tin industry, now safely housed under the American flag.

In 1873, when we had no tin factories in this country, the American people paid for coke grade tin $12 per box, charcoal grade tin $14.75. About 1875, some Welshmen who understood the tin business, under the stimulus of a tariff of 1.1 cents per pound, started small works at Wellsville, Ohio, Leachburgh and Demler, Pennsylvania. When those factories were ready to put their product on the market the British tin trust at once dropped their prices down to $5.18 and $6.25 per box, and, of course, wiped out, in short order, the capital of the much derided infant tin industries of the patriotic Welshmen, after which prices again went up, and from that period until the much abused McKinley tariff went into force, we did not manufacture a pound of tin in this country, during which time we had to pay such prices for tin as the foreigners deemed it wise to charge.

During that period we paid to foreigners from twenty to thirty millions of dollars per year for our tin, but the McKinley tariff put a protective duty on foreign tin and by reason of that duty American capital invested in tin mills and commenced producing until we have grown to such dimensions that American factories now supply the entire consumption of the country. Let us compare the results:

1873, no American factories, price of foreign tin per box, $12 and $14.75.

1892, one half consumption supplied by home factories, price $5.35.

1898, entire consumption supplied by home factories, price $2.75.

Amount of money paid by American people to foreign factories per year, when we had no tin industry, twenty to thirty million dollars.

Amount paid now that the tin industry, through protection, is domesticated, practically none.

In 1897 there were 200 tin mills in this country, with a capital of $33,836,782, employing 40,000 workmen and paying wages from 75 cents (boys) to $8.00 per day. Eighty per cent of the capital employed in the tin industry go into wages and we pay from two to three times higher wages than are paid in England for the same class of workmen. Were it not for protection, not a dollar of those wages would be paid to American workmen, not a dollar of American capital would be employed in the tin industry and the American consumer would in all probability be yet paying the old high prices for tin. The price of tin is now $4.65. I am informed it can be accounted for by the wave of prosperity that has increased the consuming powers of the home market, increased the price of raw material, and increase of wages and employment over that of the late panic years. Even wheat has risen fifty per cent in price since prosperity has again shed its happy rays on our country, and our free trade friends cannot charge the increased price of wheat to a trust.

The fact that it is the foreign manufacturers who are always spending their money and sending agents into our country, agitating for the repeal of the tariff, should convince all thinking citizens who it is that pays the duty. If the American consumer pays it, why should the foreigner spend his money to relieve us? "Beware of the Greeks, even when they come with presents."

The history of the transfer of the tin industry to this country is but a repetition of the results of protection in its influences in the transfer of nearly all our industries from Europe, and there is not a single article among the thousands that go to supply the needs of the American people which cannot now be purchased vastly cheaper than they could when we depended upon Europe for our supply. Even sugar, which is yet a revenue product, can be purchased for a third of what it could in the fifties. These facts should convince the people of this country that protection is the guardian of our prosperity and free trade is the poisoned dagger that foreign trusts continually aim at the vitals of our industries, for which reason you find the free trade agents, who spoke to you from this platform, ignoring all recommendations of regulation through American law and crying out: "The heart of the trust problem is in our tariff system of plunder. The quickest and most certain way of reaching the evils of trusts is not by direct legislation against them or by constitutional amendment, but by the abolition of the tariff duties." Pray what effect will the abolition of the tariff duties have on the sewing machine, the Standard Oil and other trusts with which the tariff has no relation? Past experience clearly points out that those people who now ask us to abolish our tariffs are not interested in crushing trusts, but they are anxious to destroy our industries and our prosperity in the interest of foreign manufacturers.

But, say our free trade friends, if we can sell cheaper than the foreigner why continue the tariffs? For the very same reason that we do not destroy our government in times of peace, or remove the side walls of our houses in summer time. We know war and winter are liable to come, so we retain our government and the side walls of our houses. Experience has taught us that the war of industry is liable to come, hence we continue protection.

The seeping of a few gallons of water through a muskrat hole in the Mississippi levee is more dangerous to the welfare of the people living in the lowland than the millions of tons of water that flow by. Open a muskrat hole in the tariff, as those agents of foreign factors and would-be haters of trusts ask us to do, and their employers, the foreign manufacturers, would swoop down on that opening, and Johnstown flood like, they would undermine the foundations of our industries and sweep us into another panic. A 10 per cent reduction of our tariffs brought on the panics of 1837, 1857, 1873, and a promise of a reduction brought on the panic of 1893.

A few illustrations, out of the hundreds, will show what we

have lost through free trade and what we have gained through protection.

In 1850 we numbered twenty-three millions of people. We had just got control of the Pacific coast. Our flag kissed two oceans and welcomed all lovers of liberty to our shores. California gave us $1,100,000,000 in gold just for picking it up. The Crimean war and European conditions gave us a plethoric market for our bounteous crops. Peace and health prevailed. Providence poured blessings beyond number upon us during that decade, but the madness of political insanity controlled our lawmakers, hence we reaped thistles instead of fruit.

The Walker tariff became a law in 1846 and struck such a blow at our industries that it paralyzed all our energy. The 1856 tariff was the last straw that turned the gifts of Providence and all our wonderful wealth making conditions into dead sea fruit. What were all these opportunities given to us for? History has recorded the hell of war we passed through soon after that period. Was it to aid us in preserving this Republic? Was it to strengthen our souls for the atonement for the crime of slavery? Whatever it was, man's unwisdom put them aside. At the close of that providential decade this nation was poor indeed. Free trade had destroyed our industries and sent all the California gold to Europe to pay for foreign goods. If we were wise, protected and developed our industries during that decade, that $1,100,000,000 gold would have remained with us and made a financial basis of $36.66 per capita, which with our increased industries would long ere this have made us the commercial clearing-house of the world. Our gold went to Europe and she now occupies that position. Hence, I assert, the crime of the centuries was perpetrated against this Republic in that decade by the sectional madness of our legislators who threw a bombshell of unwise legislation in the midst of our industries, dissipating the rich conditions that poured on our country at that time, conditions that may not again happen in ages.

At the close of President Buchanan's administration we numbered over 30,000,000 people, yet so poor were we that the government then paid 36 per cent for the use of money, and after twelve years of peace and agricultural plenty, there was a deficit in the revenues of $90,580,873. That was during free trade, when the highest expenditures of the government were only $45,000,000 a year. From 1861 to 1865 was a period of destructive war, which removed for the time being ten millions of taxpayers. During that war our expenditures were $2,000,000 per day. But then it was also an era of protection and industrial activity, during which four and a half years, the twenty millions, who remained faithful to the Union, paid into the United States Treasury $4,753,811,-777.74. I wish to specially direct your attention to those two events, illustrating the helplessness of a people living under the slavery of conditions arising from free trade, and the wealth-creating power and freedom of that same people living under the conditions which arise from protection. I wish to emphasize the fact that every dollar of that sum was paid by the people of this country. Some persons are under the impression that Europe loaned us some of that money. Not one dollar until the Union proved its stability.

Mr. Fessenden, Secretary of the Treasury, commenting on this subject, in his message, 1864, said:

"This nation has been able thus far to conduct a domestic war of unparalleled magnitude and cost without appealing for aid to any foreign people. It has chosen to demonstrate its power to put down an insurrection by its own strength, and furnish no pretense for doubt of its entire ability to do so, either to domestic or foreign foes. The people of the United States have felt a just pride in this position before the world. * * * After nearly four years of a most expensive war, the means to continue it seem apparently undiminished, while the determination to prosecute it with vigor to the end is unabated."

When this nation entered into that war we had no army, no ships, no money, no credit, comparatively speaking no factories. During the war we equipped 2,778,304 soldiers, built 700 ships of war, expended $6,000,000,000 in suppressing the rebellion. When we got through we were richer than when we commenced. Protective tariff was the ally that aided the brain and brawn of this nation to produce such marvelous results.

Thus it will be seen that protection is a law which creates an economic condition that employs land and labor in active production, establishing in our country centers of industrial activity which bring forth wealth, good money, prosperity, national power, individual happiness, education and higher civilization. Such results do not create injurious trusts, but free traders coolly come before us and ask us to abolish all these because a few men among our people would imitate the selfish class of Europe by establishing trusts in our midst. To take this advice would be as sensible as stopping the circulating of the blood for the purpose of curing a boil on one's neck.

Tinkering with the economic conditions of a great industrial nation is a serious matter. The ups and downs of our industrial history emphasize most forcibly what Sir Hely Hutchinson wrote on that subject one hundred years ago:

"Compare this period with the former and you will prove this melancholy truth, that a country will sooner recover from the miseries and devastations occasioned by war, invasions, rebellion, massacre, than from laws restraining the commerce, fettering the industry, and above all breaking the spirit of the people."

In 1892 we were in a very healthy industrial and monetary condition. A five line free trade plank in the platform of one of our political parties brought on the panic of 1893 that cost the nation more than it cost to put down the rebellion.

From 1862 to 1892, with the exception of six years, was a period of protection, during which period we brought into existence more original wealth than the entire wealth of England, and enough of wealth to purchase all the lands, houses, ships and personal property of Germany. The bringing into existence that vast sum in one generation and controlled by our people, who are human like the rest of mankind, developed the spirit of an Alexander, who sighed for more worlds to conquer. To be rich beyond precedent is a craze, species of insanity. Insanity is not held responsible by God or man, but it is subject to law. Give the people time and if trusts prove to be against the interest of the majority, the law will harness them to the people's interest, not by killing the goose that laid the golden eggs, but by regulating and correcting the evil. In the last generation we had as formidable and healthy a trust in this country as ever filched the sweat of the poor man to enrich the rich. It was a trust that made a door mat of our Constitution, it controlled the political independence of a majority of the people of this country, it used the stars and stripes as a defender of the slave barracoon. But when the conscience of the American people was awakened the slave trust went to the grave of the dead. It cost money and life. Yes, and that is the best evidence that the American people will not permit any combination to interfere with the mission of the Republic.

To the men who would create trusts I would say you are establishing the most gigantic schools of socialism the world has ever known. If a few men can run all the industries why cannot the government run them more equitably in the interest of the people? That is the lesson the trusts will teach the people, the all powerful people, who through the ballot box are peacefully revolutionizing governments every year. The people of the south tried the experiment of free trade, and as a result for a generation they have been bleeding at every pore. Previous to the Revolution they understood the principle of diversified industries, and then that part of our country controlled the centers of industrial activity. After the Revolution cotton became king, and they deemed it necessary to marry free trade to slavery, while New England and the Middle States, recognizing the coming events, laid the foundation for diversified industry in their midst, with the result that in fifty years thereafter the center of industrial activity was transferred to the north, and the people of the south had to come north to find a market for their raw produce and to borrow money, even though, as Benton says, the south in the meantime had exported raw products to the amount of $800,000,-000, a sum equal to the product of the Mexican mines since the days of Cortez.

Six years ago we entered into one of those free trade eras and expatriated our industries, our people were idle, banks and business houses toppled over like rows of bricks, commercial credit was wiped out as if the safeguards of civilization had been abolished. No talk of trust then except the trust of poverty, and protection could say, "Point not thy gory fingers at me." You all remember what a terrible time we had trying to keep $100,-000,000 gold reserve in the Treasury. Officials and business men sat up nights and generally became nervous over that fund, but it would not stay. All the power and influence of this government and people with $70,000,000,000 of wealth could not keep that small sum in the Treasury. $250,000,000 gold was borrowed and imported, but it would return to the source of confidence, centers of industrial activity, where we had expatriated our industries. The people changed the government. An American tariff was passed. Presto! the smokestacks signaled the workmen to their benches, and gold, as if some living thing, heard the click of the anvil and came over here in such quantities that we have to cry, "Hold, enough!" and a late report shows that we have in this country $1,000,000,000 in gold, a greater quantity than any other nation. With such an object lesson before us would it not be wise to look before we take the advice of free trade doctrinaires, because a few unpatriotic and selfish men have crept into the temple and seek to grasp the people's interests through the agencies of trusts? No! let us rather follow the example of Christ—whip them out who would make our temple dens of thieves. Do not unwisely pull the temples down, but let our fountains of wealth continue to flow, as they now are flowing, since we have tapped prosperity through the magic of protection, and in all our political thought let us consider the source and object, God, country, home. Then, I am satisfied, we will not kill protection for the sake of curing a wart on its face, and under the same principle of political economy, we will go on enriching the people and nation until we will have imbibed the spirit of the higher law and learn THAT WEALTH IS A GUARDIANSHIP, EDUCA-TION A MINISTRY, AND THE CAPTAINS OF INDUSTRY FATHERS TO GUIDE THE MASSES TO HIGHER CONDITIONS.

THOMAS UPDEGRAFF.

Ex-Member Congress, Iowa.

Thomas Updegraff, of Iowa, said:

It is said that nothing on earth is so utterly useless that it will not be thought of some use once in seven years. It is just seven years since the atmosphere of the whole United States was agitated with the free trade shibboleths we have just heard from this platform. Deceptive as they have proved in the past by actual experience, it was to be hoped they would not be resur-rected here.

I am not going into a speech here in favor of protection. It is too late. I shall speak only of protection as it affects trusts. If the experience of the American people during the last seven years has not taught them better than the doctrines that have just been read from this stand, then God help them! The ob-ject lesson has not been forgotten, and whoever now raises his voice before an American audience for free trade labors in vain.

The head of the trust that is taking more money out of the pockets of the people than any other has been introduced as a witness here, and he testifies on his "honor and conscience" that the tariff is the mother of trusts. I thought the witness was smarting a little with resentment because the protectionists had not given him enough in their last tariff bill. If the tariff were, in truth, the mother of his trust it is not likely he would have rushed voluntarily into so savage a denunciation of her char-acter.

That great aggregations of capital have wrought incalculable public good is not denied. A monopolistic trust I stand against; an aggregation of capital, however large, properly managed, I approve. As was said a few moments ago by the gentleman who preceded me: It is only a fool who kills the goose that lays daily the golden egg. We will not give up the tariff; if it be in any sense the mother of trusts, we will save the mother and raise her children in the nurture and admonition of the Lord.

Did any one ever see rich and fertile lands without weeds? What do sensible people who have rich and fertile soil do? Do they abandon it because of the weeds and go to raising grain among the rocks of New England? Do they not rather kill the weeds and save the soil?

It has been said there never was a paradise without snakes. Protectionists would kill the snakes and save the paradise. Free traders in America would devastate the paradise and save the snakes.

That there are abundant and sufficient remedies, within constitutional limits, for all the evils arising from those trusts or combinations which seek to extinguish competition and fix prices is not to be doubted. That the public good arising from greatly cheapened production attainable by great combinations may be saved, is equally clear. This is the work to be done. Whenever the American people have been sufficiently aroused and take the work earnestly in hand it will be accomplished. The party which hesitates may be lost; but we shall ultimately save whatever is good in aggregations of capital and control whatever is bad.

HORATIO W. SEYMOUR.

Publisher Chicago *Chronicle*.

Horatio W. Seymour discussed "Excessive Financial Energy," and said:

The trusts or combinations which should be destroyed and which can be destroyed are those which exist by reason of the protective tariff or which could not exist if there were no protective tariff, and those which either in their organization or in their methods since organization have adopted criminal practices and are therefore amenable to the criminal laws. In the one case there is need of the repeal of unwise and unjust legislation. In the other there is need of the enforcement of penalties which run against individuals hiding behind trust organizations as well as they do against individuals who stand upon their own responsibility.

These are simple remedies, and the wonder is not that they are needed, but that, being needed, they are not applied. The reason is to be found, I think, in a certain weakening of the moral fibre of the American people, partly as a result of the economic errors which have been inculcated so industriously and partly in response to the tireless propaganda of calumny and calamity which has become in a manner a public disease affecting injuriously the entire body of the people.

This habit of complaint is something more than mere discontent. It is sullen, despairing, slothful fault-finding, which quarrels with every new condition, and particularly with every new manifestation of mechanical, financial and commercial energy. It looks upon the dark side of everything. It corrects no evil because it represents every wrong as necessarily incurable. It is pleased with nothing that does not in some manner promise a gratuity. It is continually asking or expecting something for nothing. It teaches that corruption is the mainspring of all success, and that honest effort in any direction is hardly worth while. Its existence indicates quite clearly that the development of great financial energy in this country has been attended by a decided loss of tone on the part of the people.

The supporters of the protective tariff are largely responsible for this condition of affairs. One political party has taught practically nothing else during the past twenty-five years. Most of our political campaigns during that period have turned upon such selfish pecuniary interest as this party could persuade the majority of the people that they, or somebody with whom they were in touch, had in the control of government and in the making of the laws. The indiscriminate granting of pensions and the sale of franchises, grants and other special privileges by municipalities have also done much to fill the minds of the people with wrong ideas as to the relation which they hold to their own government.

Trusts need not be more objectionable than corporations or sole ownerships. They are subject alike with them to the laws. If they violate the laws, their officers may be punished. If they secure advantages under unjust laws, purchased in their interest, or if they escape the penalties of wise laws enacted to prevent and to punish crime, it is certain that representatives of the people in office have betrayed their trust and would have done it as quickly if the bribe giver had represented individuals or had represented himself alone.

The evil to be intelligently complained of and redressed, in the first instance, therefore, is more the weakness and dishonesty and heedlessness of many of the people and their agents than it is the rapacity of the trusts. There is not an unlawful combination in America to-day that does not owe its existence to some unfaithful representative of the people. There is not one that cannot be destroyed in short order by an honest enforcement of the laws. Those trusts or combinations against which the laws do

189

not run are no more to be decried than any other manifestation of business enterprise.

Aside from such trusts as might have had a dishonest origin or as may be conducted contrary to the law, the great mass of these combinations will stand or fall exactly as, under similar circumstances, individual enterprises would. If conducted wisely and economically, with due regard to public rights and public opinion, and with a sagacious comprehension of changing conditions in markets and methods of production and distribution, they will succeed and will deserve to succeed. If inflated at the start, dishonestly managed, and conducted without a decent regard to public sentiment and public rights, they will go to ruin, as they will deserve to do.

Over-capitalization, big salaries and incompetent management are practically certain to wreck a large percentage of these trusts in the course of a few years. The number of men of first-class ability who might be able to manage such combinations satisfactorily is large enough, but such men are not always selected for such positions, and if they are so chosen they do not always have the power necessary to bring about the best results.

The trust exemplifies in a broad field of action a condition which prevails in every crossroads village throughout the civilized world, wherever one man through superior industry, skill, finesse or capital may have gained some advantage over his fellows. It is the highest expression of human selfishness as applied to business affairs. It is on a grand scale, exactly the same thing that every man of enterprise is attempting on a smaller scale.

Unlawfully conducted, the trust may undertake by conspiracy to restrict trade, to destroy competition and to limit production, but numberless corporations and individuals are doing some of these things all the time, and have been doing so for years. The same law which will prove sufficient if invoked against a disorderly vendor of bananas who, by main force, drives away a competitor, will be potential, if honestly enforced, to deal with every lawless combination of capital.

Before instituting prosecution, however, it will be well to consider with some seriousness the fact that business methods in this country, whether in trade unions or in combinations of capital, are not wholly idyllic. The man who undertakes to work when a trade union decrees that he shall not work, is likely to have his head broken, unless society bravely and honestly comes to his defense, as it should.

The weak will suffer at the hands of lawless trusts in the same manner until society, through its proper agents, comes to their relief. Its failure to do so is due to the popular delusion that lawless trusts present a new phase of crime, whereas the new and novel feature that they present is the ability and the willingness to corrupt or to intimidate the people's servants. The lawless trust can be proceeded against as easily and as effectively as a lawless individual can be, and it would be so proceeded against were it not for its corrupt relations with politics and politicians.

To talk about new laws and new penalties against trusts when those now in existence are not enforced, and when it is not even seriously proposed anywhere to enforce them, is idle. If we will not or cannot enforce the laws that we have, it is hardly worth while to ask legislature or congress to enact others. This amazing manifestation of official dereliction is fittingly supplemented by the despairing and discouraging popular cry in many localities that socialism—or state and municipal ownership, as it is now called—is the only remedy for monopoly and extortion. Incapacity or worse in the officer of justice and abject helplessness in the citizen are a deplorable combination in a republic. No remedy that can be proposed will reach the unlawful trusts until this double infirmity shall have been removed.

Hence the problem to be considered in connection with unlawful trusts and combinations is not so much one of undue and criminal financial energy as it is of deplorable popular and official weakness. As a result of the appeals of ignorant or crafty demagogues, who lightly assail all progress and all prosperity, and the wretched and despairing preachments of socialistic agitators, who find no remedy for any ill except in their own miserable process of leveling, too many Americans have lost sight of the fact that the first requisite in a well ordered republic is a self-reliant, self-respecting citizenship.

It is not remarkable that we have lost some sturdiness of character of late, for we have pursued many false ideas as zealously as we formerly adhered to the wiser ones. Forty years of protective tariff legislative hypocrisy and deception have taught the average American that a wise man before entering upon any important enterprise secures a favoring law or privilege or franchise at the hands of government, local, state or federal.

The upholding of this doctrine has educated a generation of Americans to the belief that there is nothing discreditable in asking and accepting public assistance. Imitating our conspicuous public dependants, the tariff beneficiaries, we find in every walk of life that beggary is becoming a great profession, followed by a mighty host made up of every manner of man, woman and child.

In addition to our pension roll of nearly a million names, we have several millions of workingmen who, with their families, have been taught that except as government taxes all the people for the benefit of their employers, they cannot hope for work or wages. We have also a propaganda of helplessness and imbecility carried on sometimes in the name of democracy, but oftener outside of its councils, which teaches hostility to all wealth and to individual enterprise, which informs the young falsely and maliciously that every avenue of promotion is closed to them and which offers no remedy for existing ills save the enfeebling and destructive ones which are to be found in socialism and anarchy.

Under such conditions, who can wonder that every aggregation of capital, no matter how laudable, is viewed by many Americans with dissatisfaction and discontent, or that defiant lawlessness on the part of some of the rich and powerful is everywhere helplessly ignored? To enforce any law, public sentiment is needed. To maintain a republic in respectable form, it is necessary that a majority of its citizens shall be self-sustaining men who scorn pauperism, who detest robbery of every description, and who have sufficient intelligence and individuality to detect and repudiate the sophistry of socialism as well as to meet with proper rebuke the fiercer fanaticism of the revolutionists.

With a citizenship honestly and wisely inspired and officered there would be no more reason for holding a conference to consider how to deal with lawless trusts than there would be to assemble a mass meeting for the purpose of discussing the propriety of enforcing the laws against housebreaking. The unlawful trust would be punished as a matter of course. The lawful trust would be permitted to pursue its business unhindered, as a matter of course.

The need of an invigorating tonic in American political, business and social life is very great. The want of it is felt on every hand where senseless agitation merely for the sake of agitation embitters the old and discourages the young, where the corrupting influence of the dishonest rich finds a ready response on the part of the vicious poor, where demagogues mislead the idle and careless, and where designing men sow the seed of lawlessness and perhaps of revolt.

There is need of some sturdy response to the numerous irresponsible spokesmen of calamity and slander who have the floor at all seasons, and whose influence upon the thoughtfulness and inexperience is far reaching and dangerous. There is need in every section of the country of more hopeful, helpful and suggestive leadership and less of chronic and wholly useless lamentation.

192

Conditions change rapidly in these days. Public intelligence and virtue must and will keep pace with them. The most difficult problems will be solved quickly by a people actuated by rugged honesty, common fairness and a desire to see justice done for the sake of justice. The world grows better daily, presenting more opportunities than ever before, but calling all the time for greater intelligence and a stronger purpose in the pursuit thereof.

The American republic needs a tonic of sound doctrine for the instruction of youth and for the admonition of the aged, which will inculcate the wisdom of hope and the folly of despair, which will show that no abuse of power is too deep seated for correction and which will hold ever before the republic the countless shining examples of success achieved not as a result of jealousy of and slanderous attacks on the triumphs of others, nor by reason of despair and indifference because the obstacles to be surmounted seem greater than formerly, but by faithful work and indomitable courage.

One immediate and wholesome effect of such a tonic would be the impartial enforcement of wise laws against all offenders, the strong as well as the weak, and the repeal of obviously unwise laws, regardless of the protests of their beneficiaries. No unlawful trust could stand for a day in the face of a public sentiment so actuated.

SAMUEL ADAMS ROBINSON.

American Protective Tariff League.

Samuel Adams Robinson said:

We are to suppose, in dealing with this question, that those who contend that "the customs tariff is the mother of trusts," and that the surest way to kill the child is to kill the parent, are sincere in that contention. In taking such sincerity for granted we are, it must be owned, obliged to close our eyes to certain evidences which conflict with this conclusion. We must, for example, ignore the eagerness with which free-traders have sprung to the front with their anti-protective antidote for trusts, while at the same time extending to the trusts the consoling reassurance that it is not the trust, but the protective tariff, whose scalp they (the free-traders) are after. Such reassurance was not long ago conveyed in connection with the published announcement of the New England Free-Trade League of its arrangements to secure the publication of a series of articles tending to show that it is to the protective tariff that trusts are indebted for their existence primarily and their survival ultimately. In response to the gratifying assurance that the chief concern of the New England Free-Trade League was for the foreign producer and not for the domestic consumer it is to be presumed that contributions to the publication fund from trust sources were not altogether lacking. They should not be. In this connection let us note a curious fact, namely, that while demagogic theorists have been prompt to suggest the removal of the tariff when a domestic trust has increased prices, there is no recorded instance, I believe, of these gentlemen demanding that the tariff be doubled when prices have been increased by a foreign trust.

Assuming, however, for the purpose of this discussion, that the enemies of protection are also the enemies of trusts, in equal sincerity, it ought to be plain to every unbiased mind that the remedy for trust oppression is not to be found in the death of domestic competition. At least, we should not make a headlong rush for that remedy until we are sure that it is the right one. Rather let us be wise and patient and inform ourselves as to the precise character of the disease before attempting to diagnose and prescribe. When we shall have done this it is not impossible that the trust antidote will be forthcoming in the shape of effective laws born, not of guesswork and dogmatism, but of the knowledge gained from test and experience.

If experience has taught anything, it has taught that in a country such as ours, with its limitless latent resources, awaiting development, you cannot pluck the fruit of prosperity from the tree of free-trade. It does not grow there. "Do men gather grapes of thorns, or figs of thistles?" On general principles the remedy for monopoly is not the limitation of internal competition. Gasoline is not a good medium for fire extinguishment. Free-trade is not the remedy we are in search of, unless the people of the United States are prepared to enter upon an experiment certain to overthrow our industries, but not certain to "smash the trusts." So I say, for the present:

"Rather bear those ills we have than fly to others that we know not of."

Considered in the light of logic and expediency, the present time is most inopportune for striking down the economic policy which, according to the increasing testimony of British writers and thinkers, has created in the United States the great manufacturing industry which threatens British commercial supremacy. American free-traders are about the only people on earth to-day who do not concede this to be a fact.

Let us suppose a condition. In the event of the consolidation of all industries into trusts, with the protective tariff forever removed, and with its removal all incentive to new competitive enterprises wholly lacking, does any one suppose that the trusts would dissolve and their constituent companies return to unrestricted competition and price cutting among themselves? Would they surrender to foreign competition and go out of business entirely? No sane person could for a moment anticipate any of these results. On the contrary, the assured prospect of a permanent removal of protective tariff would impel every industrial enterprise in this country now operating independently to rush for shelter into a trust organization. Domestic competition would be at an end. What of foreign competition? The answer is plain. On a free-trade basis, and with the certainty that no new domestic competition could arise to complicate matters, our industrial captains, being absolute masters of the situation, would not surrender the home market to foreigners, but would make a tremendous fight for the preservation of their existence. They would fight inside the limits of a very small ring—the ring of reduced prices and reduced wages. Prices and wages must come down to approximately the European standard, to say nothing of the Asiatic standard. No use for American wage earners to rebel, for you must remember that we are now organized on a free-trade basis into a compact national trust of wage payers, and that our industrial captains, secure through free-trade from the menace of new domestic competition, are in a position to dictate the rate of wages. No such dictation is possible in the presence of such open and unrestricted domestic competition as is made possible through the operation of the protective principle. But in the condition we are now supposing, protection has been abandoned and free-trade is the order of the day. The industrial captains are organized under the new conditions, not the old, and they will know how to handle the wage question. Having reduced wages and lowered the cost of production, we are thus in shape to meet foreign competition. We can control the great home market, and, more than that, we are able to realize the free-trade dream of underselling the rest of the world in the markets of the world. To be sure, we have reached that ideal (free-trade) condition by a sweeping reduction of the American wage rate and a corresponding drop in the American standard of living. But, no matter, we have got there, and that was the main consideration. We have succeeded in bringing about a sweeping reduction of prices and values, and have done it at the expense of the American workingman. What have we to offer the lower paid wage earner in the way of compensation for his sacrifices? A lower cost of living, some one will reply. Yes, we have done that, to some extent, it may be, but to no extent that is at all commensurate with the loss of his ability to earn, buy and consume. He is still the loser by the readjustment of things —a terrible loser, I think. But he is not the only loser. What of the general body politic? Has any one ever figured out what it would mean to the business of this nation of seventy-seven millions if the average wage rate were to be reduced 25 per cent? To express such a result would require so many ciphers following a unit and a dollar mark that I shall not attempt the calculation. I don't like to imagine, much less depict, such a state of things, and I prefer to dismiss this appalling aspect of the question with the conclusion that it cannot and will not come to pass.

However, we have brought about unrestricted foreign competition by means of abolishing protective duties, and we have "smashed the trusts." But have we smashed the trusts? Have we not given them a new lease of life by the removal of the peril of domestic competition outside the trusts? Have we not opened the door to the international trust? With the American market closed against them by reason of a lower cost of production in this country, and with American competition crowding them out of the world's markets, will foreign industrial producers lie down and give up the fight? Probably not. Being already familiar with the development and operation of the trust plan, they will naturally undertake the arrangement of a *modus vivendi,* and by easy stages will reach a *modus operandi,* with the all powerful American trust. Behold the international trust, the universal trust, if you please. It is not an impossibility. It is not even an improbability. It is a certainty. In such an event will our last state be better than our first?

I have said that in the altered conditions brought about by the permanent abolition of the system of protection, the trust would find its operations facilitated, not hindered. Hard times are the best times for trusts. It is then that profits are smallest and that combination is easiest. In good times the problem is not so simple, for it is complicated by the alertness with which capital seeks employment in new ventures and by the active competition in all productive lines, which is a natural consequence of such activity in the employment of capital.

Tin plate has been selected as a bright and shining mark, a conspicuous target for the shafts of those who while pretending to aim at trusts direct their volleys at protection. Tin plate is indeed a bright and shining mark, for it is the most recent and hence the most notable exemplification of the practical workings of a policy which establishes industries by means of guaranteeing a stable market for their products. It also happens that the tin plate trust is the most conspicuous one among the trusts whose products enjoy the benefits of a protective tariff which has in any notable degree advanced its prices. It is not my purpose to defend or apologize for this action on the part of the manufacturers of tin plate, but rather to inquire into the facts with a view to arriving at an intelligent conclusion as to the merits of the question. I find, to begin with, that the difference between the present price of American tin plate and the price of Welsh tin plate laid down in this country, duty paid, is very much less than the duty of 1½ cents per pound. Recent quotations for tin plate in Wales for export are 16 shillings per box of 108 pounds, while the price in the United States is $4.52½ per box of 108 pounds. The Welsh price is equivalent to $3.89 in United States money. This price is subject to discounts for cash of 3 and 1 per cent, and a brokerage of 2 per cent is customarily paid to the foreign broker for buying the plates and inspecting them, so that the net price would be practically 2 per cent less than $3.89, or $3.81. To this must be added 15 cents for ocean freight and insurance, making the price in bond in New York $3.96. The duty on 108 pounds, at 1½ cents, is $1.62, making the price on dock in New York, duty paid, $5.58. While foreign plates would cost in New York $5.58, American plates are costing at mill $4.52½, or $1.05½ less. The price of American plates at mill is $0.56½ more than the price of foreign plates at New York, before the duty is paid, so that under present conditions just about one-third of the duty, or one-half a cent a pound, is actually benefiting the American tin plate industry. The other two-thirds is nominal. It should be noted that the comparison made is not as favorable a one as might be drawn, because the principal consuming centers of the United States are nearer the mills than they are to New York, and the freight from New York to the point of consumption would average more than the freight from mill to point of consumption. There is no question that had there been no tin plate industry established in this country, Welsh tin plates would be selling at very much higher figures to-day. The Welsh manufacturers were securing very good profits out of the American trade before the McKinley law, from the absence of competition. They would have continued to secure such profits had no competition arisen in this country, while the demand has so increased that were there no source of supply but the Welsh tin mills, there would have been an excess of demand over production of 25 to 50 per cent at the present time, and prices would without doubt have been sent much higher. It would be the height of folly to attempt to deny that with the Welsh manufacturers retaining a monopoly of the American demand, their prices would be, not $0.56½ higher than they are now, but many times this advance, and in this case free Welsh plates would cost the American consumer much more than American plates do now. The American tin plate industry is to-day indebted to the tariff for but about one-third of the protection it nominally offers, and it requires this small protection only because Welsh tin plates are selling much lower than they would be selling were there no American industry.

The advances that have occurred in tin plate in the last nine months are in great part, if not wholly, explained and justified by the advances in raw material on the one hand, and the increased demand on the other. That such influences are fully able to produce still greater advances is shown by the condition in tank plate, which early last year sold at one cent a pound and is now selling at 2¾ cents for delivery in the next two months, an increase of 175 per cent, as against an increase in tin plates of less than 70 per cent, from $2.60 to $4.37½ for 100 pound cakes. With a very few exceptions, iron and steel products, which have no trust control whatever, and on which the duty is merely nominal, have advanced much more than have tin plates. From August 1, 1898, to August 1, 1899, the standard grade of tin plates quoted by the Treasury Department in the monthly summary of the Bureau of Statistics increased in price 77 cents a box. In the same period the same grade of goods in Wales increased $1.45 a box, and that foreign increase was nearly all made in 1899. In other words, in free-trade England tin plates increased twice as much in price as in the United States under a protective tariff.

It is urged in behalf of tin plate manufacturers that they had no desire, when the Dingley bill was under discussion, to see the rate of duty advanced, and it is a fact that some of them were actually opposed to the increase. They knew that the advance would not secure them any higher prices for their product, and that the workmen would make it a pretext for demanding higher wages, and the outcome proved that they were right. The only tin plate lobby was that of the Amalgamated Association of Iron, Steel and Tin Workers, through the influence of which the duty was advanced. The price of American tin plate was not raised a particle by the increased duty, but at the next scale settlement the workers demanded an advance in wages on the strength of the higher duty, and they got it. Last summer they demanded another advance, and they got that also, the two advances amounting to about 25 per cent over the wages paid under the Wilson law. The earnings of about 54,000 tin plate operatives have been affected by these advances. Nine years ago there were no operatives in the tin plate industry; there was no such industry in existence in this country.

Contrasted with this large increase in the rate of wages among tin plate workers in the United States is the action taken by the provisional committee of the newly formed South Wales Tin Plate Masters' Association, which met representatives of the workmen in conference in Swansea recently on the wage question. A cable dispatch says:

"After two hours' discussion it was decided to recommend the acceptance of a 10 per cent reduction throughout the trade."

No one has yet succeeded in showing that prices of tin plate have been advanced in the United States to the point of unreasonable or oppressive exaction, in view of the large increase that has taken place in the cost of production by reason of higher wages, increased cost of materials, etc. It is not my purpose to either accuse or defend the tin plate trust. That organization, like all other trusts, will stand or fall on its merits. This much, however, is clear and indisputable: That to the policy of protection is wholly due the fact of the establishment of the tin plate industry in the United States; and that through the establishment of this industry, many millions of dollars have been saved to the consumers of tin plate, and many millions of dollars have been added to the gross sum of wages paid to American labor.

Enemies of protection, unable to explain away the catastrophe which has overtaken their cherished theories through the wonderful development of our export trade in manufactured products, seem to find much comfort and consolation in the assertion that this tremendous trade has been brought about by means of a general cut in prices, and that the home consumer pays more than the foreign consumer pays for the same article. There was a time, in the four years of depression following the free-trade triumph of 1892, when to a considerable extent our manufacturers were compelled to sacrifice their profits in order to find a foreign outlet for their surplus products. This was a time of national underconsumption and hence of national overproduction; a time when a reduction of prices afforded a means of obtaining ready cash for products rendered unsaleable because of the greatly diminished purchasing and consuming power of the nation as a whole. In this way manufacturers found it possible to keep their plants in operation and their labor employed during a long and

199

trying period of deadly depression. Their goods were marketed abroad at figures which left little or no margin of profit, and sometimes involved actual loss. But there was no choice. Either this, or close the factories and discharge the workpeople. But this dismal necessity no longer exists. Export prices are now much nearer on a parity with domestic prices. It would be hard to find a manufacturer to-day who is developing a foreign trade without profit or at a loss. Mills are too busy working over-time to catch up with orders. Discounts are allowed on goods sold for export, for several good reasons—such as the spot cash payment for such goods, whereas in domestic trade long credits are the rule and spot cash the exception; and the additional fact that in marketing his product through the export trade the manufacturer is at no expense for advertising, maintenance of agencies, and other items in the cost of distribution amounting in the aggregate to fully the difference between export prices and domestic prices. The domestic consumer understands this perfectly, and does not grumble at it. It is only the American free-traders who feel aggrieved at a condition which increases the use of American material, increases the employment of American labor, and increases the consumption of American food products by American workers to the enormous average of over $50 per capita, against an estimated per capita average of less than $1.50 of American food products sold to and consumed by the workpeople of Europe. Who should find fault with such a state of things? The foreign manufacturer and his American agents and friends don't like it, of course; but I think it will be found that the American farmer is not losing any sleep because Europeans get a small discount from current American prices on agricultural implements, sewing machines, or typewriters; still less is the American wage earner worrying over the practical workings of a system which gives him increased wages and increased employment. Our export trade of a million dollars per day, including Sundays and holidays, in the products of American manufacture is one of the glories of the protective policy. Foreigners know it, and recognize it as the direct outgrowth of that policy.

Mr. Havemeyer's contention that "the customs tariff is the mother of trusts" was a blessing in disguise. It was intended as a blow at the party in power at the time Mr. Havemeyer failed to get the increase of duties he wanted on refined sugar, and also failed to get a reduction or repeal of the duties on raw sugar. Its effect has proved to be exactly the opposite of that which was intended. Before Mr. Havemeyer left the witness stand he placed on record the damaging admission that the sugar trust could,

SAMUEL GOMPERS   T. B. WALKER
EDWARD Q. KEASBEY   M. M. GARLAND
U. M. ROSE   A. LEO WEIL

if assured of the absence of domestic competition outside of his trust, get along extremely well without any protection whatsoever, and that he would welcome the abolition of all protective duties on raw and refined sugars. So we may dismiss Mr. Havemeyer with the remark that in his testimony before the Industrial Commission he served his country better than he knew, and much better than he intended, by making it clear that in the case of the sugar trust protection is more a hindrance than a help.

The question of the effect of a protective tariff upon wages has been injected into this discussion somewhat gratuitously on the part of the enemies of protection; somewhat unwisely, too, it must appear, for no one, I believe, claims that a reduction in wages has yet been put in force by the trusts. The fact is that in the general advance of wages, estimated at 15 per cent for the entire country, which has taken place in connection with the phenomenal prosperity following the restoration of the policy of protection to American labor and industry, trust wage payers have thus far shown no disposition to shirk their share. So we must conclude that the free-trade claim that wages are not affected by tariffs is a proposition on general principles intended to discredit protection and not aimed at the trusts. Here again the American free-trader stands solitary and alone, a gloomy Napoleon on an economic St. Helena. His foreign fellows long ago abandoned the contention. There is at present scarcely a shade of difference among European manufacturers as to the true cause of their inability to compete with America in the world's markets. With common accord they say it is the result of the high wages paid American workingmen, and that the establishment and maintenance of the American standard of wages has been made possible only by the operation of the protective principle. The American wage earner has lately had an object lesson along the line of tariffs and wages. The lesson lasted four years, and he is not likely to forget it.

The free-trade advocate of the removal of protection as a trust antidote finds himself upon the horns of a dilemma. Either we need protection to hold the home market against outside competition, or we do not need protection and can get along equally well without it—better, our free-trade friends tell us. If we do not need protection, its removal would be valueless as a trust antidote. If we do need protection in order to maintain our hold upon a market with a consuming capacity estimated at nine billions yearly, then the removal of protection would work such havoc with our country's prosperity as the gloomiest of pessimists would find it well nigh impossible to adequately foreshadow. I am not a pessimist. I am a protectionist, a very different thing, now and always. Protectionists in the past have known how to confront a danger with a defense. They will know how to meet the trust question at the proper time and in the proper way. They have never failed in an emergency; they will not fail now. A remedy will be forthcoming whenever the pathological moment arrives. We all remember the practitioner who could cure but one disease, and who always threw the patient into a fit, and then prescribed for the fit. History does not, however, record that he was invariably successful in curing the fit. The stage of fits has not yet been reached, though some of the quacks would have us think otherwise. Their antidote is an old and a well known one. It was tried in 1892, and we all know how it worked. Do we want any more of it? I think not.

The conference took a recess until 3 o'clock in the afternoon.

AFTERNOON SESSION, SEPTEMBER 14.

The conference was called to order at 3 o'clock by Vice-Chairman Dudley G. Wooten. The chair announced that owing to the number of papers the twenty-minute rule would be enforced. He then introduced S. H. Greeley of Illinois, representing the National Grain Growers' Association.

S. H. GREELEY.

National Grain Growers' Association.

An evil from which no relief is possible seems to be an absurdity in this age of progress and discovery, but the producers and shippers of grain in the great Mississippi Valley are to-day in the grasp of a number of so skillfully managed combinations, created by secret rates and special privileges, granted them by railroads, that the brightest mind cannot suggest a practical remedy; by practical, I mean a remedy which the people are ready to apply, for I assume from the general tone of the press, that as a nation we are not yet ready to own the railroads, the very mainspring of many of the combinations and trusts, which are now crushing out the middle class in the United States, and fast hurrying us to the condition of the yellow race.

To-day capital and labor are prosperous, the intermediate

class find themselves struggling against hidden and unscrupulous foes, to maintain an independent position in society, they share but slightly in the general prosperity and are fast drifting into the employ of combinations and trusts, and disappearing as independent factors in society.

To my mind the most glaring examples of the power of the railroads to make and unmake men, is seen in the Chicago grain market of to-day; merchants no longer buy and sell grain in Chicago, but their places have been usurped by the "recipients of cut rates and special privileges," who have become as necessary an adjunct of the modern railroad, tapping the grain belt, as the general freight office—it is their business to see that the railroad favoring them gets their share of the grain tonnage, and where a merchant paying the tariff rates of freight would lose money, this specially favored class grows rich; they handle all the grain that they are physically capable of caring for on the particular line of railroad of which they are the favored dealers.

The effect of this condition has been disastrous in many ways:

1. Competition has been destroyed to a great extent, and the business of handling grain in Chicago markets, has (by force of special favors from railroads) concentrated in the hands of several large concerns, who do not bid against each other, but are known to agree on prices each day for grain in territory where their bids are liable to reach the same sellers.

Without advantages of ability or capital, over the merchants whom they have driven from the field, these concerns through employees and agents carry on a traffic, not in grain, but in freight, switching and elevator charges; incidentally the grain is transported, but if tariff rates and fixed charges were paid it would show a loss.

2. Values suffer far more than would be conceded even by a majority of the grain growers. Unnatural conditions constantly surround the movement of grain; if the business of a railroad lags, grain is forced to move by that railroad through its favored shipper, by a cut rate, thus creating a fictitious supply at a time when the demand is meager, and the result is a decline in values by reason of excessive offerings, while had the grain been permitted to remain at the country points until the demand justified its shipment, the depression in values would have been avoided and the demand would have been all the more urgent by reason of the grain not being in sight.

Another condition which tends to depress values is the piling up of vast stocks of grain in the warehouses of Chicago and by every trick and device preventing the moving of these stocks, so long as they can be sold for future delivery at a profit. The public and private elevators of Chicago have passed into the hands of the concerns specially favored by the railroads; several of them lease the terminal elevators of the railroads. The result has been that the public warehouse system of Chicago has been prostituted to the extent that the public no longer can handle grain through them, and what was once the depots for the public's grain are absolutely the storehouse of the railroad's favored dealer to the exclusion of all other persons. It is to the advantage of this favored class that low prices should prevail, so that they can fill their vast warehouses (aggregating almost 40,000,-000 bushels' capacity) with cheap grain, sell it for future delivery at a premium, buying back and selling for a still more deferred delivery as often as market conditions will permit. When it ceases to pay tribute as a speculative commodity, they then proceed to sell it in eastern and foreign markets, and having driven out of business all other grain shippers by their methods, they merchandise the grain themselves; but no matter how urgent the consumptive demand, so long as speculative sales pay best, consumers cannot get supplies from the vast stores held in Chicago.

This feature of the grain trade and its tendency toward monopoly are clearly set forth by the courts, in decisions affecting this very condition, in an action brought by the attorney-general of the state of Illinois against the public warehousemen of Chicago.

The eminent Judge Tuley, after listening three weeks to evidence, and pleadings of counsel, rendered an opinion in favor of the people, in which he used the following language:

"The great weight of evidence is to the effect that the warehousemen of Chicago did not commence to so deal in grain to any general extent until about the year 1885; that the practice has grown so rapidly that now and for two or three years last past they are the principal buyers and sellers on the Chicago market and upon the Chicago Board of Trade; that by reason of the advantages they possess, and by reason of certain changes in the grain trade, they have practically driven out of business the class of men who were before them engaged in buying and shipping grain on the Chicago market. And it is admitted that they have dealt in grain to the extent that they now own at least three-quarters of all the grain stored in the public warehouses of the city of Chicago, and it also appears by the evidence that they are fast monopolizing the business of dealing in grain in the Chicago market.

"It is in evidence that they not only own this large proportion of the grain stored in their public warehouses, and also are the principal buyers in the Chicago market, but that nearly all of them deal in 'futures.'

"It is easy to perceive the temptation they would be under as to mixing the grain of their customers, and also to control the market by the ownership of such a vast proportion of the warehoused grain. It is also easy to perceive in selling grain the temptations they would be under to abate or remit storage charges in order to effect sales.

"In the case at bar it is shown that the public warehousemen of Chicago, being licensed to carry on a warehouse, have used their capital, to wit, their warehouses and business as warehousemen, to aid them in trading in grain in competition with the public, and having a great advantage over such public in such trading, by reason of their control of such licensed warehouses, they have become the principal buyers and sellers of grain in the Chicago market and upon some lines or systems or railroads centering in Chicago, almost the only buyers.

"It is, however, contended that the warehouseman gets the grain because he pays more for it than other bidders; that the constitution of the state requires the law passed in pursuance thereof to be construed 'in the interests of the producer,' therefore it is to the interest of the producer that the warehouse be allowed to enter into the grain business. No monopoly in grain dealing can operate in the long run to the interest of the producer. There is no truer maxim in economics than that 'competition is the life of trade.' The warehousemen may be able to pay more than outside shippers or buyers until he has driven them out of the market; when he has succeeded in so doing (and the evidence shows that that time has nearly arrived) and he has practically no competition, then the producer would suffer. The law should not be so construed as to give the warehouseman the right to use his privilege, his public business as a warehouseman to crush out competition against himself as a dealer in grain."

In affirming the decision of Judge Tuley, the Supreme Court of Illinois, touching on the tendency toward monopoly, said:

"It is a firmly established rule that where one person occupies a relation in which he owes a duty to another he shall not place himself in any position which will expose him to temptation of acting contrary to that duty or bring his interest in conflict with his duty. This rule applies to every person who stands in such a position that he owes a duty to another, and courts of equity have never fettered themselves by defining particular relations to which, alone, it will be applied. They have applied it to agents, partners, guardians, executors, administrators, directors, and managing officers of corporations, as well as trustees, but have never fixed or defined its limits. The rule is founded upon the plain consideration that the one charged with duty shall act with regard to the discharge of that duty, and he will not be permitted to expose himself to temptation or be brought into a situation where his personal interests conflict with his duty. Courts of equity have never allowed a person occupying such a relation to undertake the service of two whose interests are in conflict, and then endeavor to see that he does not violate his duty, but forbids such a course of dealing irrespective of his good faith or bad faith. If the duty of the defendants, as public warehousemen, stands in opposition to personal interests as buyers and dealers in grain storing the same in their own warehouses, then the law interposes a preventive check against any temptation to act from personal interest by prohibiting them from occupying any such position.

"The public warehouses established under the law are public agencies, and the defendants, as licensees, pursue a public employment. It is clothed with a duty toward the public. The evidence shows that defendants, as public warehousemen storing grain in their own warehouses, are enabled to, and do, overbid legitimate grain dealers by exacting from them the established rate for storage while they give up a part of the storage charges when they buy or sell for themselves. By this practice of buying and selling through their own elevators the position of equality between them and the public whom they are bound to serve, is destroyed, and by the advantage of their position they are enabled to crush out, and have nearly crushed out, competition in the largest grain market in the world. The result is, that the warehousemen own three-fourths of all the grain stored in public warehouses of Chicago, and upon some of the railroads the only buyers of grain are the warehousemen on that line.

"In exercising the public employment for which he is licensed he cannot be permitted to use the advantage of his position to crush out competition and to combine in establishing a monopoly by which a great accumulation of grain is in the hands of the warehousemen, liable to be suddenly thrown upon the market whenever they, as speculators, see profit in such course. The defendants are large dealers in futures on the Chicago Board of Trade, and together hold an enormous supply of grain ready to aid their opportunities as speculators. The warehouseman issues his own receipt to himself. As public warehouseman he gives a receipt to himself as individual, and he is able to use his own receipts for the purpose of trade and to build up a monopoly and destroy competition. That this course of dealing is inconsistent with the full and impartial performance of his duty to the public seems clear. The defendants answer that the practice had a beneficial effect upon producers and shippers, and naturally were able to prove that when, by reason of their advantages, they were overbidding other dealers there was benefit to the sellers, but there was an entire failure to show that in the general average there was any public good to producers or shippers."

Would any honorable man try to override so sweeping a decision of the highest court of the great state of Illinois? Individuals would bow to this logical and equitable decision, appealing as it did to common sense and sustained by well-settled principles of law; but the railroads and their favorites, who had tasted the advantages of monopoly, immediately set to work to break the force of this victory, which had carried joy to the hearts of hundreds of small dealers throughout the state of Illinois and the great Northwest; it could not be done by honorable methods; intimidation, bribery and deception were their only tools; and by the aid of the officers of the railroads, who traveled from town to town, in the interests of this monopoly, to inform shippers it would be as well for them to submit; by the special train provided by the railroads to carry the agents of the Chicago warehouseman from town to town; by offering labor one incentive to support their methods, and grain handlers an incentive directly opposed to the one offered to labor; and finally and more effectually placing at our state capitol a strong lobby whose arguments were made in private, this combination, embracing all the public warehousemen in Chicago and almost every trunk line operating west of that city, forced through the Legislature of Illinois a bill which for the time being again placed the yoke of monopoly on the neck of the grain trade in the greatest grain market of the world and its great tributary states which produce the surplus grain crops. As a result, individual effort to succeed is no longer possible, the conditions outlined in the court decisions are intensified, that is, the monopoly has become complete and the railroads simply dictate who shall and who shall not do business. This condition, originally affecting only the business coming to Chicago from the west has now extended to shipments of grain to the east from that market, and scores of individuals and firms formerly prosperous, have disappeared or drifted into other, and in some cases, less legitimate lines.

Practically all the great railroads tapping the grain belt are in the grain business; the details of their arrangements are, of course, secrets, but it requires but very little investigation to satisfy the most skeptical that they each have one, two or three concerns handling the bulk of grain on their lines, to whom the published tariffs are simply a guide as to what the public have to pay; the public soon discover that the favored shipper can do business with an entire disregard of fixed charges and still prosper. One railroad president admitted at a public investigation that his company had organized a corporation for the purpose of carrying on a grain business at all points on their line, that it was necessary to do so to protect their interests, as their competitors had arrangements with shippers that were practically preventing the competition of the ordinary shipper. With this tendency to create a monopoly, to destroy competition, to secretly enrich a few men and destroy the business of hundreds of others, to evade laws, to override courts, to bribe legislators, to intimidate the public, to create unnatural conditions, by destroying the natural laws of supply and demand, the railroads and their creatures are making rapid strides toward a complete control of the grain markets of this country—not for the purpose of advancing the price paid to the producer or cheapen the price the consumer is compelled to pay—but to force it forward to points of accumulation to be held for speculative purposes when it is possible to collect a tax in the form of storage charges from the speculator, who is willing to pay an enhanced price for a deferred delivery.

For twelve years the federal law, known as the Inter-State Commerce Law, has been on trial, that railroads and individuals do not even respect the law, or try to obey it, shows that our so-called great men of commerce and corporations have no use for laws except to appeal to them for protection for themselves or their soulless creations behind which they hid their individuality and from whose coffers they obtain the millions to endow colleges and bribe public officials.

Money is a giant, beside which law is a pigmy; to attempt to control the present greed for wealth by laws, is like trying to make Niagara's waters turn back and climb the precipice over which they now flow. The disregard of the Inter-State Commerce Law and other laws by accumulated wealth is sufficient argument that such accumulations are a menace to the welfare of the nation; they respect neither the nation nor the individual, and have reached a point where they no longer can be tolerated except with great danger to our institutions.

We find no difficulty in conquering a foreign enemy. Wh

should we not do the same with domestic enemies, even though they are so magnificent in capitalization and water? The railroads for twelve years have given us proof of their contempt for our laws; shall they now be permitted to consummate the enslavement of a majority of the people or will our national government rise to the occasion and conquer and own the giant that threatens the liberty and happiness of its people?

With the railroads in the hands of the people, with rates equitable and alike to all, men now unable to cope with their favored competitors will be enabled to live; ability, energy and industry are useless when a cut rate of freight supplies the margin to a competitor.

Protect the value of farm products by preventing unnatural conditions, which overcome the laws of supply and demand and depress values, to the end that railroads may earn freight and elevators collect storage. Kill trusts and combinations by cutting the "tap-root," railroad discrimination.

J. C. HANLEY.

National Farmers' Alliance and Industrial Union of America.

J. C. Hanley said:

On behalf of the National Farmers' Alliance and Industrial Union of America, I desire to express the approval of our association of the object and purpose of this gathering, if that object is for the purpose of securing information and education on the subject, trusts and combines, their cause and effects upon the financial, commercial, industrial and agricultural interests of our country, and to find a remedy to apply that will be both practical and effective.

With this idea before me, I can assure this conference that I will render every possible aid to bring good out of this meeting, and will pledge the earnest and active co-operation of the officers and members of our association in carrying out any plan or policy that has for its aim the betterment of conditions for the people in general.

The marvelous development and growth of trusts and combines within the last few years, and the changed conditions which it has brought about, in all walks of industrial and social life, have brought the people abruptly to consider this new phase of conditions which are novel, significant and far-reaching. It has finally dawned upon the people that the formation and extension of the trust movement means new and changed conditions for them, and whether these conditions are for better or for worse, is determined by those who are affected by its operations.

Trusts and combines if conducted on a strict business competitive system would be a blessing rather than a curse. But the operation of many of these gigantic monopolies as conducted at present is a menace to the existence and stability of our nation.

The causes in brief are the tendencies to capitalize combinations at enormously watered values, and then exact tribute in the shape of fixed interest on this vastly over-capitalized stock. The effort to earn these fixed charges often places these trusts and combines under public disapproval. Because of the power they control, they can suppress competition, put down the price of the raw material or product, and put up the price of the manufactured article, while in the same breath they can reduce wages and reduce labor. Under these conditions the trust becomes a curse, as none but the members of the combine or trust is a beneficiary, while the producer and consumer are obliged to pay the tribute.

I am convinced that legislation cannot remedy this evil, except it strikes at the root of the evil, and that the government should own and control all means of transportation, and public utilities, and operate them in the interests of the people. I refer to such agencies as railroads, telegraph and telephone lines, mines of coal, iron, oil, etc. While I firmly believe that this will be the only correct and finally effective remedy, I am still aware that it will be some time before this condition will be realized, and the trusts themselves are hastening this day faster than the most ardent socialist ever dreamed of. But as we must offer some remedy that will meet the conditions that confront us, a remedy both practical and effective, and which can be put into operation at once, I can sum the whole thing up in one word, "competition." I will therefore apply my remarks to matters and conditions having direct bearing on the interests of agriculture.

There are many ways in which the farmer is made the helpless victim of the numerous combines through which his products pass in transit from the farm to the consumer, and every one of these combines levies tribute on him. The transportation, elevator and cotton combines are possibly the most exacting of local combines, and are of such importance that we have left it to the delegates of one of our grain growers' societies to make a special subject of investigation of this form of combine, and its cause and effect on agriculture. In order to secure competition for the products of the farm I propose four remedies which will be necessary to carry out successfully the permanent establishment of competition, which is absolutely necessary to relieve the conditions which agriculture endures, and to make the great national crops of the United States—wheat and cotton—profitable crops, instead of crops raised at a loss:

1st. The opening and extending our foreign markets in Oriental countries.

2nd. The building of our own merchant ships to carry our products to foreign markets.

3rd. The establishment and maintenance of permanent international exhibits, in the Orient, of American raw and manufactured products.

4th. The protection of American grain markets from railroad and warehouse monopoly and the encouragement of local and terminal competition.

The records of the Agricultural Department show that the average cost per pound of raising cotton was 6 2-10 cents, while the average market price was 4½ to 5 cents per pound. The enormous loss on this great national crop of nearly three and one-half billions of pounds of cotton can be appreciated.

This feature of the cotton situation last fall and winter in the south was aptly put by Col. J. P. Sossaman, of Charlotte, N. C., who said in a letter to me: "The cotton industry is in terrible plights. There is so much cotton in the south that the warehouses are full and the people are going naked, while the crop is for sale at 4½ cents, and no takers. The planters measure their loss by the amount of cotton they raise."

And the same condition applies to the wheat section. It is also raised at a loss. I have compiled statistics from every section of the wheat raising country, from all kinds of land, prairie, timber, small and bonanza farms. Rich and poor, educated and ignorant farmers, each and every one has the same story to tell, and that is that wheat raising is done at a loss. The following is a report by Mr. A. S. Stephens, of Beardsley, Minn., a well-to-do farmer, who has had nineteen years' experience as a successful farmer, 200 miles from a terminal market, but who has been obliged to make up the losses on the farm from other business pursuits. His report is an average one from many sources, and will reveal the average condition on the American farm. He says:

"My experience in producing 160 acres of wheat has been as follows:

Cost of producing 1 acre of wheat of 13 bu. per acre (a very liberal yield).

Value of land $20.00 per acre.

Interest on same at 8%	$1.60
Taxes on same	.12½
Plowing same	1.25
Harrowing and seeding	.50
Cutting and binding	1.25
Stacking	.90
Threshing at 3c. per bu.	.39
Help for threshing 75 acres, one day's work 20 men at $2.00 per acre, one day	.54
Board of crew for threshing as above and machine crew	.20
Delivering to elevator, 6 miles, 3c. per bu.	.39
Seed, 1¼ bu. at 50c. per bu.	.62
Natural wear and tear of machinery and earnings of housewife	.26
	$8.02½

Making an actual cost of nearly 62c. per bu. for production.

Average highest price paid at this station in the last past 19 years, 76c.

Average lowest in the same period, 43c.

"In finding the above average prices, I take $1.38, which was paid at this station only one day during the Joe Leiter speculation, whilst the low prices have been paid fully seventy days out of every 100 days during the above period. The above is the actual cost of producing a bushel of wheat on an area of 160 acres of land. In addition to the above, which cannot be avoided, the farmer has to pay fire insurance, usually hail insurance, road taxes, and feed horses in idle times, and other incidental expenses too numerous to mention, which will amount to at least 60 cents per acre, making a total cost of $8.62 per acre, or 66 4-13 cents per bushel, whilst the average prices in the above period have been 50 cents per bushel, or an actual loss of 16 cents per bushel, or $2.08 per acre, or $332.80 per 160 acres.

"It appears quite evident that there are several causes for the low prices, viz:

"1st. We have rings and combines of mills and line elevators that apparently make agreement to pay (especially early in the threshing season) a stated price, regardless of cost of production or prospect.

"2nd. We at present practically have but one foreign buyer or market, which is England. It is natural for human ambition to pay as little as possible for all purchases, and between the friendly feeling of American monopoly and English combines, the American producer is at their full mercy, to that extent that we have produced wheat at a loss for a number of years past.

"The result of it is that one-third of the homes that were given to the tillers of the soil by the United States government have been lost by foreclosures, one-third are now paying tribute to mortgagees, the other third have succeeded in keeping their homes by force of economy and hard work."

Now, gentlemen, I come to the matter of this paper, and that is the establishment and extension of our foreign markets and its effect on agriculture and labor. It is well known that we can raise more wheat, meat and textile fabrics than would feed and clothe a nation double our size. We have a great deal of export products that we must sell to dispose of our surplus. We raise in round numbers 500,000,000 bushels of wheat annually. We consume for home consumption about 400,000,000 bushels. We have, therefore, about 100,000,000 bushels of wheat for export annually. We are so situated that the export crop sets the price by which the whole crop is measured. If we have but one customer who will buy from us, and he is quite indifferent about what prices he pays, so long as it is the lowest possible price that he must pay, the price that he pays for our products is the price that the producer measures the profits or losses of his toil and industry by.

Now the very necessities of the farmers compel them to part with the grain in the early months of the crop year, and by the very volume of grain thus thrown on the market they assist the gamblers who are utilizing every means to "bear" the market at that time of year when the bulk of the grain is passing out of the farmers' hands. We find that of the 100,000,000 bushels of grain that is for export, 50,000,000 is on the western slope, and as a natural consequence must be loaded into ships and sent to foreign markets. The very instant that a vessel clears port it is registered on the boards of the markets of the world that a ship loaded with grain or produce containing ——— bushels of grain, destined, for instance, to Liverpool, England, has cleared. The moment that these vessels are placed on the blackboards and marked "to arrive," they know that it will arrive sometime unless it should encounter storms and go to the bottom of the ocean. But barring accidents it will arrive and the purchaser knows that he must take it at some figure, and of course he will drive as sharp a bargain as possible and bear the market to its lowest possible point.

These ships, laden with about one-half of our grain, have a long and dangerous journey, and are from four to five months at sea, making the trip around Cape Horn and crossing the equator twice. This immense volume of grain being afloat and marked "to arrive" at a time when the bulk of the farmers are parting with their grain, contributes in no small degree to the establishment of the "low prices" at which our farmers are forced to part with their grain. England is our chief and only consumer on whom we must depend to take our surplus food crops, and a natural consequence is that any agency that will create competition and give us another market for our surplus products will stimulate the prices which competitors will establish in order to secure the products that they must have. And any advance on the prices of such products gained by this agency will go to the producer and he at once becomes the beneficiary.

Let us for a moment consider the Oriental situation and draw intelligent conclusions. Here we have a vast population aggregating 400,000,000 people which would be asked to consume our 40,000,000 to 50,000,000 bushels of wheat. This would mean that each inhabitant would consume less than one-half a peck. While on the other hand this nation, with 70,000,000 inhabitants, consumes 400,000,000 bushels, or 5 5-7 bushels per inhabitant. It will thus be seen that one-half of our wheat export crop would not provide enough to make pie crust in that country. It might be suggested that the inhabitants are too poor to be able to buy wheat flour, as it would be considered a luxury, and could not afford it. To this question I would answer that there are wealthy and middle classes in that country the same as we have here, and those who could afford to buy wheat bread would do so. History has shown that where wheat bread has come in competition with rice and coarse grain it has displaced them permanently. Being a luxury, we could not expect to establish it as a stable article of food, but the demand would grow as fast as the people would acquire a taste for it, and know that they could get it when they wanted it.

It has been computed that the establishment of this market will bring from 15 to 20 cents a bushel extra for the export crop, and as the export sets the price for the entire crop the saving to the American farmer would be $75,000,000 to $100,000,000 annually on the item of wheat alone.

It has been remarked by a prominent man that he examined the records of Congress for the last thirty years, and he has not seen one single word or line indicating that an attempt has been made to establish and extend our foreign markets. This is a sad and humiliating spectacle that the law-makers of this great na-

214

tion have shown to the calling of agriculture, upon which the greatness of this nation is built.

I will quote from the address of Col. B. F. Clayton, president of the National Farmer's Congress, to show how our law-makers have disregarded the interests of the farmer, bulwark of the nation:

"A biographical sketch of a recent Congress as furnished by its members, discloses the fact that out of a membership of 444 in the Senate and House of Representatives, the farming element, representing the majority of all the people, have thirty-five members in the House and one in the Senate. The chairman of the Senate agriculture committee records himself as a lawyer. The only farmer on the committee is at the tail end. Ten of the eighteen members of the House committee, including the chairman of the agriculture committee, are lawyers. The only chairmanship held by a farmer is on the committee of "ventilation and acoustics."

This gives an eloquent but humiliating picture of the way the farmer is represented in the hall of our national legislature.

The remedy for this is to nominate farmers from agricultural districts in all political conventions, and it will make no difference which political party wins, a farmer will be elected, and a friend of agriculture will be present to work and vote for measures that will advance his calling. The remedy is in the hands of the farmer.

I will now discuss briefly another phase of this question, which deals direct with labor and the farmer, and that is the building of our own merchant ships to carry our products to market.

It is a sad and humiliating spectacle for a great nation like the United States to become compelled to permit foreign nations' ships to come to our doors and load up our products for export and watch them bear away to the world's markets the products of this great nation. Many nations boast of their greatness because of their commerce on the seas. Why cannot the United States also be rated as a maritime power? Is it because we are too weak to engage in this line of trade? Is it because we have not the capital to engage in building up a fleet of ships? Is it because we have no freight to carry when built? Is it because we lack enterprise and patriotism? Is it because we have no idle workmen to employ in such enterprises? Is it because the American sailor is afraid of the sea? To all of the above questions we can answer emphatically no.

But like all great nations and enterprises, often the most important matters of general interest are lost sight of in the mad scramble for development and wealth, and there follows the lack of organization that would give influence and backing to any demand coming from sources of recognized character and standing. This nation has recently shown that it has some claim for recognition as a power on the seas. Its splendid victories in the recent war have been a source of pride and exultant joy to ourselves and a revelation to jealous powers, who never thought the Yankee was "in it" on the sea. We have compelled the respect of the world to be laid at this nation's feet, through the achievements of our brave naval heroes, Dewey and Schley, and the "men behind the guns." No more will the face of the American blush to hear the insulting and contemptuous remarks of foreign nations about interfering in the policies or purpose of this great nation. We find instead that nations who have always in the past proved our most inveterate enemies have suddenly reversed themselves and are now proclaiming from the housetops that they are our great friends, and that we are of one blood, and all that kind of rot. Don't you believe it. Do not permit the advantage that has been achieved by the valor of the Yankee in the fields of battle and in the domain of enterprise through his own energy and bravery to be now surrendered to a nation hostile in the past, but transformed into a demonstrative friend in the present, caused by a reverence which all the world entertains for successful achievement. When we get down to business the practical common sense of the people will work out the problems that confront us, though they be new and novel to our statesmen.

One of the nation's first requirements is a merchant marine compatible with our dignity and importance as one of the leading powers of the earth. It is our first duty as citizens, from the standpoint of patriotism, to see that American ships be built. It should be the aim of every citizen to declare that our shipping shall be restored, and restored as quickly as possible. It will be seen what advantages this will give our nation and its citizens, as it will at once place at our disposal in time of war a fleet of vessels that is second only in importance to the navy itself. A great navy and auxiliary ships will be the best guarantee of peace, as no nation will be anxious to invite its own destruction by hastily declaring war. Now, as a resource of this nation, it opens up the most profitable avenue of enterprise that is now left undeveloped. Our commerce on the seas is as expansive as the surface of the earth. New markets can be found and extended that will absorb the products of the farm and manufactured products of labor. Regenerating our merchant marine will create a new industry in the United States, shipbuilding, and a new occupation, that of the American sailor. A merchant navy would be built by American labor of American material, for Americans to man and navigate. Then we can earn the two hundred million dollars which we pay annually to the owners of foreign vessels for doing our carrying trade for us. With this enterprise thoroughly established and equipped it will take half a million men from the ranks of idle labor and give them permanent and profitable employment, and to the American capitalist an avenue for investment for over $100,000,000. Owing to the generous treatment that foreign nations give their ships and commerce we will be at an immense disadvantage if we do not receive government aid in starting this enterprise for the first twenty-five years in the shape of bounties and subsidies.

Let us consider for a moment what can be done with a small appropriation of say $25,000,000 annually. Let us pay a bounty of $2 per ton on all freight of American production and manufacture. This to apply to two ships of 10,000 tons capacity which could leave our shores daily. Such ships leaving 300 days each year would give us 6,000,000 tons of American products carried in American ships to foreign markets. This would be $12,000,000. With the balance, $13,000,000, we could establish permanent national exhibits of American products which would assist in extending our trade in such countries. This small appropriation could be taken from the rivers and harbors and public buildings appropriations and scarcely be missed, while it would give to the neglected industry of agriculture a small measure of the protection which is so lavishly bestowed on all other interests. This appropriation will establish a fleet of American ships for the Pacific trade of about 100 ships of 10,000 tons capacity, which would cost about $1,200,000 each. This would call for an investment of over $100,000,000 in a new enterprise, which up to this time has remained undeveloped, and which is almost as important to the success of agriculture as a market for our surplus crops. When we have no vessels to carry our crops, we are almost as helpless as if we had no markets.

When we have to depend on the favors of foreign nations' ships to engage in the carrying of our crops to market, which may often come in competition with the products of their own country, our products suffer accordingly. Then, when such nations, with whom we have trade relations, shall be assured that communication between us and them will be speedy, regular and permanent, and that they can place orders with us for our products, they will largely increase their orders for our goods. This subsidy is absolutely necessary to permit our American ships to compete successfully with foreign ships which receive such generous aid from their respective governments.

Mr. Hanley concluded by congratulating his hearers on the uprising of independent parties, and the liberalizing of the two old parties, and reminded them that the leaders of all parties were warm advocates of trade expansion and the restoration of our merchant marine.

As Mr. Hanley sat down the chairman invited the governors in the auditorium—Stanley of Kansas, Atkinson of West Virginia, Pingree of Michigan, Scovillé of Wisconsin, and Poynter of Nebraska—to seats on the platform. The distinguished delegates were warmly applauded and loud calls were made for a "speech" from Governor Pingree. He declined to respond.

AARON JONES.

Grand Master National Grange Patrons of Husbandry.

Every citizen of this republic should be free to use his labor as will best contribute to his benefit and happiness, not, however, infringing on the rights of any other citizen.

The right to acquire, own, control and enjoy the use and income of property, is an inalienable right, that should be enjoyed by each individual. Governments are organized and laws are enacted to better protect life, liberty, and the ownership and use of property. It is the legitimate function of governments to protect its citizens in the full and free enjoyment of these rights. It is for this security of life and the ownership of property that people are willing to pay taxes for the support of state and national governments.

The tendency of the times is for conducting large business enterprises and concentration of business into the hands of a few. In the early history of this country, when individuals desired to do a more extended business than they had capital to control, partnerships were formed of two or more, and the business was conducted by them jointly. These partnerships gave them no additional powers or privileges beyond those enjoyed by the individual citizen.

As the demand for concentration and the conduct of business on a still greater scale, the laws provided for the formation of corporations to conduct certain lines of business, and the state granted them certificates of incorporation with certain defined privileges and the right to conduct business along certain lines, and in the case of canals and railroads they were granted the extraordinary power of condemning lands found necessary for the constructions of their roads or canals, and issue stock, limiting liability within certain limits defined by law, and granting absolute control of the minority of stock by the majority, and many other advantages and privileges not enjoyed by any individual citizen. These forms of corporation served a useful purpose, but within the past few years the ambitions of men to acquire power and wealth rapidly, these corporations have been consolidating many separate corporations located in one or several states, selling out their plants to a corporation organized for the purpose of buying up all these separate plants and conducting them under one management, and it has been found that the increased power possessed by these large consolidated corporations or trusts, as they are commonly known, have caused them to pursue a policy that has infringed on the rights of individuals, or have used their influences in restraint of trade, been detrimental to the rights of labor, destroyed the value of other property, and deprived other individuals of the use of their capital, and so far as this has been done, is clearly against public policy; and subversive of the best interests of the republic. The purpose of this conference, as I understand, is to consider this great question so vitally effecting the property rights of the citizens of the United States and make such recommendation to the Congress of the United States and the several legislatures as will secure such legislation as will in no wise cripple legitimate enterprise and the development of the resources of our country, and yet secure the passage of such laws as will restrain the abuses that have grown up in corporate management of the various corporations now doing business in the United States. This is one of the most important questions now confronting the American people and one that must be met, and wisely met, or the republic is drifting on very dangerous grounds, that sooner or later will subvert the liberties of the people. We believe every good and loyal citizen should wisely consider this grave question and cast their influence to secure such legislation, state and national, as will eliminate all the evil practices of these so-called trusts and combinations.

It occurs to me that the first step to be taken in remedial legislation is to pass a well-considered anti-trust law by the Congress of the United States, clearly defining what practices on the part of any corporation would be injurious to public policy, and cripple or injure individual enterprise, thrift, and the acquirement and use of the property of any citizen of the republic; and to supplement this law by equally well-considered anti-trust laws by each of the several state legislatures to reach and apply to such phases of the matter as could not be reached by the act of Congress of the United States. These laws should have such provisions for their enforcement and provide penalties for violations by fines or imprisonment or both as will insure the compliance and observance of the laws by all corporations and combinations. To make these laws effective, it is absolutely necessary to know what these trusts and combinations are doing; and as these trusts have assumed so far as appearances go, to be honest, legitimate corporations, it is difficult to ascertain which ones are operating in a way detrimental to public policy. It would therefore seem that these laws should provide for government and state inspection of their business, of their books, agreements, receipts and expenditures, and that the state may have full knowledge, the right to examine all vouchers and records of the meetings of directors and managers; in short, full and complete knowledge of all the business of affairs of the corporation. The individuals in seeking a corporation franchise have asked the state to help them to a privilege or advantage they did not possess as individuals, or they would not seek to be incorporated as a corporation; and on account of that advantage granted and to protect the public, this inspection should be rigid and full. The people must know what the specific acts are that are against public policy before the laws can be enforced as against them, and the rights of the public protected. Corporations may object to this inspection on the ground that it would expose what they claim as their private business. In answer to this it might be said that the rights of the citizens of the state who grant the articles of incorporation or allow them to do business in the state, special privileges, have a right to know that the privilege has not been used against public policy; besides, there is no law now, never has been, never can be any law compelling any one to form a corporation and invest his money in any corporation enterprise. Those who invest in corporation stock, do so voluntarily.

If the corporations are conducting legitimate business, no injury will be done them by inspection. If they are using the powers granted to them by the state, to crush out other enterprises and deprive other citizens of the use and value of their property in order to avoid competition; if they are using their power and influence in restraint of trade; if they are using large sums of money to illegitimately control political parties or to control legislation, as was testified before the Congressional investigation that the "Sugar trust made it a rule to make political contributions to the Republican party in Republican states and to the Democratic party in Democratic states." Mr. Havemeyer testified that, "We get a good deal of protection for our contributions," and when asked if his company had not endeavored to control legislation of Congress with a view of making money out of such legislation, he answered: "Undoubtedy. That is what I have been down here for," and many other cases might be cited. If they have agreements with railroad companies for rebates of freights, as has been shown to be the case in the Standard Oil trust and many others, these practices are most reprehensible and should be punished by such penalties as will effectually stop them. The agreements and conspiracies to depress the prices of raw material and staple products are equally against public policy.

In speaking for the agricultural interests of our country, that great basic industry that produces 70 per cent of the wealth of the country, and furnishes 60 per cent of the freight on all railroads, lake, river, and coastwise trade, and 69 per cent of all exports, and that make it possible for the other industrial interests of our country to prosper, I desire to say, these practices and conditions most seriously and injuriously affect it, and they demand of the legislatures of the several states and of the national Congress, well considered and effective legislation that will prevent the injurious practices of trusts and combinations.

I believe it to be the settled purpose of a majority of the people, to hold our representatives in Congress and in the several legislatures personally responsible for the enactment of such laws as will restrain and prevent the continuance of acts of trusts that are against public policy. I do not believe that the people hold any one party, as responsible for the present conditions, but I do believe that each individual member holding official position will be, and is, held for his voice and vote and action in the enactment of demanded remedial and protective legislation.

Our country is so vast, its interests so extended, and the constantly increasing wealth in its multiplied forms of the people need carefully considered laws governing the rights and uses of property, that corporations or individuals by agreements, may not be able to oppress or destroy any of the great industries of the nation. The demand of the times is for sound, sensible, good business men, with broad common sense, to frame the laws of our country, state and nation.

JOHN M. STAHL.

Secretary Farmers' National Congress.

Trusts are the latest device for doing things in a large way. They are the latest advance in a steady, persistent movement that has dominated the industrial development of the past one hundred years; that has gathered the isolated workers with tools, working alone, into shops; and then has brought a score of shops into a factory; and has then combined factories; that while thus developing the factory system until the result has been well termed an industrial revolution, has none the less worked a similar revolution in merchandising, in transportation, and in yet other lines of human activity, always resistlessly absorbing and combining to put more men and greater means under the control and direction of the masterful brain that has reached the place it occupies by a civil service indisputably based on merit, truly a "natural selection" in industry, always having for its object doing things in a larger way, because it is constantly proved that this is doing things in a more economical way (whether, all things considered, it is the best way, I cannot discuss here). Hence the trust is a logical phenomenon in this industrial development. Being such, it may be destroyed in form, but I do not believe that it can be destroyed in essence. It will doubtless be modified, in time it will be superceded, and certainly while it exists it may and ought to be directed, controlled, and made an instrument, not for private gain alone, but for the public good. I believe that it will be wiser for us, not to seek to destroy it, but to make it our servant. We have the machine; it is for us not to try to smash it, but to discover how best to use it.

I believe that anything that increases the productivity of mankind is a good thing and should work good; that if it does not work good, it is not the fault of that thing *per se*; that whatever increases the productivity of human labor gives man more to enjoy and more time for recreation; that it is a good, though to reach the ultimate benefit of the many, it may for a time hurt the few, as when a new labor-saving machine for a time throws men out of employment, and therefore the trust ought to be a good thing. If so far it has wrought ten times as much harm as good to the people, as it seems to have done, that is not the fault of the trust, which certainly can exist without being a monopoly, but because it has been misused. I doubt if any discussion of the effect of industrial combination on the individual, for example, will show otherwise.

222

But some men are greedy and hard, and have little regard for others. It has been found necessary to control many instruments of industry that man's brain has devised—machinery, factories, stores, banks, transportation facilities, corporations, insurance—in fact, very few, if any, means of industrial or commercial activity are not more or less controlled by law. To control trusts by law will not introduce any new principle. The Emperor Zeno found it necessary to decree that all monopolies and combinations to keep up the price of merchandise, provisions, or workmanship, should be prohibited, upon pain of forfeiture of goods and perpetual banishment. Blackstone tells us that "combinations also among victuallers or artificers, to raise the price of provisions or any commodities, or the rate of labor, are in many cases severely punished by particular statutes; and in general by statutes II and III of Edward VI." While the principle was early established that government had the right to take cognizance of the instruments of industry, increasing experience and wisdom showed that efforts should be to direct rather than suppress, and probably it has no more perfect flower than the law that grew out of "the Granger cases" of a quarter of a century ago, which demonstrated that the strongest corporations are the servants of the state and subject to its control. The same application must be made to the trust, which seemed to be a plant, not to be rooted out or to be allowed to grow as a weed, but to be cultivated and cared for and trained, to increase the food and clothing of mankind.

Certainly we should lose no time in taking control of the trust, which up to this time has been a great curse to the American people.

Using terms in their popular meaning, the price of an article, which roughly indicates the difficulty of enjoying it by the people, may be lowered in two ways: By lessening the cost of production, or by lessening the profit of the manufacturer.

Competition keeps down the profit of the manufacturer; and by stimulating the discovery of methods and the invention of means that economize in production, lessens the cost of production.

The trust, which is opposed to competition, lessens the cost of production apparently even more than competition does; but its avowed object has been to hold up the profit of the manufacturer. If, however, it brings the price down to the figure made by competition, it would appear to be the better, since generally it is better to lower the price by lessening the amount of energy required in production than by lessening the profit of the manufacturer below a certain point. If less labor is required to make certain things, then men, working as before, will have more things to enjoy, or, having the same to enjoy, will have more time for culture and recreation; while if the manufacturer has a fair profit he can pay fair wages and will have increased capital to be taxed and to be used for the employment of labor.

But if this profit be excessive the result must be evil, for so much capital will accumulate in the hands of the few that it can, and probably will, be used to oppress the people, corrupt public officials, and destroy good government. Certainly when trusts, instead of lowering prices, advance them, those trusts yield excessive profits while directly hurting the people. Nearly all trusts have advanced the prices of the things the production of which they control. This makes it imperative and urgent that they be regulated by law.

The nature of much of this law to regulate trusts must be decided upon after the beginning has been made. Results will indicate further actions. I will, however, take the liberty of suggesting that when a trust is favored by artificial conditions created by law, as, for example, a protective tariff (and I am and always have been a protectionist), those conditions should be removed. The very existence of a trust controlling our market as to anything removes all grounds for a protective tariff on that article.

Many trust properties are capitalized at much more than their worth. This is unjust and dangerous. It is unjust because in order that a fair return may be made on all the capitalization of the trust, the people are made to pay too much for a trust article. It is dangerous because, first, selling large plants for twice what they are worth puts into the hands of a few a dangerous amount of capital; and, secondly, because the public is led to invest in properties at an exaggerated value and collapse and panic and hardship will ensue. Hence a trust should not be allowed to put its bonds and stocks on the market until its properties have been carefully investigated by public officials, whose minute statement is open to the public, and it is found that every dollar of bonds and stocks offered to the public for investment is backed by a dollar of real value.

I will confess that I tried hard to reach conclusions not so favorable to trusts *per se*, as those stated. But I am constrained to write the truth, as it is given to me to see it, knowing that anything in any wise favorable to trusts is very unpopular, especially among farmers. And trusts have been so outrageously diverted from their proper use and have been so used to rob the people,

224

that I heartily sympathize with the public opinion of them; especially when I come to buy some trust article, fencing wire, for example. Further, I have not a dollar invested in any trust in any way; and, more, so far as I know, or have reason to suspect, no one that I know has a dollar invested in a trust.

In the weeks that I have spent in Great Britain—England, Wales, Ireland, and Scotland—and on the Continent, I have not once heard trusts mentioned in conversation, except when I spoke of them; and I have seen them mentioned only twice in the papers on this side of the Atlantic. Here they are not of public interest or concern. This has a deep significance, when one remembers that the industrial revolution has been less rapid here. There are trusts in Great Britain and in the continental countries, and apparently a protective tariff slightly favors them, but this is by no means certain. But certainly no trusts here have robbed the people as trusts have robbed the people of the United States, and I do not believe that trusts would dare, in any European country, Russia and Turkey possibly excepted, to double and treble the price of articles, while lowering wages and discharging men. Our people are greater than the trust, and when it oppresses them beyond endurance it will be roughly handled, then more wisely attended to, and ultimately it will be used for the public good.

J. STERLING MORTON.

Ex-Secretary Department of Agriculture.

In my letter to the Civic Federation July 22d I think I sufficiently indicated my opinion of the present agonizing solicitude which seems to have permeated the practical politicians of all parties as to the possible despotisms and outrageous monopolies which combinations of large capital may bring about in the United States.

But there is no reason for apprehension. There can be no monopoly if trade and commerce are free. The combination of millions of dollars in any special manufacture can do no more nor less than compete with alert individual enterprise making the same staple. And the competition may make an article of equally good quality and sell it at an equally low price, and have logically an equal share of the market. Small corporations, even copartnerships, will be free to enter every field of competitive manufacture and commerce whenever demand makes high prices and gives promise of profits. Smaller concerns will seldom be overcapitalized. They will seldom be extravagantly managed. Many of the larger combinations, however, will be threatened and jeopardized by overcapitalization and extravagant management. It will be impossible therefore to pay dividends upon their common stock. That stock will then soon have no value in the market, and the "trust" will speedily go into bankruptcy. The whisky and other trusts that failed from these causes verify this prognosis. There are, however, no "trusts" in the United States, as trusts in their obnoxious sense are defined, but there are many very large corporations. It is impossible to prevent such great corporations, unless each state repeals its general incorporation laws.

Forty-five years ago I came to Nebraska. It was then more than three hundred miles from any point within its boundaries to a railroad. All capital was individual. There was no corporation anywhere within the limits of the territory. There were very few corporations in Iowa or Missouri.

The first corn planted on the farm where I lived in 1855, and have lived ever since, was dropped by hand and covered with a hoe. So was the second crop. But the man with the hoe has departed. The village blacksmith who made hoes has been crushed out by the cruel competition of combined capital. There are to-day ten million acres planted to corn in Nebraska. It promises an average yield of thirty bushels to the acre. This will make an aggregate of 300,000,000 bushels for the state. If the hoe and the man with the hoe who dropped the corn with his fingers had never been supplanted by the double-rowed, two-horse corn planter and, in tillage, crushed out by the double-rowed cultivators, such a breadth of corn would have been an impossibility. Combinations of capital made the corn planters, made the cultivators, crushed out the village blacksmith, and relegated the man with the hoe to everlasting inutility.

But the great multitude of mouths which consume food made from corn get this food at a less price than they ever did before and for a very small per cent of what the cost of corn food would have been at this time if it had continued to be planted and cultivated by a man with a hoe.

These examples are illustrative of the fact that all these great combinations of capital, while they may put out of employment a vast number of traveling men and others differently employed, they also reduce competitive waste. The traveling men and all their expenses have been paid invariably by the consumers of the goods which they sold. The entire advancement and improvement of the industrial world are marked by the wrecks and ruins of individuals, but illuminated and glorified by the advantages which they have given to the multitude.

The West has been opened up by combinations of capital. The means of production, all the improved implements for planting and tillage, all the perfected machinery for the speedy harvesting and storing away of crops, together with their accelerated cheap distribution by rail, make this fertile West inhabitable and prosperous. But if there had been no incorporation of money out of which to evolve manufactories for improved and cheaper agricultural implements and machinery, these crops, which now astound the world with their magnitude and money value, would never have been grown west of the Missouri river. And even if they could have been grown without the direct power and influence of improved machinery, they could never have been cheaply distributed to the markets of the world, unless there had been further incorporations of capital to build and operate railroads.

The state of Nebraska is swiftly paying off all of its land mortgages. These mortgages largely represent the purchase money. Originally, prior to the alleged "crime of 1873," mortgages upon these farms carried from 40 per cent down to 12 per cent interest per annum. The latter figure was regarded exceedingly low and quite favorable to the borrower. But to-day, upon the same number of acres of land, three times the amount of money can be borrowed that would have been loaned on the same security in 1870 and 1871, and the rate of interest is now 6 and 5 per cent per annum.

By combinations of capital the railways have been doubled as to their mileage in the last fifteen years. Instead of their mortgage bonds bearing 8 per cent, they now carry only 4 per cent. Thus, instead of seeing great possible evils in incorporations of capital for the future, it is better to contemplate and verify the great good which has come to the country because of capitalistic combinations in the past.

The word "trust," as used by partisans, particularly those who are endeavoring to organize the discontent of the United States against the courts, and the laws as construed by the courts, is given a sinister significance. Without any attempt at analysis, definition or explanation, every combination for investment of capital, of whatsoever kind, is denounced as a "trust." This is merely an appeal to envy, malice, and the other meaner characteristics of humanity. Originally, however, the word "trust" was defined as "a beneficial interest in land or other property, the legal title to which is in another, recognized and enforced by the courts of equity."

Having observed individual capital carrying on business in Nebraska prior to its invasion by a single corporation; and subsequently having experienced the change of cost made in the same business when taken up by incorporated capital, and noted particularly the reductions in transportation as charged by stage coaches and ox and mule trains, when compared to rates charged by passenger and freight trains on railways, one is rejoiced at the advent of the money power and the agents of capital into this wilderness. The cost of carrying 100 pounds of freight from Nebraska City to Denver by mule or ox trains was from $5 to $12. Freight between the same points to-day is 50 cents per hundredweight. Passenger fare from Nebraska City to Denver by coach was $150; by rail to-day it is $17. For a seat in the coach from Nebraska City to Salt Lake City one paid $300; the rate by rail to-day is $30. Steamboat rates from St. Louis, by the Missouri river, were, on freight, from 75 cents to $4 per hundredweight (the steamboats, however, were not owned by corporations), and passenger fare was $30.

Combinations of capital for vast production and distribution, while they may have destroyed small dealers in great numbers, have, as a rule, ultimately benefited the great majority of mankind. The present tendency toward large aggregations of money for the purpose of carrying on manufacture, commerce, and transportation, may therefore be not dangerous to the millions of consumers who may thus be furnished more bread and more clothing for less hours of labor.

The consummate perfection of civilization will be realized in the lowest possible prices for all the staples of life. The cheaper all staple commodities become, the less hours of efforts and exertion will each member of the human family be obliged to put forth in order to maintain and clothe himself. The more leisure the mass of mankind may have from bodily effort, the more time they may bestow upon intellectual development and moral culture. High prices are not a boon to mankind. High prices always prevail in newly-settled and crude communities. The lowest prices will be at hand when, by combinations of skill and capital, mankind shall have reached the *ultima Thule* of cheap production combined with speedy and cheap distribution.

By protective tariff advocates, paternalism has been preached in the United States for many years. Out of protection many monopolies have been evolved. When protection shall have been abolished many will die.

Free trade will not compel anybody to trade anywhere, but will permit everybody to trade everywhere. Under free trade monopolies can not be long-lived. Under free trade the homeo-pathic maxim that "like cures like," may be verified by killing off one combine with another combine, and by organizing syndi-cate against syndicate for intense competition, thus keeping prices and profits at a minimum.

Trusts which are over-capitalized are born of the machinations of shallow and impractical men. They will fail and no one be harmed except those whose credulity led them to invest in their securities.

There is much misapprehension as to incorporated capital in the United States. Oratorical vagarists have endeavored to make common people believe that incorporations are not subject to economic laws of competition and that the relation of supply to demand is not the sole regulator of values. The fact, however, re-mains that money invested in manufactories or in railroads be-longing to incorporations is no stronger, no better and no more exempt from the operation of commercial laws than the money which is owned by individuals. There need be, in my judgment, no apprehension as to the trusts crushing out all competition. With the exception of the oil trust and the sugar trust, failure among trusts has been universal. The whisky trust, the tobacco trust and all the other trusts of any importance up to date, except those that have been formed very recently, have been complete failures. These failures have come, firstly, from over-capitaliza-tion; and, secondly, from mismanagement. Intelligent competi-tion can enter the field against any trust on earth except one which has a natural monopoly (by this I mean one which, like the Standard Oil Company, owns the only oil-producing lands in the country), and successfully put its products upon the market with the sympathy of the consumer all on its side. By this I mean that outside of the trusts co-partnerships and stock companies may be formed with capital, energy and ability to successfully take the market against any and all trusts' products, except those which are the result of a natural monopoly.

Enactments will not cure the tendency toward combines. Economic laws will rectify their errors and protect the people. Whenever legislatures invade the domain of economic laws with statute laws, they merely show the power and majesty of the former and italicize the feebleness and littleness of the latter. Too much legislation begot all the real and all the possible evils which combinations of capital, even under a protective tariff, are capable of inflicting. "Let alone" trade, manufacture and dis-tribution are good servants to all the people. Favored by special privileges they may become servants to the few and masters of the many. The less legislation—after repealing the protective tariff—about restraining capital, the better.

Of course, it is fashionable, it is epidemic, to denounce all large aggregations of capital as "trusts." This mania will at last exhaust itself and the country will find that those who have been damaged by trusts were those who bought their securities for more than they were worth.

CYRUS G. LUCE.

Ex-Governor of Michigan.

As a lifelong farmer I crave a few moments of your valuable time to present the interests of that great portion of the American people that are engaged in agricultural pursuits.

Much attention has been given by this conference to schemes and methods that are intended to increase our exports. With all proper efforts in this direction we are in hearty sympathy. Our enormous exports of the last few years have been the wonder of the civilized world. We have surprised ourselves by their magnitude. We have forced a great balance of trade in our favor. We have loaded ships with gold coming from other nations to our shores. These conditions have contributed largely to the present prosperous condition of our own country. It is well to pause and reflect upon the sources from whence these exports come. Beginning with 1892, and coming down to the present hour, nearly eighty per cent of the products that have produced these vast sums have been wrung from the brown soil. In faith the American farmer has sown and planted. He has with industry cultivated and with rejoicing harvested the wheat, cotton and corn that has gone abroad to feed and clothe the people of other nations. He has reared, watched, cared for and fed the herds and flocks that have, together with the grain and cotton, loaded the cars and the vessels that have brought profits to the owners of railroads and steamships. He, with the necessity of his products, stands as a breastwork against the dangers of foreign wars. In the consideration of questions that affect the welfare of the nation none are entitled to greater or more candid attention, and yet during all the discussions here he, with his great contribution to the general welfare, has occupied just twenty minutes of your time. His interests were championed and his views presented grandly and nobly by the master of the National Grange, and that was all. His interests have not been directly attacked, but by all others quietly ignored. I do not say this to complain,

230

but to intimate to you the modesty of those engaged in this giant pursuit. But with all this modesty we are not disinterested listeners to the discussions of the trust question, nor are we ignorant of the tendency of the times nor of the inclination to unite corporation with corporation until they have become a threatening menace to their interests. We are not unfriendly to the ordinary corporation where other corporations can exist as competitors in the production of goods, articles and implements in the same line. While human nature remains the same we do not and can not believe that it is safe to lodge in the hands of one man or set of men the power that would be given him by union of all the corporations under one management engaged in the production of any one line of goods. It is idle to claim, as some men do, that these men, clothed with such unlimited power, would suddenly become so good, just and humane that he would mete out even-handed justice to all. He would create a monopoly in his line; he would force down the price of articles that he must purchase and put up the price of products that he makes for sale. This prophecy is made with some knowledge of human nature and the policy pursued in this and other generations. But more than this, we have the evidence of practical demonstrations by every day's occurrence at the present time. The modern trust is comparatively new in its existence and operations, but in all cases where it is fairly on its feet it is doing and undertaking to do the very things that we have predicted it will do. Of the hundreds of articles that the trust has been able to control, prices have been advanced in nearly all cases; still it is claimed with great confidence that the advance in price grows out of the general tendency of events. But is it not a singular coincidence that the price so suddenly advances as soon as the trust secures control? It is freely and gladly admitted that labor is securing an advance in wages, but this is slight compared with the advance in the price of trust-made articles. Now, if it is true (and more than possibly it is) that these mammoth combinations produce and place on the market their goods, wares and implements at lower prices than the ordinary corporation can where competition exists, where do all the increased profits go? Who is getting them? They very likely save enough by their improved methods in making and selling to pay all the advances made to the laborers, and this would leave the enhanced prices secured for products to pay increased dividends to the stockholders. Among all who have made a defense or a quasi defense no one has given any other solution of this question, hence the conclusion reached is a safe one. All corporations have not yet formed themselves into trusts, but it is safe to conclude that all who can, seeing the increased profits secured by those who have united their forces, will be inclined to do so, and others will be compelled to do so or die. And this justly causes great apprehension upon the part of the American farmers. I do not see how it is possible for them to unite in a counter trust these great producers of the world's wealth. I know that some with a more vivid imagination than I possess have conceived the project. I can readily see how labor can respond to the appeals made here and elsewhere to unite and join forces with the great productive combinations, but how the farmers can do so is beyond my imagination. But even if they can form one so comprehensive and so perfect in its operation that they shall be enabled to absolutely control production and prices, with my present ideas of human nature I am afraid that in too many cases the children of the poor would go supperless to bed. It is neither here nor there a safe power to place untrammeled in the hands of any one man or set of men. But if the trust reaches the height of its ambition, the great army engaged in agricultural pursuits will be driven to desperation. The tendency will inevitably be to force them through a trust or otherwise to reduce production, to cease in their efforts to load the cars and vessels as bounteously as before, they will cease to purchase as generously as in the past. In this many others will suffer as well as they. This is no fancy picture, and far be it from a threat, but it is believed to be the inevitable result of operating causes, and the conclusion is drawn from the fact that in all the relations of life and positions occupied men usually exercise all the power and authority lodged in their hands. This is just as true in America as in any other land. We do not clothe the President or the Governors of states, the Congress or state Legislatures, or even the courts, with unlimited power. We do not permit any of these to discharge duties at their own sweet wills, but they are hedged about by constitutional provisions and by legal enactments and somehow or in some way these mighty corporations known as trusts must be checked, trammeled, restrained. In all my acquaintance I know of no farmer who feels safe in the prosecution of his calling without placing restraint upon them. In the incorporation of corporations they make bold claims not for the public, perhaps, in relation to what they can and expect to do. No better or more dangerous illustration can be given than the one presented to the woollen manufacturers, and the same claim is made and presented as an inducement to the manufacturers of leather and of its products. They or their promoters claim that when they are properly organized and in working

HOWARD S. TAYLOR   WILLIAM FORTUNE
AZEL F. HATCH   EDWARD C. AKIN
FRANCIS B. THURBER   JEREMIAH W. JENKS

condition that one man can buy all the wool in America, fixing their own prices without fear of competition. Another man can sell all the cloth made by all the factories, limiting the products and fixing prices. All this may never be realized, but it is the scheme desired and presents a glowing, fancy picture. We conceived the difficulty in devising and executing remedies for these present and prospective evils. Absolute publicity and oversight is good as far as it goes. Absolute prevention of discrimination in freight rates will help in some cases. A modification or repeal of the tariff on trust-made articles will aid in other cases. But in spite of these suggested remedies the trust will continue to live, thrive and monopolize. Nothing short of a united, determined public opinion in opposition to the monopolizing power of the trust will conceive and execute efficient remedies. While the farmers themselves entertain decided opinions in relation to the central question, yet because of their generally isolated condition and want of organization they do not contribute toward molding public opinion in proportion to their numbers and the magnitude of their contributions to society. They seldom secure seats in Congress, and only occasionally anything like a majority in Legislatures. Hence we make an earnest appeal to all the agencies that contribute so largely to forming public opinion for the enactment and enforcement of just laws. We ask no special favors, but demand even-handed justice and exemption from threatened dangers. We desire to live and let live. Our purpose is not to tear down, but build up. We ask for no acts of incorporation for ourselves or our interests, but we do insist that if other interests are incorporated that ours shall be sacredly guarded and safely protected. This claim is not made solely for ourselves, but in behalf of all the great interests of the republic. Without reasonably prosperous agriculture other interests can not prosper. Farmers are quiet, unobtrusive citizens, but they are not cowards, as has been attested in peace and in war. The farmers fired the first shot in the great conflict that gave to us liberty, independence and power. That liberty they still enjoy and highly prize. They do not believe that the trust has or will become so great in strength and power that it can not be overthrown, hence they have no sympathy with the sentiments that it has come to stay and can not be dislodged from power. And the more speedily and effectually attempts to carry out its purposes the more certainly will it be overthrown. The ballot box is the natural place for the American people to fight their battles, and I am sure that the farmers will be there.

MARTIN A. KNAPP.

Chairman Interstate Commerce Commission.

The purpose of this brief paper is to suggest a phase of the general subject which is quite commonly overlooked. In dealing with the trust problem there is frequent failure to distinguish the activities engaged in private pursuits from the agencies employed in public service. The restraint of competition among railway carriers, for example, is often opposed on the same grounds and with the same arguments as are relied upon to prove the dangerous consequences of restricting competition in the fields of industrial production.

But there is a fundamental difference, I maintain, between those combinations in private business, the formation of which is of such recent and rapid growth, and associated action by those who furnish the means of public transportation. This difference may be stated in a single paragraph. As regards actual property, the products of labor and skill in any vocation, the things we eat and wear and use, we do not want—under present economic conditions at least—uniformity of price. Every producer should be perfectly free to sell for all he can get, every purchaser equally free to buy just as cheap as he can. The dealer should always be at liberty to make one price to one person and another price to another person, or to vary the price to the same person as and when he sees fit. That is to say, in the exchange of goods there should be the utmost freedom of contract between the parties. As between buyer and seller the power to bargain should be unrestrained, for in that power is the essence of commercial liberty. Therefore, speaking in general terms, whatever tends to abridge this freedom of contract and so to bring about uniform or non-competitive prices, whether by limiting production or controlling the markets, is to be deprecated as on the whole against the public interest. For this reason, legislation which checks this tendency and promotes industrial freedom may well be regarded as defensible and necessary.

But as respects public transportation, which is not property at all, but a service, not a commodity, but a function or agency of government, we do want uniform charges—under like conditions —without preference or exception to any person. Rightly considered, the tolls paid to the public carrier are in the nature of a tax, and the relations between carriers and the public are not contract relations, save in a very limited sense and for special purposes. I do not procure transportation as the result of a bargain with the carrier, but in the exercise of my political rights. The right to that transportation is primary, indispensable and inalienable. The essential element of this right is equality. The privileges I enjoy as a citizen in this regard are precisely the same in every respect as those possessed by any other citizen under like circumstances, and impairment of those privileges is a deprivation of like character and scarcely less serious than restraints upon my personal freedom or the denial of protection to my property. Therefore, whatever promotes stability and uniformity of charges by public carriers, whatever tends to secure equality of right in the use of transportation agencies, should be encouraged and promoted. Indeed, I go to the extent of saying that we cannot have that free and fair competition in the fields of production, which is the condition of industrial freedom, without methods and charges for public transportation which amount to a monopoly.

The benefits supposed to result from railroad competition I believe to be greatly exaggerated. Those who honestly uphold the present policy—to say nothing of those who oppose a change from unworthy motives—apparently assume that the public gets the same advantage from competition between carriers as from competition between producers and dealers generally. That this is a mistaken and fallacious view I am fully persuaded. I do not see how any one can derive benefit from competition in the matter of his daily wants, unless he is in a situation to choose freely between two or more persons who are each able to supply those wants. The objective value of competition, I submit, rests in the power of selection, and he who is debarred from choice must be deprived of any direct advantage from the rivalry of others.

As to most of our ordinary wants—broadly speaking—every person in every place has the opportunity to choose. If the only merchant in a remote hamlet charges more for his wares than his customers are willing to pay, there is another store at a near-by cross-roads where they can purchase the same commodities; and, like liberty of selection, is commonly enjoyed as to the various needs of social life, whether simple or complex. But in respect of railroad transportation only a few people comparatively are so situated as to have any available choice between carriers. So that, without amplifying the argument, the simple fact is that only a small percentage of population, and an exceedingly small fraction of territory, are so located as to have any practical opportunity for selection in the matter of public conveyance. To the great majority of people railway transportation is now a virtual monopoly. I do not mean to say that the competition between railroads connecting great cities by different lines has not had an indirect and important influence upon railroad charges at intermediate points which are dependent upon one of those lines alone; but I venture the opinion—again speaking broadly—that the limit of such indirect advantage has already been reached, and that further benefit from that source cannot reasonably be expected. The result is that a few commercial centers and a few large shippers, having this power of choice, and finding their traffic indispensable to the carriers, secure enormous advantages, either by evasion or violation of law, of which the masses are deprived. It is entirely plain to me, therefore, that co-operative methods, the general discontinuance of competition in rates between rival railroads, would tend strongly to remove the inequalities which now exist, and prove a positive and substantial advantage to the great majority of producers and consumers. And I firmly believe that while there is a popular objection to railroad pooling, as it is commonly called, founded largely upon ignorance of its purpose and misconception of its effects, the principal opposition to legalized co-operation, the opposition which has thus far prevailed, comes from the favored few who are reaping unearned profits by the discriminating practices which they virtually compel and of which they are the sole beneficiaries.

In harmony with this view, as I conceive, is another suggestion. The opposition to trusts, so far as it is sincere and intelligent, seems to be based largely upon belief that they do, or apprehension that they will, so use their combined power, and the degree of monopoly thereby secured, as to obtain extortionate prices from the consumer, or at least higher prices than would otherwise prevail. The demand for laws to prevent these combinations arises from our inability to control by legislation the prices of industrial products. We cannot by law fix the price of sugar, petroleum, cotton cloth or any other commodity. And if we could we should be powerless to compel their sale in any case at the price so fixed. Therefore, since the apprehended evils cannot be reached by direct legislation, we seek to accomplish the desired end by the indirect means of preventing the combination, and these indirect means must be resorted to because no others are available.

But this difficulty does not exist in respect of prices or charges for public transportation, for those charges are under direct and complete legislative control. Within limitations which secure to the owners of railway property the equal protection of the laws and prevent the taking of such property without due process of law, being the same limitations as are applied to all legislation, the power of Congress and of the several states in their respective spheres—either by direct action or through the medium of commissions—to control and prescribe the charges for public carriage is plenary and exclusive. This being so, the above mentioned objections to industrial combination are mainly, if not wholly, untenable in the case of railway combinations. The end desired, viz., protection of the public against unreasonable charges, can be secured by direct legislation, and hence there is no occasion for employing the indirect method of preventing the combination. And if the right to equal treatment in all that pertains to transportation service will be better secured, as unquestionably it would be, by allowing and legalizing association of public carriers, our legislative policy should be shaped accordingly. So far as railway service is concerned, the practical choice lies between competition on the one hand, with the inevitable outcome of discriminations which favor the few at the expense of the many, or like charges for like service, which can be realized only by permitting and encouraging co-operative action by rival roads. The power to compete is the power to discriminate, and it is simply out of the question to have at once the absence of discrimination and the presence of competition.

For these reasons I regard as fundamental and of the greatest practical importance the distinction I have endeavored to draw.

H. T. NEWCOMB.

United States Census Office.

Before beginning an examination of the nature and results of railway combinations it is desirable to consider some of the facts that differentiate combinations in transportation from combinations in manufactures and trade.

First in point of time: A strong tendency toward the combination of originally separate corporations has characterized the railway industry during its entire history; in manufactures and in trade such combinations were practically unknown prior to 1870.

Again, one of the methods of railway combination, formerly most effective—I allude to the practice popularly known as "pooling"—has been illegal, so far as interstate traffic is concerned, since 1887, and even agreements to maintain reasonable rates were forbidden by the anti-trust law of 1890 which does not appear to have been applied successfully to any other industry.

The years subsequent to 1887 have witnessed a stronger movement toward the consolidation of manufacturing and trading establishments than was ever previously known.

Further, combinations among railways can directly affect rates on but a portion of the transportation furnished to the public, for there are comparatively few points served by more than a single railway and a large portion of the aggregate traffic must traverse a particular route or it cannot be moved; manufacturing and trading combinations, if they affect prices at all, must affect those on the entire output of the establishments combined.

Railway combination has assumed three distinct forms. The first involves the actual merger of several properties through corporate consolidation or practically perpetual leases. Nearly every great railway in the country is a result of this process. The line of the New York Central from Albany to Buffalo is formed of ten originally separate roads, the Atchison, Topeka and Santa Fe railroad, which terminates in this city, operates lines that were formerly the property of more than one hundred distinct corporations. Such consolidations have been welcomed by the wiser section of the public, for they have improved the service and lessened the cost and difficulty of travel and of moving freight.

Another form of combination is effected by the purchase of the control of separate corporations in a common interest. Combinations of this character do not affect the corporate organizations which remain legally separate, and they may be brought about without publicity. Until recently the only connection among the lines composing the great Vanderbilt system was of this character and at present most of the lines in that system are held in this manner. The system controlled by the banking establishment which is headed by Mr. J. Pierpont Morgan has no other connection and probably very few individuals outside of the firm know exactly what properties compose the system.

The third form of combination is by agreements between corporations which remain legally separate and continue to exercise most of their functions independently. Such agreements may provide for through tickets, the forwarding of baggage, through billing of freight, interchange of cars, and many other incidents of modern methods of operation that are essential to the efficient organization of transportation. Without them the production of utilities of place would be much more difficult and costly and territorial division of labor, which permits the assignment to each locality of the particular industrial function to which it is best adapted by natural resources, climate, and location, could not exist in its present state of development.

Another form of combination by agreements among otherwise independent railway corporations has probably furnished the occasion for more debate and has been less understood by the general public than any other incident of railway development—I refer to agreements concerning the rates to be charged on traffic for which two or more routes are available.

As soon as the railway system of the United States had reached the point of development at which the same localities were connected by rival and competing lines, some peculiarities incidental to rate-making began to attract attention. The business of railway transportation is not and can not be competitive, in the ordinary sense, at more than a few points and with regard to but a small portion of the aggregate traffic. Railways cannot be, in many instances or for long distances, exactly parallel. At points not served by more than one railway or possessing facilities for transportation by water railway business is from its nature a monopoly. The business of such points can often be made to pay the entire fixed charges and a large proportion of the operating expenses and the railway is left free to accept traffic at the competing points at rates that barely pay train-expenses. In the absence of express or tacit agreements concerning such charges this result was found to occur very frequently. It involved discriminations, apparently unjust, against traffic from and to local points which artificially accentuated the tendency toward the concentration of population and industry at large cities.

But the case was even worse than this. Competition in this form practically placed the rate-making power in the hands of the most reckless, incapable, or unscrupulous officials connected with any line. Such an official could force rival lines to meet rates far below the remunerative point or to witness the possibly permanent diversion of important traffic to the lines of their competitors. He could bankrupt his own road or that of his rivals and at the same time profit greatly by the manipulation of the securities affected in the stock market. The competition of rival routes seeking to secure the same traffic therefore produced unjust discrimination in rates, artificially stimulated the tendency toward concentration of population in cities, and was an effective and dangerous instrument in the hands of railway-wreckers. Few have failed to recognize these facts, but many have supposed that such competition has resulted in lower railway charges. An argument in favor of this contention can be plausibly supported by the common assumption, that too frequently passes undetected, that coincidence of time and place prove a relationship as between cause and effect. The decline in railway charges in the United States has been continuous and extensive. The average rate per ton of freight carried one mile, measured in gold, has declined from nearly two cents in 1867 to less than eight mills in 1898, the last year covered by the reports of the statistician to the Interstate Commerce Commission. The price of wheat at the port of New York during 1867 would pay for the transportation of but 2.84 bushels of wheat, from Chicago to New York at the rates of that year; in 1897 the price, though considerably lower than in 1867, would pay for moving six bushels. In other words, the decline in the railway rate from Chicago to New York was twice as great as the decline in the price of wheat. The decline in passenger rates from 1871 to 1898 amounts apparently to 25 per cent; but, unlike that in freight rates, is not susceptible of satisfactory statistical presentation. The substantial identity of the service necessary to permit the use of the statistical method, has not, however, been preserved. The dollar that purchases transportation in a modern train, provided with automatic couplers and air brakes, traversing at sixty miles per hour, a track composed of Bessemer steel rails weighing 100 pounds to the yard, and guarded by block signaling apparatus, purchases vastly more than did the dollar paid for personal transportation a few decades ago, even though the distance traversed be but little greater at present. The public has preferred to have improved accommodations and better service rather than very much lower charges and, as usual in America, has had its way. The same rise in the standard of living that has given the American farmer his top-buggy, his piano in the parlor, his Sunday suit, and Brussels carpet, has given him the luxurious coaches and well-ballasted roadbeds, the safety and the speed of modern passenger service.

But has the competition of rival routes produced these reductions in rates and improvements in the quality of service? I think not.

Such competition has caused numerous extravagant expenses —it has made railway business unnecessarily costly, and some one must have paid the bills. Let us examine some of these expenses, though it is not easy to secure authentic statistics, and those available serve to suggest, only, the possible aggregates. The Interstate Commerce Commission has reported that nine roads paid out an aggregate sum of more than one million dollars in a single year as commissions for securing competitive passenger business, and it is known that as much as $20.70 has been paid to secure a single second-class passenger from this city to San Francisco. The multitude of outside agencies and traveling agents maintained solely for the purpose of securing business for their respective lines that might otherwise traverse those of their competitors involves an expenditure so great, even during periods of comparative harmony, that it has been deemed necessary to restrict their number by contract. An agreement in force for a considerable time limited to eight the number of agencies that might be maintained in New York City by each of the nine roads competing for westward bound traffic from that city. As it is a fact of ordinary observation that such agencies always cluster in particular regions and around particular corners, it is obvious that a system of joint agencies would afford the public equal accommodation at lower cost.

During the periods of unbridled competition, popularly known as "rate wars," each participating carrier sends its freight and passenger agents to every important city in the country at a total expense for rents, clerk hire, advertising, etc., that must be enormous. Four roads operating westward from Chicago are known to have expended $1,283,585 for outside agencies and advertising in a single year, during which rates were fairly maintained, while during an equal period one road terminating at New York City expended $871,291 for similar purposes.

The competition of long circuitous and commercially illegitimate routes for traffic that would naturally traverse cheaper and more direct lines is another gross extravagance too frequently observed. The president of an important line has said:

"Illegitimate business is always the pride of the average traffic manager. To secure a share of some competitive business not naturally or fairly belonging to a carrying line, always appears to inspire heroic efforts and to be regarded as meriting special commendation."

Illustrations are numerous. Between Chicago and St. Paul traffic is regularly forwarded over a route practically double the length of the shortest; from this city to New York there are twenty-one routes varying from 912 to 1,376 miles in length; from New York to New Orleans, beside many water carriers, there are more than ninety all-rail routes, one of which involves carrying the freight nearly to this city. As an example of the waste of competitive train service, it is not necessary to add to the bare statement that forty-four trains leave this city every day for New York and that practically similar duplication of service exists wherever the same cities are connected by competing railways.

The construction of unnecessary lines is another gross

extravagance involving an expenditure from the store of energy available for the satisfaction of human wants that produces no good result. The West Shore, the Nickel-Plate, and many other wholly superfluous routes will occur readily to any one as illustrations.

If competition, while involving these wastes, has still reduced railway charges, these extravagant expenditures must have been met by investors in railway property. If this were the case would it have been possible to secure the capital necessary for the rapid development of the American railway system, for the new construction that has gone on during the years· subsequent to 1870?

But the arguments are by no means all of a negative character. The decline in rates has affected those from and to points served by single carriers as well as those served by one or more. There is no important point and no article of traffic that moves in considerable volume that has not felt the effects of reduced charges.

A little thought will suggest a cause that may have produced the decline, in spite of, though somewhat hindered by, the wastes just discussed.

For lack of a better phrase this cause may be designated as the competition among producers for the privilege of selling in the dearest markets and that of consumers for the privilege of purchasing in the cheapest markets. This needs to be qualified by the suggestion that railways must be considered as producers for the reason that the productive process cannot be regarded as complete, in connection with a particular article, until that article is available for consumption. In more technical words, that are however perfectly clear in their meaning, production consists of the creation of utilities of place as well as of utilities of form.

Railways, therefore, are partners in the production of the commodities that they carry. Partners with whom? The answer is with every separate productive establishment, farm, or factory, workshop or mine that exists along their lines and furnishes traffic for their trains. Each railway forms in effect a separate combination (the word combination is here used in a clearly innocuous sense) with each separate productive establishment and, as either place or form utilities might be useless without the other, these combinations are essential to the completion of the productive process. Obviously, any railway may participate in many such combinations which produce the same article. These combinations may compete among themselves and as most producers of form utilities have a definite cost of production per unit of product while most of the costs of producing transportation

242

cannot be assigned to particular services it is not difficult to force railways to assume the greater shares in the sacrifices which such competition involves. There is no other possible explanation of the decline in rates that will account for the fact that while railway mileage is now three times as great as in 1871 the aggregate amount of dividends paid on railway stock has been lower during every year of the present decade than it was in that year.

The student who will carefully and impartially investigate the circumstances attending the decline in railway charges, its relation to prices and cost of production, its effect on the competition among the producers of form utilities, and its consequences as expressed in rates of interest and dividends, will find convincing evidence that competition of railways as partners in the business of production is always powerful enough to force railway rates to the lowest point at which the revenue derived from them will pay operating expenses, under whatever methods of operation are for the time being in force, and afford the lowest return to the capital invested which in a developing country will induce capitalists to provide the additional facilities from time to time required and to maintain those existing in a state of satisfactory efficiency.

The foregoing analysis shows that the substitution of effective agreements in regard to rates for the competition of rival routes prevents unjust discriminations in charges, and permits economies in operation which inevitably accrue in the form of reduced rates to the benefit of shippers and travelers.

I say "*effective* agreements" for experience has shown that such arrangements are frequently of little use. How can such agreements be made effective? The history of American railway practice affords a ready answer. To give effectiveness to such arrangements has been the aim of nearly every practical railway manager since, at least, the year 1870, but no scheme ever devised has been even moderately successful unless it has provided for the distribution of traffic between points connected by two or more routes in shares fixed in the agreement or determined in accordance with its terms. Popular will has attached to such arrangements the name "pool," and though it is in many respects inaccurate and misleading, not much can be gained by quarreling with an accepted designation. We shall not be terrified by the name for we have discovered that the thing to which it refers is nothing more than a device for giving effect to agreements which are in themselves wise and beneficial, which tend to secure justice in the distribution of the cost of transportation and also to reduce its aggregate.

Those who are only superficially acquainted with the history of railway administration in the United States will inquire how it happened that so beneficent a practice was prohibited by congressional enactment. The interstate commerce law was intended to prevent unjust discrimination in railway charges, yet it was weighted down and some of its most salutary features rendered nugatory by the anti-pooling clause which is in irreconcible conflict with every other substantial provision that it contains. The *"power to compete,"* in the words of the statesmanlike chairman of the Interstate Commerce Commission, who is an honored member of this conference, *"is the power to discriminate."* Why, then, did Congress attempt to perpetuate competition while endeavoring to prevent its natural results? One might answer, not incorrectly, that this action was in obedience to a "Texas idea" not unlike that which refuses here to consider the nature and consequence of industrial combinations while vehemently demanding their statutory condemnation and prohibition, for the anti-pooling clause was actually forced into the interstate commerce law by a faction led by a member of the House of Representatives from the state of Texas and against the judgment of the most enlightened members of both houses of Congress; the alternative presented being the defeat of the measure under consideration and the indefinite postponement of all regulative legislation.

When the committee on Interstate Commerce of the United States Senate conducted the exhaustive investigation which preceded the passage of the act to regulate commerce, pooling had been an important feature of American railway practice for at least fifteen years. Yet objections to the system are infrequently found among the large number of opinions gathered in the public hearings and explicit expressions of approval are numerous. Students of transportation and public officers charged with the duty of studying railway methods had previously declared in favor of agreements for the division of traffic. A member of this conference, Dr. Joseph Nimmo, Jr., who was for many years at the head of the Bureau of Statistics of the United States Treasury Department, declared in the course of an official report published in 1879 that railway pooling was then favored by the general public because it had proved to be the means of "arresting discriminations" and the Iowa Railroad Commission in its report for 1878 expressed the same opinion by declaring that it considered "the pool as the only agency that can compel the through traffic to bear, as it should, its proportion of the interest on the cost and expenses of maintaining and operating the roads."

Whatever public condemnation the pooling system received aside from that inspired by the irresponsible utterances of demagogues, who found attacks upon railway corporations, just as their prototypes a few decades earlier had found the enthusiasm for railway construction, an easy and convenient means of attaining office, was due to the fact that those arrangements were never permanent and in consequence never wholly eradicated the evils they were intended to correct.

Indeed at almost the same time that the officials referred to gave their approval of the pooling system, Mr. Albert Fink, the originator, organizer, and official head of the most complete pooling association ever established, was complaining of their lack of permanence and stability and urging the necessity of legislation that would give them legal sanction and effect.

In fact all railway pools in the United States were extra-legal arrangements dependent for their execution upon the good faith of the parties, upon the violation of which none of them would venture to appeal to the courts for redress. So lacking were these arrangements in the necessary cohesive qualities that each railway considered their abrogation an inevitable incident, pending which constant vigilance was necessary in order that the day of dissolution should not find it an unready or tardy contestant in the struggle for traffic. The period during which a pooling contract was in force was consequently one of armed neutrality, and, as in many cases between nations, that relation was regularly disturbed by the depredations of irresponsible members of the rival forces. As the apportionment of business in any pool which should follow a period of warfare would probably be based upon the proportion offered (if a tonnage pool) or carried (if a money pool) prior to the disruption of such an agreement, there was a strong incentive to take advantage of every opportunity to gain traffic by its violation which promised immunity from detection.

Thus there was never an entire abandonment of the baneful practices of competition, there were always discriminations in favor of competitive traffic, and there were frequent periods during which all the evils of unjust discrimination operated to their fullest extent. Nevertheless, as indicated in the quotation from the Iowa Railroad Commission, the evils of excessive competition were in some degree mitigated and the pooling arrangements, unstable and unsatisfactory as they too frequently were, indicated a means of securing, in a large measure, that substantial identity among the interests of the carrying corporations which is a prerequisite to the lowest and most equitably adjusted rates.

When the interstate commerce law became effective all pooling contracts were discontinued and there is evidence that the railways generally sought in good faith to observe its provisions.

Railway associations were formed which announced as their objects the maintenance of reasonable rates and the enforcement of the regulative provisions of the law. The co-operation of the weaker lines was in many instances purchased by permission to charge slightly lower rates than those collected by their stronger rivals. Subsequently other efforts were made to effect the satisfactory division of traffic without its actual transfer from one line to the other after consignment and without resorting to the methods technically characteristic of tonnage pools. The practical failure of these measures is generally recognized, and most railway patrons now agree with railway owners and managers in urging a modification of the interstate commerce law that will permit agreements for the apportionment of traffic; operations thereunder to be conducted under the supervision of federal authorities.

This change has been recommended by several annual conventions of national and state railway commissioners, by the National Board of Trade, by a conference of representatives of boards of trade and other commercial organizations of the principal cities of this country; it has been approved by members of the Interstate Commerce Commission and by the author of the anti-pooling section of the present law. A bill embodying it and including also several very desirable amendments to the interstate commerce law which had been strongly urged by the Commission passed the House of Representatives during the last session of the Fifty-third Congress, and would unquestionably have received the support of a large majority of the Senate had not the rules of that body and the early approach of the end of the session, combined with the obstructive tactics of a numerically insignificant minority, made it impossible to secure a vote upon its passage.

It should be observed that whatever pooling measure may finally be adopted by Congress, operations under it will certainly be free from objections such as those growing out of the instability which characterized pooling arrangements prior to 1887. The contracts permitted will have the express sanction of a federal statute and any railway corporation that may be injured by the failure of another to observe the terms of a pooling agreement to which both are parties may invoke judicial aid in securing the particular redress that is found to be adequate and suitable.

Such agreements will naturally provide for a definite period of operation, with possibly continuance thereafter subject to notice of the intention of any party to withdraw. The possibility of unjust personal discriminations will, it may reasonably be hoped, be minimized by the discontinuance of separate soliciting for traffic, and the substitution of joint for independent ticket and freight agencies.

Mr. President, I believe it only reasonable to assert that the facts to which I have directed your attention establish the existence of a natural tendency toward combination in the railway industry, that they demonstrate the futility and the fatuity of legislation intended to prevent such combinations, and establish beyond controversy the advisability of restoring the pooling privilege with federal supervision and legal effect and sanction added. It would be almost superfluous to introduce evidence, as would be easily practicable, that the prohibition cf pooling—such prohibition being itself a restriction upon freedom of contract—artificially stimulates the tendency toward other forms of combination. All are familiar with the facts which amply prove this to have been the case since 1887.

It remains to consider the relation between railway combinations and combinations in other lines of industry. Nearly every one who has addressed this conference has alluded to discriminations in railway rates as one of the causes of industrial combinations and perhaps the most important public contribution made by this body will, when in the lapse of time its results can adequately be summarized, be found to be the classification of combinations with regard to whether they are the result of superior efficiency in production, whether of machinery or organization; or of special privileges at the hands of government or the agents of government.

Whatever may be held as to the consequences of the first class there can be no doubt that those combinations that are dependent upon special favors of any kind are harmful in the extreme.

Railway corporations are agents of government in the sense that they are empowered thereby to exercise functions usually and properly regarded as governmental. If these agencies unjustly discriminate among their patrons those receiving unfair advantage may be able to dominate markets and destroy competition. In the words of the present chairman of the Interstate Commerce Commission, whose clear and vigorous English is always quotable:

"The ultimate effect of preferential rates is to concentrate the commerce of the country in a few hands. The favored shipper, who is usually the large shipper, is furnished with a weapon against which skill, energy and experience are alike unavailing. When the natural advantages of capital are augmented by exemptions from charges commonly imposed it becomes powerful enough to force all rivals from the field."

We have found, therefore, in unjustly discriminating rates a primary cause of a dangerous and harmful industrial growth. Wise statecraft will seek to remove the cause. But how? Can this be accomplished by making it a felony to grant special rates as suggested by the great orator from New York (Hon. Bourke Cochran) who has preceded me in indicating this cause of industrial combination? Apparently not, for it is now nearly a decade since the interstate commerce law was so amended as to provide the penalty of imprisonment, not only for the railway official who makes, but for the shipper who accepts any concession from the open published rates. Nothing could be more drastic, yet discriminations so accomplished have been a conspicuous feature of the railway situation during nearly the entire subsequent period, the existence of the evil has attained public notoriety and its magnitude has alarmed and amazed the nation, yet no prison door has ever opened to receive an individual convicted of violating the statute.

These practices are not contrary to the ethics of modern business; selling or buying at lower than the usual prices, or giving or accepting special rates are not recognized evidences of depravity, the methods of making concessions are easily hidden, and those interested in their detection are, as compared with their beneficiaries, too frequently inexperienced and powerless.

A little while ago I endeavored to show that discrimination is the natural result of competition among railways seeking the same traffic. These concessions are not voluntarily granted by railway officials, but are wrung from them through fear of losing important traffic; they are grudgingly and reluctantly given to those who control traffic that is vitally important. To quote Chairman Knapp once more:

" * * * it is simply out of the question to have at once the absence of discrimination and the presence of competition." And:

" * * * the choice lies between competition on the one hand, with the inevitable outcome of discriminations which favor the few at the expense of the many, or like charges for like service, which can be realized only by permitting and encouraging co-operative action by rival railroads."

Mr. President, I can add nothing to this extract from one who has been for years charged with the duty of attempting to enforce a statute that in its present shape is unenforceable. To prevent railway discrimination, to destroy many of that evil class of combinations which is based upon illegitimate advantages, it is necessary to restore to railway corporations under federal supervision, the power to divide competitive business. Then the possibility of unjust personal discrimination will, it may reasonably be hoped, be minimized by the discontinuance of separate soliciting for traffic, and the substitution of joint for independent ticket agencies. The temporarily divergent interests of separate bodies of stock and bondholders will be subordinated to the general interest of all the carriers in the satisfactory adjustment of the railway system to the ends for which it exists, and the latter will constitute a powerful agency for the elimination of unjust discriminations including those among competing localities and communities. Whenever the exact proportion of competitive traffic which will fall to each particular route is as certain as that it will receive all of the non-competitive traffic, both will be treated with equity, for there will be no reason for favoring localities served by more than one railway. The selfish interests of carriers will then make powerfully for justice, while such regulative instrumentalities as may be established by the public, will have the advantage of dealing with a railway system that has become practically unified. , Until then the existence of unjust discriminations must not be charged against railway corporations or railway officials, but against the public agencies, legislative or otherwise, which have insisted upon the continuance of the uneconomic, wasteful and socially detrimental form of railway competition.

PAUL MORTON.

[Third Vice-President A., T. & S. F. R. R.

Industrial combinations or trusts are very similar to other commercial enterprises. Some will fail, others will succeed. Success or failure depends, first, on whether they are constructed on a good foundation, or whether they are built upon sand and inflated with wind and water. Second, whether they are intelligently managed or not.

In most instances, the efficient men are being retained by the trusts which have been recently formed. This augurs well. Upon intelligent management depends the question of prices which should be quite reasonable at all times. No citizen denies the right of the manufacturer or producer to make a reasonable profit, and it is manifestly best for the welfare of the community at large that the nation's commerce should make a fair return to those engaged in it, for capital, time, brains and labor employed.

I am one of those who believe that the United States possesses great advantages over most other countries of the world. We raise our own food products, and yet have much to spare for export. There is no such fertility of soil under cultivation in the universe as that found from the Atlantic coast extending west to the Rocky Mountains.

In addition to the cheap food supply, there are districts here and there immensely rich in coal, timber, oil, natural gas, iron and other metals. In the Rocky Mountains themselves, which have as yet been barely scratched, are gold, silver, lead and copper. West of the Rocky Mountains is California with its wonderful climate and soil that is capable of producing anything that Italy does. One is not startled at the wonderful production of this Pacific coast state until it is learned that in one season California has shipped 15,000 car loads of oranges, over 10,000 cars of deciduous fruits, 5,000 cars of raisins, and 6,000 cars of prunes.

For a long time we have been the granary of the globe, and we are now ambitious to become the factory of the world. The raw material, the inventive genius and the business ability are here and it seems to me that with these colossal industrial institutions the opportunity for trade expansion is to be grasped. Through the agency of these much condemned combinations, I believe the control of the markets of the world will be much more easily and quickly secured, and by their operations we will make such rapid strides in the next twenty years that we will all look back and wonder why the wisdom of their incubation was ever questioned.

The new trusts are largely organized with ample working capital, and can afford to employ the best salesmen to explore and capture the far-away markets. Small firms or industries cannot do this. It requires a great deal of money to work up a foreign trade. One of the chief reasons why the merchants of Mexico and South America do not trade here, is because they are given twelve months' credit or longer by French, German and English traders. It will be an easy matter for our new industrial institutions to meet this kind of competition, but private industries and corporations could not do so.

Some of us that are very much in touch with the railroads are very earnest in the belief that the railroad service of the country could be very much improved and cheapened, provided the transportation lines of the country were permitted by law to contract with each other for a division of business.

It is without doubt the aim and intention of all those in favor of or opposed to railroad pooling that there should be no preferential rates in favor of large shippers as against small ones; that there should be no discrimination in transportation charges as between individuals or communities and that, generally speaking, there should be stability in freight rates.

I contend that the present interstate commerce law, which without doubt was conceived with the idea of no discriminations of any character to any one, prevents by its anti-pooling clause, precisely what it seeks to attain.

The transportation of the country is a public service and a tax upon its inhabitants. None escapes from it. It is with many indirect and invisible, but even to a greater extent than a protective tariff, it is always with us. This tax should be levied with the greatest care, and should neither favor the largest shipper nor the greatest city. The small shipper and infant industry and the village should have every reasonable opportunity to grow. Even though it be of great consequence in the operation of a railroad whether it handles one thousand car loads of freight for one man, or for one hundred men, it is the inherent right of the small shipper and the small village that they should be treated with justice. Certainly the railroads can better serve one hundred customers shipping ten cars each at tariff rates, than to serve the one thousand car man at a cut rate. There should be no injustice or unreasonable discrimination in rates.

Distribution is the handmaid of production, and the greatest prosperity will come from the most perfect stability in transportation charges. Rates should be so fairly adjusted as between shippers and between localities as to work no injustice. They ought to be so adjusted that the small shipper in the small town will have the same relative right and opportunity that the big shipper in a metropolitan city possesses. I believe the price of railroad charges should be as unfluctuating as the price of postage stamps. How would a Chicago or a Kansas City merchant feel if his New York competitors were buying postage stamps at a lower price than he? How would interior merchants take it if it was generally understood that business houses in cities located on the sea coast were obtaining lower import duties? Would they not be indignant and resent such a condition with all the vigor and energy that they could muster, and yet the price of postage stamps and the import duties of the country cut a very small figure in the commerce of our country, when compared with its transportation.

I believe that railroads should be authorized by law to com-

251

bine under proper supervision of the Interstate Commerce Commission, and I think that this is more desirable and will bring more prosperity and satisfaction to the country at large than unrestricted competition. Unrestricted competition is sure to lower wages and beget inferior service.

One-fifth of the wealth in the United States is invested in railroad properties. The transportation lines are the greatest purchasing power in existence. When they are doing well and freely buying goods at fair prices, the country is prosperous Destroy that purchasing power by unrestricted competition and you at the same time strike a blow to the industry of the country that will stagger it.

There have already been great consolidations of railroad properties in this country. What has been the effect? Are wages any lower, or rates of freight any higher? Is not the service rendered the highest type produced in the world? Statistics will show that the large roads of the country pay higher wages than the small ones do, and they generally receive less pay for the services rendered than the small ones do.

Rates of transportation in the United States are much lower than anywhere else in the world. The fact is playing no small part in the position that this country is now assuming in the commerce of the world. The true interest of the United States is in properly protecting its transportation lines, and one of the things that should be done in this direction is to enact a law legalizing pooling. Much has been said about the trusts keeping down the young man without capital, it being claimed that under these colossal industrial combinations, the poor young man will have no opportunity to advance. I take the other view of the case. The more colossal the combination, the more requirement there is for brains and the higher the compensation that is offered for it. Big railroads and large combinations of industry are always on the lookout for good men. It is often claimed that eighty men out of every hundred that go into business for themselves make failures of it. If this is true, will not the twenty men who have succeeded heretofore be in much greater demand as executive officers of these large institutions and at greater remuneration than heretofore? Will not the other eighty be happier in finding employment at good wages where they do not have to risk their capital? I do not think that any radical regulation of trusts is necessary. I believe that when securities are offered for sale to the public, too much publicity cannot be given by the officers of the company selling the securities, although people who buy in-

dustrial or other stocks without careful investigation before purchasing, are not entitled to much sympathy.

I believe that trusts will regulate themselves. Any attempt
to keep prices higher than they ought to be is a direct bid for
competition, and capital always stands ready for new industries
to manufacture products which can be sold at abnormally high
prices. Many of those who have tried it, say they like nothing
better than to compete with a combination that is trying to get
unreasonable profits.

Permit the railroads to pool their earnings under the supervision of the Interstate Commerce Commission, or some other
similar body, and you will take a long step toward doing away
with preferential rates in favor of a select few, and this is the
one reform that all the speakers at this trust conference are emphatically united in saying is an evil that should at once be
stopped.

BENJAMIN R. TUCKER.

Editor New York *Liberty*.

A warm reception was extended to Benjamin R. Tucker of
New York, who, speaking on "The Attitude of Anarchism Toward Industrial Combinations," said:

Having to deal very briefly with the problem with which the
so-called trusts confront us, I go at once to the heart of the
subject, taking my stand on these propositions: That the right
to co-operate is as unquestionable as the right to compete; that
the right to compete involves the right to refrain from competition; that co-operation is often a method of competition, and that
competition is always, in the larger view, a method of co-operation; that each is a legitimate, orderly, non-invasive exercise of
the individual will under the social law of equal liberty; and that
any man or institution attempting to prohibit or restrict either,
by legislative enactment or by any form of invasive force, is,
in so far as such man or institution may fairly be judged by such
attempt, an enemy of liberty, an enemy of progress, an enemy of
society, and an enemy of the human race.

Viewed in the light of these irrefutable propositions, the trust,
then, like every other industrial combination endeavoring to do
collectively nothing but what each member of the combination
rightfully may endeavor to do individually, is, *per se*, an unimpeachable institution. To assail or control or deny this form of

co-operation on the ground that it is itself a denial of competition is an absurdity. It is an absurdity, because it proves too much. The trust is a denial of competition in no other sense than that in which competition itself is a denial of competition. The trust denies competition only by producing and selling more cheaply than those outside of the trust can produce and sell; but in that sense every successful individual competitor also denies competition. And if the trust is to be suppressed for such denial of competition, then the very competition in the name of which the trust is to be suppressed must itself be suppressed also. I repeat: the argument proves too much. The fact is that there is one denial of competition which is the right of all, and that there is another denial of competition which is the right of none. All of us, whether out of a trust or in it, have a right to deny competition by competing, but none of us, whether in a trust or out of it, have a right to deny competition by arbitrary decree, by interference with voluntary effort, by forcible suppression of initiative.

Again: To claim that the trust should be abolished or controlled because the great resources and consequent power of endurance which it acquires by combination give it an undue advantage, and thereby enable it to crush competition, is equally an argument that proves too much. If John D. Rockefeller were to start a grocery store in his individual capacity, we should not think of suppressing or restricting or hampering his enterprise simply because, with his five hundred millions, he could afford to sell groceries at less than cost until the day when the accumulated ruins of all other grocery stores should afford him a sure foundation for a profitable business. But, if Rockefeller's possession of five hundred millions is not a good ground for the suppression of his grocery store, no better ground is the control of still greater wealth for the suppression of his oil trust. It is true that these vast accumulations under one control are abnormal and dangerous, but the reasons for them lie outside of and behind and beneath all trusts and industrial combinations—reasons which I shall come to presently,—reasons which are all, in some form or other, an arbitrary denial of liberty; and but for these reasons, but for these denials of liberty, John D. Rockefeller never could have acquired five hundred millions, nor would any combination of men be able to control an aggregation of wealth that could not be easily and successfully met by some other combination of men.

Again: There is no warrant in reason for deriving a right to control trusts from the state grant of corporate privileges under which they are organized. In the first place, it being pure usurpation to presume to endow any body of men with rights and exemptions that are not theirs already under the social law of equal liberty, corporate privileges are in themselves a wrong; and one wrong is not to be undone by attempting to offset it with another. But, even admitting the justice of corporation charters, the avowed purpose in granting them is to encourage co-operation, and thus stimulate industrial and commercial development for the benefit of the community. Now, to make this encouragement an excuse for its own nullification by a proportionate restriction of co-operation would be to add one more to those interminable imitations of the task of Sisyphus for which that stupid institution which we call the state has ever been notorious.

Of somewhat the same nature, but rather more plausible at first blush, is the proposition to cripple the trusts by stripping them of those law-created privileges and monopolies which are conferred, not upon trusts as corporate bodies, but upon sundry individuals and interests, ostensibly for protection of the producer and inventor, but really for purposes of plunder, and which most trusts acquire in the process of merging the original capitals of their constituent members. I refer, of course, to tariffs, patents, and copyrights. Now, tariffs, patents, and copyrights either have their foundations in justice, or they have not their foundations in justice. If they have their foundations in justice, why should men guilty of nothing but a legitimate act of co-operation and partnership be punished therefor by having their just rights taken from them? If they have not their foundations in justice, why should men who refrain from co-operation be left in possession of unjust privileges that are denied to men who co-operate? If tariffs are unjust, they should not be levied at all. If patents and copyrights are unjust, they should not be granted to anyone whomsoever. But, if tariffs and patents and copyrights are just, they should be levied or granted in the interest of all who are entitled to their benefits from the viewpoint of the motives in which these privileges have their origin, and to make such levy or grant dependent upon any foreign motive, such, for instance, as willingness to refrain from co-operation, would be sheer impertinence.

Nevertheless, at this point in the hunt for the solution of the trust problem, the discerning student may begin to realize that he is hot on the trail. The thought arises that the trusts, instead of growing out of competition, as is so generally supposed, have been made possible only by the absence of competition, only by the difficulty of competition, only by the obstacles placed in the way of competition—only, in short, by those arbitrary limitations of competition which we find in those law-created privileges and monopolies of which I have just spoken, and in one or two others, less direct, but still more far-reaching and deadly in their destructive influence upon enterprise. And it is with this thought that anarchism, the doctrine that in all matters there should be the greatest amount of individual liberty compatible with equality of liberty, approaches the case in hand, and offers its diagnosis and its remedy.

The first and great fact to be noted in the case, I have already hinted at. It is the fact that the trusts owe their power to vast accumulation and concentration of wealth, unmatched, and, under present conditions, unmatchable, by any equal accumulation of wealth, and that this accumulation has been effected by the combination of separate accumulations only less vast and in themselves already gigantic, each of which owed its existence to one or more of the only means by which large fortunes can be rolled up, interest, rent, and monopolistic profit. But for interest, rent, and monopolistic profit, therefore, trusts would be impossible. Now, what causes interest, rent, and monopolistic profit? For all three there is but one cause—the denial of liberty, the suppression of restriction of competition, the legal creation of monopolies.

This single cause, however, takes various shapes.

Monopolistic profit is due to that denial of liberty which takes the shape of patent, copyright, and tariff legislation, patent and copyright laws directly forbidding competition, and tariff laws placing competition at a fatal disadvantage.

Rent is due to that denial of liberty which takes the shape of land monopoly, vesting titles to land in individuals and associations which do not use it, and thereby compelling the non-owning users to pay tribute to the non-using owners as a condition of admission to the competitive market.

Interest is due to that denial of liberty which takes the shape of money monopoly, depriving all individuals and associations, save such as hold a certain kind of property, of the right to issue promissory notes as currency, and thereby compelling all holders of property, other than the kind thus privileged, as well as all non-proprietors, to pay tribute to the holders of the privileged property for the use of a circulating medium and instrument of credit which, in the complex stage that industry and commerce have now reached, has become the chief essential of a competitive market.

Now, anarchism, which, as I have said, is the doctrine that

in all matters there should be the greatest amount of individual liberty compatible with equality of liberty, finds that none of these denials of liberty are necessary to the maintenance of equality of liberty, but that each and every one of them, on the contrary, is destructive of equality of liberty. Therefore it declares them unnecessary, arbitrary, oppressive, and unjust, and demands their immediate cessation.

Of these four monopolies—the banking monopoly, the land monopoly, the tariff monopoly, and the patent and copyright monopoly—the injustice of all but the last-named is manifest even to a child. The right of the individual to buy and sell without being held up by a highwayman whenever he crosses an imaginary line called a frontier; the right of the individual to take possession of unoccupied land as freely as he takes possession of unoccupied water or unoccupied air; the right of the individual to give his I. O. U., in any shape whatsoever, under any guarantee whatsoever, or under no guarantee at all, to anyone willing to accept it in exchange for something else—all these rights are too clear for argument, and anyone presuming to dispute them simply declares thereby his despotic and imperialistic instincts.

For the fourth of these monopolies, however,—the patent and copyright monopoly—a more plausible case can be presented, for the question of property in ideas is a very subtle one. The defenders of such property set up an analogy between the production of material things and the production of abstractions, and on the strength of it declare that the manufacturer of mental products, no less than the manufacturer of material products, is a laborer worthy of his hire. So far, so good. But, to make out their case, they are obliged to go further, and to claim, in violation of their own analogy, that the laborer who creates mental products, unlike the laborer who creates material products, is entitled to exemption from competition. Because the Lord, in his wisdom, or the devil, in his malice, has so arranged matters that the inventor and the author produce naturally at a disadvantage, man, in his might, proposes to supply the divine or diabolic deficiency by an artificial arrangement that shall not only destroy this disadvantage, but actually give the inventor and author an advantage that no other laborer enjoys—an advantage, moreover, which, in practice, goes, not to the inventor and the author, but to the promoter and the publisher and the trust.

Convincing as the argument for property in ideas may seem at first hearing, if you think about it long enough, you will begin to be suspicious. The first thing, perhaps, to arouse your suspicion, will be the fact that none of the champions of such property propose the punishment of those who violate it, contenting themselves with subjecting the offenders to the risk of damage suits, and that nearly all of them are willing that even the risk of suit shall disappear when the proprietor has enjoyed his right for a certain number of years. Now, if, as the French writer, Alphonse Karr, remarked, property in ideas is a property like any other property, then its violation, like the violation of any other property, deserves criminal punishment, and its life, like that of any other property, should be secure in right against the lapse of time. And, this not being claimed by the upholders of property in ideas, the suspicion arises that such a lack of the courage of their convictions may be due to an instinctive feeling that they are wrong.

The necessity of being brief prevents me from examining this phase of my subject in detail. Therefore I must content myself with developing a single consideration, which, I hope, will prove suggestive.

I take it that, if it were possible, and if it had always been possible, for an unlimited number of individuals to use to an unlimited extent and in an unlimited number of places, the same concrete things at the same time, there never would have been any such thing as the institution of property. Under those circumstances, the idea of property would never have entered the human mind, or, at any rate, if it had, would have been summarily dismissed as too gross an absurdity to be seriously entertained for a moment. Had it been possible for the concrete creation or adaptation resulting from the efforts of a single individual to be used contemporaneously by all individuals, including the creator or adapter, the realization, or impending realization, of this possibility, far from being seized upon as an excuse for a law to prevent the use of this concrete thing without the consent of its creator or adapter, and far from being guarded against as an injury to one, would have been welcomed as a blessing to all— in short, would have been viewed as a most fortunate element in the nature of things. The *raison d'être* of property is found in the very fact that there is no such possibility—in the fact that it is impossible in the nature of things for concrete objects to be used in different places at the same time. This fact existing, no person can remove from another's possession and take to his own use another's concrete creation without thereby depriving that other of all opportunity to use that which he created, and for this reason it became socially necessary, since successful society rests on individual initiative, to protect the individual creator in the use of his concrete creations by forbidding others to use them without his consent. In other words, it became necessary to institute property in concrete things.

But all this happened so long ago that we of to-day have entirely forgotten why it happened. In fact, it is very doubtful whether, at the time of the institution of property, those who effected it thoroughly realized and understood the motive of their course. Men sometimes do by instinct and without analysis that which conforms to right reason. The institutors of property may have been governed by circumstances inhering in the nature of things, without realizing that, had the nature of things been the opposite, they would not have instituted property. But be that as it may, even supposing that they thoroughly understood their course, we, at any rate, have pretty nearly forgotten their understanding. And so it has come about that we have made of property a fetich; that we consider it a sacred thing; that we have set up the god of property on an altar as an object of idol-worship; and that most of us are not only doing what we can to strengthen and perpetuate his reign within the proper and original limits of his sovereignty, but also are mistakenly endeavoring to extend his dominion over things and under circumstances which, in their pivotal characteristic, are precisely the opposite of those out of which his power developed.

All of which is to say, in briefer compass, that from the justice and social necessity of property in concrete things we have erroneously assumed the justice and social necessity of property in abstract things—that is, of property in ideas—with the result of nullifying to a large and lamentable extent that fortunate element in the nature of things, in this case not hypothetical, but real—namely, the immeasurably fruitful possibility of the use of abstract things by any number of individuals in any number of places at precisely the same time, without in the slightest degree impairing the use thereof by any single individual. Thus we have hastily and stupidly jumped to the conclusion that property in concrete things logically implies property in abstract things, whereas, if we had had the care and the keenness to accurately analyze, we should have found that the very reason which dictates the advisability of property in concrete things denies the advisability of property in abstract things. We see here a curious instance of that frequent mental phenomenon—the precise inversion of the truth by a superficial view.

Furthermore, even were the conditions the same in both cases, and concrete things capable of use by different persons in different places at the same time, even then, I say, the institution of property in concrete things, though under those conditions manifestly absurd, would be infinitely less destructive of individual opportunities, and therefore infinitely less dangerous and detrimental to human welfare, than is the institution of property in abstract things. For it is easy to see that, even should we accept the rather startling hypothesis that a single ear of corn is continually and permanently consumable, or rather inconsumable, by an indefinite number of persons scattered over the surface of the earth, still the legal institution of property in concrete things that would secure to the sower of a grain of corn the exclusive use of the resultant ear would not, in so doing, deprive other persons of the right to sow other grains of corn and become exclusive users of their respective harvests; whereas the legal institution of property in abstract things not only secures to the inventor, say, of the steam engine, the exclusive use of the engines which he actually makes, but at the same time deprives all other persons of the right to make for themselves other engines involving any of the same ideas. Perpetual property in ideas, then, which is the logical outcome of any theory of property in abstract things, would, had it been in force in the lifetime of James Watt, have made his direct heirs the owners of at least nine-tenths of the now existing wealth of the world; and, had it been in force in the lifetime of the inventor of the Roman alphabet, nearly all the highly civilized peoples of the earth would be to-day the virtual slaves of that inventor's heirs, which is but another way of saying that, instead of becoming highly civilized, they would have remained in a state of semi-barbarism. It seems to me that these two statements, which in my view are incontrovertible, are in themselves sufficient to condemn property in ideas forever.

If, then, the four monopolies to which I have referred are unnecessary denials of liberty, and therefore unjust denials of liberty, and if they are the sustaining causes of interest, rent, and monopolistic profit, and if, in turn, this usurious trinity is the cause of all vast accumulations of wealth—for further proof of which propositions I must, because of the limitation of my time, refer you to the economic writings of the anarchistic school—it clearly follows that the adequate solution of the problem with which the trusts confront us is to be found only in abolition of these monopolies and the consequent guarantee of perfectly free competition.

The most serious of these four monopolies is unquestionably the money monopoly, and I believe that perfect freedom in finance alone would wipe out nearly all the trusts, or at least render them harmless, and perhaps helpful. Mr. Bryan told a very important truth when he declared that the destruction of the money trust would at the same time kill all the other trusts. Unhappily, Mr. Bryan does not propose to destroy the money trust. He wishes simply to transform it from a gold trust into a gold and silver trust. The money trust cannot be destroyed by the remonetization of silver. That would be only a mitigation of the monopoly, not the abolishment of it. It can be abolished only by monetizing all wealth that has a market value—that is, by giving to all wealth the right of representation by currency, and to all currency the right to circulate wherever it can on its own merits. And this is not only a solution of the trust question, but the first step that should be taken, and the greatest single step that can be taken, in economic and social reform.

I have tried, in the few minutes allotted to me, to state concisely the attitude of anarchism toward industrial combinations. It discountenances all direct attacks on them, all interference with them, all anti-trust legislation whatsoever. In fact, it regards industrial combinations as very useful whenever they spring into existence in response to demand created in a healthy social body. If at present they are baneful, it is because they are symptoms of a social disease originally caused and persistently aggravated by a regimen of tyranny and quackery. Anarchism wants to call off the quacks, and give liberty, nature's great cure-all, a chance to do its perfect work.

Free access to the world of matter, abolishing land monopoly; free access to the world of mind, abolishing idea monopoly; free access to an untaxed and unprivileged market, abolishing tariff monopoly and money monopoly—secure these and all the rest shall be added unto you. For liberty is the remedy of every social evil, and to anarchy the world must look at last for any enduring guarantee of social order.

The announcement of the chairman that the remainder of the afternoon would be devoted to five-minute talks in open discussion of the day's papers was met with calls on Governor Pingree for a "speech." After several minutes of applause, the governor stepped forward and said:

"Most of you know where I stand in regard to trusts. I am opposed to them; always have been. I claim it is a cowardly way of doing business. If you cannot do business without being in a trust, I haven't any use for you. Get out. I will be here this evening, and I have a short paper I will be pleased to read to you. I want to thank you for this invitation right now."

The conference took a recess until 8 o'clock.

EVENING SESSION, SEPTEMBER 14.

Third Vice-Chairman Corliss called the session to order at 8:05 o'clock, and Secretary Easley read the nominations for membership on the Committee on Resolutions as follows:

ALABAMA.—Eyre Damar.
ARIZONA.— W. C. Campbell.
ARKANSAS.—B. J. Brown.
CALIFORNIA.—C. D. Willard.
COLORADO.—Henry V. Johnson.
DISTRICT OF COLUMBIA.—H. T. Newcomb.
DELAWARE.—Henry Allaway.
FLORIDA.—John F. Forbes.
IDAHO.—Judge Claggett.
ILLINOIS.—W. R. Jewell.
INDIANA.—A. P. Kent.
IOWA.—Geo. E. Clark.
KANSAS.—W. J. Bailey.
KENTUCKY.—P. W. Hardin.
LOUISIANA.—W. W. Howe.
MAINE.—A. E. Rogers.
MARYLAND.—Geo. R. Gaither, Jr.
MASSACHUSETTS.—John Graham Brooks.
MICHIGAN.—Cyrus G. Luce.
MINNESOTA.—W. B. Douglas.
MISSISSIPPI.—J. W. Cutrer.
MISSOURI.—E. C. Crow.
MONTANA.—H. H. Swain.

NEBRASKA.—Edward Rosewater.
NEVADA.—Francis G. Newlands.
NEW HAMPSHIRE. — Henry W. Blair.
NEW JERSEY.—Edward Quinton Keasbey.
NEW MEXICO.—C. J. Gavin.
NEW YORK.—Albert Shaw.
NORTH DAKOTA.—Wm. T. Perkins.
OHIO.—I. F. Mack.
OREGON.—E. Hofer.
PENNSYLVANIA.—W. P. Potter.
SOUTH CAROLINA.—A. C. Kaufman.
SOUTH DAKOTA. — Freeman Knowles.
TENNESSEE.—C. E. Snodgrass.
TEXAS.—Cecil Smith.
UTAH.—George W. Bartch.
WEST VIRGINIA.—Geo. W. Atkinson.
WISCONSIN.—John Nagle.
WYOMING.—J. Dana Adams.

NATIONAL ASSOCIATION OF MANUFACTURERS.—Theodore C. Search, President.
NORTHWESTERN TRAVELING MEN'S ASSOCIATION.—D. K. Clink, Secretary and Treasurer.
AMERICAN FEDERATION OF LABOR.—Samuel Gompers, President.
BROTHERHOOD OF RAILROAD TRAINMEN.—P. H. Morrissey, Grand Master.
UNITED GARMENT WORKERS OF AMERICA.—Henry White, General Secretary.
SINGLE TAX LEAGUE OF THE UNITED STATES.—Louis F. Post.
ORDER OF RAILWAY CONDUCTORS.—E. E. Clark, Grand Chief Conductor.
BROTHERHOOD OF LOCOMOTIVE FIREMEN.—W. S. Carter.

NATIONAL GRANGE PATRONS OF HUSBANDRY.—S. H. Ellis.
ILLINOIS COMMERCIAL MEN'S ASSOCIATION.—R. A. Cavenaugh.
NEW ENGLAND FREE TRADE LEAGUE.—Byron W. Holt.
AMERICAN ACADEMY OF POLITICAL AND SOCIAL SCIENCE.—John H. Gray.
NATIONAL ALLIANCE THEATRICAL STAGE EMPLOYES.—Lee M. Hart, General Secretary and Treasurer.
NATIONAL BUSINESS MEN'S LEAGUE.—John W. Ela.
AMERICAN ANTI-TRUST LEAGUE.—M. L. Lockwood, President.
KNIGHTS OF LABOR.—J. G. Schonfarber.
UNITED STATES EXPORT ASSOCIATION.—Francis B. Thurber, President.
COMMERCIAL TRAVELERS' NATIONAL LEAGUE.—P. E. Dowe, President.
NATIONAL GRAIN GROWERS' ASSOCIATION.—S. H. Greeley.
NATIONAL FARMERS' ALLIANCE AND INDUSTRIAL UNION OF AMERICA.—John Hill, Jr.
NATIONAL TAX LEAGUE.—Lawson Purdy.
NATIONAL SOCIALISTS' LEAGUE.—Thomas J. Morgan.
BRICKLAYERS' AND MASONS' UNION OF AMERICA.—M. R. Grady.
MILLERS' NATIONAL ASSOCIATION.—F. H. Magdeburg.
FARMERS' NATIONAL CONGRESS.—B. F. Clayton.
ASSOCIATION OF WESTERN MANUFACTURERS.—Walter Fieldhouse.
AMERICAN SOCIAL SCIENCE ASSOCIATION.—C. R. Henderson.
INTERNATIONAL TYPOGRAPHICAL UNION.—Samuel B. Donnelly, President.
TRAVELING MEN'S PROTECTIVE ASSOCIATION.—M. W. Phalen, President.
EX-OFFICIO.—Franklin H. Head, President Civic Federation of Chicago.
Ralph M. Easley, Secretary Civic Federation of Chicago.

A motion was made by P. E. Dowe of New York that the names of all persons who had been admitted to the floor since the organization was effected be stricken from the rolls. There was no second, and on calls for the regular order of business Chairman Corliss introduced as the first speaker of the evening, Governor Hazen S. Pingree of Michigan, who was obliged to wait several minutes for the applause to subside before he could speak. His subject was,

"The Effect of Trusts on Our National Life and Citizenship":

HAZEN S. PINGREE.
Governor of Michigan.

In all that has been said about trusts, scarcely a word has been written or spoken from the standpoint of their effect on society.

In this busy, rushing, feverish world, everything is ruled by the commercial spirit. The dollar seems to be the standard for measuring all things.

In gathering material for the use of this conference, the Civic

Federation of Chicago sent out circulars containing in all sixty-nine questions. These inquiries were addressed to trusts, whole-sale dealers, commercial travelers' organizations, railroads, labor associations, contractors, manufacturers, economists, financiers, and public men.

Only one of these sixty-nine questions related in any way to the effect of trusts upon society. I do not call attention to this in order to criticise the Civic Federation.

I do so for the purpose of showing that in all the discussion of trusts, there is no indication that any thought whatever has been given to their effect upon our national life, upon our citizenship, and upon the lives and characters of the men and women who are the real strength of our republic.

I think that this is the most important consideration of all.

Everybody has been asking whether more money can be made by trusts than by small corporations and individuals—whether cost of production will be increased or decreased—whether investors will be benefited or injured—whether the financial system of the country will be endangered—whether we can better compete for the world's trade with large combinations or trusts—whether prices will be raised or lowered—whether men will be thrown out of employment—whether wages will be higher or lower—whether stricter economy can be enforced, and so on.

In other words, the only idea nowadays seems to be to find out how business or commerce will be affected by trusts. The "Almighty Dollar" is the sole consideration.

I believe that all these things are minor considerations. I think that it is of far greater importance to inquire whether the control of the world's trade, or any of the other commercial advantages claimed for the trust, are worth the price we pay for them.

Will it pay us either as individuals or as a nation to encourage trusts?

Instead of discussing the question from the standpoint of commercial gain, let us view it as patriots.

I believe that a conference of this kind should not attempt to judge a question so important to our national welfare as this, by the selfish standard of commercial greed. I think that loftier motives should rule us in this discussion.

The commercial and financial aspects of the trust problem are important. I believe, however, that there are considerations more important to us as a nation.

In this republic of ours we are fond of saying that there are

GEORGE R. GAITHER, JR.   JOHN W. HAYES
EDWARD W. BEMIS   LOUIS F. POST
GEORGE GUNTON   JEFFERSON DAVIS

no classes. In fact, we boast of it. We say that classes belong to monarchies, not to republics.

Nevertheless, none of us can dispute the fact that our society is divided into classes, and well defined ones, too. They are not distinguished by differences of social standing. That is, we have no aristocratic titles, no nobility.

The distinction with us is based upon wealth. The man is rated by the property he owns. Our social and political leaders and speakers deny this. In doing so, however, they ignore actual conditions. They discuss what ought to be under our form of government—not what is.

The strength of our republic has always been in what is called our middle class. This is made up of manufacturers, jobbers, middle men, retail and wholesale merchants, commercial travelers and business men generally. It would be little short of calamity to encourage any industrial development that would affect unfavorably this important class of our citizens.

Close to them as a strong element of our people are the skilled mechanics and artisans. They are the sinew and strength of the nation.

While the business of the country has been conducted by persons and firms, the skilled employee has held close and sympathetic relations with his employer.

He has been something more than a mere machine. He has felt the stimulus and ambition which goes with equality of opportunity. These have contributed to make him a good citizen. Take away that stimulus and ambition, and we lower the standard of our citizenship. Without good citizenship our national life is in danger.

It seems to me, therefore, that the vital consideration connected with this problem of the trust is its effect upon our middle class—the independent, individual business man and the skilled artisan and mechanic.

How does the trust affect them? It is admitted by the apologist for the trust that it makes it impossible for the individual or firm to do business on a small scale.

It tends to concentrate the ownership and management of all lines of business activity into the hands of a very few. No one denies this.

This being so, it follows that the independent, individual business man, must enter the employment of the trust. Self-preservation compels it. Duty to his family forces him to it.

He becomes an employee instead of an employer. His trusted foremen and his employees must follow him.

They have been in close and daily association with him. The new order of things compels them to separate. They are both to become a part of a vast industrial army with no hopes and no aspirations—a daily task to perform and no personal interest and perhaps no pride in the success of their work.

Their personal identity is lost. They become cogs and little wheels in a great complicated machine. There is no real advance for them.

They may perhaps become larger cogs or larger wheels, but they can never look forward to a life of business freedom.

A very select few may become heads of trusts, but such opportunities will be rare indeed. They will, therefore, be entirely useless as incentives to the ambition of the army of those employed by the trusts. As a result of the ceaseless and heartless grind of the trusts, in the almost insane desire to control trade, ambition, and perhaps inventive genius, will be deadened and killed.

The middle class of which I speak will lose their sense of independence. They are already being deprived of that equality of opportunity which has made this nation what it is. It is equality of opportunity which has attracted to this country the millions of people of other nations who have helped make American citizenship and American institutions the greatest and best in the world.

The trust is therefore the forerunner, or rather the creator of industrial slavery.

The master is the trust manager or director. It is his duty to serve the soulless and nameless being called the stockholder. To the latter the dividend is more important than the happiness or prosperity of any one.

The slave is the former merchant and business man, and the artisan and mechanic, who once cherished the hope that they might sometime reach the happy position of independent ownership of a business.

Commercial feudalism is the logical outcome of the trust. The trust manager is the feudal baron.

These may perhaps be harsh characterizations, but who can deny their truth? Honesty to ourselves and loyalty to our country and its free institutions compel us to face and recognize the situation.

We cannot be true to our republic by ignoring these things. We cannot be honest to the people, either at this conference or in our legislative assemblies by confining our deliberations to the commercial advantages and disadvantages of the trust.

It is better to be forever poor, but independent and happy as individuals, than to lay the foundations for industrial tyranny and slavery.

Personal liberty is rather to be chosen than great riches.

Equality of opportunity to all men is better than the control of the world's trade.

The effect of the trust upon our national life and our citizenship will not be sudden perhaps. It will rather be a silent and gradual change. It may not be observed, at once, but its influence will nevertheless be felt.

The warning with which the history of the decadence and downfall of other nations furnishes us may not be heeded now. If not, we may pay the usual penalty of slavery to commercial avarice and greed.

Increase of the wealth of the country is greatly to be desired, but if the people are to be degraded to industrial slaves, wealth under such conditions is a curse.

If our independent and intelligent business men and artisans are to be crowded out of existence as a class by the trust, there is no remedy too drastic for the trust.

Some may think it is too early to sound a note of warning of this kind, but the time to check an evil tendency is when it first shows itself.

We have given the private corporation "too much rope." Some say give it more rope and it will hang itself. In other words they claim that the trust problem, if left alone, will work out its own solution.

I do not believe in such a policy. There is too much at stake. The most important element of our citizenship is in the balance. We cannot afford to sap the strength of our democracy in order to forward an experiment.

I favor complete and prompt annihilation of the trust,—with due regard for property rights, of course.

I care more for the independence and manliness of the American citizen than for all the gold or silver on or in the world. It is better to cherish the happiness of the American home than to control the commerce of the globe.

The degrading process of the trust means much to the future of a republic founded upon democratic principles. A democratic republic cannot survive the disappearance of a democratic population.

CHARLES FOSTER.

Ex-Governor of Ohio.

Speaking on "The Desirability of Trusts," ex-Governor Charles Foster of Ohio said:

This conference, so unique in its conception, responded to so universally, resulting in a gathering of distinguished representatives of all the states of the nation, attests the deep concern of the people in the subject, which we have voluntarily consented to deliberate upon.

An intelligent and imposing body of men are here assembled; and it may also be said that no economic subject of such far reaching importance, was ever before deliberated upon. How very important that our deliberations should eventuate in a line of suggestion (we can only advise) that will, when sanctioned by law, conserve the greatest and best interests of the greatest country on earth.

We are considering the great question of the combination of capital as it relates to, and effects all of the interests of the country great and small. These combinations are popularly known as trusts, and by a common impulse, the whole country has assumed the position of antagonism to them.

The gentleman from Texas who so eloquently entertained us yesterday, stated that his state had no industrial development, that they sold raw material, and bought their supplies, as the reason for their fierce opposition to trusts.

He also eloquently portrayed the superiority of manhood over money.

It strikes me that if the Texas people had sufficient enterprise to establish industries, to consume their cotton, wool and other raw material, their manhood would not deteriorate, their opposition to trusts would be less vehement, and they would have more money.

The evolution in business from the individual to the partnership, and from the partnership to the corporation was no more natural and necessary than is the evolution from the corporation to the trust. Let us look the situation squarely in the face.

Denounce it as we may, it has come to stay. Why? Because the gigantic business operations of the present and future cannot be carried on without it.

Through the trust, the enormous waste that is entailed upon business operations by competition, is saved; the product and the service performed is cheapened. Labor will have the better opportunity to enhance wages and shorten the hours of toil, as is so signally illustrated in the railroad service of the country.

Through the trust, the superior inventive genius of our people (because of universal education) will have improved opportunity.

It is a gratifying fact that we are making rapid progress in securing the markets of the world for our manufactured products. For this, we are first indebted to our economic policy of protection that gave the incentive to an enterprising people; and secondly, to the much abused trust. With a settled policy in relation to them, it is not a wild prophecy to make that in the near future our foreign trade will be largely increased, and that in less time than many of us imagine, this country will become the money center of the world. Not only will our foreign trade be greatly enhanced, but the greater consumptive power of our people will largely increase our home business.

The enormous increase of wealth in this country has already lowered the rate of interest, and the end in this direction has not been reached.

When the trusts shall have been properly safeguarded by law their securities will furnish a means of safe investment, at a somewhat higher rate of interest than will be paid by government, state, or municipal bonds, thus affording the opportunity for investment for savings banks and people of moderate means.

It is certain that the amount of idle money in the hands of our people will be very great. How valuable, then, will be the opportunity to safely invest it, even at moderate rates.

We must not neglect to take note of the fact that the history of this country has been that of great growth territorially; of great expansion, if you please. Up to the present, every addition to our territory, however much misguided people have opposed these additions, has proved to be a blessing in added power, glory and manhood.

So now, whether the present large acquisitions shall prove to be blessings (as they will be, even greater than some of the acquisitions of the past) or not, it is clear that by an energetic appreciation of the new conditions, we shall add greatly to our material interests without any deterioration of the manhood of our people.

The isthmus canal is certain to be constructed, and then, with naval stations at Honolulu, in the Ladrones, and in the Philippines, with the powerful aid of the trusts, who can match us in facilities for conducting the commerce with seven hundred millions, or more, of people on the other side of the Pacific ocean?

Seward's dream that the Pacific side of our country was likely to become the most important, may prove to be a reality.

The trusts will prove to be the great reliance of our country in successfully conducting the great industries that are to supply the greatly enhanced foreign commerce, that the opportunities of the near future are opening to us.

Have no fear that the trusts will seriously impose upon the people in the prices that will have to be paid for their products. The germs of death are in them and their only method to prevent an early demise, is to avoid extortion.

It may be a debatable question as to whether the Standard Oil Company has been, and is a blessing to the country or not. Certain it is, however, that it has developed an industry in something more than thirty years, from practically nothing, to an annual volume of perhaps more than $150,000,000, of which it retains about $25,000,000 and gives $125,000,000 to the people of the country. It has greatly lessened the cost of light; it is paying more than a hundred millions of dollars annually for oil and labor, and pays labor more than any other employees receive.

It has added more than one thousand millions to the wealth of the country, and contributes sixty millions a year to our credit in its exports.

But there are reasons for the control of trusts by law. Overcapitalization must be guarded against.

While I have always been, and am yet, a thorough believer in the protective policy, I regard the appropriation of the tariff to enhance the price of any product of the country, as a misuse of the purpose intended. When any trust shall avail itself of a tax upon imports to enhance the price of the product, then the tax should be modified or wholly removed.

A bureau of government, or a board, similar to the interstate commerce commission, should be established, to whom all trusts shall apply for license, after being incorporated, and to whom reports as exhaustive as is required of the national banks, should be made. The terms of the license should not be illiberal, but it certainly should provide against overcapitalization.

All profits beyond 6 per cent should be taxed for the benefit of the government.

As probably the power does not exist in Congress to make the requirements suggested, it seems then, that it is the plain duty of this conference to request Congress to submit amendments to the Constitution, giving it necessary power, not only to control the trusts, but as the suggestion is made to tax their profits, also to provide for an income tax.

It is evident now, that the country hereafter must rely upon internal taxation for revenue to support the government. An income tax is the most equitable form of taxation and can be paid with less hardship than any other. It is objected to on the ground that it exposes the secrets of business, and because it is generally evaded. If the return is honorably made, I apprehend there will be little ground for this objection.

It may be that our powers do not give us jurisdiction over the latter subject.

If this view should be taken, then let us appeal to the wealthy people of the country to take it up and move for its adoption. It is certain they could not render themselves a better service.

It seems to me that as both those who oppose, and those who favor trusts are in accord in favoring the assertion of a power strong enough to either destroy or regulate them, that we ought to be able to get together on the proposition to amend the Constitution of the United States.

I apprehend but for the inherent support of the doctrine of state rights by our Southern friends the proposition would be readily agreed to. It is evident that the states acting independently cannot successfully deal with this great question.

As the country expands the weakness of state control of great questions becomes more apparent, and the need of the use of federal power becomes greater.

The law of this country has been one of expansion and growth, and I may appropriately say, that when we cease to grow our decline will begin.

I believe the great mission designed by Providence for this country has only begun; that it will go on evangelizing and civilizing the world until all lands and all peoples will be in the full enjoyment of free institutions.

JEFFERSON DAVIS.

Attorney-General of Arkansas.

Following Mr. Foster, Attorney-General Jefferson Davis of Arkansas spoke extemporaneously on "Arkansas Anti-Trust Law," saying:

Coming as I do from a land that lies to the South, it is with great gratification that I accepted your invitation and have come here from the Southland to give you my ideas, crude as they are, on the subject before this convention, one that is threatening to sap the very life blood of our American institutions.

It is with a feeling of trepidation that I enter upon this discussion, and I was very glad indeed when I received notice from your secretary that this meeting should not be political. Had it been otherwise, I should not have attended, because beyond and above all things else I hold and pride my democracy. If in this discussion I should unwittingly say anything that would be improper, or transcend the proprieties of this occasion, I ask that you attribute it to my zeal, and not to a willful desire to infringe on the proprieties of this convention.

The subject, ladies and gentlemen, that has been assigned to me is "The Arkansas Law as Applied to Trusts."

Before entering upon that discussion, ladies and gentlemen, permit me to say that I am surprised at some of the sentiments expressed here to-night by the last gentleman who has taken his seat upon the platform. He tells us that trusts have come to stay. That may be true—I doubt it sincerely. But if it be true, ladies and gentlemen, that trusts have come to stay, and if the withering blight of trusts is to overshadow our fair land, then away with American liberty, American patriotism, the God of the American people. Mr. Chairman, we all know—at least the legal fraternity who face me in this convention—know that any conspiracy to control prices—and that is but an epitome of trusts—is a crime at the common law, and that wherever the common law prevails in this broad land of ours, under that, without federal interference and without any legislation, under the common law alone, the crime of conspiracy to control prices may be punished criminally. We know, ladies and gentlemen, that the trust is but a conspiracy to control prices. What is the trust? You have had it differently defined during the sitting of this convention. I say to you, ladies and gentlemen, a trust is but the ripened fruit of misused tariff legislation, as the robbery of the people upon the silver question was. We know, ladies and gentlemen—and while I do not intend to invade the province of politics, and while I never in my life prepared a speech for any convention, perhaps you have observed that ere this—I say to you that a trust is but the ripened fruit. We know, ladies and gentlemen, that money is the blood of commerce; we know, like the blood that flows from the heart to the extremities and helps the circulation, money should flow from the centers to the extremities and back again, to help the circulating commercial life. But we know that by a system of tariff taxation, by representations, that the money has flowed from the extremities to

272

the centers, and has not returned again, but it has been congealed and it is only in the center. Not only that, but the money of the constitution, the money of the people, the money of our fathers, the money that we all love so well, not by law but by precedent, has been taken from the people, and it, too, has congealed in the east and in the north, and with this great mass of wealth, fellow-citizens, you know full well that men are attempting to-day, with this great mass of wealth they are attempting to control the price of products, and the trust is but the outgrowth, but the ripened fruit, as it were, the outgrowth of these two gigantic evils—and this distinguished gentleman tells us it has come to stay! It means that its father and mother came to stay, and it is but their offspring, ladies and gentlemen.

Now to the discussion that has been assigned to me. Applause is always permissible at any part of this discussion, ladies and gentlemen, and in the few brief moments for the discussion of one of the best laws, I think, upon the statute books of any state in the Union, I find in the few moments I will be unable to go over the field as I would like, and point out to you, as I see it, one of the best remedies on earth to destroy the thing which this gentleman has told us came to stay. I say to you, ladies and gentlemen, that we cannot destroy it successfully without federal interference and state legislation in harmonious action. We do not need so much legislation. It is not the legislative branch of our government that in my brief experience as attorney of one of the best states in the galaxy of states that I have the honor to represent here—it is true we raise more corn and cotton and pretty women in Arkansas than any place on earth—it is not of the legislation department of my state or this beautiful Southland of which I would complain, but it is with another function of government—it is with the judicial department of this great commonwealth of ours that I would complain to you to-night. What! they say. You should not criticise the judiciary! There isn't a man, fellow-citizens, in all this broad land of ours that would pay greater tribute to the honorable, to the just, the upright and conscientious judge, than I. But do you remember, ladies and gentlemen, that Abraham Lincoln, one of the greatest patriots this country has ever produced, in the Dred Scott decision he criticises more severely than it is possible for me to do a decision of the Supreme Court of this land of ours, and do you remember, ladies and gentlemen, just a short time ago, in the income-tax decision to which my distinguished friend referred so learnedly, that Justice Harlan criticises more severely than it is possible for me to do the most infamous decision that has ever been handed down by a court of last resort in any country or time?

I have not lost my faith in God and man. The saddest fate that can befall a human soul is when it loses its faith in God and man, and had I lost that gem, though the thrones of this world stood empty in my path, I would go wandering back to my childhood in tears till I found it. It is not of the legislative department that I would complain, but of the judicial department. I hold in my hand a copy of one of the best laws, in my judgment, that was ever enacted in a state upon the subject of trusts. This law provides in a few words, "Any corporation organized under the laws of this or any other state or country and transacting or conducting any kind of business in this state, which shall create, enter into, or become a member of or a party to any pool or trust or agreement to regulate or fix the price of any article of mechanics or merchandise or any article or thing whatsoever, shall be deemed and adjudged guilty of a felony, and subject to the penalties of this act." I come from a people that is in no humor to temporize with one of the most monstrous evils that has ever "come to stay." Gentlemen—excuse me, but I have been talking politics—ladies and gentlemen, do you remember in the 158 United States Supreme Court, the case of Hall against Virginia, where the United States Supreme Court says that a corporation is but a creature of the law, and that the creature cannot control the creator? This law provides that a corporation so created cannot migrate to another sovereignty unless by the consent of that sovereignty; and it goes further, and says that that sovereignty may prescribe any condition upon which it may enter its borders and transact its business. Now, taking that as a basis, if a corporation is considered by the ultimate authority, the government, but a creature of the law, then it remains for you to say whether the creature shall control the creator, or whether the creator shall control the creature.

Now, ladies and gentlemen, the Federal Court of this land has said that these creatures can only exist in the land of their creation, and they can migrate to another sovereignty only upon the will of that sovereignty, no matter how cautious that will may be. Now, fellow-citizens, we know that a trust is but a combination of wealth formed for the purpose of controlling prices; we know, fellow-citizens, that it is a corporation; we know that it is a creature of the law, and I am here to say to-night that the only remedy, in my judgment, for its extermination—because exterminate it we must—the only remedy for its extermination is to bring upon it the strong hand of the law, and I am surprised to

274

hear the sentiment expressed before this vast and intelligent audience that the trust is a good thing. I say to you, ladies and gentlemen, that this is not a political subject—it is a question of economics. We have come to the divide of the waters; we have come to the point, ladies and gentlemen, where we must stand up like patriotic American citizens and meet the conditions that confront us to-day.

Now, fellow-citizens, Arkansas started the agitation, but Texas went us one better, and Texas has to-day possibly a better law than that. Do you know, ladies and gentlemen, do you know that the Supreme Court of the State of Missouri has decided, and that decision has never been questioned by any lawyer of ability—the Supreme Court of Missouri has absolutely decided that you cannot collect a bill rendered for trust goods? Then if that is true, fellow-citizens, if that is true, ladies and gentlemen, then you see that this trust is an outlaw in the land. And, gentlemen, when I speak the word "trust" I use it as it is known to-day—they ought to have called it "octopus," or something that symbolized its character—but they have stolen the livery of heaven to serve the devil in.

I find that my time, twenty minutes, has long since expired, and I have just fairly started the discussion of the Arkansas law as applied to trusts. Now, fellow-citizens, now I'll say why I forget myself and call you fellow-citizens: I have been speaking for the last sixty-five days in Arkansas on this very proposition, and I only caught the train by a forced drive to make the train to come here, and hence you will excuse me when I greet you as "fellow-citizens." I say, ladies and gentlemen, that I find my time has expired, and of course I will not ask this intelligent audience to bear with me further, and I shall submit the question with just one other consideration. Ladies and gentlemen, the only way to grapple with this matter, as I have stated before, is by the strong arm of the law.

A Voice: State or national?

Mr. Davis: State and national combined, and in order to carry to a successful issue, I am here to tell you, ladies and gentlemen, that we have got to reconstruct our judiciary. I am here to say, ladies and gentlemen, that if we ever have another civil war—and God grant we may not—it will be brought about, in my humble judgment, by judge-made law. I say to you, ladies and gentlemen, that it is one of the great evils that threatens this republic to-day—judge-made law—the judiciary of the country invading the province of the legislative department of this country.

Now, fellow—ladies and gentlemen, if I have unwittingly in these few scattering remarks said anything, I am glad at least I have furnished some amusement for this conference, and if you'll just come down to Arkansas, the home of the red apple and the pretty women, I'll treat you as nicely as I can.

GEORGE GUNTON.

Publisher *Gunton's Magazine.*

During the remarks of Professor George Gunton of New York, who spoke on "The Public and the Trusts," the spectators became so demonstrative over the speaker's pro-trust views that the chairman had to threaten to have the galleries cleared. Professor Gunton's paper was as follows:

The trust question is only a new phase of an old problem, the problem of free industrial enterprise. Notwithstanding that everybody knows that the marvelous progress of the last three quarters of a century is mainly due to the introduction of improved methods of industry, every improvement since Wyatt's spinning frame and Hargreaves' spinning jenny has had to fight its way against the popular prejudice of the time. The hand loom weavers marched through England and broke the power looms. Hargreaves, Arkwright and Crompton were driven from their homes for inventing new methods of spinning.

Now, after three quarters of a century's experience, in which the fallacy of this policy has become notorious, we are face to face with another movement of the same character. The present agitation against trusts has all the characteristics of the anti-machinery riots of a century ago. It pervades the attitude of both laborers and business men alike. Workingmen give about the same reasons for opposing the introduction of new machines as did the neighbors of Crompton and Arkwright for breaking their spinning frames. The business men who twenty-five years ago were among the hated organizers of corporations are now among the agitators against trusts. And now the movement is taking on a political form. Men of national repute and leaders of great political parties, candidates for the highest and most responsible positions in the nation, are asking the people to reverse the policy of industrial freedom and return to the doctrine of arbitrary paternalism, specifically to suppress large corporations. Are the American people ready for such a step?

There is only one point of view from which this subject can properly be considered—the interest of the public; the public as representing the consumers who are interested in superior commodities at low prices; the public as representing the laborers who are interested in permanent employment and good wages; the public as representing the farmers who are interested in cheap transportation and the advantages of the modern products of science, art and literature. It is in these aspects of the subject, and not in the confusing clamor and sensational subterfuge of campaign oratory, that the American people are interested. The question for this conference to ask, the question for the people of the United States to ask, is: Are trusts inimical to public welfare in all or any of these respects?

It must be remembered, first of all, that the trust, be it good or bad, is only one among a large number of experiments in industrial organization, which the progress of the last fifty years has evolved. One of the marked features of the economic development of the century is the radical change that has taken place in the character of competing units. Under the primitive hand labor method, the competing unit was the individual. With the development of factory methods, the individual as a competing unit was superseded by partnerships, because they could more economically employ the new methods. With the growth of invention, partnerships were superseded by corporations. With the growing completeness of machinery and magnitude of business, corporations grew larger and larger, until the corporation is now the prevailing form in the most advanced countries.

Nor is this limited to the capitalist side of industry. It is equally characteristic of the labor side. The competing unit in the labor market is no longer the individual laborer, but the group, the union. The factory system has made it impossible for individual laborers to be competitors, because it is impossible for them to make individual contracts. In all matters pertaining to wages, hours of labor, conditions of work, whether by piece or by the day, it is the group and not the individual that is considered. Each factory, and in most instances each industry, pays uniform wages, works the same hours, and has substantially the same conditions, and when they are altered for one they are altered for all. In short, the progress during the nineteenth century has irrevocably established the group as the competing unit; the union as the unit on the labor side, the corporation as the unit on the capital side.

Now the trust was one of the experiments in the evolution of this group unit. Numerous forms of organization and association were tried. Corners, associations to fix prices, were tried. But these were uneconomic and failed, usually wrecking somebody in the collapse. The trust was another form. It differed from these in that it was an attempt to integrate productive forces. Corners and trade associations were mere manipulators of prices, not producers. Trusts were bona fide producers.

The difference between the trust and the ordinary corporations was not economic, but legal. The trusts are a formal merging of a number of corporations or firms under one management, which holds the property in trust for its original owners, giving certificates for their respective claims. There have been very few bona fide trusts; the Standard Oil trust, the sugar trust and a few others. But through the intense popular opposition, resulting in adverse legislation, these have all disappeared. They have been disbanded and converted into simple corporations, with capital stock owned by whomsoever chooses to invest, and governed by the majority vote of the stockholders. So that, if there was anything peculiar or alarming in trusts, the evil has disappeared, because the trust is gone.

In reality, then, what we have are simply corporations. The whole question which this conference is called to consider is: What is the influence of large corporations upon public welfare?

First, then, what is the effect of large corporations upon the quality and price of the community's supply of commodities? This question is one of fact, and can only be adequately answered by experience. The history of corporations on this point is almost too obvious to need reciting. The evidence abounds on every hand. While experience differs in different industries, as it necessarily must, the tendency is universal that with the growth of large corporations the quality of the commodities improves, and the prices fall. It was in obedience to this principle that corporations came into existence. A long series of experiments taught that under certain conditions large capital could be used to greater advantage than small capital. It could produce more at the same cost, give a larger aggregate profit, by selling the products at lower prices. As the experiments proved successful they were increased, and so from small individual concerns to partnerships, then to corporations, the process went on and on, and if not arbitrarily interrupted will continue to go on just so long as it will yield any advantage. Just so long as adding another million to the plant will increase the earning capacity of both the old and new capital, the additions will continue to be made, and as soon as the point is reached where to increase the size fails to increase the economy, it will stop. Clearly, the history of industrial growth and prosperity is the history of corporate development. Without corporations productive efficiency could not have progressed beyond the economic status of the small individual concerns of the last century.

The era of corporations in this country is since the war. It is during that period that our industrial expansion has been so enormous and the great corporate interests have developed. If we take the groups of industry in which the commodities are produced by corporations, by individuals or small capitalists, we get a fair view of the difference in the influence of the two types of industrial effort upon prices and public welfare. These data are easily found, already classified, from 1860 to 1891 in the Senate report on wholesale prices and wages, which is the most exhaustive collection of industrial data ever printed in any language. In the table given in Part I (pp. 30 to 52) the prices of over two hundred articles are given every year from 1860 to 1891. Of these 58 had risen in price, some 100 per cent, and a very large proportion from 30 to 70 per cent. With one or two exceptions these were all agricultural or raw material products, in which little corporate capital was employed. On the other hand the tables give 140 groups of manufactured products, mostly produced by corporations, and some of them by very large corporations, using most modern machinery, and in all these prices had fallen varying from 6 to 40 per cent. At the same time wages rose, chiefly in the manufacturing and mercantile industries, 68 per cent. That is to say, through the economies of corporate methods, from 1860 to 1891, the purchasing power of the day's work was increased over 72 per cent, which is equivalent to an absolute increase in public welfare of 24 per cent every ten years.

While this is true of corporate industries in general, as compared with non-corporate industries, it is most markedly true of very large corporations. If we take the concerns where millions are invested by a single corporation, like the Standard Oil Company, the American Sugar Refining Company, the great railroads, the Carnegie Steel Company, we find that their products have undergone the greatest improvement in quality and the greatest reduction in price. Without the immensely large capitals invested by these great corporations, many of the great improvements accomplished during the last twenty years would have been absolutely impossible. Take for instance the Carnegie Company. Nothing short of tens of millions invested under one management could have developed the extraordinary improvements which have revolutionized both the quality and price of iron and steel products. With small concerns of less than a million each, that could not have been done. The same is true of our great railroad systems. No small or individual enterprise could have given us the marvelous development in railroading of the last twenty-five years, which has constantly improved the service and so greatly reduced the cost to the public. In 1873 it cost 2.21 cents a mile to transport a ton of freight. Through the increased investments and improved facilities, the price has been gradually reduced year by year until now it only costs 75-hundredths of a cent a mile per ton. The surface railroad systems throughout this country are another illustration of what large corporations can and do accomplish. It used to cost ten cents to ride a few blocks in a dingy, dirty horse car, in every city in this country. With the development of large corporations, electricity has superseded horses, large, light and wholesome cars have replaced dingy boxes, and fares have been reduced one-half, with transfers to nearly all connecting lines, a result that could not have been accomplished under small separate concerns.

The Standard Oil Company, the most hated of all large corporations, is another conspicuous illustration of this fact. The immense investment involved in thousands of miles of pipe line and millions of gallons of storage capacity, which takes the oil from the wells and delivers it at the seaboard without the touch of human hand, and the immense sums expended in experimentation for an improved quality of the product, which have resulted in reducing the price of oil (in gold) 75 per cent since that corporation was organized, required tens and even hundreds of millions of capital, which only a colossal corporation could furnish. This corporation, by its immense capital, preserves the oil industry to this country. But for it the American market for petroleum would be supplied by Russian producers. Russia protects its oil producers by a 200 per cent tariff; we put ours upon the free list. Only the competition of the Standard Oil Company, through the immense economies it has developed, of which the smaller concerns now have the benefit, keeps Russian oil out of the American market. That company furnishes an unlimited cash market for every barrel of petroleum that it produces in this country. Moreover, it gives employment to 35,000 American laborers, pays $100,000 a day in wages, and exports, in competition with Russia, into Europe and Asia, nearly 1,000,000,000 gallons of oil a year, bringing about $60,000,000 in gold into the country. Here is an industry, all told, which furnishes employment to about 45,000 American laborers, paying about $125,000 a day in wages, bringing a balance of $60,000,000 of gold a year into the country, all of which would be lost to this country but for the economic energy and superiority of the Standard Oil Company. Small refineries, such as those now outside the Standard, could not hold the American market a month in competition with the Russians. In short, it has preserved the industry to this country, and at the same time improved the quality of the people's light and reduced its price 75 per cent; and all this without government aid, purely as a highly developed productive enterprise competing against the government-aided capital of Russia. I could go through the whole list of industries where great improvements have been made and large reduction in prices accrued, and substantially the same facts will be found.

Next, what is the influence of corporations upon the conditions of labor? It is commonly asserted that large corporations tend to destroy the laborer's liberty and individuality by making him a part of a productive machine. Mr. Cleveland sounded this note in his last message to Congress. A little touch of fact would show this to be a pure phantom of the imagination. Nothing could be more contrary to the whole history of wage labor. If there were any truth in this, we might expect to find that laborers had more freedom and greater individuality before the wage system began. Yet everybody knows that then they had neither liberty nor individuality; that it was not until long after the wage system came that laborers acquired any liberty, political rights or social individuality.

The laborer's freedom and individuality depend upon two things—permanence of employment and good wages. Wherever the employment of labor is most permanent and wages are highest, there the laborer is most intelligent, has the greatest freedom and the strongest individual identity. Where do laborers get these conditions? It is not where capital is small and employers are poor. On the contrary, it is where large corporations prevail that wages are highest and employment most continuous, and everybody knows it is there where the laborers are most independent. It is notorious that large corporations have the least influence over the opinions and individual conduct of their laborers. Let it be known that a large corporation is trying to influence the election of candidates for office, and that is the signal for the working men to vote against them. Instead of being controlled by the corporations they act almost uniformly on the rule of defying and opposing them.

Nor is there any loss of individual liberty in becoming a fractional part of a large productive concern. What society wants is not individuality as producers but individuality as citizens. What we need is that the laborer should give less and less of his personal energy to earning a living and more and more to his social and individual improvement. A permanent stipulated income is the first step toward real individual freedom for the laborers. Nothing is so depressing to manhood, nothing makes the weak so cowardly, as precariousness of income. The small business man who does not know from quarter to quarter, and sometimes from month to month, whether he can meet his obligations, is neither as brave, as intelligent nor as free a citizen as the wage laborer in the safe employ of a large corporation. As a matter of fact, the corporation and banker have far more influence over the votes of small business men whom they have befriended or patronized than they have over their own laborers. A laborer's freedom does not depend upon the fact that he works for wages, but on the amount of his wages. With high wages and permanent employment the laborer's freedom and welfare is secured. The laborer has not a single interest, social, economic or political, in the existence of employers with small capital.

How do large corporations affect the interest of the farmers? There is probably no class in the community who derive more benefit from the economic improvements of large corporations than do the farmers. All the great improvements in tools, architecture, sanitation, domestic appointments, art, literature and general refinement, are the products of industrial centers where large capitalistic enterprises abound. Every form of commodity outside of food which enters into the farmer's life has been immensely improved and greatly cheapened by the efforts of large corporations. Transportation, which is an important item in the farmer's economy, has been reduced 50 per cent during the last twenty-five years, as will be seen by the following table:

Year.	Average rate per ton per mile. (cents.)	Year.	Average rate per ton per mile. (cents.)
1873	2.210	1886	1.042
1874	2.040	1887	1.034
1875	1.810	1888	0.977
1876	1.855	1889	0.970
1877	1.524	1890	0.927
1878	1.401	1891	0.929
1879	1.201	1892	0.941
1880	1.348	1893	0.893
1881	1.264	1894	0.864
1882	1.236	1895	0.839
1883	1.224	1896	0.806
1884	1.125	1897	0.798
1885	1.036	1898	0.753

While the farmer has received all the advantages produced by large corporations in lower prices of everything he buys, and lower transportation, the price of what he sells has undergone very little fall, and of many products no fall at all, and some have even risen.

What is the influence of large corporations upon business stability and prosperity? This is one of the most important features of the subject. The greatest menace to modern society is business depressions, which usually are the result of ignorant eagerness among competitors. A slight boom in business leads to a rash increase of output. Without any general knowledge of what is being done elsewhere each hopes to fill the new void, with the result of an increase of output wholly disproportionate to the demand. For instance, the Illinois farmer, when the price of corn is high, will double his acreage for corn, and next year finds that he can hardly sell the corn at any price, and is compelled to use it for fuel. Large concerns tend to remedy this evil on the same principle that they invest heavily in experimentation. They take pains to gather accurate information of the condition of their business throughout the world. They find it pays to be informed as to what next year's demand is likely to be. Their investments are so large that they could not afford seriously to miscalculate the demands of the market. With their comparatively accurate information, they adjust their production with great precision to the present and probable future demand. As a matter of fact, in lines of industry where the very largest concerns are organized there is the least perturbation. If the raising of corn were in the hands of a few well informed corporations instead of thousands of uninformed small farmers, the erratic ups and downs in corn farming would be largely avoided. Industrial depressions can never be eliminated until the relation of productive enterprise to general consumption is reduced to some degree of precision, which the small go-as-you-please producers can never do.

Large corporations are superior to small concerns; first, because by the use of large capital and superior methods they improve the quality and reduce the price of commodities; second, they are more favorable than smaller concerns to high wages, and individual freedom of laborers; third, by introducing scientific precision into industry they tend to increase the permanence of employment and reduce the tendency to industrial depressions, all of which are vital elements in the nation's prosperity and progress.

In studying the literature against large corporations one is impressed by the marked absence of careful presentation of facts and rational discussion of the case. There seems to be no attempt to apply economic principles or recognize the great law of societary evolution. The only hint thus far of a policy to be adopted is the proposition of Mr. Bryan, which is that Congress pass a law forbidding all corporations to do business outside the state in which they are incorporated without a license from the federal government. It is difficult to imagine a gentleman who is about to be for the second time a candidate for the Presidency of the United States, seriously making such a proposition. Yet he recently presented this to the Nebraska Democratic convention, and repeated it to this conference. This is so contrary to the spirit and traditions of democracy, which is usually opposed to any trade restrictions whatever, and so contrary to the American idea of free intercourse between the states, and so contrary to Mr. Bryan's previous declarations, that one has difficulty in taking him seriously. If this is really the best that his mind can suggest on the subject, it is a depressing gauge of his statesmanship. It would hardly be possible to invent a proposition that would be more fertile in creating corruption, injustice, favoritism and business demoralization. A license might be granted by one administration and refused by another, for purely political reasons, which would be equal to confiscating the property of the corporation, since it would destroy its business value. There is not a single aspect of this proposition which is not surcharged with economic and political iniquity. It partakes neither of economic sense, political wisdom, fair statesmanship, nor even party shrewdness.

It is not to be assumed, however, that large corporations are always wise, or good, or fair. They are born of the same spirit and partake of the same attributes as the small business venders. Their main ambition is to make profits. It is the duty of the state, therefore, to see to it that the conditions shall be such as to make dishonesty, unfairness, oppressive dealing, difficult and as impossible as any other offenses against the welfare of the community. This cannot be accomplished, however, by the petty nagging and corruption-creating license-granting proposed by Mr. Bryan. The federal government if it acts at all should act in exactly the other direction. It should surround industrial enterprise with the maximum freedom and the maximum protection to all, and no uneconomic privilege to any.

To this end it might be well for Congress to enact a law empowering the government to grant national charters to corporations, which should give them the right to do business over the entire territory of the United States, against which no state should have the right to interfere. This would be economic, in that it would give the market of the entire country to every business enterprise. National charters could have the proper qualifications subjecting the corporations to a certain supervision and compelling annual reports to be made. Second, it might also be provided that companies using a public franchise, like railroads, should not be permitted to make uneconomic discriminations in their rates of traffic, that they should be subject to public accounting, and that all contracts with shippers should be accessible to all other shippers. The general influence of publicity and inspection by the national government, coupled with the corporations' protection in its right to do business throughout the United States, would tend to create a wholesome influence around corporate conduct. While affording corporations the full support of the national government in their business rights, it would free them from the petty uneconomic nagging of partisan legislation in the different states. It would carry out the true idea of protection—that the American market should be open to every American producer and that the interests of the laborers and the public is safeguarded by the national government; at the same time leaving the essential features of business to be determined by the free action of economic forces, which are more permanent, more sure and more equitable than the wisest statutory enactment would ever be.

GEORGE R. GAITHER, JR.

Attorney-General of Maryland.

The day's program was closed by the reading of a paper by Attorney-General George Gaither, Jr., of Maryland, on "Maryland and the Trusts," who said:

The phenomenal growth of trusts, as the consolidations of great business interests into central corporations are currently designated, has excited the deepest interest in the minds of the people of this country. The meaning of this tremendous change in the economic relations of the nation is being earnestly considered by every thinking citizen, and some effective remedy for the evils which the growth of this new system threatens to produce is eagerly looked for. It is peculiarly fortunate that this new problem has developed so rapidly that it has not as yet been complicated by political antagonisms, and no partisan spirit should be allowed to enter into the present serious discussion of the great question. The evils attendant upon the present and the threatened development of these combinations in the manufacturing, producing and transportation interests of the country are universally recognized. For four hundred years the English-speaking races have abhorred monopolies, and since the reign of the Tudors every bill of rights has prohibited the sovereign power from granting any privileges in trade or commerce which were in their nature exclusive and preventive of competition. There is scarcely a constitution of a state of the Union which does not contain this prohibition, and in the constitution of Maryland it is expressly stipulated "that monopolies are odious, contrary to the spirit of a free government and the principles of commerce, and ought not to be suffered." Abhorrence of monopolies is therefore one of the most deep-seated convictions of the English-speaking races. Our modern form of monopolies differs, however, most radically from the form which our ancestors fought against. Ancient monopolies owed their existence to the exclusive privileges with which they had been invested by the royal prerogative. Modern monopolies or trusts claim no protection from the law,—on the contrary they simply ask that they shall not be interfered with, relying upon the crushing power of the exclusive privileges, which their own control of great aggregations of capital has obtained, for their flourishing existence. The old monopoly was a creature of the law, the modern trust seeks to establish itself without legislative assistance, and in many instances in defiance of express enactments. It is manifest, therefore, that present constitutional prohibitions against monopolies do not touch the modern type of these dangerous elements in the business world— that a prohibition on the sovereign power from creating an exclusive privilege in business cannot prevent such privileges from being exercised when acquired by means independent of the sovereign itself. We must consequently look for the machinery to properly deal with these new creations of modern industrial life in new legislation applicable to the new phenomena, and not in any attempt at adaptation of old principles which were meant to apply to practically opposite conditions.

Before considering the remedial legislation which should be applied to these new monopolies in business, it is of paramount importance to determine whether the development of those combinations, in their colossal proportions, is due to sound economic laws. Whether their growth is the result of the evolution of modern business conditions, or of a mania for manipulating the possible profits of a combination of conflicting interests so as to create an aggregation of fictitious wealth and unload its shares upon a speculative public. If the latter view of the origin of trusts is correct, the country need not concern itself much about remedial legislation. The inexorable law of economics that values must inevitably find their true level can be safely relied upon to disintegrate and destroy the false combinations which have been formed, and the creation of trusts may be regarded as only a temporary disturbance of the business world.

But is the tendency of all economic undertakings, under the well recognized laws of modern business affairs, toward a disintegration of business enterprises into smaller establishments, or to a concentration under greater and ever greater combinations? A casual observation of the tendencies of business conditions for the past forty years must convince everyone of the trend of economic forces, and furnish unanswerable proofs of the sources from which our modern colossal combinations have flowed. Before the late Civil War the tendency of the numerous small railroad corporations throughout the country to consolidate into larger companies was manifest, and these corporations have since that time been merged into a few great trunk lines, which lines by traffic agreements and pools have practically been united in a common undertaking. Then, too, manufacturing interests have been concentrated and combined. Factories have been placed in close proximity to the raw material which was to be used, until the great corporations engaged in producing the finished products of industry have owned practically every factor entering into their business. So, too, the shoe manufacturer and clothing manufacturer have sought through their own stores to place their products in the hands of the consumer without the intervention of any third parties. The consolidation of gas companies, street railways and electric companies in our municipalities, or their agreement as to price or territory (which is practically the same thing), are experiences with which we have been familiar for many years. Whilst the great department stores which have developed in every city to their present proportions have demonstrated the economies and conveniences which the public enjoys from a concentration and consolidation of interests. The savings in the cost of production by the cutting down of competing expenditures, the economies of purchases in great bulk and of transportation, are realized by everyone, and the saving in the cost of the article to the consumer from these new channels of trade is universally recognized. Such has been the tendency of business methods for many years.

We have viewed consolidation and concentration in all of these manifold phases of industrial and commercial life for many years with complacency, and in most instances with satisfaction. It is only when the tendency reaches the acute stage, and a consolidation of the great businesses which deal in the necessaries of life, and with the callings in which we are vitally interested, threaten us with a great economic revolution, that the country becomes aware of the dangers which are threatening. In the first paroxysm of fear the cry is raised that this tendency of modern business life must be checked, that these combinations must be destroyed, and men must be forced by legislation to return to the business methods and ways which their intelligence has discarded. As well might we attempt to turn back the forces of nature as the forces of economic social conditions. It would be as reasonable to endeavor by legislation to restore the days of the stage-coach, or to prohibit electricity from usurping the sphere of steam. The attempt of ignorant bigotry to compel Galileo to recant his masterly exposition did not prevent the earth from revolving about the sun. The truth is rapidly dawning upon humanity that co-operation is the highest form of industrial activity that civilization can develop. When this great economic axiom is being accepted by the capitalists of our nation, it is imperative that the great working masses should not blindly oppose its adoption. Competition is no longer the life of trade, it is a destroying force to those engaged in it. Then, too, the country should profit economically from the great benefits which these combinations and consolidations must confer. The favorable conditions under which the production of commodities will take place must minimize the cost price of the finished article, and enable the consumer to enjoy at least a percentage of the saving. The use of the most approved machinery, and of the most scientific methods which the best intelligence can devise, necessarily minimize the amount of human labor which is to be expended, and at the same time insure greater purity for the product. The stability of business which will be the outcome of the new order of things will be of lasting benefit to the country. Under the competitive system men will sell to firms of doubtful credit rather than be deprived of business, and the solvent merchant is always at the mercy of a cut in prices by his recklessly insolvent neighbor. Under the new system the thousands of active country merchants, who cover every hamlet of our great continent with their wonderful distributing· facilities, will be able to purchase their standard articles at a uniform price, and one which they can reasonably rely upon being maintained. The advantages of such stability in business to the entire people will in the near future prove enormous. Then, too, after the fictitious capital in most of these combinations has been squeezed out by receiverships and reorganizations, as must inevitably be the case with many of them, the shares of these great industrial combinations will furnish as safe an investment for the savings of the people as the standard railroad securities of the country now afford. In this way co-operation in the industrial enterprises of our nation will be practically established, and the grip of the great capitalists upon every business enterprise will be, in practically a brief period, permanently loosened. Shall all of these benefits be given up, shall the attempt be made to reverse the great tides of industrial and commercial development, simply because the American people declare themselves otherwise unable to avert the evils which the present system threatens to bring upon the body politic? Shall we burn down the house in order to get rid of the vermin which infest it? Must we destroy all modern development by a wild and relentless crusade against the existence of these so-called trusts? I would readily admit that if destruction was the only remedy for the threatened evils, then those evils are so injurious to the great masses of the people that such a radical remedy would be justifiable, but I do not concede for a moment that such extreme measures are necessary.

Every evil which is attendant upon the present development of trusts can be restricted and finally eliminated by wise legislation under which the management and development of these corporations can be controlled and directed. The control and direction of such corporations can be affected with absolute certainty. The giant of capitalistic greed has bound himself with thongs which cannot be loosened, the genius of monopoly has placed itself in the bottle which has been tightly sealed. Experience has shown that old forms of trust, such as the Standard Oil trust originally was, cannot exist for an indefinite period in an incorporeal stage, that pools and agreements are not sufficiently binding or legal to be effective. The modern form of combinations for every purpose is therefore the corporation. Such a form is the only legal one, and in the form of a corporation nothing is easier than control by the law. A defiance of the creator by its creature, the corporation, can be followed with such penalties of forfeiture and confiscation that every act of the trust can be ascertained and directed by the law, and every officer compelled to do his duty. It is only necessary to have an enactment of a law by a competent body to compel its observance by the corporation, and such has been the result of legislation in restraint of corporate action even in this period when corporate wealth is so arrogant and aggressive. The manner of obtaining that competent authority will be discussed later, its use is now referred to. By this legal control and direction all of the evils of trusts can be successfully eliminated. The evil tendencies of these consolidations may be considered under three heads: First, an unreasonable and excessive increase of the price of the article or service, due to the stifling of competition; secondly, a wholesale discharge of employees, whereby the opportunities of mankind to earn a livelihood are seriously diminished, and, thirdly, a fictitious creation of capital values whereby the public are victimized. First as to the excessive price. The propriety of a law regulating the price to be charged for a commodity or a service, controlled by a trust, cannot be questioned. For half a century the courts of this country have been upholding the right of legislatures to regulate the reasonable charges of railroad and express companies, and of gas, water, electric light and street railway corporations. It is true that this right has been sustained on the ground that these services so regulated were of a quasi-public nature, but although this is the theory of the law, the basic principle is that the people are at a disadvantage in dealing with the corporation, because they must employ the company (it having practically a monopoly) or go without the service, and therefore the sovereign power steps in and makes a just regulation for their protection. It must be remembered that this advance has been made by the courts under existing constitutions and under present theories of industrial relations. Assuredly if it is just and proper that the citizen should be protected in the price that he should pay for the gas or water which he consumes, or for his transportation on the street car or railroad, how much more imperative that he should not be required to pay an exorbitant price for the sugar, beef or flour which his family consumes, or for the fuel or clothing which they require. This regulation of prices should be intrusted by Congress to commissions for each industry to be regulated, and such commissions should be selected from the skilled and trained employees in the several businesses or vocations, who have been deprived of employment by the consolidation of enterprises. Secondly, as to the discharge by corporations of a trust character of a number of its employees. Under the power to control and direct it would be within the province of Congress or of the states to vastly ameliorate the present semi-barbaric relationship between great corporations and their employees. If the resources and the conditions of the corporation should warrant it, the hours of labor might be shortened in a particular trade or business and thereby the number to be employed increased. Then again an inspection of the goods furnished, or the service rendered, so as to insure their quality and adequacy would be a source of employment for a number of those who have had experience in the particular industry. Moreover, a system of compulsory arbitration could be established, whereby the unfortunate strikes, which have been in the main most prejudicial to the common interests of employer and employee, might be permanently avoided. And again, by a wise system of taxation, levied upon these new great aggregations of wealth, a sufficient fund could be secured by the nation, and the municipalities, to establish channels of public enterprise in which everyone deprived of employment by the ever-changing conditions of the economic world could secure temporary employment until a footing could be obtained in another branch of industry. As to the remaining evil, that of overcapitalization, taxation and the weakness inherent in its organization would in a comparatively short time eliminate the inflation, or as it is now termed, liquid capital, and through receiverships and reorganizations this fault eventually would be cured. Through these methods, simply offered as suggestions, and which in practice would probably be vastly amended from the imperfect outlines which have been set forth, the system of trusts or combinations could be relieved from all the dangers which are now apparent. There may be other deleterious tendencies, but if so they are of a minor character, and can be successfully regulated and controlled.

We have so far considered the method of dealing with combinations or trusts which would appear to be most efficacious; the remaining question is as to the machinery by which the necessary control and direction of trusts can be made effective. The control, regulation and direction of all trusts, whose business either directly or indirectly is carried on in more than one state, should be placed under the jurisdiction of Congress. A similar jurisdiction over such combinations operating in a single state should be reposed in the respective State Legislatures. It would be almost suicidal to attempt such legislation under the present constitutional limitations both of the nation and the states. Let us cut the Gordian knot of endless constitutional discussion by adopting immediately an amendment to the federal Constitution which will confer the broadest power to deal with the subject upon Congress and the states in their respective spheres. The decisions of the Supreme Court in the Sugar Trust ·case, and in other cases, demonstrate the inability of the federal government to deal with the subject under the powers conferred by the interstate commerce clause of the Constitution. Every lawyer is familiar with the tendency of the court to destroy the effect of all state legislation affecting business or commerce between the states, by invoking the force of this same interstate commerce section. To allow this most momentous subject, under either federal or state legislation, to be the victim of narrow legal construction or baffling technicalities, or to be robbed of its efficacy by conflicting decisions of numerous state and federal courts, would be a blunder worse than the crimes which might be perpetrated under the trust system. The amendment should be couched in the most comprehensive terms. It should expressly confer adequate powers upon the states to legislate concerning trusts operating wholly within their borders, so that there may be no restraint upon state action on account of restraints imposed upon the states in certain clauses of the Constitution as it now stands. Then, too, the constitution of the state should be amended wherever there is any doubt as to present powers being adequate. This latter step is not so necessary at the present moment as the amendment to the national document. The proposed amendment should be passed by the present Congress at its first session. Then it can be submitted to the State Legislatures to be chosen in the year 1900, and in the present attitude of both parties to the subject should receive the approbation of the necessary three-fourths vote before the meeting of the Congress which will be elected at the coming presidential election. That Congress should be composed of men who will be ready and willing to take up the necessary legislation to make the control, regulation and direction of these combinations a lasting benefit to the entire people.

With this plan our beloved country can commence the twentieth century with a hope of a triumphant solution of the greatest of industrial problems. It is idle to attempt to forecast the ultimate results. The dreams of socialism may be realized, or cooperation may work out the destinies of mankind in an industrial and social republic differing widely from the fancies of imagination. But whatever may be the outcome, the substitution of the control of the people for the control of the trusts will make the future of the nation under the guidance of intelligence and lofty purpose forever secure.

JAMES R. WEAVER.

Professor of Political Economy, De Pauw University.

By economic limitations is meant all such checks or restrictions that a sound, enlightened study of economics should bring to bear upon trusts, to prevent them from becoming social evils, by appealing to the self-interest of the parties or corporations combined. By way of introduction, and to a clearer understanding of the subject, it should be borne in mind that all trusts, whether of labor or capital, possess two distinct sides or phases: First, that of co-operation, recognized as a natural right, only to be restricted when clearly detrimental to the welfare of society. This is its beneficent side. It stands over against excessive competition, being the corrective to destructive competition, hence is fundamental and deserves our highest praise; but, like all good things, when carried too far, it becomes an evil, taking on the form of monopoly, which not only regulates competition, but practically destroys it. It now in turn becomes injurious to society, if not limited to its proper functions. Possessed of despotic power, the monopolistic trust may become the source of great social evil. It may strive to levy tribute on smaller industrialists and consumers, much as did the feudal lords upon their serfs during the Middle Ages. This phase justly arouses social apprehensions, and merits our condemnation. The only or chief difference between capitalistic and labor trusts is one of power; but small despotisms may be as galling as great ones, as frequently revealed by labor organizations.

To distinguish in practice between the good and evil phases of trusts is not an easy task. To find a solution or remedy for the monopolistic phase, even when distinguished, may well baffle human ingenuity, from the fact that it depends so largely upon conditions and limitations, and frequently upon a hidden purpose of those combining. Hitherto, all social appliances have fallen short of the demands of society to regulate monopolistic trusts, and this conference witnesses with great emphasis the general unrest in regard to the recent manifestations and expansion of trusts in general. Again, as trusts are competitive as well as monopolistic, it is rather of the former that this paper seeks to deal, since the latter can often, at least for a time, violate the laws of political economy without suffering the penalty of such violation. Hence while monopolistic trusts must generally be more rigorously controlled or even prohibited by law, competitive trusts may be generally sufficiently restricted by the operation of economic laws. This latter phase is especially considered.

Like all social questions, the elements of the trust are so multiform as to preclude the hope of ever discovering any single satisfactory remedy. Doubtless the solution must be as complex as the evil to be remedied; that is to say, while rational economics and ethics must in the end prevail, legislation and public opinion must frequently enforce their behests. But great caution should be used in the exercise of legal restrictions, lest individual initiative be crippled and discouraged, resulting in a serious check to our present industrial progress. Hence I firmly believe that the economic checks should be primary and fundamental, since these appeal directly to the self-interests of the trusts themselves, and as yet neither science nor art nor philosophy has found a substitute for that original incentive to human industry, viz., self-interest.

But what can reasonably be hoped from the application of the soundest principles of economics in regard to trusts? Much, I affirm; though doubtless not everything desired, and to formulate these is my self-imposed task. The principal dangers from trusts and especially from those in which competition is still possible, which I denominate competitive or semi-monopolistic trusts for which we seek a remedy, may be categoried briefly under four heads: But in noting them in order, and proposing certain checks thereto, space permits only the broadest generalizations, mere suggestions without specific statistical or other satisfactory proofs, to supply which everyone must test them for himself by means of his best philosophy and experience, supported by the most reliable statistical data available.

The first one to be mentioned is that these colossal organizations have created a great displacement of labor, that is by these combinations many employees have been thrown out of employment, which is undoubtedly true; for while some expansion of labor may follow, for the present many are stranded by being dropped from the pay-rolls of the absorbed firms, being no longer needed. Here economics affords relatively but little consolation, for no effective arguments can be given for the employment of useless labor, just as when the skilled artisan finds himself supplanted by an ingenious labor-saving machine. We certainly pity him in his sacrifice for the welfare of society, but the machine must neither be boycotted nor destroyed. In like manner, when in consequence of the better organization of productive agencies, middle-men and commercial travelers are dropped, and thousands of small entrepreneurs are subordinated to the powerful centralized combination, great sympathy is felt for the suffering, but progress must not be stayed, even if some sacrifice attend the process. However, even here one check against the arbitrary actions of the trusts is found, in the fact that if these capable men be unjustly treated, or not somehow provided for, to the limit of the possible, dangerous competitive rivals are sure to spring up, detrimental to the prosperity of the trust, on the general principle that only by distributing power can power be accumulated; hence these higher organizations dare not unduly subordinate the elements out of which they are composed, as injurious competition would arise, to meet which would be more expensive than considerate treatment.

The second danger from trusts is financial, viz., overcapitalization. This is so manifest, however, that it may in the main be left to individual correctives. The undue confidence of investors, and especially those of small means, may permit speculators to unload upon innocent parties much inflated or watered stock. Then later the business is wrecked, sometimes purposely, not only to the destruction of the victims, but to the creating of a general mistrust that may lead to a general financial crisis. Still it must be said that trusts are no more likely than many other forms of speculation to deceive the unwary; and the public, particularly banking institutions, are so keenly alive to this danger that being forewarned is forearmed. A wise precaution against over-speculation is one of the elementary tenets of economics. If this self-interest be supplemented by due publicity, but little, if any, social damage would likely follow from overcapitalization of trusts. At any rate, such danger is not confined to trusts, but exists as well in all corporations, partnerships, and even individual enterprises. That is, overcapitalization is not confined to trusts, and ordinary care or economic provisions should be sufficient protection against abuses, but if not, where legislative regulation can avail, the latter should be employed.

But the third danger from the modern trust which is uppermost in the minds of all is generally regarded as the danger par excellence, for this threatens our entire industrial régime. It concerns every consumer, for, if true, it enhances the price of his morning meal and his lamplight by night. It has become the nightmare of politicians, thrusting upon them the greatest of all political issues. This threatening danger is formulated in the question as to its effect upon prices and the rate of wages. It would seem that here we have the crux of the whole matter. If political science and organic society are incapable of furnishing an answer to this question, and supplying a remedy for the supposed evil, both are doomed from imbecility in the hour of great need. Here is where we need light rather than heat, for practical experience has by no means answered in the affirmative this query as to the injurious effect on prices and wages. Investigation, if possible, must yet supply the practical data to test economic law in respect thereto. Fortunately, however, as we believe, economic theory permits us to prognosticate, viz., that a potent check is found in the self-interest of the trusts themselves against inflating prices or lowering wages, but that the opposite tendency should be found in any rational and wisely administered trust or combination. This conclusion follows from the two following considerations. Briefly stated, they are: First, any undue advantage taken of the consumer by the superior power of the trusts is bound sooner or later to react upon them detrimentally, and, if not corrected, will finally overthrow them totally. It can hardly be questioned that trusts steady market prices, thus preventing ruinous fluctuations and possibly crises greatly destructive of our industrial well being, and it is generally realized by the trusts themselves, with but few exceptions, probably, that a safe business must be conducted rationally and in conformity with the best principles of legitimate trade. Therefore, we should expect that the folly of raising prices which would react against their prosperity could only be temporary or exceptional. Further, the reduction of expenses by these combinations is very evident. In most instances this has been the producing cause. Competition, by becoming so sharp as to be almost destructive, demands co-operation as a corrective. This is the highest manifestation of the trust. The two poles of industrial activity are fair competition and free co-operation. These must mutually check each other if a wise harmony prevails.

It must not be forgotten that the chief elements of effective competition are complete knowledge and perfect mobility of the competing factors, and that although labor may not possess these two elements equally with capital, that small capitalists usually possess them with great capitalists; hence the effect of capitalistic competition is always powerful if not absolutely perfect, and should result in securing equal returns to last increment of energy employed, that trusts are largely combination of capital to reduce the sharp competition of capital, that the conflict is between capitalists, rather than between capital and labor.

But even when trusts take on their monopolistic or semi-monopolistic form, they must conform still under general conditions to the laws of trade. To do this they must offer to society, the consuming public, at least a portion of their profits, and for

JAMES B. DILL   EDWARD ROSEWATER
J. G. SCHONFARBER   JOHN BATES CLARK
EDWARD P. RIPLEY   M. L. LOCKWOOD

very good reasons. Their success depends generally on the magnitude of consumption, and any unfair treatment of the public would arouse such resentment that patronage would necessarily be lost. This can be done by refusing to buy, and further by boycotting the product of the offending trust, wherever found. Even trusts must court public favor by offering a better and a cheaper article, and this they can do best through the magnitude of their production and the superiority of their appliances. Now, as trusts, as a rule, are dependent on increased rather than diminished consumption, public opinion can whip them into line should they demand too high a price for their products, to the end that the legitimate outcome of the trusts must be lower rather than higher prices. The same argument may be applied to wages.

But, secondly, in case the consumer cannot influence the trust in this manner, there is another economic factor that rarely fails in accomplishing the same end, and I believe facts will always bear out this position, if carefully examined. This corrective may be dominated technically the potential competition of capital, and it is a well-known fact that at present a great mass of idle capital exists in the hands of enterprising men ready to enter any specific field of production, whenever the profits of that industry offer sufficient inducement. So that, to avoid this new competition, prices must be lowered or profits shared with the consumer. True, their gains may be for a time concealed, but in these days of enterprise and publicity that is next to impossible. Therefore, are we not justified in concluding that economic law of itself supplies at least these two potent checks against any material permanent rise of prices by the trusts? Where freedom to enter any industry is full and free, and where monopolistic franchises have not been foolishly or fraudulently granted, which is becoming less now every day, individual initiative and competition may be largely trusted to counteract any tendency to raise prices, but must in the very nature of the case force them to the lowest practicable point. The same law would hold in respect to wages. But here, moreover, the combinations of labor and the higher standard of living reinforces the other tendencies.

An additional danger may be mentioned, though variously regarded by its advocates and enemies, viz., that trusts are a long step toward state socialism. It would seem an easy matter to reassure those who fear the socialistic tendencies of trusts. They rather, if anything, lead in the opposite direction, viz., to anarchy, the extreme antithesis of socialism. Should trusts finally become so politically powerful as to take the government by the throat, then the masses, in the absence of any other remedy, should revolt, and bring about a social revolution. Still, we are rather upon the eve of a social evolution than revolution, for never in the history of the world has the common man counted for so much in politics. No, they need not resort to revolution, but wisely and conservatively operate through economic competition and combination, and finally through legislation, to secure any wise and needed reform. Again, the advocates of socialism should readily understand the difference between the trusts and the socialistic state. Their purposes are diametrically antagonistic; for one is individualistic, or co-operatively individualistic, based upon the egoism of human nature, while the other is altruistic, based on the sacrifice of self. Hence, what under present competitive individualistic conditions proves a success for the trust, which is a co-operation of the most capable organizers, the great captains or leaders of industry, limited in number, so that unity of purpose can be preserved, and all for their personal gain, why should these not succeed? But contrast with this the socialistic program, even the highest and most ideal, where is any ground of hope for success from any analogy? Socialism must organize the whole mass, capables and incapables alike, and not for the welfare of self, but of the whole. Beautiful ideal, certainly, but too angelic for this world of human passions and selfish hearts. Is it too much to affirm that any rational comprehension of the fundamental principles of political economy scientifically based on human nature as we find it, must preclude both the fears of the enemies and the hopes of the friends of state socialism? That is, no logical analogue is found in the trust.

Still, while these various checks upon the trust have been emphasized, we dare not conclude that all men, or even the majority of them, are subject to such checks, for all do not act rationally or even wisely for their own self interest, much less the common good. Until men are controlled from within, they must be regulated from without. Hence, legal compulsion must reinforce public opinion based on economic and ethical law. Legislation, therefore, must not abdicate its function, but at the proper moment and in the wisest manner see to it that trusts, like any other agencies—yea, more so, on account of the power they yield—are not permitted to sacrifice public welfare; that is, place themselves beyond the laws of political economy. Some propositions are self-evident here; all trusts made monopolistic by franchises or public favor should be destroyed by being nationalized or otherwise; freedom of competition must be guaranteed, hence all other trusts may be regulated by publicity and taxation. The great difficulty, however, is not so much in the form of the combination as in the mass of the capital. This mass may be even more detrimental to society by being in the hands of one individual. Then what? Must we check individual power by limiting the amount of capital in any one enterprise, whether in corporate or individual hands? We are not ready for this yet, but as trusts are in the line of economic progress, how is it possible to check them other than by legal restrictions as to amount of capital, as well as by publicity, etc.?

But I would first exhaust the economic checks before resorting to legislative authority; would plead for individual liberty, limited, of course, by the higher rights of society; I would strive to educate morally and economically before calling in the extreme rigor of the law. For these reasons personally I am still optimistic, even in regard to the trusts, believing that the economic checks here briefly suggested cannot fail to operate substantially upon a wisely educated body of industrial organizers; for if this can be made effectual, we save untrammeled individual initiative, that mainspring of progress, that God-given lever to push the race onward in the path of civilization. Let us, therefore, only regulate and rationalize, and not destroy the trust when not monopolistic. But if these economic checks fail, then, for the time being, force must reinforce moral suasion, and the highest principles of self-interest for society must be saved. It is not the function of this paper to point out the specific method of legal restriction, but leave that to the conservative wisdom of statesmen and other members of this conference to formulate.

W. P. POTTER.

Member of Pennsylvania Bar.

In order to understand the present situation, it is necessary to look back a little. During the period of time extending from 1892 to 1898, the business community throughout this entire country was suffering as it had never suffered before, from what seemed to be chronic overproduction.

The result of this was to bring about excessive competition in all lines of business. In the anxiety to find purchasers, prices were cut below the limits of reasonable remuneration. This evil of excessive competition seemed to prevail everywhere. Discouragement marked every department of trade. In the effort to obtain relief the wages of labor were reduced. This only led to additional complications. The workingmen strove by the only means at their command, to save themselves, and strikes and lockouts were instituted, with the usual distressful accompaniments.

The only effective means of overcoming this condition seemed to be the obvious one of an understanding among the producers in various lines, as to the prices to be asked for their commodities.

Regulation in this respect was possible only through a union of interests upon the part of those engaged in the same line of business. Ordinary trade agreements were hard to enforce, and were readily disregarded in the effort to obtain business.

Naturally the next step, in the effort to regulate production, and sustain prices at reasonable levels, was to combine the holdings of the various parties interested, and concentrate the capital engaged, so far as might be feasible, into one corporation. No reasonable objection could be made to this action, for the uniting of different properties under one management, and under one control, upon a fair valuation, could not be harmful to the general public.

In this connection I desire to say that during the progress of this whole movement, the result of trade combinations has thus far not shown in a single case that the operation has been prejudicial to the rights of the public.

It is but the statement of a simple fact to say that the present tendency toward combination and co-operation is the reaction from the keen and excessive competition of the past few years. Whether this movement for co-operation is justifiable or not, depends upon the facts in the case. Whether for good or evil is to be determined by an examination of the results. "By their fruits ye shall know them," and in arriving at a conclusion, calm and careful consideration is called for, and the subject should be approached in a spirit of fairness, and not in bitterness or with blind denunciation. An impulse so general, and so widespread in the business world, must have cause for its existence.

The rights of the public are not to be ignored in any event; but so long as these rights are respected, the individual is certainly at liberty to concentrate his capital and combine his resources with his fellows in the same line of business for their mutual benefit.

The demand for commodities of all kinds at the present time is greatly in excess of what it has ever been, and it is required, too, that they be furnished more cheaply than ever before. Experience has shown that these demands can be met only by the employment of large capital, and upon a most extensive scale of working.

Civilization has advanced, and a comfortable scale of living has been brought within reach of the average man, just in proportion to the development of business along these lines of cooperation and combination. First, it was the individual working by himself in his particular line. Then came the union of two or more individuals into a partnership. This was followed by the formation of the small corporation, and from that grew the larger corporation, and the last and present stage of development is the union or partnership of the smaller corporations, into the grand aggregation, often miscalled a trust.

As a matter of fact most of the business combinations of the day are not trusts at all. They are simply large corporations. The so-called "anti-trust" attacks are not really attacks upon trusts, for the reason that but very few real trusts are in existence in this country. The hue and cry that has been raised is really an attack upon large corporations. If the people of this country are determined to wipe out all corporations, of course they can do so. No one would claim, however, that such an extreme measure is desired by anyone who has the prosperity of the country at heart. Such action would be to turn backward the hands upon the dial of human progress, and 90 per cent of the country's industries would stop.

To the community as a whole, large corporations are neither injurious nor dangerous. On the contrary, the economies effected by the concentration and combination of capital and its direction by competent management means always the cheapening of commodities to the public.

During the process of reconstruction, there may be individual cases of hardship. Certain men may lose their positions, but this grows out of the economy effected by the new organization, and is one of the things which tend to cheapen the cost of production under the new circumstances. In this respect, there is no difference in the effect from that caused by the introduction of labor-saving machinery, and yet the day has long gone by when remonstrance is effectual against the introduction of appliances for saving labor upon the ground that certain operators will be thrown out of employment thereby.

It is admitted upon all hands that when the general result is for the good of the public, individual cases must be met and adjusted as best they may. In the old days of teaming over the mountains of Pennsylvania, the building of a canal was opposed by the teamsters on the ground that it would hurt their business;

at a later day, the canal boatmen in turn opposed the building of a railroad for the same reason, but boatmen and teamsters alike had to give way for the advance of the new and improved mode of transportation. Oftentimes, too, the injury was more apparent than real, as in the case cited, the drivers of the teams, and captains and crews of the boats, many of them, at least, found employment as railroad employes, and so were really not injured by the change.

Following along the line of the thought just suggested, in the early days of railroad building, the companies were small and the roads were short, and their capital was limited. Independent railroad corporations dotted the country here and there, with short lines. Rates of freight and passenger fares were high. No contract for through or continuous carriage could be made. Now note what happened in the case of the projection and development of the Pennsylvania Railroad system. Freight rates were about five cents per ton per mile. The process of combination of the little roads into one great system began. One road after another was taken in, until the Pennsylvania system now is made up of more than two hundred and fifty companies, which were formerly separate and independent organizations. The result has been that with a continued and steady improvement in the service, the rates of freight have steadily fallen, until now the cost of moving a ton of freight per mile, instead of being five cents, is less than one-half of a cent.

Can anyone say that any harm has resulted to the interests of the public from the consolidation in this case? Here is one of the largest combinations in the country, and, next to the Standard Oil Company, possibly railroads are the subject of attack more than any other class of corporations. I submit that the facts do not warrant it. The Pennsylvania Railroad furnishes employment for more than one hundred thousand men, and these men probably support upon an average, each of them five persons, so that five hundred thousand people depend for their subsistence upon the prosperity of this one great corporation. And this is not all—for, in addition to the wages paid employes, we must remember that a large proportion of its earnings go steadily back to the community for the purchase of supplies. More than forty millions of dollars a year are poured from this one source into the channels of commerce. The amount is widely distributed too, as the articles purchased range from soap and matches to monster locomotives and steel bridges a mile long.

This is a striking instance, but it is by no means an isolated one, of the good accomplished by means of great combinations of capital. The larger the scale upon which an industry is carried on, the better as a rule is the provision made for the health and comfort of the workers. Here again the experience of the Pennsylvania Railroad is an instance in point. It has from time to time reduced the hours of labor of its train crews, and as its last and crowning effort in behalf of its employes, it is now putting into operation a system of retiring them at the age of seventy, upon a pension sufficient for their support. Surely there is nothing in the action of this company to justify the assertion that corporations have no souls.

Take another familiar illustration of combinations upon a large scale, which appears in almost every large city in the country. It has been notably effective in my own home in the city of Pittsburgh. The street railway system. A few years ago we had perhaps a dozen different lines in the vicinity. The cars were small, and were drawn by horses, and a separate five-cent fare had to be paid on every car boarded. With the introduction of electric motive power, larger capital was needed to accomplish the best results, and consequently the small roads were combined, and complete and extensive traction systems were organized, with arrangements for transfers, so that to-day, for the same five-cent fare, you can ride from one extremity to the other, several times as far, and twice as fast, and in cars in every way more commodious and comfortable.

Is a combination producing such a result to be hastily condemned, or destroyed?

It is only when work is carried on upon a small scale that long hours of labor, low wages, and unsanitary conditions are found to prevail. Individual employers are the ones who run the sweat shops and employ child labor. In large corporations, the rule is that hours of labor are shortened, and with them there is a general acknowledgment of the rights of the employees. The larger the concern is, the greater, too, is the steadiness of employment, and the more influential in the public opinion is the standing of the employee.

With the good management which they are able to employ, and the immense amount of business which they can handle, the average rate of wages rises, while the price of the service, or of the product, as a rule continues to fall.

There are instances where the prices in certain lines of business owing to the fact of unregulated and excessive competition, have for long periods been continuously too low to afford reasonable remuneration. Let me cite an instance which has come under my own observation. It is that of the production of bituminous coal. The city of Pittsburgh is in the center of the bituminous district. For the past twenty years, the firms engaged in the production and shipment of coal have struggled along in keen and sharp competition and have been unable to make anything in the business. Many of them have succumbed to the pressure and been driven out altogether. Almost constant disputes and friction with the miners has been the inevitable result. The employers simply have been unable to pay a living rate of wages. During the past few months the influence of the present tendency towards combination as a check upon excessive competition has reached this industry, and to-day a combination is in process of formation, which already has enabled the employers to effect a slight advance in the selling price of coal, and this, with the various economies which co-operation can effect, will enable them to obtain a fair return for their capital, and at the same time permit of an increase in the wages of the miners.

Here again is a practical instance of great good accomplished, and its characteristics are those common to all similar combinations. There can be no denial that they carry with them certain positive economic advantages. They decrease the cost of the product, first, by doing away with the wasteful methods of competitive business, and, second, by the introduction of improved methods of work.

They are also enabled by the exercise of intelligent and skilled oversight of the business, to prevent overproduction, by means of their ability to ascertain the state of the markets, and regulate the supply in accordance therewith. By constant study of the conditions of the business in all its phases, as in the case of the Standard Oil Company, they are enabled to increase the demand for a product, and thus enlarge the consumption. They are able also to provide vastly increased facilities for transportation, and by reason of all these conditions are enabled to furnish goods at lower prices than would otherwise be possible.

If abuses should arise, these organizations are at all times amenable to the law; and the states are able to provide against violation of reasonable statutes. No combination will ever be able to maintain abnormal prices, for the reason that such a course would call into play the possibility of practical competition, and this possibility will always operate as a check. Another thing which will prevent any undue increase in price is the fact that any great advance in price tends to lessen the demand. Nothing is better known to experience, than the fact that the profits of any business are more easily and permanently increased by the cheapening of cost, and not by the raising of prices.

In all the combinations that have thus far been made, prices have been but slightly advanced by reason of the consolidation. The rise has been the result of the unusual demand, and has been as great, if not greater, in lines where no combination exists. As an example, pig tin has advanced 75 per cent; steel plates 127 per cent; refined bar iron 82 per cent; steel rails 94 per cent. Yet in none of these is there a combination. In all these commodities and many others, prices have gone up simply because of the physical inability of the manufacturers to meet the demand.

I affirm, therefore, that the movement toward consolidation is the outgrowth of natural conditions, and opposition to it is based upon a misunderstanding of the fact that it is the application of a great and effectual remedy, to the demoralization of business, which was the result of unlicensed and excessive competition. Any attempt to crush out or interfere with the proper and reasonable workings of this remedy is utterly hopeless. The movement is bound to continue until practically all industrial activities are brought into a system of co-operation.

You can supervise, and you can regulate, if desired. You can establish a national board of supervision over corporations doing interstate business. You can limit the amount of capital in any one corporation, if thought wise. You can correct abuses if, and as, they arise. But the people who have learned from bitter experience in the past the effect of the competitive system, will not give up the right to co-operate in the conduct of their business, in the future.

FRANCIS G. NEWLANDS.

Member Congress, Nevada.

First.—The term "trust" is a misnomer as applied to the combination of capital which has aroused so much solicitude. The old trust was a combination of independent producers to fix the price of a particular commodity. Such a combination could be annulled through the courts as an agreement in restraint of trade. To-day the same object is accomplished in a legal way, viz.: by a union of capital in one great corporation which purchases the property of the independent producer and makes them all stockholders in a common enterprise. Capital has learned from labor unions the wisdom of co-operation, and co-operation is now largely substituted both in labor and capitalistic unions for the old principle of competition.

It is contended with much force that, if the right of laborers to combine and fix the price of labor by preventing the individual laborers from competing for a job by the acceptance of lower compensation is conceded, it must also be conceded that capital has the same right. It must be recollected, however, that the labor union is formed for the purpose of obtaining for labor an increased share of the profits of production, and that the accomplishment of such a purpose is a distinct advantage to society, and should be favored, whilst the capitalistic union may so exercise its power as to depress the price of labor and to unduly raise the price of products, and as this power can only be exercised through an artificial being called a corporation, which is the creation of the state, it is the right and duty of the state to limit and control it.

Second.—Tariff legislation will not reach the difficulty, for whilst it may be true that the field of competition is restricted by the tariff wall, thus making the organization of a domestic trust easier by reason of the lack of foreign competition, yet it must be recollected that combinations of capital exist in England, France and Germany to-day, and that the effect of lowering the tariff wall would simply be to substitute a foreign trust for a domestic trust in the control of our markets. This would be at the expense not only of American capital but of American labor. The laborers now employed by our domestic trusts would be idle; their places would be taken by laborers employed abroad by the foreign trusts; the remedy would be worse than the disease. The American union of capital might be destroyed, but with it would go down the American union of labor.

The prosperity of the republic is founded upon the prosperity of American laborers. All legislation should place the American man above the American dollar, but it should not, in its endeavor to rectify the abuses of American unions of capital, take away the employment of the American laborers. What we should do is to maintain for American laborers and American capital the practical monopoly of American markets, and at the same time by domestic legislation inside of the tariff wall, so restrain unions of capital as to prevent them from oppressing the laborer on the one side and the consumer on the other.

Third.—All attempts to regulate capital by state legislation will fail simply because it will be impossible to produce voluntary co-operation among the various states. Some states will welcome the advantages which capital extends to them for permitting their territory to become the spawning ground of trusts, and as long as one state fails to co-operate, trusts will multiply.

Fourth.—The only adequate remedy is through federal legislation, the operation of which will be uniform throughout the republic. It is true that the federal government cannot prevent the organization of state corporations, nor is this desirable; but it can, through its power regarding the regulation of interstate commerce, restrain their operations, and it can use its taxing power in such a way as either to destroy or to regulate and control. The power relating to the regulation of interstate commerce is hardly sufficient to meet the evil, as evasion would be easy. Any trust could restrain its operations to the limits of the state under the laws of which it was organized; at the same time purchasers from other states could buy in such state. The sale would be domestic, the transfer of the product would be interstate, and legislation aimed at the trust in its interstate business might thus be evaded.

Fifth.—The power of taxation of the federal government is ample to meet the difficulty, and it is much more far-reaching than the power exercised under the interstate commerce section of the Constitution. The power of taxation can be used either to destroy or restrain, and it has been so used within our experience.

Thus, for instance, as to the undoubted right of state banks to issue currency under state statutes permitting it, the federal government does not deny the right, but it has seen fit to impose a tax of ten per cent upon state bank currency and thus practically to prohibit its issue.

So, also, with reference to oleomargarine. The beef trust had organized for the production and sale of oleomargarine upon a great scale. Oleomargarine was innocuous and resembled in appearance and taste the genuine butter. The use of this material was threatening the destruction of the dairy interests of the country, in which large amounts of capital were invested, and hundreds of thousands of people were employed. The states took hold of the matter and by legislation within their own boundaries sought to protect the dairy interests and restrain the oleomargarine interests. Their legislation was, in the main, ineffective, and so recourse was had to the federal government for a far-reaching law. The result was that the power of taxation was so exercised by the federal government as to restrain the oleomargarine interests and to protect the dairy interests. Thus, oleomargarine was made a subject of revenue to the government and the tax imposed upon it served to limit its competitive efficiency.

Here, then, we have two illustrations of the power of federal taxation; one the power to destroy, the other the power to regulate and restrain. Why cannot this power be used with reference to the modern trust, and in a most efficient way? Through it two evils can be reached—one, the monopoly of production by unions of capital, and the other the escape of organized wealth under present conditions from the burthens of federal taxation. The latter is one of the crying evils of the times. The whole tendency of federal legislation has been to exempt accumulated wealth. The wealth of the country has been for years rapidly drifting into corporations. Stocks in corporations represent, more than any other class of property, the surplus wealth of the country, for the man who has a share of stock has something which he has accumulated over and above his current wants and expenditures, and the best method of reaching the surplus wealth of the country is to tax corporations. It is true that the income tax decision has in a measure restricted the field of federal taxation. It practically exempts real property and its income, and personal property and its income, from internal revenue taxation; yet the field of federal taxation is still a large one, for it embraces all the transactions of business and though the real and personal property of a corporation and the income therefrom cannot be directly reached, yet every transaction in which such corporations engage may be made the subject of taxation by the federal government, and the taxes imposed may be classified in such a way as to restrain unions of capital in their monopolistic tendencies.

Now, it is well understood that the great monopolies of production can only be accomplished through the formation of gigantic corporations. The formation of those gigantic corporations means concentrated control, diminution of the number of officials, improved economies in every line. From the standpoint of economics it is hard to point out any danger to which society is subjected by their creation, so long as their only purpose is the conservation of energy; but they go further than this. If allowed to go unchecked they will undoubtedly attack labor itself by the diminution of its wages. The ordinary producer, having but one factory, cannot afford to get into a controversy with his employees for that would involve an absolute cessation of the work of his enterprise. A corporation owning a dozen factories can easily operate eleven whilst it is engaged in bringing the operatives of the twelfth to its terms, and thus step by step can bring about a reduction of wages throughout all of its twelve factories. So, also, having destroyed competition, it can raise the price of its products and thus increase the profits of capital both by diminished wages of its employees and increased prices charged to its consumers. It can also destroy all competition by selling its products below cost within the territory of competitive operation, retaining its prices in the field of its monopoly, and thus, without loss in the aggregate, yield to a localized loss which will destroy all competitive enterprises. Thus the individual stands no chance against the corporation, and individualism is practically destroyed.

The purpose, then, of federal legislation upon this subject would be to reach accumulated wealth, and at the same time protect individualism. Taxes, therefore, imposed upon the transactions of corporations, will accomplish both purposes. They will reach accumulated wealth and they will protect individualism, for the individual, freed from the handicap of such taxes, may be able to hold his own and thus the handicap of the tax will preserve the equilibrium between individual enterprises on the one hand and corporate enterprises on the other.

It is true that it will take time to work out this problem wisely and justly, but I see no reason why progressive legislation advancing with conservatism, step by step, should not ultimately reach every difficulty. The first step should be the organization of a Bureau of Industry, somewhat resembling that of the Bureau of the Controller of the Currency, to which report should be made by all corporations, showing the amount of their capital stock, their bonds, their income, their transactions, the number of operatives employed, the wages paid and all the other data which in time will present a mass of statistical information that will aid and guide legislation. Publicity itself will do much in the way of correcting evils, for definite statistics will suggest definite remedies. The tax at first inaugurated should be moderate. It should reach at first only those great organizations whose evil effects upon modern individualism is conceded, and reliance should be placed upon the statistics accumulated later on, to furnish suggestions for additional tax legislation.

The powers of the federal government relating to taxation and interstate commerce in connection with published reports should be ample to meet every difficulty. No time should be wasted in academic discussion as to the precise evils that may result from unions of capital, or as to whether such evils have as yet been realized. Accumulated wealth should contribute more than it does to the federal revenue. This is a sufficient reason for commencing immediately with corporations, even if, as is claimed, the evil of unions of capital are imaginary. The machinery being prepared by law, the evils can be taken hold of as they arise, and taxation so levied as to restrain if that only is desirable, or to destroy if relief is otherwise unobtainable.

U. M. ROSE.

Little Rock Board of Trade.

Reference may be made to the Arkansas statute of March 6, 1899, restraining trusts, as a piece of experimental legislation. It provides, in short, that all persons and corporations that shall become a party to any pool, trust or combination, for the purpose of fixing prices of merchandise, commodities, premiums of insurance, etc., enumerated at great length, "shall be deemed and adjudged guilty of a conspiracy to defraud," and subject to a punishment of from $200 to $5,000. For every offense, each day of the continuance of such pool, etc., to be a separate offence, and it was declared that offending domestic corporations should forfeit their charters, and that offending foreign corporations should forfeit their privilege of doing business in the state. Moreover, foreign corporations were made subject to the same penalties as domestic corporations.

It will be observed that the statute did not specify the place where the combinations were made in order to render parties to them subject to its penalties. The attorney-general at once brought about one hundred and fifty suits against foreign insurance companies and foreign manufacturing companies for a forfeiture of privileges of doing business in the state, and for the recovery of the penalties denounced by the statute.

Some of the defendants demurred because the complaints did not allege that the alleged combinations were not formed either in the state or with a view to fix prices of commodities, etc., in the state; while others answered, denying that they had entered into any combination in the state, or having for its object the fixing of prices in the state.

The cases went to the Supreme Court, where it was held that where a criminal or penal statute does not purport to have been intended to have an extra-territorial operation it must be held to apply only to offences committed within the state; consequently that the answers set up a valid defence. The decision in the matter is to be found in State vs. Lancaster Fire Ins. Co., 51 S. W. R. 633. As soon as it was rendered the attorney-general dismissed all of the pending suits.

There is nothing novel about the decision; the principle is elementary and axiomatic. Indeed, the same court had decided the same thing in 1856, in State vs. Chapin, 17 Ark. 561.

It remains to be said that as soon as this statute was passed all of the foreign insurance companies doing business in the state, with one exception, I believe, closed their doors and declined to do any business until the question of their liability under this severe statute should be settled. As soon as it was settled they resumed.

It must be obvious that legislation along this line does not reach the heart of the matter. Of course it is possible to drive all foreign corporations out of any state by legislative enactment; but while such a course would cause a great shock to public business as now organized, the real evils would not be affected. We might expel foreign corporations engaged in manufacturing nails, for example, but people would still have to buy nails, as they are articles of necessity; while the nail trust would continue to duplicate prices as heretofore. The same thing is true of nearly all other manufactured commodities. Laws against monopolies are of very ancient origin, based on principles of public policy that have found expression in some of our state constitutions, and which have for long periods lain as disused weapons in the armory of the law; until now, when something of the kind is needed, it is found that they are quite inadequate to the occasion. Our government has survived so many perils, and our confidence in its ability to overcome all difficulties has become so robust, that any one who ventures to express any distrust of the future is apt to be considered as a modern Cassandra, indulging in groundless forebodings; but the admitted fact that within a few years past we have undergone a social revolution of a kind and a magnitude wholly unknown to history, one that places power in the hands of comparatively a handful of individuals to control the prices of most articles of manufacture, thereby enriching themselves at will, while they impoverish the vast multitude of consumers; that various corporations representing fabulous wealth are in a position to exercise exclusive dominion over nearly all of the industries of the country, and to impose excessive burdens on the rest of their countrymen precisely as does the patentee of a new invention, except that their dominion acknowledges no limitation in respect of time or law, must surely afford food for the gravest reflection.

If the recent and enormous aggregation of wealth under corporate control, running into billions, and putting to shame the budgets of the most powerful nations on earth, were alone to be regarded, the present emergency is full of suggestions of a sudden collapse exceeding in its disastrous consequences those that resulted from the inflictions of John Law in France, or of the South Sea Bubble in England. The speedy growth of this extraordinary development, like the conquests of Alexander, Cæsar and Napoleon, foretells its sudden collapse, whose ruinous effects must, as usual in such cases, fall chiefly on the innocent, the inexperienced and the unwary. During the Middle Ages, when there were neither bonds nor stocks, and but little personal property of any kind, a monopoly of lands led to the establishment of the feudal system, the most blighting and desolating that ever afflicted mankind. In a time of ignorance it managed by mere physical force to perpetuate its existence for centuries, and to check the evolution of progress, which, in the present period of enlightenment, travels with lightning speed, so that no such exceptional longevity can be expected for a new feudalism based on vast accumulations of corporate wealth, which has no armed castles for defense, and is condemned by principles of public policy equally immemorial and indestructible.

As a people and as individuals we have been nurtured in convictions that are hostile to monopolies, and those convictions will hardly be weakened by the present exigencies. Never since the controversy growing out of African slavery have the people of this country been confronted with any question of equal importance and of equal difficulty. The question of slavery was settled by England, Russia, Spain and Brazil without any great expenditure of money, and without the shedding of blood; but American statesmanship, inadequate to cope with the situation, had to resort to a war in which, considering its incalculable expense in money and the destruction of property, more was lost than would have paid for the slaves many times over, to say nothing of the fearful loss of life.

The present situation contains, I believe, all of the elements of socialism, anarchy and that *deus ex machinâ*, imperialism, that always emerges at the proper moment. The question as to the suitable remedy to be applied is one that has exercised and baffled the strongest minds. The proposal to drive foreign corporations out of particular states, and thus to build around them a Chinese wall of exclusion, will not attain the desired end. We shall still have to buy everything almost that we require at prices arbitrarily fixed by the monopolies which, intrenched behind charters granted by other states, defy legislation of that kind, saying, "If you do not buy of us you cannot buy at all."

We are told that if all of the states and the federal government will concur in the proper legislation pending evils may be corrected, and future ills may be prevented; but the principle of unanimity, which in Poland was sometimes tempered by assassination, is not practicable in our government. At no time since its organization has uniformity of legislation been secured; and the prospect of such uniformity at present seems slim and remote.

As it has been decided by the federal court of last resort that Congress has no delegated power to restrain the organization of trusts and combines between manufacturing companies, it is needless to expect efficient aid from a body which it is incompetent to grant. To hope for remedy or redress from the mere lapse of time would seem to be madness. By amendment to the Constitution of the United States, Congress can be invested with power to deal with the evil in all of its phases, just as the English parliament dealt with it as long ago as the reign of Edward VI.; but this step is one of such profound and far-reaching importance that it will necessarily excite the distrust and opposition of many that view the present situation with unfeigned alarm, and whose hostility to monopolies is sincere and lasting.

The problem is one that will be exploited by the political demagogue, whose words darken counsel; but violent and inflammatory declamation can avail nothing. What is needed is the deliberate wisdom of the statesman who will act with an eye single to the public security and welfare.

I am not of the opinion that laws requiring publicity in the keeping of corporate books and accounts will meet the objects in view. Similar laws have been often passed, and have been constantly evaded with impunity. The search for truth in the intricate maze of corporate documents has proved to be extremely discouraging.

In the meantime the problem clamors for solution. Every day we hear of new combinations, extending in their range from steam engines to peanuts. If the public prints are to be believed, millions are sometimes paid to agents who succeed in effecting these trusts or pools, however created. It can hardly be doubted that much of this money entrusted to "promoters" is used for purposes of bribery and corruption. Every day we hear that superfluous factories or mines have been closed, and that hundreds of men have been thrown out of employment. The same thing happened in England when railroads and improved spinning machinery were introduced; but the whole country was enriched and benefited by these inventions; not so with monopolies, which have always proved to be mere festering cancers on the body politic. The watered stock and bonds which attend their modern creation only enhance their power for evil.

At 10:15 o'clock the conference adjourned to 10 o'clock Friday morning, September 15.

MORNING SESSION, SEPTEMBER 15.

COMMITTEE ON RESOLUTIONS MEET.

The committee on resolutions met at 9:30 o'clock and organized by electing ex-Gov. Luce, of Michigan, chairman, and Ralph M. Easley secretary. The same doubts and differences on the subject of resolutions which had agitated the conference when the question of the committee was debated, prevailed in the committee meeting. On motion of Howe, of Louisiana, the chair was instructed to appoint a sub-committee of five on resolutions, and after a general debate of an hour's duration on the policy to be followed by the committee an adjournment was taken until 2 o'clock.

William Wirt Howe was in the chair and called the conference to order at 10:30 o'clock. A delegate called the attention of the chair to the fact that many more delegates were present than at any previous meeting, and suggested that the credentials of all persons in the delegates' seats should be examined. No formal motion was put and the suggestion was not acted upon. Louis F. Post, of the National Single Tax League, was the first speaker.

LOUIS F. POST.
Single Tax League of the United States.

My only purpose in speaking on this occasion is to contribute to these deliberations a brief statement, in bare outline, of the position of single tax men on the subject of trusts. By single tax men I mean those men the world over—and women, too—who are proud to be known as followers of Henry George.

We recognize that there might be such a thing as a good trust. There might be commercial combinations that would reduce prices by economizing. They would indeed displace men, as all labor-saving machinery and methods do; but under just and normal conditions, there would be abundant opportunities for all who were displaced. Immediate demands for them in kindred occupations would constantly exceed the supply. Such trusts would tend to improve social conditions instead of making them worse. Those are the kind of trusts which our pro-trust

314

friends have in mind when they defend the trust. But in fact there is no such trust in existence to-day, and under prevailing industrial conditions there can be no such trust.

The trust question as it faces us is not a question of business combination. It is a question of legal monopoly. If competitive conditions prevailed, combinations of competitive businesses would do no harm. They would have to do good, or they couldn't keep the combination alive. But when businesses control legal monopolies and form combinations of these, then you have harmful trusts. And that is the kind of trust we have to-day—the kind of trust of which we complain. The trust question, I repeat, is at bottom not a question of business combinations, but a question of legal monopoly. It is not to be dealt with by restrictive laws, operating upon methods and effects. That would only make bad conditions worse. You have got to go beneath the methods and effects and get at the causes of these bad trusts. You have got to strike at the monopolies which give them their power. Abolish the legal monopolies that underlie trusts, and trusts will disappear. Without these monopolies no business combination could be injurious to the public. Without them every business combination that came to stay would be able to stay only if it proved to be really and wholly beneficial. But if those monopolies be perpetuated, all trusts will be tainted, all trusts will be bad; and by no system of restriction can you either destroy them or regulate them for the public good.

Take any trust which on its face seems to be a combination of mere competitive interests. If it were so in fact, it would be a good or at least a harmless trust. But scrutinize it, and you will find that somehow, directly or indirectly, it depends for its power upon monopoly. It may have no monopoly by name. It may simply be taking advantage of general laws that prevent free competition. It may depend, for example, upon the restrictions upon free competition which are imposed by tariffs. To the extent that the tariff narrows the field of competition, to that extent it fosters trusts. One of the very objects of the tariff is to produce that condition of strangulated competition without which trusts could not live. If we wish to get rid of the trust, we must sweep away the tariff and make trade as free between the people of the world as it is between the people of our States.

While single tax men demand the abolition of the tariff—offering in its place for revenue purposes an infinitely wiser and juster system of taxation—while they would have no tariff at all, yet they do not suppose that the abolition of the tariff would abolish all trusts. It would abolish a good many, and weaken the foundation of a good many more. But other and more direct systems of legal monopoly would still foster trusts.

There are the highway monopolies. Take the railroads, for instance. That is a highway, and in private hands is a highway monopoly. The monopoly is not in the cars, or tracks, or tunnels, or buildings, or anything of that sort. It is in the right-of-way—in the land that constitutes the "way" as distinguished from the structure. These highways connect places, and to control them is to control traffic. Railroad corporations can form oppressive trusts because they can control their highway monopolies.

They can and do do more than that. Give this monopoly of highways to railroad corporations, and they make exclusive contracts with business concerns, which form trusts upon the basis of special railroad privileges. One of the most familiar examples of this subletting of railroad highways is furnished by the case of express companies. Express companies have monopolies, because they get special privileges from railroads. No outsider can compete in the express business. The existing express companies have monopolies of right-of-way. And they can form oppressive trusts by combining these monopolies. Express companies are only one class of concerns deriving monopoly privileges in that way. There are others. The Standard Oil trust built up its power in precisely that way. The cracker trust is said to have privileges of this kind. And doubtless, if you inquire closely, you will learn that many a trust with an innocent face derives its power from railroad privileges.

Highway monopolies, then, must be abolished, if we would free ourselves from vicious trusts. But even if that were done, trusts would still have a firm foundation to build upon. The fact is that even to-day no trust can perpetuate itself unless it gets its feet upon the ground. All the advantages of tariffs and railway privileges and other monopolies will not avail trusts in conflict with hostile trusts which monopolize sources of supply and distributive points. Monopoly of land is, after all, the ultimate basis of the trust. It is an absolute condition to success that the trust have its feet upon the earth. This has been discovered by the great trusts. The steel trust and the copper trust go back to the land and make ore mines part of their property, while the coal transporting trust of the anthracite region is careful to secure not only highways but coal mines; and railroad monopoly in itself is being subjected to the more powerful monopoly of land at terminal points.

Let me follow this idea a little further. The control of trusts by trusts is clearly among the possibilities of trust development. As partnerships have merged into corporations and corporations into trusts, so will trusts merge into trusts of trusts, and finally into one all-powerful trust. That is the tendency. It is already manifest, and will be a thing accomplished unless we kill the trust system. ∖

Suppose, for example, the steel trust should reach out until it controlled all the steel business clear back to all the ore mines. It would then have its feet upon the ground, and no competitor in the steel business could cope with it. But it must use coal, and here, let us suppose, is one coal trust which has reached out until it controls all the coal mines. It, too, has its feet upon the ground. Suppose, now, that the interests of these trusts collide, and what could be the outcome but the consolidation of the two into one. That illustrates the trend of trusts. And if not stopped, that trend will persist until the organization of trusts and their absorption into trusts of trusts eventuate in the ownership of all businesses by some gigantic combination.

To that triumph of the trusts most socialists look forward with satisfaction. They see in it the opportunity of the people to take possession not only of the earth, but of the artificial instruments of production also, by dethroning the single trust under whose control all business will have come. They are satisfied, because in this trend they discover signs of the evolution of public ownership of all the instruments of production and distribution. But there is little real cause for satisfaction in that. As the evolution of the trust proceeds, trust employes become in greater and greater degree mere voting machines. It is not their convictions as citizens that they register at the polls. They vote as they are ordered to. This condition would be enormously worse if the development of trusts proceeded even approximately to the point of a universal trust. And when the time came to dethrone trusts, the voice of the people would be stifled. The trusts themselves would decide the issue. They would do it through the army of dependent voters whose livelihood they would control. It might be that they would decide in favor of the substitution of such a government trust as the socialists look forward to. But if they did, they themselves would fix the terms. All land and all machinery might by their consent and with the votes of their dependents, be turned over to the government, but it would be for a price which the trust magnates would dictate and to a government which they would continue to con-

317

trol. It is not by waiting until trusts own everything and then taking it from them that the trust question must be met.

We must kill the trust by securing in time the point of vantage toward which it is advancing. We must keep its feet off the ground. It would not be enough to abolish secondary monopolies. We must also abolish the monopoly of sources of supply and points of distribution.

Since trusts, in order to survive, must get their feet upon the ground, must control the earth at the points of supply and the points of distribution, the abolition of all monopolies except land monopoly would fail to abolish them. By acquiring control of the land they would control everything else. So it is that single tax men, though they would abolish the tariff, though they would abolish highway monopolies, though they would repeal every law that creates or supports monopoly, they would not stop there. They would strike at the mother monopoly of all. They would abolish the monopoly of land. To do that they propose nothing revolutionary. Revolution is not necessary. All that is necessary is to tax into the public treasury the peculiar value that attaches to especially advantageous locations. If that were done, no man or combination of men, whether incorporated or not, could monopolize the sources of supply or the points of distribution without paying annually to the public the full value of their privilege. That would deprive them of all advantage over others. It would lift their feet off the ground.

You remember the classic fable of Hercules and Antæus. Hercules with all his strength could not conquer Antæus so long as Antæus could touch the ground. But when Hercules discovered wherein the power of his adversary lay, he lifted Antæus from the ground and then destroyed him with ease. The trusts are the modern Antæus. Let the people lift them from the ground and the battle against them will be won.

While Mr. Post was speaking the committee on resolutions entered the hall and filled every seat reserved for the delegates. The other portion of the auditorium had been filled with auditors long before.

THOMAS J. MORGAN.

Socialist.

Mr. Post was followed by Thomas J. Morgan, of Illinois, who, speaking on "The Trust from a Socialist Point of View," said:

We see, from the socialistic view, not the special interest of this or that trade, of this or that business, of this or that state, of this or that nation, of this or that particular race, but we see the interest of the whole human race, as it is involved in the development of modern industry and modern commerce.

We socialists look into the past and see the end of the feudal system. We see the domination of the landed aristocracy destroyed and the rising importance of the new manufacturing and business interests. We see the employer and the merchant stepping into the imperial parliaments and taking charge of the nations. We see, following the individual employer, a partnership; following the partnership we find a corporation, and following the corporation in its logical order, we see the introduction of the trusts. We welcome the appearance of the trust as one of the natural and inevitable products of our industrial and commercial system.

The socialist sees that you are totally impotent to prevent the operation of trusts. You are impotent to interfere with its growth in the states or in the Union. It overrides your state and national laws in its progress.

The socialist sees what you fail to perceive; that is, that industry and commerce has long ceased to be mere local, state, and national interests, and that the limits of the workshop, the farm, and the market are co-extensive with the boundaries of the habitable earth, and hence that the controlling influences are world-wide, and above and beyond the reach of all your puny efforts.

It is very interesting to note the very high stand that is taken by those who are opposed to their natural offspring, the trust. They pose before the American people as the guardians and champions of personal liberty, of good citizenship, of manhood, and they tell us that unless the trust is destroyed we must go back to the individual methods of industry and business of the past, or we will become slaves; that our dependence in the future must be, not upon gigantic organizations of property owners, but upon the single individual property owners. We socialists go back and look over your records, and we ask you to listen to what the individual employer and business man did before the corporation came and before the trust was dreamed of. You individual employers, you individual business men, you opened the doors of the orphan asylum, and you took out of it the fatherless children, and put them into your individual factories, and ground their lives into dollars; you took the man and his wife; you took the mother and the child, and you put them into the bowels of the earth to bring out your black diamonds so you could enrich yourselves. You sent your old rotten ships to sea with worthless cargo, so they might sink with their crews, so you could enrich yourselves with the fraudulent insurance. And an act of Parliament was required to prevent you from continuing this murderous method of enrichment.

This spirit of murderous greed is not dead. It is seen in Africa, where the Kaffir is down in the diamond mines and the gold mines. It is seen in the effort to subject the Boers. Not alone there, but here—you freed Cuba, didn't you? Oh, the poor Cubans, they must be freed from Spain! But what do you do with the negro down South? You disfranchise him. Then you individualistic business men, your spirit goes out into the Philippines, and will reduce the Filipinos to the level of your negroes down South.

You go down to your sunny Southland here, and what do you see? From Virginia and Arkansas, and all these other places where these men have addressed you about personal liberty and about the enormous resources of their states as one of the inducements to the individual capitalization, they tell you there is no restriction for child labor down South.

And in the North, in this state, the Supreme Court, at the request of the Manufacturers' Voluntary Association, has declared that an individual employer may drive the hardest bargain with a starving woman or girl, and work her twelve or twenty-four hours for a day's work and pay 50 or 75 cents as compensation, and that all laws that interfere with this "right" of the individual employer are unconstitutional.

In the face of such a record as this, you individual employers and business men come here and pose as champions of liberty, guardians of manhood, and saviors of society.

The corporation is a legal personality, but it has no soul; the trust has neither personality nor soul, but soulless as the first is, and bodyless and soulless as the trust is, it is utterly impossible for either or both to exceed in inhuman cruelty the record you individual employers and individual business men have already made.

We have been regaled here with delightful descriptions of the vast natural resources of the particular states from which the respective speakers hailed, others have attempted to picture in words the creative forces of machinery, steam, electricity, harnessed and operated by the "dignified" millions of American workmen, and of the enormous wealth which has and can be produced. You all agree that if as yet America may not be able to feed, clothe, and house the world it certainly is able to do more than that for its own people. In other words, if we but look about us at our bursting granaries and warehouses, and our productive power, we must see that the problem of production has been solved, and that not one single human being in this land need suffer for lack of the necessaries, comforts, and even luxuries of life, because of any inability to produce them.

And yet, plain as this is, it is still more plainly seen that want, gaunt and dreadful, ever stalks beside millions of our American workmen, and that the shadow of this monster of modern civilization is now spreading over the great middle class.

We socialists clearly see that as the little workshop and small factory and mill had to give place to the larger and larger manufacturing institutions, so the little business is absorbed by the ever increasing corporations, and they in turn into trusts, and the many trusts into still larger and fewer trusts, till it requires no prophetic eye to see the form of the one all absorbing and controlling trust. Cannot you, business men, see with the socialist in this inevitable line of development of the private ownership of the earth—the means of production and distribution—the end of the principle of private property?

The fetich of private property in the mines, in the soil, in the forests, and in the fields, and everywhere else, an idolatrous worship of the millions of propertyless workers as well as of the propertied classes, is the bane of civilization, is the illusion of civilization, and must be wiped out of the intellect. We socialists rejoice that the trust has come to show you that the logical sequence of the ownership and control of what is now known as private property and the resources of the earth, that the private property of this great country and others like it, will be organized into trusts until there will be one trust, and you will not be in it.

You can send bands of music to your legislatures, you can pass resolutions, you can hold your demonstrations everywhere; but the concentration of private property, the right of man to own all he can get and hold all he gets, will go on with irresistible force so long as the principle of private property in the things by which we live is maintained by you men.

It is very interesting and somewhat amusing to the socialist

321

to watch your actions as you feel this resistless pressure you try to escape in every conceivable way but cannot, and this conference proves beyond a doubt that as a class you are in great distress— are very sick—and we, socialists, seek to comfort you by the assertion that the disease which afflicts you is fatal, that in the very near future you will die, and we shall be present and rejoice at your funeral.

With this condition confronting you, with this outlook before you, will not you business men look above the present system of production for profit and consider the better principle of production for use?

Will you still continue trying to tear the corporation and the trust to pieces, so that each of you individuals may have a little and begin again in the "good old way," or will you not see that these great trusts, with their organized methods of production in which all waste is eliminated, in these great corporations for distribution which are being perfected, a means to be used and not destroyed? Will you not see that with these perfected mechanical methods of production and distribution, the mythical "self-made-man," the assumed superiority of the employing and business class disappears in this bodyless, soulless thing called a trust, but which still can supply all the necessaries, comforts, and luxuries of the world?

Will you not see with the socialist, that in these forms of combination the warfare of competition must cease, a warfare in which man is at war with man, and man with woman, and both with the child in every place of industry and commerce in the world?

Will you not lift your eyes, your thoughts, your aspirations from the low groveling plane of inhuman, stupid warfare in which the prize for you is profit and the prize for the worker at best only a "living wage"?

Will you not lift your heads and hearts above this and realize that in the higher, peaceful relations of fraternal co-operation you must seek and will find that commonwealth in which alone the people rule, in which alone there can be liberty, in which alone there can be manhood; manhood which can exist only in a state where the trust perfected includes the whole people, where private property which once belonged to the individual employer and business man, next to the corporation, and last to the trust, has become in the very nature of things the common property of the common people, and makes the commonwealth a fact instead of a mere abstraction?

HENRY WHITE.

General Secretary United Garment Workers of America.

Henry White, of New York, general secretary of the United Garment Workers of America, was next introduced and said:

The industrial combination known as trusts have so entrenched themselves in our economic system, that it is not so much a question now as to how they can be suppressed, but what the public attitude should be toward them, and whether or how they should be regulated for the public benefit. They are already a phase of our industrial development, and being here have at least some presumption in their favor, but they are not yet sufficiently established to give them the sanction of time and experience. They have just forced their way into the arena of public activity. The benefits derived by the community from them still requires demonstration, likewise adequate proof as to the dangers attending their existence. Simply citing cases showing abuses is no indictment against the method itself. We must distinguish between the use and abuse of a thing, otherwise no human institution could stand. Discrimination is the soul of an argument. While pointing out the evils of trusts we must not forget the serious grievances of competitive business—its limitations, its wastes, its uncertainties. Workingmen are only too familiar with the disheartening reply when asking for an increase of wages, "Can't afford it on account of competition." The trust method, at least, changes that situation as far as ability to concede better conditions are concerned.

If the success of the trusts has been to the detriment of the people society, always supreme, can harass it, tax away its profits and even outlaw it, but as to whether it can be destroyed under a system of private enterprise or whether society can prevent competing concerns from consolidating or being operated under a mutual agreement without undoing the work of progress and establishing medieval trade restrictions, that is the question.

National incorporation, if that were possible under the Constitution, suggests a way of uniformly regulating corporations, by limiting their operations to the definite purpose for which they are chartered, instead of the unsatisfactory state regulation which has led to such grotesque results. Government ownership and control of all monopolized industries is one way of dealing with the subject, but we are not evidently prepared to seriously consider so vast and revolutionary a proposition, there being nothing in all history or in our own experience to support it. Society cannot be moulded at will to fit any scheme no matter how well thought out.

The real reason why trusts have grown so wonderfully in this country is really due to the American genius for doing things upon a large scale, and putting natural forces to the best use. Favored legislation, tariffs, discriminating railroad rates, or the many other things, commonly ascribed as being the cause of their growth, reminds me very much of the fly upon the wheel, which exclaimed, "How fast I am making it turn." These things may accelerate their development and enable them to exact undue profits, but they do not account for the phenomena itself. It is Yankee enterprise rather which quickly utilized the advantages which centralization gives just as it applied electric energy immediately after its secrets were known. We frequently hear men of business experience expressing themselves disparingly upon this subject as though the well established law of trade, viz.: that money for investment will flow in the direction of the most profit and greatest security had ceased to operate and that the trusts charged with exacting exorbitant profits had preëmpted all claims and forestalled the formation of rival corporations. Can it be that the spirit of rivalry has ceased to assert itself? Is it not more likely to do so in another form through competition between great combinations? As soon as present industrial tendencies have evolved from the present formative state there can be no doubt that, that force in business which has never failed will be made manifest. In a fair free field would not superior service more likely be the only means by which a corporation could continue to dominate the market? Where a monopoly is supported by the obtaining of favored freight rates, legislative privileges, patent rights, or the tariff, this beneficent process would be hampered or even counteracted and all of our energies therefore should be directed toward removing such impediments instead of vainly striving to prevent the natural and inevitable movement toward concentration. This is the pith of the whole question.

That the tariff in some cases enables a combination in control of a product to put up the price based upon the difference in the customs duty, there can be no question. I mention as an instance the case of woolen cloth. Where a monopoly is due to the control of a necessary invention it is improbable that inventive genius will have exhausted its resources, and that such a monopoly will be long continued. In America competition has reached a condition of intensity unknown anywhere else. Every device of a fertile and ingenious people is resorted to in order to enable one rival to obtain an advantage over another, and the principal weapon used is the cutting of prices. Instances can be cited where production has been carried on in some large industries at practically no profit, simply with the hope that conditions would improve and because of the inability to withdraw invested capital. Against such destructive warfare, combination has come as a relief. This tendency is but the fruition of such competition. While in the very nature of things competition, under private enterprise, cannot be avoided, in the long run it can at least be carried on in a form other than in the ruinous way.

While this evolution continues there are some important industries which escape this tendency. I refer, for instance, to the clothing trade which I am identified with, where manufacturing can be carried on just as cheaply upon a small scale as upon a large one. To this is due the sweating system which is a survival of the old domestic workshop method transplanted from Europe, fed by immigration, and exploited by American capital. The sweatshop has managed, therefore, to prevent that industry from drifting into the ways of the trust. Our trade is even denied the privilege of choosing between a real evil and a possible one. In the clothing trade free competition of a certain kind has reached its last ditch and any change would be gladly welcomed as an improvement. This is the sort of free competition which follows the throwing of a bone among hungry animals. There is a competition to emulate, to excel, to build up, and another which devours and destroys.

On the problem itself I confess I have formed no positive convictions, because of the suddenness in which this industrial reorganization has come upon us and the difficulty of grasping its true meaning. I have, however, a few fundamental questions to ask in the course of my address, which require a convincing answer in order that public alarm may be allayed that the trust institution may establish itself in the public confidence, prove that it is necessary to progress, show that it widens the sphere of human endeavor and adds to the happiness of mankind. The opposition to trusts, it is claimed by them, is due to the incidental but temporary disarrangement and that this opposition is similar to the antipathy manifested toward improved machinery and better business methods. Their advocates claim the following advantages for them:

That it gives the consumer the benefit of increased economy in production by lowering prices and by which consumption is increased. That it makes employment more regular and enables higher wages to be paid. That it creates more certainty and system in business, thus making panics less likely. That it opens up foreign markets on account of the superior productive methods.

Now if the soundness of all these claims be admitted, and there are no serious evils, associated with the trust, then it ought to be hailed as a benefactor of mankind for it brings results compared with which all other improvements in human history become as naught. But, alas, for the ungrateful public. It can only see the forked tongue and gleaming eyes of a monster.

This deep-rooted antagonism cannot be solely attributed to the squeezing out of the middlemen, the displacement of labor or the work of the alarmist, but if analyzed is found to be due to the fear that these great financial institutions are establishing an irresponsible, impersonal and selfish despotism. That this power tends to control legislation, that it reaches out for public franchises by special privileges and so intrenches itself that it can successfully keep out competitors.

Now, to what extent is this so? And is there some compensating or balancing power in society? An active public opinion must, of course, be always relied upon to remedy abuses, but it is roughly formed and proverbially slow, and is frequently thwarted by the compactly organized few. History has some warning to give in this regard, and surely those who control great wealth have not usually acted as though they were its steward. Have we been encouraged into believing that the trust managers will use their power for good, rather than for evil?

Is it possible for a trust to keep in control only so long as prices are kept down to a point which would shut out competition? Numerous cases can no doubt be cited, if the current newspaper reports can be credited, where prices keep going up and the trust holds the fort. Are such cases isolated and due to the general advance in prices and have no bearing upon the larger results, or do they indicate the real character of the trusts and what we may anticipate from them?

On this serious problem, where does labor stand? I have been invited to speak from the point of view of the wage earners, or rather, the organized portion of them, for the unorganized have no voice, and like "the man with the hoe," have always been mute.

I feel justified in saying that the general attitude of the trade unions toward the industrial corporations is neither trust nor anti-trust. They have a position of their own. They are not making any leaps in the dark. Hard experience has taught them caution. Trade unions, the creation of modern social evolution, have no quarrel with the progressive forces in society, but they demand for the workers a share in the benefits.

While organized workingmen may disagree, somewhat on the general question, they agree in this, that improved means of protection is more vital to them than improved methods of production, as important as the latter is. They want some say as to the terms of employment. Even though the trusts may concede higher wages and shorter hours, it is the recognition of the right to make terms through the agency of the union that concerns them most. Employers will often voluntarily grant concessions as a means of offsetting the demand for recognition, knowing that such recognition would enable the men to deal with the employer more like an equal. Will it be the policy of these corporations to recognize the function which organized labor fulfills in society and treat with them as such? Or, will they deny to the workers advantages which they themselves enjoy? Will they insist upon ignoring the necessity of workingmen acting in groups in view of the impossibility of the individual making satisfactory terms of employment in a great factory, where uniform conditions are fixed?

What will the policy be toward united labor when the trusts are more fully established? Will the unions have to meet a more unyielding foe? That is the question which a million organized mechanics are asking and an assuring answer cannot be given by words alone. · It might be said that necessity would stimulate and strengthen the movement of the workers, and no doubt it will, because years of struggle and sacrifice made for economic independence have trained and nerved the American toiler for a greater trial and the test must soon come, for the organization on the other side is proceeding at such a pace that labor will have to make great strides in order to catch up. To meet one single employer who speaks for the entire trade is quite different than coping with one who figures on the advantage his competitor will gain in the event of a strike.

Now, suppose the unions are overcome and destroyed. Instead of the natural and orderly methods of trade unionism the discontent would express itself through wild and revolutionary uprisings, or it might give way to a dull deadening passiveness, the very worst fate which could befall society. Professor Brooks has well said: "If the growth of the trust would end in the crushing of the unions, it would be a great human tragedy." Trade unions have often been likened to trusts. True, they are alike in respect to the features of organization and the desire to eliminate a detrimental competition; but they differ in this, that trade unions depend for effectiveness upon admitting all crafts-men to membership; they enjoy no privileges and represent the movement of the mass for economic justice and social advance-ment.

The whole purpose of the human race is not alone to produce goods cheaper. A visitor to a great factory may be delighted with the order and system which he observes, but when he mingles with the workmen he often finds them sullen and discontented. True prosperity is not so much a question of superior production as that of more equitable conditions. In that I agree with the delegate from Texas, but there is no occasion at the same time to ignore social growth and change. The essence of civilization is the doing of justice and a nation's standing must be measured by its ability to administer justice, likewise with a system of industry. The element of fair dealing must always be paramount or its fruits will become like dead sea apples, sour and bitter to the taste.

The golden age of labor is supposed to have been in the fifteenth century. Gibbons, in his work on "The Industrial History of England," says: "The cost of living was not more than one-tenth of that at the present day. Food was abundant and cheap. Three pounds of beef could be bought for a penny. A pig cost about four pence. Employment was fairly constant and regular, and in addition to their wages the laborers still possessed valuable old manorial rights to common pasture and forests. Artisans earned about three shillings a week, which should certainly be worth more than thirty shillings a week at the present. Industry was organized into craft guilds"—a form of trade unionism.

Yet, this was in a state of primitive industry, in the days of the domestic handicrafts, and was alone made possible by the social harmony which prevailed, when the master and journey-man met in common fellowship. With that kind of harmony combined with the economic effectiveness, which the trust makes possible, the human race would advance with mighty bounds. The trust managers have magnificent opportunities; will they avail themselves of them? Will they show the necessary large-mindedness? Judging by our knowledge of human nature, which we know has not changed perceptively for a thousand years under varying conditions, we have reason to be anxious, but the people of America have never failed to successfully meet a great issue when once they grappled with it. The vigorous manner in which the trusts were opposed here but indicates the feeling out-

A. M. COMPTON   HENRY D. BAKER
DAVID ROSS   GEORGE A. SCHILLING
WILLIAM H. TUTTLE   PAUL J. MAAS

side and with such sentiments aroused no possible power can prevail against the people's might.

In the lowering clouds of social strife I see a welcome light. The mere fact alone of such a gathering as this shows that the age of reason is dawning, and when men reason everything is possible.

Other speakers of the morning were, M. M. Garland, former president of the Amalgamated Iron and Steel Workers; Samuel Gompers, president of the American Federation of Labor, and John W. Hayes, secretary and treasurer of the Knights of Labor. The latter remarked that as some of those who had been assigned to talk on the side of labor were not present, he felt that he should be accorded more time than that allotted other speakers.

Cockran moved unanimous consent to an extension of the speaker's time. Mr. Hayes declined to accept an extension as a concession. He demanded it as a right. There was confusion in the galleries, and without any formalities, the chair closed the incident by intimating to Mr. Hayes that he would probably find the ruling in his case sufficiently elastic.

SAMUEL GOMPERS.

President American Federation of Labor.

Mr. Gompers' subject was "The Control of Trusts." He said in part:

We are all conscious of the giant strides with which industry during the past decade has combined and concentrated into the modern trust. There is considerable difference of opinion, however, as to what is regarded by many as an intolerable evil.

Organized labor is deeply concerned regarding the "swift and intense concentration of the industries," and realizes that unless successfully confronted by an equal or superior power there is economic danger and political subjugation in store for all.

But organized labor looks with apprehension at the many panaceas and remedies offered by theorists to curb the growth and development or destroy the combinations of industry. We have seen those who know little of statecraft and less of economics urge the adoption of laws to "regulate" interstate commerce and laws to "prevent" combinations and trusts, and we have also seen that these measures, when enacted, have been the very instruments employed to deprive labor of the benefit of organized effort while at the same time they have simply proven incentives to more subtly and surely lubricate the wheels of capital's combination.

For our part, we are convinced that the state is not capable of preventing the legitimate development or natural concentration of industry. All the propositions to do so which have come under our observation would beyond doubt react with greater force and injury upon the working people of our country than upon the trusts.

The great wrongs attributable to the trusts are· their corrupting influence on the politics of the country, but as the state has always been the representative of the wealth possessors we shall be compelled to endure this evil until the toilers are organized and educated to the degree when they shall know that the state is by right theirs, and finally and justly come to their own while never relaxing in their efforts to secure the very best possible economic, social and material improvement in their condition.

There is no tenderer or more vulnerable spot in the anatomy of trusts than their dividend paying function, there is no power on earth other than the trade unions which wields so potent a weapon to penetrate, disrupt, and, if necessary, crumble the whole fabric. This, however, will not be necessary, nor will it occur, for the trade unions will go on organizing, agitating and educating, in order that material improvement may keep pace with industrial development, until the time when the workers, who will then form nearly the whole people, develop their ability to administer the functions of government in the interest of all.

There will be no cataclysm, but a transition so gentle that most men will wonder how it all happened.

In the early days of our modern capitalist system, when the individual employer was the rule under which industry was conducted, the individual workmen deemed themselves sufficiently capable to cope for their rights; when industry developed and employers formed companies, the workmen formed unions; when industry concentrated into great combinations, the workingmen formed their national and international unions, as employments became trustified, the toilers organized federations of all unions—local, national and international—such as the American Federation of Labor.

We shall continue to organize and federate the grand army of labor, and with our mottoes, lesser hours of labor, higher wages, and an elevated standard of life, we shall establish equal and exact justice to all. *"Labor Omnia Vincit."*

JOHN W. HAYES.

General Secretary and Treasurer Order Knights of Labor.

Mr. Hayes, speaking on "The Social Enemy," said:

The question which we are invited here to discuss—"Trusts and Combinations"—is fast pressing itself for solution before the highest tribunal in the nation, the court of final resort, for all questions of public policy, the court of public opinion. It is too vital, too important, to be confined to the narrow limits of commercial affairs, of mere business operation, or mercenary speculation. It touches the very foundations of our free institutions, involves the liberty of the people, the comfort, happiness and prosperity of millions of free men, and the stability of our governmental system, established by the fathers to defend and protect coming generations in their inherent rights, which rights were declared by them to be the gift of nature to all her children.

This question, then, involves more than the trivial matter of production and prices. It goes far beyond the profitable operation of the manufacturer. It rises to the high plane of a government policy, involves the question of human rights, of individual liberty, of the status of the citizen, of the dignity of citizenship, the right of defense, a limit to the power of wealth, a point at which the encroachment of mercenary greed must stop, and a barrier created that will enable us to defend our liberties, our manhood, and our independence.

I shall, therefore, discuss this question only as it bears upon the broad field of human rights, and deny at the outset the moral right of any individual, or combination of individuals, to so monopolize any natural field of industry to such an extent as to be able to dictate the conditions which govern the lives of that portion of society which gains its maintenance by the exercise of productive industry in that particular field. I assert that it is contrary to the best interests of society—indeed, that government has not the constitutional power to enact such legislation as will make it possible for any combination of individuals to so limit the volume of production in any natural field for its own particular advantage, or so create conditions that any individual or combination of individuals may have despotic power over the lives of any citizen or number of citizens.

I further assert and maintain that these great combinations are an assault upon the inherent and constitutional rights of the citizen, and that the real and vital advantage to be gained is the despotic control over labor. Virtually to own and command the labor engaged in any particular field, and consequently it is an assault upon that portion of the people. If one field may be invaded and reduced to despotic dictation, all may be, and the logical outcome must be the conquest of all fields of production, the establishment of a despotism in each, the enslavement of the people, the overthrow of our free institutions, and the erection of moneyed aristocracy. Thus would our boasted free institutions become a fraud and a pretense, our government perverted, and only used as a machine to enforce the will of the dictators.

The term "trust" is so indefinite, so vague and uncertain, being used many times without a clear conception of its scope or exact reference, that we must secure a definition for it. Webster defines a trust to be "a combination to control production and prices." This definition furnishes us with sufficient grounds to attack them constitutionally, as the control of production involves our inherent rights, the liberty of our citizens—in fact, the very existence of our form of government. Not only does the trust dominate and control production and prices, but it controls and cuts off our opportunity to labor, which is one of our inherent rights, and thus the very right to live is denied us, or we are doomed to involuntary servitude for the benefit of a more favored class. This, you see, places the question beyond the profitable operation of the manufacturer and raises one of equity, of justice, and of the rights of man. An analysis of the character and objects of the trust cannot but convince any unbiased and patriotic mind that they are inimical to our popular form of government, subversive of our institutions, tyrannical in their methods, antagonistic to the common welfare, the common enemy of society, and should be treated as an invader or armed revolutionist aspiring to dictatorial power. Arms are not the only resort of the invader, the despot, or the conqueror. Violence is not the only means of making conquests and enslaving the people, and it can be proven beyond any question of doubt that the methods of the trusts are the methods of the invader, the conqueror, and the despot, and the ends to be accomplished by the instigators of the trusts are exactly those intended to be accomplished by arms directed by military genius. Taking this view of the trusts, which I hold is the correct one, I assert boldly that they are the enemies of society, and as such should be destroyed as any common enemy, and that the financial phase of the question should not come into the subject for consideration, as the liberties of the people are far above the mere question of money.

The definition that a trust is an aggressive combination of private individuals leads naturally to the inquiry, against what or whom this aggression or assault is to be directed? Is it an organization of private individuals formed to attack some similar organization in a competitive rivalry, the result of which will affect the private interests of those immediately concerned, leaving the unsuccessful and unfortunate the ability to recover from any injuries they might suffer from the contest, with their social status unaffected and their capacity and ability to produce unimpaired? Or is it possible that this aggression is against society, against the established social and political conditions, which guarantees to every citizen the right and opportunity to labor in any field of industry he may find most favorable to his pursuit of happiness and the enjoyment of his liberty? What more nearly concerns the happiness of man than the enjoyment of the full return of his industry, or his liberty, more than the access to any field of industry nature has provided, from which he may gather the necessities and comforts which minister to his happiness and the happiness of those depending upon him? It is the duty of society and government to foster and encourage production, to guard every field of industry for the common good of society, and to develop the producing energy to the greatest extent possible.

There is no fear that a people can produce too much of anything that is serviceable and useful to the community; that the people can become too comfortable or too industrious. The good of society demands that the productive energy be developed to the greatest degree possible; that the fields of industry be not circumscribed, and that free access be guaranteed and preserved to all who require or desire to exercise their productive labor in such fields. The controlling of any field of industry by any individual or combination of individuals is contrary to the declared spirit of our institutions, for it recognizes the power of such individual or combination to restrict production, even to absolutely close the field of opportunity against the citizen, if they consider their personal interests will be benefited thereby.

The great corporations, the trusts, with their capital, their machinery, special privileges, and other advantages, are overwhelming the individual, reducing him to the condition of a mere tool, to be used in their great undertakings for their individual profit, and of no more consequence than a piece of dumb machinery. Man is the slave of necessity, and he who controls the necessities has the power of a despot. The first and prime necessity is the opportunity to exercise his industry in some productive field where he can secure the means of existence. To close this field, to cut off this opportunity, is to sentence him to death. To restrict the exercise of his productive ability, or limit the terms of his access to the opportunity by the will of another, is to make him the slave of another. It is claimed by short-sighted, selfish, and mercenary men that if the opportunity is closed in one field there are others to which the individual may turn. This is too silly and childish an assertion to merit notice. First, because no such possibility should be allowed to exist under our free institutions; and next, because were it possible for one field to be monopolized, it is possible for all to be, and the individual would turn from the field closed against him to find all others in the same condition. Even were this not so, his skill, experience, and training in that field would be lost to him, and he would enter a new one at a disadvantage in the competition with trained minds and skilled hands already employed, and an injustice would be done on the one hand, and undue favor extended on the other. The trust, by monopolizing the field, becomes the dictator of the conditions which govern the life of every individual engaged in the field monopolized. By limiting the extent to which he may exercise his productive energy, limiting his wage, or the possible amount of his earnings, it dictates the quality and quantity of food the worker may eat, the kind of clothes he may wear, the kind of shelter he may provide for his family, the opportunity for education and improvement his children may have, and, by cutting his opportunity to labor, it denies him even the right to live.

The great danger from these great combinations is the fact that they step in between the citizen and the government and levy such tribute as they may choose, imposing the most severe penalties in the form of enforced idleness, destitution, and suffering for refusal to comply with their demands. The individual is thus subjected to the dominition of two distinct powers— the one the political government, which taxes him and controls his relations to his fellow-citizens, and which power is of his own creation and is submitted to voluntarily; the other controls the necessities by which he exists, and only by permission of the combination which controls his field of industry can he exist at all. This latter is, in its nature, compulsory, and is only submitted to because he is unable to resist it. In this sense he is a slave.

Each field of industry is looked to to supply whatever demand may be made upon it by the necessities of the people not only of our own country, but throughout the world. A larger demand gives greater activity to such industry as is already employed and opportunity to such energy as may at any time be unemployed, the supply being naturally adjusted to the demand and a just and equitable return made to the producing energy. The operation of the trust interrupts this natural adjustment, arbitrarily fixes the volume of production, and demands whatever price necessity may compel the unfortunate consumer to pay, and thus an unjust tax is levied upon all society to fill the purses of the greedy dictators, who dole out whatever pittance they may choose in the form of wages to those unfortunates whose labor they are enabled to command. In this way society is compelled to pay tribute to this speculative freebooter, and submit to his dictation as to the quality and quantity of whatever product he controls which its necessities may demand.

It may be said in reply that this is never done. I answer that it is possible it may be, and it should be so arranged that such a thing would not be possible in any civilized society. The trust, then, is the enemy of society, as well as of the individual.

This surely is enough to condemn it, for whatever is the enemy of society should be exterminated without thought of mercy or charity. But the trust is worse. It is the enemy of free institutions, a breeder of treason against the government, involving the overthrow of our system and the destruction of our liberties. This is a severe charge, but it is capable of clear and undisputable proof.

The great object of human endeavor is the achievement of the greatest degree of human happiness. This is the great aim of all human society, all human governments; and this is the declared and recognized purpose for which our free institutions were devised and established, and the machinery of our government was designed and constructed for the purpose of accomplishing this result in the most effective manner. By preserving the inherent rights and liberties of the individual and defending the dignity of citizenship, it is hoped that the citizen may be protected from the tyranny of more fortunate individuals and classes, and the operation of unjust conditions and influences which may assail him, and he be left untrammeled in his pursuit of that degree of happiness to which he may aspire.

The establishment of the trust renders impossible this preservation and defense, because it transforms the citizen into a servile dependent upon the despotic will of the corporation, which is governed only by mercenary greed and selfish desire, the trust becoming in its very nature a power far more effective in all things directly pertaining to the individual's comfort and happiness than the government. In this way it usurps the power of government, which it nullifies and overthrows, and so far as the individual affected is concerned, assumes the functions of government. The object and aim of the trust being purely mercenary and selfish, naturally it will seek to establish and maintain conditions which will give it absolute control of the productive energy employed in its field, regardless of the rights of individuals or the common welfare of society.

The legislation enacted by the government, if uninfluenced, naturally would be the expression of the popular will in the interests of individuals and society. This legislation it becomes the interest of the trust to influence and pervert to its own profit and advantage. This opens the door to corruption of the legislative branch of government and the oppression and overawing of the popular will. The representatives of the people are corrupted, and the class dependent on the trust for its employment and maintenance intimidated and practically disfranchised through fear of loss of employment and enforced idleness. They are compelled to support the methods of the trust or neglect to exercise their rights as citizens. In this way the independence of the citizen is destroyed, his manhood degraded, his right to give free expression to his opinions upon public affairs abridged. He becomes a sycophant, a moral coward, a helpless dependent upon the will of his master, and the will of the trusts becomes the only voice heard. Legislation in this way becomes merely the dictation of the trust, and the pretense that it is the emanation of popular will is false and fraudulent. In this way the power and machinery of government are gradually transferred from the people to the corporation, and that which was founded and intended to protect the citizen and defend his natural and civil rights becomes the means of his oppression. This is unquestionably treason, a conspiracy to usurp and pervert the government, to overthrow free institutions, and to establish a despotism and a favored and dominant class, practically autocratic in its use of power. That this is not only possible, but practically in operation at the present time, is proven by the history of our political campaigns for the past two decades, and a review of the legislation enacted in the interests of corporations, which constitute the great bulk of all legislation, municipal, state, and national. It is universally admitted that legislation emanates from the class benefited by it, and, looking over the mass of legislation, one is at no loss to decide what class is benefited. Therefore, there can be no doubt as to what influence brought about its enactment. The fraud, corruption, and bribery of legislatures, the open defiance of executive authority, the corruption of courts and their officials, the usurpation of power and the legal assumption of rights, the ready appeal to the military and arrogant overriding of the civil authority by this power in controversies between corporations and employes; the defiance of municipal authorities in questions between corporations and municipalities, the employment of armed mercenaries to enforce their decrees, the constant and never-ceasing struggle of corporations to compel as many hours of labor and as low a rate of wages as is possible to enforce, are all clearly indicative of the character, desires, and purposes, and show beyond any question such combinations to be the enemies of society and of any form of government which tends to abridge or control their power over the citizen, or the exercise of their will in any undertaking their greed and avarice may suggest, regardless of the rights, interest, liberties, or happiness of the people, or even the interests of the people's government. Their intents are unquestionably treasonable, and if carried to their ultimate results will certainly cause the overthrow of our institutions and government.

In this world all things work in a circle. So it will and must be with trusts if carried to their logical culmination. The inspiring motive which called them into being will prove their destruction, as well as the destruction of our government. They will end by destroying themselves, as well as the government which gave them birth. The very nature of the system proves this.

The trust being an aggressive combination for purely selfish objects, attacks the individual, and by overthrowing his natural rights seizes upon his field of opportunity and production, appropriating them to its own advantage. This field having been conquered, and the trust strengthened in its financial power, the aggressive spirit of selfish greed looks for conquests in allied fields, which are soon invaded and monopolized, or other combinations, seeing the success of the first attempt, enters upon the same campaign of conquest. Soon the individual is overwhelmed and every field of production is monopolized by a trust. Individual enterprise, opportunity, liberty, and individual energy are destroyed, competition for the individual is impossible, and the war between the trusts begins.

The strongest combination in one field attacks the weaker in allied fields, and the overthrow and absorption of this strengthens the victor and makes further conquest possible, which finally ends by the overthrow of all opposition and the monopolizing of all fields of production by one colossal, irresistible combination, instigated by mercenary greed and utter selfishness, which will issue its autocratic decree to a cringing mass of dependent slaves, whose very right to live would depend upon the imperial will of the corporation, which would hold the power of life and death over its subjects. These would represent the citizenship of the pretended republic which might stand for the sham of civil government, for should even a pretense remain, the laws enacted would be merely the will of the corporation. But would such an aggregation of power and wealth be content to allow even a pretense of its subjection to any recognized authority? It is scarcely reasonable to suppose, but it is far more probable that all sham and pretense would be thrown aside and the victor openly declare his power, brush aside any futile opposition, set up his aristocracy, and free institutions, the popular government erected by patriotic fathers, would disappear from the face of the earth, and in its stead would arise a despotism born of greed and selfishness, subservient to the interests of an utterly irresponsible group of heartless speculators, ruling their slaves with an iron hand in order to secure to themselves the greatest profit and advantage, and to whom the common welfare would mean only their own mercenary advancement. Besides such conditions the despotism of Russia would be liberty, hereditary monarchy liberal, the condition of the black slave of the South enjoyable. No more deplorable fate could possibly befall any people than that, which in this case is possible, as the logical outcome of recognizing this heartless, this heathenish and selfish system.

I do not hesitate to proclaim that in recognizing it at all we are nourishing a serpent, fostering treason, giving aid and comfort to the enemies of society, welcoming an invader, assisting in the overthrow of free institutions and popular government, inviting a dictator, and laying the foundation of despotism. We are sowing the seed of revolution and may reap the harvest upon the bloody fields of civil strife or amid the groans and sighs of fettered slaves, bereft of manhood, wallowing in moral degradation, ignorance, and vice, degraded from the exalted dignity of citizenship in a free and mighty nation to a condition of sycophantic dependence upon the despotic decree of an autocrat.

The slums of Europe have been raked to secure a horde of the most ignorant, the most servile, the most depraved, the lowest element of the most oppressive aristocracies of modern civilization, and these purchased slaves, dependents upon the will of an autocrat, without even the rudiments of education, without even a faint conception of liberty or of human rights, with no conception of the character of our institutions and government, have been injected into our population and employed in the development of some of our most productive fields, where they are worked under conditions almost identical with those under which the convicts of Siberia exist, conditions which no free American citizen could submit to and no man worthy of citizenship should. Thus are these great fields of industry, the inheritance of American children, closed against our own people for the profit of a few speculators, and the industry in these fields ruled despotically by force, and practically a system of slavery established.

Nor does the wrong end here. This mass of ignorance and depravity has been degenerating for centuries under the most iniquitous tyranny, and cannot by any means hope to reach the plane of intelligence our people occupy. They submit willingly and with no sense of humiliation to methods and treatment our own people would not brook, and thus gradually their masters introduce and usurp authority similar to that of European potentates, which, being accepted, gradually comes to be looked upon as legitimate, and so usurped authority comes gradually to be recognized as legal, and our government the executor often of the will of the corporation. Further than this, the influence of this degraded and vicious element upon our own population is bad in the extreme, tending to degrade and lower our own citizens, rather than to elevate those too dense and ignorant to be impressed by moral influences. The result is rather to Europeanize our own people than to Americanize the stolid mass which exists under such degrading influences.

However, it is plain that this grand inheritance of the American people, these great fields of opportunity and production, have been closed to their rightful owners and absorbed by a greedy few, who operate them with foreign labor under the most servile and degrading conditions.

That the unrestricted competition of centralized wealth against individual enterprise is fatal to the individual and against the best interests of society is further proven in the commercial field. The small merchant has been forced into the position of a paid servant of the combination. Formerly young men enjoyed the opportunity of entering this field of occupation with the hope of advancement, if not fortune. Beginning as clerk, they could gain a knowledge of the business and qualify themselves to conduct a business of their own or become partners of their employer, in either case becoming independent, self-reliant, self-supporting, and valuable citizens, maintaining their family in comfort. Now this opportunity is closed. The field is monopolized by combinations of wealth. The clerk must remain a clerk, without hope in the future, except such increase in his pitiful wages as his master may in his magnanimity see fit to dole out to him. His opportunity is further limited by his being forced into competition with helpless women, driven by necessity to accept any wage in order to exist.

To sum up the whole, this policy of the trusts is an aggressive invasion organized against the best interests of society and destructive to our free institutions and popular government. It is too often the instigator of fraud, corruption, bribery, and treason. It is the ally of despotism, tyranny, mercenary selfishness, and slavery, and is an enemy to the elevation of the race and the equality of man.

JOHN B. CONNER.

Chief Indiana Bureau of Statistics.

It is said that the germ of the corporation idea had its origin in Rome in the ecclesiastical organizations and combinations, and that the English law in respect to corporations was fashioned by these ancient impressions, when taking civil instead of ecclesiastical form. Then followed the organization of guilds in trade and commerce, and universities. To a great extent in these times of combinations and trust organization, the corporation has taken on the idea wholly of corporate personality, instead of that of public utility. More than a century ago Blackstone said: "When it is for the advantage of the public to have any particular rights kept on foot and continued, to construct artificial persons, who may maintain a perpetual succession and enjoy a kind of legal immortality," the law authorizing corporations seems necessary and proper. Note that he predicated the need of this form of organization "for the advantage of the public." In the early history, and indeed till recent years in this country, the idea and principle of advantage to the public were both the purposes of law authorizing corporations and their limitations. The decisions of many high courts go to confirm this view.

But in recent years legislative bodies have on one account and another extended the rule under which corporations have been organized, till the persons participating in their organization, and not "public benefit" are the only conceptions of their being. Maintaining this view, recently the well-known head of one of the great trusts said: "It is not material to the public how business is transacted, whether by a corporation or by a trust, as the object is the personal interests alone of those who participate and invest for profit."

And so practically many states in their legislation seem to have drifted away from the purpose of the early law creating corporations, and herein lies the uprising against trusts which have taken advantage of this condition. No class of the people can say to any other class that "You did this." The stream never rises higher than its source. Year after year the people of all parties have been electing and re-electing to legislative bodies of the states those who, under misapprehension, or otherwise, enacted the laws perverting the true idea of public advantage in corporate bodies. The real remedy lies in a complete revision of these laws, and in a return to functions held to be for the "public advantage." It is not hard to discriminate or to determine what is included in such organizations. Great railway lines could not be constructed by single individuals for want of necessary capital, but in the development and growth of the country natural waterways and canals became totally inadequate in transportation, and it was and is greatly to the public benefit that railways be constructed, and associated capital and privileges of bonding and stocking became imperative under the conception of the corporation. And the same is true of other transportation, commercial, and the numerous manufacturing enterprises requiring great capital to meet the requirements and demands of the public. None of these obstruct free competition, for both in the matter of great transportation lines and manufacturing, the country has witnessed how public demand has called one after another into being, and competition has been left free along these lines of enterprise.

But state legislation in behalf of corporations in the past thirty years, in some of the states, losing sight utterly of the principle of public benefit, and looking only to private or personal advantage, have paved the way to combinations and trusts having in view the restraint of trade and destruction of competition, and it is this that has now precipitated the movement toward a remedy.

The old form of trust, in which one corporation held stock in another, was stamped out some years ago by the courts, but a new form of combination has appeared lately in which a corporation under a new name absorbs industrial organizations in given lines by purchase, and issues of stock, evidently having for its object such abridgement of the law of competition and limitations on production as threaten public interests. It is this new order of combination to which state legislatures must address themselves in the way of such revision of corporation legislation as will meet and defeat personal ends having no conception of public good.

It is held by some that the economic policy of this country promotes the organization of trusts. This is best answered by the facts, that Great Britain maintains a totally different policy, and yet that country is where trusts originated and where they yet abound. Great Britain has corporate and trust combinations capitalized up into the billions of dollars. There, as here, the fundamental provisions of law, originally intended to extend corporate privileges only in consideration of public benefit, have been perverted to recognize personal and private advantage largely. And so, eager always to avail themselves of such personal advantages, this condition has been seized upon by many, and thus far acquiesced in by all classes and parties, and only in the past few years have the people begun to realize that there was a wrong somewhere underlying the possibilities for such a condition. The note of warning sounded by the Sherman act passed by Congress in 1890 touching this question in its interstate relations should be made available in state revision of corporation law, and legislation that would stamp out trusts under state jurisdiction and authority.

It is readily seen that by such revision of the laws respecting corporations as would embrace the conception of advantages to the public, would of itself make impossible the organization of corporate trusts having the tendency toward restraint of trade, which is contrary to the interests of the public. At least such combinations would have no lawful status. The possibility of such combinations operating under the laws of states not so revising their codes, might readily be met and prevented by like proper requirements. There could be no breach of the amity between states under the recognition of such just provisions as put both home and foreign corporations on the same footing. It may readily be supposed that the action of a few state legislative bodies in this direction would soon influence all the others to a return to the original conception of corporate authority and privileges.

It has been said that revolutions never go backward. That is true of revolutions in the right direction, and when they tend toward higher and better conditions, but not applicable in fact or observation to industrial, commercial and social conditions of a state or nation possessing the power of imparting higher and better aspirations to all whom they touch. The fears and impressions of fatalism for the most part have their origin simply in misapprehension of the facts and want of ability to discriminate.

Take an illustration at point in the matter of commercial organization: When the numerous lines of railway from the central west to the seaboard began to consolidate, many believed that it was the beginning of capitalization of such power as would eventually bring ruin to great interests and great industries. That such consolidations have resulted in shortening transit three-quarters in time, and very greatly reducing expenses of travel and freights, these fears are now seen to have been without foundation. If it was then believed that such powerful capitalization would eventuate in combinations that would overthrow the law of competition and result in restraint of trade, the Supreme Court decisions of 1897, under the law of 1890, already referred to, show how strong the country is at the first appearance of possible danger. If the revolution in railway consolidations set its face for strides beyond the limit of public good, we had in the court decisions of 1897 a very marked illustration of the fact that such revolutions do go backward, and of the power of the nation to put limitations on corporate greed.

The philosophy of Mr. Jefferson, that the possibility of error might be tolerated where truth was left free to combat it, is applicable in business and commercial affairs under free competition and natural laws of trade. The law of the nation and the courts have shown how they stand for truth, so far as interstate commerce is concerned. The states may exemplify the power of truth over error in state relations in the same way.

J. G. SCHONFARBER.

Executive Committee Order Knights of Labor.

Thirty years ago the great organization known as the Knights of Labor issued its first public declaration of principle and intents, and the writers of that declaration must have been profoundly prophetic in the scope of their thought. The first paragraph in that declaration predicted exactly the conditions which have made it necessary as a patriotic duty for the Civic Federation of Chicago to call together these men present to confer as to the public welfare. The Knights of Labor is not a combination of private individuals bound together for the purpose of furthering their personal individual interests, regardless of any other individuals, or the common welfare of society. It is a popular combination, formed for the purpose of maintaining and defending the best interests of society as a whole, and guarding and advancing the general welfare. It has chosen as its slogan in this great social contest, "the greatest good to the greatest number," as follows:

"The alarming development and aggressiveness of the power of money and corporations under the present industrial and political systems will inevitably lead to the hopeless degradation of the people. It is imperative, if we desire to enjoy the full blessings of life, that a check be placed upon unjust accumulation and the power for evil of aggregated wealth. The much desired object can only be accomplished by the united efforts of those who obey the divine injunction, 'In the sweat of thy face thou shalt eat bread,' therefore, we have formed the order of Knights of Labor for the purpose of organizing, educating, and directing the power of the industrial masses."

Calling upon all who believe in securing the greatest good to the greatest number to aid and assist us, we declare that our aims are:

1. To make industrial and moral worth, not wealth, the true standard of individual and national greatness. 2. To secure to the workers the full enjoyment of the wealth they create; sufficient leisure in which to develop their intellectual, moral and social faculties; in a word, to enable them to share in the gains and honors of advancing civilization.

This is the general purpose of the organization, and the declaration goes on setting in detail twenty-four measures by which it is hoped the declared objects may be attained; all of these depend upon legislation directed by the popular voice, as our Constitution provides, and all are consistent and in harmony with the spirit of our free institutions and methods of our government.

It will thus be seen that the object of the Knights of Labor is moral as well as economic, fostering independence, pride of character, dignity and manhood, and endeavoring by precept and action to elevate mankind to that plane upon which it can share in the gains and honors of enlightened advancing civilization. Having thus called your attention to the character of at least one great reform labor organization and the basis of its work, I shall only briefly attempt to discuss its relation to trusts and combinations, our reasons for opposing the same, and a suggestion of remedy not so radical as to cause revolution.

We have long looked for and expected the conditions that now confront the people, but I trust we are not so blind as to confound all combinations of capital looking to economy of production and distribution with those especially detrimental to the interests of society. Trusts should be divided into two classes

344

at least; one class, that which find their being and profit in the franchises or special privileges granted by city, state and nation; receiving legislation which enables them to mortgage the unborn babe of the American citizen, as well as burden him by taxation to the point of bare subsistence. The other class is that which finds its profit solely by combination of capital, and performing useful functions in society, such as partnerships usually perform. Where this latter class are not enabled by the aid of an iniquitous and discriminating tariff or alliance with other corporations, that enables it to restrict production, it can do little harm in the field of individual competition. We believe the remedy for the first class of trusts is so simple and patent to all that there need hardly be a discussion of it now. It has almost passed from the field of discussion to the field of actuality. Over three hundred American cities have in part or wholly given us an example by municipal or state ownership of public utilities how these trusts can be eliminated from the field. If the power to oppress the people, to burden society and mortgage futurity has been given by law, it can be taken away by law, and that, too, without injustice to anyone. Public utilities, such as railroads, telegraph, water, electric light, gas, street railways, are among the principal trusts or combinations that oppress the people which can be easily and safely remedied. Our organization pointed this out at the same time it warned the people of the "alarming development and aggressiveness of the power of money in corporations," by suggesting in its preamble that all things which can be best done for the whole people by the whole people, should be so performed. At the bottom of the success and the main example for nearly all the combinations of to-day has been that given by gas and water corporations and municipal and state railways generally. Having gradually eliminated competition, they have watered the stock and distributed the same so as to make it almost impossible to secure local legislation that would restore to the people the valuable rights foolishly given away, lost or stolen.

It remains to be seen whether the national government is beyond the reach of a quickened public conscience, and can be induced to enact such legislation as will gradually pump the water out of these inflated capitalizations of inter-state roads, telegraphs and telephones, and restore to the people by taxation those rights which are as essential to the perpetuity of the state and nation as is the repelling of a foreign foe or the maintaining of the so-called public credit. Over-capitalization has been productive of higher charges for all these services to the public, and has opened the door for the speculator and the promoter, until, like England, we are on the verge of a South Sea bubble bursting, which can but bring misery and poverty to the entire country. As stated, we believe the remedy lies in the hands of the city, state and national governments to destroy this kind of trusts. They had their being in law, and should find their power for evil eliminated by law, that is, by condemnation and payment to the holders of the actual value of the property condemned, not including the franchise value, which has never become the actual property of the corporation, for the reason that even the state cannot give or deed away the rights of future generations.

The other kind of trusts, the commercial combinations, have little power for evil if deprived of the support and assistance of the special privileged corporations. Take away the railroads and their discriminating power between shippers, and where would be your Standard Oil Company? With railroads transporting one gallon of oil as cheaply as a hundred, as would be the case under government ownership, we could safely leave to individual effort the development of competitive enterprises that would keep down prices, while enlarging the field for employment.

In the mass of evidence presented before the Industrial Commission it was shown that enormous sums were paid in the form of rebates by the railroads of the country to the favored trusts, which favoritism alone appears to guarantee them the power to crush all opposition and establish a monopoly for each in its respective field. Had I the time, many instances in this evidence could be cited, namely: The Atchison, Topeka & Santa Fe Railroad case, and the great case of Mr. George Rice before the Inter-State Commerce Commission, in his endeavor to do business in oil on equal terms with other citizens. It would be only multiplying evidence to repeat these cases. The extent to which this favoritism goes in the discrimination against the competitors of trusts is almost impossible to estimate, but it is sufficient to maintain these monopolies, and let it be remembered that this discrimination is exercised upon the highways of the nation, upon which all citizens are supposed to have equal rights and advantages.

It is claimed by the railroad management that they are moving the freights of this country cheaper than the freights of any other country are moved. Statistics show that the average cost of moving freight is 0.85 cents per ton mile, including everything, and yet it was shown before the Industrial Commission that individual shippers had paid and were paying from 4.32 to

13.57 cents per ton mile. If this is true, and the average for all is the 0.85 cents per ton mile, then how much less than 0.85 cents per ton mile does the trust pay in order to bring the average of all freights of the country down to 0.85 cents? This has only been set out to show what an enormous advantage the trusts have under the present railroad system; indeed, with most of us this seems to be the key to the trust situation. With competition in the market shut off by the railroads, the trusts are the masters of the situation; the roads are not hurt, but merely get the freight from one shipper instead of many, thereby decreasing the employment of labor, and yet not decreasing the price of the product carried.

Now, what is the remedy? Take these railroads, these highways of the people from the corporations. By such legislation as will insure the payment of the actual value of the roads, less the over-capitalization of the franchise value and other water in the stock, re-establish the equality of all the people in the access to the highways of the nation. When this is done, the cornerstone which supports the trust superstructure, and the main edifice, will fall. With absolute equality over the railways of the country, so that every butcher could ship a car of cattle just as cheap as the beef trust, the beef trust could not hold the monopoly of the beef trade; with a like condition every owner of coal lands could reach the coal market on the same terms as the monopolistic combination of coal owners, and this is true in regard to nearly every industry monopolized by trusts. Their control of the means of access to the markets or their connection with those who do control these means of access is the principal source of their power.

To-day, by means of a postal system operated by government, the letter of the individual, pauper, or workman, miner or butcher, oil producer or farmer, goes to its destination just as quickly and at as little expense as the letter of an Armour, a Rockefeller or any king of industry. Send their coal, their oil, their iron, their meat, their wheat to market upon the same terms of equal speed and cost, and these great combines will soon lose their power for evil, and the increase of healthy competition will give increased employment to labor and higher wages because of demand.

Corporate ownership of railroads is the backbone of the trust and a protective tariff its right arm. It is within the limit of possibilities for the government, by the right of eminent domain, to come into the ownership and control of the railroad, and also to repeal the tariff tax upon every article controlled by a trust.

Do both these things, and it is scarcely probable that trusts could exist at all.

The withholding of opportunity to labor out of use through iniquitous tax systems in the cities and states has restricted opportunity and restricted trade. Tax idle land out of the hands of the monopolizer, or let him pay the people for the special privilege of controlling the land just the same amount as his competitor pays for utilizing the land, and we will have opportunities for labor galore, the demand for labor will soon raise wages. Coal mines and the farms, the building sites and the water fronts will resound with the ring of the pick, the hammer and the noise of the plow, for it will be unprofitable to hold the opportunities for labor out of the market. Our present system of taxation is so much to blame for the present industrial conditions that men who are seeking the remedy to correct must have the courage to apply the knife of legislation to the sore, even if it cuts to the quick.

I have grave doubts about the American legislator having arrived at that point of courage; probably his constituency have not suffered quite enough yet to make them forcibly prod him into action, and I am justified in this belief by the attitude of the last Congress toward the Dockery amendment to the tariff bill. It is now hardly disputed that the high tariff act has enabled various trusts and manufacturers to levy tribute on the American people to the full extent of the tariff, while only in one or two isolated cases dividing even a small portion of the result of the robbery of the whole people with their employees. The tariff tax has helped the industrial trusts to put up prices and enhance the cost of living to the consumers, and when we remember that the consumers are composed of seven-eighths of the people of the country and the employees of protected industries hardly the other eighth, it will be seen clearly how injustice is done by this iniquitous tax. It has not compelled the manufacturer to raise wages, nor to reduce the working hours, for both of these results wherever secured have been forced at the point of the strike by the organizations of labor, while the condition of the consumers, the larger mass of wage earners and farmers, has been lowered in the scale of civilization. No tariff tax ever helped the farmer to pay off the mortgage, nor the unskilled laborer to get over $1.25 a day, and only a beneficent God who ordained a famine or short crop in one country and smiling plenty in another has shifted the starvation point from one hemisphere to another temporarily, while the brain of man conceives and invokes measures that will eventuate in poverty for the millions all around and plenty for the few everywhere.

Let us summarize: The Knights of Labor are opposed to trusts and to restrictions upon trade, commerce and industry, because we believe that, firstly, trusts are an evil when allied with corporate monopoly, or when receiving special privileges from municipality, state or nation, and to secure these special privileges they resort to the corruption of councils, legislators, and Congresses, corrupting the body politic and lowering the standard of morality and liberty among the people. We believe this evil can be cured by municipal, state and national ownership of the means of transportation of passengers, freight and intelligence, and the absolute freedom to sell in the highest market and buy in the lowest. Secondly, restrictions upon trade by means of tariff tax is governmental aid to the trusts and a special privilege to levy tribute upon the consumers; and thirdly, because these trusts not only lead to legitimate economies in manufacture and distribution, but to abuse of legislation, corruption of courts and legislatures, and to the oppression of the masses, as well as shutting out the opportunity for employment for the industrial masses. Our platform in its fifth, seventh, seventeenth, and twentieth planks has for twenty-five years been offered as the proper remedy for these evils under our form of government, and until the people of this country are aroused thoroughly to the dangers to their liberty lurking in a continuance of the present system and demand at the hands of their law-making power the radical legislation needed, our work as the Knights of Labor will go on, organizing and educating the industrial masses to a realization of their rights and the need for real liberty.

M. M. GARLAND.

Ex-President Amalgamated Association of Iron and Steel Workers.

Mr. Garland, in "An Iron and Steel Worker's View of Combination," said:

With a full realization that this conference is made up of many of the brightest minds of the country, and being neither a constitutional lawyer nor a professor of economics, it would be the height of egotism on my part to say anything on this great question now under consideration, except from the standpoint of actual experience, and that must be by the humble experience of an iron and steel worker. And while this observation is from that source, yet it may, in application, fit most of the other branches of business and interests affected by the trusts and combinations. The whole life of the men employed in the iron and steel rolling mills must, from the very nature of his labor, be of the practical. Years of such toil leaves no room in his life for theory. With him is first to realize results; he reckons the probability of a question from actual experience with it.

The trust question is an old one. It has been the instigator of much attempted anti-legislation, and has formed the target for campaign speakers in almost every kind of elections, from ward aldermanship to the highest office in the land. Its influence was used as one of the exhorting features for organizing labor among the iron and steel workers more than a quarter of a century since, and now it works a most active development of organization among workingmen because of example from employer.

When the iron and steel worker became convinced that capital at all times had been used by some possessing it to monopolize particular branches of business, until the vast and various pursuits of the world were becoming centralized under the immediate control of a comparatively small portion of mankind, he realized that to secure for himself an equivalent for his labor sufficient to maintain him in comparative independence and respectability—to procure the means with which to educate his children and qualify them to play their part in the world's drama, it was absolutely compulsory that he form a combination with his fellow worker to control, as far as possible, wages and fair treatment. This organization was immediately formed, and is now termed a trust by many, but the fair mind cannot consider the open trade union as such under the general acceptance of the term; but in deference to a number of decisions by the eminent judges of both local and superior courts in the several states of the Union and the decision of an attorney-general of the United States, all of which declare us at least amenable to whatever penalties would occur to a trust violating the statutes of present enacted anti-trust legislation, to that extent we are compelled to accept the onus. But it is the recent rush of corporations, doing business in the same line of manufacture or interest, into one or more immense corporate combinations, usually termed trusts, that has challenged widespread comment and occasioned the discussion of the question by this conference. No corporation desires to lose its identity, and there can be no doubt that much of this, in the iron and steel industries, has been caused by the same elements that forced the workmen to organize—that of self-preservation. The corporation of many years' standing had grown with the increased uses of iron and steel, until in some branches of the trade several firms were more powerful and held more assets, each within themselves, than any of the trusts that have yet been formed in the same line of business.

The discovery of immense mountains of Bessemer steel ores in the Mesaba and adjoining ranges, together with the ductile and malleable qualities of steel, have made possible the introduction of machinery on a large and costly scale, and large capital rapidly gained an ascendency over the smaller and lesser equipped plant until one of two options against absolute dissolution only remained. One to try to eke out an existence on what orders might be left over after the larger plants had taken all that it could attend to, and the other was to combine capital with other plants that were at the same disadvantage, and form the corporate combine, the trust. Already the mighty change has taken place. We had passed the point where corporations in iron and steel were of great moment, whose capitalization was limited to thousands or hundreds of thousands of dollars, and we had entered the era of millions and hundreds of millions of dollars capitalization. The recent years of business depression furnished many examples of this truth. For instance, one of the largest steel firms in the country in the winter of 1893 and 1894, and at a time of dearth in orders, taking advantage of a glutted labor market, reduced the wages of employees, and then sent agents out with the open declaration that they were to take orders irrespective of price. The hope of citizens in many towns and villages, which depended on rolling mills and factories, was taken away, and thousands of workmen were bereft of even the broken time and small pittance that had served to keep them from want, while the boast of the large corporations went abroad, that they had given their employees steady work.

The possibility of an employee becoming a steel magnate, as insinuated by some of the speakers here, has long since become as scarce as the proverbial "hen teeth."

The trusts can avoid reducing wages wantonly. They can divide work among employees in times of depression in any line of trade, as the employees would then be in the employ of one or but few firms. But the inclination to better the condition of the employee will be no stronger with the trust than it has been with the corporation, but the endeavor to apply this legislation will find a more fertile field in this direction than any other.

But in considering the subject of legislation, so strongly urged by some against trusts, care should be exercised that the bills hold no ulterior meaning. The working people are appealed to in almost every state to urge the passage of some pet measure of certain representatives to law-making bodies, which propose to crush out trusts and combinations; and while it may be that labor unions do not possess the skill, cunning and capability of trusts to defeat the aim of the enactment, it is certain that the application of such legislation has found its final and only target to be labor unions. The record of neither city councils, state legislation or national Congress ever contained one breath of intimation that anti-trust, restriction of combination or interstate commerce laws passed by these could, in the least, interfere with the free and full exercise of the right of workmen to organize, yet, I make the assertion, without fear of successful refutation, that every one of these laws that have been passed upon and found constitutional by the courts have been found to apply to organizations of labor, and that every such law now on the statutes, not yet passed upon, will be so decided when adjudged, not excepting the much mooted conference called for, state law of Texas, nor the one that came from the home of the "red apple," Arkansas, or if either or both of them become federal enactments there would not be one small cluck left in the workingman's eagle that has soared so valiantly through this hall for the past two days.

Future anti-trust legislation must be drawn with a full knowledge of whether it is intended to cover the evil, claimed by this title, or whether it is to restrict the efforts of workmen in the organization of their fellowmen.

The position of the worker may become easier as the operation of the trust proceeds; the example is set and the necessity widened for every man in their employ to unite in common organization. The farmer, mechanic, laborer and business man alike will feel its effects for good or evil.

While it is with a true sympathy that springs from the actual experience of loss to the thousands of our men of remunerative positions by reason of the introduction of machinery that we behold the almost entire discharge from positions of that valuable class of citizens, commercial travelers, yet by their presence to the realm of the wage-worker will be added another element that gave but passing thought as to whether goods sold by them were made under fair or unfair conditions, and that the brain that could command a large commission will of necessity be used in the council halls of the labor and farmer organizations, and the horror with which, all too many, have held up their hands in beholding men in organizations of labor resorting as their last remedy to strike and stoppage of work in resisting unfair conditions which have been imposed upon them will have passed away, by reason of a fuller knowledge of these wrongs, brought about by the magic touch of concerted cause, and property rights will then be commingled with human rights by common consent. The right of workmen, by conference, to be heard through their own selection of representatives as to the rate of wages and hours the condition of trade warrants will become in fact, and the farce meeting now so often employed by capital as a prelude to the lock-out in order to enlist public sympathy will disappear under the melting rays of peaceful relations, forced by a wider field of legitimate trade unions, and the conference settlement will take the place of strike and lockout between employee and the corporate combination.

Thus far in this new day of trusts the workmen in rolling mills find their inclination is to treat with organization. The annual wage scales and agreement were presented by our representatives and conferences arranged promptly. An advance in wages, ranging from ten to twenty-five per cent in different departments, was secured, and further advances in wages seems assured by reason of advance in prices of material and product, which is one of our agreements. A number of plants that had been operating non-union and at unfair wages, were unionized by the wage rates applying to them since they had become a part of the trusts. I would not be understood to infer that there would not have been an advance in wages if the trust movement had not been on, nor do we think the price of material would have been less, for we note that in branches where trusts do not control the greater rate of advance has occurred in material. That in this country a trust, or the trusts, could long maintain an unnatural or inordinate price for material or product is a remote contingency, for not alone would other capital interested in the consumption of product combine on as large a scale and become their competitor, but the fact remains that there is not an article produced in these modern times, but there are, or can be, adopted several substitutes for it, and the cost, as a rule, will not vary enough to permit any very great or long-lasting extremity to our needs.

That this new form of trusts will bring, voluntarily, any new virtues to the business world is a doubtful question. They are organized for the purpose of making money, and will certainly attempt to operate to that end; but they have awakened more powerful watchers in the interests of the great mass of common people, and in this country the majority of the privileges of the people and interests cannot long be trampled on. The action of the trusts within themselves will soon decide whether they are to be tolerated as useful members to the nation's household, or whether the show of hands raised against them will relegate them to oblivion.

WILLIAM H. TUTTLE.

Member Illinois Bar.

At the present time, while the subject of trusts and combinations of capital is under discussion, and particularly while there is a general demand that such combinations and aggregations of wealth be regulated by law, a correct understanding of the legal status of combinations of labor becomes quite important. Such a knowledge is all the more important because it has received comparatively little attention. The legislator, who would regulate trusts, and at the same time not embarrass trades unions should understand the distinction, or lack of distinction, so far as the policy of the law is concerned between combinations of capital and combinations of labor. If the two are so closely allied in principle as to be separated with difficulty, every one interested should understand the matter, and be prepared to meet the difficulty, otherwise many radical measures, intended to root up the tares in the industrial field, will pluck up the wheat also. Striking examples of this have occurred, leading to unjust criticism of our judiciary and executive officers, because laws that were aimed at one class in industrial life, hit another class as well, and perhaps hit the other class first. We will take time to mention one illustration. In 1890 a law was passed by Congress, entitled "An act to protect trade and commerce against unlawful restrictions and monopolies." It provided that "every contract, combination in form of trust, or otherwise, conspiracy in restraint of trade, or commerce, among the several states or with foreign nations, is hereby declared to be illegal." The law was unquestionably aimed at railroads and monopolies, and intended to relieve the middle classes and laboring men. The laboring man, however, was the first to be affected by it, and it has even been so far-reaching as to make the railroad strike illegal, which subject we will discuss more at length hereafter. It can readily be seen that unless we understand the situation our somewhat frenzied demand, for radical legislation to help the laboring man, may cause him to pray for deliverance from his would-be friends.

This fact, with which a layman may not be familiar, should

be borne in mind in this discussion, as in all other similar discussions, that is, that most of the law principles involved are not found in the statutes, but belong to the realm of the common law, or unwritten law. The common law is a set of legal principles which courts have declared to be the law because the good of society, technically known as public policy, demands it. Public policy therefore plays an important part in our laws. It is the basis of the common law and the sanction of our statute laws. Indeed, statute law may be declared void because it opposes public policy. Story says: "What constitutes public policy is difficult exactly to determine. It is in its nature uncertain and indefinite, fluctuating with the change of habits and opinions, with the growth of commerce and with the enlargement of international intercourse, but the rule may be safely laid down that whatever contravenes an actual rule of policy or which interferes injuriously with the true interests of society is against public policy." Notwithstanding the fact that public policy changes with the times, no principle has remained more deeply rooted and unchangeable than the requirement that trade and competition shall be free from restrictions. It is the legal basis of our whole industrial life under the competitive system.

We now come to the important question in our discussion. Is there a distinction between capital and labor so far as concerns the requirements of public policy that there shall be freedom of competition? Is it against public policy for capital to combine in trusts and monopolies and artificially control the price of commodities which it has to sell, and not against public policy for labor to combine in trades unions to artificially control its wages? It may be safely stated as a general proposition, that the policy of the law recognizes no distinction between capital and labor in requiring freedom of competition. This was the rule of the English common law without exception, and is the rule of the present common law made up of decisions based upon principles of public policy. In recent years, however, certain distinctions have been attempted by statute law, which we will notice later. A leading case, State vs. Stewart, speaks in common of labor and capital as follows: "The principle upon which the cases, both English and American, proceed, is that every man has the right to employ his talent, industry and capital as he pleases, free from the dictation of others; and if two or more persons combine to coerce his choice in this behalf, it is criminal conspiracy. The labor and skill of the workman, be it of high or low degree, the plant of the manufacturer, the equipment of the farmer, the investments of commerce, are all in equal sense property. If men by overt acts of violence destroy either they are guilty of crime." Mr. Tiedman, in his text book on commercial paper, says: "All combinations of capitalists, or of workmen, for the purpose of influencing trade in their special favor by raising or reducing prices, are so far illegal that agreements to combine cannot be enforced by the courts." In the case of Doremus vs. Hennessy, recently decided by the Illinois Supreme Court, this general language was used: "No persons, individually or by combination, have the right to directly or indirectly interfere with or disturb another in his lawful business or occupation, or to threaten to do so for the sake of compelling him to do some act, which, in his judgment, his own interest does not require." These decisions, with many others, indicate that in the field of industry, capital and labor are partners of equal importance, endowed with the same privileges and subject to the same restrictions. We can only take time to discuss, somewhat disconnectedly, certain phases of the law of competition and apply the principles involved to both labor and capital, hoping thereby to at least illustrate the identity of these principles.

Free competition, whether involving capital or labor, deals with the unit and abhors a multiple. The law gives each person the greatest freedom of individual action in his business relations with others. Such freedom is the life of free competition. In this discussion we leave out of consideration all cases where one is bound by contract to work for a certain time, or to do a certain thing. Such cases are comparatively few, however. Likewise there are certain employments and lines of business charged with a public duty, which are required to furnish certain services to every one and treat all alike. The business of railroads, and other common carriers, keeping hotel, furnishing light and water to a municipality are examples. With these exceptions always in mind we may accept this as a general proposition, that every one may enter into or refuse to enter into, may continue or refuse to continue business relations with each and every one else.

This is true of both capital and labor, as proven by many decisions that use language which may be applied to both. It is so important that the action of the individual shall be perfectly free, that the courts will not inquire into the motive that actuates him in entering into, continuing or discontinuing business relations with others. So true is this that the courts frequently reiterate the statement that in this regard a person's actions may be governed by "whim, caprice or malice."

In emphasizing the freedom accorded to the individual, we have demonstrated the abhorrence of the law for any combination, or agreement, or other restriction that will deprive the individual of his freedom, whether voluntary or otherwise. If the law, to secure freedom of competition, accords to individuals unusual freedom, it likewise, for the same purpose, greatly restricts their actions when they pass from the relation of so many units to an association or combination. All agreements between two or more persons the object of which is to control the price at which the parties to such agreements shall sell their commodities, the amount of goods which they shall produce or sell, or generally to restrain trade and commerce are illegal and void as against public policy. The law is exceedingly strict in this regard. It insists that the determination of all these things shall be left to individual discretion. Under the common law, however, the penalty for making such an agreement consists in the refusal on the part of the courts to enforce them. It results therefore that the parties thereto may each individually carry out such an illegal agreement, without suffering any criminal liability. If one fails to carry out such an agreement, however, the other parties to the agreement cannot, compel him to do so. They cannot enforce against him any fine or secure damages for any loss to them caused by his failures. The court will help neither party in such a transaction, but will treat the illegal contract as void. Many contracts of this sort, involving capital, have been the basis of litigation, and the courts have again and again condemned them as against public policy. It is apparent that when such agreements between laboring men are disregarded by the parties thereto they may be deprived of further advantages and privileges under the agreement or association, but the other parties to the agreement would not be likely to consider it worth while to sue the violators of the agreement for money damages. The courts have therefore but seldom passed upon the legality of contracts to raise or regulate wages. The fact that comparatively few decisions can be found condemning contracts restricting free competition in labor has led some writers to question whether the law did not consider associations of labor more favorably than combinations of capital. We believe, however, the case of More vs. Bennett, decided by the Illinois Supreme Court, is directly in point, and correctly expresses the law. In this case one member of the Chicago Law Stenographic Association sought to recover damages from another member because the latter had broken the rules. The court said of the association: "It clearly appears, both from its constitution and by-laws, and from the averments of the declaration, that one of the objects, if not the leading object, is to control the prices to be charged by its members for

stenographic work by restraining all competition between them."
The court cites cases of which it says: "The determining circumstances in all of them seems to have been a combination or conspiracy among a number of persons, engaged in a particular business, to stifle or prevent competition and thereby to enhance or diminish prices to a point above or below what they would have been if left to the influence of unrestrained competition," and says: "All such combinations are held to be contrary to public policy and the courts will therefore refuse to lend their aid to the enforcement of the contracts by which such combinations are sought to be effected."

From the nature of things, very seldom can trusts and trade combinations on the one hand or labor organizations on the other. secure the co-operation of all competitors; and those outside the combination or association are a constant menace, whom the parties on the inside usually seek to coerce in whatever manner may appear effectual. This is the source of much litigation, and is the danger ground of the strike and boycott, to which are applied precisely the same principles as those that control in trusts and combinations. The strike and boycott are of such importance in this discussion of labor combinations as to require somewhat extended treatment.

The law encyclopedia says: "The term strike is applied commonly to a combined effort on the part of a body of workmen employed by the same master to enforce a demand for higher wages, shorter hours or some other concession by stopping work in a body at a prearranged time and refusing to resume work until the demanded concession shall be granted." The attempt of laboring men when on a strike to prevent others from taking their places has been so frequent that it has given rise to many decisions which have more or less clearly defined the rights of the strikers in the premises. One in sympathy with a strike may argue with one who is about to take his place, or who has taken his place, and try to persuade the latter that he would best serve his own interests and the interests of his fellow men if he refused to work and aided in making the strike effectual; but such argument and persuasion must not be accompanied by circumstances and such a showing as will amount to intimidation.

The general and prolonged labor trouble on the various railroads in 1894 gave rise to many instructive decisions relative to strikes, in many of which the courts discredited the strike and rendered decisions against the railway employees. From a legal standpoint the struggle was unfortunate for the laborer. As conducted by Eugene V. Debs, and the American Railway

Union, it was wrong in principle and could not succeed in law. The decisions of the courts were therefore favorable to the railroads. The strike of 1894 was fought out in the courts on the legality of the sympathetic strike, and the sympathetic strike lost. No other results ought to have been expected from a legal standpoint. As we have previously seen the workmen on the various railroads had the right to quit their employment as individuals, although their quitting was in the nature of a boycott, and was for the purpose of coercing the railroads to help them in their fight against the Pullman company. The law could not inquire into their motive as long as they acted as units, but they passed out of the realm of individual action and confederated to act as a union. As a confederating body they were without the immunity granted them as individuals. Right here the strike of 1894 failed and left the labor unions demoralized by an inevitable defeat.

The law will not, if it can help it, tolerate indirection or allow damages to be done on the excuse that it indirectly will be an advantage in competition. The labor unions were doing that which was injuring the railroads. It was incumbent upon them to show that their action in thus doing what would injure capital and inconvenience the public, was justified by some reasonable excuse. Their excuse was an indirect one. Employees of the Pullman company were on a strike for higher wages. The various railroads throughout the country were carrying Pullman cars under contract. Employees of the railroads entered into the strike, not because of their own wages, or to better their condition. Helping another body of employees in their struggle is too remote a reason for inflicting the damage to the railroads and the public that was necessarily contemplated. There was no element of legitimate competition, such as an attempt to secure their own higher wages. That this position was taken by the courts is indicated in the decisions in cases growing out of the strike.

In one of the cases it was said: "All the employees had the right to quit their employment, but they had no right to combine to quit in order thereby to compel their employer to withdraw from a mutually profitable relation with a third person for the purpose of injuring that third person, when the relation thus sought to be broken had no effect whatever on the character or reward of their service. "In the celebrated case against Eugene V. Debs, when carried to the Supreme Court, while the court would not grant relief to Debs, who was sentenced to imprisonment, Justice Brewer, in the course of a lengthy opinion, said specifically: "The right of any laborer, or any number of laborers, to quit work was not challenged."

In the heated conflict of the railway strike of 1894, where new phases of legal action were developing, and where it was necessary to cope with aggravated conditions, under the stress and hurry that usually attends cases requiring an injunction, some of the courts overstepped their rightful bounds. Judge Jenkins, during that time, in the United States Circuit Court, took the position in passing on the right of employees to quit service of a railroad that "one has not the right arbitrarily to quit service without regard to the necessities of that service," and held that "the duties of an employee of a public corporation are such that he cannot choose his own time for quitting the service," and held that the right of employees of a railroad "as the right of bond-holders and shareholders are subordinate to the rights of the public and must yield to the public welfare." This was a case where the employees of the Northern Pacific Railroad Company, operated by its receivers, had threatened to strike, if their wages were reduced, as contemplated by the receivers. An injunction was granted whereby such employees were enjoined from doing many things, such as disabling engines, interfering by force, and threats with those who desired to continue in the employment, and were also restrained "from combining and conspiring to quit with or without notice the service of said receivers with the object and intent of crippling the property in their custody, or embarrassing the operation of said railroad, and from so quitting the service of said receivers, with or without notice, as to cripple the property or to prevent or hinder the operation of said railroad." In other words, they were enjoined from striking to prevent a reduction of their wages. In his discussion, he says "This part of the motion presents the issue whether a strike is lawful. * * " "A strike is essentially a conspiracy to extort by violence. * * " "I know of no peaceable strike; I think no strike was ever heard of that was or could be successful unaccompanied by intimidation and violence. * * " "The strike has become a serious evil, destructive to property, destructive to individual rights, injurious to the conspirators themselves and subversive of republican institutions." "Whatever other doctrine may be asserted by reckless agitators, it must ever remain the duty of the courts, in the protection of society, and in the execution of the laws of the land, to condemn, prevent and punish all such unlawful conspiracies and combinations." This opinion was not upheld, but it contains an element of truth that can not well be disregarded. The higher court did not take this view of

G. W. NORTHRUP, JR. LAWSON PURDY
P. E. DOWE JOSEPH NIMMO, JR.
BYRON W. HOLT JOHN F. SCANLAN

the strike, and so reversed the case. Suppose, however, in view of the violence and lawlessness that frequently accompanies the strike, the courts should take the view of strikes in general expressed by Judge Jenkins. If our contention is correct that the law only gives great liberty to the individual and looks with disfavor upon the association or combination that seeks to destroy individual discretion, the courts could at once punish the confederating together as a conspiracy without any change of time-honored principles.

So far we have been dealing with the strike in its relation to the public policy of the common law. None of the cases above cited were based on the federal statute of 1890, and they must be considered and read with that fact in mind. We now must consider the effect of some of the statutes, and particularly the effect of the federal anti-trust law of July 2, 1890, on the status of the railway strike. Judge Thayer, in granting a temporary injunction during the strike of the American Railway Union in July, 1894, made use of the following language: "A combination whose professed object is to arrest the operation of the railroads whose lines extend from a great city into adjoining states until such roads accede to certain demands made upon them, whether such demands are in themselves reasonable or unreasonable, just or unjust, is an unlawful conspiracy in restraint of trade and commerce among the states within the act of July 2, 1890, and acts threatened in pursuance thereof may be restrained by injunction under section four of the act." This language is broad enough to cover all railway strikes. The Circuit Court to which the case was appealed quoted with approval the language of Judge Thayer above noticed, but followed with comments on the circumstances of the particular case that would indicate that the idea of the boycott was strongly in the mind of the court as well as the violation of the federal law. Another case in the federal court affords a still more sweeping statement. In Waterhouse vs. Comer it is stated: "It is true that in any conceivable strike upon the transportation lines of this country, whether main lines or branch roads, there will be interference with and restraint of interstate or foreign commerce. This will be true also of strikes upon telegraph lines for the exchange of telegraphic messages between people of different states in interstate commerce. In the presence of these statutes which we have recited, and in view of the intimate interchange of commodities between people of several states of the Union it will be practically impossible hereafter for a body of men to combine to hinder and delay the work of the transportation company without becoming amenable to the provisions of these statutes. * * * " "It follows, therefore, that a strike or boycott, as it is properly called, if it was ever effective, can be so no longer." The several courts, except the United States Supreme Court, that heard the case involving the injunction against Eugene V. Debs and others engaged in the railway strike of 1894, and the proceedings taken to punish Debs for violation thereof, base their authority in the premises upon the federal anti-trust law of 1890. The Supreme Court considered it unnecessary to discuss the effect of this law, for it held that the federal court had authority to issue the injunction under the general powers committed to the United States government over interstate commerce and the transmission of the mail, regardless of the act of 1890. We know of no case where the United States Supreme Court has passed upon this relation of the strike to the law of 1890, but we see no reason to believe that the lower federal courts have not correctly stated the effect of this law upon the strike. The authority which this statute has added to the common law is set forth in a recent leading case as follows: "Contracts that were in unreasonable restraint of trade at common law were not unlawful in the sense of being criminal or giving rise to a civil action for damages in favor of one prejudicially affected thereby, but were simply void and were not enforced by the courts. * * " "The effect of the act of 1890 is to render such contracts unlawful in an affirmative or positive sense and punishable as a misdemeanor, and to create a right of civil action for damages in favor of those injured thereby, and a civil remedy by injunction in favor of both private persons and the public against the execution of such contracts and the maintenance of such trade restraints."

In observing the important effect of the federal anti-trust law of 1890 on labor organizations we must not conclude that combinations of capital have been less seriously affected, or the equality of labor and capital in the law has been impaired. Beginning with a case decided less than a year after the passage of the law to the effect that "a combination between coal producers in one state and coal dealers in another to regulate prices of coal in a certain city * * * " "is in violation of the act of Congress of July 2nd, 1890," this law has been successfully invoked against many such industrial combinations, and through the decision of the United States Supreme Court has been used to destroy such powerful railway organizations as the Trans-Missouri Freight Association and the Joint Traffic Association.

The fact that labor organizations have not suffered under state anti-trust laws does not prove that these laws have been more carefully drawn to protect labor than the federal anti-trust law. Although about thirty states have passed anti-trust laws neither capital nor labor has been affected by them, for there has been no earnest effort to enforce them; and for this reason there are few, if any, decisions of the courts defining their application. Without such decisions, however, we can arrive at fairly definite conclusions concerning the application of some of these statutes with their accompanying penalties. We must keep in mind that public policy, outside of statute laws, shows little or no inclination to favor combinations of labor to regulate wages more than combinations of capital to control prices. We will commence with Kansas. We may presume the legislators there would be as careful not to injure the laboring men as in any state. The Kansas law contains the following provisions: "A trust is a combination of skill or acts by two or more persons, firms, corporations or associations of persons, or either two or more of them, for either, any or all of the following purposes: First, to create or carry out restrictions in trade, or commerce, or aids to commerce, or to carry out restrictions in the full and free pursuit of any business authorized by the law of this state." Such combinations are "declared to be against public policy, unlawful and void. * * " "All persons, companies or corporations within this state are hereby denied the right to form, or to be in any manner interested, either directly or indirectly," etc., "in any trust as defined in section one of this act," and prescribes the following penalty: "All persons, companies or corporations, their officers, agents, representatives or consignees, violating any of the provisions of this section, either directly or indirectly, or of abetting or aiding, either directly or indirectly, in any violation of any provision of this decree, shall be deemed guilty of a misdemeanor and shall be fined not less than $100 nor more than $1,000, and confined in jail not less than thirty days nor more than six months, and shall forfeit not less than $100 for each and every day such violation may continue." The language of the federal law, above mentioned, which the courts decided applied to labor organizations is, "Every contract combination in the form of a trust, or otherwise, or conspiracy in restraint of trade or commerce," etc. The Kansas law broadens this and in addition to "restrictions in trade or commerce" adds "or aids to commerce," and then makes it general and sweeping by including "restrictions in the full and free pursuit of any business authorized by the law." If, therefore, the court was correct which declared that "in any conceivable strike upon the transportation lines of this country, whether main lines or branch lines, there will be interference with and restraint of interstate or foreign commerce," and that the federal law applies to such strikers, then the Kansas law applies not only to strikes that effect trade and commerce, but all such organizations or movements of workingmen that restrict the free pursuit of any business authorized by law. The Kansas law was evidently patterned after the Texas anti-trust law of 1889, but the latter was amended in 1899, leaving out these features, which we have mentioned. The anti-trust law of Louisiana, New Mexico, Nebraska and Mississippi also include among the prohibited agreements and combinations those that are in restraint of trade and commerce.

Again it is possible that the anti-trust laws of several states may be used against labor organizations for the reason that in regulating the wages of labor they effect the price of commodities. In People vs. Fisher it was said: "Whatever disputes may exist among political economists upon the point, I think there can be no doubt in a legal sense but what the wages of labor compose a material proportion of the value of manufactured articles * * " "If journeymen bootmakers by extravagant demands for wages so enhance the price of boots made in Geneva, for instance, that boots made elsewhere, in Auburn, for example, can be sold cheaper, is not such an act injurious to trade? * * " "Combinations and confederacies to enhance or reduce the price of labor, or of any article of trade or commerce, are injurious. They may be oppressive by compelling the public to give more for an article of necessity or of convenience than it is worth; or on the other hand of compelling the labor of the mechanic for less than its value." The laws of Arkansas, Indiana and Georgia, which are all practically the same, include among the "arrangements, contracts, agreements," etc., which are declared illegal, those "designed, or which tend to advance, reduce or control the price or the cost to the producer or to the consumer of any such article or product." This provision of the law may be found to be as far reaching in its effect on the laboring man as the provisions of the federal anti-trust law. We have pointed out these items in the anti-trust laws of different states as perhaps the most conspicuous examples of some provisions that may be made to apply disastrously to labor associations.

In some of the anti-trust laws combinations of labor are specifically excluded from their operation, and in Illinois there is this exception made to the operation of the law: "Provided, however, that in the mining, manufacture or production of articles of merchandise, the cost of which is mainly made up of wages, it shall not be unlawful for persons, firms or corporations, doing business in this state, to enter into joint arrangements of any sort, the principal object, or effect, of which is to maintain or increase wages." But the United States Circuit Court in the North Division of Texas in 1897 decided the Texas anti-trust law of 1889 unconstitutional, as class legislation, because, among other things, it excepted from its provisions, restrictions of competition in "agricultural products or live stock while in the hands of the producer or raiser," which provision, or substantially the same provision, is also found in the laws of Arkansas, Georgia and Indiana. The decision last referred to we believe in certain particulars to be somewhat erroneous and we do not consider it conclusive, but the court seems to support that portion of the decision mentioned above by good argument. The court emphasizes the fact that "One of the most sacred rights of liberty is the right of contract," which these anti-trust laws seek to abridge. The court says, "The merchant, the manufacturer, the agriculturist, three great classes of the world, each dependant upon the other, each entitled to the same protection before the law, each justly claims alike, under the Constitution, the right of life, liberty and property." The Texas law was declared to be class legislation, because it allowed the agriculturist to make a contract restricting competition but did not allow the merchant or manufacturer to do so. If this is good law, might not the court by analogous reasoning divide industry into two classes, the laborer and the capitalist, and say that a law that allowed the laboring man to make contracts restricting competition, but punished the capitalist for doing the same is class legislation and unconstitutional?

We have discussed certain phases of the law governing all agreements and combinations that seek to prevent freedom of individual action in order to show in a general way the legal status of labor organizations, and also to prove that labor and capital in this particular occupy the same position before the law. It is true certain expressions, very comforting to the laboring man, appear in some of the decisions emphasizing his privilege to combine against the oppression of employing capital, which might indicate that the policy of the law outside of statute law is changing so as to allow labor organizations more rights than combinations of capital to control the individual actions of their members; but such dicta lose most of their force when it is noticed that they occur in decisions that really find against the labor organizations on the vital issues in the case, and appear to be included in the decisions largely for the purpose of making the actual findings in these cases less disappointing. We have not noticed anything in the law that indicates any important distinction in public policy so far as it relates to such organizations and combinations between labor and capital.

I. D. CHAMBERLAIN.

Executive Committee Order Knights of Labor.

We read that a certain man on the road from Jerusalem to Jericho fell among thieves (Christ used that word instead of kleptomaniacs). The priest and the Levite, representing the prosperity, aristocracy, religion and legal ability, passed by on the other side, too holy and so far above the common herd that it was profane, vulgar and irreligious to soil their clothes and fingers and spotless reputations by mixing with common people who work, and who should have brains enough to take care of themselves. But there passed a stranger, that hated Samaritan, who saw the man-brother was robbed, wounded and half dead; and he bound up the wounds, took him on the Samaritan horse to the inn, and paid the bills. What a fool! The modern man would ask: What office is he running for? Christ hit the evasionist with his interrogative: "Who was neighbor to him who fell among thieves?" In imitation of the organized labor leader of Nazareth, the Carpenter's Son, who was crucified between two thieves, because he "went about doing good," the order of the Knights of Labor builded upon the maxim: "That is the most perfect government, in which an injury to one is the concern of all," and have gone out teaching the rights of man, the republic of our fathers; and that a government of the people, for the people and by the people should not perish from the face of the earth. It is the only prominent organization on earth that has fearlessly taught opposition to all forms of violence; and labored to promote an intelligent and independent use of the ballot, instead of the strike and the gun. This is why it has been the target for the trust, and becomes the enemy of legal robbers. These little bands are organized throughout the country. They meet in the school houses of Kansas, in the vacant corn cribs of Nebraska, in the miners' cabins of the Rockies, and in the lodge rooms of the East.

The handful of speculators and absorbers of labor products are not the people to rescue labor, or correct economic ills. The four million wage-workers have been so long on the treadmill, and in the clash of greed against greed, that they are losing sight of the Goddess of Liberty, and their eye fails, except where the labor union holds the light of hope. But the thirty millions of farmers have remained closer to the foundation principles of the republic, and are the last to forget the landmarks of human liberty. They are the great producing element of society, and, therefore, the chief feeding grounds of the trusts. When their hogs, cotton and wheat must go on the market, "the market is off." When the corn is all in the hands of wealth, the market and rates are "fixed," and the speculator makes more than the farmer got for his crop. He sells his corn as "rejected corn," too low to be even graded, and it turns up in the next state as a prime quality of seed. I spent two days in a Nebraska county seat watching a battle to prevent a car load of flax being shipped to a customer outside the elevator pool, and followed for months the crushing out of an independent grain buyer, because he gave honest weights. No cars and an effort to assassinate came into the contest, and he was helpless in the courts. Milltown, near New Brunswick, N. J., with 2,000 people, workers in a rubber shoe factory—closed by the trusts, and the homes were only worth farm values. The 2,000 were homeless, but the wealth was transferred to the trust. Overton, Col., had one of the finest oil refineries, until the Standard harvested it, and they are now tearing down the brick buildings and the thriving young city is deserted. The farmer saw a large corn crop on top of a surplus, and ten million bushels in sight, and it went on the Chicago market for 70 to 75 cents. Ten years later with a crop failure, and a foreign demand, and only a half million in sight, corn sold in Chicago for 40 to 45 cents. When he asked the reason, he got soup, flavored with over-production, and charged it to religion, saloons, the agitators, high and low tariff, or anything that would be a soothing syrup, so he could be worked for another crop; and after a few such games got a mortgage on his farm. Few people seem to understand that one of the secrets of the fight on silver, including the shut-down of the western smelters, is to bear the mines, so the great syndicate can buy them in. The farmer sees the practice of law going to a few corporation lawyers, the practice of medicine rapidly concentrating to the company doctor; they see what the average merchant does not see, until too late, the department store to become the distributer, and the old merchant driving a mule team. He sees this meeting to-day talking of "palliatives" and "control" instead of an open war on a giant evil. The genius who influenced the county board to build a bridge with public money and license him to collect toll, and keep up repairs, got the other bridges condemned by dividing the profits with the chief spirit on the board. But for the guns of the citizens he would have had a fat job, and when he suddenly quit, a valuable financier had left the country, who might have adorned the halls of Congress.

Attorneys for these combinations simply ridicule or deny the general facts. They appeal to your patriotism; they ask us to worship the flag, even though we are hungry, and they look at us as cranks, and our proofs as merely isolated cases, that have no bearing in discussing the question. We, therefore, call up a single witness, divesting it of all possible personality and in great brevity.

Think of a business man going to New Mexico and Texas to hire fifty men on this agreement: "We will pay you $5 a day, pay all expenses, furnish transportation, food, guns, dynamite, and to each one an insurance on his life. Here is a list of forty-two men, in Wyoming, that we want killed, because they have taken homesteads and planted their cabins where we want to feed our cattle. For each and every one of these men you kill, each of you shall have $50. We will go along and defend you in the courts." They went, and the wires were down, until the sheriff and three hundred deputies cornered the gang, and then the wires worked all right. The president ordered the regular army to rescue the invading army from the sheriff. The two witnesses who saw the murder of two peaceable citizens were paid $1,500 and $1,700 to fly to British possessions, with the trust attorneys, who furnished horses. But a snow storm turned them to Nebraska, where they were arrested on a trumped-up charge of selling whiskey to Indians and the government sent a special train to rush them east, where the courts could not find them. One of the prominent counsel for the defense said to me, "The whole power of the government will be used to clear these men," and they went clear. But the trust papers and trust politicians never refer to it. I give it as it has been told on many a platform, and oft repeated in the press, but never challenged. Silence is the safest policy. Many of the farmers and miners of the Rockies are witnesses with myself. A generation ago the Senate Commission warned us of a deliberate attempt to make the governing power a function of commerce, and we notice this case as evidence that the trust has clandestinely entered the citadel of the nation, and seized the reins of government. The government must, therefore, take possession of the trust and use it or die.

In this conference we discuss "at" trusts, and daintily talk all around them, of classifying and placing them under control; and philosophize on molecules, and evolution of trade, and the benefits we can derive from stealing and murder, and the plunder of a people, all of which is as ineffectual as a penal statute in governing a cyclone. The trusts are all related, and fully understand that an injury to one is the concern of all—see Vanderbilt's holdings. This family of trusts owns the nation. It has control of nearly every line of industry, manufactures, the higher courts, carrying trade, the channels of thought, and pockets the products of the soil. It has made money the god, and labor the slave. While somebody, on this floor, favoring one of these engines of modern commerce, may deny my statements, and call it rot, the proprietors will laugh at the man who is hired to defend them. As a whole, labor, the foundation of all national wealth and greatness, is sinking into decay, while the political doctors seem to imagine that transferring wheat from the Armour elevators to the Leiter transports is a process of producing more breadstuff, and that the collection of labor products is a process of creating wealth. The wise men of the East assume not to see that the homes are fast becoming unproductive, and drifting into syndicate farms, like English estates, to be operated by menials. All our so-called industrials are in the trust family, now registering at the New Jersey Hotel, and there seems to be a trust on patriotism. You notice we are closing out our stock of man's inalienable rights, and we will soon be prohibited from speaking of our inheritance—a right by contract under the Constitution.

What is the quality of American manhood, politics and morality when our physicians of economics must call a thief some softer name, and when the home is going, and independent thought on these lines is strangled in the back yard, to prevent alarm? You may call it a dark picture that should be concealed. When your neighbor's house is on fire, don't tell him, for fear he calls you an alarmist or a pessimist. We do not yet accept as the only remedy Senator John M. Thurston's solution: "No great reform comes but by the sword."

The trust embodies all the evils that make a nation the pest-house of humanity, and is rapidly changing the republic to a monarchy. It was generated in greed and special privileges, defended by falsehood, animated by robbery, sanctioned by deception and fattens on the sweat and toil of honest industry. It is fed and prospers on the blood of humanity, and its natural food is the wreckage of decent government. It was conceived in a desire to defraud. It was born of illegitimate parentage. Its existence, in the broad sense, is in defiance of the genius of the republic, and a blot on the flag of our country. To shield and defend a monopoly is to give aid and comfort to an enemy in time of public danger, and to treat them as factors of advancing civilization is to compound a felony. "Pushing foreign trade" may be as selfish and murderous as highway robbery. The so-called trust or monopoly of to-day is a mutiny in society, an enemy of the nation and a conspiracy against civilization. The good secured to us by the trust method is small, incidental and only for the benefit of the legal monster. The evils are great, universal, national, loaded with decay, and fatal to a free people. They are made legal by statute, defended by official dignity and for the sole purpose of stealing the products of labor—the only source of national wealth and greatness. Are we to offer "palliatives" and decree where the monster may feed next, or dare we call a spade a spade? Europe and America are looking at the quality of the patriotism assembled in Chicago to-day.

A recess was taken until 3 p. m.

COMMITTEE ON RESOLUTIONS.

The committee on resolutions met at 2 o'clock, and Chairman Luce announced a sub-committee of five as follows: Edward Keasbey, of New Jersey, chairman; Cecil Smith, of Texas, Attorney-General Gaithers, of Maryland, S. H. Greeley, of Illinois, and Edward Rosewater, of Nebraska. There was a long discussion over the propriety of the conference adopting any resolutions. A large majority of the members expressed the opinion that no resolutions could be passsed by the gathering under the call issued by the Civic Federation. Albert Shaw, of New York, and W. W. Howe, of Louisiana, were the only members who spoke in opposition to this argument. The call was read and discussed at length. Finally Louis Post, of Illinois, moved that the committee report to the conference that under the provisions of the call issued it would be improper for the body to adopt a resolution of any kind touching on the subject under consideration. This was agreed to, and Chairman Luce was instructed to so report to conference.

AFTERNOON SESSION, SEPTEMBER 15.

The conference was called to order at 3:20 o'clock by Vice-Chairman H. V. Johnson, and David Ross, of the Illinois Bureau of Labor Statistics, took the place of E. E. Clark, of the Order of Railroad Conductors, on the program.

DAVID ROSS.
Secretary Illinois Bureau of Labor Statistics.

Whether this conference can accomplish anything beyond the interchange of opinions, or whether the process of consolidating industrial interests can be interrupted, or whether it is wise to attempt to interfere, are problems which, for the present at least, will probably remain to be solved.

Whether right or wrong, the opponents of the new system of industrial activity have acquired a temporary advantage in the odium they have succeeded in attaching to the modern definition of the term "trust." Eloquent tongues and brilliant imaginations are enlisted in the work of coining new words in which to picture the frightful calamities which await us.

Through our own neglect we have become the victims of villainy, the playthings of power. Nothing can save us now except an appeal to our neighbors who may happen to be members of law-making assemblies, and the enactment of a law, according to some, defining the ratio for the free and unlimited coinage of silver; according to others, through the confiscation of rent, as proposed by the advocates of the single tax; still others favor the nationalization of all industry and the municipal ownership and control of local monopolies.

We are not requested by our reformers to consider the economic causes which make necessary the reorganization of industry upon a stronger and broader basis. We are only asked to believe that these vast combinations have been and are being formed for the fiendish purpose of preying upon the necessities of the people, and, while robbing them, secure in the majesty of might, can afford to laugh at the law and the courts.

The present improved industrial condition of the world is the result of centuries of toil, energy, and enterprise. Mechanical and inventive genius, encouraged by great commercial opportunities, has made possible during the past few years such rapid changes in trade methods as to fill the minds of all with wonder and some with fear. Genius, like air, knows no limitations, and while the American brain has proved most potent in the performance of modern miracles, it is not entirely alone in this respect. The federation of labor and the combination of wealth go hand in hand and are found in their most complete and forceful form only in those countries where the people are the most advanced.

There is a destiny that shapes our ends, and the evident fate of the young republic is to become the future master and helper of the world. Industrial evolution traces its history from the small workshop to the factory, and from the factory to the great corporation, and from the corporation to the so-called trust of the present day.

Men who profess to betray great apprehension for the rights and liberties of the people cannot truthfully contend that these various transformations have operated to abridge any of their privileges. On the contrary, there has been a steady and substantial forward movement. It has been further demonstrated that with each succeeding change there has come, not only a reduction in the cost of life's necessities, but also an increase in the wages of human labor, with other improved conditions of employment. It would seem that our latest form of industrial organizations will prove no exception to the rule, so far as toil's compensation is concerned, as wages in the skilled and unskilled occupations have recently advanced fully 25 per cent. This upward movement in wages has not been entirely confined to products manufactured by the trusts. In a few lines of industry prices have been advanced considerably beyond the increase in wages—not on account of any trust influence—but due to the inability of manufacturers to fill orders, many of them for foreign markets. When productive capacity is more fully developed prices will again decline, but, under the new system, not so as to seriously impair profits or affect wages.

Engaged in a contest for the trade of the world, and believing that present combinations are the inevitable incidents of our industrial situation, there is no particular duty I would impose on our legislative assemblies beyond the reasonable regulations which every civilized state requires. As a state enactment, the Illinois anti-trust law, as amended, is the best I have seen. It makes lawful an advance in prices only where it can be shown that such action was taken for the purpose of maintaining or increasing wages.

The sympathetic public has always professed its willingness to pay if assured that labor gets its share. Men talk of destroying such combinations by legal enactment, on the supposition, presumably, that it is possible and desirable to return to the simpler systems of the past. Our development as an industrial state is the result of trade conditions and opportunities which no legislative power could anticipate or control. Even those charged with the management of great enterprises are seemingly powerless, and appear to be urged on by some unseen and irresistible force, and yet an influence which makes for better conditions.

While this question is distinctly an economic one, the indications now are that it will be given political significance. The peculiar feature about this phase of the case is the attitude of certain party leaders who, in the national contest of 1896, ascribed the horrors of that period to low prices. Men who had formerly favored free trade as a means of reducing prices became the most vigorous advocates of free silver, claiming that unlimited coinage would immediately enhance values. In the confusion of theories the wonder is that more people were not deceived.

The past two years have been noted for exceptional activity in all industrial and commercial lines. Great organizations have been formed for carrying on the growing business of the country. During this period the wages of workingmen have been increased and the hours of labor shortened. The application of sound principles in governmental affairs has aided in placing increased comforts within the reach of every wageworker in the land. In many departments of industry there is a scarcity of labor. Yet in the face of these encouraging indications—and they present the appearance of permanency—we are asked by certain discontented disciples to believe that the method of the new business era constitutes the greatest danger that confronts our republic.

This class of industrial pessimists have put upon their fear and fancy the duty of destroying their judgment.

> " Imagination bodies forth the forms of things unknown,
> * * * * And gives to airy nothing
> A local habitation and a name. "

Much of the public feeling against so-called trusts is the result of misconception. Certain people have been educated to think that the combination of capital, like the organization of labor, is to consummate the schemes of plunder and oppression. This opinion not only reflects unjustly upon our motives as civilized beings, but it has arrayed against it all the laws of trade.

It is impossible for any combination of employers to permanently fix the price of any product where the field is open to face competition. The only sense in which a trust could be maintained is where, by reason of greater economy in production, the product is placed upon the market at a price so low that others would have no inducement to compete. Against this form of "price fixing" the people who consume would certainly have no reason to complain. In spite of all our prejudices, has this not been the tendency?

When the great railroads organized years ago the apprehension prevailed that rates would be advanced, and the calamity prophets of that day, like the present, were painfully realistic in describing the fate that was to destroy us. Transportation charges for freight are less by two-thirds now than they were prior to the organization, with a corresponding improvement in the service.

The independent refiners of petroleum will unite in declaring the Standard Oil Company a monopoly, and yet it cannot be disputed that it was powerless to maintain prices. The reports show that the wholesale export price of oil has declined from 25 cents per gallon in 1871, to less than 6 cents in 1899. The people are getting a better article for nearly one-fifth the former cost; changes in the process of refining have saved the people millions of dollars, without, it is fair to presume, impairing the profits of the company.

The oil and railroad interests of the country have been singularly free from labor disturbances. As a matter of recent history, our most serious conflicts have been with interests that neglected to federate. Labor leaders will agree that better terms of employment can, as a rule, be obtained from large than from small employers. Why, then, should we fear the results of consolidation? It is the part of reason to encourage a tendency that will make possible higher wages, lower prices, and less hours of labor.

Workingmen who will be expected to join the crusade against so-called trusts should have a care lest they become the victims of designing demagogues who would invoke the law to punish those who favor the restrictions which labor unions impose.

M. L. LOCKWOOD.

President American Anti-Trust League.

M. L. Lockwood, president of the American Anti-Trust League, spoke on the subject of "Property Rights and Human Rights," saying:

We are confronted by great questions, greater, I feel, than have ever confronted any generation of men. Slowly and by tortuous route man has pulled himself up to the present stage of civilization, and we now live in the most important age of all the centuries; in an age in which the capability of this man for self-government will be put to a new test, tested in that crucible of absolute unlimited supply of corrupt corporate money in our public life. Absolute unlimited corrupt money, because if they may be allowed to destroy competition and plunder the people, the trusts and monopolies and railroad combines can afford to make it absolutely unlimited. From a money standpoint it will pay them.

We live in an age of the most marvelous development, in an age in which man has come nearer to unlocking the secrets of nature than ever before, in an age in which he has harnessed, blocked and unloosed the lightning and has invented labor-saving machinery so perfect in its mechanism that it can almost think and actually talk. Man has more than doubled his power to produce. He has invented compressed air drills that can strike five hundred blows a minute, when he could once strike only twenty-five a minute.

And yet corporations have claimed it all. Corporations say, "This is ours." "That the marvelous inventive genius of man in the creation and production of labor-saving machinery shall not lighten the burden of man at all." Yes, and when multiplicity of factories create competition for man's labor and competition developed in the supplies to man so that he was commencing to realize a benefit, then corporations further combined created trusts and monopolies, destroyed competition, combined to force man to become a cog, a commodity, a serf to their grind for money. And when with the help of the compressed air drill and with steam and electric power it had become possible for man to mine enough of the precious metals with which to pay his honest debts in the coin of the contract and walk uprightly and free of debt, then the shylocks of the world in secret and by corrupt means demonetized one of the precious metals, thereby

375

doubling the value and purchasing power of the other, chaining man to the rock a more helpless slave to debt.

My friends, do you recognize that under this system of monopolies and trusts that all of man's inventive genius and marvelous creation and production of labor-saving machinery has only heaped on him a heavier burden, that a few by the organization of trusts and monopolies are becoming multi-millionaires, while the burden upon the back of man is becoming heavier and heavier for him to bear? Do you recognize that these great captains of monopoly and finance under this system to-day are absorbing all the wealth produced by the people: and more, that they are annually absorbing a part of the accumulated wealth of the nation? Do you recognize that annually tenant farmers in America are increasing by thousands; that the property of this great nation is slowly but surely being concentrated in a few hands,—the rock upon which old Rome and Greece and Carthage were wrecked? Is there no way to call a halt and turn back from this road to ruin?

To-day we have men with fine-spun theories telling of the advantages of trust combinations, telling us that trusts and monopolies can lop off here and lop off there and make more money. Money everything! Man nothing! My friends, they have gone money mad. Can it be possible that man, man made in the likeness of God, has become so cheap that he shall be ground under this juggernaut of monopolies and trusts that a few may become rich in money, rich in millions that have already become a curse on their hands, a curse to their sons and to their daughters, a hindrance to the development of that kind of noble manhood and womanhood of which they and the republic may justly be proud?

My friends, we are confronted to-day by two great forces, property rights and human rights. And now when property rights assume the new relations of perpetual corporate ownership, an entail, without human heart or human conscience behind it, what is its power for evil? We eulogize Jefferson for his delivering us from the curse of propinquity and entail, and we find ourselves now in the grip of a greater monster. England charged the old East India Company four hundred thousand pounds, two millions of dollars, annually, for the right to plunder the people of India; and they would only give fifteen years at a time, at that. But this great republic of ours gives the Standard Oil Company, the Sugar Trust, the Big Four Beef Combine, and the rest of these little trusts the perpetual right to plunder the producers and consumers of America, and doesn't charge them a cent. If the

Standard Oil trust could be secure in the monopoly they now have, they could well afford to pay the government thirty millions of dollars annually for the privilege, and cheap at that.

And here I must digress for a moment.

I was somewhat surprised last evening to hear a gentleman upon this floor tell an American audience that Russia had put a protective tax of $2 a barrel on oil to keep American oil from driving the Russian oil out of Russian markets, and in the very next moment he tells us that if it had not been for the organizing genius of the Standard Oil Company people that Russian oil would have flooded the American markets and dried up the American oil wells and shut down American refineries. Now that is spreading it on pretty thick—thicker than I have been used to, and I have been used to a good deal. The gentleman would have us believe that the Standard Oil Company have a monopoly of the brain and business capacity of America, but I want to tell the gentleman and you that if it had not been for railway rebates and discriminations that there would never have been a Standard Oil trust monopoly. I want to say to the gentleman and to you that if he will re-establish and maintain equal rates over the railways of America (that in spite of this legitimate evolution of business that we hear so much about), that the energy, enterprise, courage and business capacity of the American people will drive the Standard Oil Company, with its extravagant methods, into a secondary position in the oil trade of America in less than ten years. Oh, but they say that that would be waste, that that wouldn't be evolution of business, that that would be competition, but I want to say to you, my friends, that competition is a good thing for the people and a bad thing for monopoly.

Yes, we are confronted by two great forces, property right and human right, for the last two hundred and fifty years. For the last two hundred and fifty years whenever property rights have encroached upon the rights of man, man has moved onward. He came to America. Along the Atlantic coast for the last one hundred and twenty-five years, when property rights have encroached upon man, the brave and the true went west, and they have gone on and on until they can go no farther. And they have turned back, and to-day property rights and human rights have met upon the highway and are combatting for the mastery. The echoes of dynamite from Shoshone County, Idaho, from Cleveland, Ohio, and from Brooklyn, New York, admonish us that the battle is on. It is not of our choosing, but the battle is on.

My friends, do you recognize the gravity of the situation?

Do you recognize that a new issue is upon us, the solution of which will take great men, "sun crowned, who live above the fog," men prompted by the noblest impulses, no money-worshiping men, no corporation, railroad-controlled men, will do; but statesmen broader than the world had ever known, noble men, brave enough to hold the scales, appreciating the mighty issues of the hour; men who can weigh and weigh justly human rights, human flesh and human blood, human heart and conscience, human hopes and human aspirations in the one scale, and property rights in the other. This is no work for pigmies. This is a work for giants, filled and prompted by the divine spirit of God. Such men and such men only can meet and solve this issue and carry the republic upward and onward in its mission for mankind.

My friends, there has been so much cold, cruel, corporate cash crept into our public affairs that I want to call your attention to the fact that while manhood and land and all unmonopolized commodities are becoming cheaper and cheaper, that almost all corporate capital has nearly doubled in value in the last three years. Why is this? It is because corporations have been given free rein to combine, to create monopolies, to create freight traffic and passenger associations, to destroy competition and to plunder the producers and consumers of America. That's why.

My friends, a freight traffic association, a trust or monopoly create no wealth. Freight traffic associations and trusts are organized to take from other men the wealth they produce without giving them any adequate recompense in return. Wealth is not created by trusts. Wealth is created by labor, by hard, untiring application of brain and muscle upon the raw resources of nature. Trusts create no wealth. Trusts and monopolies, by the destruction of competition, obtain power to fix prices to the producers and consumers and then plunder all producers and consumers of wealth.

Let me illustrate: Every man, woman and child in America that works, works, and as a result of this labor a certain enormous amount of wealth is produced in one year. Don't get away from the fact that freight traffic association and trust combines created none of it, that labor created it all. Now then: Let us bring all this wealth that has been created in one year together in an enormous pile before us. Now, then, if, under this system of monopolies and trusts, the Standard Oil Company can come in and take from this pile of wealth that the people have produced, say, fifty million dollars' worth of it annually; and if, under this system the Sugar Trust can come in and take, say, two hundred million dollars' worth of this wealth that the people have produced annually; and if, under this system, the Big Four Beef Combine can come in and take twenty millions' worth of this wealth that the people have produced annually; and if, under this system, the freight traffic and passenger associations can destroy competition and take from this pile of wealth that the people have produced three hundred millions annually more than the law of competition would give them; and if, under this system, all of these innumerable trusts which now control nearly every necessity of human life can come in and take from this pile of wealth that the people have produced all they can get under this infamous system, there is practically nothing left for the people. This system must not go on. It must stop. It is ruining our institutions of government. It is undermining the foundation stones of the republic. It is uprooting the tree of liberty and there is no virgin soil in which to plant it again. Can we not join in the restoration and maintenance of the doctrine of equal rights to all and special privileges to none? Cannot we join in rescuing our dear land and country from the curse of a corporate oligarchy of wealth upon the one hand or the horrors of a French Revolution upon the other?

Mark you, it was the lion-hearted, the cream of the world, who faced old ocean's roar that they might be free and equal. If we fail now, popular government as our fathers planned it, is gone and gone forever. Mind you, the brave are not the small. They would move onward before they would stop and quarrel, but drive them to the wall, and then look out. My friends, the brave are at the wall now. The monopolies, the trusts and the shylocks have put them there, and they are fighting back. But this military power, this 100,000 of a standing army they want; my friends, these questions cannot be settled with a standing army. This standing army has already been allowed at the behest of this corporate conspiracy against American rights to arrest innocent American citizens in Shoshone County, Idaho, and put them in a bull pen without any warrant of law. And this in free America under the Declaration of Independence and bill of rights and the Constitution of the land! My plea is not for criminals. My plea is for the rights of American citizens, for there is nothing so sacred between heaven and earth,—aye, there is nothing more sacred, even at the holy altar of God than the right of American citizens. And yet we have seen these rights trampled under foot by this military power. An outrage against an American citizen in Idaho is an outrage against you. An outrage against an American citizen in Idaho is an outrage against every American citizen everywhere. If they can do this thing in

Idaho to-day, they can do it here to-morrow. This power grows from that upon which it feeds. The power that is behind it is the selfish greed of corporate capital. "Onward and onward they go, determined, it seems, to drive the American people to destruction; to give their roofs to the flames and their flesh to the eagles." I see men before me who have been reared in an atmosphere of luxury who look upon these words as extravagant. My friends, you do not know the heart beats of the masses as I know them. Now, then, what is the remedy?

One of the most important remedies is national ownership of the highways of the people, the railroads. For railway discrimination has been the father of it all. But how can this great corporate conspiracy against equal rights and equal opportunities be checked and driven back? That is the question of the hour. My friends, there is not a monopoly in America to-day but has been created and maintained by railway discrimination—some system of favoritism. These trusts and combines do not have a monopoly of the brains and business capacity of the country. Under the great law of evolution, keener brains and brighter minds and men with more intense capacity for application to business are being produced. It is only when trusts and monopolies are hedged behind some condition of advantage that they can expect to monopolize. No one knows this better than the great leaders of the trust-monopolies. They know it so well that their greatest energies have been directed, not to a matter of the superiority of their goods, but as to how they can best manipulate the men who control the highways of the people so that they can go over these highways with their goods to the practical exclusion of their competitors.

The bludgeon that has created all exporting monopolies and trusts is railway discrimination, secret rebates, manipulation of cars and a general effort on the part of the railway managers to hinder, humiliate and discourage all men whose tastes and inclinations lead them into the channel of business occupied by their favorites and co-conspirators. This power is also an important factor in maintaining manufacturing trusts that do not export. The fear of railway discrimination, the fact that all moving spirits in these great industrial combinations stand close to the men who control the highways of the country, deter men from putting their money into enterprises against such desperate odds as those created by railway favoritism.

Then what is the remedy? Take these railways away from these corporations. Let the government own and run them.

Under the power of eminent domain, take them. Pay for them just what they are truly worth. Run them under a department of government just as the postoffice is run now. Then every man can go to market with the products of his labor just as cheap as any other man. Then equal rights and equal opportunities can be reëstablished. But, says one, how can the government pay the interest on this enormous public debt which the purchase of these roads will create? My friends, the people, who are the government, are paying it now. In excessive freight rates charged by these corporations they not only pay the interest on the bonded debt of these roads, all dividends on watered stock, but they are paying hundreds of millions annually for the benefit of monopolies, trusts and favored shippers.

One great advantage of national ownership is that the bonded debt necessary to purchase all these roads could be placed by the government at from one and one-half to three per cent less interest annually than is now being paid by these corporations on their bonded indebtedness. And this great saving of interest would be an important factor in cheapening the cost of transportation to the people. By government ownership, the people are only changing the managers of their highways. And the present managers have shown themselves unworthy to perform such a great public duty. By government ownership, only, can the equal rights of the public over these highways be guaranteed to the people.

Guarantee absolute equality over the highways of the country so that every butcher can ship a carload of cattle just as cheap as the Big Four Beef Combine, and the Big Four Beef Combine cannot hold a monopoly of the meat business of America twenty-four hours. Guarantee absolute equality over the highways of the country so that the independent oil producers and refiners of America can go to market just as cheap as the Standard Oil Company people and the wrongs of the Standard Oil Company will soon be a thing of the past.

How can this reform be brought about? How? By creating a great political force, independent of party, independent of party bosses, strong enough to drive from public life, from legislative halls, from senatorial chambers, from executive chairs and judicial benches the subservient tools of the trusts and corporations and put in their places men whose hearts beat in sympathy with God's toiling millions. When you have done this, the rest is easy.

How can this great political force be created? By all men of all parties who are opposed to trusts and monopolies, organizing in their respective counties and townships American Anti-Trust Leagues, an organization interfering with no man's politics, an organization the religion of which is to vote against men who are controlled by trusts and corporations and to vote for men who are prompted by impulses for the public welfare. Let the old parties nominate their candidates and the men of the American Anti-Trust League will elect the good ones and defeat the bad ones.

Let all men of all parties, religions and creeds, who are opposed to trusts and monopolies and who are in favor of the great basic principles of equal rights to all and special privileges to none, join in the defense and maintenance of these great fundamental principles of the American republic. This is no time for the friends of the principles to divide their forces. Let all men who love their country better than they do their party, come. Let all Democrats, all Republicans, all Populists, all Prohibitionists, come. Let all Knights of Labor men come. Let all Farmers' Alliance men come; let all American citizens come and fight for the maintenance of the great principles of equal rights for that great principle of the brotherhood of man for which the lowly Nazarene suffered upon the cross, that He might inculcate it into the hearts of men. Come and create a great power strong enough to drive from public life all men, be they Democrats or be they Republicans, who are opposed to these principles, and re-establish equal rights and equal opportunities to the American citizenship. Divided, you are but as egg shells in the hands of the enemy. United you are omnipotent. These questions are above party. They are as broad as our common country.

The weapon is in your hands. The greatest weapon in all the annals of time. It is greater than gatling guns, greater than dynamite—aye, the thirteen-inch guns may thunder from all the battlements and they are but puny compared with your weapon, the ballot. Use it, and see that it is honestly counted. He who would use dynamite and vote wrong will be damned through all eternity.

This precious weapon, it costs oceans of blood to wring it from the kings and emperors and the aristocrats of the old world. Use this weapon earnestly and prayerfully—this weapon before which legislators, congressmen, senators, presidents and judges are but as chaff in the whirlwind.

Organize the American Anti-Trust League. Stand shoulder to shoulder with all the sons of toil. Rescue our land and government from the curse of a corporate oligarchy of wealth. Rescue popular government from the grave opening to receive it. Carry the republic onward and upward in its mission of giving to man an equal show in the battle of life.

Do this and you will be blest of all generations of men.

A photographer was given possession of the stage and took a flash-light picture of the assemblage.

EDWARD QUINTON KEASBEY.

Member New Jersey Bar.

Edward Keasbey, of New Jersey, spoke on "New Jersey and Trusts," saying:

New Jersey has been called the mother of trusts. I have not come here to maintain or defend them, for although many of them are only a few months old, they are all big enough to take care of themselves. I have come to hear what is said about them outside of their home, and to carry back to people of my own state any suggestions you may have to offer for their regulation and discipline. At the same time I would like to say a few words on her behalf, and to state as clearly as possible the principles upon which she is acting in dealing with the corporations for whose existence and conduct she is in a measure responsible.

It is true that many large corporations have been formed during the last few years under the laws of New Jersey, and that these are called the trusts. The names of many of them are well known. In name and in form they are merely ordinary corporations organized under an old statute in New Jersey that makes provision for the formation of manufacturing companies, but their capital stock is very large and their names will be recognized as those of some of the most notorious of the trusts. There is the Standard Oil Company, with a capital of $100,000,000; the American Sugar Refining Company, with a capital of $75,-000,000; the American Woolen Company, with a capital of $65,000,000; the Amalgamated Copper Company, with a capital of $75,000,000; the Distilling Company of America, with a capital of $125,000,000; the Federal Steel Company, with a capital of $200,000,000, and many others. The whole number of corporations organized between the first of January and the first of August of the present year is 1,636, and the aggregate of their capital stock is more than two thousand million dollars.

New Jersey, indeed, is not the only state in which large corporations are formed for the purpose of carrying on business throughout the whole country. West Virginia and Kentucky have for a long time afforded especial facilities for the formation of companies intending to exercise their powers in other states, and Delaware has lately offered peculiar inducements for the creation of such companies. In fact there is hardly any state in which corporations cannot be formed with capital enough and powers enough to become formidable rivals of the greatest of the companies that have been organized in New Jersey, and yet it cannot but be interesting in a conference of this kind to inquire what it is in the laws or policy of New Jersey that leads men to turn to that state for the organization and protection of the capital invested in such great enterprises.

Combinations of capital for the purpose of controlling the market are no longer made in the form of trusts. They are no longer made by means of agreements to refrain from competition, and by placing the stock of rival companies in the hands of trustees. When the courts declared that such agreements and conspiracies were invalid and the legislatures of many states declared combinations in the form of trusts or otherwise to prevent competition to be unlawful the agreements were annulled and the combinations were dissolved, and men who desired to unite their interests under one control formed corporations and transferred to them the stock or property and business of existing companies. It is these corporations that we have to deal with and not with agreements in restraint of trade or conspiracies to prevent competition and maintain prices.

The results intended and accomplished by the corporations may be the same as those intended by the trusts, but the difference is vital in its legal effect.

The corporations are in form like other corporations and they exercise the rights of property which are common to all corporations, and indeed to all individuals. They differ from other corporations only in that they are larger and more powerful, in that they have more capital, and have acquired the control of many separate enterprises under a single management, and as a consequence they do in effect prevent competition among the several enterprises under their control, and tend to monopolize, so far as is possible, the trade of those enterprises. It is in these points of difference that they resemble the combinations made in the form of trusts, and it is in these points of difference that they are regarded as dangerous, but in discussing the dangers and the remedies it is important to bear in mind, first, that it is not trusts or agreements in restraint of trade that we have to deal with, but large corporations, and secondly, that it is not corporations as such

384

chat have aroused this anxiety, but only the fact that the form of organization has been used to avoid the effects of excessive competition and to control so many individual enterprises as to create a single ownership and create what is called a monopoly of the trade in which they were engaged. It is the attempt to prevent competition and create a monopoly that has alarmed the people and provoked antagonism. It is for these that remedies are demanded.

It is in view of these facts that I wish to inquire why it is that so many large companies commonly called trusts have been formed under New Jersey's laws, and to consider whether she owes it to her own people, or to the country at large to make changes in those laws. There has been no legislation in New Jersey against trusts as such. No statute has been passed declaring combination and agreements by way of trusts or otherwise in restraint of trade to be unlawful. When combinations of industrial enterprises became so large as to be formidable, it soon became apparent that it was not easy to find words which would apply to the really formidable combinations of capital without affecting the freedom of contract between individuals and making illegal a great number of perfectly harmless arrangements with respect to the conduct of their trade. It seemed best to leave it to the courts to declare invalid contracts which were found to be really against public policy rather than to pass laws in general terms which might hamper the liberty of individuals and restrict the natural tendency of organized society toward combination of effort. This tendency among the workingmen had been recognized and encouraged by the repeal of the laws making it criminal for them to combine to obtain higher wages and this was followed some years after by removing from the conspiracy act all reference to acts injurious to trade or commerce. The question what acts are injurious to trade or commerce was considered too difficult a question of political economy to be left to a jury in a trial for conspiracy.

The first fact to be noted in the inquiry into the policy of New Jersey with regard to corporations is that there is nothing of much consequence that is new in her existing laws. The large companies lately incorporated were organized under a general law which, in its substantial features, has been in force ever since 1846, and which has been unchanged in any very important particulars during the last twenty-five years. From a very early time it has been the policy of New Jersey to encourage the combination of capital for the promotion of industries, and charters were freely granted for that purpose. There is one that is still in force that was drawn, or at least revised, by Alexander Hamilton, for the formation of a society for the establishment of useful manufactures, with a capital of one million dollars and with power to hold property to the amount of four millions, and with authority to create a city government which was to take the name of the great New Jersey lawyer who took part in the formation of the Constitution of the United States and which became the great manufacturing city of Paterson. Special charters, however, created special privileges, and a general act, as I have said, was passed in 1846, and the power to grant special charters was abolished in 1875, and in that year a revision of all the general acts concerning corporations was made and permission was given to any persons to form corporations for any lawful business or purpose whatsoever. The provisions of that act were substantially the same as those of the earlier statutes, and these provisions have remained substantially unchanged until the present day. The act was drawn with the purpose of carrying out the settled policy of the state to encourage the aggregation of capital for promoting manufactures and developing the resources of the state. It was recognized that the efforts and the means of individuals were inadequate to large undertakings, and that provision must be made for combining the resources of many without risk of individual liability, and corporations were regarded as a means of accomplishing this result.

The earlier acts contained a provision for filing statements every year of the condition of the companies, and their assets and liabilities, but this was omitted from the act of 1875. It was considered that the publication of such a statement might, under many circumstances, be disastrous to the business and that such a requirement would not be tolerated with respect to the business of individuals. Provision was, therefore, made that stockholders should have access at all reasonable times to the books of the company, and they were given power to make such regulations as they saw fit for the conduct of the business, but no obligation was laid upon the company to make known to the public or its rivals the precise condition of its affairs. In this respect the policy of New Jersey differs from that of many other states, and in this conference publicity is suggested as a safeguard against the dangers of the large corporations called trusts. Without argument now, I wish only to emphasize that the policy of New Jersey was adopted nearly twenty-five years ago with a view to the government carrying on business within her own borders. It is a part of her policy of treating corporations as associations, of individuals for business enterprises and dealing with them as it deals with individuals and partners in the conduct of their affairs; seeking rather the protection of stockholders and creditors and the security of the money invested than the regulation of the business in the interest of the general public. If now, under changed conditions, when her corporations have become so large as to affect the industries of the whole country, it shall seem best to make special provisions for the protection of the interests of the public, New Jersey will be glad to join with other states in such provisions as shall be found best to accomplish this purpose.

New Jersey from the earliest times has adopted the policy of promoting rather than hindering the aggregation of capital for business purposes and from the beginning corporations have been regarded not as hostile to the public interests, but as a means of combining the efforts and resources of individuals to accomplish large undertakings.

It was the same under the act of 1846 as it is to-day. No public notice of the intention to form a corporation need be given. No petition need be presented to the governor nor to any official for leave to incorporate, nor was it made necessary, as in Pennsylvania, for example, to obtain letters patent from the governor. No limit was placed upon the amount of the capital stock. It was not until 1883 that any tax was imposed upon the franchise or privilege of incorporating, and then the tax was a moderate one, imposed not for the purpose of restricting the corporations, but rather to compel them to contribute to the payment of the expenses of the government. It was in 1884 that an annual tax was first laid upon the franchise of corporations of certain classes and both of these acts have remained substantially unchanged. The amount of the tax was fixed with reference to the needs of the state and the conditions of corporations organized for business within her own borders, and it is certain that it had no reference to the organization of the so-called trusts, which did not begin until many years afterwards.

It was assumed in the earlier statutes that the business of the company would be carried on within the state, but there was no requirement that any of the directors except the president should reside there, and as early as 1865, it was expressly declared by statute that any company might on certain conditions carry on a part of its business, and have offices and hold property outside of the state, and it was in 1875, when special privileges of every kind were abolished, that the act was passed that made it easy for persons residing beyond the borders of the state to associate themselves for business purposes as a corporation under the laws of New Jersey. This act declared that, if the by-laws should so provide, the directors of any company might have an office and keep the books (except the stock and transfer books) outside of the state, on condition, however, that they should always maintain a principal office within the state and have an agent in charge thereof, and the chancellor and the judges of the Supreme Court were empowered, upon good cause shown, to make a summary order for bringing all the books within the state upon pain of contempt and forfeiture of the charter.

There is one provision of the present statute of New Jersey which is regarded as responsible for the combination of many companies in one and the existence of the so-called trusts under her laws. This is the act which declared that it shall be lawful for any corporation organized under the laws of the state of New Jersey to purchase, hold and sell the stock or bonds of any other corporation in the same manner as an individual may do.

This act, moreover, was not passed until 1893, a year after a similar act was passed in New York, and some of the largest of the trusts came to New Jersey from New York before 1892, on the advice of counsel that corporations in New Jersey under their general power to hold such property as was proper for the purposes of their business, might purchase and hold the stock of other corporations engaged in a similar business.

Another important feature in the laws of New Jersey in view of the present tendency to the undue inflation of capital is the fact that stock may be issued for property purchased and that in the absence of fraud in the actual transaction the judgment of the directors is accepted as conclusive. The issue of stock for property was authorized by the act of 1875, which required that the property should be taken at a fair and *bona fide* valuation, and it was the courts that established the rule that in deciding whether the stock was fully paid or not, the question is whether the transaction was an honest one or not, judged upon the facts as they appeared to the directors at the time the purchase was made and not in the light of subsequent experience. The courts will have still the power to declare that a gross overvaluation of property is not *bona fide* and to set aside the purchase for fraud.

Other features of the corporation laws of New Jersey are in the main not unlike those of the other states.

The chief points of difference in actual policy between New Jersey and a majority of the states relate to the supervision of the business in the interest of the public, and the modes and extent of taxation. On both of these points the policy of New Jersey was established many years ago, and it was not until the opposite policy in other states had been carried so far as to become oppressive that persons began to seek the benefit of organization under the laws of New Jersey.

The chief characteristic of this policy of New Jersey is that it is a policy of encouraging rather than discouraging the aggregation of capital. It regards the corporation as a means of bringing the savings of many into efficient use as capital for the development of resources and the promotion of industry. It treats the corporation as an association for the purposes of business, deals with it as it deals with individuals and partnerships in the conduct of their affairs and holds that the largest possible freedom of the individual is for the best interest of the community. It is this settled policy of the state, and not any recent legislation intended for the purpose, that has caused the formation of so many corporations in New Jersey.

Another important fact in determining the choice of the domicile of a corporation is the permanence or stability of the legislative and judicial policy of the state. Few changes have been made in the statutes of New Jersey during a long period and these were made along the lines of development already laid down. The decisions of the courts also have been consistent and uniform.

I may add that, perhaps, the convenient situation of New Jersey between two great cities may be the real reason why many corporations come to her instead of to other states having a similar policy.

It is perfectly clear that the corporations called trusts are merely associations of individuals in joint stock companies purchasing and owning property and carrying on business under the ordinary powers that have been freely granted to all who chose to organize as corporations and under laws that have been in force for many years.

In any practical discussion of the question of the nature and effect of these combinations and of the remedies to be applied it is necessary to consider the laws under which the large corporations are formed and to ask what changes, if any, should be made in the laws that govern them. In view of the fact that so many of them have been organized in New Jersey, it is natural that New Jersey should be asked how she can justify the fact that she permits and even encourages the formation of corporations which apparently accomplish the same result as the forbidden trusts?

The fact is that New Jersey has not attempted to give an answer to this question. She has simply acted under the well established policy of encouraging the aggregation of capital for business purposes, and has found herself suddenly confronted with a new condition arising out of an unexpected development in the world of trade and industry.

The difficulty is that there is nothing really new in the situation, except the extraordinary size of the corporations, the large amount of property controlled and the vast extent of their enterprises. Their appearance is alarming, but after all the size is only the result of unduly rapid growth, and it is not easy at once to devise means to check over-growth without risk of destroying the life. Combination of capital has become a necessary part of the social organization, and it is hard to stop it at any particular point in its development.

It is true that every state may limit the sphere of the action of its corporations. It may decline to give them power to hold property or carry on business outside of its own borders, it may confine the privileges of incorporation to its own citizens, it may compel their directors to hold their meetings and transact their business within the state, it may even limit the amount of property which they shall acquire, but unless it is willing to adopt this policy of close restriction, it cannot control the extent of the business that they shall carry on, or the number of rival manufactories that they shall absorb.

New Jersey might insist on the close supervision of corporate business, require the filing of detailed reports of debts, assets and earnings. She might levy taxes in such a way as to expose the company to the extortion of officials, or to make its business uncertain and the burdens oppressive, but these are questions of local policy which concern her dealings with all her corporations and they are not to be settled with a view only to the effect of her policy upon the acquisition of property and the control of business in other states.

On this point I may say, moreover, that the state tax is not unusually low, and that under her laws as they now stand, imposing a moderate and certain tax on the capital stock issued, few companies survive which are not engaged in actual and profitable business, and many apparently large companies formed merely for the purposes of the promoters, are wound up every year and their franchises declared at an end.

With respect to the publication of reports of debts and earnings, she may well take the ground that the requirements of the stock exchange are more efficient than statutes in securing to the public a proper acquaintance with the condition of such corporations as are of public concern, but if it be found that there are companies that in fact have become so large as to control any large branch of industry throughout the country and whose stock is purchased for investment by a very large number of persons who have not ready access to the books of the company, so that the condition of the company is in fact a matter of public concern, it would be wise for the state itself to require that the condition of its affairs and the methods of its management should be made known to the public not merely in reports made to the annual meeting, but also in detailed statements filed in the office of the Secretary of State and printed in some public journal.

One of the most important provisions of the laws of New Jersey in its relation to the formation of large combinations is that which permits the purchase of stock of other corporations. It was under this that the Standard Oil Trust and other trusts were reorganized as corporations in New Jersey, but, as I have said, the same provision was adopted in New York as early as 1892 and has since been adopted in many other states, and this privilege is not necessary to the combination of several companies into one.

One of the inducements to the promotion of large corporations and the combination of industrial properties is the inflation of stock, and the creation of fictitious stock is one of the most serious evils of the whole movement. This can be discouraged, though not wholly prevented, by the requirement that nothing but money shall be taken in payment of capital stock. The laws of New Jersey provide that stock may be issued for property purchased, and the property must be put in at a fair and *bona fide* valuation, and in such a case it is impossible wholly to prevent undue inflation of the stock, but the true remedy is not in forbidding the issue of stock for property purchased, nor even in limiting it strictly to the value of the property. Some allowance must be made for the earning power of the property and business under the control of the new corporation and some inducement of a speculative nature must be given to tempt capital into new and doubtful enterprises. It is stockholders and creditors that are chiefly interested in knowing what the property for which the stock is given is really worth, and they have full protection if they can ascertain what that property really was. The English plan is to punish promoters severely for issuing a false prospectus, and to require the contract for the purchase of the property to be written in detail and give to anybody the right to obtain a printed copy of it for sixpence.

Holding promoters strictly to account would go far toward preventing fraudulent prospectuses and if every creditor or purchaser of stock could demand and have a full statement of the basis of the issue of the stock, he would have no just cause to complain if he remained in ignorance of the facts. If these should not be sufficient, there remains the Massachusetts plan of requiring the contract for the issue of the stock to be submitted to a public officer for his approval, but there are dangers in this and it is not in keeping with the New Jersey democratic idea of freedom from official intervention in business affairs. When the issue of stock is based upon public franchises, as in the case of companies using the public streets, stringent provisions should be made against inflation of the stock, and this has been attempted in the statutes of New Jersey relating to street railways, but the provisions have been evaded by taking advantage of certain statutes providing for combination of existing companies and the fixing of the amount of the stock of the new company without reference to the actual stock of the old ones. These acts I think ought to be repealed.

Whatever the remedies may be for the undue growth and increasing power of corporations they must be directed to the precise evils which it is sought to remove and not to the general principle of combination of capital in joint stock companies We must be careful that in removing the evils we do not destroy what is good. We cannot attack in this stage of the world's history the principle of combination or corporation.

We cannot follow the suggestion that was made upon this floor that since the trusts are in fact corporations, we must abolish corporations for the purpose of putting an end to the trusts. It is by means of corporations that we are able to combine the resources of many for the great undertakings that are necessary to commerce and industry, and until we find some better means of combination we cannot destroy those that we have.

For the same reason we shall not, if we are wise, adopt as a remedy against the evils of the trusts, such regulations of corporations as are merely vexatious and harassing and tend to cripple or to discourage combinations for proper purposes. And certainly we cannot adopt the remedy suggested by a speaker who has preceded me, making every stockholder responsible for all the debts of the company. This would make combination in corporate enterprises possible only for the very rich or those who have nothing to lose.

If the size of the corporations and the amount of the property they control are the sources of the dangers that are feared, these can be limited by law.

The purposes for which corporations may be organized may be restricted and the business they are authorized to carry on may be strictly defined. Legislation in this direction may be taken without striking at the principle of combination in discouraging the organization of corporations for proper purposes and with reasonable powers.

Legislation against the large corporations as combinations in restraint of trade is of little avail. It has failed to reach the corporations already organized.

In New Jersey it has been held that in a collateral proceeding the court of chancery has no power to restrain a corporation organized under the forms of law from performing acts within its corporate power merely because the purpose of its incorporation may have been to prevent competition and establish a monopoly, and in a very recent case in the court of errors, it has been held that although contracts in restraint of competition in the production of some commodity in the production and sale of which the public have an interest are contrary to public policy, yet when such agreements result in the formation of a corporation with the powers conferred under the liberal statutes of New Jersey, it may lawfully buy the business of its competitors and the courts cannot pronounce a contract for such permitted purchases invalid, although it may tend to produce, and may temporarily produce a monopoly.

The court assumes that an agreement among independent dealers to combine for the purpose of maintaining prices by avoiding competition and limiting production is against public policy, but while it is well settled that contracts in general restraint of trade are void and not to be enforced, it is not true that at common law such contracts are unlawful, and if this be so then, even though the agreement by which it is formed be against public policy, it cannot be said that the corporation is the result of an agreement that was unlawful.

It has been insisted that corporations which control the market may be held to be illegal as creating monopolies, but no ordinary corporation, however large, possesses a legal monopoly, and the monopolies that were declared illegal at common law were the royal grants giving special privileges to individuals or corporations. The truth is that there is no real monopoly without special privilege, and so long as there is perfect freedom of competition, no actual monopoly can be obtained. There may be an appearance of monopoly, but the courts cannot deal with an appearance, and it will be found in the long run that competition, or at least the possibility of competition, will prevent any group of individuals, however they may combine themselves together, from obtaining the actual and permanent control from an open market.

Before asking that a radical change should be made in a long established policy of law relating to corporations, it should be shown clearly that these results do follow the organization of corporations under those laws. When definite action is demanded, the burden of proof is upon those who assert that it is required, and for want of the statement of such facts I am inclined to think that we exaggerate the dangers of the situation.

The conditions of trade and manufacture are very different from what they have been. The extent of the territory that can be profitably occupied has become much greater and larger undertakings can now be more easily controlled under a single management.

The great combinations of capital are new, and there has not yet been time to ascertain by experience what is the actual effect of uniting many enterprises for the purpose of reducing the cost of production and regulating the prices of commodities.

The obvious effect is to reduce competition and it is competition that has been the ruling force in the struggle for existence in the commercial and industrial world. We have not yet had experience of the effects of combination on a large scale. Nor do we know whether in the removal of competition there may not come the saving of ill-directed energy, the regulation of supply in accordance with the demand both in place and in time, a saving in the cost of production and a steadiness and a certainty of industrial effort and result and the command of all the capital needed for any useful enterprise, and that out of all these there will not come an increase of actual wealth, a wider distribution of it among the people as stockholders in the great corporations, and a decrease of the cost of commodities to the individual man.

EDWARD W. BEMIS.

Bureau of Economic Research.

Prof. Edward W. Bemis, of the New York Bureau of Economic Research, was the next speaker. He said :

Many speakers at this conference have sought to remove all anxiety as to the future of the problem before us, by referring to the scare and suffering attendant on the introduction of machinery and of the corporation, with their displacement of the individual hand worker and of the small partnership. As those changes have on the whole worked to the advantage of society, though introducing tremendous and still unsolved problems of the distribution of wealth and of how to secure continued prosperity and markets for farmer and manufacturer, and steady employment for labor, so it is argued we should smile at the ignorant fears of the fast growing number of those that are truly alarmed over the wonderful growth of the trust.

Now so far as this relates to the department store, so often classed with the trust, the argument is sound. The department store does not, like so many trusts, ruin the business of its smaller rivals by cutting prices, even below cost, in one portion of the community, while keeping them up for the residents of other sections. It furnishes alike to all the advantages of lower prices, which are rendered possible by the economies of a big business, while it gives its patrons opportunity to buy all their goods, from bonnets to flour, from needles to lawn mowers, in one store at a great saving of time and cost of delivery. It permits one payment, one delivery, and one ringing of the door bell, one payment and that only on delivery of all perishable goods, as the result of a day's shopping, and by reason of its rapid sales can often afford to furnish a fresher and more attractive assortment of the things desired by the buyer.

The department store, however, differs from the trust vitally in the fact that having once secured a large market by reason of its accommodation to the customer, it does not, like the trusts, raise prices above those that would naturally exist with small competitive stores. The essential feature of the trust, however, is its monopoly character. While legally it is only a large corporation, since the technical trust has been changed to the corporate form, yet in fact there is all the difference in the world between the change from hand tools to machinery or from the partnership to the corporation, or from the small store to the department store, throughout all of which the keenest competition continues, and the change from the group of competing corporations to the one giant consolidation, which is possessed of monopoly features by virtue of its enormous size and of the large proportion of the business of the country in its hands along the special line of its work. It is virtually a monopoly of large capital, or a capitalistic monopoly. Professor Jenks has well defined it as such a monopoly as "so controls the business, whatever it may be, as practically to regulate competition and to fix the price of its products on the whole with little reference to competitors, or to the cost of production, but mainly with reference to securing the greatest net results." The trust differs from the so-called natural monopolies, which I prefer to call monopolies of situation, such as gas, street railways, water, electric light, the telephone, the telegraph and railroad, in that while equally natural in its development, the trust does not primarily depend on specially favored and limited locations of land, but on the enormous amount of capital requisite for entering upon successful competition. It is not denied that the trust is often favored by affiliation with monopolies of situation, or by a grip upon such natural resources as anthracite coal mines and oil wells, but in a broad way the distinctions given above will hold.

I cannot subscribe to the roseate view of Mr. Gunton that wages have been rapidly rising during this trust movement. The so-called Aldrich or United States Senate financial report of 1891, upon which Mr. Gunton relies for his statement that wages have risen in a certain period 68 per cent or thereabouts, has been utterly discredited by all careful students who have examined it. Not only does this report ignore many industries in which wages have fallen and base its conclusions in other industries upon the three or more clerks of a single store or employees of a single business, but throughout it follows a method of averaging which can be best illustrated in this way: Suppose in the course of ten years the foreman of a given shop has had his pay increased 20 per cent, while the dozen men under him have not gained any rise in wages. This Aldrich report argues in such a case that the average increase of wages in that enterprise is found by adding 20 per cent rise of the foreman to the zero rise of the men and dividing by two, giving thus an average increase of wages of 10 per cent. Such absolutely dishonest, or certainly deceptive methods of averaging render the conclusions on wages altogether valueless. A more recent report in a United States Bulletin of Labor within the current year shows that in a large number of representative occupations in our leading cities there has been practically no rise in wages during the past twenty years and an actual fall during the last ten years. It is not denied that in the building trades and a few others where labor has been well organized the rise has been considerable.

Without, however, attempting to connect the wage movement thus far with the trust question, which is too recent in its development to permit of conclusions, it will be noticed that the present indictment of the trust takes four forms: First, either a direct rise of prices on the formation of the trust, or in its subsequent history, as apparently in the case of the Standard Oil, an interception of many of the benefits of invention and progress in the arts, cheapening of transportation, etc., which would normally have had great tendency to reduce the prices of trust goods further than the trust has permitted, as has been so fully the case in the competitive market. Mr. Byron W. Holt, who appears to have made the most careful statistical examination of trusts thus far published, for example in the June *Review of Reviews*, has informed us during this conference that of four hundred trusts studied by him, he has thus far only found two that have failed to raise prices, and believes there are but very few others. Those two have lowered the quality of their product. Following in much of this paper the article which I contributed July 20th, to the *New York Journal of Commerce*, I would say that in the twelve years prior to the formation of the Standard Oil trust in 1882 the charge for transportation of oil to New York and for refining it fell from 17.16 cents to 5.52 cents per gallon, or 62 per cent, while the fall during the next fifteen years from 1882 to 1897 was only from 5.52 cents to 4.04 cents, or 27 per cent, and nearly all of this fall was due to cheaper transportation through pipe lines which were first developed by rivals of the great oil company. During the five years, 1883 to 1887, preceding the formation of the Sugar trust, the average difference between the cost of raw and refined sugar was admitted by Mr. Searles before the Lexow trust committee to have been less than the average of the subsequent nine years by .128 cent, i. e., the formation of the trust was followed by an increased charge for refining of one-eighth cent a pound, or $3,584,000 a year on the 2,800,000,000 pounds of annual output. The public was, however, blinded to this by the greater fall in the price of raw sugar, which permitted some fall in the charge for refined sugar, despite the increased toll of the trust. Mr. Searles defended the increase of price after 1887 by the claim that the previous five years' business had been conducted at a loss. He found it difficult, however, to explain in this view of the case how, on the formation of the trust, the capitalization of the component companies was swelled from $6,590,000 to $42,-000,000, or over six-fold. The fact that large dividends have been paid on such an enormous amount of water is merely another proof of the extortionate charges.

Mr. Henry O. Havemeyer, president of the American Sugar Refining Company, testified before the Lexow trust committee: "It goes without saying that a corporation that controls 80 per cent of the product does control the market price up to the importing point, if it chooses to exercise that power." The question was then asked: "You do, in fact, control the product and price in the United States?" To which Mr. Havemeyer replied: "We undoubtedly do."

Even better proved is the charge against the trust of over-capitalization and consequent deception of investors and the public as to the amount of its exorbitant charges and as to its prospects for a continuance of these profits. No student of the problem doubts the evils of this situation, or of the stimulation given by the trust to a dangerous concentration of wealth and purchasing power in the hands of the few. When these do not care to buy the products of our mills and the many can not do so, frequent depressions and a feverish demand for foreign markets at no matter what cost of property and life are inevitable.

Much might be written of how the trust often clubs competitors till it drives them from the field. An ordinary competitive business has similar tendencies, it may be, but it is the trust which boldly approaches a would-be rival and declares that it will sell goods below cost until it ruins him unless he will join the great combine.

Most ominous of all is the danger in the trust to political purity and personal liberty. Whether we like it or not we are beginning to see vigorous efforts of our law-making bodies to regulate city monopolies of light, heat and transportation. The latter effort has thus far had its most visible result in many cities in raising the price of the alderman and the legislator. It is to be feared that this and some malodorous events in the United States Senate are but a forecast of what awaits us in any really serious attempt to control the trust. Yet public control in some form of trusts is the mildest demand of every speaker on this floor. The support of the trust is so necessary to the bar and the press, its donations so eagerly desired by the university, the library and the hospital, that freedom of speech is already endangered.

The entire manufacturing capital of the country in 1890 was only $6,500,000,000, and may now perhaps be $10,000,000,000, while the true valuation of our trusts to-day is conservatively estimated at over $2,000,000,000. The nominal capitalization, according to Mr. Holt, in the June *Review of Reviews*, is about $8,000,000,000. If, aside from all their water, trusts now control one-fourth or even one-sixth of the manufacturing capital of the country, what a political influence they must be able to exert over their employees. Taken in connection with the fast consolidating power of our railroads these aggregations of capital probably employ to-day one-fourth of our non-agricultural voters.

It was said last night that the most independent class of men are the organized laborers in well paid employments, but this ignores the well-known fact that organized labor at present in America, outside of the glass business, is almost entirely confined to the railroad employments, the building trades, cigar making and printing, though there are a few other well organized trades. The vast mass, however, of the machinery industries, such as are being acquired by the trust, are almost entirely unorganized, and are likely to remain so for some time to come, for reasons which I cannot stop to enumerate. The power of employers to influence the political action of their unorganized employees is too well known to need discussion.

The economies of the trust, however, are not to be despised. Prof. Henry C. Adams and some large manufacturers here present believe that the possible economies from this form of organization are mostly confined to the selling department, but they admit that here the chances for economy are great. Some of the largest manufacturers in their respective lines in the United States are authority for the assertion that the price that the consumer pays is often 100 per cent in excess of the cost and of a fair profit for the manufacturer. Through a saving in the number of traveling salesmen, in advertising and in the distribution of goods from the nearest source of supply, and in many other ways, this cost of distribution might well be reduced one-half. One of the greatest criticisms of the competitive system is the waste involved, for example, in the journey through the same street of a dozen different milk carts or ice wagons, stopping at as many different houses. The manager of the trust adopting unconsciously this socialist view of the matter, familiarizes us with the arguments as to the advantages of combination. We are then face to face with our problem, given on the one hand a new form of organization, which has in it vast possibilities of social economy and advantage, but on the other hand is now being selfishly used to work great social harm.

What shall we do about the trusts?

First—We may leave the entire matter alone in the belief that many of these trusts will soon go to pieces. The revival of the copper syndicate in stronger form than ever, despite the failure of the previous one, and the history of many other such experiences show that while many trusts will doubtless go to the wall from time to time, the trust movement is likely to become stronger and stronger if left undisturbed.

Second—We may favor the solution which is attracting some attention in England, where, if I understand the matter aright, the trust of capital allies itself with a strong labor combination, and the two together agree to rob the consumer of all they can, the monopoly profits to be divided in the proportion of two or more parts to capital to one part for labor. This is the meaning of the contention of Mr. E. J. Smith, of Birmingham, that when a combination of capital raises prices 10 per cent, it should raise wages, which are but one factor in cost, only 5 to 10 per cent. That such a solution, if really being tried across the water, will ever satisfy our people for any length of time is incredible, although it may be an improvement over the American method of denying the right of labor to form its own organization and deal as a unit with the trust.

Third—We may smash the trust, or endeavor so to do. The trouble with this is two-fold—it cuts us off from any possibility of securing the advantages which under a better social organization the general public might derive from the trust, and in the second place it seems to fly in the face of industrial evolution. There is more and more evidence that Henry D. Lloyd is right when he says that "monopoly is business at the end of its journey." The world is face to face with a new type of competition, because the development of machinery has required a large amount of capital and its extreme specialization. Since it is no longer possible to regulate competition by the easy withdrawal of unprofitable capital to other employments, competition is changing to a struggle to the death. The public appreciates the change by designating it as "cut-throat" competition, or a "war" of rates. In an industry where all goods are of the same kind and quality and not known by the brand of the maker, and where the capital required is very large, there is a tendency for competition to become so keen as to allow no margin for interest on the necessary capital. Particularly is this true where the competitors have the corporate form, and the managers who set the prices do not feel that it is interest on their own capital that they are imperiling. Suppose that a given quantity of sugar or oil or matches is sold for a dollar, and that 75 cents would cover labor, raw material and other operating expenses, and that 25 cents would be a fair allowance for return on capital, due allowance being made in this 25 cents for depreciation, etc. Under these circumstances it is quite natural for some factory to try to secure business from its rivals and obtain command of the market by cutting the price to, say, 90 cents. Rival establishments will rightly argue that if they also sell for 80 cents, they will lose 10 cents on every article that they sell, but if they do not reduce and so lose their trade, they will lose 25 cents on every article they do not sell, since their fixed charges continue when business stops. Consequently one cut in prices follows another, with general resulting demoralization, and injury to the public, for it increases the hazards of business, and this renders higher prices necessary in the end, in order to tempt capital into business, while opportunities for securing investment for idle capital are lessened. Where, however, the capital necessary to start a factory is small, competition will not long reduce prices unduly, without such a quiet lessening of capital in the business as will bring back the prices of products to their normal level. Where the capital required is enormous, it cannot be so easily transferred.

Where an industry requires special skill and its goods have made famous the brand of the maker, as in the case of the Elgin watch and the Columbia bicycle, there is less need of union with other establishments, although even here combination is beginning to enter. It has been easy at times to consolidate the alcohol manufacturers or makers of proof spirits, but it has been more difficult to form a trust among the whisky manufacturers of Kentucky, whose individual brands are famous. If the trusts would confine themselves to restoring prices when unduly low to the level which would leave merely reasonable profits, such as the same investment, risk and ability would secure in competitive business, and if the other abuses above mentioned could be eliminated, the trust must be looked upon with comparative favor. But the tendency of any monopoly in private hands to abuse its position is beyond question, and the difficulties before us are enormous.

In some respects the trade union resembles the trust, since it seeks to secure a monopoly of the labor market, and in order to secure it adopts many trust methods, such as refusal to deal with rivals who will not join it. The labor world, like the capitalist world, is divided into two divisions—those who sell their products by reason of special superiority, or well established qualities of the seller, as for example, the teacher, lawyer, physician, artist, and, on the other hand, the great mass of workmen, even in the so-called skilled trades. In the latter, one workman is usually considered about as good as another, and the question of wages is the chief factor with the employer. The men thus are tempted to cut under each other in an effort to secure employment, until wages fall below such a point as will properly keep up the standard of living and provide for their children and for old age. The labor trust is as inevitable as the trust of large capital, but the former, unlike the latter, gives equal vote to all its members, independent of their capital; it admits every good workman on equal terms with the organizers of the union, and is an engine, not of the well-to-do and the wealthy, but of the weak against the strong. The many points of similarity, however, between trades unions and trusts render it very difficult to pass laws preventing the latter that shall not at the same time be interpreted by the courts as preventing the former.

Fourth—A more hopeful attack upon the abuses of the trust

consists in the removal of tariffs upon such products as Congress shall decide to be of trust make. It will not do to leave to the courts the determination of what are trusts. Congress must make its own decision of what tariffs to repeal. This has been sufficiently discussed already to render further consideration unnecessary at present.

Fifth—The notorious and widespread granting of secret rebates and other privileges by railroads to large shippers and particularly to trusts and combinations must be checked in the most summary and speedy manner, although we are probably forced by the conditions of public opinion to approach the subject through public regulation, rather than through ownership by the people, which I believe will be found in the end the only satisfactory solution, as has been the case recently in Switzerland. The railroads cannot very well be controlled by commissions, for these giant corporations regulate their regulators—they insidiously weaken or control the bodies appointed to control them. The independent shipper, the average business man, is likely ere long to recognize that the door to the trust problem lies in a solution of the railroad question. The Interstate Commerce Commission in its last report declares: "There is probably no one thing to-day which does so much to force out the small operator and to build up these trusts and monopolies, against which law and public opinion alike beat in vain, as discrimination in freight rates. This problem is so serious that it will soon attract an attention that has never hitherto been given to it."

Sixth—The conference has been several times invited to consider direct public regulation of the trust. This will require in a large measure preliminary constitutional changes, so as to give more opportunity than we now have for national regulation of industries that through their wide area of operations are superior to state control. Prof. Jenks has urged for the protection of the investor that we should require sworn returns to the stock exchange, when stocks and bonds of great combinations are listed there. This report should relate to value of physical plants, cost of operation, etc. Prof. Henry C. Adams goes farther, and urges government reports on all the details of business of these trusts and the fullest publicity with regard to their accounts and conduct, while the attorney-general of Maryland last night even went so far as to urge public control of wages, hours of labor, and the prices of goods. This all sounds very good theoretically, and it is quite likely that we should work in this direction, for a while, but in practice it will be found that, as the Massachusetts Railroad Commission once declared, the placing of ownership in private hands and management in public hands, is sure to result in great political demoralization. We shall have to devote the most strenuous efforts to purifying and strengthening government, if it is to undertake this vast task.

Seventh—Prof. Adams has urged that we restrict the right of incorporation in the case of all industries which are not, like railroads, of quasi public character. Further explanation by Prof. Adams may win us over to endorsement of this proposition, but at present it looks like taking a backward step, and depriving society of the almost universally recognized, but perhaps exaggerated benefits of the corporate form of organization.

Eighth—There is an increased number, though still but a minority of very intelligent people who believe that the only way ultimately of treating the trust in an adequate manner is for all of us to join it, by public ownership and operation of oil refineries, match factories, anthracite coal fields, etc., just as in a somewhat indirect manner the people own many sugar refineries in the great province of Queensland, Australia. While the writer finds himself in growing sympathy with such a solution, it seems still only a remote possibility. The people must first become habituated to public operation on a civil service reform basis of city monopolies, the railroads, telegraph and express business before they can ever wisely undertake forms of business now absorbed by the trusts.

Ninth—Finally, there is no quick and royal road to the settlement of the trust question. Even Henry D. Lloyd, whose book on this question is known the country over, when asked by a recent congressional committee for a bill dealing with the trust problem, replied that he had no legislation as yet to propose, although he would suggest that a good introduction to more constructive legislation could be made by opening our prison doors as readily to receive the rich as the poor criminal, and by punishing the corporate violators of the laws we now have.

We conquered at Santiago and Manila by building our Oregons on a far-off Pacific coast, and training our Deweys in rocky Vermont, which does not even touch the sea; so before we can wisely deal directly, or at least adequately, with the trust problem, we will have to build our battering ram back in the hills, and gradually move it up to the walls of Jericho, getting practice and preparing for the final struggle by overthrowing many obstructions as we move along. There must be such a change in our attitude that we will not merely envy the trust, because we are not fortunate enough to be in one, and the time must come when it will no longer be possible for our state universities to receive a paltry three or five thousand dollars a year for the investigation and teaching of all these great economic and social questions, as is the case in most of our states to-day where monopoly magnates think nothing of securing to their universities ten times as much a year for the same purpose. Our American states will have to cease to be contented with commissioners, state attorneys, etc., worth two or three thousand dollars a year, and going out of office with every change of administration, while a sugar refinery or a railroad is ready to pay five to ten times that amount for its talent wherewith to oppose or checkmate public control. The trust problem, like the slavery question, will take a generation or more to settle, and like the slavery question will entail endless trouble unless approached intelligently and with deep conscientious devotion to the public weal.

JOHN BATES CLARK.

Columbia University.

The session closed with an address on "The Necessity of Suppressing Monopolies While Retaining Trusts," by Prof. John B. Clark, of New York, who said:

I shall confine myself to a single one of the questions asked by Professor Jenks in his admirable introductory paper, the one, namely, that referred to the relation of trusts to competition. I accept and use the loose definition of the term trust that is current in popular thought and speech. It is any corporation that is big enough to be menacing. There is, indeed, an intermediate form of the trust which allows the companies or firms that compose it to retain a separate existence, though they form a combination, or pool, for the purpose of limiting production and raising prices. Such forms of the trust can probably be crushed by law; but the result of this will be to cause many of them to take the shape of monster corporations; and it is in this form that you will finally have them to deal with.

I claim the immunities of a theoretical student when I enter the realm of prophecy, and, on the basis of laws and tendencies that are plainly discernible, make a somewhat confident assertion concerning the type of trust legislation that is likely to be permanent. Very unlike the sweeping prohibitions with which the statute books of many states have been supplied, is the law that will survive and will accomplish what we all have in view, the protection of the public from the extortions of monopolies.

It will do in reality what the ordinary anti-trust law fails to do, for it will have on its side what the ordinary statute has against it, namely, the power of economic law.

Three distinct things are often confounded and indiscriminately attacked: The first is capital as such; the second is centralization, and the third is true monopoly. Popular attacks on monopoly often take the shape of attacks on capital itself. I am happy to say that this has not happened in the present conference, for we have heard again and again, in the utterance of speakers who have opposed trusts, expressions that show that they are not assailing capital. They are assailing aggregations of capital. They oppose centralization because of the element of monopoly that at present inheres in it. Poor as is the opinion that I entertain of many existing anti-trust laws, I must, in fairness, say that they also strike not at capital itself, but at the centralized form of it. The present effort of the people is to stop centralization in order to preclude monopoly, while their effort will ultimately be to crush the element of monopoly out of massed capital and let massing continue. The line of cleavage between what is good and will abide, and what is harmful and must go, is not between capital and centralization, but between centralization and monopoly.

If it were impossible to have capital in great masses without having true monopolies, I would favor a heroic effort to stem the current of natural progress and keep the general capital of each branch of business in the shape of separate smaller and competing capitals. Monopoly is evil, and almost wholly so; and if the massing of productive wealth necessarily means monopoly, farewell to centralization. We shall do our best to get rid of it, and shall suffer the loss of productive power that this entails, as the price that we are willing to pay for being rid of a great evil. The fact is that massed capital does not need to bring with it a régime of true monopoly. We shall soon see why this is true, and before doing so it is well worth while to notice how much will be gained if we can safely allow the natural and centralizing tendency to go on. It means the survival of the most productive forms of business. It is first and chiefly because it can give more for a dollar than little establishments can give that the great establishments supplant them. They out-do the small ones in serving the public, and this power of superior service is soon to have a new and unique field in which to display itself. We are entering on an era of world-wide industrial connection. Asia and Africa are incorporating themselves into the economic organism of which Europe and America are the center. There is coming a neck-and-neck contest between European countries and the United States for lucrative connections with the outlying regions. There is also coming a later and grander contest between both America and Europe, on the one hand, and Asia and Africa on the other, for the command of the traffic of the world. In this contest victory involves more than any hurried expressions of mine can indicate. It means a leading position in the permanent progress of the world. It means positive wealth, high wages, and intellectual gains that cannot be enjoyed by those who develop less power.

In the momentous struggle that is before us and that will yield to the successful the greatest of mundane prizes, I want my country to come uppermost. To that end I wish it to have every advantage that it can have in the way of productive power. I wish it to be able to meet the fiercest competition, not by accepting low pay for its labor, but by creating the largest possible product. Do you suppose that this is possible if it reverts to the plan of multiplying little shops, with the wastes that this system entails? Mechanical invention, on the one hand, and organization, on the other, can save us in the sharpest economic contests.

There is a competing power that comes from poverty. Pauper labor is a dangerous antagonist. We have perceived this at times, in the rivalries of America and Europe, and shall see it more plainly when the poorly paid dwellers in Asia shall enter the manufacturing field and try conclusions with us in an effort to command the largest markets. If they under-bid us it will be because they take less than we do for their labor; while if we under-bid them it will be because we produce more by our labor. Against the competing power that rests on poverty is to be arrayed the competing power that rests on economic strength, and this strength can come, in a decisive measure, only to that country that combines with inventive genius an organizing genius, and so adds to the power of the engine, the dynamos and the automatic machine, the power of centralized capital. I wish that successful country to be ours. I wish that our workmen may excel not in power to live on a little, but in power to create much, and to offer what they create for a correspondingly large reward.

Is this possible under a régime of great combinations? I firmly believe that it is so; though it will not be possible without the wisest laws, honestly enforced, and backed by all the moral energy that the present anti-trust campaign is developing.

Why is it that trusts have not raised the prices of their products to an undeniable and startling extent? Why has it, until lately, been almost a debatable question whether they raise them

406

at all? Are their managers filled with an enthusiasm of humanity and a desire to scatter gifts among the people? Have they conscientious scruples against making undue profits? They do not raise prices very much because they cannot. Why they cannot do it the public does not altogether understand.

In the lucid intervals in which they tell the truth to the people, managers of trusts say that they cannot greatly raise prices without bringing new competitors into the field. As has been said, the foundation of a combination is liable to "build mills," and so to defeat the purpose for which the combination is formed. To keep the new mills from coming into existence a wise policy keeps prices at a moderate level. Within limits it is safe to raise them, but beyond such limits it is not safe. The competitor who is not now in the field, but who will enter it at once if prices are unduly raised, is the protector of the purchasing public against extortion. He is also the protector of the workmen, for the fact that he will begin his operations if too many of the old mills are closed, prevents the closing of them. In technical phrase it is potential competition that is the power that holds trusts in check. The competition that is now latent, but is ready to spring into activity if very high prices are exacted, is even now efficient in preventing high prices. It is to be the permanent policy of wise and successful peoples to utilize this natural economic force for all that it is worth.

At present it is not an adequate regulator. The potential competitor encounters unnecessary obstacles when he tries to become an active competitor. There are abnormal difficulties and dangers in his way, and the consequence of this is that he is often reluctant and tardy in his action; and the fear of him is a far less potent influence with the managers of trusts than it easily might be made to be.

The European competitor is usually a potential competitor because of the tariff which deters him from becoming an actual one. Shall we sweep away all duties on trust-made articles? That would make this latent competition active, and would do much to keep trusts in check. As a theoretical economist I am not prepared to favor so sweeping a measure; but where there are duties that are not at all necessary for the protection of an industry as such, but are necessary for the protection of a trust in an industry, these particular duties should go.

A domestic competitor is sometimes only a potential one because of patents. A trust often sustains itself by securing a monopoly of the kinds of machinery that are needed in an industry. Shall we abolish patents? Far from it; but we should reform our patent laws, and while making them afford a greater incentive than they now do to invention, should prevent patents from being instruments of extortion or oppression.

Railroads have the power to handicap the potential competitor, and it is an open secret that they are doing it. Discriminating rates for carrying freight are an intolerable evil, and they tend distinctly to build up real monopolies. If legal acuteness backed by popular energy can secure it, this evil must be suppressed.

These measures have already received attention in popular discussions and in the discussions of this conference. There is another type of law that, as I venture to affirm, is of even greater consequence than any that is before the public. The ability to make discriminating prices puts a terrible power into the hands of a trust. If in my small field it can sell goods at prices that are below the cost of making them, while it sustains itself by charging high prices in a score of other fields, it can crush me without itself sustaining any injury. If, on the other hand, it were obliged, in order to attack me, to lower the prices of all its goods, wherever they might be sold, it would be in danger of ruining itself in the pursuit of its hostile object. Its losses would be proportionate to the magnitude of its operations. Many a small competitor is in a position to beat a trust in a contest of cutthroat competition, if only the trust were compelled to make its low prices uniform for all customers. There is no saving power in a great capital, if a ruinous competition entails losses that are proportionate to the capital.

Akin to the power to make prices low in one locality and high in many others is the power to reduce the prices of one grade or variety of goods, and to sustain them on other varieties. My mill may make only one specialized product, and the mills of the trust may make that kind of goods and twenty others. If it is willing to lose money for a time on the goods that I produce, and to make money on all other kinds, it can ruin me if it will.

Akin to these resources for predatory warfare is the power to boycott customers who will not give their whole patronage to the trust, or to make special rebates to those wholesale or retail merchants who will refuse to buy any goods from independent producers. Such producers may find most markets closed against their goods, however cheap and excellent they may be.

The power to do all these things gives to the trust a great and abnormal advantage which the law can take away.

Predatory competition that is evil and that crushes producers who have a right to survive rests mainly in one of these three methods of discriminating and unfair treatment of customers. That power must be destroyed. With a fair field and no favor the independent producer is the protector of the public and of the wage-earner; but with an unfair field and much favor he is the first and most unfortunate victim. Save him, and you save the great interests of the public. You can do this if you find or make a way to success in that type of legislation that will prevent the single evil, discrimination in the treatment of customers. Put them all under what in diplomacy would be called a "most favored nation clause"; secure to all of them the benefit of the best treatment that the trust gives to any of its customers, and you may forego all other attempts to regulate their charges. Economic law that acts even now in a way that limits their exactions, will act far more efficiently. It will keep prices and wages at or near their natural levels and that, too, without sacrificing the prosperity that a high organization of industry insures. Carry that policy to success—conquer the difficulties that lie in the way of it—and you will secure for our country a happy union of productive power, that will give us the command of the markets of the world, and justice, that will develop the manhood and insure the contentment of our citizens.

A. E. ROGERS.

University of Maine.

In the preparation of this paper which I now have the honor to present to this convention, it has seemed to me unnecessary to discuss at any length the results of the present tendency in the industrial and commercial world towards concentration of power and control.

It must be admitted at the outset that competition is not always an unalloyed blessing, that there are cases, especially in the great business of railroad transportation, where the advantage to certain individuals resulting from the struggle for patronage is more than offset by the disadvantage to the people as a whole consequent upon the demoralization of a service that is essentially public in its nature. But that the great combinations ordinarily termed "trusts" are an evil in our social and economic life is admitted by the great majority of those who are not the beneficiaries of them, and who are not the advocates of state socialism. The latter see in these organizations but the prelude of the destruction of competition of every kind through the public ownership and control of all means of production.

Indeed, there is no argument in favor of these combinations, organized to crush competition, to limit production, and to control prices, which cannot logically and consistently be turned by the socialist to support his doctrines. If avoidance of waste resulting from competition is to outweigh any and all considerations of individual initiative and enterprise, and is to be a determining factor in our social and economic life, then, the more perfectly our people are organized as a great industrial machine, the more completely shall we realize our ideal. If this is to be the condition, however, the socialist is right in his contention, for it will be safer and better to entrust the control of this machine to the government, which is responsible to the people, than to place it in the hands of irresponsible combinations, where, as both history and recent experience demonstrate, it will not only be susceptible, but liable, to grievous abuse.

In the social and industrial world, a great and growing evil is to be checked and destroyed only by striking at the very roots of it. Spasmodic legislation, however drastic, will generally prove not only useless, but harmful. In the majority of cases, such legislation will be circumvented by skillful lawyers employed for this purpose by interested parties and when, as often happens, some of its provisions in their application conflict with fundamental principles of our jurisprudence that have been made a part of our national or state constitution, the very evil that the legislation was intended to check tends from this fact to assume a legitimate character to which it has no claim. Even in those cases where legislation of this nature effects the purpose of its framers and reaches the abuses at which it is aimed, it is apt, from its radical nature, to involve such an excess of inconvenience and harm as to lead to its early repeal, and thus to create in the minds of many the dangerous feeling that such evils are irremediable under present social conditions.

Trusts, as they are commonly called, whether in the form of trusts proper, or of great corporations, as well as corporations organized for the purpose of fraud and swindling, are but the natural results of the vices and deficiencies in our corporation laws, and it is here that the remedy must be applied, if this disease in our social and political organism is to be treated rationally.

Investigation of many economic questions, such as rate of wages, interest, profits, labor-saving machinery, division and specialization of labor, and the like, often leaves us, after our facts have been obtained and our theories framed, helpless in the face of these facts and theories. A careful study of the conditions of corporate organization, however, cannot fail to be fruitful in positive results, for this all-important factor in our social and economic life is of our own voluntary and immediate creation, the product of the law. If abuses exist, and intelligence be not lacking, these abuses can be remedied by the same means that gave opportunity for their existence; and not only this, but the usefulness of the organizations themselves may be greatly increased as we come to understand and appreciate more fully their legitimate purposes and functions.

Although the life of our common law has been, as Judge Holmes says, experience, the organism through which this life manifests itself is precedent. As is the case in the evolution of the animal body, some parts of the legal organism that once served a useful purpose persist after their usefulness has disappeared and become a source of disease and danger by impeding functional activities, essential to life and growth under new and more complex conditions of existence.

The development of the law of corporations in England and this country affords a striking illustration of this fact. The fiction of the personality of these organizations served its purpose in an age when the conditions of business and industrial life were comparatively primitive and searching legal analysis was unnecessary and unknown; in those days, it was easier, perhaps better for the sake of simplicity and clearness of thought, to attribute to a single fictitious person the special rights and obligations of several individuals associated for certain purposes, than to consider such special rights and obligations as pertaining to the individuals themselves.

So long as this question remains a merely academic one, a theme for legal scholastics, we can look with good-natured tolerance on such solemn nonsense as the following, even though it appears under the guise of a judicial opinion: "None can create souls but God; but the king creates corporations; therefore they have no souls;" a syllogism whose conclusion has been of the greatest use to many reformers in making up for a deficiency of ideas. But when we find modern legal conceptions and rules, and modern legislation concerning economic policies of the greatest moment, influenced and shaped by deductions from this ancient fiction, and also see reasoned out of practical existence from the same premise the fact that the historic, legal, and moral justification for the existence of the corporation lies in the advantage to the public to be gained thereby, we may well be excused for an intellectual revolt on a small scale, and believe that in some respects, at least, our present corporation laws are the development, not of fundamental truths, but of fundamental errors.

It is quite unnecessary to discuss here the importance of corporations in our present economic system, for it scarcely need be said that without them this system could not exist. Until we go back to the days of the hand-loom, of the sailing-vessel, and of travel by stage-coach, or come to governmental socialism, pure and simple, corporations will remain indispensable. The building and maintenance of railroads, the establishing and operating of vast manufacturing plants, in short, the thousands of enterprises of a like character and magnitude that have made the past fifty years the most wonderful period in the history of the human race, demand, from the very nature of these undertakings, such a continuity in the consistent prosecution of plans and purposes as cannot be measured by the life of an individual. The immense amount of capital, also, required in such enterprises, must ordinarily involve co-operative investments on the part of a large number of persons; of these, the great majority are necessarily excluded from any direct interference or control, must entrust the management of the undertaking to others; hence, to effect the aggregation of this capital there must be, to a greater or less extent, limited liability on the part of the investor.

The theory that corporate organizations had their origin in ancient Rome has of late been questioned by some investigators, who are inclined to look for their sources in the history of the early Greeks. A comparative study of institutions leads me, however, to believe that in the solidarity and continuity of the family, not only among the early Greeks and Romans, but among many, if not all, of the races ethnically related to them, is to be found the source of corporations of every kind, governmental, ecclesiastical, and lay, aggregate and sole. Whether trusts originated in Rome or, as has been contended, among earlier races, it was in Rome, as the power of the central governing authority became greater, and as the family lost more and more its autonomic character, that the conception of the unity and continuity of a group of persons extended from the association united by bond of kinship to other organizations, naturally at first to those exercising some of the functions of the family, such as colleges of priests, and afterwards, as opportunity for great enterprises of a private nature resulted from the increasing wealth and commerce of the city, to organizations whose main purpose was private advantage.

Fortunately, it is not necessary in this connection to discuss or to attempt to discuss in detail the development of the Roman corporation. The main fact here to be noted is, that in this city, whose laws and whose legal conceptions concerning corporate organizations have had so much influence in shaping our own views and our own policy, these earlier forms of corporations precluded the idea of private gain or individual advantage.

In early England, the nearest approach to the modern corporation is the church. But the early ecclesiastical organization, even, did not consciously base its unity or continuity upon the succession of individuals; God or the different saints to whom the church establishments and lands were dedicated were individually held to be their actual owners, and the ecclesiastics were regarded as administering the property in the character of agents or stewards. But the ecclesiastical law, derived as it was from the Roman law, on the revival of the study of the latter, easily appropriated its maxims and doctrines and, as a consequence, the proprietor-saint was gradually supplanted by a vague personification of the church; the lay courts had only to recognize this fiction to clear the way in the English law for the being so forcibly described in later times as having "no body to be kicked, and no soul to be damned."

Side by side with the ecclesiastical organizations in England there had existed the local political and administrative organizations,—counties, hundreds, boroughs, towns, and manors, which Pollock and Maitland in their "History of the English Law" designate, "for want of a better term," as "land communities." Under the influence of these, to represent which no fictitious person had been imagined, and of the ecclesiastical organizations, we find a new kind of corporations coming into existence, partaking of the character and tendencies of both of the earlier forms. The most important examples of this new type are the trade and merchant guilds and the universities, the latter showing the natural predominance of the ecclesiastical influence in the very name, the word "universitas" being but a Roman law term for corporation.

In discussing these new organizations the learned writers above referred to say:* "The English temporal corporations when they first appear as ideal persons, appear not in the character of mere private persons, but in the character, we may almost say it, of governmental officers and magistrates who hold property in the right of their offices. Their lands, their goods, are few; what they own is jurisdiction, governmental power, and fiscal

*Pollock and Maitland, Hist. of the Eng. Law, Vol. 1, p. 493.

immunities. This is a characteristic feature of our temporal corporations in the first stage of their existence; the artificial person comes into being in order that he may govern and do justice—that he may govern and do justice to the profit and ease of the members of the corporation, no doubt, for no one governs or does justice without gaining thereby; but it is as much within the sphere of the public as within the sphere of the private law that the nascent corporation becomes active."

As in ancient Rome, so in England, with the increase of commerce and wealth, the private character of these organizations was correspondingly developed, but the extinction of all idea as to their public nature is practically a thing of our own day.

Within the past fifty years, as the result of tremendous economic forces that have been called into existence, and of legislative action facilitating the establishment of corporations, these organizations have assumed a character in our industrial life that is almost revolutionary. Seventy-five years ago, the number of corporations in this country, aside from banks, was so small that as an economic factor they might be safely disregarded. The conditions to-day are well set forth in an address delivered by Justice Field at the centennial celebration of the organization of the federal judiciary:

"Nearly all the enterprises requiring for their successful prosecution large investments of capital are conducted by corporations. They, in fact, embrace every branch of industry, and the wealth that they hold in the United States equals in value four-fifths of the entire capital of the country. They carry on business with the citizens of every state, as well as with foreign nations, and the litigation arising out of their transactions is enormous, giving rise to every possible question to which the jurisdiction of the Federal courts extends."*

Legal rules and conceptions wherein transitions and modifications may gradually take place are easily adapted by the courts to changing social and economic conditions. But when the rule or conception is of such a nature that modification or transition is impossible, if it have the sanction of age it is exceedingly tenacious of existence. Courts must adhere to precedent if legal development is to be orderly and consistent, and legislation must be in accord with the spirit of the legal development of a country as it finds expression in the decisions of its courts if the law is to remain an organic whole.

Through this wise and necessary conservatism, however, an erroneous legal conception or rule, harmless, perhaps, under the

*134 U. S. 742.

conditions in which it was first formulated or came into existence, may be perpetuated under new conditions that will render it not only an evil in itself, but a source of other evils that will survive the death of the parent error. The early ecclesiastics of England introduced into their canon law the Roman fiction of a corporate entity, which was soon transformed by them into a corporate personality. The lay courts grafted upon the English law this branch, alien not only in origin, but alien in character and alien in development. Much of the law of ancient Rome has been made a part of the English law and completely assimilated. But this conception of the legal entity, or the artificial personality of an organization, as such, was not and is not capable of assimilation or of beneficent tendencies in a system of jurisprudence whose very essence lies in the fact that it contemplates the individual as the legal and political unit.

A corporation is a collection of individuals to whom, as individuals, special powers and privileges are granted by the state, the most important and characteristic of these powers and privileges being limited liability and capacity to transmit the special rights so granted under the same conditions as those under which they were received. As Judge Finch, of New York, so well said in giving the opinion of the court in the case of the People vs. North River Sugar Refining Company (21 N. Y. 582): "The state gave the franchise, the charter, not to the impalpable, intangible and almost nebulous fiction of our thoughts, but to the corporators, the individuals, the acting and living men, to be used by them, to redound to their benefit, to strengthen their hands and add energy to their capital."

Wherein do we find the justification for such a grant, in other words, for the existence of the corporation? Certainly not in the advantage accruing to its members from the fact that they are endowed with special legal powers and privileges by the state, for it is a fundamental principle of our jurisprudence that all our citizens are equal before the law. A departure from this fundamental principle is warranted only when an advantage to the people as a whole, to the public, is to be secured thereby; hence, in the securing of such a public advantage must lie the justification for the existence of each and every corporation.

Blackstone, when writing his famous Commentaries at the beginning of the latter half of the last century, could say of the organization of corporations: "—it has been found necessary, when it is for the advantage of the public to have any particular rights kept on foot and continued, to construct artificial persons, who may maintain a perpetual succession and enjoy a kind of legal immortality."*

Chief Justice Marshall, speaking in 1819 for the Supreme Court of the United States in the famous case of Dartmouth College vs. Woodward, declared: "The objects for which a corporation is created are universally such as the government wishes to promote. They are deemed beneficial to the country; and this benefit constitutes the consideration and, in most cases, the sole consideration of the grant."**

It is clear from the context of this opinion, with succeeding clauses, that the term "benefit" as used here by Judge Marshall does not signify the benefit that accrues to the public from the establishment of any legitimate and honorable enterprise, but only such benefit as cannot ordinarily be secured through the undertakings of an individual or of individuals exercising only such legal powers and enjoying only such legal privileges as pertain to citizens generally. This is clearly shown by the subsequent declarations: "Charitable or public spirited individuals, desirous of making permanent appropriations for charitable or other useful purposes, find it impossible to effect their design securely and certainly without an organizing act. The benefit to the public is considered as an ample compensation for the faculty it confers."

Again, as late as 1850, we find the Supreme Court of North Carolina using these words: "The purpose of making all corporations is the accomplishment of some public good. Hence the division into public and private has a tendency to confuse and lead to error in investigation; for unless the public are to be benefited, it is no more lawful to confer exclusive rights and privileges upon an artificial body than upon a private citizen."†

Unfortunately, however, in Dartmouth College vs. Woodward, which was to have so great an influence in shaping the corporation laws of this country, the court held to the ancient fiction of legal personality, declaring: "A corporation is an artificial being, invisible, intangible, and existing only in contemplation of the law. Being the mere creature of the law, it possesses only those properties which the charter of its creation confers upon it, either expressly or as incidental to its existence."

Here the court denies, by necessary implication, the very principle on which is based the doctrine that benefit to the public is the consideration which gives the charter of incorporation the nature of a contract. If we assume that the corporation is an entity, a legal person, then the theory that special powers are

*Bl. Com., Bk. 1, p. 467.　　**4 Wheat. 518.　　†Mills vs. Williams, 11 Iredell.

416

conferred upon it by the state is manifestly illogical, for it is the very grant of these powers that creates this entity, this person, prior to the grant, the corporation does not exist; the grant, then, must be made to the individuals taking part in the act of incorporation; hence, upon these individuals and their successors the responsibility to the public must logically rest. If we accept the idea of a legal personality, we can reach the final conclusion of the court that the charter of incorporation is a contract only on the assumption that a grant of special powers and privileges to certain individuals has for its consideration a benefit to the public, to be derived from, and resting as an obligation upon, a distinct individual created by this same grant, hence coming into existence subsequently to it; a proposition condemned by the elementary principles of logic as well as of law.

This shunting of public responsibility into space, upon the man supposed to live in the moon, "artificial, invisible, and intangible," has had its deplorable but logical result in the complete disappearance of the idea of any public responsibility whatever on the part of these organizations, for of the two inconsistent doctrines, that of the responsibility of the corporation to the public was ultimately to go to the wall, while that of its legal personality was to endure and shape not only future judicial opinions and future legislation, but, through its apparent simplicity, to mould even popular ideas and conceptions. Had the Supreme Court in this, I had almost said fateful, opinion, looked beyond the fictitious person to the real persons, whose rights and privileges and responsibilities arising through the corporation were to be affected, its reasoning would have been, as its conclusion is, incontrovertible, the fundamental doctrine that the justification of the corporation lies in the fact that an advantage to the public is to be secured thereby, might have remained a guiding and formative principle, and many of the evils now existing might well have been avoided.

It is a legal maxim that where the reason ceases the law ceases, but at present, in the great majority of cases, either the doctrine that charters of incorporation are contracts must form a notable exception to this rule, or the public advantage as a consideration supporting such contracts must be a fictitious creature of the law, even more vague and unsubstantial than the intangible and invisible personality of the corporation, that has existed so long in the imagination of learned jurists.

Mr. H. O. Havemeyer, speaking before the United States Industrial Commission a short time ago, expressed the logical consequence of present conditions, if not the generally accepted idea of to-day, when he said: "I maintain that it is immaterial to the public in what form business is done,—whether by an individual, firm, corporation, or even a trust. They are merely forms of conducting a business, in other words, machinery for the operation of business."

Compare this with the following words, spoken for the Supreme Court of the United States in 1865:

"The purposes to be attained [by incorporation] are generally beyond the ability of individual enterprise, and can only be accomplished through the aid of associated wealth. This will not be risked unless privileges are given and securities furnished in an act of incorporation. The wants of the public are often so imperative, that a duty is imposed on government to provide for them; and as experience has proved that a state should not attempt directly to do this, it is necessary to confer on others the faculty of doing what the sovereign power is unwilling to undertake. The legislature, therefore, says to public-spirited citizens: 'If you will embark, with your time, money, and skill, in an enterprise which will accommodate the public necessities, we will grant to you for a limited period, or in perpetuity, privileges that will justify the expenditure of your money, and the employment of your time and skill.' Such a grant is a contract with mutual considerations, and justice and good policy alike require that the protection of the law should be assured to it."*

The idea that corporations are purely private organizations in which the public has no concern is the offspring of the ancient fiction of their legal personality, and its predominance, to the practical exclusion, if not extinction, of the doctrine that they are formed to secure some advantage to the public, is due to patent causes. Enterprises whose main object, at least from the standpoint of an increasingly large and increasingly influential body of our citizens, have increased in number and magnitude during the past fifty years in an almost incredible manner. Legislation, shaped in part by questionable means, and for questionable ends, and in part by desire to encourage great enterprises, has too often thrown conservatism to the winds; and, finally, the character itself of our people has had a tendency in the same direction, for we are inclined to look upon loose corporation laws as democratic in their nature, inasmuch as they apparently offer equal privileges to all persons for all purposes; we are apt to lose sight of the fact that the very essence of these laws is discrimination, the granting to some individuals of rights and privi-

*Binghamton Bridge, 3 Wall. 51.

leges which the sound policy of the laws denies to our citizens generally.

Scarcely less harmful in its results than the trust evil, and resulting from the same conditions, is the organization of corporations for fraudulent purposes. With but few exceptions, our different state legislatures have opened the door wide for abuses of this nature. Every pretense of public need or public benefit is openly discarded, and we have corporations organized to conduct clothing stores, to sell groceries, to sell drugs, and, in short, for enterprises that could just as efficiently be undertaken without the grant of special legal powers and privileges. The sole object in the great majority of such cases is to limit personal liability and to avoid that responsibility which the members of the community should bear, and generally must bear. The fact, also, that the corporation may be organized without any capital being actually paid in is an abundant source of evil. Undoubtedly, there are cases where the funds for a great enterprise can be more easily and advantageously secured after the corporation has been organized. Ordinarily, however, the record, "nothing paid in," or the fact that the promoters of the enterprise have not sufficient confidence in it to lead them to invest more than a nominal amount, is a fairly sure indication that the corporation laws have been invoked to further speculative or fraudulent designs.

As an illustration of the conditions existing in the state of Maine, I find in a newspaper taken at random that in this state there were recently filed on two consecutive days the certificates of organization of nine corporations whose total capitalization was $2,220,000, while the amount actually paid in was $1,093, or less than one-twentieth of one per cent. One of these corporations was to deal in drugs and medicines, and of the sixteen officers whose names and residences were given, eleven were from another state, where the laws pertaining to the organizations were more stringent.

A newspaper published the same day on which this is written gives a list of three corporations whose certificates were filed in this state the day before. Of these, one was organized and incorporated to conduct a sporting lodge. Their total capitalization, $360,000, of which "nothing is paid in."

It may be that every one of these corporations was organized for a legitimate purpose, but the fact remains that corporations for fraudulent or swindling purposes might just as easily have been organized. The sovereign power of the state of Maine, if it has not been, may easily be, prostituted to further the dishonest schemes of dishonest men through its present system of loose corporation laws; and this, I suspect, might be said of nearly every state in the Union.

In our country at large, such a thing as a system of corporation laws can scarcely be said to exist. From the national standpoint, we have a vast tangle of heterogeneous statutes which the legislatures of our different states are constantly making more inconsistent and more confusing.

In general, interstate comity has thus far been sufficient to prevent any state from excluding corporations organized in another from transacting business within its limits, its powers, of course, not extending to that business which is strictly commerce between states and with foreign nations, but the tendencies of an opposite nature are to be seen; it is certainly becoming a question, how long a state that is endeavoring to establish a rational system of corporation laws should continue, to its own detriment, to respect a sister commonwealth that has no respect for its own sovereign power.

Though the question as to the nature of corporations is, in a certain aspect, a purely legal one, it is in another and vastly more important aspect a matter of grave economic and social interest to us all. Many of the evils resulting from these organizations had their origin in an erroneous legal conception, but so completely have deductions from this conception, the immediate causes of these evils, become established as a part of our legal system, to a certain extent by frequent judicial recognition, and still more by positive legislation, that they are practically beyond the controlling influence of the courts. Reform must come through legislation, and that this legislation may be effective as well as conservative, it must be based on clear conceptions as to its subject-matter—on an appreciation of the fact that a corporation is but an association of individuals, to whom, as individuals, the state makes a grant of special legal powers and privileges, of the fact, also, that this grant can be justified in our system of jurisprudence only on the ground that a definite advantage to the public is secured thereby.

Trusts and fraudulent corporations are the results of vices and imperfections in our corporation laws. When these are remedied, and not until then, will the evils of which they are the cause disappear. In the domain of law, which is that of ideas, and principles, and reason, ultimate truths are the only safe foundation on which to build. Legal fictions often have highly important functions in unifying legal rules; they serve, so to speak, as a scaffolding, useful in raising the structure of our jurisprudence, but constituting no real part of it. In determining and shaping important economic conditions, however, fictions, legal or otherwise, have no place; we must be guided by the absolute facts of human life and human experience.

As civilization advances, and as science, and wealth, and trade increase, the public and private relations of the different members of society become more complex and the problems that our legislative bodies are called upon to solve necessarily demand on their part increasing skill and intelligence. To understand even a branch of our legal system has become the business of a learned and laborious profession. But the great principles, along whose lines the development of our substantive law should proceed, must be the business of all enlightened and thoughtful men, if we are to realize in our jurisprudence that justice so well described by the Roman jurist as "the set and constant purpose that gives to every man his due."

Assuming that the views set forth in this paper embody correct principles, the next question is: How can we make these principles dynamic, render them effective in shaping actual legislation?

The first step in this direction is, I believe, an organized effort to secure uniformity of the corporation laws of the different states.

At present the great difficulty in the way of the application of correct and rational principles to the development of our corporation law, especially in the all-important matter of organization, lies in the fact that certain states are ready to prostitute their sovereign power for sake of revenue, and to enter into competition to secure patronage in this shameless traffic, regardless of their own honor and of what is rightfully and justly due to other commonwealths.

From such a traffic and such a competition not only does there result a continuous leveling down on the part of the states engaged in it, but almost insurmountable obstacles are placed thereby in the way of those states seeking to maintain or establish proper and rightful standards. A general and strongly sustained effort to secure uniformity would, above anything else, counteract these demoralizing influences, and tend to substitute public welfare in the place of short-sighted selfishness as a determining factor in our legislation. Undoubtedly a few states might be disposed to resist efforts looking towards reform, but concert of action on the part of the others in regard to corporations organized under the laws of these recalcitrant commonwealths would reduce their power for evil to a minimum.

Approximate uniformity of the corporation laws of the different states being secured, national legislation, also, could be more intelligently framed for the purpose of complementing state legislation, and made much more effective in meeting those evils which because of the exclusive control of Congress over interstate commerce the state legislatures cannot reach. Federal legislation, however, as affecting the evils resulting from the abuse of corporate power and privileges can be nothing more than complementary, the reform must be essentially worked out by state action.

The American Bar Association has already done most excellent work in securing uniformity of state legislation along certain lines, notably that of commercial paper, and commissions on uniformity of state laws have been provided for in a majority of the states. It seems certain that if this conference with its great influence should make an earnest and organized effort in conjunction with these bodies to secure uniformity of corporation laws throughout the Union, a high degree of success would be assured from the outset.

To claim, however, that even the complete success of this effort would abolish all the evils arising from corporate organization would be absurd. Abuses and evasions of the law and imperfections in the law itself will continue to exist until human nature and human foresight have reached a far higher stage of development than that of to-day. The surest way, however, to meet and minimize these evils is through a rational and intelligent application of the fundamental principles of right and justice and next in importance to a clear appreciation of these principles and of their relation to the problem before us, is the removal as completely as may be, of the obstacles which obstruct the application of them.

HENRY D. BAKER.

Associate Financial Editor New York *Evening Post.*

Literal accomplishment of what Mr. W. J. Bryan has termed the "Democratic idea that if you make the masses prosperous their prosperity will find its way up and through every class," was responsible for the increased resources and confident venturesomeness of the financial and investing classes, such as caused the recent rapid multiplication of corporations known as "trusts." The fine crops and high prices of 1897 and 1898 brought vast wealth to the masses, while the relief from silver agitation pu vast sums of money that had been hoarded, into the channels of circulation. Some of the phenomena which arose during 1898 out of the same conditions so favorable to the growth of trusts were witnessed in the magnificent success of the popular war loan of $200,000,000 hurriedly raised without a ripple of disturbance to general business, the war bonds soon selling at a premium of 9 above par. The United States became a creditor instead of a debtor nation in its relation to the general world of finance. Savings banks reduced long established rates on deposits, and clients of banks of deposit were notified that balances no longer carry interest. Some localities bought foreign exchange for an investment; some communities in the far West became lenders of money in Europe.

The promoters of trusts were not in evidence, however, during the period between the blowing up of the Maine on February 14th and Dewey's victory at Manila on May 1st of 1898. Deals that had not been successfully finished before the catastrophe in Havana harbor were sent up the spout.

The glorious news from Manila not only put the nation in ecstasy of patriotic joy, but it also brought the promoter of trusts out of the woods. The destruction of Cervera's fleet in July and the end of the election uncertainty in November marked further stages in the growth of investment and speculative confidence. Toward the close of the year not only was prosperity extremely pronounced in all branches of business, but also millions of dollars had become added to the value of all kinds of securities. Newspapers were announcing new trusts at about the rate of three a day; time and call money ranged from $3\frac{1}{2}$ to 4 per cent. Such conditions of extreme public confidence, of cheap money, of rising security values, all essential to the successful promotion of trusts, continued for about the first month and a half of the present year. Tremendous profits became shown in the underwriting of industrials. In a great many instances, underwriters sold their rights and made fortunes before it was necessary to pay a cent of cash on their subscriptions. The belief became prevalent that by simply signing subscription lists it would be possible to realize profits of from 10 to 20 points on the rights before there could be any call for cash. It was the policy of promoters to foster the preliminary speculations in rights by hints or announcements to the effect that the heavy over-subscriptions would necessitate the proportionate cutting down in the allotments of stock to subscribers. The purchase of rights by those who wanted to be sure of full allotments of stock usually more than offset sales of the rights by those who wanted to take profits before it was necessary to meet the call for cash. Often advances in the underwriting premium would be accelerated by the scrambling endeavor to buy back rights after it was discovered or feared that only a part of the stock would be received which had already been sold for delivery "when issued." The economics due to consolidation, natural growth of business, cheapness of money, increase in general prosperity and absence of political disturbances in all parts of the world, were argumentative features to which the speculative public eagerly listened.

Toward spring of the present year the "trust" movement had become greatly overdone in the opinion of those who looked at it purely from the financial standpoint. Despite the unprecedented plethora of money in the country, money was growing dearer, owing to the absorption of enormous sums of capital in the flotation of the new industrial issues. Bankers began to entertain misgivings, and their discrimination against industrials as collateral began to hurt their progress in the stock markets. Several big promotions then pending became conspicuous failures. In one or two instances underwriters, fearing losses on their subscriptions, forced the closing of the deals before they could become consummated by payment of cash. The sudden death of ex-Governor Flower, who had been the most potent bull leader in the market for industrials, hit his own specialties hard and sympathetically wrought injury to industrials as a class. The plan for effecting the most gigantic combination of the age to include the Carnegie properties, the Federal Steel Company, the American Steel and Wire Company, the National Steel Company, the American Tin Plate Company and lesser concerns, fell through. The stock issues of the trusts already created now show losses in value of from 10 to 50 per cent. The trust promoter to-day admits that future attempt at trust creation will be exceedingly uphill work.

It is thus shown that the trust movement has owed its immediate origin to an unprecedented plentifulness of money and to an exceedingly high state of public confidence such as always tends to make capital venturesome. Tariffs, railroad discrimination and lack of publicity may serve to perpetuate the existence of at least some of the trusts lately created, but have had little or no relevant connection with their origin. The trust motive has been the speculative motive to make big profits in quick time. Perhaps the American people would rather now enjoy prosperity in which great trusts share with themselves, than endure hard times in which neither great trusts nor themselves can find meat whereby to grow and thrive. The nation was sad and horrified over the blowing up of the Maine, notwithstanding the fact that the disaster interrupted for a time the promotion of trusts. Equally jubilant and thrilled with patriotic spirit were the American people on hearing of Dewey's triumph at Manila, which was not diminished by the fact that the victory was the sunlight which brought the promoters of trusts out of their holes, so to speak.

Payments through the principal clearing houses of the country are now about 37 per cent greater than a year ago, and 57 per cent greater than in 1892. East bound railroad tonnage is nearly double that of a year ago. The number of business failures is about half of that of a year ago, and a third as great as in 1896. The country's gold reserve to-day stands above the $250,000,000 mark. Generally advancing prices in manufactured lines of goods have attended the increasing prosperity. Although such advances have not been confined to articles produced by trusts, but have included furniture, products of the packing house, and other articles in which trade is unquestionably regulated by conditions of competition and of demand to supply, yet there is a good deal of complaint that practically all late advances in prices have been produced by the trust arbitrarily and for their own profit, and that therefore they afford no indication of conditions benefiting the country. It is true that the trusts in nearly every instance after their recent formations, have marked up prices, and yet considering the increased cost of raw material entering into production and the fact that wages have been generally advanced, it cannot be correctly said that the trusts have made unfair use of their trade opportunities. Where they have advanced prices more than would seem to have been warranted by advances in raw materials, such advances seem usually to have effected simply an adjustment of prices to some basis of fixed profits such as had existed before the hard times period, or as in the case of the Biscuit Consolidation for instance, before a competitive war had brought earnings down below the cost of production, and had threatened practically the whole business with bankruptcy.

In the case of the best managed industrial companies the policy has been to keep prices of products high enough to allow reasonable profit on capital invested, but low enough to offer no inducements for competitors to enter the business. In the case of the Glucose Sugar Refining Company, which is the oldest of the recent industrials,* President Matthissen, at the annual meeting of stockholders last year explained as follows the application of this policy: "There is not at this time a bushel of corn being ground by any concern except those in our company. We do

*Organized August, 1897.

not intend to pursue the policy of making spectacular profit in the beginning and dwindling at the end. We are in business for a long pull. For instance, on a ten-year run we might have raised prices, made $5,000,000 the first year, $2,500,000 the next, $1,000,000 the next, and down to nothing at the end of ten years. It is better business to be moderate and earn $2,000,000 a year for ten years, which would be $20,000,000 in profits, against a loss of $10,000,000 the other way. We did for a short time make the mistake in the beginning of putting the price too high, but it did not last long. If we had maintained that policy, we would have had sixteen or seventeen competitors, against none as it is now." Generally speaking, from the standpoint of the investor, it is considered better to own securities of a trust which makes its money by saving money through especial economies, than it is to own securities of a trust which is known to make its money through practicing extortion on consumers. In the case of long-lived industrial corporations like the Standard Oil Company, success seems to have been at least in large measure due to a policy of lowering rather than raising prices. This fact investors are beginning to appreciate, and is causing them to discriminate. Considerable blame has been thrown on the iron and steel trusts owing to the enormous advances which have taken place in prices of products in the iron and steel industry. Quotations on steel billets are about $37 per ton to-day as against $14.50 per ton one year ago, while various steel products are quoted relatively the same. As pig iron, however, is now $24 per ton as against $10 per ton one year ago, it is evident that the advances in finished steel products have been legitimate. Practically all the companies engaged in the iron and steel business now have contracts ahead which will keep their furnaces active at full capacity for six months to come. If the general prosperity had not caused an enormous demand for steel products, the price of pig iron could hardly have advanced, for manufacturers would not create a demand for more pig iron than they would expect to sell as finished product from their foundries.

Owing to the fact that the American Tin Plate Company is about the most conspicuous example of a protected trust, the sharp advances it has made in prices have drawn down upon it much aggressive criticism, which seems to be unfair in the extreme, as shown by the following data furnished me by President Reid of the company late in the month of August. Since the organization of the company pig tin had shown an advance from $12\frac{1}{2}$ cents to 33 cents per pound; 15 per cent more was being paid for skilled labor, and 20 per cent more for unskilled labor; the price of acids used in making tin plate had gone up 25 per cent; steel billets, of which about 10,000,000 boxes were figured as the company's probable consumption for the year, had advanced one dollar per box; the increases in the bill for castings, etc., to keep the plants in repair, would, it was estimated, be about double what they would have amounted to a year ago. Yet despite these great increases in the cost of supplies and labor, finished tin plates were quoted at only $4.37½ as against $2.50 one year ago. As the protection on tin plate makes the price which would induce imports of tin plate $5.58, it is therefore evident that the company has not by any means availed itself of the full opportunity allowed it by the tariff.

The increase in legitimate business in this country during the past year has resulted in the establishment of a fairly normal ratio between the supply and demand for money. It has put a limitation on trust promotions, practically ending the movement before it could cause a financial crash. At the present time the prosperity of the country allows opportunity for unlimited business development of all legitimate kinds. The trust movement was an early incident of our present prosperity. Trusts are, however, no longer the product of our prosperity. Whether or not we would be more prosperous without the trusts is a question concerning which views and theories now may differ and which can only be definitely and thoroughly settled by the economic data of the next few years.

JOHN I. YELLOTT.

Member Maryland Bar.

The "trust" problem is of that character to-day that the American people are called upon to deal with a condition, rather than with theories on the subject. The consideration of facts as they exist in consequence of what the "trust" and the "combine" are doing with the masses of the American people, is of more practical importance than any indulgence in nice and finely wrought-out theories as to what the "trust" ought to do—as to what it can do, as to what minor laws found in the trade and financial circles of business may compel it to do, and what it may be expected to do for the public good in the future—if let alone. To me, the competent theorist is always entertaining, but I am ever slow to adopt theories that I know to be contrary to certain fixed laws, and unsupported by present or past facts.

In the matter of production and distribution, there is one law regulating both the buying and selling interests of civilized man so fixed and so unvarying in its long operation, that it has been looked upon as a natural law. It is the law of competition. It, in conjunction with the recognized laws of supply and demand, is the one great force all the time at work for the healthful regulation of production, distribution, and values. Any system of production, or of distribution, including the commanding industry of transportation, that is in contravention of, or, at variance with this great law can have but one result, to-wit: injustice and wrong to the weak and undue imposition upon both the consumer who must buy in the market and the producer of the raw material who must sell! When you destroy competition in the production of the finished article required for the use of man, you destroy two open markets—that in which the consumer may buy to advantage, and that in which the seller of the raw article may sell to competitors. You do more, you give to the producer the right to dictate the price which the consumer must pay for the finished article, and the power to say to the producer of the raw material what he shall take for the product of his labor; you give to that producer the right to dictate and fix the price that shall be paid for the labor required to convert the raw material into the finished product. You do what is worse, you make a favored class of the few chartered producers and transporters, and give to that class unlimited authority to say to the millions of our population what they shall pay for food, raiment and everything used by them for comfort, luxury or necessity, and what every man shall receive for the product of his labor. A condition of things abhorrent to the common law, before the American Constitution was thought of.

No legal authorization for, or acquiesence in, any system of production or class favoritism can be, under the American form of government, without violation of its every valued principle. Our government is founded upon the eternal foundation of human equality. When organized after the vindication of this principle in the war of the Revolution, the object of the Government was declared to be: "To establish justice"; "to promote the general welfare"; "to secure the blessings of liberty". Later in our history the fourteenth amendment to the Constitution was adopted, which embodied all that statesmanship of the country had ordained for accommodating the organic law to our then condition. It provides, "No state shall make *or enforce* any law which shall abridge the privileges or immunities of citizens of the United States; nor shall any State deprive any person of life, liberty, or property, without due process of law, nor deny to any

person within its jurisdiction the *equal protection* of the law."
The meaning of these privileges and immunities has been defined by the courts as those rights which are fundamental under every free government, including the right to acquire and possess property of every kind, and to pursue and obtain happiness and safety, subject to such restraints as government may prescribe for the *general good of the whole.*

All monopolies in any trade or manufacture are an invasion of these privileges, for they encroach upon the liberty of the citizen to acquire property and pursue happiness, and were held to be void at common law as long ago as the reign of Elizabeth.

No State of the Union can have the power to create a monopoly in any industry by incorporating a number of men into one body, without doing violence to the Constitution of the country. What it cannot directly do it is without power to do by indirection. The incorporation of any body of men with monopolistic power is in contravention of the spirit and the letter of our form of government and its written Constitution. If the organized trusts and combines are possessed of monopolistic powers and have monopolistic tendencies, then they should be abolished or brought within legal control, without regard to the fact whether they be advantageous or disadvantageous. They are an un-American institution, though flourishing in America only, and should not for that reason be allowed to grow and multiply.

Now, Mr. Chairman, it would seem that the all-important questions involved in the trust subject, are:

First: Are trusts and combines as now existent in the United States monopolies, or of monopolistic character and tendency?

Second: Are they of such character in their operation and modes of business as to infringe upon the Constitutional rights of the American citizen?

Third: If monopolistic and an invasion of the rights of the citizen, what is the proper remedy to apply?

I desire to discuss briefly the first two propositions, and in doing so I hope to be pardoned for dealing in facts more than theories. The origin or birth of the "trust" in our general industries is a mystery, but necessary to be inquired into in order to discover the laws that are likely to control its existence and growth.

One, and perhaps the greatest trust magnate of the land, has solemnly affirmed that the protective tariff is the mother of the "trust," but when we remember that it was that magnate's ox that was gored by the tariff of which he was speaking, this charge of

429

maternity must be accepted with some allowance. I believe this "Protective Tariff" has enough sins to answer for at the bar of public opinion without being charged with the motherhood of this monster.

Protection is but the foster mother, if mother at all, and I am disposed to yield to it the rightful claim only of being wet-nurse to the trust; it has surely kept it in vigorous life and possibly aided at the birth. Others, with plausibility, have advanced the theory that the "trust" is the result of evolution in trade and manufacture into which so many improved methods have been injected. Some ascribe to the great prosperity of our people in the last few years the life-giving cause, whilst still others claim the concentration of wealth in the productive industries to be the result of natural laws of business which demand some saving in the wastefulness of the competitive system. A few days ago I read an able article in one of our most valued monthlies, from the pen of an apparent advocate of the "trust"—the Hon. George E. Roberts, Director of the United States Mint, which came nearer to my views of the causes constituting the true parentage of the American "trust" than anything I have elsewhere seen. I beg to quote briefly from the article, page 305, "Review of Reviews," for September. The writer says: "Let us inquire about the forces that have brought on this general movement of the industries into combinations. It is a primary fact that the impelling motive has been the low returns recently earned by capital. It has been difficult to *make profits when competition has been open and active.*" The writer then proceeds to assign other causes for concentration, but the first of the forces at work, as stated by him, is the one great power, which is, in effect, that money, finding it could no longer get satisfactory returns from its accustomed user, determined to concentrate in the form of the trust or the combine for the purpose of nullifying the natural law of competition, and exacting from the masses of the people such profit as it might dictate. Practical monopoly only, can destroy competition, and if that be the object of combination in the industries, it follows that whatever the trust of to-day be, the very law of its existence will develop it into "odious" monopoly.

Again, the trust of to-day, which is doing its work of ruin amongst the masses, is an incorporated body, and is made up of the smaller corporations generally. It is a man-made machine sent forth into the world of the industries to compete with the human being, with unlimited power to acquire wealth and seek gain in the particular field for which it was made, without one of the finer instincts with which the natural man is endowed;

430

without soul to be saved or body to die, or conscience to restrain, it is actuated by one human instinct only—greed for money!

I am the friend of the corporation honestly created for a legitimate purpose. For centuries it has been a necessity in civilized society, and has done and is destined to do more for its advancement and full development, but none is blind to the fact that the corporation needs to be properly regulated and controlled by law. It has little regard for individual right and individual privilege unless conscious of the fact that the violation of the one or the invasion of the other invites inevitable legal responsibility.

Such being the constituent parts of the five hundred or more giant corporations which have taken control of about all the industries of the land, it follows that if absolute monopoly will give them greater gains for their stockholders, there will be no hesitation in establishing it. If the smaller corporations can combine for monopolistic purposes, the larger ones will not be slow in combining for the establishment of actual "monopoly" in all industries.

I do not contend against the belief, or the fact, that as a general rule production on a large scale is cheaper than on a small one. This is a rule of general application, but, sir, I do contend that if the producing agency, by reason of its great proportions, be removed from the field of competition, there is no incentive to the economic saving in production that is required in the competitive field. Economic improvement and invention result from the necessities growing out of competition. Destroy this necessity, and you banish the incentive to improve and invent and adopt cheaper modes of production. It is less trouble, easier and safer to profit by increase of price or adulteration, when it is known the consumer must buy your article, whatever its cost or its quality.

But, sir, conceding the trust and combine can produce cheaper than the individual, or company on a smaller scale, there is no known law of unvarying application by which the consumer will be benefited, or the seller to the combine be protected. The buying market must depend solely upon the conscience of the trust producer for any share in the benefits of cheapened production. The producer, of monopolistic character, has no interest in allowing the general public to share in such benefits. If it be an incorporated producer, there is no conscience to regulate the selling price, except loyalty to the stockholder in its concern, and that conscience points with constant finger to fat dividends, be the stock *bona fide* or fictitious! The advance in the price of nearly all trust productions, from the moment the trust got full control of the production, may be cited in support of the truth and the soundness of what I have said.

Coming to a consideration of a legal remedy, for the correction of the trust evil, it is passing strange, in the light of the history of monopoly in England and France, that an invention is to be sought in America where the individual and the protection of his every right are the boasted purposes of government. When we recall what English courts, an English parliament, a French statesman, sustained by a French king, have done to correct and restrain the evils of monopoly when concentrated money capital oppressed the individual; when we recall the fact that the English common law is the boasted inheritance of the American people, there is awakened a train of thought resulting in conclusions by no means flattering to American legislation and American courts! As far back as the case of Hurdis in 11th Coke, an English court, without republican sympathies or democratic bias, adjudged in the case of a corporate company, by no means so monopolistic as our Sugar Trust, that the citizen had the right to have his cloth dressed by whom he pleased, and in that, he could not be restrained to certain persons, *"for that in effect would be monopoly and therefore void."* It has been determined by a long list of our State courts, and by the Supreme Court of the United States as well, that whatever tends to injustice or oppression, restraint of liberty, or trade or commerce, and natural or legal right, when made the object of a contract, is void. It has also been determined by many State courts that all combinations between men or bodies of men to elevate or depress the market, or increase prices, are injurious to the public interests and in restraint of trade.

Chief Justice Fuller, delivering the opinion of the Supreme Court in the Sugar case, 156 U. S. Rep., p. 16, says: "Contracts, combinations, or conspiracies to control domestic enterprise in manufacture, agriculture, mining, production in all its forms, or to raise or lower prices or wages, might unquestionably tend to restrain external as well as domestic trade." The court says on same page: "All the authorities agree that in order to vitiate a contract or combination it is not essential that it should be a complete monopoly; *it is sufficient if it really tends to that end and to deprive the public of the advantages which flow from free competition.*"

In what precedes, we have the concession of the highest court in our Nation, that, if the facts exist, as conceded by more than 69,000,000 in a total of 70,000,000 of people, the American trust is an illegal thing and cannot exist! Yet we find it growing in numerical and individual strength, and oppressive power. How can a thing that is under the bane of public condemnation and the bane of the law as well, so flourish and multiply? On the hustings, inflammatory but conclusive answers could well be given—in an assemblage of this character, a briefer, and one subject to less criticism can be supplied, and that answer may be thus framed: Great moneyed wealth by means of unhealthy economic legislation has been concentrated in a few hands, and it can, if allowed, secure greater gains by means of the trust and combine, than by investment in more legitimate enterprise; that the Supreme Court of the United States, having declared and adjudged in the case just cited, that there is no law existing, and can be none under the Constitution as it now stands, to prevent the concentration of capital for the purpose of having the few wealthy exploit the many not so fortunate, by means of the trust and combine, those means of multiplying wealth will be naturally resorted to.

Is it true? On the 2d of July, 1890, Congress passed "An Act to Protect Trade and Commerce against Unlawful Restraints and Monopolies." That *act* was apparently drawn so as to prevent any form of trust or combine in restraint of trade, or, that would destroy competition. Sec. 3 of the Act declares—"Every contract, combination in form of trust or otherwise or conspiracy in restraint of trade   *   *   *   is hereby declared illegal," and a severe penalty was fixed upon any person who should make such contract, or engage in such combination.

This far-reaching act of Congress, as shown by the record, restrained the formation of trusts and combines from the date of its passage, and the addition to the number of existing trusts was small until January, 1895, when the Supreme Court, not without protest from a sitting member, judicially declared that whilst the act was not unconstitutional, it was ineffective, and that the Congress of the United States was without constitutional power to attain the purpose sought. This was, for reasons strongly stated by Justice Harlan in his dissenting opinion, a startling decision, and has given birth to the hundreds of trusts that now afflict the American people. The decision is one to which the American citizen must bow in submission, though with some feeling of shame and humiliation, inasmuch as the court admits the trust to be an evil thing, and an *unlawful* thing, but a thing which the United States Congress is unable to deal with under our Constitution as it now exists! In this case we have the judicial declaration of our highest court, that the United States government is not strong enough to control the trust and the combine, and will not have the strength until there is a constitutional revision!

The English Parliament in the time of James I. declared: "That all monopolies and all commissions, grants, licenses, charters, and letters patent to any person or persons, bodies politic or corporate, of or for the sole buying, selling, working or using anything within the realm * * * were contrary to law and utterly void." By this act the Englishman was protected against the imposition of the trust and combine. The courts before that had held such bodies to be void under the common law of the realm, and that same common law is the basis of all American jurisprudence, our Congress of the united colonies having, in 1774, declared it to be a part of our "indubitable rights and liberties." But in the matter of trusts, our Supreme Court has decided that the people have no remedy either by statute or common law, and that all the remedy they can hope for under the Constitution as now framed, must be through state legislation and state courts!

When concentrated wealth and monopoly invaded the rights of the Frenchman, that great French statesman, Turgot, prepared an edict which was issued by Louis XVI. in the year of the declaration of American Independence, which reads: "God, in creating man with necessities, has compelled him to resort to labor, and has made the right to labor the sacred unproscribable right of man. Therefore, it is ordained that the arbitrary institutions which prevent the indigent from living by work; which extinguish emulation and industry, and make useless the *talents of those who do not belong to a corporation or company;* which load industry with burdens onerous to the subject without benefit to the state; which by the facility which they afford to the combination of the rich to force the poor to submit to their will, and to create conditions that enhance the price of the most necessary articles of subsistence, be abrogated."

It is impossible to draw a more exact picture of the American trust than that given by Turgot, and which the French king banished from his kingdom because of its injustice to and hardship upon the citizen! The American government is powerless to do so much for the protection of the citizen as the French king did for his subject.

The decision of the Supreme Court in the Knight case, determines that we must have a constitutional change if the general government is to deal with the trust problem. This enabling amendment must be made, or we must rely upon state legislation for a remedy. What view the Supreme Court may adopt as to the constitutionality of any State legislation that undertakes to deal effectively with the subject, remains to be seen. There are now pending one or more cases in which this problem may be solved.

Recent litigation and observation leave no room to doubt that the trusts of the country have in operation a cunningly devised system of what can be termed nothing milder than corruption. The head of one of the largest of these bodies unblushingly admitted before a recent investigating board that his company freely contributed to the campaign funds of Democrats and Republicans alike—to Democrats in Democratic States, and to Republicans in Republican states. This is one grievous evil of the system working in a dangerous direction, and should be curbed by comprehensive and well digested state legislation that would prevent the evil.

Under the almost undefined and limitless police power of the State, the states of the Union can do much to restrain if not destroy the oppressive power of the trust and the combine. Under the general law the corporation formed in any one state is a resident of that state, while it has power to do business where it pleases. West Virginia and New Jersey, notably, create corporation of any character where the projectors are willing to pay the required fees.

Such corporation can claim the judicial protection in any state where it may do business, but so far as its existence is concerned, no court outside of the State where it is created can affect it. If a corporation doing business in States other than where created should be required to become a resident of such other States for all purposes, and on equality with other citizens of the State, as a condition precedent to doing business therein, the State courts, governed by the principles of the English common law, would exercise a healthful control over them. Such legislation could be framed without violation of the restrictive provisions of the Federal Constitution, and would tend to give more general effect to such legislation as has been adopted in Illinois and other States.

Again, the taxing power of the state is a large one, and a wise exercise of this power would do much to control the too powerful trust, including the department store.

Public policy ever favors fair dealing, enterprise, and free competition, and the courts have declared all combinations whose object is to destroy or impede free competition in business as void.

In such cases there must be some evidence of the object and purpose of the combination. Change the rules of evidence so as to make shown the effect of the combination, or of the trust that has taken its place, evidence of the purpose for which formed, and the trust will be made more amenable to the law, both in civil and criminal proceedings.

In the light of State attempt to successfully deal with the trust evil it may be concluded that the question should come within the domain of the general government, and to accomplish this there must be one or more amendments to the Constitution. The further increase in the number of monopolistic aggregations may be easily met by state legislative action in the future; but it is with the evil that now exists with its power for future development without increase in numbers, that the people are called upon for decisive action.

It is argued that the whole subject will settle itself to the mutual advantage of capital and the people if left alone. No evil will correct itself so long as its intended purposes are attained by growth and development! There is no law of trade or production that will cure the trust evil by its inherent force. One of the great authorities on the trust subject has voiced general sentiment in this language: "It has come with none of the careful deliberation that usually attends the investment of great aggregations of capital. It has been guided by no precedent experience. It is no gradual result of a natural evolution. It is a reversal of all that economists have accepted as fundamental axioms of trade. It is an undeliberate revolt against the most essential force in the regulation of production, distribution, and values—the natural law of competition."

It being true that the trust is a thing born in defiance of law, no known law can cause it to develop into a good thing in business that must be controlled by natural laws or legislation.

I admit that in the business affairs of men there is at work a leveling force which brings about a reciprocity of benefit and a sort of equality; but this is a natural force, and there is no place for its operation when the business belonging to the natural man is turned over to the unnatural monopoly. The condition then becomes too abnormal for the application of natural laws and usual forces. And when we know that the abnormal condition has its birth in the purpose of the powerful few to impose upon and oppress the millioned many, we know, without close reading from cause to effect, that the law of birth will develop strength and power in the purpose of origin.

If the trust evil as it now exists is to be corrected, if the future evils that must ensue, are to be averted, there must be legislation that can come from one source only—and that is a legislature, State and National, composed of men who are truly American and above all undue corporate influence!

E. C. IRWIN.

President National Board of Fire Underwriters.

As a proper understanding of this question involves more or less technical or expert knowledge, possessed only by those engaged in the business, it may be well, for the benefit of those of other callings, briefly to explain those fundamental principles of underwriting which are indispensable to a correct conclusion from a community standpoint.

It is perhaps unnecessary to explain that the "premium" is the price paid an insurance company for assuming the risk of fire; that the "rate" is the charge per $100 of insurance, fixed according to the construction of the building, its occupation, environment and facilities, public and private, for extinguishing fires; and that the "policy" is the contract, a unilateral one, written and issued by the insurance company to the property-owner.

It is not generally understood that a policy of insurance is not an agreement to pay a stipulated sum by way of liquidated damages in the event of the destruction by fire of the subject insured, which would be a wager; and contrary to public policy, but is simply an undertaking on the part of the insurance company to indemnify the owner to the extent of his loss in actual value damaged or destroyed; the amount of insurance named in the policy and paid for at the rate of premium being the limit of claim, and not a measure of it.

The rate of premium or price charged by the company is not based upon the expectation of burning of a particular risk insured, but upon the number of risks of like kind which would be burned or damaged out of say a thousand in any single year. At a rate of 1 per cent, for illustration, a thousand risks, each insured for $1,000, would yield $10,000 in premium. If ten risks out of the thousand should burn in a year, the entire amount of premium would be required to pay the loss. It is evident that a smaller number than ten must burn, or a higher rate than 1 per cent must be obtained, to provide for expenses as well as losses.

The proper rates of premium for the various kinds of property

—dwellings, churches, schools, stores, and manufactories—are based, therefore, upon the observed number of risks and amount of loss in each class which burn out of a thousand of like kind in a single year. If the business of fire insurance is conducted on proper lines, the element of luck or chance does not enter into it. While nothing could be more uncertain than the probabilities of escape from loss by a single risk, nothing can be more certain than that the average loss in thousands of risks of the same hazard, environment, and conditions will be the same year by year; but to ascertain this average percentage of loss, a comparison of the experience of all, or nearly all, of the companies engaged in the business is necessary, certainly in the case of most hazards, for the obvious reason that no one company would have enough of most classes on its books, outside of such large classes as dwelling houses, farm buildings, etc.—especially in single states—to indicate the expectation of what might be termed the fire mortality, or the loss on any one class.

This consideration indicates the twofold mistake of confining the business of an insurance company to a single city or limited territory, as it would deprive the company of a sufficient average, and, therefore, any legislation prohibiting the conference of companies for comparing their experience in other states, in order to ascertain an adequate rate, would be subversive of the principles of insurance. It might happen that a single company in a single state, or, for that matter, a single company throughout the United States, would show a loss on a certain class of hazards, while the experience of all companies put together would show a fair profit at the rate obtained. The co-operation of insurance companies in order to ascertain correct rates is, therefore, necessary.

Take the risk of whisky in brick warehouses, for example. A large company, having an exceptionally broad general experience, incurred losses on this particular class during a five-year period in the two states of Kentucky and Tennessee in excess of the premiums taken. Such an experience would seem to indicate that the rate obtained of 90 cents per $100 was too low, whereas the experience of all the companies doing business in the two states named proved that it was sufficiently high, and the rate was not raised. This same company during the same period in another section of the country—the Middle States—lost nothing on the same class; an experience which, taken alone, would seem to indicate that the rate obtained was for that locality too high, which was not a fact, however, for the experience of all the companies doing business in the territory showed the rate had been properly fixed and that the experience of this single company was simply exceptionally unfortunate in the one territory and exceptionally profitable in the other.

The argument so frequently made by some property-owners, that they have paid insurance for a long term of years without collecting a single loss, and should, therefore, have a lower rate, is based upon ignorance of the principles of fire insurance, and overlooks the fact that at a rate of 1 per cent it would take nearly forty-one years for a sum of money like the premium paid at the beginning of each year to equal the amount insured and a total loss, compounding the interest at 4 per cent, and this without any allowance for the expense of conducting the business. Anyone can verify this computation for himself, and cannot afford to be ignorant. It is best for the individual to entrust this branch of his worldly affairs to those who understand it, for the same reason that he entrusts the erection of his building to the mason, carpenter, and architect. Cannot the state safely conduct the business of insurance for its citizens?

Theoretically, yes; but practically nothing would be gained, the chances being largely in favor of a higher cost to citizens and poorer management than would result from the conduct of the business by men engaged in it for a livelihood. The state would need the same executive and clerical labor as an insurance company. It would require inspectors, adjusters, bookkeepers, and men qualified for the various branches of the business to the same extent that insurance companies would, but with this difference, that they would too often be appointed for political reasons, rather than because of personal qualifications for the duties to be discharged. There is no more reason why the state should conduct the business of insurance than why it should conduct any other business—that of groceries, dry goods, or manufacturing. It is safe to say that in the distribution of labor in a community the community will regulate itself. No single calling can secure an undue amount of profit without attracting to it enough competitors from other callings to keep the prices at a proper level.

What would have been the burden of the citizens at large of the two states of Illinois and Massachusetts if they had been called upon to pay the losses of their two cities of Chicago and Boston in the years 1871 and 1872? Fortunately for them, the citizens of the entire country, almost of the entire world, contributed, through the fire insurance companies, to pay the millions that were required for the purpose.

Co-operation in fire insurance is not a "trust" in the modern acceptation of the term. There is not and never has been any "pooling" in the business of insurance. The rates obtained are sufficient simply to insure the payment of losses and a moderate profit on the capital. No combination, in any business, can possibly be injurious to the public which furnishes to the public the article produced at the lowest price consistent with fair return upon the capital invested and proper remuneration for the labor employed. The statistics of all the companies engaged in the business through a long series of years show that the profits of the business of insurance have been less than 3 per cent of the premiums collected, and dividends in excess of that per cent made to stockholders have been received from interest returns on capital and invested surplus—an increment which would have come to the owners of such assets without placing them at the risk of fire.

The laws of the various states require detailed statements on the part of insurance companies, showing every item of income and every item of expense; the amount of their premiums received and of losses paid. There is, in fact, no other business whose methods, income, expenses, losses, and profits are thus exploited for the information of the public. There are no trade secrets in fire insurance. If the business is conducted at unnecessary expense or with undue profit, the result will be known, and invite other companies to enter into competition, especially from foreign countries, and it is impossible for any single company, or any number of insurance companies, to maintain any form of monopoly.

It is doubtful if any mercantile or manufacturing business could live if obliged thus to publish at the end of each year, for the information of competitors and customers, the fullest details of its transactions. Indeed, if the laws now in force for the regulation of the business of fire insurance—the compulsory publication of accounts, etc.—were applied to other branches of business, manufacturing and mercantile, the present war against so-called "trusts" and combinations in those branches would be unnecessary.

What, then, has been the protection of the business of fire insurance that it has been able to survive this public exhibit of all the details of its methods and its exact profits? It has been the fact that the profit of the business has been so low as not to encourage the organization of companies. Does not the simple fact that the public shows its unwillingness to invest in insurance stocks on other than a 6 per cent basis indicate what the published figures of the business clearly prove, that there is no abnormal profit in it and that investors recognize the element of risk and have an apprehension of the facts, or surely the stocks would find purchasers on a better basis than 6 per cent? The stocks of well-managed railroads are selling to-day on a 4 per cent basis.

In connection with this should be taken into consideration that new companies can be easily organized. They have to acquire no "right of way," no franchise, or the construction of a valuable building plant; there are no patent rights or copyrights involved; the necessary capital—and the law does not require a large one—with a little office furniture and stationery, is all that is needed to launch a new fire insurance company. Surely the written and unwritten law of trade and the rules of competition can be relied upon to regulate the profits of such a business without legislative interference.

As already stated, the ascertainment of the average percentage of loss, to be correct, involves comparison of experience, in the interest of the property-owner as well as in the interest of the insurance company, for an inaccurate estimate would be as likely to be too high as too low. If it is too high, the property-owner will be called upon to pay an excessive rate of premium; if it is too low, the company will lose money; and as capital is simply an incident of security, grossly inadequate if the premium should prove insufficient for the risk run, the property-owner would not secure the indemnity he is paying for. The total capital of all the fire insurance companies, domestic and foreign, reporting to the New York Insurance Department at the close of 1898, was less than ninety millions ($89,476,981), while the amount of premiums held by them for their insurance in force was one hundred and two millions of dollars ($102,872,081), whereas, the losses paid for the single year named were seventy-one millions ($71,781,247), a sum, it will be observed, which was nearly seven-eighths of the total capital of all the companies engaged in the business.

This simple computation shows how important it is for the community at large that the average rate of premium of the companies should be high enough to pay the losses and expenses, and that it would not do to rely upon the capital invested as a security. State laws recognize this fact, and require that whenever the reserves of a company are not equal to its liabilities and its capital becomes impaired, the company must immediately make its capital good or retire from business.

Competition, which is claimed by some to be the life of trade, is the death of insurance if it results in inadequate prices or rates. The proper conduct of the business, therefore, in the interest of all concerned, involves accurately ascertained and equitable rates; a cheap price for insurance always implies reduced security, or the absence of that which it is intended to purchase, and inadequate rates must sooner or later result in worthless policies.

It should not require argument to demonstrate that, since all the companies having policies on a burned property must incur the same percentage of loss, and also the same percentage of expense, they should get the same rate, and that the property-owner may well be suspicious of a company offering to write at a lower rate than the majority of companies are willing to accept. The buyer of merchandise, who secures possession when he acquires title of an article of whose value he is a competent judge, may felicitate himself on a good bargain if he gets it below cost. With the merchandise in his possession, and sure of its value, he has no reason to care whether the seller lost money on it or not, but it is not so with insurance. Insurance is not a "good delivery" until the policy has expired, or, in case of fire, until the loss has been collected; and he who secures it at a rate below cost and flatters himself that the other customers of the company do not secure the same terms, or overlooks the fact that, if they do, his insurance is likely to be worthless, would do well to keep his money in his pocket or deposit it in a savings bank.

It should be borne in mind that the payment for a fire by an insurance company simply distributes the loss of the individual upon the entire community; it does not restore anything. Such drains upon the resources of the country are to a large extent preventable, and intelligent inspection and discriminating rating by insurance companies would secure this end.

Any system of insurance rating which does not discriminate between safe construction and unsafe construction and between carefulness and negligence, is an injury to the community and a gross injustice to that better class of citizens who build securely and manage their affairs prudently.

It may safely be asserted that the enormous fire waste of the country, costing at present at the rate of more than one hundred and twenty-five million dollars per annum, or more than ten millions a month, would be materially increased but for the inspections and suggestions of insurance companies, enforced by higher rates charged to those property-owners who are careless or indifferent as to fire, and would be materially decreased if legislative restrictions in various states did not prohibit the co-operation of insurance companies for so laudable a purpose directly in the interest of the community.

It is as short-sighted to compel companies to write at inadequate rates as it would be to require savings banks to pay 6 per cent interest and invest their deposits at 3 per cent.

Animosity toward corporations grows largely out of misapprehension in regard to them. The individual citizen does not and should not lose his rights by becoming a member of a corporation any more than by becoming a member of a partnership firm. It is in the power of any citizen to become a shareholder, even though his means are limited. One hundred dollars will buy a share in a new insurance company. He is thus enabled to engage in a business which he may not understand and to secure intelligent management and expert knowledge which he does not himself possess.

Corporations thus enable people of small means, by joining forces and uniting their savings, to secure the same advantages for business purposes that millionaire capitalists enjoy, and a corporation thus becomes a poor man's opportunity. Among the stockholders of insurance companies, thousands in number, are widows and orphans, who are thus enabled to keep their modest capital employed and to have an active partnership in commercial undertakings.

It is, perhaps, not unnatural that property-owners, having in mind only the simple process of writing a policy of insurance by an agent of an insurance company and the delivery of it by him to the assured or property-owner, should regard the expense of transacting the business as merely nominal. They overlook the fact that a greater number of persons of various qualifications must be employed and remunerated before the policy of insurance can be written and delivered, and that the percentage of the premium required to pay the expenses of the business (about 35 per cent), is not greater than that involved in the sale of merchandise, a piece of calico, for example, which includes the profit to the planter who raises the cotton; to the compress that presses it; to the commission merchant who sells it; to the common carrier that carries it to the mill; to the mill-owner who manufactures it into cloth, including his operatives; to the dye and print establishment that prints it; to the commission merchant in the distributing center of a great city who sells it; to the wholesale merchant, who in turn sells to the retailer, who in turn delivers it to the consumer. All of these processes involve separate remunerations and an aggregate percentage of expense fully equal to that of the insurance business, which requires the agent in the town, who writes and delivers the policy of insurance; the expert who inspects the building from time to time during the term of the policy; the rating expert who fixes the rate, recognizing every point of construction, occupancy, and environment; the adjuster who must adjust the losses; the accountants and bookkeepers in the offices of the company, and, lastly, the executive officers, who must employ all of these men, supervise their work, and attend to the investment of the assets and reserves of the company, not forgetting office rent, stationery, blank books, printing, postage, and last, but not least, taxes—the latter seldom less than 2½ per cent of the premium, to be paid whether the company makes money or not. So that it is doubtful if any business involves greater necessary outlay or requires higher executive ability or a broader education as to the methods and hazards of all other occupations.

Charles Sumner, when United States senator, wisely said, "a tax upon insurance is a tax upon a tax, and, therefore, a barbarism." As the insurance company must collect enough from property-owners to pay its losses and expenses and yield a living profit, it is clear that the citizens of a state, after all, have to pay the tax, with the expense of collecting it added—which is a farce. A tax upon the profits, on the other hand, is a tax upon the insurance company, and one that it should pay without complaining. A tax upon the premium is a tax upon the assured property-owner, and one he ought not to pay. No insurance company would complain of being taxed 2½ per cent on that portion of the premiums taken out of a state after paying the losses and expenses, and this should be the basis of taxation everywhere.

This may be expected to be 55 per cent of the premium. The largest and most successful companies have experienced not less than this percentage of loss as the result of the years they have been in business. If this percentage be added to the 35 for expenses, there will be left 10 per cent—5 of which should be accumulated, as already stated, for sweeping conflagrations, and the remaining 5 per cent will probably not be regarded by those engaged in any other business as an abnormally high profit, leaving out of consideration the great risk run by those whose capital is invested.

No legislation more inimical to the interests of the community or injurious to the business of fire insurance has been enacted of late years than so-called "Valued Policy Laws," which require, in the event of the destruction of a building, that its owner shall receive the full amount for which he has effected insurance upon it, even though it be more than the actual cash value of the property destroyed. As already stated, an insurance policy is not an undertaking to pay a stipulated sum in the event of loss, but a contract of indemnity or protection, so that when a property owner pays, say, $50 for a $5,000 insurance policy, he is paying $50 for $5,000 worth of protection against loss by fire for a given time—the term of the policy, one year, three years, or five years. If during that period a loss occurs, he will receive the amount of the loss, not exceeding the amount named as the limit of insurance. He may have five or more partial losses on the same property during the time for which the policy is written and receive pay for each of them, and still not exhaust the whole amount of protection, unless the aggregate sums paid equal the amount of limit in the policy.

The standard, legal form of an insurance policy contracts to insure the property-owner in the following words:

"Against all direct loss or damage by fire to an amount not exceeding five thousand dollars."

Overlooking these unmistakable terms, some property-owners and legislators infer that the agreement is to pay $5,000 in the event of the destruction of the property, though it might not be worth more than $1,000. They also overlook the fact that the policy may be written for one year, or, as is often the case, for five years, and the value of the building, by age, use, decay, etc., may be greatly less at the end of the term than at its beginning. A "valued policy" law would in such case work most unjustly.

The argument is made by those advocating such laws that insurance companies should investigate the values of the properties they insure if they do not wish to pay for the full amount of the insurance, and that it will be their own fault if they are mulcted an undue amount. This argument overlooks the fact that to properly ascertain the actual cash value of a building requires a careful examination by expert builders, masons, carpenters, etc., who would charge for their services in many cases—especially in the case of the buildings of small value of the poorer classes, and particularly farm buildings in the country, which they would charge extra to visit—as much as, or more than, the whole premium paid for the insurance. Such expensive expert examinations ought to be necessary only in case of a fire to ascertain the amount of loss, and, therefore, only in the one case of a burned property out of the hundreds which do not burn. A "valued policy" law, therefore, works most oppressively upon the property-owner of small holdings, and least oppressively upon the properties of larger value, whose owners do not, as a rule, obtain an undue amount of insurance, and the requirement entails that the same labor and expense shall be incurred as to each of hundreds of risks to prevent the single property-owner who may have a loss from collecting more than he is entitled to receive.

445

The argument in favor of valued policy laws also overlooks the obvious fact that an honest claimant is sure to receive the full amount of his loss in any event, since no intelligently managed insurance company would be so short-sighted as to refuse to pay an honest claim, realizing that, in case it should, it would be forced to do so at law, for courts and juries never sympathize with corporations, but always with the individual. Moreover, all insurance policies contain a clause which provides that in case of differences between the owner and the insurance company, the matter in dispute shall be left to disinterested appraisers, chosen by each, who in turn shall select a third as umpire. A man is thus entitled to have for his appraiser any neighbor in whom he trusts. It would with this provision be impossible for an insurance company under its policy to escape paying all to which any claimant is entitled. Insurance companies are not litigious; they cannot afford to go into courts except with clean hands and with claims of unmistakable justice. The statements of the companies reporting to the New York Insurance Department show that a sum less than 2 per cent of the amount of losses paid by them during the past year was in suit at its close, and as those losses in suit were the result of an average of at least three years' business, it follows that the losses contested by companies are less than 1 per cent of the whole amount of the losses incurred. When it is remembered how many fraudulent claims are made upon insurance companies, it becomes a serious question, not whether too many claims are contested by them, but whether enough are resisted to protect the interests and insure the security of their more honest claimants.

The man who insures his building knows better than anyone else what it is worth; he is not obliged to pay for more insurance than would protect him for its full value. If he does, he contemplates a fraud upon the insurance company, and should not be assisted in consummating it by the operation of law on the plea that he should receive the full amount of the limit named in the policy simply because he voluntarily paid for more than he knew was necessary to protect him against honest loss. A valued policy law is in reality a premium upon fraud and an incentive to incendiarism or burning for gain, imposing unnecessary burdens upon honest citizens, who must be taxed in higher rates of premium to pay for the exaggerated claims of an unprincipled few.

Few persons realize to what importance insurance has grown as a factor in the commercial world. It is to-day the security on which most enterprises rest, without which their projectors

446

would hesitate to engage in them. The lender could not afford to trust the borrower if the ability of the latter to pay the debt was liable to be cancelled by a fire. The last census report showed that the real estate mortgage loans of the United States amounted to more than six thousand million dollars ($6,019,679,985.) Of this enormous sum the citizens of Illinois alone had borrowed three hundred and eighty-four millions; Massachusetts three hundred and twenty-three millions; New York sixteen hundred and seven millions; Pennsylvania six hundred and thirteen millions. It is safe to say that all of these loans are based upon insurance policies held as collateral security. Can anyone estimate the consequences if these mortgages should be called in by the lenders, deprived of their insurance collateral and unwilling to trust their money to the contingencies of fire! Can anyone doubt that such action would be taken if fire insurance capital should be withdrawn from a business made unprofitable by the burdens which mistaken legislation is increasing year by year!

There is probably to-day not an enterprise in the business world which does not depend upon the security of fire insurance. It protects alike the dwelling of the laborer and the palace of the millionaire; the business of the retail dealer and the aggregated values of the largest manufacturers. Without the assurance which its protection affords it is doubtful if the enterprise of those possessing capital would be exerted sufficiently to give employment to the wage-earner or to keep the wheels of trade and manufacture in motion. Commerce would be paralyzed, for credit would be withheld where confidence would be wanting in the ability of the purchaser to pay. It is the handmaid of commerce and the guardian of industry. Ventures are made without hesitation which would appall those embarking in them if liable to miscarry through a single fire; large values are boldly collected to meet the requirements of commerce where an accidental conflagration might destroy them in a night, merchants sell their goods on extended credits, knowing that although the misfortune of fire may overtake the purchaser, his insurance indemnity will enable him to pay for them not less readily than before; vast industries giving employment to thousands of operatives and supporting whole towns by their enterprise, testify not more to the courage of their projectors than to the confidence they repose in the protection which insurance gives to their undertakings; and, to-day, insurance is as certainly a necessity of commerce and manufacture as is the railroad or telegraph or steam power itself; it is as essential to the commercial system of the world as the woof thread to the fabric of the loom.

447

Probably no more eloquent tribute to the spirit of insurance is to be found than the utterance of the French jurists, at the close of their report to the council of state, on the subject in the code of commerce:

"Insurance may justly be deemed one of the noblest creations of human genius. From a lofty height it surveys and protects the commerce of the world. It scans the heavens; it consults the seasons; it interrogates the ocean, and, regardless of its terrors or caprice, defines its perils and circumscribes its storms. It extends its cares to every part of the habitable globe, studies the usage of every nation, explores every coast, and sounds every harbor.

"To the science of politics it directs a sleepless attention; it enters the council of monarchs, watches the deliberation of statesmen, weighs their motives, and penetrates their designs. Founding on these vast materials its skillful calculations, secure of the result, it then addresses the hesitating merchant: 'Dismiss your anxiety and fear; there are misfortunes that humanity may deplore but cannot prevent or alleviate. Such are not the disasters you dread to encounter. Trust in me, and they shall not reach you. Summon all your resources, put forth all your skill, and with unfaltering courage pursue your adventures. Succeed, and your riches are enlarged; fail, and they shall not be diminished. My wealth shall supply your loss. Rely on me, and for your sake, at my bidding, the arm of your enemies shall be paralyzed, and the dangers of the ocean or the flaming pile cease to exist.' The merchant listens and obeys, and is rewarded. Thousands, tempted by his success, follow his example. Those whom it had long separated, the ocean now unites. The quarters of the world approach each other and are bound by the permanent ties of mutual interest and mutual benefit."

We trust we have explained the relation of insurance to the community in such manner as to secure a negative to this important question. We trust we have established as facts:

First—That fire insurance is a commercial and community necessity.

Second—That a policy of fire insurance is a contract of indemnity; and

Third—That the reliability of the indemnity depends upon the sufficiency of the rate of premium, because

1. State laws properly require that if the capital is impaired it must be made good, or the company must cease doing business. If companies cannot pay their losses and expenses and secure a fair profit return on the capital adventured they will neither be

organized nor continue in business if already organized; therefore, capital is only an incident of the business and an adequate rate is indispensable.

2. Adequate and equitable rates are necessary for the protection of the policy-holder as well as for the protection of the stockholder. Otherwise the burden of insurance will be unequally distributed and one man's property will be protected, if insured below a proper rate, at the expense of another. Insurance capital must and should have a fair return for the risk run—a law of community.

3. As inspection and supervision necessary for the ascertainment of correct rates can be as cheaply performed for one hundred companies insuring a single building or risk as for any one of them, co-operation is advisable to reduce the expense percentage. At the same time it would reduce the loss percentage by securing correction of faults which would cause fires and by encouraging proper construction which would tend to prevent their spread, and so result in cheaper insurance to property-owners. In this view, co-operation of insurance companies is directly in the interest of the community and should be encouraged and not prohibited. Laws which prevent companies from co-operating in this way, and compel each company to inspect each building for itself, must increase the expenses of transacting the business and result in unnecessarily higher rates of premium.

4. As the labor required to ascertain and fix proper and equitable rates for a building and its contents can be performed by the same expert in the same time for one hundred companies who insure it as for any one of them, co-operation to ascertain and fix rates would result in a saving of this expense also, and so further cheapen the cost of insurance to the property-owner and be directly in the interest of the public.

5. As rates of insurance are based upon the experience of the companies through terms of years on the various classes of hazards, most of which are so few in number that there would not be enough of a class in a single state to determine the experience cost of insuring them, the statistics of experience should be collated from the whole country, in justice to the owners of such risks, and not based upon the abnormal loss rate of a small class in a single state, which would indicate the necessity for an exorbitant rate on the class in such state, when in fact it might not be necessary.

6. The burden of insurance rates should be graded according to the percentage of insurance carried to value, just as municipal and state taxes are based upon uniform assessments of the same

percentage of value, and the property-owner who insures a proper percentage of his value is entitled to a lower rate than one who insures a small percentage on the same principle that wholesale prices should be lower than retail prices. Otherwise one class of citizens would be securing insurance at a lower cost than another. Co-operation of companies, therefore, is necessary to provide for this in percentage co-insurance clauses in all policies.

It follows, therefore, since co-operation is necessary

To ascertain cost;

To ascertain and secure adequate rates for indemnity;

To prevent fires and thus cheapen the cost of insurance;

To divide and lessen expense and so to further cheapen the cost of insurance;

To secure that the same percentage of insurance should be carried by all owners or a difference in rate made—the principle of co-insurance or average which has always been a feature of marine insurance;

That the conference of companies and co-operation must be in the interest not only of the insurance companies themselves, but of their customers, the insuring public.

Insurance is, therefore, not a "trust," in the modern and ordinary acceptation of the term, by which is meant a combination of those engaged in a particular business to extort improper prices from their fellow-members of the community and so to obtain an undue share of community benefit. The ease with which any number of citizens can organize an insurance company will always prevent a monopoly of the business, and those engaged in it can always be relied upon, in their own interests, to regulate their prices with reference to this important fact. Exorbitant rates and abnormal profits always attract competition, which results in inadequate rates, and those engaged in the business thoroughly understand this. Managed on true underwriting lines, an insurance company is simply a great machine for distributing the burden of the fire loss of the individual citizen among his neighbors throughout the entire country, so that the burden of helping one who is unfortunate will be lightly felt by all. It is the truest and most sensible method of carrying out the scriptural injunction, and it is amenable to the laws of trade which automatically regulate the profits of all commercial enterprises so that no one class of citizens can long retain any undue advantage of their neighbors or any improper share of the community wealth.

EVENING SESSION, SEPTEMBER 15.

With W. Bourke Cockran and William Jennings Bryan announced as speakers of the evening, the conference on trusts was the one event of importance in the city of Chicago Friday evening. The afternoon session had not adjourned before the doors were besieged by ticket holders anxious to secure their places for the evening. By 7 o'clock State street was packed with a struggling crowd working toward the doors of the hall where the conference was to convene an hour later, and when Chairman Howe's gavel fell at 8 o'clock the auditorium was packed from the parquette to the outside edge of the upper gallery and there were ten thousand people clamoring in the street for admission. The boxes were filled with a brilliant audience of society people, and the delegates made way in their seats for scores of gaily dressed women, while the aisles were utilized to accommodate as much of the overflow as possible. Altogether the audience was as brilliant and intellectual a gathering as ever assembled in Chicago, and bore testimony to the interest of all classes in the question under debate.

While the audience expected to hear both Mr. Bryan and Mr. Cockran speak, the program was changed after the arrival of Mr. Bryan that afternoon, and he was assigned Saturday morning.

In spite of the crowd and the trouble of seating it, there was no delay in opening the evening session, and the chairman introduced William Dudley Foulke, of Indiana, who spoke on "The Problem of Trusts and Some Proposed Remedies."

WILLIAM DUDLEY FOULKE.

I confess I have not yet been able to see my way clearly through the whole labyrinth of complicated questions which arise in connection with this problem of the trusts. Nay, more, I believe that if anyone to-day thinks "he knows it all"—that he has found a complete remedy for every evil involved—he will learn that he is mistaken; and if he could awaken sometime far into the next century and look upon the great transformation wrought by the mighty agencies that are being organized at the present time, he would perhaps be as much surprised as if he had arisen in paradise and found that the gates were not of pearl, and the streets were not of gold, and that the angels were playing upon instruments with which he was wholly unacquainted.

The question we are called to consider dwarfs in importance all other issues now before the country or the world. When Dreyfus shall have been forgotten, when the war in the Philippines shall be regarded only as one of the episodes of history, when men shall speak no longer of the tariff or the currency, the present era may well be remembered by coming generations as the epoch of that great organic change when the system of competition began to give way to the system of co-operation—a change leading inevitably (whether for good or ill we cannot clearly see) to the radical reconstruction of the world's industrial and social life.

The organizers of the trusts, in their eagerness to put a stop to wasteful and ruinous competition, have been rushing in headlong haste to realize the immediate, personal benefits of increased economy and power offered by these great unions, with little regard to ultimate consequences. Their thought has been, "After us the deluge."

On the other hand, those who have been thrown out of employment or ruined by the suppression of competition, together with that vast conservative element in our population which fears a leap into the dark, are lifting their voices in warning, and some, it may be added, in rather indiscriminate abuse.

Let us consider first the competitive system which seems to be diminishing in importance in our industrial life, and next the co-operative methods which are so largely taking its place. First, what has competition done for the world?

It has been, perhaps, the most prominent factor of our industrial progress. Competition between buyers has enhanced the price to the producer. Competition between sellers has stimulated improvements in the quality of the product, has quickened invention and skill, has reduced the cost to the consumers and multiplied their number, and thus stimulated production to supply the enlarged demand. It has increased the employment of labor, enhanced the wages of the workmen, and improved the condition of the laboring classes.

But competition, although immensely valuable and necessary as a phase in industrial development, has certain grave disadvantages. Essentially based as it is upon the principles of self-interest, it promotes the development of selfish characteristics of skill and energy, indeed, but often also of heartlessness and indifference to the welfare of others. It is part of the great struggle for existence. It follows the law of organic life—the survival of the sharp eye, the swift wing and the keen talon and the merciless beak. And it has resulted just as natural evolution results, in the destruction of lower and feebler forms of existence and in the survival of those only who are best fitted to carry on the work of the world. But this has been accomplished, like the development of organic life, at immense waste and sacrifice. Thousands of smaller creatures have perished to make the food of one. A far greater effort than that which is required for production itself is often expended in the mere fight for a market.

Each year the struggle has grown more intense. By steam and telegraph distant points became united, and the industry which originally feared no competitor outside the limits of its own town was perhaps overthrown by some rival in a distant part of our country, or even beyond the seas. The margin of profit became smaller, the outlay for putting goods on the market constantly increased, vast sums were spent in advertising or paid to commercial agents and travelers, or consumed in the useless reduplication of plants and of expenses of administration, all of which could be saved under a more perfect system. The very thing to be developed by competition—cheap production—was in a measure defeated by the struggle which competition required. The only remedy then was for industries engaged in the same branches of business to unite so as to reduce the cost of production, if not also to increase or maintain the price of the product. The law which led to this is as much a natural law as that which brought about the competitive system itself.

But there are evils incident to these combinations which may outweigh their advantages. When the aggregations of capital become very great, when competition is virtually suppressed, and when the combination becomes practically a monopoly, it may exercise its powers to the injury, not only of competitors, but of the public. It may dictate terms to the world. Whenever there is only a single buyer of the same material, he dictates the price to the producer. Wherever there is a single seller of the finished article he makes his own price with the consumer, perhaps an exorbitant one, and diminishes thereby the numbers of consumers and thus restricts production and curtails the employment of labor and the wages paid for it.

In practical experience, the actual economic evils are indeed less than are generally supposed, far less indeed than those which are theoretically possible. In point of fact monopolies do not often increase the cost of the product very greatly, since if they do this they will curtail the consumption of their goods too much, or their extravagant profits might often induce new competitors to enter the field. The monopolies which are under the wisest management have therefore kept prices at figures which are not unreasonable, and they often show, as in the case of the Standard Oil Company, and the Sugar Trust, that there has been an actual decrease both in the price of the product and in the cost of the manufacture. But there is reason to doubt whether this diminished cost is due to monopoly, or is indeed anything like as great as it would be under a free system of competition with the improved methods which the progress of civilization continually introduces.

Therefore, while the monopoly may pay somewhat less for the raw material and may charge somewhat more for the product than would be possible under competition, this evil is by no means the greatest which is involved. The restriction of the output and the displacement of labor by these new organizations also occurs, but this is not an unmixed evil when their greater economy is considered. It is of much the same character as that which follows the introduction of labor-saving machines and of labor-saving organizations of industry everywhere.

Indeed, monopoly may often be of advantage to labor organizations. Under the present system a demand for increased wages may fail, or wages may be reduced because the employer cannot afford to pay them without destroying his business, and depriving himself of the power to meet his competitors on equal terms. To pay the higher rate of wages he must carry on his business at a loss, hence he suffers his plant to lie idle.

But a monopoly can always afford to pay the increased wages. It can always recoup itself by increasing the prices of its product. So the only question to be considered is whether labor of the same kind can be procured on better terms elsewhere. The workmen skilled in certain branches of industry are often limited in number, and under proper organization such workmen are likely to receive a continually larger proportionate share of the product.

But the political and social effects of monopoly are far more menacing to society than its economic results. The great consolidations of capital are fast seizing the avenues of power that lead to the control of the government, and are seeking to rule the states and the nation, often through procured legislatures and corrupted officials.

Yet the monopolies are here. A great part of our manufacturing industries and a considerable fraction of our commercial business is already in their hands.

When the Sugar Trust controlled 98 per cent of the production of the country it was idle to say that the remaining 2 per cent could offer any substantial competition. And the present tendency is for all these great organizations to draw closer and closer to the ideal of a perfect monopoly, though none of them has yet entirely reached it.

If this present tendency remains unchecked, it is easy to see that each of the important branches of manufacture will be controlled by a single company, and the people naturally look forward with alarm to the time when in each branch of industry a single monopoly shall control the trade.

Nay, the combining and recombining will not stop even here. A single company is likely to control many branches of industry. The department store already absorbs nearly all the branches of retail trade. The great anthracite coal fields are practically under the control of two or three railway companies, and it is impossible to say that even the wheat fields of the Northwest, or the cotton fields of the South may not in the future share the same fate. The railroads indeed have undertaken many other branches of industry as feeders for their great lines. The summer hotel business seems to be passing largely into their hands, as well as much of the grain elevator business, the shipping and other agencies of transportation. Who can say indeed what branch of industry may not be the feeder for a railway?

As the great nations of the globe are becoming fewer and fewer until now there are four or five at most which control the future destinies of mankind, so the tendency of industrial organizations to aggregate is such that I can see in fancy four or five great companies which shall control practically the whole output of the country.

Nay, since all industries are now indissolubly united, who can say (if the present movement should go on unchecked) that a single gigantic organization may not sometime control all production?

This will be a form of socialism, and yet it may not be at all the socialism which fancy pictures in the dreams of the disinherited.

Socialism may take many forms. The industrial organization of society may be for a time separated from its political organization, but not permanently. Socialism does not necessarily mean equal shares to all in the joint property, or returns. These may be divided according to the services rendered or capital contributed either by the actual stockholders or their predecessors in title, just as private property to-day consists of that which a man earns and acquires as well as that which has come to him by gift or inheritance. It is, however, clear that the mass of the people must have a sufficient interest in the co-operative commonwealth to give the structure a broad base and prevent its toppling over. That it should remain in possession and control of only a few millionaires would not long be tolerated. And yet equality might be found as impossible in a co-operative state as under the competitive system. So long as men are unequal in skill, industry and ability, the greatest prizes will always be won by comparatively few.

Most of us would look with great apprehension upon such a radical change in the social order, although we cannot fail to see that many steps toward this change have already been taken. Our chief apprehension comes from two sources:

First, we realize how inadequate are our government agencies even for the smaller problems which confront us in city, state, and national administration. How utterly impotent then will they be for the management of our whole industrial life!

But perhaps one of the reasons why they are so inefficient at present is owing to the very fact that they are not important enough. The great prizes which the world offers to-day are generally to be found in industrial life, and our best and ablest men will therefore not devote themselves to politics. But if the power of the commonwealth embraces all things, if it becomes the only agency through which men can reach success, our best life must inevitably flow thither.

But the second great objection to the socialistic form of government resides in the fact that men believe that it will be destructive of individual independence, that it will take away a great part of the incentive to exertion, that it will be fatal to the development of character by making each individual, in the words of Governor Pingree, only a single cog or rivet or bar in the great machinery of the state, rather than an independent being with aims and interests of his own. Has this not already been the effect upon the great masses of workmen in many of the vast industries heretofore established? Each laborer has become the producer of an infinitesimal part of some great product. He has been turned from a man into an automaton. Will not this be the case in a much greater degree when all society is organized for the development of a common industry? But I am advancing further into the future than is permitted to human foresight. Of one thing, however, we may be sure, that the present tendency

456

HENRY WHITE   JOHN I. YELLOTT
W. P. POTTER   JOHN W. SPENCER
A. E. ROGERS   F. E. HALEY

toward the combination of capital, if it be not arrested somewhere in its course either by natural law or by artificial means, will lead in the end to some form of socialism.

But is the present tendency to continue indefinitely? Will the operation of this law be like that of the law of gravitation, which has condensed the vast nebulous mass of the solar system into one great central orb, with a few planets and their satellites? Or will it be like the motion of the pendulum, like the current of the waters to the sea, coming always back to their source? Will we return again to the competitive system, or even to the industrial periods which have preceded it?

Many of our profoundest thinkers believe that our present industrial development will take care of itself. Following the analogies of organic life, they say that wherever an organization becomes too bulky to do its work successfully, that it will give way in the struggle for existence to smaller and more efficient organizations, just as the monsters of the Saurian era have vanished from the world, while so many of the minuter forms·of life still remain in healthy activity. Some of these men have even shown us what they consider the law which will guard society against the evils of accumulated capital. I was much impressed with a recent article in the September number of the *Review of Reviews*, entitled, "Why the Trusts Cannot Control Prices," from the pen of Hon. George E. Roberts, Director of the Mint. He insists that there is in the world a leveling force which continually operates to reduce the value of what has been inherited or accumulated in the past, and to enhance the importance of the ability to do things in the present; that the profits and earnings of capital have been declining on account of the rapid accumulation of capital itself, and that this loss has been distributed by means of lower prices to the multitude; that the amount of wealth seeking investments will constantly and rapidly increase, and that all efforts to fence up the several fields of industry for quiet possession by a few with extraordinary returns, are inevitably doomed to failure; that accumulating capital can only find employment through the increased purchasing power of the masses; that the abnormal profits of the successful trust must be invested and the beneficiaries would constantly encroach upon their neighbors' preserves; that therefore these new combinations, if they seek extraordinary profits, are opposing a force greater than themselves, that will persist forever; that the trusts are therefore bound to divide their profits with the consumers rather than sacrifice them in a hopeless attempt to buy off an endless succession of new competitors; that the more rapidly capital increases in the hands of investors, the greater the pressure to find employment at even nominal terms, and the more difficult to maintain a profitable monopoly; and that the new capital coming into the market to-morrow will protect the public against the combinations of the old.

But even if we do not concur in the conclusions of Mr. Roberts, even if we see in the present tendency a menace to our social life, still I fear that it will be found impossible entirely to eradicate the present tendency of our great industries toward combination and monopoly.

The numerous laws which have already been enacted to break up trade agreements, pools, and technical trusts, have been ineffective. They have resulted in the organization of larger corporations which are more permanent and more dangerous in their character than the things which are prohibited by statute. If it were possible to break up these corporations, which may well be doubted, the men who compose them would unite perhaps in partnerships or other forms of union to accomplish the same objects. If you break up these there are infinite varieties of organization which will take their place. The tendency of men to associate for the accomplishment of a common purpose is like the law of gravitation, and no statute will be found effective against such a tendency.

I should like to consider in greater detail the reasons why the trusts cannot be entirely overthrown. But you have not come here to-night to hear me, but to listen to a far abler and more distinguished gentleman, and I will close.

I wish, however, to refer to another fact which has passed into history, and which may guide your judgment. Trades unions were illegal at the common law just as the monopoly of consolidated capital is to-day. Every combination of laborers to advance wages was punished as an offense against the so-called law of free competition in the labor market. But competition had to give way to co-operation, and who shall say that the condition of the workingman has not been improved? Will not the legal barriers which failed before organized labor be found equally ineffective against organized capital? Organization is part of the world's progress, even though we cannot fully see whither that progress tends. This much is surely evident, that if legislation cannot overthrow the present tendency to combination, it is worse than useless to enact for that purpose laws which shall cripple the productive agencies of the country while they fail to accomplish the end they have in view.

The present consolidating tendency of our industrial life is largely beyond our control. We can guide it only a little way upon its journey, for the most part we shall have to stand aloof whether we will or no, and see the salvation of the Lord. And if better things develop than we dream, it will not be the first instance in the evolution of our race where good has been the final outcome of apparent evil, and where the agencies which seemed to portend disaster and ruin have been in the end the ministers of prosperity and happiness.

Mr. Foulke was in the midst of his paper when Mr. Cockran entered and made his way to the seat reserved for him on the platform. The audience made a demonstration of welcome, while the speaker smilingly suspended his remarks. He resumed, but had not concluded when Col. W. J. Bryan entered and another outbreak of applause followed. Smiling at the interruption, Mr. Foulke said:

"I perceive you have come to hear some one else."

There were prolonged applause and cheers for the speaker with cries of "Go on! go on!" and Mr. Foulke concluded without further interruption.

EDWARD ROSEWATER.

Publisher Omaha *Bee*.

Edward Rosewater, of Nebraska, was the next speaker, and said:

We are confronted by grave problems generated by the industrial revolution of the nineteenth century. The trust is but the outgrowth of natural conditions. The trend of modern civilization is toward centralization and concentration. This tendency is strikingly exhibited in the congestion of population in large cities, the building of mammoth hotels, tenement blocks, skyscraper office buildings, the department store and colossal manufacturing plants.

The monopolistic combination of corporate capital known as trusts has its origin in overproduction and ruinous competition. Honestly capitalized and managed with due regard for the well being of their employees and operated economically for the benefit of consumers of their product these concerns would be harmless. Within the past decade the trusts have, however, for the most part, degenerated into combinations for stock jobbing. Nearly every trust recently organized had its incentive in the irresistible temptation held out by the professional promoter to capitalize competing plants enormously in excess of their actual value. This fictitious capitalization constitutes the most dangerous element of the modern trust. In nearly every instance overcapitalization becomes the basis for raising the price of trust products and invariably lays the foundation for bank failures, panics and all the ills that follow in their train.

It has been asserted from this platform that fraudulent capitalization is an evil that will cure itself and at the very worst concerns only the stock speculators who voluntarily assume the risk of investment in over-valued trust securities. Experience has exploded this delusive theory. Nearly all the so-called "industrials" are on the market and the owners of over-valued plants either dispose of their holdings or place them in banks as collateral for loans negotiated for speculative schemes financiered on the baloon plan. The inevitable outcome in cases of money stringency or panic is shrinkage and collapse of the concerns involved. Banks rarely loan their own money, but that of their depositors, and when the banks go to the wall the whole commercial and industrial fabric is involved in wreck and ruin. This means the destruction of confidence and wide-spread distress to the toilers in every field of industry. Fraudulent capitalization is, moreover, not merely a menace to the well being of the present generation, but also endangers the future of generations yet unborn. It is an open secret that life insurance funds held in trust for the widows and orphans of policyholders are invested in industrial securities resting on a foundation of sand and water.

It is a matter of history that every panic that has ever occurred in this country was brought about by inflation. The panic of 1837 was caused by wild land speculation and inflation of land values. The panic of 1857 was precipitated by the enormous inflation of paper currency issued by wildcat banks and consequent overspeculation and inflation of values of all classes of property. The panic of 1873, ascribed to the failure of Jay Cook and the collapse of the Northern Pacific, was in reality due to the inflation caused by an almost unlimited issue of greenbacks and consequent reckless speculation in railway stocks and other securities that had been fraudulently inflated. The panic of 1893 was again caused by the enormous inflation of securities issued by railroads and industrial concerns of every description, among which the trust securities were quite prominent.

The imperative duty of this conference is to devise measures that will make the trusts harmless. With this end in view it should recommend:

First—The creation by act of Congress of a bureau of supervision and control of corporations engaged in interstate commerce with powers for its chief similar to those exercised by the comptroller of the currency over national banks.

Second—Legislation to enforce such publicity as will effectually prevent dishonest methods of accounting and restrict traffic and competition within legitimate bounds.

Third—The abrogation of all patents and copyrights held by trusts whenever the fact is established before a judicial tribunal that any branch of industry has been monopolized by the holders of such patents or copyrights.

Fourth—The enactment by Congress of a law that will compel every corporation engaged in interstate commerce to operate under a national charter that shall be abrogated whenever such corporation violates its provision.

Fifth—The creation of an interstate commerce court with exclusive jurisdiction in all cases arising out of the violation of interstate commerce laws.

Sixth—The revision of the Constitution of the United States by a constitutional convention to be called by two-thirds of the states at the earliest possible date, as provided by article V of the federal Constitution, which reads as follows: "The Congress, whenever two-thirds of the states shall deem it necessary, shall propose amendments to this Constitution, or on the application of the legislatures of two-thirds of the several states shall call a convention for proposing amendments which in each case shall be valid to all intents and purposes, or part of this Constitution when ratified by the legislature, if three-fourths of the several states or by conventions in three-fourths thereof as the one or the other mode of ratification may be proposed by the Congress."

It will be noted that the initiative for the adoption of separate amendments to the Constitution must be taken by Congress while the initiative for a revision of the Constitution can be taken by the states through their legislatures and when two-thirds of the states have endorsed the proposal it becomes mandatory on Congress to call a constitutional convention and submit its work for ratification. Manifestly, the revision of the Constitution is more certain by a convention called by the states than would be an amendment proposed by Congress, which is not likely to pass the ordeal of a two-thirds vote of the United States Senate so long as its members are not elected by the direct vote of the people. In my judgment, the time is ripe for such a revision of our fundamental law as will make it conform to the changed conditions wrought by more than a century's marvelous industrial evolution, commercial growth and territorial expansion.

While the trusts might be reached by a single amendment to the Constitution, I doubt very much whether anything could be gained by such patch-work, since the Constitution contains many other provisions that would constitute a bar to effective enforcement of the interstate commerce law. The mode of procedure for securing a single amendment is, if anything, more cumbersome and ratification thereof more difficult to obtain than would be a complete revision of the organic law of the land.

If you will examine the Constitution you will see that it lies within the power of the states to call a national constitutional convention whenever two-thirds have concurred in such call, whereas the ordinary amendment requires the concurrence of two-thirds of each of the houses of Congress, which is very difficult to procure in view of the tremendous influence exercised over the Senate by the confederated corporations.

Take, for instance, an amendment to elect United States senators by popular vote. Do you believe that the Senate will ever vote for an amendment that would bar out two-thirds of its members? Do you believe that a trust-made Senate will ever vote a constitutional amendment that would abolish the trusts?

W. BOURKE COCKRAN.

Perhaps twice or thrice in the lifetime of a brilliant and popular speaker does he receive such an ovation as was accorded Bourke Cockran when he stepped to the rostrum and bowed his acknowledgments of Chairman Howe's introduction. It was several minutes before he could do more, but finally the cheering, applauding, handkerchief waving assemblage became calm and Mr. Cockran began:

No person who has listened to the papers read from this platform during the last three days can doubt that the object of this gathering is an honest search for truth. I think the country is to be congratulated upon some of the contributions to this discussion, particularly those from the representatives of the trades unions, and of the National Grange.

As I realized the sound conceptions of economic law which distinguished many of the addresses delivered by delegates from labor organizations, I became convinced that the laborers who spoke to us understood these laws much better than their employers. Indeed, I believe some recent events in our history would have been impossible if every element engaged in production understood the true relations of employer to employee as well as one element showed that it understood them this very day.

The precise question which we have been called to consider is the effect produced by combinations, whether of capital or of labor, upon the general prosperity of the community. The first step towards a solution of this problem is to ascertain just what we mean by prosperity. One of the great difficulties in the way of philosophical inquiry into economic subjects is a very general tendency to use vague, sonorous and misleading phrases, which instead of making a difficult problem clearer serves to becloud it, obscuring its outlines, and magnifying its dimensions. In the controversies which have arisen over this industrial question, certain expressions have become perverted from their original significance and have acquired a strange power of provoking men to excitement, if not belligerency, so that oftentimes we find ourselves embarrassed in discussing facts which concern us by words which excite us. The word "trust," for instance, a word originally of highly respectable significance, has become discredited—apparently by association with millionaires —so that its application to a business enterprise is now the signal for discarding the sober language of argument and for invoking the violent epithets of denunciation.

For the purpose of establishing an intelligent basis of discussion, free from terms likely to provoke passionate declamation, I shall define prosperity as an abundance of commodities fairly distributed among those who produce them. Now, this is not to state two separate and distinct conditions, but rather two aspects of one condition. For, my friends, I hope to establish before I conclude that there cannot be abundant production of commodities without an extensive distribution of them in the form of wages wherever industry is based upon freedom. Whether that distribution be as general as we might wish, is a question which we will consider hereafter; meanwhile we can all agree that distribution can be extensive only where production is abundant. We must have commodities in existence before we can distribute them in the form of wages or of profits. If this definition of prosperity be correct, it must follow that any industrial organization or system which operates to swell the volume of production should be commended, and any that operates to restrict it should be condemned. For my part, I could never understand why a sensible man should grow excited either to approval or resentment over a combination as such. A combination may be good or bad, according to its effect. A combination for prayer is a church. All good men would subscribe to the success of it. A combination for burglary is a conspiracy. All good men would call out the police to prevent it.

Whether combinations of capital operate to raise prices or to reduce them is a subject about which there has been a wide diversity of opinion, not merely in this hall, but wherever economic questions are discussed. While I am fully conscious that the movements of prices depend upon many forces; or perhaps I should rather say, upon every force,—upon the fertility of the soil, upon the sun that quickens the seed, upon the rains that refresh it, upon the rivers which facilitate the transportation of the crop harvested on the surface of the earth, and of the minerals yielded from its bosom,—upon every element of nature as well as upon the industry of man. I think it is beyond question that some combinations of capital operate to cheapen commodities and some operate to make them dearer.

Ladies and gentlemen, I believe there is a very simple test by which we can always determine the effect on prices of any successful industrial organization, and that is to ascertain whether it flourishes through government aid or without it. You must see, my friends, that an industrial enterprise which dominates the market without aid from government, must do so by cheapening its product, or, as it is commonly described, by underselling competitors. An industry which at one and the same time reduces the price of its product and swells its own profits can accomplish that result in one way, and one way only, and that is by increasing the volume of its production. On the other hand, an industry which flourishes through the aid of government, direct or indirect, cannot, in the nature of things, be a force to lower prices, because if it could dominate the market by underselling competitors in a free and open field it would not need government favor. In that case, any interference of government with its business would be an injury, not a benefit. The prosperity of an enterprise enjoying government favor, depends not on the excellence of its service, but on the inability of people to purchase elsewhere. Such a corporation, or combination, never operates to stimulate the volume of production, but always to restrict it, because a government's aid to industry is effective only when it is exercised to extort from the public a volume of profit which without it could be gained only by a larger output. Whatever may be our opinions of industrial enterprises dominating the market by cheapening products, I believe we are unanimous in condemning as detrimental to prosperity every concern whose revenues derived from consumers forced to deal with it on its own terms are not profits earned by substantial service, but tribute exacted from a community made helpless in its hands.

There are three ways by which in this country government interferes with the trade of individuals. One is by patent laws. It is not my purpose, ladies and gentlemen, to intensify differences of opinion among us, but to emphasize the points on which we can agree, and, if possible, to extend the field of our agreement. Questions which cannot possibly be settled or even affected by anything which this conference might do or advise, it would be utterly useless to discuss. I will not waste time, therefore, in considering the effect of exclusive patents on industrial conditions.

Another method of government interference with trade is by tariff laws. Every person must concede, whether he believes in high tariff or free trade, that a protective tariff fosters combinations to control the market in one way. It restricts competition in any commodity to those producing it in this country. Under a condition of free trade every article seeking a market, wherever produced, is exposed to the competition of the whole world. Obviously the control of a market by a combination or trust is facilitated where the field of competition is artificially limited, since it is easier to combine the producers of one country than those of all countries; to that extent the tariff encourages trusts.

It is proper to say, however, that according to the protectionist the exclusion of foreign competition develops a domestic competition much keener and in some mysterious way, more beneficent. I do not understand his logic, but I think that is a fair statement of his proposition. The tariff has been discussed in this country for some eight or ten years, and the question is still unsettled. As it has become a party question we cannot hope to settle it here, and therefore we will relegate it to the forum in which all political issues must be decided.

There is a third and very serious form of government interference with trade which I think we can discuss profitably and which in my judgment has had a wider influence in promoting industrial combinations than the tariff. I refer to special favors extended to certain industries by great corporations exercising public franchises. I call this form of discrimination government favor, because these corporations are essentially agencies of the government although their stocks are owned by private individuals.

465

No person can enjoy a favor at the hands of any company exercising a public franchise except at the expense of another. This is true in every instance where government extends special favor to an individual. I have said in many places, and I say here, that government cannot at one and the same time be a fountain of generosity and of justice. Government cannot of itself create anything. It cannot by any exercise of its own powers, compel the boards that constitute this desk to become a useful article of furniture; it cannot summon the elements of this building from their original places and command them to become a durable edifice; it cannot cause two blades of grass to grow where one grew before; it cannot make a barren field fruitful. Now, if government cannot create anything it has nothing of its own to bestow on anybody. If then it undertake to enrich one individual, the thing which it gives him it must take from another. A government cannot be just and generous at the same time, for if it be generous to one it must be oppressive to another. If it have a favorite it must have a victim, and that government only is just and beneficent which has neither favorites nor victims. Government is always just and always beneficent when it is absolutely impartial. Not merely must its own hands be impartial, but, to paraphrase Lord Bacon, the hands of its hands must be impartial; not merely must its laws be impartial, its courts impartial, its executive officers impartial, but the agencies which it empowers to discharge functions essentially public, must be impartial in their service to every human being within the limits of the state.

It must be clear that if one person obtain rates of transportation unusually favorable, in other words, if his goods be transported for less than the service costs, other men using the same means of transportation must make good the loss. Discrimination of this character is destructive of free competition. The producer who gets the benefit of it is able to undersell his competitor, not by the superiority of his product, but by the favor of the government agency. Profit is the object of all industrial effort. If the favor of a corporation be a shorter pathway to it than efficient service to the public, the ingenuity, enterprise and talent of men will be diverted from the wholesome competitions of industrial skill to debasing and corrupting intrigues for corporate favor. Is there any remedy for this form of oppression? Some gentlemen have suggested municipal ownership as a cure for corporate misconduct. Ladies and gentlemen, I have no irreconcilable quarrel with that suggestion. I concede the principle of municipal ownership.

Any public service which the government can authorize a corporation to perform, it can perform itself. The only excuse for empowering a private corporation to discharge a public function is the belief that it will perform the service more efficiently. The question of municipal ownership then is a mere question of expediency.

Can a government through the machinery of its civil service, administer a railway, a gas company or a telegraph system, as efficiently as private individuals inspired by hope of extensive profits, and with the peculiar capacity developed by years of experience in a particular calling? I won't debate that question here, because if municipal ownership of public franchises be a remedy for existing evils, it is such a remote one that to discuss it would be to discuss the interests of our children rather than of ourselves.

There are many grave obstacles to be overcome before municipal ownership could be reduced to practical operation, even though we should set about establishing it to-day. On what basis of valuation would we compute the interest of the present owners? Should it be fixed on the basis of what these enterprises can earn or on what it would cost to reproduce them? To take them on a valuation fixed according to their present earning power would be a very hazardous speculation. It is exceedingly doubtful if under the administration of public officials they could be managed as economically as they are now under the management of specially trained experts. But if the cost of operation be increased, the rates charged for service must be raised. If the rate of fare from New York to Chicago were increased or the quality of the service impaired, the result would be none the less a public calamity because it was a feature of municipal ownership.

If it should be decided to limit the compensation of the present owners to the cost of reproducing existing railway, telegraph or gas plants, another and more difficult question would arise. Has the state, after allowing and encouraging the original grantees of these franchises to dispose of them to innocent holders on a valuation based on their earning power, any right to take those franchises back upon a different valuation?

Moreover, questions involving the powers of municipalities under special constitutional provisions would have to be settled, before one step could be taken in the reduction of this plan to practical operation. On the whole, while the theory of municipal ownership is highly ingenious and highly interesting, yet, like the suggestion of a convention to frame a new constitution for the United States, as a remedy for pressing evils it is somewhat remote.

Can this conference, then, suggest any practical remedy which could be put in force to-morrow, by any legislature that may be in session? My friends, it seems to me there is a very effective remedy and a very simple one. It would not be necessary to frame a law prohibiting special privileges to individuals from public corporations; that is the law to-day. The remedy is simply to prescribe a definite penalty for violation of it, and to provide for publicity in all the transactions of a corporation exercising public franchises. No fines, no judicial rebukes, no denunciations from platforms, no legislative enactments merely declaring things to be reprehensible will eradicate the evil, but a simple statute giving every shipper, every person using a public franchise of any kind, the right to have disclosed to him at any time every contract and agreement made with any other person for a similar service and declaring the grant of a special rate by a corporation a felony punishable by a long term of imprisonment, will cure it effectually.

My friends, there is no disproportion between the offense of which we complain and the remedy suggested. Discrimination in the rates charged for a service essentially public is a crime of the first magnitude. The corporation, exercising powers conferred by the state for the benefit of all which denies one man opportunities enjoyed by others, robs him, if not of property in his possession, of the opportunity to acquire property.

Publicity of corporate proceedings would accomplish more than the prevention of discrimination in rates. It would go far towards curing the most conspicuous and the most crying evils of corporate management.

We have heard much about the evils of over-capitalization. Indeed, it is one of the subjects which this conference is called to consider. In one sense, I do not regard over-capitalization as a matter of importance; in another sense, I think it has a serious aspect. The nominal capitalization of an enterprise in itself is a matter of little moment. If an enterprise earning ten thousand dollars a year is capitalized at one hundred thousand dollars, the stock would probably sell at two hundred; if it were capitalized at four hundred thousand dollars, the shares would sell at fifty. In either case, the actual value of the stock would be two hundred thousand dollars. That value is established not by the rate of capitalization, but by the opinion of the public, and that value would remain undisturbed no matter what the nominal capitalization might be.

The gentleman who opened this conference, Professor Jenks, in his admirable statement of the questions to be considered, presented this question of over-capitalization by means of a very striking illustration. He mentioned the case of a newspaper earning one hundred thousand dollars a year, and pointing out that according to its earning capacity it represented a capital of at least one million dollars, although one hundred thousand would reproduce its presses, its building and its entire plant,—all except the editor, he asked this conference to say at what sum would it be fair to capitalize such an enterprise. It seems to me the answer is very simple. Tell the public to whom you offer the shares candidly and frankly the whole truth about the property, and capitalize it as you please. If you capitalize it for more than the public believe it to be worth, your shares will sell at a discount; if you capitalize it for less they will sell at a premium. The nominal capitalization is the asking price of the seller, the market value of the stock is the price actually paid by the buyers. If I ask a million dollars for a building and take one hundred thousand for it, nobody is injured by the price demanded, and nobody has a right to question the price which I receive provided no element of fraud or misrepresentation has entered into the bargain.

A high rate of capitalization even of a corporation exercising public franchise, is not necessarily an injury to the public. I can imagine a case where an increase of capitalization without any investment of additional capital might be a great public benefit. Assume for a moment that the Western Union Telegraph Company should reduce its rates to five cents per message, and that instead of being diminished its profits were doubled thereby, should anybody object to an increase of its capitalization based on such an improvement of its service? If it undertook to swell its profits by increasing the cost of telegraph service, then every weapon, legislative and executive, should be invoked to prevent it. The injury to the public would not be the increase of capitalization, but the increase of rates.

The idea that high capitalization forces corporations to charge excessive rates in order to pay dividends, is wholly erroneous. A corporation always strives for the maximum profit, regardless of its capitalization. An attempt to exact excessive profits defeats itself by discouraging consumption and encouraging competition. Skill in business management is shown by capacity to fix that rate for a product which yields the largest margin of profit consistent with the greatest stimulus to consumption. The rate of capitalization has no relation to the cost of the product, and, therefore, it in no way affects the consumer. It concerns merely the holders of the stock, that is to say, the owners of the enterprise. It is, therefore, a question between partners, in which the community as a whole has no interest.

In all this, however, I am assuming that the public have been treated with absolute candor, and that the property capitalized has been truthfully described. There are instances, too common, unfortunately, in which over-capitalization of corporations has been made an effective engine of fraud. The capitalization, for instance, at five millions of an enterprise which cannot pay dividends on one, by men whose names are accepted as guarantees of solvency, honesty, and capable management, often leads the public to buy the shares at a fictitious value without any direct or specific misrepresentations. To deceive by indirection or suppression is as much a fraud, as to mislead by positive falsehoods. A false pretense by which a dealer on the Bowery is cheated out of a pair of shoes, is called a swindle, but misrepresentation on Wall street by which the public is cheated out of millions, is often called a financial operation. When a swindle is called by its proper name and punished as such, whether it be perpetrated on the Bowery for a few cents, or in Wall street for millions of dollars, whether it be in the crude form of breaking a window to abstract valuables, or in the more dangerous form of inducing thousands to part with money for worthless certificates, swindling will become rare.

If in every instance the promoters of a corporation were compelled to state the whole truth about the enterprise offered to the public, it is plain that swindling by over-capitalization would be impossible. For this species of fraud, as, indeed, for all other frauds growing out of corporate management, the remedy, I repeat, is publicity, publicity, publicity.

While on this subject I may dwell for a moment on what to many seems an unaccountable phenomenon—the public dislike and distrust of corporations. Ladies and gentlemen, I don't share that hatred and dislike, but I understand it. While I don't think it is wholly justified, yet I believe the history of corporate management in this country explains it. Indeed, I hold it is indisputable that whenever in America a general opinion on any subject is found to prevail, there is always pretty good ground for it.

The distrust of corporations arises not, in my judgment, from a general opposition to corporate organizations, but from profound distrust of corporate administration. My friend from Texas whose eloquent periods moved this body profoundly on the first day of our session, was careful in his denunciation of corporate oppression to distinguish between corporations which served the public faithfully and those which oppressed the public. I am not quite sure that I understood all his words, but I think he and I sympathize in our feelings. We do not object to the principle of co-operation. The corporation is the natural evolution of the partnership. It is a scheme by which many men, strangers to each other, can co-operate in various fields of industry with a limited risk to each, while partnership is essentially the co-operation of a few men well known to each other, who are compelled to devote all their time and pledge all their resources to the success of their joint enterprise. A man by holding stock in different corporations may participate in many enterprises without risking all his capital in any one, while the liabilities and conditions of partnership are such that few, if any, men could afford to be concerned in more than one. As every device which facilitates the industrial co-operation of men promotes the volume of production, corporations possess enormous capacity for swelling the tide of human prosperity, and they have promoted the well-being of every community in which they have been encouraged, in spite of the fact that the management of corporations has been the blackest page in all our history.

You need not look further back than the panic of 1893 and the corporate management which preceded it to find abundant cause for indignation, distrust, and alarm. It is a dreary, shameful story of trusts betrayed, of stockholders deceived and plundered, of corporations wrecked and looted—their treasuries emptied by faithless officers through devices ingeniously fraudulent, until, deprived of property, of resources, and of credit, they were driven over the precipice of insolvency in a condition so rotten that their fall was almost noiseless. But this is not all. The corporations which trusted these faithless agents were not the only sufferers. The people at large were defrauded of untold millions. Worthless securities were marketed not, it is true, by specific misstatements, but by devices still better calculated to defraud. Interest was paid upon bonds where it had never been earned. Dividends were declared upon preferred stock when the actual revenues showed deficits instead of profits. The people, deceived by these evidences of prosperity, bought the securities, only to find when the collapse came, when the ruin was complete, that in nine cases out of ten the architects of these frauds were appointed by the courts receivers of the enterprises which they had wrecked, enabling them to control the process of reorganization and to conceal the proofs of their crimes. The worst feature of this miserable story is that all these perfidies, all these frauds, all these infamies, have not brought one hour of shame or punishment to those who perpetrated them. These engineers of ruin are walking the streets to-day, their heads high in the world of finance. Their misdeeds bring upon them no popular condemnation, because their operations have been shrouded in secrecy. To the best informed the story of their crimes is only partially known, to the vast mass of the people it is a sealed book. The masses of the people feel instinctively that corporate management has been frequently a fountain of oppression, of fraud and of corruption, but the lack of specific information has caused the public indignation which ought to be visited upon the officers responsible for this shame to be turned on the corporations who have been its victims.

We hear much about the corruption of municipal corporations. Well, probably they are corrupt; certainly they cannot be more so than they are believed to be. But the government of industrial corporations has largely escaped public censure, notwithstanding the recklessness and fraud which have characterized it. What we punish as corruption in politics, we are inclined to encourage as talent in finance. The courts of nearly every state record prosecutions of public officers for bribery. I don't believe that in the whole history of our jurisprudence an officer of a corporation has been compelled to answer at the bar of a criminal court for corruption or fraud perpetrated by the indirect and insidious methods which I have endeavored to describe.

Mr. Gompers mentioned to-day the complaints which labor organizations make against the courts for interfering in disputes between employer and employee by the writ of injunction. The expression "government by injunction" has become a political phrase, and so we must exclude it from these discussions. But, ladies and gentlemen, I will say that to me it has always been a source of profound regret that the courts which have displayed so much ingenuity in devising methods to prevent corporations from being disturbed by their employees have not shown half that ingenuity in devising methods to prevent them from being robbed by their officers.

Wherever we discover corporate abuse we find that it originates in secrecy, that it is developed in secrecy, and that it is maintained in secrecy. Special favors could never be granted in the light of day. Misrepresentations would be useless if all the facts within the knowledge of corporate officers were imparted to the public. Fraud upon corporations by the directors would never be attempted, if their operations were conducted within full view of the stockholders and of the public.

Everybody who has discussed corporate misconduct on the

platform has agreed that it is encouraged by the secrecy surrounding corporate management. Surely, then, we may hope that this conference will be unanimous in recommending publicity.

What objection can there be to publicity? We are told that corporate management is private business. This certainly is not true of corporations engaged in operating public franchises. Such corporations are government agencies, and the right of the people to full information concerning the operations of public agencies cannot be questioned under a republican form of government. Corporations of every kind are created for the purpose of encouraging industry and promoting prosperity. Wherever they become engines of fraud or oppression they are perverted from their original purposes. Secrecy being the source of evil, publicity is its natural antidote. An officer of a corporation acts not for himself, but for others. Whoever acts for others will not shun publicity but court it, if his conduct be governed by honesty. The desire for secrecy is the infallible badge of fraud. The pretense that publicity would injure the interests of stockholders is a device to plunder them. Under the cloak of secrecy stockholders have been robbed quite as extensively as the people have been oppressed. No man who seeks to render another a service fears the light of day. It is only the rogue who seeks the cover of darkness for his operations. Whenever any person seeks to lure you up a dark alleyway on the pretense that he wants to serve you, be sure that he means to cheat you. Do not parley with him for a moment. Call a policeman on the spot if you want to preserve your property and your character.

The final argument in favor of publicity as a remedy for corporate misconduct of every character is its simplicity. It is not a suggestion of new laws, but of more efficient machinery to enforce existing laws. Before leaving this branch of the subject I will venture to outline a system for securing such publicity of corporate administration as would effectively prevent favoritism to individuals, oppression of the public, and fraud on the corporations themselves.

Every person using a public facility should have the right to know the terms on which the same service is enjoyed by every other person. Every stockholder should have the right to examine the books of a corporation and to learn every detail of its operation. If it be objected that to allow the holder of a single share in a corporation capitalized for millions, to examine its books at pleasure, would disturb its business, the answer is simple. If a corporation doesn't want a great number of stockholders it need not have them. It has but to divide its capital stock into shares of five hundred or a thousand or ten thousand dollars each in order to reduce the number of its shareholders. Corporations divide their stock into a great number of shares because it is easier to raise money from many persons contributing each a small sum, than from a few persons each contributing a large amount. If the corporation enjoy the advantage of such a subdivision of its capital, it should accept a corresponding responsibility to every individual shareholder. Indeed, under existing laws, every stockholder has a right to examine the books of a corporation, if the courts would enforce it. In this respect the only new legislation necessary is an act compelling the courts to grant as a matter of right, what to-day they grant as a matter of discretion.

Every corporation should be compelled to file with the secretary of state at its organization a statement of all the property, franchises, goodwill, and assets of every description on which its capitalization is based.

It should be compelled to make a full report every year of all its business to some department of the state. This is the law to-day in nearly every state, but I believe that it is evaded in all of them. The reports are invariably misleading, when they are not incomprehensible. It would not be difficult to make provision for such clear, specific statements as would enable everybody to understand the exact financial condition of every company doing business under a corporate charter. The public could then estimate the value of its shares and no man need be defrauded, no matter what its nominal capitalization might be.

The powers now exercised in almost every state by the department of insurance and the department of banking should be extended so as to make it the duty of some public authority to examine the condition of every corporation, to scrutinize its operation, and to institute criminal proceedings against any officers attempting to practice fraud or concealment in preparing the reports exacted by law. The failure to place the law in motion against them would then be accepted by the public as proving the honesty of their management.

Finally the violation, evasion or disregard of any of these provisions should be punished by long terms of imprisonment. Where great sums are to be gained by disobeying the law, fines will not secure obedience to it. Under such circumstances fines are too often regarded as mere taxes on financial operations, to be collected subsequently from the public.

With these simple remedies prescribed and rigidly enforced, no form of corporate corruption or oppression could be practiced, and I promise you that when honesty governs corporate officers the distrust and dislike of corporations now so general will disappear from the minds of a liberty-loving people, who are always seeking justice even through their prejudices.

In prescribing the limits of publicity a distinction must be observed between corporations which enjoy no favor from the state, except the right to do business under corporate forms, and those specially chartered to perform public functions. To compel a private corporation to disclose its processes of manufacture would be to confiscate its property. The methods by which such a corporation conducts its business concerns itself alone; the results of its business, that is to say, the nature and extent of its property, concerns the public; they should be disclosed so that the people to whom its shares are offered could form an intelligent judgment of their value.

Corporations exercising public functions should have no secrets whatever. They are public agencies. Every feature of their possessions, every detail of their administration should be public property.

I have discussed government interference with the affairs of the citizen at this length because I want it understood that to monopoly dependent upon government favor in any shape or form I am as firmly opposed as any gentlemen in this body—even from Texas. I confess that I envy Texas its breezy rhetoric, when I want to denounce that form of government oppression. But, my friends, when we come to consider an industrial organization which dominates the market not through government favor but through the cheapness of its product, we are face to face with a force in production which is of a radically opposite character.

To denounce any organization as a trust or a monopoly is neither to state an objection to it nor to suggest a method of dealing with it. Avoiding the use of all such exciting and misleading phrases, I will state simply that any form of industrial organization which cheapens a commodity necessary to my comfort commends itself to my approval. I confess that I would rather pay forty dollars for a good suit of clothes to a large industrial organization, than fifty dollars for an inferior suit of clothes to an individual dealer. Now, this may be a confession of total depravity. If it be, ladies and gentlemen, I hope you will regard the candor which impels the confession as some extenuation of the offense. I am so constituted that I prefer good service to bad service, and I cannot quarrel with any organization or system which improves my condition, even though you call it a monopoly. Monopoly is a word which suffers from a very bad name, and deservedly so. It has been associated for ages with the very worst form of governmental practice. During nearly all the history of the world, indeed, I may say until this generation, monopoly meant control of the market by some favorite of the government through a patent conferring upon him the exclusive right to deal in certain articles of general consumption. This was practically a license to prey upon the necessities of the community. In operation it led to such abuses, oppressions and infamies, that the word used to describe it very naturally acquired an evil significance, which to this day awakens the indignation of every justice-loving freeman.

I do not believe there is an organization doing business in this country without government favor which can be called a monopoly, in any fair interpretation of that term. The Standard Oil Company, which is generally deemed a monopoly, supplies only about 62 per cent of all the oil consumed in this country. Such concerns have been described here as "partial monopolies." I confess I am unable to understand that term. A "partial monopoly" is about as intelligible an expression as a "partial whole." It seems to me corporations of this character would be better described as dominating industrial enterprises, than as monopolies. Each may be said to dominate the market for its product, because, although it does not furnish the total amount consumed, it does furnish the larger proportion of it. However, I will not quarrel with words. I don't object to the institution which gives me clothes or food the cheapest, even if you call it a monopoly. I care little about the terms in which it may be described, while I am deeply concerned in the service which it renders.

Let us examine the objections to these industrial enterprises which through aggregations of capital or efficiency of management, or any other cause independent of government favor are able to dominate the market. It is said such an organization destroys competition, but this is manifestly illogical. It does not destroy competition; it is itself the inevitable fruit of competition. It is not possible to have competition without competitors, and if there be competitors, one must prevail. Where a number of persons engaged in the manufacture of shoes, or cloth, or machinery, compete in a perfectly open field, and one succeeds in producing his commodity cheaper than the others, and offers it to the public at a lower price, he will always be the first to dispose of his product. While he can supply the demand no one will pay a higher price for the same article to another producer. He will therefore have a monopoly. He who sells cheapest must always dominate the market, for in economics the domination of the cheapest is the survival of the fittest. If the man who prevails in the competition is not allowed to enjoy the fruit of his victory, that is to say, the control of the market, he will not compete; nobody else will; and then there will be no competition whatever.

The competition of men in any department of human endeavor, if it be absolutely free, always develops excellence. But excellence is monopoly. It would not be excellence if it were not. Surely you would not call that excellence which is shared by many. As the producer of the best commodity must dominate the market for his product, so will the possessor of conspicuous excellence dominate any other field of endeavor. At the bar the most capable lawyer obtains the best clients. In medicine the most skillful physician obtains the most desirable patients; in literature the best writer obtains the widest circulation; each dominates his calling and in that sense he is a monopoly. The leading orator always draws the largest audiences,—indeed, there is a gentleman here present who in this respect is an absolute monopoly, as many of us know to our cost who have attempted to divide public attention with him.

Ladies and gentlemen, I am reminded by the presence of the gentleman—whose name has evoked this great demonstration, as, indeed, it provokes enthusiasm everywhere—that his prominence is itself the direct result of free competition, and the most striking illustration of its essential tendency.

Three years ago a convention met in this town, and as the great majority of delegates were strangers to each other, a few among them who had already attended many similar gatherings, hoped through their wider acquaintance to manage its proceedings and to control its conclusions. They succeeded in directing its preliminary stages, but differences over the platform led to a struggle so fierce that each side was compelled to call on its strongest champions. Factional exigencies thus threw the debate open to free competition, and a young man unknown to the majority, so outshone all rivals that in an instant he was lifted upon the shoulders of shouting, excited delegates into the absolute and unquestioned leadership of his party.

The views which he represented were not mine, but without undertaking to discuss their soundness everybody must admit that the leadership most capable of expounding and maintaining them was developed from the open competition of that debate. While the convention was controlled by the management, as it was during its preliminary proceedings, that young man could not have been chosen a temporary officer. It was then a field of restricted competition in which prominence was to be achieved not by ability but by the favor of the leaders. When it became a field of free competition, its leadership passed to the man who had shown himself able beyond all others to voice its hopes and to defend its opinions.

Wherever free competition prevails, pre-eminence must be achieved as Mr. Bryan achieved it—by shining and conspicuous merit in that particular field. And the preëminence established by merit must be maintained by merit. The lawyer must establish eminence and maintain it by excellence in advocacy; the physician by skill in checking the ravages of disease; the orator by supporting the popular side of every public question, with the most persuasive arguments, clothed in the most attractive words, just as the successful producer must maintain his control of the market by affording the public at all times the best article at the lowest price.

If, however, prominence at the bar depend on the favor of the court, the leading lawyer will not be the man who excels in forensic ability, but the one who is most proficient in the base and servile arts of the courtier. If patients must be secured through social influences, the leading physician will not be the man who labors most assiduously in the laboratory or the hospital, but the one who cultivates most successfully the favor of the drawing-room; if the largest audiences must be secured through flattering the follies of the crowd, the leading orator will not be the man who displays the most eloquence in defense of truth, but the one who shows the greatest aptitude for the wiles of the demagogue. If the control of the market depend on the favor of government, the successful manufacturer will not be the man who excels in production, but the one who excels in corruption.

The same enlightened sense of interest that impels us to defend monopoly based upon excellence, should lead us to overthrow monopoly based upon favor, because while free competition leads to the domination of the best, restricted competition develops the domination of the baser, if not of the basest.

It is objected, however, to the great industrial combinations which dominate the market through the cheapness of their products, that their success in serving the public operates to throw men out of employment. To this there are two answers. First, it is not true, and in the second place, if the statement were true, it would not be a sufficient reason for suppressing an industrial development of great benefit to the body of the community that it worked hardship to a few individuals. The man who says that

478

any system of organization deprives him of employment because he cannot compete with it successfully, admits that somebody else can perform his job better than he can, and if that be so he should be ready to surrender it.

It has been said here by one gentleman that these combinations of capital have been so effective that thirty-five thousand commercial travelers are no longer necessary to the sale of commodities. We have no particular evidence that his statistics are accurate, and we must take his word for the statement that his single voice expressed the feelings of such a multitude. Suppose it to be true, must we hold back the car of progress until every human being can get aboard? If so we must diminish its speed from the rate of the lightning express to that of the lumbering ox-wagon. It seems to me it would be cheaper for the community to pension middlemen directly from the treasury than to restrict the efficiency of the capable in deference to the lamentations of the incapable. I may add that until there is a prospect of a pension, I doubt very much whether we could find thirty-five thousand unemployed commercial travelers in the country. I know of nothing that prolongs life or multiplies a species so effectively as a pension or a prospect of a pension.

As a matter of fact, industrial organizations which increase production have never thrown anybody out of employment even for an hour, and, in the nature of things, they never can. Production has never been increased without increasing the number of hands engaged in it, and to increase the number of laborers cannot operate to throw anyone out of employment.

A period of industrial transition is always a period of apprehension, vociferously expressed but never realized. While the substitution of steam for hand labor was impending, loud lamentations were heard on all sides from laborers who believed that it meant their ruin. After it had been effected, nobody was found to be injured and everybody realized that he had been benefited.

While the application of machinery to manufacturing was in course of preparation and before it was completed, operatives of every description bemoaned their fate, believing the change would reduce them all to starvation. The cobbler in his cellar, the weaver in his back room, both believed that the scanty crusts on which they supported existence, would be filched from their mouths by this new force in production. Now the only way by which machinery displaced hand labor was by placing goods in greater abundance on the market, that is to say, at cheaper rates. But to make these goods human hands were necessary, and no hands were so efficient as those which had already acquired familiarity with the articles to be manufactured. Hence the first person employed to operate the machine for making shoes was the cobbler who had dreaded its advent. The first to manage the steam loom was the weaver who had believed it would be the engine of his destruction. The cobbler was displaced from his cellar by himself, and the weaver from his back room by himself,— each was taken from miserable, fetid, degraded surroundings into a well-lighted, wholesome factory, where he earned better wages, and where in a short time he organized unions and demanded still better wages.

The stage coach drivers believed to a man that the establishment of railroads would deprive them all of occupation, but as a matter of fact, railroads from the first hour of their operation increased the demand for drivers. By the time the railroad had reached such a degree of efficiency as to preclude competition with the stage coach the necessity of distributing the greatly increased traffic in passengers and merchandise from railroad stations had created a wider demand for drivers and horses than had ever been known before. It is quite true that occasionally a man who had been accustomed to drive a coach with four horses thought there would be some loss of dignity in consenting to drive a less splendid but more useful vehicle drawn by one or two horses, even at better wages, but surely it would not be contended that the progress of the human race should have been blocked out of sympathy, not for the necessities, but for the vanity of an occasional stage coach driver.

And so I take leave to doubt the statement that thirty-five thousand commercial travelers have been reduced to idleness by increased efficiency in business management. The object of consolidating corporations must be to increase sales. But an increase of sales involves an increase in salesmen, and as these commercial travelers are considered the best salesmen, they will be the first beneficiaries of the change. Of course, I speak of those who promptly seek employment under the new system, not of those who spend their days bemoaning discarded methods.

It has been said that competition is cruel, pitiless, and destructive. Our friend, the socialist, whose interesting address delivered this morning should make his name familiar throughout the country declared that competition was warfare. Let me protest against that statement. Competition is not warfare in the sense of being destructive. Competition is the best method of ascertaining the place of greatest utility for each individual. Believe me, every man has special aptitude for some occupation. A man who is defeated in one field of competition is not excluded from the whole field of production, but he is transferred from a field of lesser to a field of greater efficiency. Competition prevents a misdirection of powers. A man qualified to be a farmer might wish to be a lawyer. Competition by depriving him of bread if he persisted in following a profession in which he would be useless, drives him to agriculture, where he enjoys greater chances for achieving prosperity and efficiency.

A few days ago, in the waters around New York, a number of boats competed for the honor of defending America's cup against the foreign challenger. In that competition the Columbia was successful. Did they break up the Defender as useless because another by outsailing her had excluded her from the international races? No, the Defender is retired from that particular field, but one of wider usefulness is open to her. She will cease to be a racing craft, but she will remain a swift and useful boat. She will join the Puritan, the Vigilant, and the other vessels which formerly were champions, but which are now ministering to the pleasures and the necessities of men. This competition has not caused the destruction of any craft. It has assigned each to the field in which it will be most useful, while it has determined the one which in point of speed is best fitted to defend for our country the trophy she has held so long of supreme excellence in making ships and in sailing them.

Attempts to excel otherwise than by superiority are not competition, although that word is often used to describe them. If in that preliminary competition of boats which I have mentioned, one of them had undertaken to succeed by fouling, that is to say, by running into another, or if an industrial organization undertook to outstrip a rival by throwing obstacles in the access of its product to the market,—by imposing penalties on retail merchants who offered its goods to the public,—or by any means whatever except the superiority of its product,—it would not be engaged in a competition, but in a conspiracy to prevent competition.

If predominance—monopoly—call it what you will, resting on excellence be reprehensible, how are we to prevent it? The distance between excellence and mediocrity can be obliterated only by reducing the superior to the level of the inferior. The process cannot be reversed. It is impossible, by any device of legislation, to make the unskillful equal to the skillful man, but it is entirely possible for government to limit the efficiency of the skillful by hampering his industry. But if it be advisable to obliterate the difference between efficiency and inefficiency in material production, it must be equally advisable to obliterate distinctions between capacity and incapacity in other fields of human endeavor. If I must be prevented from obtaining a good suit of clothes from a large concern for thirty dollars and forced to pay fifty dollars for an inferior suit to a smaller but less efficient dealer merely to maintain him in business, why should a litigant be allowed to employ the best lawyer while a number of inferior lawyers are eager for the retainer and ready to give everything in return for it except equally good advice? Why should a sufferer be permitted to consult the leading physician while the neighborhood abounds with practitioners less skillful, but fully as virtuous, and who are ready to experiment on his system with greater enthusiasm, though probably with less success? Why should the leading orator be allowed to crowd the largest hall with delighted auditors, while hundreds of others equally patriotic are bursting with noble sentiments to which nobody will listen?

If the preëminence or monopoly of merit be reprehensible in itself, every attempt to establish it must be equally reprehensible. If it be wrong for a manufacturer to strive for control of the market by the superiority of his product, it must be equally wrong to contend for preëminence in the learned professions. Must the capable lawyer, then, sacrifice a certain number of cases deliberately,—that is to say,—betray a certain number of his clients,— lest he excel the incapable attorneys who lose causes through stupidity? Must the physician who possesses skill use it to destroy a few lives, lest he be more successful than others who destroy them through lack of skill? Must the leading orator reduce the splendor of his periods lest he outshine duller speakers?

If we are to suppress monopoly resting on excellence we must begin by suppressing the excellence which establishes it, and this would be to arrest all human improvement.

To ascertain conclusively the effect of any industrial system upon the condition of a country, we must examine its effect on wages. In my judgment, there is but one test of prosperity absolutely infallible, and that is the rate of wages paid to labor. I beg you to believe that this statement is not made through any profession of special love for the man who works with his hands. I don't claim to hold the laborer in any greater affection than the lawyer, or the doctor, or even the capitalist. I say the condition of the laborer in any country is an infallible test of its prosperity, because wages, being that part of his own product which the laborer receives in compensation for his toil, it is plain that the more he produces, the greater the fund from which he draws his compensation. If a laborer engaged in making chairs produce five chairs worth twenty dollars every day, and his wages be four dollars a day, the rate of his compensation is equivalent to one-fifth of his product. In effect he receives one chair out of the five which he produces. Instead of taking home with him every day a chair which he could not divide among the various persons on whom he depends for the necessaries of life, he takes its equivalent in money, which he can divide, that is to say, he takes four dollars. If by an increase in his own efficiency, by a better system of organization, or any other cause, that laborer produced ten chairs every day instead of five, and his wages were still a fifth of his product he would receive two chairs or eight dollars a day. The difference between the larger product and the amount of his wages being thirty-two dollars, while the difference between the smaller product and his wages was but sixteen dollars, it is clear that the more highly he is paid the greater the profit of his employer. This explains why those industries are the most prosperous in which the highest rate of wages prevails.

But the laborer cannot increase his own product without causing an increase in the production of others. An increase in the production of chairs involves a corresponding increase in the production of all the articles that enter into its manufacture, in the production of lumber, of glue, and of tools. Nor is this all. The manufacturer would not increase the production of chairs without an increase in the demand for them. Demand for an article in the economic sense does not mean a mere desire for it. It means that people are ready to offer other commodities in exchange for it. An increase in the production of one article would be unprofitable unless there be a corresponding increase in the production of other articles. Abundance of chairs would not profit me if there be not an abundance of clothes, an abundance of shoes, an abundance of tables, and other things which could be exchanged for them. Abundance, therefore, is impossible, unless it is general. An abundance of commodities necessarily causes an extensive demand for labor to produce them. An extensive demand for labor always causes a high rate of wages, and that is what I meant when I said in the beginning that there cannot be abundant production of commodities without an extensive distribution in the form of wages.

As it is impossible to increase profits and at the same time lower the price of a product in any other way than by increasing the volume of production and as an increase in the volume of production must increase the rate of wages, all industrial combinations which operate to lower prices; or, in other words, those which flourish through excellence are powerful forces to promote the general prosperity.

Mr. Gompers said to-day that the movement of industry has steadily tended to a higher rate of wages, and I am glad to concur in that statement. The movement of wages is upward and must be upward under the immutable laws governing production. Any discussion of wages would be incomplete which did not embrace the effect of Trades Unions on industry, and, therefore, if you will bear with me I will say a few words on that subject. What I am about to say will sound strange to most of you. It may perhaps shock a great many who approved what I have said before, but with opinions an honest man must do one of two things—express them or change them. I can't change mine, so I must express them and explain them. Labor unions, in my judgment, have no direct effect whatever upon the rate of wages. I am aware this proposition conflicts with an opinion which is almost universal, yet, I believe it will be justified by a very slight examination of economic laws. I do not mean by this to say that trades unions have not exercised a great, even a decisive, influence on social conditions. They are the most effective agencies yet discovered for facilitating the intercourse between employers and employes concerning the conditions of their common industry. The loyal discharge of this function helps to maintain industrial peace, upon which depends, in a large degree, the industrial efficiency through which this republic is destined to exercise a wider, a better, and a more lasting influence upon mankind than the great republic of antiquity. The rate of wages, however, does not depend on agreements between employers and employees or upon concessions by one to the other. It is fixed by immutable laws which neither the employer nor the employee nor both combined could disturb. The wages of the laborer depends on the value of his product and nothing else.

The employer cannot pay the laborer any more than the value of his product and he cannot pay him any less. Recurring to the illustration of the chair, it must be plain that if I undertook to pay the laborer who finished it any more than the value of his product, in a very short time I would be reduced to bankruptcy, when I would be unable to give him any employment or pay him any wages whatever. If I succeeded in inducing him to accept less than the value of his product, the only effect would be an increase in my profits. But if capital engaged in the chair-making industry showed unusual profits, other capital would be attracted to it from different fields of industry. It would compete with my capital. Its competition would take the form of drawing away the best laborers by offering higher wages. I must meet this competition by offering equally high wages or I must abandon the industry.

The standard of wages then is fixed by two forces acting on each other; the competition of laborers for employment, operating to make wages lower, and the competition of capital for profit operating to make wages higher. It may seem strange to many, but it is nevertheless true that the competition of capital for profit is keener than the competition of laborers for employment, because it is easier and cheaper for capital to move from place to place in search of higher profit than for a laborer to seek a field of higher wages.

It would cost a laborer at least fifteen dollars to move from Chicago to New York, but you can send millions of dollars from Chicago to Hong Kong for a postage stamp. It would take a laborer two days to go from here to Boston, but you can send any amount of capital to the other side of the globe in an instant by a cable dispatch. Moreover, capital has no family affections; it is indifferent to climate; all languages are alike to it. But the laborer has domestic ties deeply implanted in the fibers of his being which none but very powerful motives can induce him to disturb. It is doubtful if a difference of 15 per cent in the rate of wages would be enough to cause a movement of laborers from Chicago to New York, but a difference of an eighth of 1 per cent in the rate of interest would start capital all round the world.

The competition of capital for profit being keener than the competition of laborers for employment, the force which operates to advance wages is stronger than that which operates to lower them; the result is a steady rise in the rate of wages, and a steady fall in the rate of interest.

Wages being fixed by the operation of these two forces, it is plain that the rate cannot be determined, altered or changed by any agreement between the employer and the employee. If I be a capitalist engaged in the production of chairs, the wages of the laborer who finished that chair and the profits of my capital must both be paid from its proceeds. Not merely must he be paid his wages and I my profits, but every person who has furnished any of the materials or who has contributed in any degree to its production must be paid from the sum realized by the sale of it. There is no other fund from which their compensation can be drawn. The wages of each laborer who contributes to it is determined by the proportion which his labor bears to all the labor expended in its production. My laborer and I cannot by any agreement between ourselves change the proportion of that chair to which each of these other laborers are entitled. We cannot even change our own proportion. That is fixed, as we have seen, by the competition of laborers for employment on the one hand, and of capital for profits on the other. But while we cannot by any agreement between ourselves change the proportion of this particular chair to which each is entitled, there is one method, and only one, by which we can both increase our earnings—he his wages and I my profits—and that is by increasing the number of chairs produced by our joint industry.

Nothing can be further from the truth than the degrading notion—so widely entertained—that wages are a species of alms depending on the moral attributes of the employer—that good employers pay high wages and bad employers low wages. The wages of the laborer depend on his own efficiency. Wherever a man labors, he creates the fund from which he must be paid. Before his wages can be increased that fund must be increased and by his own hands. Whether he be driving a locomotive, handling a brake, mending a track, or guiding a ship across the sea, making chairs, tables, or shoes, building houses or planting crops, arranging for the sale of commodities in the market, or for the distribution of their proceeds among those who produced them, the only method by which his wages can be increased is by an increase in the efficiency of his own labor.

It is quite generally believed that there is an essential and irreconcilable conflict between employer and employee—that the laborer cannot increase his wages except by reducing the profit on capital, and that capital can increase its earnings only by decreasing the rate of wages. If the amount which human industry could produce were a fixed and immovable quantity, the theory that the share of the laborer could be increased only at the expense of the employer, and vice versa, would have some basis of justification. But the whole history of the world shows that the productive capacity of man is practically limitless. It has increased from day to day. It is greater now than it was a year ago. It is probably ten times greater at the close than it was at the beginning of this century. In the course of the next century it is likely to grow beyond our capacity to conceive at this moment. Wages have never increased except as production has increased. An increase in wages is but the distribution of an increased production. A reduction of wages is the distribution of a diminished production. Employer and employee cannot prosper separately, or at the expense of each other. The prosperity of each flows from the same fountain. The rate of wages cannot be increased at the expense of capital, and the profits of capital cannot be swelled at the expense of wages, but the prosperity of both can be increased by an increase in the yield of human industry and the division of that increase between them. We have been called to consider the effect on industry of combinations of labor as well as of capital, and yet little, if any, attention has been bestowed on the strike,—that most dangerous form of civil war,—ever threatening industrial communities,—most threatening where prosperity is widest. The disasters of war have at least the compensation that those who suffer from them are brought together in bonds of closer union by the recollection of calamities which they have shared, and by the necessity of coöperating to repair them; but the strike leaves behind it no memories except those of hate and injury, leading to wider distrust, further recriminations and fresh disturbances. War arrays nations against each other, but it draws the people of each nation closer. The strike tends to resolve society into its original elements—each hostile to all others. It is more dangerous than foreign invasion or domestic insurrection, as the cancer which corrodes the vitals is more deadly than any injury to a single limb.

Compulsory arbitration has been suggested as a remedy for industrial disturbances. Ladies and gentlemen, compulsory arbitration is inconsistent with a condition of free labor. That man is not free who cannot decide freely whether he will work or whether he won't, without any semblance of coercion. Arbitration to be effective must be binding on both sides. If the tribunal have power to fix a rate of wages, it must have the right to enforce obedience to its decree by the laborer as well as by the employer. To compel laborers to work upon any terms would be to reduce them to servitude. To compel an employer to pay higher wages than his business will permit would reduce him to bankruptcy, and deprive him of the power to pay any wages. I know of no means by which a court could determine the exact value of a laborer's product. Moreover, elaborate devices for the suppression of strikes are wholly unnecessary. Strikes must be prevented by removing the causes which produce them, and I think it can be demonstrated that strikes spring not from inherent and irreconcilable difficulties between employers and employees, but from a misconception of their true relations.

This misconception can be traced to the very general but none the less erroneous idea that employment involves the relation of master and servant. The word "service" has come down to us from the days of the old Roman Empire, when all labor was slave labor. The capacity of a mere word for mischief has no stronger illustration than the train of evil consequences which have flowed from the application of this word "service" to free labor. It has bred contempt in the employer for the employee, and distrust in the employee for the employer. We have seen that the one source of prosperity for employer and employee is the prosperity of the industry in which both are engaged. That being so, the relation between employer and employee is not one of service, but of partnership. The partners may be changed, but the partnership must continue while industry is active. The employer may discharge his laborers, that is to say, he may change his partners, but he cannot prosecute his business unless he employs other laborers who at once become his partners. The partnership of all free men engaged in industry cannot be changed. It is fixed by laws as immutable as those which regulate the movements of the planets, or the course of the seasons.

If employers and employees realized that they were partners with common interests—as they are—it is impossible to believe that either could ever be led to interrupt the operations of the industry on which the prosperity of both depends. The gravest disturbances to industry have arisen, not from disputes about wages, but from the refusal of employers to discuss conditions of employment with agents selected by their employees, or, in other words, with labor unions. These refusals have been based on various pretexts, but I think they all sprang from the same source—a feeling on the part of the employer that there would be some abasement of dignity in treating a laborer not as a servant to be commanded but as a partner to be consulted.

Conceding for the sake of argument that the organization of unions or the appointment of walking delegates be unwise or unprofitable, the fact remains that the laborers insist upon dealing with their employers through these agencies. We have seen that the laws governing industry fix the rate of wages according to the value of the product. The employer must determine that value at the peril of bankruptcy,—or at least of loss. While he alone determines the rate of wages, what difference can it make to him whether he announces his conclusion to A or to B, to each workman separately, or to a labor union representing all his workmen?

If the employer and the employee could be induced to reason together, they could not quarrel. It is true that the demands of laborers are often unreasonable, but the best way to defeat an unreasonable demand is to insist that it be formulated. The striker has but one weapon, and that is public opinion. If he be compelled to state his grievance before the public and his position be unreasonable, public opinion would be as quick to condemn him as it has been to support him when the attitude of his employer was believed to be unjust or intolerant. We hear much about the boycott. It may be a good weapon or it may be a bad one. It may be justifiable or it may be unjustifiable, but certain it is that a boycott depends absolutely on an overwhelming public opinion. A mere majority could not make it formidable. It is effective only when the whole population is practically unanimous in enforcing it. The day that industrial issues are discussed in public,—the workingmen compelled to define their demands and employers forced to deal with these specific demands, excluding all collateral questions, strikes will become impossible and boycotts will be unknown.

I say that discussion will obviate strikes because it would be difficult to unite employees in an unjustifiable demand, and impossible to enlist public opinion in support of it. A laborer who demands more than the value of his product is invading, not the rights of his employer, but the rights of all the other laborers— his unknown partners scattered all over the globe—who have contributed to the industry in which he is engaged. If one laborer gets more than his share of a product to which many have contributed, some other laborer must get less. If the man who finishes that chair obtains an undue proportion of the proceeds, the man who felled the trees in the forest, or who transported the materials or who furnished the tools, or the glue, must get less than his share, for there is nothing to divide between them except the proceeds of the chair. On a railway system everybody must be paid from the earnings. If one gets more than his share somebody else must get less. If the locomotive engineer is paid more than his fair proportion, the switch-tender, the brakeman, or the fireman, must get less than his share of the fund produced by them all. These principles are so plain that if expounded with frankness and good temper an attempt by any class of employees to obtain unwarrantably high wages would appear at once to be a raid not on the profits of the employer so much as on the wages of other laborers. A public discussion would make this plain and would enlist against them on the spot the unanimous opinion of the community. No laborer could make an effective appeal to force—either the active force of weapons or the passive force of the boycott—when the question between himself and his employer had been fully discussed with the entire community for a tribunal and an audience.

Let no man think that in what I say here I undertake to excuse violence under any circumstance. I believe that the laborer and his employer are partners, and that full and fair discussion of all questions between them is essential to the prosperity of the partnership. But if one of the partners undertake to become violent, I would be the first to condemn him, to restrain him, if necessary, to punish him. There is something more important than the success of any particular partnership, and that is the preservation of the public peace, on which depends the industry of the whole community.

Having said this, I hope I will not be misunderstood if I add that, in my judgment, whenever a strike occurs the master should be held responsible to public opinion. I don't say this because I believe workmen are always reasonable, always loyal, always obedient, or always industrious. I say it simply because the existence of a strike on any industry shows that the person in charge of it is unable to manage men. This is not necessarily a reflection upon his moral character. His inability to manage his employees may proceed from the excellence of his moral qualities, but the fact remains that no man should be suffered to remain in control of laborers who is unable to manage them. This is but applying to the management of men the test now applied by all owners of industrial enterprises to the management of mules or horses. If a man engaged to drive a pair of mules repeatedly allowed his animals to become entangled with the wagon which they were harnessed to draw, do you suppose he would be maintained in his employment, however unimpeachable his moral character? Would he be heard for a moment to charge the failure of his industry upon the perversity of the mules? No; his employer, recognizing his sobriety, his truthfulness, his honesty, and his general excellence, would nevertheless replace him by some person, perhaps of inferior morality, but of greater dexterity in the handling of mules. And surely a test of capacity applied to the management of animals should be applied more rigidly to the management of men.

The person in charge of a great industry, like the captain on the bridge of a ship, should be held responsible for the safety of his charge no matter what the peril which may beset it.

When some years ago the St. Paul ran ashore on the New Jersey beach, a passenger undertook to console the captain by saying it was well understood that the accident was caused by a mistaken report of the officer in charge of the soundings, but that loyal seaman answered, "I am the captain of this ship. I am in control of every member of the crew, from the stoker in the hold to the lookout at the masthead, and responsible for all of them. I alone must bear the blame for this disaster." So when a great industrial enterprise lies paralyzed through the quarrels of those whose coöperation is essential to its efficiency, the man in charge of it, the captain on the bridge, should not be allowed to divide his responsibility with any one; the collapse of his industry should be taken as conclusive proof that he is unable to manage it.

We have seen that compulsory arbitration is not a remedy which can be enforced in a free country. Can the state, then, do nothing to promote among employers and employees a proper conception of their relations, and prevent these industrial disturbances which by interrupting all production, work irreparable injury to them and to the whole community? Directly the state can do nothing, indirectly it can accomplish a great deal. In a free country where an enterprise is of a private character, whether conducted by individuals or corporations, the state cannot interfere with the management of its business. But where a corporation chartered to discharge public functions is forced to suspend its service by a strike of its employees, it is the right and it should be made the duty of the state to bring proceedings for the revocation of its charter, while every citizen inconvenienced by its breach of duty should be given a right of action against it for substantial damages.

Where, however, it could be shown that the corporation at all times had been ready to discuss with its employees through any agency which they thought proper to select, all questions at issue between them that fact should be a complete defense to any actions by the state or by individuals. No matter what the subject of dispute might be, whether it were a question of wages, or hours, or anything else, so long as the corporation could show that it had been ready to discuss it fully with its employees directly or with anybody designated by them, it should be held blameless.

With such a law on the statute book discussions would be certain to precede hostilities between corporations exercising public franchises and their employees. For the reasons already stated this in itself would be sufficient to maintain industrial peace between them. The fear of strikes is a spectre which constantly haunts industry, causing capital to hesitate and enterprise to lag. Corporations exercising public franchises are the largest employers of labor. Any system of managing employees imposed on them which proved effective in avoiding labor disputes would be adopted voluntarily, aye, eagerly by private employers and the gravest danger to civilized society would be greatly reduced, if not wholly averted. This remedy would not be a radical innovation on our system of jurisprudence, but merely a provision for the better enforcement of fundamental principles. A distinguished judge in New York some years ago entertained an application for a mandamus against a railway company, the operation of whose system had been suspended by a strike among its freight handlers, and the principle on which he acted would justify such a law as I suggest.

These, then, are my suggestions for the cure of such evils as affect the body politic: equal rights to all men in the enjoyment of all facilities furnished by the government directly or by agencies of its selection; publicity of every detail in corporate management affecting the community; penalties for the interruption through strikes or other industrial disturbances of any public service which a corporation is chartered to perform, unless the corporation can show that it had always been ready to discuss matters in dispute with its employees through agents of their own selection.

These remedies are not ambitious plans for the reorganization of society, but merely suggestions to promote the industrial coöperation of men by a fuller recognition of certain immutable and eternal laws governing the human race. It is said that the closer coöperation of man, tends to destroy individualism. Individualism is another of those phrases which appear to have been invented for the special purpose of bewildering the mind. It disguises an argument for barbarism under an expression with a humanitarian sound. Individualism in its last analysis is savagery. The savage depending on himself alone for his shelter and his food, treating all his fellows as foes to be shunned or killed, is the most complete instance of individualism conceivable. Individualism is isolation or savagery. Association or coöperation is civilization. The badge of savagery is the weapon of destruction by which the savage maintains his isolation. The badge of civilization is the implement of production by which each man enlists the coöperation of many men for the benefit of all. All civilized men are engaged in a great scheme of coöperation, in which the activity of every man's hands is of vital importance to all the rest.

If socialism would result in a more abundant yield of the earth I would be a socialist. I don't believe that in the present condition of the race a man would labor as zealously or as effectively for the common good as he does now for his own profit and therefore I believe socialism would restrict rather than promote the volume of production.

Again, we are told that closer coöperation among men tends inevitably to socialism. This conference will not have been held in vain if it result in dispelling to some extent that fog of phrases which so often overhangs economic discussions, causing men to lose sight of the object which they have undertaken to consider. The matter that concerns us is the system which best

492

promotes the fruitfulness of industry, not the term in which that system may be described.

Socialism and individualism are features of our existence now. No one can attempt to gratify individual desires without serving society at large. Wherever a man labors to improve his own condition, he contributes to the welfare of the entire race. Can you or I do one thing for individual benefit without benefiting all our fellows? Can vanity indulge itself, can pride gratify itself, can appetite satisfy itself, without paying a tribute to the universal partnership in which we are all engaged? The man who builds a palace to gratify pride, must employ ten thousand hands in every quarter of the globe. The woman who buys a robe to indulge vanity, must employ hundreds of her fellow-creatures throughout the world. The miser, seeking to raise the rate of interest on his capital from 5 to 6 per cent must serve his fellows in doing so. There is but one way in which he can increase the profits of his capital, and that is by an increase of its productivity. If his capital be employed in making tables, more tables must be produced; if in building, more houses must be erected; if in agriculture, the area of tillage must be increased. In doing all these things more labor must be employed, and thus hundreds of dollars will be distributed in wages for every one that is gained by capital. Our pride, our hopes, our fears, our ambitions are but illusions which spur us to activity in the service of others,—traces that bind us to the car of human progress, making of all our activities forces to move it onward and upward. The questions which perplex the civilization of this age arise from freedom and the ever-swelling tide of prosperity, of which freedom is the fountain. The triumph of Christianity led inevitably to the establishment of this republic. A government based on the equality of all men in the eye of the law was the necessary fruit of a religious belief in the equality of all men in the sight of God.

The economic effect of Christianity was the substitution of free labor for slave labor. The removal of manacles from the hands of man has worked an extraordinary change in his condition. It has wonderfully increased his productivity, extended the scope of his powers, multiplied his possessions, lengthened the span of his days, widened the horizon of his ambitions. But out of the very prosperity which it has created, a difficulty has sprung. The slave was willing to accept from the hands of his master a crust of bread as a reward for his labor, glad to escape the lash, but the free laborer demands a fair share of the property which has been created by his toil. The adjustment of this demand, the fair distribution of the commodities created by the coöperative industry of every man, is the problem of this age. I do not think it is an insuperable or even a very difficult question. Its solution in my judgment, will be found by recognizing in our industrial systems, the partnership of man as we have recognized in our political system, the equality,—the brotherhood of man. While the relations of men are governed by the principles of justice and morality which underlie this government, and indeed the whole fabric of Christian civilization,—I have no fear of the future. Words cannot disturb me while every fact in history encourages me. This civilization which has created our marvelous prosperity, will defend it and maintain it. I have no sympathy with those timid souls who see in our splendid growing civilization a dizzy eminence from which the race is in constant peril of falling back into the darkness and ignorance from which it has risen. I prefer to regard man as a reasonable being, pursuing by the light of experience an ever-ascending pathway of progress, proving by what he has done, his capacity for greater deeds,—surveying from the heights which he has achieved, with courage, with determination, and with confidence, the still nobler heights which are accessible.

WILLIAM JENNINGS BRYAN.

Several times during his address the speaker was interrupted by bursts of applause, but especially was this noticeable when he referred to Col. Bryan in a brief but glowing eulogy. As he took his seat the demonstration was punctuated by calls for the noted Nebraskan who, after much pressure, stepped forward and said:

I am denying myself a great pleasure when I refuse to respond to your very cordial invitation. When I came this afternoon and found that Mr. Cockran and I were to speak together this evening, or it had been so announced, I consulted with him and with those who were in charge, and it was the decision that anything like a debate would not be in keeping with the purpose of this conference.

"We are not here to arouse partisan feeling by standing as representatives of different ideas. We are here to take part in a conference, to give expression to our views, and to gather as much information as we can from the views expressed by others, and it was decided that it was better that Mr. Cockran should have this evening by himself and that I should speak to-morrow at 10 o'clock and give my views. And while, as I say, I am denying myself a great pleasure in refusing to speak to this magnificent audience, I am sure that you upon reflection will agree that our decision is the correct one and that the purpose of this conference shall be carried out and that we shall avoid as far as possible anything that might seem like partisanship or an attempt to array one part of the body against another part.

"I don't know to what extent Mr. Cockran represents the views of the delegates here. I don't know to what extent I represent the views of the delegates in what I shall say, but to-morrow at 10 o'clock I shall submit some remarks in regard to the subject of monopoly and make some suggestions as to methods by which monopoly can be eliminated. I am one of those who believe that monopoly in private hands is indefensible in a free country.

"While I agree with much that Mr. Cockran has said to-night, agree with some of the remedies proposed, I cannot fully agree with all that he has said, and to-morrow instead of attempting to answer any part in which I may differ, I expect to present this subject as it appears to me in order that I may contribute my part toward the solution of this great question."

At 10:50 o'clock the conference adjourned until 10:30 o'clock the following morning.

MORNING SESSION, SEPTEMBER 16.

It was 10:05 o'clock when Chairman Howe called to order the first of the two last sessions of the conference. In anticipation of Col. William J. Bryan's reply to Mr. Cockran's address of the preceding evening the hall was again packed to the doors, and many of the scenes of the previous evening were reënacted.

Moved by Gaines, of Tennessee, seconded by Davis, of Arkansas, that a committee of five on finance and publication be appointed by the chair. Carried.

W. E. STANLEY.

Governor of Kansas.

Chairman Howe introduced Governor Stanley, of Kansas, who said:

More than three years ago in this city a great political party met in convention, and in less than an hour changed their policy and entrusted their banner and chances of success into the hands of a new and untried champion. The campaign that followed was one of the most memorable—aye, the most memorable in the history of American politics. We did not all agree with the wonderful man who led over 7,000,000 voters with him in that fight; but we did all admire his matchless eloquence and brilliant leadership.

It is not necessary for me to introduce him to any American audience. I take pleasure, however, in presenting to this audience Col. W. J. Bryan, who will now address you.

WILLIAM JENNINGS BRYAN.

Col. Bryan was as enthusiastically received as he had been when he entered the hall on the preceding evening. As soon as the applause, which was long and vigorous, had subsided he began his address, saying:

I appreciate the very kind words spoken by Governor Stanley in presenting me to this audience. I am glad I live in a country where people can differ from one another, differ honestly, express their convictions boldly, and yet respect one another and acknowledge one another's rights. I am not vain enough, however, to think that any good will which has been expressed by the people toward me is due to personal merit. If I have had political friends it is because people believe with me in certain ideas or rather because I believe with them in certain ideas. It is the idea that makes the man. The man is only important as he helps the idea.

I come this morning to discuss in your presence a great question—a question of growing importance to the American people. The trust principle is not a new principle, but the trust principle is manifesting itself in so many ways and the trusts have grown so rapidly that people now feel alarmed about trusts who did not feel alarmed three years ago. The trust question has grown in importance, because within two years more trusts have been organized, when we come to consider the capitalization and the magnitude of the interests involved, than were organized in all the previous history of the country, and the people now come face to face with this question: Is the trust a blessing or a curse? If a curse, what remedy can be applied to the curse?

I want to start with the declaration that a monopoly in private hands is indefensible from any standpoint, and intolerable. I make no exceptions to the rule. I do not divide monopolies in private hands into good monopolies and bad monopolies. There is no good monopoly in private hands. There can be no good monopoly in private hands until the Almighty sends us angels to preside over the monopoly. There may be a despot who is better than another despot, but there is no good despotism. One trust may be less harmful than another. One trust magnate may be more benevolent than another, but there is no good monopoly in private hands, and I do not believe it is safe for society to permit any man or group of men to monopolize any article of merchandise or any branch of industry.

What is the defense made of the monopoly? The defense of the monopoly is always placed on the ground that if you will allow a few people to control the market and fix the price they will be good to the people who purchase of them. The entire defense of the trusts rests upon a money argument. If the trust will sell to a man an article for a dollar less than the article will cost under other conditions, then in the opinion of some that proves a trust to be a good thing. In the first place I deny that under a monopoly the price will be reduced. In the second place, if under a monopoly the price is reduced the objections to a monopoly from other standpoints far outweigh any financial advantage that the trust could bring. But I protest in the beginning against settling every question upon the dollar argument. I protest against the attempt to drag every question down to the low level of dollars and cents.

In 1859 Abraham Lincoln wrote a letter to the Republicans of Boston who were celebrating Jefferson's birthday, and in the course of the letter he said: "The Republican party believes in the man and the dollar, but in case of conflict it believes in the man before the dollar." In the early years of his administration he sent a message to Congress, and in that message he warned his countryman against the approach of monarchy. And what was it that alarmed him? He said it was the attempt to put capital upon an equal footing with, if not above, labor in the structure of government, and in that attempt to put capital even upon an equal footing with labor in the structure of government he saw the approach of monarchy. Lincoln was right. Whenever you put capital upon an equal footing with labor, or above labor in the structure of government you are on the road toward a government that rests not upon reason but upon force.

Nothing is more important than that we shall in the beginning rightly understand the relation between money and man. Man is the creature of God and money is the creature of man. Money is made to be the servant of man, and I protest against all theories that enthrone money and debase mankind.

What is the purpose of the trust or the monopoly? For when I use the word trust I use it in the sense that the trust means monopoly. What is the purpose of monopoly? You can find out from the speeches made by those who are connected with the trusts. I have here a speech made by Charles R. Flint at Boston on the 25th day of last May, and the morning papers of the 26th in describing the meeting said he defended trust principles before an exceedingly sympathetic audience, and then added: "For his audience was composed almost exclusively of Boston bankers." "We thus secure," he says, "the advantages of larger aggregations of capital and ability; if I am asked what they are the answer is only difficult because the list is so long."

But I want now to read to you a few of the advantages to be derived by the trusts from the trust system. "Raw material bought in large quantities is secured at lower prices." That is the first advantage. One man to buy wool for all the woolen manufacturers. That means that every man who sells wool must sell it at the price fixed by this one purchaser in the United States. The first thing is to lower the price of raw material. The great majority of the people are engaged in the production of raw material and in the purchase of finished products. Comparatively few can stand at the head of syndicates and monopolies and secure the profits from them. Therefore, the first advantage of a monopoly is to lower the price of the raw material furnished by the people. Note the next advantage: "Those plants which are best equipped and most advantageously situated are run continuously and in preference to those less favored."

The next thing, after they have bought all the factories, is to close some of them and to turn out of employment the men who are engaged in them. If you will go about over the country you will see where people have subscribed money to establish enterprises, and where these enterprises, having come under the control of the trusts, have been closed and stand now as silent monuments of the trust system.

Behold the next advantage: "In case of local strikes and fires, the work goes on elsewhere, thus preventing serious loss." Do not the laboring men understand what that means? "In case of local strikes or fires the work goes on elsewhere, thus preventing serious loss." What does it mean? It means that if the people employed in one factory are not satisfied with the terms fixed by the employer and strike, the trust can close that factory and let the employees starve while work goes on in other factories without loss to the manufacturers.

It means that when the trust has frozen out the striking employees in one factory and compelled them to return to work at any price to secure bread for their wives and children it can provoke a strike somewhere else and freeze the workmen out there. When a branch of industry is entirely in the hands of one great monopoly, so that every skilled man in that industry has to go to the one man for employment, then that one man will fix wages as he pleases and the laboring men will share the suffering of the man who sells the raw materials.

"There is no multiplication of the means of distribution and a better force of salesmen takes the place of a large number." That is the next advantage named. I want to warn you that when the monopoly has absolute control, brains will be at a discount, and relatives will be found to fill these positions. When there is competition every employer has to get a good man to meet competition, but when there is no competition anybody can sit in the office and receive letters and answer them because everybody has to write to the same house for anything he wants. There is no question about it. A trust, a monopoly, can lessen the cost of distribution. But when it does so society has no assurance that it will get any of the benefits from that reduction of cost. But you will take away the necessity for skill and brains. You will take away the stimulus that has given to us the quick, the ever alert commercial traveler. These commercial evangelists, who go from one part of the country to the other proclaiming the merits of their respective goods, will not be needed, because when anybody wants merchandise all he has to do is to write to the one man who has the article for sale, and say, "What will you let me have it for to-day?"

And here is another advantage: "Terms and conditions of sale become more uniform and credit can be more safely granted." The trust can not only fix the price of what it sells, but it can fix the terms upon which it sells. You can pay cash, or, if there is a discount, it is just so much discount, and you have to trust to the manager's generosity as to what is fair when he is on one side and you on the other. I have read some of the advantages which a great trust magnate thinks will come to the trust.

What is the first thing to be expected of a trust? That it will cut down expenses. What is the second? That it will raise prices. We have not had in this country a taste of a complete trust, a complete monopoly, and we cannot tell what will be the results of a complete monopoly by looking at the results that have followed from an attempt to secure a monopoly. A corporation may lower prices to rid itself of competitors; but when it has rid itself of competitors, what is going to be the result? My friends, all you have to know is human nature. God made men selfish. I do not mean to say that He made a mistake when He did, because selfishness is merely the outgrowth of an instinct of self-preservation. It is the abnormal development of a man's desire to protect himself; but everybody who knows human nature knows how easy it is to develop that side of a man's being. Occasionally I find a man who says he is not selfish, but when I do, I find a man who can prove it only by his own affidavit.

We get ideas from every source. An idea is the most important thing that a man can get into his head. An idea will control a man's life. An idea will revolutionize a community, a state, a nation, the world. And we never know when we are going to get an idea. Sometimes we get them when we not want to get them, and sometimes we get them from sources which would not be expected to furnish ideas. We get them from our fellow men. We get them from inanimate nature. We get them from the animals about us. I got a valuable idea once from some hogs. I was riding through Iowa and saw some hogs rooting in a field. The first thought that came to me was that. those hogs were destroying a great deal in value, and then my mind ran back to the time when I lived upon a farm and when we had hogs.

Then I thought of the way in which we used to protect property from the hogs by putting rings in the noses of the hogs; and then the question came to me, why did we do it? Not to keep the hogs from getting fat, for we were more interested in their getting fat than they were; the sooner they got fat the sooner we killed them; the longer they were in getting fat the longer they lived. But why did we put the rings in their noses? So that while they were getting fat they would not destroy more than they were worth. And then the thought came to me that one of the great purposes of government was to put rings in the noses of hogs. I don't mean to say anything offensive, but we are all hoggish. In hours of temptation we are likely to trespass upon the rights of others.

I believe in self-government. I believe in the doctrines that underlie this government; I believe that people are capable of governing themselves. Why? Because in their sober moments they have helped to put rings in their own noses, to protect others from themselves and themselves from others in hours of temptation. And so I believe we must recognize human nature. We must recognize selfishness and we must so make our laws that people shall not be permitted to trespass upon the rights of others in their efforts to secure advantages for themselves.

I believe society is interested in the independence of every citizen. I wish we might have a condition where every adult who died might die leaving to his widow and children enough property for the education of his children and the support of his widow. Society is interested in this because if a man dies and leaves no provisions for his wife and children the burden falls upon society. But while I wish to see every person secure for himself a competency, I don't want him to destroy more than he is worth while he is doing that. And I believe the principle of monopoly finds its inspiration in the desire of men to secure by monopoly what they cannot secure in the open field of competition. In other words, if I were going to try to find the root of the monopoly evil I would do as I have often had occasion to do—go back to the bible for an explanation—and I would find it in the declaration that the love of money is the root of all evil.

I will not ask you all to agree with me; we have not met here as a body of men who agree. We have met here as a body of men who are seeking light and each ought to be willing to hear what every other person has to say, and each of us should desire the triumph of that which is true more than the triumph of that which he may think be true.

Let me repeat that the primary cause of monopoly is the love of money and the desire to secure the fruits of monopoly, but I believe that falling prices, caused by the rising dollar, have contributed to this desire and intensified it, because people, seeing the fall in prices and measuring the loss of investments, have looked about for some means to protect themselves from this loss, and they have joined in combinations to hold up prices to protect their investments from a loss which would not have occurred but for the rise in the value of dollars and the fall in the level of prices.

Another thing that, in my judgment, has aided monopoly is a high tariff. Nobody can dispute that a tariff law, an import duty, enables a trust to charge for its product the price of a similar foreign product plus the tariff.

Now some have suggested that to put everything on the free list that trusts make would destroy the trusts. I do not agree with this statement, as it is made so broadly. I believe that the high tariff has been the means of extortion and that it has aided trusts to collect more than they otherwise could collect. But I do not believe you could destroy all trusts by putting all trust made articles on the free list. Why? Because, if an article can be produced in this country as cheaply as it can be produced abroad the trust could exist without the aid of any tariff, although it could not extort so much as it could with the tariff. While some relief may come from modifications of the tariff, we cannot destroy monopoly until we lay the axe at the root of the tree and make monopoly impossible by law.

It has been suggested that discrimination by railroads has aided the trusts. No question about it. If one man can secure from a railroad better rates than another man, he will be able to run the other man out of business. And there is no question that discrimination and favoritism secured by one corporation against a rival have been largely instrumental in enabling the favored corporation to secure practically a complete monopoly. Now that can be remedied by laws that will prevent this discrimination, but when we prevent the discrimination, when we place every producer upon the same footing and absolutely prevent favoritism, monopoly may still exist. The remedy must go farther. It must be complete enough to prevent the organization of a monopoly.

Now what can be done to prevent the organization of a monopoly? I think we differ more in remedy than we do in our opinion of the trust. I venture the opinion that few people will defend monopoly as a principle, or a trust organization as a good thing, but I imagine our great difference will be as to remedy, and I want, for a moment, to discuss the remedy.

We have a dual form of government. We have a state government and a federal government, and while this dual form of government has its advantages, and to my mind advantages which can hardly be overestimated, yet it also has its disadvantages. When you prosecute a trust in the United States court it hides behind state sovereignty, and when you prosecute it in the state court it rushes to cover under federal jurisdiction—and we have had some difficulty in determining a remedy.

I believe we ought to have remedies in both state and nation, and that they should be concurrent remedies. In the first place, every state has, or should have, the right to create any private corporation which in the judgment of the people of the state is

502

conducive to the welfare of the people of that state. I believe we can safely intrust to the people of a state the settlement of a question which concerns them. If they create a corporation and it becomes destructive of their best interests they can destroy that corporation, and we can safely trust them both to create and annihilate if conditions make annihilations necessary. In the second place the state has, or should have, the right to prohibit any foreign corporation from doing business in the state, and it has or should have the right to impose such restrictions and limitations as the people of the state may think necessary upon foreign corporations doing business in the state. In other words, the people of the state not only should have a right to create the corporations they want, but they should be permitted to protect themselves against any outside corporation.

But I do not think this is sufficient. I believe, in addition to a state remedy, there must be a federal remedy, and I believe Congress has, or should have, the power to place restrictions and limitations, even to the point of prohibition, upon any corporation organized in any state that wants to do business outside of the state. I say that Congress has, or should have, power to place upon the corporation such limitations and restrictions, even to the point of prohibition, as may to Congress seem necessary for the protection of the public.

Now I believe that these concurrent remedies will prove effective. To repeat, the people of every state shall first decide whether they want to create a corporation; they shall also decide whether they want any outside corporation to do business in the state, and if so, upon what conditions; and then Congress shall exercise the right to place upon every corporation doing business outside of the state in which it is organized such limitations and restrictions as may be necessary for the protection of the public.

I do not believe that the people of one state can rely upon the people of another state in the management of corporations. And I will give you a reason. I have here a letter that was sent out by a Delaware corporation with an office in New York. It is a most remarkable document, the most remarkable document on this subject that has ever fallen under my observation. We have talked about the state of New Jersey having a law favorable to trusts. I have a letter here which shows that in Delaware they adopted a law for the purpose of making Delaware more friendly to the trusts than New Jersey. Let me read the letter. It is a little long, but it will repay reading.

"The state of Delaware has just adopted the most favorable of existing general corporation laws, one marking a forward step in the evolution of corporations. It does not encourage reckless incorporation nor permit the existence of wild-cat companies, but it furnishes at the least expense ample rights to stockholders, and reduces restrictions upon corporate action to the minimum. The enactment is not the result, as in the case of most states, of hesitating, halting, enacting, amending and repealing, but is a logical and systematic measure framed by a committee of able lawyers appointed by the legislature to examine the various statutes of the various states and prepare a bill which should embody the good and eliminate the bad points of existing law. The law is based broadly upon that of the state of New Jersey, and embraces all the beneficial provisions and safeguards found in the laws of that state. It has, however, in many respects advanced far beyond New Jersey, and makes Delaware a much more attractive home for business corporations. In the following salient provisions the Delaware and New Jersey law are substantially identical, namely: Any three persons may organize a corporation; second, it may engage in any lawful business excepting banking; third, its existence may be perpetual or limited; fourth, it may purchase and deal in real or personal property wherever situated and to any desired amount; fifth, it may be a mortgagee or mortgagor; sixth, it may conduct business anywhere in the world; seventh, stock may be issued for property purchased (and in Delaware for services rendered) and in the absence of fraud the judgment of the directors as to the value of such property or services is conclusive; eighth, it may easily wind up its affairs and dissolve itself; ninth, its authorized capital stock need not be more than $2,000 and only $1,000 of this need be subscribed for; tenth, the amount of capital stock which it may issue is unlimited; eleventh, it may file its certificate of incorporation and even commence business before any sum whatever is paid in; twelfth, it may have different classes of stock, with different privileges or restrictions; thirteenth, the charter may be easily amended; fourteenth, only one director need be a resident of Delaware; fifteenth, the capital stock may be easily diminished or increased; sixteenth, the corporation may be readily merged or consolidated into other corporations; seventeenth, it may own and vote upon the stock of other corporations; eighteenth, the incorporators may or may not limit the authority of the directors as to the liabilities.

"The Delaware law possesses the following decided advantages: First, the original fee to be paid for incorporation is small—about three-fourths of that in New Jersey, for instance; second, the annual tax is very small, one-half that in New Jersey.

Delaware is a small state, and does not need a very large revenue. Third, stockholders and directors may hold their meetings wherever they please, and need never meet in the state of Delaware. (New Jersey stockholders must meet in that state)." You see it is a decided advantage over the New Jersey law in that respect. "Fourth, the original stock and transfer books (which in a New Jersey corporation must be kept in the state), may be kept in or out of Delaware in the discretion of the company. Fifth, the examination of the books by intermeddlers is much more difficult under the Delaware law than under the laws of any other state.

"Sixth, the liability of the stockholders is absolutely limited when the stock has once been issued for cash, property or services. Seventh, stock may be issued in compensation for services rendered, and in the absence of fraud in the transaction, the judgment of the directors as to the value of such services is conclusive. (In New Jersey authority is given to issue stock for property, but not for service). Eighth, for certain important classes of corporations, as, for instance, railroads, railway, telegraph, cable, electric light, steam heating, power, gas piping lines, and sleeping car companies, the advantage is still more marked."

I wish we had some way of knowing what the additional advantages are after having read the ordinary advantages.

"Ninth, the annual report of a Delaware corporation is required to give no secret or confidential information.

"Tenth, the certificate need not show nor need public record be in any way made of the amount of stock subscribed by any incorporator."

And then the letter adds: "This company is authorized to act as the agent and trustee of corporations organized under the Delaware law. It will maintain the principal office of the company in Delaware and keep an agent in charge within the state. It is formed for the purpose of facilitating the incorporation of companies in Delaware, and of aiding them to comply, at a minimum expense, with the requirements of the Delaware law. We are ready to aid and give full information to incorporators or their counsel. We do not interfere between attorney and client. We do not conduct a law business. Copies of the Delaware law, blank forms of information concerning Delaware corporations furnished on application.

"All communications to us are confidential."

A voice from the gallery—Colonel, Delaware and New Jersey are both Democratic states, are they not?

Mr. Bryan—They were not in 1896.

Another voice from the gallery—Has the gentleman any more questions to put?

Mr. Bryan—I am very glad to have questions asked, because we are seeking the truth.

I have read you this letter in order to show you that where a state can gain an advantage from the incorporation of these great aggregations of wealth, it is not safe to place the people of other states at the tender mercies of the people of such a state as may desire to collect its running expenses from the taxation of corporations organized to prey upon people outside.

I read the letter to show how impossible it is for the people in one state to depend for protection upon the people in another state; and while, as I say, I believe the people of every state should have the power to create corporations and to restrain, to limit, and, if necessary, to annihilate, yet I believe that no complete remedy will be found for the trust until the federal government, with a power sufficiently comprehensive to reach into every nook and corner of the country, lays its hands upon these trusts and declares that they shall no longer exist.

I am here to hear, to receive information, and to adopt any method that anybody can propose that looks to the annihilation of the trusts.

One method has occurred to me, and to me it seems a complete method. It may not commend itself to you. If you have something better I shall accept it in the place of this which I am about to suggest. But the method that occurs to me is this: That Congress should pass a law providing that no corporation organized in any state should do business outside of the state in which it is organized until it receives from some power created by Congress a license authorizing it to do business outside of its own state. Now, if the corporation must come to this body created by Congress to secure permission to do business outside of the state, then the license can be granted upon conditions which will, in the first place, prevent the watering of stock; in the second place, prevent monopoly in any branch of business, and, third, provide for publicity as to all of the transactions and business of the corporation.

A voice—Colonel, would such a law be constitutional?

Mr. Bryan—I was going to come to that. I am glad you mentioned it. What I mean to say is that Congress ought to pass such a law. If it is unconstitutional and so declared by the Supreme Court, I am in favor of an amendment to the Constitution that will give to Congress power to destroy every trust in the country. The first condition which I suggest is that no water should be allowed in the stock. I do not agree with those who say it is a matter entirely immaterial whether a corporation has water in its stock or not. It may be true that in the long run, if you are able to run as long as the corporation can, the stock will fall to its natural level, but during all that time the harm goes on; during all that time the trust demands the right to collect dividends upon capital represented by no money whatever. I do not believe that any state should permit the organization of a corporation with a single drop of water in the stock of that corporation. The farmer cannot inflate the value of his land by watering the value of that land. The merchant in the store cannot inflate the value of the goods upon his shelves. Why should the corporation be permitted to put out stock that represents no real value?

Why, there are instances where there are $4 of water for $1 of money.

A voice—Seven.

Mr. Bryan—Yes, a man suggests seven. Do I hear a higher bid? I have known it to be twelve—but I am a conservative man, and I must maintain my reputation. No man can defend stock that does not represent money invested, and only in the case of a monopoly can you secure dividends upon stock that does not represent money invested.

We had a law in Nebraska that was intended to regulate railroad rates. One railroad in our state was capitalized and bonded for more than five times what it would cost to duplicate the road, and yet the judge held that in fixing rates and in determining what was fair compensation for the railroad, we had to consider the watered stock as well as the actual value of that road, and when the case went to the Supreme Court, the Supreme Court rendered a decision which, while I cannot quote its exact language, was in substance this: That in determining what was a reasonable rate we had to take into consideration a number of things besides the present value of that road, measured by the cost of reproduction. If the watering of the stock is permitted, then the cry of the innocent purchaser is raised, and you will be told that you must protect the man who bought the stock. No man ought to stand in the position of an innocent purchaser who buys stock in a corporation, if that stock does not represent actual money invested, because he can find out what the stock stands for if he will only investigate, but, as a matter of fact, the holders of watered stock are able to collect dividends. Now, if this license is granted, then the first condition can be that any corporation desiring to do business outside of the state in which it is organized shall bring to that board or body proof that that stock is *bona fide* and that there is no water in it. In my judgment, when you take from monopoly the power to issue stock not represented by money, you will go more than half the way toward destroying monopoly in the United States.

The law should provide for publicity. As has been well said by men who have spoken here, corporations cannot claim that they have a right, or that it is necessary, to cover their transactions with secrecy, and when you provide for publicity so that the public can know just what there is in the corporation, just what it is doing, and just what it is making, you will take another long step toward the destruction of monopoly.

But I am not willing to stop there. I do not want to go one or two steps, I want to go all the way and make a monopoly absolutely impossible. And, therefore, as a third condition, I suggest that this license shall not be granted until the corporation shows that it has not had a monopoly, and is not attempting a monopoly of any branch of industry or of any article of merchandise—and then provide that if the law is violated the license can be revoked. I do not believe in the government giving privileges to be exercised by a corporation without reserving the right to withdraw them when those privileges become hurtful to the people.

Now, I may be mistaken, but as I have studied the subject it has seemed to me that this method of dealing with the trusts would prove an effective method, but if you once establish the system and require the license, then Congress can, from year to year, add such new conditions as may be necessary for the protection of the public from the greed and avarice of great aggregations of wealth. I do not go so far as some do and say that there shall be no private corporations, but I say this, that a corporation is created by law, that it is created for the public good and that it should never be permitted to do a thing that is injurious to the public, and that if any corporation enjoys any privileges to-day which are hurtful to the public those privileges ought to be withdrawn from it. In other words, I am willing that we should first see whether we can preserve the benefits of the corporation and take from it its possibilities for harm.

A delegate—Would you apply that to rich individuals also, suppose Rockefeller did it on his own account?

Mr. Bryan—We have not reached a point yet where an individual has been able to do harm, and, in my judgment, if we would abolish those laws that grant special privileges and make some men the favorites of the government, no man, by his own brain and muscle, could ever earn enough money to be harmful to the people.

A delegate—What will you say to the banks reporting five hundred millions of money in the vaults and four billions of loans?

Mr. Bryan—Well, I would say it would not be safe to have all the loans collected at once.

Following out the suggestion the gentleman has made, I want to add to what I have said to this extent: My contention is that we have been placing the dollar above the man; that we have been picking out favorites and bestowing upon them special privileges, and every advantage we have given them has been given them to the detriment of other people. My contention is that there is a vicious principle running through the various policies which we have been pursuing; that in our taxation we have been imposing upon the great struggling masses the burden of government, while we have been voting the privileges to a few people who will not pay their share of the expenses of the government.

Every unjust tax law is an indirect form of larceny. If, for instance, a man who ought to pay $10 only pays $5, and one who ought to pay only $5 pays $10, the law that compels this contribution from these two men virtually takes $5 from one man's pocket and puts that $5 into the other man's pocket, and I have claimed that when we collected our taxes we were making the poor people pay not only their own share, but the share of the men whom they have no chance to meet at the summer resorts. I have been gratified to note the progress that you have been making in Illinois towards more equitable distribution of the burdens of government. I heard it stated that there was a time only a few years ago when the agricultural implements owned by the farmers living within the city limits of Chicago were assessed for more than all the money in Chicago returned for taxation by private citizens. I do not know whether it was true or not, but I saw it stated as a fact. There are some people who have visible property, others who have invisible property, and the visible property is always taxed. The invisible property has too often escaped, and as a result the people owning visible property have not only paid their own taxes, but the taxes that should have been paid by the owners of invisible property. I have advocated an income tax because I believe it the most just tax. I do not mention it to argue the question here, because I want to avoid the discussion of any questions that might be considered partisan. If the government will quit picking out favorites and follow the doctrine of equal rights to all and special privileges to no man—I have no fear that any man by his own brain or his own muscle will be able to secure a fortune so great as to be a menace to the welfare of his fellow men. If we secure a government whose foundations are laid in justice and laws exemplifying the doctrine of equality before the law, if we can secure such a government and such laws, and wealth is then accumulated to a point where it becomes dangerous, we can meet that question when it arises, and I am willing to trust the wisdom of society to meet every question that arises, and remedy every wrong.

Sigmund Zeisler (Attorney, Chicago)—What will you do, colonel, with the multi-millionaires that already exist? Suppose they should hold and acquire all the industries, all the factories, and particularly industries?

Colonel Bryan—Do you mean before our laws go into operation?

Mr. Zeisler—The multi-millionaires that already exist.

Colonel Bryan—In the first place, private individuals have not been able to secure monopolies, and are not likely to do so. As to the multi-millionaires now in existence, I would wait and see whether they would die off soon enough to relieve the country of danger. Life is short. If, however, their accumulations should become a menace, I would then consider what measures would be necessary for the protection of society. And this brings me to what I regard as a very important branch of this subject. I am glad the question was asked; it calls attention to the difference between an individual and a corporation. Every trust rests upon a corporation—at least that rule is so nearly universal that I think we can accept it as a basis for legislation. Every trust rests upon a corporation, and every corporation is a creature of law. The corporation is a man-made man.

When God made man as the climax of creation he looked upon his work and said that it was good, and yet when God finished his work the tallest man was not much taller than the shortest, and the strongest man was not much stronger than the weakest. That was God's plan. We looked upon his work and said that it was not quite as good as it might be, and so we made a fictitious person called a corporation that is in some instances a hundred times—a thousand times—a million times stronger than the God-made man. Then we started this man-made giant out among the God-made men. When God made man he placed a limit to his existence, so that if he was a bad man he could not do harm long, but when we made our man-made man we raised the limit as to age. In some states a corporation is given perpetual life.

When God made man he breathed into him a soul and warned him that in the next world he would be held accountable for the deeds done in the flesh, but when we made our man-made man we did not give him a soul, and if he can avoid punishment in this world he need not worry about the hereafter.

My contention is that the government that created must retain control, and that the man-made man must be admonished: "Remember now thy Creator in the days of thy youth"—and throughout thy entire life.

Let me call your attention again to this distinction. We are not dealing with the natural man; we are not dealing with natural rights. We are dealing with the man-made man and artificial privileges.

What government gives, the government can take away. What the government creates, it can control; and I insist that both the state government and the federal government must protect the God-made man from the man-made man.

I have faith that these questions will be settled and settled right, but I want to protest against this doctrine that the trust is a natural outgrowth of natural laws. It is not true. This trust is the natural outgrowth of unnatural conditions created by man-made laws. There are some who would defend everything good or bad, on the ground that it is destiny—and that you cannot inquire into it. The fact that it is, proves that it is right; the fact that it is, proves that it has come to stay, and the argument most frequently made in defense of a vicious system is not that it is right and ought to stay, but that it has come to stay whether you like it or not. I say that that is the argument that is usually advanced in behalf of an error—it is here, it has come to stay—what are you going to do about it?

I believe that, in a civilized society, the question is not what is, but what ought to be—and that every proposition must be arraigned at the bar of reason. If you can prove that a thing is good, let it stay, but if you cannot prove that it is good you cannot hide behind the assertion that it is here and that you cannot get rid of it. I believe that the American people can get rid of anything that they do not want—and that they ought to get rid of everything that is not good. I believe that it is the duty of every citizen to give to his countrymen the benefit of his conscience and his judgment, and cast his influence, be it small or great, upon the right side of every question that arises. In the determination of questions we should find out what will make our people great and good and strong rather than what will make them rich. "A good name is rather to be chosen than great

511

riches." Shall we decide the ethics of larceny by discussing how much the man is going to steal or the chances of his getting caught? No, my friends, we must decide questions upon a higher ground, and if you were to prove to me that a monopoly would reduce the price of the articles that we have to purchase, I would still be opposed to it for a reason, which to my mind overshadows all pecuniary arguments. The reason is this: Put the industrial system of this nation in the hands of a few men, and let them determine the price of raw material, the price of the finished product, and the wages paid to labor, and you will have an industrial aristocracy beside which a landed aristocracy would be an innocent thing.

I may be in error, but, in my judgment, a government of the people, by the people, and for the people, will be impossible when a few men control all the sources of production and dole out daily bread to all the rest on such terms as the few may prescribe. I believe that this nation is the hope of the world. I believe that the Declaration of Independence was the grandest document ever penned by human hands. The truths of that declaration are condensed into four great propositions: That all men are created equal; that they are endowed with inalienable rights; that governments are instituted among men to preserve those rights, and that governments derive their just powers from the consent of the governed. Such a government is impossible under an industrial aristocracy. Place the food and clothing, all that we eat and wear and use, in the hands of a few people, and instead of it being a government of the people, it will be a government of the syndicates, by the syndicates, and for the syndicates. Establish such a government, and the people will soon be powerless to secure a legislative remedy for any abuse. Establish such a system, and on the night before election the employees will be notified not to come back on the day after election unless the trusts' candidate is successful. Establish such a government, and instead of giving the right of suffrage to the people, you will virtually give the right of suffrage to the heads of monopolies, with each man empowered to vote as many times as he has employees. I am not willing to place the laboring men of this country absolutely at the mercy of the heads of monopolies. I am not willing to place the men who produce the raw material absolutely in the hands of the monopolies because when you control the price that a man is to receive for what he produces, you control the price that he is to receive for his labor in the production of that thing.

The farmer has no wages, except as wages are measured by

the price of his product; and when you place it in the power of the trust to fix the price of what the farmer sells, you place it in the power of the trust to lower the wages that the farmer receives for his work; and when you place it in the power of the trust to raise the price of what he buys, you do the farmer a double injury, because he burns the candle at both ends and suffers when he sells to the trust, and again when he buys of the trust.

Some people have tried to separate the laboring man who works in the factory from the laboring man who works on the farm. I want to warn the laboring men in the factories that they cannot separate themselves from those who toil on the farm without inviting their own destruction. I beg the laboring men in the factories not to join with the monopolies to crush the farmer, for as soon as the farmer is crushed the laboring man will be crushed, and in a test of endurance the farmer will stand it longer than the laboring man.

I come from an agricultural state, one of the great agricultural states of this nation, and I want to say to you that while our people are, I believe, a unit against the trusts, we can stand the trusts longer than the laboring man can; we can stand all the vicious policies of government longer than the laboring man can. The farmer was the first man on the scene when civilization began, and he will be the last one to disappear. The farmer wants to own his home; he ought to own it. I think that this nation is safer the larger the proportion of home owners. I want every man with a family to own his home, the farmer wants to own his home, but if you will not allow him to own his home he can rent. He will have to be employed to work the farm.

Take his farm from him by mortgage if you like, but the man who forecloses the mortgage and buys the property will not work the farm. He will need the farmer to work for him, and he will have to give the farmer enough to live on or the farmer cannot work. When prices fall so low that the farmer cannot buy coal he can burn corn. But when prices fall so low that the coal miner cannot buy corn, he cannot eat coal. You can drive the farmer down so that he cannot buy factory made goods, but his wife can do like the wife of old—make the clothing for the family off of the farm, but when you close your factories it will take all of the accumulated wealth of the cities to feed the people brought to the point of starvation by vicious, greedy, avaricious legislation.

But, my friends, why should we try to see who can hold out the longest in suffering? Why try to see who can endure the most hardships and yet live? Why not try to see who can contribute most to the greatness and to the glory and to the prosperity of this nation? Why not vie with each other to see who can contribute most to make this government what the fathers intended it to be? For one hundred years this nation has been the light of the world. For one hundred years the struggling people of all nations have looked to this nation for hope and inspiration. Let us settle these great questions; let us teach the world the blessing of a government that comes from the people, let us show them how happy and how prosperous people can be. God made all men, and he did not make some to crawl on hands and knees and others to ride upon their backs. Let us show what can be done when we put into actual practice the great principles of human equality and of equal rights. Then this nation will fulfill its holy mission and lead the other nations step by step in the progress of the human race toward a higher civilization.

Twice after he had finally pushed his way through the crowd which rushed forward to congratulate him, did Mr. Bryan have to rise and bow his acknowledgments of the applause which ensued when he had finished speaking. It was some minutes before the chair could restore quiet and introduce James H. Raymond, of Chicago, who speaking on "Monopolies Under Patents and the Industrial Effects Thereof," said:

JAMES H. RAYMOND.
Chicago Patent Law Association.

General and unlimited propositions with reference to our present existence and to proper governmental relations, no matter how glittering, are quite unsafe to follow.

To cite Garfield, it must be remembered that the dead level of the sea, from which all heights and depths are measured, still remains.

The subject assigned to me is: "Monopolies under Patents and the Industrial Effects Thereof."

The broad statement that "all monopolies are odious" has been oft repeated, but, since the days of Magna Charta, has been little less than obnoxious to all well informed and right thinking men.

A corollary to this proposition, which is a little aside from my subject, yet worthy of note, is this: Modern history has abundantly demonstrated and the established law of this and of other lands is this, that all laws, regulations and established customs, which are, in a general sense, in restraint of trade and are restrictions upon free and unlimited competition, are not illegal and are not unwholesome. Only such laws, regulations and established customs as, either temporarily or permanently, are contrary to the general welfare of society, and are clearly shown so to be, should be prohibited.

Certain theorists to the contrary notwithstanding, from the days of tribal relations to the present day, all society or association of human beings, all laws and all governments are, in the very nature of things, and for all time will be, based upon the difference between *meum* and *tuum* or upon the fundamental idea of personal possession and exclusive property rights.

I can have no argument with, and it is difficult to exercise even a mental sympathy for, those iconoclasts, who, traversing these historic truths and denying all doctrines of exclusive rights and privileges, are attempting to pull down the pillars which sustain the framework of all civilized society. In all right basic theories of sociology, the foundation of the structure is human nature as we find it to have been, to be and to continue. The pillars upon this foundation are three: First, the individual consent to be associated with others for common purposes; second, the reservation of individual rights and liberties, which shall not interfere with the personal rights and liberties of the associates or traverse the necessary police powers of government; and, third and foremost, as to industrial or commercial considerations, the right to individual property and exclusive privileges.

All right economic conclusions have a common dual premise, clearly sounding in two questions, namely: First, What are the basic conditions of our present existence as they have been throughout historic times and are likely to be? And, second (those conditions being truthfully stated), What do the laws of thought require as conclusions concerning any plan for the future? The stern facts of our present existence and our experiences are the lamps which must, with honest thought, rather than with vagaries and theories and fads which have no relation thereto, guide our individual and our cosmic future.

My next proposition, which certainly is self-evident, is this, namely, that progress in science and in the useful arts is desirable.

For the purpose of promoting progress in science and in the useful arts, the framers of our federal Constitution, with characters which came from the cradle of suffering and were molded by pious purposes, fully familiar with the then effete institutions of the Old World, where monarchy or imperialism, in one form or another, then prevailed, and at a time when the most civilized nation on earth, our mother country, old England, was operating under an unwritten constitution, instead of the code, with which it is now struggling—at such a time inspired men compiled and created an instrument greater, broader, deeper, higher and more lasting in its effects than Magna Charta, because it dealt less with temporary conditions and more with the uttermost of the principles of individual sovereignty and personal liberty—at such a time and under such conditions these inspired men in the United States Constitution, as a paragraph in Section 8 of Article I, gave to our Congress the following legislative power:

"To promote the progress of science and the useful arts. by securing, for a limited time, to authors and inventors the exclusive right to their respective writings and discoveries."

That written Constitution remains to-day as the safeguard of our liberties and as the basis of all our political and social institutions.

Many amendments have been made to it, but none have, even indirectly, affected the provision I have quoted. It has been embodied and emphasized in many acts of Congress, which have been uniformly in furtherance of its purpose and provisions; but its purposes have been thwarted and its provisions have been disregarded by foolish resolutions of mass-meetings and by some decisions of our federal courts containing "judge-made law."

A proper and a profitable answer to any question depends upon the proper putting of the question. Let me ask some questions, and leave them with you to answer:

Was this constitutional provision a wise one?

Has the first century of our existence demonstrated that operations under it have contributed to our progress in science, in arts and in comforts?

Has our patent system aided us in our competition with other groups of humanity under other governments?

Has it markedly contributed to all of the other governmental institutions of which we boast; and

Can we separate it from any line of our progress since the time when George Washington, Thomas Jefferson, and the attorney-general signed the first letters patent for an invention, which pertained to "Matrices in Printing," on the 31st day of January, 1791?

There can be no equivocation as to the proper answers to these questions.

Our present internal disturbances require, and especially on occasions like this, that such fundamental questions should be asked, rather than questions which relate to this temporary association of capital or to that union of particular interests in some line of labor, dominated, as most of the unions are, by a brainy individual or two.

Temporary irruptions have, from time to time, appeared upon our body politic, some of which have affected our patent system. New ones are there now. They itch and are distressing and, for the most part, are promoted by doctrinaires and theorists, by seekers for office, or by others who have no visible means of support. We may, however, congratulate ourselves that, as a rule, these irruptions cure themselves without the aid of the administration of violent drugs, and they purify the blood.

In connection with my subject, I specially refer to the "granger movement," which began in 1870-71 with an onslaught upon the railroads and which provoked, and was immediately followed, by the "Grangers," with an onslaught upon our patent system.

Blackmailers put up at hotels at county-seats throughout the middle and the then western states. They sent their "walking-delegates" throughout the county to find farmers who had driven a pipe into the ground to reach water. The agent then sent formal notices, couched in legal cant, to the farmers that they had infringed the "Driven Well Patent" granted to Mr. Green (who really was an inventor and was entitled to a reward), and the notice was that the farmer must appear at the hotel and pay so much per pipe or he would be sued in a United States court twenty, and, in some cases, one hundred and fifty miles from his habitat.

The walking-delegates of those days in those matters were called "patent sharks." That race has become extinct, and we do not now even hear that name any more.

The frown of public sentiment stopped the nefarious practices, of which I have cited an example, and, during the decades ending with 1890, they practically ceased to exist, because the irruptions were cured by their own virus and our patent system has remained during the present decade, with constitutional foundations, as a permanent institution of our social fabric and as a primary factor in our industrial progress.

Is not this part of our history a demonstration of the conclusion that all monopolies, which are contrary to the public good and are really obnoxious, are necessarily so exercised as that they, without unnecessary agitation and public disturbances, are buried by their own weight or are killed by their own virus, leaving behind them purified business conditions?

Certainly no monopolies in the world have such sure foundations as the ones of which I am speaking, and history shows that, if they be abused in their exercise and thereby become obnoxious, they individually die a natural death, leaving the institution which created them for the public good, quite intact.

Let us now pause to state two facts and to ask two questions concerning them, which further questions also need not be now answered in words:

First—In 1873 the balance between our exports and our imports was a balance against us of one hundred and twenty million dollars, and on June 30, 1899, the balance was five hundred and thirty million dollars in our favor.

Has not the encouragement of our patent system been a prime factor in bringing about this marvelous change?

Second—Our inventors have been taxed by fees for the support of the patent office in an excess over the expenditures allowed by Congress for that office, with this result, that there now remains in the federal treasury a balance of these fees, as of December 31, 1898, of $4,972,976.34, and the Congress continues to treat that department most niggardly, and unintelligent and uninformed people are carping at its work.

The question, which I leave unanswered, as to this plain statement of facts, may be stated in a homely manner thus:

Has not Congress and some of our courts and some of the associations of our people, in a very midnight of darkness of information and thought, made staggering blows, blindly and insanely attempting to kill the goose which has laid most of our golden eggs?

The first patent law under the constitutional provision cited was enacted by Congress in 1790. Up to 1836, tinctured somewhat by the old theory of a royal prerogative and grant, the practice was for an inventor to petition and for the officers of the government to pay attention simply to the form of the grant. So patents were then issued.

Although, to some esthetic minds and to some wild theorists and to some associations, it is obnoxious to say that the hope of reward or gain (either in money matters or in the manner of living) is the main incentive to human endeavor, it plainly remains that our history from 1790 to 1836 shows that perfunctory performances under the constitutional provision which I have cited, did not meet its purposes. In 1836 the patent laws were revised, the patent office was organized, a corps of skilled examiners as to what, in the world, was really new and useful was installed, and provisions of law were added by Congress, which were intended to give to real inventors real monopolies.

The nations of the earth are very slowly following the example set by us in 1836. England, though tardy, was the first to follow our example in organizing a corps of examiners as to what was new and useful in her realm. She still lacks the wisdom to give to her inventors some *prima facie* exclusive property rights.

Germany, with great severity as to details, is now traveling on our lines as to inventions, and is about, in this regard, where we were in 1870, at the time of the second revision of our patent laws.

What is the monopoly which an inventor obtains under our laws? This question I shall answer briefly.

The constitutional provision gives him an exclusive right for a limited period. Our court of last resort, the supreme court of the United States, has said in an unbroken line of unanimous decisions, as to which there has been no modification, that, under the Constitution and under the acts of Congress, letters patent for inventions confer upon the recipient of the grant three monopolies, namely, one to make, another to use, and still another to sell. The recipient of the grant, that is, the person or persons to whom the patent may issue, has, under the plain meaning of our laws, the right, for seventeen years, to own, retain, and control his invention, even if he put it in a corner closet behind a Yale lock, or he may "farm out" the same upon such conditions and terms, as to the proper use of his invention in manufacturing, as to the character of the output produced, in whole or in part, by his invention, as to the location where his invention may be used, and as to the prices which shall be charged for that which involves his invention, just as to him may seem meet and profitable. I am not unmindful of recent decisions in federal courts of inferior jurisdiction, which seem to militate, upon their face, against the broad propositions just made. It remains, however, in my opinion, that he who, in this country, has made an invention which has been properly patented, may, for seventeen years, either retain it to himself or "farm it out" upon such terms and conditions as to making, as to using, and as to selling as he may elect, so long as his election shall not be contrary to some great and general public purpose.

Such is the nature of the grant, such is the constitutional provision upon which it is based, and I feel safe in saying that, for the purpose of promoting progress in science, in arts, and in our civilization, this form of monopoly will remain until after the provisions of our national Constitution preserving the right of trial by jury, preventing the deprivation of property except "by due process of law," and prohibiting enactments by State legislatures impairing the obligations of contracts, shall have been worn worse than threadbare.

My further words will be few, and they will relate to the industrial effects of our patent system.

We have received beautiful theories from the savants of other countries, but the practical inventions have been made in this country, and with this result, as to which I challenge contradiction, that in ninety per cent of the artificial and useful products of the world, the Yankee to-day produces, as compared with all other human beings, a better article, at a less cost of production, and he still pays the highest wages. This result, nay, this fact, may possibly in some part be due to tariff laws or to monetary regulations, but I do not believe it, and I do believe that it is the sole result of the encouragement of our patent laws.

It should also now be specifically remarked that, as conceded by all competent writers and economists, the principal reason why greater wages are paid in the United States than anywhere in the world is the fact that, by virtue of the encouragement of our patent system, minor improvements, relating frequently to the smallest details of processes, methods, and machines, have enabled us to reduce the cost of production and to improve the character of the article produced beyond that which producers in any other nation have yet been able successfully to accomplish. And I pause to say that, in view of this plain and prominent fact, any disposition to discourage the patenting of what are sometimes ironically called trifling improvements, and a disposition to annul patents therefor, if the improvement be, in the broadest sense of the terms, new and useful, should be affirmatively and earnestly opposed as being more threatening than any condition of war or any results of war can be.

I venture the statement that more than seventy per cent of the blades in the pocket-knives in this great audience were made and tempered in this country, shipped abroad, stamped, encased in handles and boxes, and reshipped to this country. I forbear to comment upon this fact.

Looking backward through the years of authentic history, we find "the quarry slave scourged, at night, to his dungeon." We find the Oriental, bound, as it were by the queue of his hair to the pole of unintelligent labor, and, in modern times, we find women, both in the domains of England and in continental

THOMAS UPDEGRAFF J. C. HANLEY
T. S. SMITH   AARON JONES
JOHN M. STAHL   JOHN HILL, JR.

Europe, used as mere beasts of burden, not only about the mines, but also where the pig-iron is carried to the furnace.

In our colonial days our grandmothers walked miles per day in winding a thread about a spindle with which they weaved cloth to clothe their children, while to-day our machines, the product of Yankee inventions, register in a few minutes a thousand miles of our grandmothers' tired walks.

Illustrations could be multiplied by ten thousand times ten thousand. We do not for a waking minute of our lives either dress or eat or work or play without using some product of an American invention.

What, then, has brought these distinctive conditions to pass in our country? The plain answer is this:

The workman in our country, be he the carrier of a hod which does not balance on his shoulder, or a bricklayer whose trowel is not handy, or the steamfitter who in his daily toil recognizes the relation between area and pressure—be he laborer, artisan, mechanic, or engineer, unless he be a recent importation or a natural loafer or one who is under the thumb of some irresponsible walking-delegate, either with or without his dinner pail, goes to his work through an atmosphere which makes him think.

The burden of the thought of the American laborer is as to how, possibly, his tools or his machine may be improved, how manual labor may be lessened, how the cost of production may be cheapened, how the product may be bettered—in short, how the dignity of labor may be increased by the continuous addition of the elements of intelligence, thought, experiment, and improvement, with resulting benefits, first, to himself and to his family, and, secondly, to the now very rapidly increasing, shifting, and uncertain cash capital held by the bankers and by the employers.

That the encouragement of our patent laws and the monopolies thereunder have dignified and enriched daily toil ten thousand fold is way beyond any intelligent or honest disputation.

In conclusion, I ask another question, and cannot forbear to give its necessary answer.

What has brought it to pass that the workman, the artisan, the mechanic, or the engineer in our country begins his daily work with such thoughts and with such ambitions?

The plain answer is, the encouragement and the hope of reward, by way of a monopoly for a limited period or of a full and speedy compensation for parting with the monopoly, in whole or in part, which the patent laws of the United States, in no equivocal terms, promise to its people.

I must add that any material interferences in the carrying out of these promises, whether by Congress, by the courts, or by the communes, will degrade labor, will widen the breach between capital and labor, will tend to destroy our mechanical and industrial supremacy, will tend largely, whatever the conditions of peace or war may be, to reverse the balance of trade between our nation and other nations, and will work havoc in all of our boasted institutions.

G. W. NORTHRUP, JR.

Member Illinois Bar.

G. W. Northrup, speaking on "Practical Remedies for Industrial Trusts," said:

It is well worth considering whether the popular belief in the futility of federal legislation, as applied to industrial trusts, and the declarations to that effect so generally made by prominent men, are well founded. At least it is important to inquire upon what, if anything, in the past history of legislation and judicial decision on this subject, such sweeping opinions are based. It would seem as though such conclusions would not have found general acceptance until repeated efforts had been made by the federal government to legislate on the subject, and until all such legislation had proved ineffective on account of some inherent defect in the powers of Congress. But such is far from being the case.

The so-called Sherman anti-trust act of July 2, 1890, constitutes, practically, the only federal legislation on the subject of trusts, monopolies and combinations in restraint of trade. The act makes illegal and prohibits, under penalty of a fine not exceeding five thousand dollars, or imprisonment not exceeding one year, or both, "every contract, combination in the form of trust or otherwise, or conspiracy, in restraint of trade or commerce among the several states or with foreign nations," and every attempt "to monopolize any part of the trade or commerce among the several states or with foreign nations." This language is calculated to create the impression, in the mind of a "layman," that every trust, combination and monopoly which, in the course of its business, dealings, engages in commerce in more than one state, is within the prohibitions of the act. But further consideration demonstrates clearly that this is not the fact. The phrases "among the several states" and "with foreign nations" are copied from the commerce clause of the Constitution, which declares "the Congress shall have power to regulate commerce with foreign nations and among the several states." Long before the passage of the Sherman act, long before the modern trust had made its appearance, this commerce clause had been the subject of repeated judicial consideration, and the phrase "commerce among the several states," had become fixed and crystallized as equivalent to "commerce between the several states"—those acts, dealings and transactions directly involved in effectuating the transfer of persons, property or value across one or more state lines; in short, "interstate commerce," as distinguished from "that commerce which is completely internal, which is carried on between man and man in a state or between different parts of the same state."* It is manifest, then, that the only conspiracies or combinations within the purview of the Sherman act, are conspiracies and combinations to restrain or monopolize either interstate commerce *per se*, and as thus defined, or foreign commerce, or both.

Notwithstanding these obvious considerations, the practical failure of the Sherman act as a repressive measure, has not been generally ascribed to its own inherent limitations. On the contrary, this failure has been charged up with equal vehemence to the indifference or hostility of the executive department on the one hand, and on the other, to adverse "judicial legislation" by the federal courts. If the former charge be well founded, the remedy is obvious. We are satisfied, however, that the judicial decisions which have been rendered involving the scope and application of the Act of 1890, are not justly open to criticism. On the contrary, we assert with confidence, that an examination of these decisions is calculated to inspire a renewed respect for the federal judiciary, and to afford substantial encouragement for the future. It is specially significant that the Supreme Court itself, as late as 1897, denounced in sweeping and emphatic language, the modern trusts, as "combinations of capital, whose purpose in combining is to control the production or manufacture of any particular article in the market, and by such control, dictate the price at which the article shall be sold, the effect being to drive out of business all the small dealers in the commodity and to render the public subject to the decision of the combination as to what price shall be paid for the article." Said the Court: "In this light it is not material that the price of an article may be lowered. It is in the power of the combination to raise it, and the result in any event is unfortunate for the country, by

*Gibbons vs. Ogden, 9 Wheat. (U. S.) 1.

depriving it of the services of a large number of small but independent dealers who were familiar with the business and who had spent their lives in it, and who supported themselves and their families from the small profits realized therein. Whether they be able to find other avenues to earn their livelihood is not so material, because it is not for the real prosperity of any country that such changes should occur which result in transferring an independent business man, the head of his establishment, small though it might be, into a mere servant or agent of a corporation for selling the commodities which he once manufactured or dealt in, having no voice in shaping the business policy of the company and bound to obey orders issued by others. Nor is it for the substantial interests of the country that any one commodity should be within the sole power and subject to the sole will of one powerful combination of capital."*

In the face of these trenchant declarations, the Court can hardly be charged with extreme partiality to trusts. Moreover, whenever a contract or combination, which could be fairly said to lie within the scope of the Sherman act, has come before the Supreme Court, the latter, disregarding the plausible constructions and ingenious objections of eminent counsel, has not hesitated to enforce the provisions of the act in their entirety. In this connection, the Court has declared in forcible terms, the power of Congress to legislate in its own discretion, on the subject of interstate commerce, and the duty of the courts to enforce this legislation, in accordance with the will of the legislative body as expressed in the terms of its enactments.

Most important of all, perhaps, is the express decision in the "Joint Traffic" case, that the Sherman act violates no constitutional guaranties, not even those of the fifth amendment, which declares that no person shall be deprived of life, liberty, or property, without due process of law, and that private property shall not be taken for public use without just compensation. "The latter limitation," said the Court, by Mr. Justice Peckham, "is, we think, plainly irrelevant. . . . The question which arises here is, whether the contract is a proper or lawful one, and we have not advanced a step toward its solution by saying that the citizen is protected by the fifth or any other amendment, in his right to make proper contracts to enable him to carry out his lawful purposes. . . . Notwithstanding the general liberty of contract which is possessed by the citizen under the Constitution, we find that there are many kinds of contracts which, while not in themselves immoral or *mala in se*, may yet be prohibited by the

*United States vs. Trans-Missouri, etc. Assn., 166 U, S. 290.

legislation of the states, or, in certain cases, by Congress. The question comes back whether the statute under review is a legitimate exercise of the power of Congress over interstate commerce and a valid regulation thereof. The question is for us one of power only, and not of policy. We think the power exists in Congress, and that the statute is therefore valid."*

So far, everything seems most favorable, but the concrete fact remains that the Supreme Court, while steadily refusing to fritter away the statute by forced constructions, has also with equal steadfastness declined to enlarge its prohibitions beyond the plain limitations expressed in the wording of the act itself. The Court has twice decided that associations formed to regulate freight rates for interstate traffic, are clearly within these prohibitions. But it was held in the E. C. Knight Company case† that the Sherman act did not apply to contracts by which the American Sugar Refining Company had secured all the corporate stock of four Pennsylvania sugar refining companies, which, together with the American Company, controlled all the sugar refineries of the United States, except one, and manufactured 98 per cent of the refined sugar produced in the country, although it was charged by the government that by means of these contracts, the defendants had secured a complete monopoly of the manufacture and sale of refined sugar throughout the United States, and that in so doing they had combined and conspired to restrain trade and commerce in refined sugar among the several states and with foreign nations. The essential point decided in the case was, that the particular contracts under examination did not constitute a direct restraint or monopoly of interstate commerce, but merely contracts by which the defendants aimed to secure a monopoly of the manufacture of refined sugar in Pennsylvania, and that the effect of this monopoly in manufacture on interstate commerce was indirect and incidental, and therefore not within the purview of the Sherman act.

This decision, and others which have followed it, are practically the sole authorities relied upon in support of the proposition that the federal government has no power or authority to restrain or suppress industrial trusts. It is, however, perfectly clear from the case as a whole, that the Supreme Court did not say anything to that effect, but on the contrary, carefully confined itself to the particular question presented, which was limited and defined at the outset of the opinion, as follows:

"The fundamental question is, whether, conceding that the

*United States vs. Joint Traffic Assn., 171 U. S. 571.
†United States vs. E. C. Knight & Co., 156 U. S. 1.

existence of a monopoly in manufacture is established by the evidence, that monopoly can be directly suppressed under the act of Congress, in the mode attempted by this bill."

And so in a later decision, the Court said:

"In the Knight Company case it was said that this statute (the Sherman act) applied to monopolies in restraint of interstate or international trade or commerce, and not to monopolies in the manufacture even of a necessary of life."*

But it may be conceded that an industrial trust, as a mere monopoly in manufacture, and without violating the particular provisions of the Sherman act, can secure practically as complete a monopoly in its product throughout the United States, as it would have secured had it combined with its monopoly in manufacture and local sales a further monopoly of interstate commerce, *per se*. It may be conceded further, that it is not within the constitutional powers of Congress to fine, imprison or enjoin the existence of monopolies in mere manufacture as monopolies, because manufacture being necessarily a local matter, a monopoly in manufacture is, under our dual system, to be prohibited and penalized as such monopoly, by the authorities of the state of its habitat only. Conceding all this, it by no means follows that no effective remedies for evils of this class can be afforded by federal legislation.

Although the federal authorities may have no control over industrial trusts as monopolies of manufacture, yet as soon as these manufactures start in a movement destined to carry them across the boundary line of any state, they become the subjects of interstate commerce, and come within the jurisdiction of Congress, to remain within its jurisdiction until they have actually passed the state line, and become intermingled with the general mass of goods in the state of their destination. Further, not only the actual transportation of such manufactures across state lines, but all transactions and agencies directly connected with accomplishing that end, are within the plenary power and control of Congress, by virtue of its constitutional power to regulate interstate commerce.

Power to regulate interstate commerce involves, in its very essence, among other powers, the power to determine and prescribe what agencies shall be permitted to engage in interstate commerce. Doubtless under the constitution, this determination cannot be exercised in a purely arbitrary manner, or be the result of mere whim. But where a given determination can fairly be said to rest on an intelligible basis, having some conceivable rela-

*United States vs. Trans-Missouri Freight Assn., 166 U. S. 326.

tion to the promotion of national interests, the discretion of Congress in making that determination, in the exercise of the powers granted by the commerce clause of the constitution, must, under all the decisions, be treated by the courts as an absolute discretion.

Starting with the propositions announced by the Supreme Court in the decisions referred to, i. e., that these modern combinations of capital are injurious to the real prosperity and substantial interests of the nation; that, if not in themselves immoral or *mala in se*, they are proper subjects of adverse and hostile legislation on the part of Congress in the spheres in which it can constitutionally legislate; that as subjects of such legislation, they are, owing to their injurious character, not within the protection of the Constitution; that where Congress speaks on a subject over which it has constitutional power to legislate, public policy in such a case, is what the statute enacts. Starting with these propositions, it is perfectly competent for Congress to enact legislation declaring the injurious character of industrial trusts, their dangerous effects upon the country at large, and for that reason, imposing restraint or prohibition upon their enjoyment of those fields of commercial action which are within the jurisdiction of the general government.

If it be constitutional for Congress to punish a monopoly of interstate commerce by fine and imprisonment, under the powers granted by this commerce clause, it is assuredly constitutional for Congress, under the same provisions, to prohibit a monopoly in manufacture from employing or engaging in interstate commerce to further and effectuate its injurious aims.

Indeed, the conceded fact that the individual states are deprived of power to interfere with interstate commerce on the part of monopolies in other states, even for the purpose of protecting their own citizens from destructive competition, is a sufficient demonstration that this power is possessed by Congress. Having absolutely no jurisdiction over interstate commerce, a state is unable to prevent the industrial trusts domiciled in other states from shipping their products into its own territory, nor has it any power to enact laws which have the effect of rendering unsalable, in its own territory, manufactures and products of other states which are harmless in themselves. It is clear, therefore, that the individual states are helpless to protect their own manufacturers and dealers from the destructive competition of industrial trusts in other states; that this kind of protection can only be afforded by the regulation of interstate commerce *per se*. But no powers of sovereignty are lost or destroyed by our dual system of government, and powers which are clearly not possessed by the states, must necessarily inhere in the federal authorities.

In addition to this broad jurisdiction over interstate commerce *per se,* Congress is expressly vested with the exclusive management and control of one of the most important instruments of commerce—the post-office. It is well settled that this power embraces the regulation of the entire postal system of the country, and the power to designate what shall be carried, and what shall be excluded, from the mails.* In recognition of these principles, the Supreme Court has uniformly upheld acts of Congress making it a criminal offense to deposit in the mails not only obscene matter, and letters or communications connected with the formation or execution of schemes to defraud, but also lottery "literature" of all kinds. In passing on the constitutionality of the Lottery Act, the Supreme Court said:

"When the power to establish post-offices and post-roads was surrendered to the Congress, it was as a complete power, and the grant carried with it the right to exercise all the powers which made that power effective. It is not necessary that Congress should have the power to deal with crime or immorality within the states in order to maintain that it possesses the power to forbid the use of the mails in aid of the perpetration of crime or immorality.

"The argument that there is a distinction between *mala prohibita* and *mala in se,* and that Congress might forbid the use of the mails in promotion of such acts as are universally regarded as *mala in se,* including all such crimes as murder, arson, burglary, etc., and the offense of circulating obscene books and papers, but cannot do so in respect of other matters which it might regard as criminal or immoral, but which it has no power itself to prohibit, involves a concession which is fatal to the contention of petitioners, since it would be for Congress to determine what are within and what without the rule; but we think there is no room for such a distinction here, and that it must be left to Congress in the exercise of a sound discretion to determine in what manner it will exercise the power it undoubtedly possesses."†

The application of the principles here announced, to the subject under discussion, is obvious, and needs no argument.

As we have already seen, the Federal Supreme Court has declared that these monopolies are necessarily injurious to the best interests of the country, and inimical to its prosperity. Substantially every court in the Union has made repeated and even more emphatic declarations to the same effect. The status of indus-

Ex parte Jackson, 96 U. S. 727.   †*In re* Rapier, 143 U. S. 134.

trial trusts as *mala prohibita* is now further established by the criminal statutes of more than a score of states.

In view of the foregoing considerations, it is confidently asserted that Congress is clothed with power to deprive trusts and monopolies of all kinds and descriptions, not only of the right to engage in interstate commerce, but also of the right to use the United States mails in the promotion and effectuation of their monopolistic aims.

The practical effect of measures of this character is obvious. The destructive results accomplished by analogous legislation upon the lottery evil, is a matter of recent history. The ability freely to import raw materials and supplies from other states into the states where their manufacturing plants are located, the ability freely to transport and distribute their product throughout the Union, is vital to a perpetuation of their monopolistic powers, and as a necessary consequence, vital to the very existence of industrial trusts as business enterprises.

Free use of the mails is essential to the successful prosecution of commercial enterprises, in direct proportion to the magnitude and territorial extent of their operations. Deprived of the use of this instrument of commerce, industrial trusts would practically be compelled to cease their operations.

Prohibitory legislation of this kind cannot, in the long run, be successfully evaded. So far as the element of postal exclusion is concerned, the existing postal laws and regulations furnish ample precedents for the practical enforcement of prohibitive measures of that character. Exclusion from interstate commerce can be accomplished by statutes imposing heavy penalties upon the transportation by industrial trusts of any property or values from one state to another; by the imposition of like penalties upon any common carrier or other agency which may take any part in such transportation; by the forfeiture of all property or goods in transit; by injunctive relief and by other methods.

It is true, such measures would not affect the right of industrial trusts to dispose of their product in the state of its manufacture, but property sold to dealers acting in combination, or under arrangement with, or in the interests of the trusts, would still remain within the prohibitions of such legislation, and be barred from transportation to other states so long as it remained in such hands or control. So likewise, property sold by any exclusive arrangement to a single dealer, or to two or more dealers acting in combination with each other, would continue within these prohibitions. The single dealer, when vested with such exclusive rights to the entire product of an industrial trust, would constitute a monopoly in itself. Indeed, such an arrangement could hardly be effectuated without practically creating a new monopolistic combination, composed of the trust and the dealer having such exclusive rights. Two or more exclusive dealers, acting in combination with each other, would likewise constitute a monopoly, irrespective of any connection with the trust from whom they obtained their product. In short, until any trust or combination should have absolutely and *bona fide* parted with all the interest and control of its product to independent dealers in its own state, that product would remain within the prohibitions of such legislation. But when manufactures or other property have become thus distributed among a number of independent dealers acting independently, the monopoly in that product is *ipso facto* destroyed, and it comes into the market subject to the laws of competition which govern the product of the ordinary small independent producer.

Legislation of this character is consonant with the spirit of our institutions. Under our system of government, the several states are left to deal with their own domestic, social and business problems. Every state has ample power in the exercise of its own sovereign authority, to punish and exterminate trusts and monopolies in its own borders. The practical difficulty with the present situation consists in the fact that, owing to their inability to interfere with interstate commerce, the several states are unable to prevent the practical invasion of their own territory by trusts domiciled in other states. It is idle for a state to punish and extirpate its own domestic monopolies, so long as its manufacturers, dealers and consumers remain practically subject to the destructive competition of foreign monopolies. Legislation like that suggested, leaves the states free to deal with the trusts in their own borders as they see fit. If any state prefers trusts and monopolies, it is at liberty to encourage their growth within its own limits. On the other hand, states hostile to these modern developments, are left free-handed to deal with them in their own territory as they see fit, without finding their efforts rendered nugatory by the aggressive action of monopolies in other jurisdictions.

DAVID KINLEY.

Prof. David Kinley, of the University of Illinois, presented to the convention a report on the information gathered by the Civic Federation concerning trusts. The report was in part as follows: Questions were sent to wholesale dealers, commercial travelers, railroads, combinations, labor organizations, contractors and manufacturers, and economists, financiers, public men, etc.

According to these replies the following articles cannot be bought outside of trusts:

Anthracite coal, bagging, brass goods, cigarettes, copper, (rolled), coffee, glass, iron and steel, (certain iron and steel products, such as chains, nails and shovels, pipe, etc.), glucose, kerosene oil, liquors, (domestic distilled except some Kentucky whisky), matches (certain makes), raisins, roofing (felt and slate), powder and ammunition, stoves, sardines, starch, snuff, solder, scythe snaths, tin plate, tinware, tobacco (certain brands, as Battle Axe, Horse Shoe, Duke's Mixture, and Durham), white lead, white pine, lumber, woodenware, and yeast cakes.

In answer to the question what effect combinations have on the distributor, 110 say it is injurious because it decreases their business and profits and tends to eliminate them.

Forty-nine wholesale dealers think they have been benefited by the formation of combinations.

In answer to the question what effect combinations have on the consumer, 105 think consumers are injured, while only 24 think they are benefited, and 41 think there is no difference.

The items of information about prices aggregate 506; 452 were to the effect that prices rose after combinations were made; 24 that they fell, 15 that there was no change, and 15 that they were fluctuating; 210 do not specifically assign a cause, 189 assign trusts as the cause of the change (increase, in most of these cases); and 40 assign other causes, usually "increased demand," "rise of raw materials," or the tariff.

Of the 452 answers that prices rose, 294 were from wholesale dealers, 105 from manufacturers and contractors, and 53 from commercial travelers.

Circular "H," sent to lawyers, economists, public men, etc., nominally contained eleven questions. The first question asked, "Should a combination of producing agencies be expected to increase or decrease the cost of production; if either, ought it therefore to be beneficial to society or the reverse?"

Four hundred and thirty-two of the writers think that combinations "should" decrease the cost of production, and 17 that they "should" increase it. Two hundred and eighty-nine think that the decrease "ought" to be beneficial to society, and 74 that it "ought" to be a detriment. The rest do not answer.

To what extent will the consumer gain by the decrease in cost of production? Forty of the 444 answers to the question say it will depend on competition; 110 think the consumer will eventu-

531

ally get most or all of the gain; and 101 think his gain will depend on the trusts; while 75 think the consumer will gain nothing and the rest are doubtful.

Is there any danger to the individual investor and the financial system of the country from large aggregations of capital? Two hundred and ninety-three think that there is danger for the individual investor, because of his inability to judge of the safety of the investment, or because of the widespread evil that would result if a crash should come. Sixty-three say there is no element of danger to the individual investor. In the opinion of 266, large capitalization is dangerous to our financial system, and is not so in the opinion of 79.

What effect have combinations on wages and conditions of labor?

One hundred and eighty writers say that combinations increase wages, and 148 that they reduce wages; 51 that they decrease the number employed, 3 say that they increase the length of the working day, and 3 that they decrease it, 25 that they have no effect, and 67 are doubtful.

As to the effect of combinations on middlemen, 313 are of the opinion that these will be wholly or partially eliminated; 114 think that this will be to the advantage of society.

The tendency to combination is regarded with "apprehension" by 270 on the ground that it may create monopolies contrary to the public weal, while 149 think there is no danger, and 34 are doubtful.

Three hundred think that our foreign trade would be benefited by combination, 59 that it would be injured, 64 are doubtful, and 2 think that the benefit will be to the foreigner. The nature of the benefit is variously described; most mean thereby simply an increase of trade.

Are labor organizations trusts?

Of the 459 who expressed themselves on the subject, 243 think that labor organizations are to be classified with other forms of combinations, while 165 take the opposite view, and 53 are doubtful.

Is railway consolidation desirable?

Two hundred and twenty-eight think it desirable, and 41 think it desirable under government control or ownership; 70 think it desirable if restricted by law, 11 desirable except in the case of parallel lines, making 350 who answered in favor of consolidation with or without restrictions. Sixty-seven think railway consolidation undesirable, 16 are indifferent, and the rest are either indefinite in their statements or do not answer at all.

Considerable information was received about prices, from wholesale dealers, contractors and manufacturers and commercial travelers.

What shall be done with combinations?

In answer to the question asking for suggestions on this topic, a large number of opinions were brought out, and are tabulated as follows:

	Business Men	Clergymen, Col. Pres'ts and Prof's.	Lawyers	Economists, Statisticians, etc.	Others	Total.
Answers Indefinite	8	4	10	2	6	30
Federal Commission to Supervise	3	2	4	8	3	20
Government Ownership or Control of Natural Monopolies	5	3	5	8	5	26
"Legislation," not Otherwise Specified	11	8	15	2	25	61
"Legislation," Cong. and States	2	3	5	--	1	11
"Let alone"	10	5	24	1	20	60
No answer	12	13	13	2	5	45
Prevent Over-Capitalization	14	9	16	9	9	57
Publicity of Accounts	7	7	8	16	11	49
Stricter Limitation of Corporate Powers	--	--	3	--	7	10
Tariff Revision	20	1	13	2	19	45
Taxation	6	2	3	5		17
	98	57	119	55	102	431
Miscellaneous	29	23	29	20	22	123
	127	80	148	75	124	554

JOHN W. SPENCER.

In presenting my ideas upon the remedy for the evil effects of organized wealth, I take it for granted that all owners of wealth will be reasonable enough to concede that the remedy is only to be applied to the evil effect of wealth that is concentrated and organized for purposes that are not for the benefit of the major portion of the people.

As a delegate at large from the state of Indiana, I come from the First Congressional District, which has within it the county of Posey, my birthplace, where they produce more cereals, good people, soldiers, and wealth from the soil, than any agricultural county in the United States of like area and population, notwithstanding the sneering snobs and would-be humorists, whose thoughts emanate from a brain apparently nourished by bad alcohol and raw meat. The city of Evansville, which is the second city in our state, is the commercial center of that district, and produces so much hardwood lumber that it is known as the largest market for that product on this continent. That district produces more lumber, bituminous coal, wheat and corn than any six counties of the same area in the United States. Hence, I do not hesitate to say that I come from a people who produce more than their share of this country's wealth, when compared with the amount they are able to retain, and consume their full share of the country's products of organized wealth; therefore, they as a class are more affected, and consequently more interested in the results of the organization and centralization of wealth than those who are east of the Alleghanies, who gather the wealth of the nation, a portion of which is produced by the people of my state.

I think it is everywhere a conceded proposition that wealth is centralized and industrial trusts are organized for the sole purpose of making money for those who invest therein; if this is conceded, then the prime motive prompting such organizations is human avarice and greed; or, put it another way, it is an effort to profit the few at the expense of the many, in total disregard of the rights of the many. I know that some of the later day magazine writers characterize such statements as a "crusade against prosperity," but they fail to state the prosperity they refer to is the prosperity of but the few holders of trust certificates, and not the prosperity of the great mass of people who consume the products of the industrial trusts and produce the wealth to declare the dividends on first, second, common, preferred, fluid, solid, and all other classes of stock issued by the trust; I know it is said that by concentration of business interests they cheapen their product to the consumer and enhance the price of labor that produces them, but is that true? We are constantly referred to the Standard Oil trust, and the Sugar trust, as examples. Now, while the crude oil has decreased in price since the organization of this infant industry, the price of the refined oil, such as is consumed by the people, has been very successfully maintained. We find that from 1894 until 1897, crude oil declined 6 per cent, while refined oil advanced 14 per cent; notwithstanding the fact that since the organization of the Standard Oil trust there has been developed and put into use as against its product, that greatest of all of nature's product, so great that it has been called, and perhaps correctly so, the law of gravitation, electricity, to say nothing of the development of natural gas, and the fact that demand for light has so whetted the inventive genius, that artificial gas from bituminous coal is now produced at a cost of about 16 cents per 1,000 cubic feet, and the people have learned to make a "pillar of fire by night" from the two-thirds formative substance of the earth, water; and so with the Havemeyer associates and sugar—they seem to think that some of us do not know that they are the refiners of sugar, and that the prices paid for refined sugar has never been so cheap as they were in 1885, and the Sugar trust was first organized in November, 1887, since which time the price of sugar has been steadily maintained, while the price of raw sugar has materially and steadily decreased; so on analyzing all of them, we find that their every effort has been to strike down and kill all competition, so as to gratify their apparent insatiable avarice, so that they really reap unearned profits and injure the public; that the so-called "economic evolution of our industries" injures the public, will be readily seen from a few extracts taken from the testimony of Mr. Havemeyer, given before the Senate investigating committee in 1894.

"The Sugar trust makes it a rule to make political contributions to the Republican party in Republican states, and to the Democratic party in Democratic states."

"We get a good deal of protection from our contribution."

"Our company has made considerable money out of the McKinley bill."—(Byron W. Holt in June *Review of Reviews*.)

Such statements as these drive one to the irresistible conclusion that the sugar trust is an injury to the public. That they reduce the number of positions for active and energetic citizens to fill, is no longer in dispute, since reports from all commercial travelers' associations testify to that fact; that they control the output of articles which they produce and handle is a conceded fact, that they control the price of raw material, assisted by "protection for protection's sake" legislation, is no longer disputed; that they fix and regulate the prices paid by wholesaler, jobber, retailer, and finally by the consumer is an agreed proposition.

It strikes me that a few master minds have successfully managed politics and business from a financial standpoint, until now the industrial trusts propose to make the people pay tribute to them for all the necessities of life, from the soothing syrup age to the shroud.

The manufacturing interests have told and repeated to us, that they wanted protection to give them a home market: they got it and the market, and now they are committing the old common law crimes of forestalling and regrating, until they control that home market from the raw material to the consumed article.

Up to the day of the application of the protective tariff by the industrial trusts, we had a fair competitive system of production and distribution. If it is possible, let us take up again the interstate commercial policy, that materially assisted us in developing the greatest union of states that is known to the history of man.

My method of regulating and restraining the substance eating and never earning trusts would be to first have the Congress of the United States, as soon as possible, put upon the free list every article that is made, sold or controlled by a trust, and every one of the component parts of all articles manufactured by them. The answer to that would be or is, their magnitude is such that they break over any or all nations' barriers, and become international; but "sufficient for the day is the evil thereof," by the elimination of the protective tariff, we would not necessarily destroy or disintegrate them, but it would in a great measure relieve the people from paying the enhanced prices to them for such necessities of life as coal, salt, petroleum and its products, sugar, matches and the like; and then let the American Congress pass licensing or taxing act, in the exercise of the police power of the government, under the implied general welfare clause of the Constitution, as interpreted by Justice Marshall, the definer and defender of the Constitution, notwithstanding the opinion of Attorney-General Griggs to the contrary.

Are the people to be informed that it does not lie within the power of the general government to protect the government itself from the avarice and greed of some of the members of society? If such is the only power of the government, what is there to prohibit a combination of capital or wealth from buying up all the world's output of coal, or salt or any other necessity, and they saying to the other members of society, you cannot have a pound of either, unless you pay our price?

Ah! Greater than Griggs have been in error. The people will stand by the declarations of John Marshall in preference to Griggsology. Place upon all corporations a graduated tax, the rate of taxation increasing with the capitalization. You tell me it cannot be done under the Constitution. I tell you that at one time in the interest of organized wealth, the national banks, this government placed a tax upon their competitors, the issue of the state banks, that drove them from the fields of finance. Why can not that same power be exercised in the interest of the people and against aggregated wealth? Here is a way that I believe is safe and sure. One of the great political parties that is now in complete control of all branches of the national government, will next year in its declaration of principles, declare its opposition to trusts, we are told by leaders of that party. We say, "act your opposition before you declare; you have the opportunity, give the people some performance and not so much in promise, for by 'their fruits ye shall know them.' "

HENRY H. SWAIN.

Montana State Normal School.

There is no thought of entering in this paper into a comprehensive survey of the trust problem. Nor is there any attempt to seek some one simple cause for the growth of trusts. The rise of trusts has resulted from a combination of various influences, and no one cause alone is sufficient to account for all these phenomena. We have heard how an unwisely adjusted tariff has fostered the growth of some trusts, how others have profited unduly by the operation of patent laws, others have thriven because of unfair discriminations in railroad rates. No one of these causes tells the whole story, but all are important, and if the trust question is to receive any truly scientific treatment, all these, as well as many other phases, must be fully taken into account.

The case is very similar when we come to the relation between trusts and the currency. There is no disposition to claim that our currency system is the sole cause of the rise of trusts, nor that currency reform would, all by itself, settle the matter. It is maintained, however, that the relation between the trusts and the currency is so intimate that no consideration of the trust problem which overlooks this view of the matter can be other than partial and inadequate.

If we should ask any plain, intelligent business man what is the one matter of vital importance under our profit system of doing business, he would certainly reply that it was mainly a question of prices. It is utterly impossible for any enterprise to keep on if the prices obtainable on the market fall for any reason whatever below the cost of production. If the fall of prices comes about from causes wholly outside the business itself, the result is quite as disastrous as if it came from internal causes.

During the last quarter-century or so, while we have been trying the experiment of gold monometallism, the usual course of general prices has, as a result of that experiment, with occasional temporary fluctuations, tended steadily downward. There was once a time when certain persons professed to be unconvinced of this fact. I think that time is past. I have in recent months read efforts to show that this fall was not without its partial compensations, but I think the fact of the fall is itself no longer seriously disputed.

Now what is the bearing of this upon the trust question? It touches it at two points. In the first place, the fall of prices resulting from an unstable currency has tended to magnify every disadvantage against which a weaker competitor was struggling. Does one enterprise sustain itself with difficulty because of unfair discrimination in railroad rates—then the possibility of success is still further diminished by the burden of falling prices. Is one competitor heavily handicapped because of a rival's possession of exclusive patents—then the additional weight of constantly falling prices breaks down the competitor altogether.

In a superficial view of the case it might seem that such a condition would affect all competitors alike, and so not prejudice the race at all. But while the effect upon all is similar in kind, the weight upon each is not necessarily in equal proportion. Under normal conditions a small advantage in draft of river vessels is only of slight importance, but in a stage of low water the importance of this advantage is greatly enhanced and a very slight difference of draft may make all the difference between complete success and hopeless failure. So, under stable prices, many competitors may remain in the field even in spite of unfair discrimination. But when prices continue downward for a long period, there is less hope for all competitors, and the enjoyment of some exceptional favoritism may prove the absolute *sine qua non* of survival.

An appreciating currency accelerates the development of trust combinations in the second place, because it greatly increases the stimulus to strive for a complete mastery of the market. Under these circumstances even the possession of unfair advantages may not suffice unless these advantages are such as to create a practical monopoly. Now, if an industry can be so monopolized that, while general prices are falling, the products of this industry can be made actually to increase in price, or even to fall less rapidly than the average of general prices, it may be possible not only to escape from the mire of general business depression, but even to attain exceptional prosperity. All depends, however, on securing practical control of the market. Hence all energies which, under normal conditions, might be given to improving the product and cheapening the process are now bent to combine the strongest competitors and crush out all others by whatever means may appear necessary.

Thus all causes tending to the growth of monopoly combinations have been stimulated by an appreciating currency. Now let us note what occurs when this unstable currency takes a turn in the opposite direction. In the last few years gold-mining has increased so rapidly that the production of gold in 1898 exceeds in value the production of both gold and silver for any year prior to 1891. This increase in gold production which, under an established system of general bimetallism, would scarcely have disturbed the general price level at all, now occasions a decided rise of general prices, giving a bonus at the expense of the public to producers generally. In so far as industry is controlled by a trust combination, this combination of course also gathers its bonus from this source. While therefore the long-continued appreciation of the currency has been of material benefit to the trust combination in its efforts to crush competitors, the combinations which have survived and have freed themselves from effective competition, now find an unstable currency beginning to depreciate just in season to enable them to reap an extra profit at a time when they are prepared to monopolize it.

Hence, while a currency which will keep prices always at an absolutely unvarying level, is something not yet discovered, still it can be seen that any plan for dealing with the trust problem must be at best but partial and inadequate if it does not contemplate as one of its features such changes in our currency system as will tend as much as possible toward stability of prices. Still worse would it be if, by the retirement of our national paper currency and the substitution therefor of currency of private issue, the power should be given to any private combination not only to control the prices of its own specific products, but even to manipulate the general price level in behalf of special class interests.

T. B. WALKER.

Minneapolis Board of Trade.

J. W. Gaines, of Tennessee, was called to the chair, and introduced T. B. Walker, of Minnesota, who spoke on "Trusts from a Business Man's Standpoint":

To intelligently consider the question of the modern trusts it is necessary first to examine and analyze the principles and practices on which the trust is based. Not a prolonged discussion of the meanings of words, but to know what the object, aim and intent is in forming these combinations and to trace the practical results reached by them.

The general foundation principles of the trust and that which if taken away would entirely obliterate all the trust methods, is the intention to combine together, under one central control so much or so large proportion of any industry that the production of that particular commodity can be so limited that prices can be fixed arbitrarily and maintained at any price within certain limits which the trust may determine to fix.

If this result could not be reached in the expectations of the formers and investors in the trust, there would be none organized. This is the essential object in forming the combination. The question of the intention is evident from the fact that people will invest their money in these trusts under an excessive capitalization, where it is known undoubtedly and unquestionably that without the advantage of fixing and maintaining high prices dividends could not possibly be earned or paid on such an enormous amount of capital stock.

For instance, the tin-plate trust was organized from plants which with their good will under legitimate valuation would probably not exceed ten million dollars, or twelve million dollars at the outside, was organized for fifty million dollars. Twenty million dollars of preferred stock, drawing a good rate of interest, and twenty million dollars of common stock were paid for the plants. Ten million dollars of common stock was distributed to the promoters and others who were influential in forming the combination. Before the company was formed, tin-plate was worth $2.75 per box. It is now worth $4.25. Earnings of fifteen to twenty per cent are estimated as being made on this fifty million dollars of capital stock.

As another instance, it has been proposed to me several times to organize a lumber and timber trust. A trust that is formed and can handle and control the supply of raw material has a better chance for permanency than one where the supply of raw material can be produced by competing producers to an unlimited extent. It was urged upon me that the pine timber of Minnesota and northwestern Wisconsin might be put into a deal where the lumber prices would be controlled to such an extent that the trust could afford to pay the timber owners a large price for their timber, mills and lumber stock, and very readily add enough to the lumber price to cover the excessive purchase price and to make dividends on the enormous amount of stock that would be issued. It was the general proposition to pay us a large sum of money, if wanted, and a large block of stock, and it was intimated that a portion of the promoters' portion would also be paid over.

The only object whatever in proposing to form this trust was to put so much of the timber together that the prices could be controlled and maintained at a high price. If it had been shown to these promoters and investors that prices could not have been controlled by means of the control of the supply and the limitation of the output, it would not have been considered for a moment at even much lower figures than they were willing to pay. In order to provide against competition the trust, when organized, makes it a practice to pay to those from whom the plants were purchased, as large an amount of stock as they can be induced to take as payments, in order that their interests may induce them not to build competing plants. They also give employment to as many of them in the new deal as they can conveniently manage, in large part for the same purpose, namely, to prevent competition.

Another method of destroying competition, which is practiced by some of the large trusts, for instance, the Diamond Match Company, the National Biscuit Company, and the Sugar Company, is to give to the wholesale dealers a certain discount to each one that will buy exclusively of the trust and in no instance to any extent from any competitor.

The Sugar Company, for example, pays one-eighth of one cent, and all of the wholesale grocers in Chicago are in the deal, with one exception. This places the competitors where they cannot sell goods to these firms even though they would discount a much larger amount than that offered by the trust, as the agreement prohibits any such purchases. As this, then, drives the competition to seek trade among the retail dealers, the trust follows up and offers to sell to the retailers at a competitive price.

Perhaps the friends of the trust will say that this is competition for the benefit of trade. On the contrary it is the throttling of trade to prevent or destroy competition. The competitors are not able to sell goods at even less prices for a better quality, for these trusts control so large a proportion of the output that the wholesale dealers are not able, or feel that they are not able, to maintain their trade without accepting these demands. The trust is, then, in a position to control the market without recourse on the part of the public.

Competition cannot, then, be looked for excepting there should come into the field a powerful organization of experienced competitors with modern methods and machinery and sufficient capital to meet the trust in the contest for trade. The measures taken by the trust to prevent such results and the prospect of a final collapse of trusts and all other business interests with them, are likely to make the public a heavy bill of expense before relief is reached.

We are told that a trust is a corporation. That corporations and large aggregations of capital have been the essential means through which our industrial progress and great advance in wealth and prosperity has been made. Those who understand the business world are readily agreed on these general facts. The organizations of capital under the laws of the different states has enabled small capitalists to perform the work that could be performed only with large capital, but it is begging the question when we are urged not to oppose corporations and aggregations of capital because such organizations have been of great value in the past. An invading army might be a combination and we could say that combinations are beneficial and hence we should not defend ourselves against the invasion. Trust methods were applied in other ways until the laws of the states trying to prevent these combinations drove them in defiance of public sentiment to seek protection under laws intended only for the organizations of legitimate business corporations.

The ordinary corporation in the industrial world is to bring new capital, new plants and new competition. It is for the interest of the commonwealth and the general prosperity.

The trust, however organized, is essentially a combination for throttling, and in many cases the destruction of plants that otherwise would be competing one with the other and furnishing goods at a relative price proportioned to the amounts received by others for their work or the use of their capital.

An eloquent appeal made by Mr. Cockran in favor of corporations in general and the vast advantage received from the use of capital and the necessity for peace and good will between capital and labor in our industrial affairs, while very fine, and to which all could agree, is not only unfair as an argument in favor of the trust, but when rightly applied will justify the most extreme measures to wipe out and prevent the organization and operation of trusts in this country. Mr. Cockran also appealed strongly for the protection and maintenance of competition and excellence. Now what excellence there is in the combination to defeat competition and what competition there is in the excellence of the trust methods and practices seems very ludicrous to consider. There has not been one single excuse or argument presented in favor of the trust. It is a method so opposed to fairness and equal individual rights that the most stringent laws and rigid enforcements are justifiable and necessary to protect the plain, unquestioned rights of the community at large. The fact that many who are hostile to all combinations of capital and to the use of large aggregations of capital, are arrayed against the trust, is used to show that the opposition to these combinations is essentially from this class of people.

This is not true. There is a very strong undercurrent and in many cases unexpressed hostility to this form of business over-reaching, and many who have even taken part in these combinations where they have thought that they could not avoid it without heavy loss, are strongly opposed to such combinations.

Mr. Cockran recommends as a method of regulation and to provide against the encroachments of the trust upon the public interests and to expose their unfair methods, that full and specific annual reports should be required from them and these subject to public inspection and publication. This he dwells upon largely as a specific remedy for the evils which he by inference admits are the result of the trust combinations.

This is a very plausible theory, an excuse and a make-shift which would be practically worthless as a remedy against the evils of these combinations. Most of the large corporations do make annual reports which the public is not sufficiently interested in to consider more than as to the summary of the year's receipts and expenditures.

To trace with any degree of certainty the unfair methods of the trust it would be necessary to examine in detail all the accounts and all items of expenditures. To authorize the examiners to demand explanations and to investigate under oath the officers of the company to find out the actual considerations for moneys expended, for rebates made, and the object and motive of many proceedings and work of employees. This would require a perfect army of auditors and an inquisitorial intermeddling with the business management that could be justified only by a knowledge of the wrong motives, intent and practice of the combinations, that would justify direct legislation to prevent the formation or continuance of such combinations; and the rigid enforcement of such acts.

All the publications that could be squeezed out of the trust without the application of laws that would be less justifiable than in prohibiting of trust organizations would result in no material public advantage.

Others have recommended heavy reductions of duty or free importation of all goods and manufactured products, the domestic production of which is controlled more or less by the trust.

This would be somewhat like burning a city to drive out the criminals. All business interests would collapse with the trust. In the early part of this century it was the custom of the medical fraternity to apply the lancet to every patient to take away a sufficient amount of blood to reduce the vitality of the patient below the danger point of the disease. Our tariff is the key to our prosperity. We have never had prosperous times under low tariff or free trade and we have never established and maintained for any considerable time a sufficient protection that did not result in prosperity. The old system of blood-letting and withdrawing the vital force of the body would be a discreet act compared to the destruction of our tariff to wipe out the trust.

Trust legislation should be so specific and direct that legitimate business and fairly established vested rights shall not be infringed upon or destroyed by it. Legitimate business interests are being sufficiently disturbed by the trust now without having it stand responsible for the bad methods of the trust.

J. DANA ADAMS.

After having listened to the many valuable papers presented to this conference by men so eminently qualified to enlighten and instruct, it is with much hesitation that I venture to trespass upon the limited time of this assembly by offering a few suggestions upon those fundamental principles which underlie this whole question of trusts and combinations, and which perhaps from their very nature have been overlooked or not fully brought out in the presentation of the subject already made.

The first of these is that human labor is the true measure of value in measuring the cost of production and distribution of commodities.

And the second is the great economic law that cost of production ultimately fixes the market or exchangeable value of commodities.

Taking labor as the measure of value, and for convenience a day of average labor as the unit of value, material prosperity is enhanced and progress in civilization is promoted by a decline in value of the products of labor measured in this unit.

In other words, the cheapening of the cost value, which is simply the labor value of commodities, is an unmixed blessing to humanity.

Therefore, any agency which lessens the amount of human labor which enters into the production and distribution to the consumer of a commodity, must be regarded as desirable and of benefit to mankind.

For if it is well to cause two blades of grass to grow where only one grew before, how much more is it to produce two bushels of wheat with the same expenditure of human labor as it required to produce one bushel before, or two pairs of shoes with the same amount of labor as it required to produce one pair before?

Now if, under the unrestricted operation of the economic law referred to, a commodity cannot long be furnished at a market value below its cost value, or its market value cannot long be maintained much above its cost value, then the question of primary importance in ascertaining the economic value of any agency is not whether it will directly reduce the market value of the commodity to the consumer, but whether it will reduce the cost value or the actual amount of labor necessary to produce and distribute it to the consumer, leaving to the effect of this law the ultimate reduction in its market value.

If the principles thus briefly outlined be accepted as correct, every agency claiming a right to exist under the universal law of the survival of the fittest must be able to demonstrate its ability to accomplish greater results with the same amount of labor, or the same result with a less amount of labor. And the fact that in accomplishing certain results it is able to dispense with a part of the labor formerly employed in producing them. will count in its favor, instead of constituting an argument against it.

C. D. WILLARD.

Los Angeles Board of Trade.

The foremost topic in the political and economical discussion of to-day is the rapid development of the principle of combination in all industrial lines. These combinations the public calls by the general name of trusts, although they are, for the most part, not trusts at all, if we hold that word to its original meaning as a commercial term. The question has not as yet developed into a definite issue, but the lines along which the issue is to form may already be dimly distinguished through the haze of conflicting argument and assertion. On its face, the problem seems to be one of mammoth proportions, affecting the fundamental principles upon which the business edifice has rested since trade first began; and yet this may all be an illusion. Men have been deceived before by economic mirages. It certainly concerns all classes of people—the workman, who is himeslf in a trust, or union, and who perhaps works for a trust; the housekeeper who uses trust-made articles; the investor who will handle trust securities; the statesman who must make and administer laws that deal with trusts, and the manufacturer who is forced either to join a trust in his line of production, or to fight for his commercial life. That it should be the great issue of the day is not strange; on the contrary, we may well wonder that we have waited so long to look it squarely in the face.

As a rule, the consideration of a question of the immediate present is rendered difficult by the fact that its very nearness throws it out of perspective and leads us into error. This difficulty is in a measure removed in the case of the trust, for the principle of combination is not new, nor is its application in the trust form. It has been before the American people as a minor issue for over thirty years. The developments of the past ten months, astounding as they seem, nevertheless involve no essentially new problem for consideration by economists and law-makers. All that is happening in 1899 was predicted ten years ago; the only cause for wonder lies in its delay in coming to pass.

There are four stages in this evolution down to the latest form of combination, which, as I have said, is falsely called a trust. The first of these is the pool, which originated among the railroads, and which, in spite of adverse legislation, is still widely practiced, although in a modified form. It was a limited form of trust, for it covered not the whole business of the roads that entered, but only certain specified lines of work.

The constitution provides that Congress shall have power to regulate the traffic between states, and under this prerogative the Cullom-Reagan bill, now known as the interstate commerce act, was framed and passed in the year 1887. It forbids pooling in every form, under severe penalties. The constitutionality of the law has been tested and it stands. Pooling as an open deliberate practice has ceased, but identically the same result is achieved by a different process. There is no law that can compel a railway to go out after business if it prefers to sit still and allow another road to take it. The A Route and the B Route parallel each other from X to Y, and there are ten million tons of freight to be carried annually between those two points; the roads are not parties to a pool; that would be unlawful; but at certain intervals the managers get together and compare notes on the amount of business done in certain lines, and if one is getting more than his share, he will, during the period that follows, refrain from soliciting for those commodities, or by any one of a dozen methods manage to throw the business to his competitor, thus accomplishing exactly the same result as the pool, but without violating the law. The legislation which was intended to abolish the primary trust has merely driven it into a new and utterly impregnable position. This we shall find to be the inevitable tendency with reference to all anti-trust legislation.

Next comes the real trust, which is the second stage of the development. It varies somewhat as to details, but in the main is as follows: there are a dozen large factories producing the same article, working in competition with each other, and covering all, or a large part, of that particular field. They are tired of fighting, and are ready to go into an equitable arrangement. A schedule is drawn up, showing the value of each plant, to each is assigned a just proportion of the final organization, and trust certificates are issued to each in proportion to his share as determined by the schedule. The management of the several factories is placed absolutely in the hands of the directors of the central organization. History does not record the name of the genius that devised this plan, but the first man to put it into practical and extensive operation was John D. Rockefeller, of the Standard Oil Company. That famous trust was organized on a permanent basis in 1882, and the agreement includes the total stock of fourteen companies, the partnership or individual rights of forty-seven men and women, and the majority stock of twenty-six companies. It was incorporated in all the states where the trust was to do business. Having under its control all the principal pipe lines, and mining and refining the great majority of the entire oil product, it was in a position to command special rates from railways, which it received by devices that successfully evaded the interstate commerce law. It could and did dictate to retailers, forbidding them to purchase from other producers, under fear of having their local market demoralized by competition direct from the Standard refineries. One rival after another was singled out for treatment, until all were ruined or driven into the combine.

The brazen iniquity of this performance roused Congress to action, and the Sherman law was passed in 1890, which declared that all interstate combines of corporations engaged in the same or similar lines of industry, having for their object the suppression of natural competition, were unlawful and should be punished by a fine and by the imprisonment of their chief officers. This put a stop to the formation of genuine trusts, and drove those already in existence into a different form of organization. As far as effecting the purpose it had in view, viz., the re-establishment of competition, the Sherman law was utterly worthless.

The third stage of this development was reached by a natural and easy route in the effort to evade the Sherman law. The trust organization was abolished. In its place arose a genuine corporation, having for its purpose the operation of a number of factories, mines or whatever might be chosen, a corporation which buys the various subordinate enterprises outright, and owns and runs them. The transfer is supposed to be absolute and irrevocable, and the man who parts with his factory, or the stock company that disincorporates and gives up its plant, receives in return a lump of preferred stock in the new company.

The very latest phase of the trust organization, which is the plan under which the present trusts are largely forming, differs from the one last described only in that the purchase of the plant is a bona fide cash transaction. It would seem at first glance that this difference is not material, and possibly the distinction is not important from a legal point of view; but it serves to complicate the political or legislative side of the question, as it introduces an innocent third party in the shape of the ultimate holder of the trust securities. The whole transaction is thus one of straight business, with nothing in the nature of a quibble or a makeshift about it. In cases where the factory owner had accepted stock in the new organization, there was always the question as to whether the transaction was genuine or not. In the event of the liquidation of the corporation, or a wind-up of its affairs, the preferred stock was to operate as a first mortgage lien on the tangible assets, taking precedence over any outstanding common stock. In other words though the factory was theoretically sold, there was a string tied to it, by which it could be hauled back if the scheme failed to accomplish all that was expected of it. But the latest form of the trust presents no such rough edge on which the law may fasten its clamp. The elements that enter into the transaction are simple, and are so fundamental in their character that to affect them in any way the law must tear up the whole business fabric and precipitate the country into financial convulsions.

It is quite impossible to obtain accurate figures of the trust development of the year 1899, which exceeds in gross capitalization all that which had preceded. The figures given in newspaper articles are contradictory and evidently full of error. A large part of the alleged capital of the new concerns is admitted to be fictitious, or water, as it is commonly called. The capitalization totals are therefore of no particular value as showing the real extent of the movement. But the question whether the trusts now in operation embrace one-third, one-half or nine-tenths of all industrial enterprises is, after all, not material. The important facts are: First. That certain trusts do cover certain articles in their entirety. Second. That new trusts are constantly forming, and the field rapidly widening. Third. That they have demonstrated by long periods of success the entire feasibility of the plan. Fourth. That a scheme of organization has been devised that is practically invulnerable from destructive attack either through national or state law.

It is questionable whether any form of law will ever be devised which shall put an end to these combinations. Laws may be passed which will correct certain of their attendant evils, as, for example, over-capitalization, which is not an essential of the trust nor is it peculiar to it. But how is it possible to frame a law which shall prevent men from widening the scope of their business, along natural and logical lines, until it includes all the factories or mines or stores that are concerned in any one product? Unless the government adopts socialistic measures, and itself enters the field of manufacture or mining or exchange, how can it create competition, when those who are directly concerned in the matter decline to have it? If all the shoe men of the country choose to get together, and unite as one corporation, by what kind of a legal process is the government to gain a footing among them, and compel the existence of competition?

The trust is of necessity an interstate affair, and hence is to some extent under the control of the Federal government. While we can conceive of no constitutional legislation which shall effect its abolition, it is probably feasible to frame a law governing interstate corporations which shall require them to take out a charter under Federal authority, and this charter, which is in the nature of a franchise for a semi-public utility, may lay down certain requirements. For example, the amount of stock to be issued should be exactly in accord with the value of the company's real assets. The tax to be paid might be graduated on the company's income, increasing as the profits passed a certain percentage. The tendency of such a law would be to forestall the effort to earn unreasonable dividends, and to abolish the obtaining of money under false pretenses that now prevails in the sale of watered stock.

But would such a law drive the Standard Oil monopoly from existence, and distribute its business among a number of individual firms and corporations? No; nor would any other law of a general character, such as all our laws must be, accomplish that result. There is a plain, definite reason why this is so, and it lies in the fact that the trust, much as it is berated and deplored, has its foundations deep down in the common sense and experience of the race. In the last analysis the trust is logical, and competition foolish. Here is the world to be supplied with a certain article, and here are we, the producers of it. Which is best, that we should each blunder on by himself with inadequate facilities, alternately flooding and starving the market, and using a large part of the finished product as ammunition with which to fight each other, or that we should come to an intelligent, amicable understanding, combine our efforts, stop the waste, cease fighting, and, as we say, get right down to business? As in the case of nations, so with individuals, peace is a thousand times better than war. The world never permanently goes back. When it has learned a good lesson, it abides by it. We understand the folly and waste of international conflict, and, as far as the mistakes and passions of men will admit, we will abolish war. Similarly, the business world has learned the great advantage to be gained by combination; and while certain limitations on human nature make it impossible to carry it to the ultimate lengths, it will grow and extend and strengthen until it becomes, in spite of all we may say, or do, or enact, the controlling force of production and trade.

We are now face to face with the one essential and vital issue of the trust; and it is a problem so stupendous that we pause for a moment almost in terror before we cross the threshold of inquiry. · What is to be the effect of this change in the world's business methods upon the people? It cannot be doubted that the change is of a most radical character, amounting to a veritable revolution in the world's economics. Thus far in the history of the race the natural laws of supply and demand and of the competition of producers and of distributers one with another, have prevailed, subject only to such limitations as governments have seen fit to apply.

The world has passed through a number of minor industrial revolutions—the general substitution of free labor for slave, the abolition of government monopolies, the discovery of steam, and of labor-saving machinery, the development of quick transportation, etc., and we are not ignorant of what it means to readjust man and all his affairs to a change of economic conditions. But here is a revolution so profound and far reaching in its character as to make all that have gone before it seem insignificant by comparison. Understand, I do not refer to the mere formation of individual trusts, but to the inevitable substitution of the principle of combination for that of competition. The next general movement in the trust field will be the swallowing of some combinations by others, until all are practically in a harmonious whole. It may take a quarter of a century to accomplish this; it may be done in five years. But it is coming—who can doubt it? And this period of adjustment will be one of discontent, distress, failures, panic, and disaster.

But this is the darkest hour that is just before the dawn. The worst will have passed, and that which is to follow will, I am convinced, be a vast improvement on any condition of affairs that the world has hitherto beheld. The general rule which applies to all labor-saving devices must hold good here. The scale is larger, but the principle is the same. Gradually work will be found for hands that are ready to accept it, in new lines of development which the several trusts, or the one great central trust, as the case may be, will throw open. Indeed, there is hope that the long period of disaster may be shortened by the fact that the trusts themselves will find it greatly to their advantage to provide work for the discontented and dangerous element. The producer, moreover, must have a market for his manufactured commodity, and that can come only with prosperity among the working classes.

The industrious and intelligent people of this globe have certain problems which in the divine scheme of things they must either solve or suffer a certain loss of happiness. We are coming to understand the problems that concern the production of wealth—and by wealth we mean the things that contribute to human comfort—but we have not learned even the primary lessons of its distribution, one of which is that every man should have an opportunity to work and to earn what is necessary for his family's support. Until we have mastered this most elemental principle, upon which the whole fabric of a self-respecting and generally contented community must rest, it is folly for us to attempt the solution of more difficult questions, such as the scheme for an equal division of wealth must involve. Neither have we succeeded in solving the problem of the panic and the waves of elation and depression, which at intervals sweep across our ocean of commerce and throw frightful wreckage to the shore. With the aid of science we have met and withstood the ravages of disease, we have harnessed the forces of nature to our command, we have explored the heavens and we have carried into the commonest household knowledge which a few centuries ago was restricted to the monks and the clerks. We have accomplished miracles; but the poor starve almost at our doors. We have piled up great masses of wealth, but at intervals of less than a score of years, we are all affected by a madness, that causes us to throw this wealth

551

about and destroy it. Terrible as these things are, we have at least become hardened to them. We dare not think of the sufferings of others, lest it fairly poison our own cup. We have become fatalistic; these evils are inherent in human nature, we say, and can never be eradicated. That same sentiment has, in the world's history, prevailed with regard to the tyranny of kings, and slavery, and duelling and punishment by torture; but these have all passed. Because we have operated our business affairs under the competitive system from the beginning, that system is not necessarily God-given, for all eternity. Centuries of experience have demonstrated that the panic, over-production, bad distribution and uncertainty of employment are inevitable accompaniments of competition. A plan has suddenly developed which, without overturning our laws or our social order, without war, and with nothing worse than a protracted period of industrial depression—which we have learned by hard and bitter experience to endure with patience—will do away with competition and give us co-operation in its stead—not that ideal co-operation which the socialist paints with colors so brilliant that they dazzle us unto disbelief, but a tangible, reasonable, practical condition of commercial peace. If the trust is the instrument through which the change of the world's affairs to a common sense basis is to be accomplished, then God speed the trust, let us say.

EDWARD P. RIPLEY.

President Atchison, Topeka & Santa Fe Railway System.

The Atchison, Topeka & Santa Fe Railway System is composed of something over one hundred corporations controlling all the way from one mile to one thousand miles each at the time of lease or consolidation, and the total now controlled is, roughly, 7,500 miles.

The result to the public of the consolidation as to rates has been to lower them—the force of public opinion and legislation demand more of a large corporation in all directions than is expected of the smaller companies, and the larger roads are held to a more strict account in all directions. The same is true as to convenience of service. The system now being operated as an entity was formerly disjointed and disconnected, besides being in some cases irresponsible.

The result to employees' wages has been to advance them. It is a well known fact that wages on the smaller roads are in almost all cases lower than on the larger systems. The result of consolidation on the number of employees is not considerable in any direction. Naturally the consolidation does away with a few officials and some accountants, but as a rule does not affect the number of men required for the physical operation of the properties, and the reduction in the official and accounting staff is trifling.

The conditions of service on the consolidated lines are in no respect inferior, and in some respects superior, to those on the smaller roads. As before stated, the larger roads pay higher wages, and the employees are, as a rule, less subjects of favoritism and are more justly treated.

It is difficult to say what have been the results to investors of the various consolidations and absorptions that have taken place, but it may be stated as a general proposition that the owners of the smaller properties have made more money than those of the road by which the smaller properties were absorbed, and more than they could have made had they remained independent. The small road is often worth more as an adjunct or feeder of the large road than as an independent proposition. In the latter case it is worth only the sum on which it can earn a fair rate of interest, while to the larger road it is worth what it can earn plus the profit on what business it can bring to the larger road.

The intrinsic values of the properties absorbed have not been changed by the absorption. It is difficult to say whether the process of consolidation has resulted in the diffusion or concentration of capital. Since the securities of the absorbing company are so widely distributed, it is fair to presume that there has been no radical change in that respect.

With few exceptions each absorption or consolidation has both relieved and intensified competition. That is, it has relieved us of competition at one point, only to bring us into competition at another; and as there is no part of the United States where railway competition does not exist either in its direct or indirect form, it is fair to say that competition has been restricted but slightly, if at all, by the consolidations that have taken place.

Unquestionably the result of strong trade combinations has been that the railroads have been compelled to discriminate in their favor. The railroads being mistakenly prohibited from organizing to prevent such attacks, are individually to some extent at the mercy of large combinations controlling immense volumes of tonnage, and the interstate commerce law and other equally unwise legislation on the part of national and state bodies has fostered the very evil it was intended to prevent. This is not to be construed as an admission that the railroads have been or are violating the letter of the law: there are legal ways of "protecting" the large shipper, and it may be laid down as an axiom that until the railroads are legally permitted to combine to resist such attacks, the shipper having the largest amount of transportation to buy will buy it cheapest; this is rendered the more probable because the mercantile interest as a rule maintains that such is the correct principle and that the "wholesale and retail" idea should govern in transportation as in the sale of commodities, and that interest is not in the least in sympathy with the principles of the law. On the other hand, the railroads are generally in sympathy with the objects of the law, but are deprived by its terms of the only means by which they can enforce its main principles.

It should be stated in justice, however, that some of the strongest "combinations," or so-called "trusts," have consistently refused to accept cut rates, or become parties to, or beneficiaries of, any infraction of the interstate law.

For the same reason that a legalized combination among railroads would tend to do away with discrimination in favor of large combinations of capital or trusts, the competition of roads is even still more potent in the same direction. It is quite safe to say that were all the roads of the country under one management, there would be no discrimination whatever, and it is probably equally safe to say that rates would be lower and the service better. But this is not to be construed as a suggestion in favor of government ownership, than which few greater calamities could overtake us. This is evidenced by the conduct of the post-office department, which, after paying the railroads for transportation about 28 per cent of its gross receipts, shows a deficit of sixteen millions a year, though without any competition; while the express companies, paying the roads for transportation about 50 per cent of their gross receipts and subject to severe competition, make satisfactory returns to their stockholders.

There have been in all ages and in all countries those who saw in the introduction of labor-saving devices the destruction or degradation of the workingman. Yet his condition has constantly improved.

And some of us have been taught to believe that the great economic principle is, free and unrestricted competition. The weaver displaced by the power loom, the retailer displaced by the department store, the traveling salesman displaced by the trust, are all alike the relics of a *régime* that has passed away for good in spite of sentiment and in spite of legislation— a *régime* which was wasteful, in that it forced the consumer to pay more than a fair profit or forced him to pay profits to middlemen.

The economic tendency to larger combinations is irresistible, and to my mind not dangerous, but whether dangerous or not, there is no stopping it.

Labor has by combination been able to greatly improve its condition, and labor organizations are neither more nor less than a trust. Why deny to capital the rights accorded to labor?

The average individual laborer has found that, as an individual it is difficult for him to obtain recognition, or what he conceives to be his share of the results of his work; hence he combines with his fellow-laborers that they may jointly command a respect and exercise a force, that to the individual is impossible.

For precisely the same reason the individual merchant or the individual corporation finds itself forced to seek the co-operation of its fellows.

The labor organization succeeds when wisely handled and not unreasonable in its demands; when that limit is exceeded it fails. So also the trust succeeds only when it reduces costs and is content with fair returns; to exceed this limit is to invite the competition it most dreads.

STUYVESANT FISH.

President of the Illinois Central Railroad Company.

The Illinois Central Railroad Company is not a consolidation of any other companies whatever, but is precisely the corporate entity created by the act of the state of Illinois to incorporate that company, approved February 10, 1851. The railroad contemplated by and built under that charter is 705.5 miles in length, and lies in Illinois. The Illinois Central is, however, operating, as lessee or agent, other railroads in connection with its own, aggregating all told 3,769.74 miles, located in eleven different states.

The early history of all the leased lines is not as clear as it might be, but from the records and from a personal knowledge which dates back to 1871, I can say that the number of railroad companies absorbed by or consolidated into the various lines now operated by the Illinois Central have been at least as many as fifty-five. Reference is here made only to distinct corporations, and no account is taken of mere changes of name, nor yet of mergers, consolidations, and the like. On the other hand, it should not be assumed that the Illinois Central Railroad Company has dealt directly with each of these companies. It has, in some cases, leased railroads which had previously been formed by the consolidation of smaller ones.

Having had occasion to go quite thoroughly into the matters germane to the field of inquiry of the conference on trusts, in an unpublished report made to the board of directors of the Illinois Central Railroad Company May 18, 1897, some figures there given I shall here employ.

It was not until after the Civil War that the consolidation of railroads into large systems began to make itself felt. Poor's Manual for 1869-70, after making, at page xxix, under the heading "Construction, Organization and Management of Railroads," some interesting remarks as to their control by the government, goes on to say, at page xxx, "The company having control of the longest line with us is the Chicago & Northwestern, which has a mileage of 1,257 miles. The Pennsylvania Railroad Company operates 538 miles, the Reading 807, the Erie 774, the New York Central 692." The Illinois Central was then operating 895 miles, as shown on page 319 of the same book, although it is not mentioned on the page quoted from.

The effect of the amalgamations of railroads which have since taken place is well shown in a report, entitled "Changes in the Rates of Charge for Railway and Other Transportation Services, Prepared under the Direction of John Hyde, Statistician, by H. T. Newcomb, Chief of the Section of Freight Rates in the Division of Statistics." All the figures there given are in gold, or its equivalent, and they cover, with regard to substantially all the railroads in the United States, the long period from 1867 to 1896:

In 1886 the average revenue per ton was _____ $ 2 06
In 1896 "   "   "   "   "   " _____   1 56

    Decrease _____ $ 0 50 or 24.27%
In 1886 the average rate per ton per mile was _____ ¢1.160
In 1896 "   "   "   "   "   "   "   " _____ ¢.745

    Decrease _____ ¢.415 or 35.78%

Information as to later dates down to June 30, 1898, can be obtained from the reports of the Interstate Commerce Commission on "Statistics of Railways." In using the latter it must be remembered that as the net earnings of the railroads are given without deducting taxes, there is in them a gross and constant over-statement. The steady fall in the rate per ton per mile from 1.925 cents in 1867 to .753 cents in 1898, shows the effect of consolidation on freight rates.

That the rate per passenger per mile has not fallen, if at all, in like proportion, is due to the better accommodations, higher speed, and greater comfort now afforded. No one would to-day consent to travel as all had to travel formerly, without sleeping cars, parlor cars or dining cars, without through connections and subject to repeated delays and constant changes, including the rechecking of baggage and the purchase of a ticket at the end of each short railroad.

In 1886 the average fare per passenger was _____ ¢41.39
In 1896 "   "   "   "   "   " _____ ¢34.30

Decrease _____ ¢7.09 or 17.13%

In 1886 the average rate per passenger per mile was____ ¢2.208
In 1896 "   "   "   "   "   "   "   " ____ ¢1.979

Decrease _____ ¢.229 or 10.37%

As to the convenience and efficiency of the service resulting from consolidations, a comparison of time tables, and especially of freight schedules, in force before and after consolidations would be instructive, or, better, the testimony of shippers and consignees at distant points as to the time which is now, and was then, actually consumed in delivering freight. Their testimony as to adjustment of claims against one consolidated corporation and those against a number of small, independent ones would be instructive.

The time of merchandise freight trains has been reduced:

Chicago to New Orleans, from 80 hours to 55, saving 25 hours.
Chicago to St. Louis, from 30 hours to 16, saving 14 hours.
St. Louis to New Orleans, from 59 hours to 38½, saving 20½ hours.
Chicago to Sioux City, from 43 hours to 33½, saving 9½ hours.

The average time in which freight trains are actually moved has been decreased in a much greater ratio, owing to better track, improved engines, passing tracks and other facilities, and a much better organization and *esprit du corps*.

As an illustration, showing the present possibilities, a train consisting of twenty-five Illinois Central standard refrigerator cars, containing 11,250 bunches of bananas, was moved from New Orleans to Chicago on February 20, 1894—912 miles—in 35 hours and 45 minutes, or an average speed, including stops, of 25.45 miles per hour. This was done without any unusual preparation or interfering with the regular service. Our banana trains are run from New Orleans to Chicago on established schedules of 47 hours and 30 minutes. Our manifest freight trains daily make, with great regularity, schedules nearly as fast as those set for the banana trains.

In 1886 the number of tons of freight carried one mile
  per mile of railroad operated was-----------------344,564
In 1896 it was --657,890
                                                          _____
    Increase --------------------------------------313,326 or 90.93%

Showing that, notwithstanding the increase in mileage, the intensity of service in the carriage of freight has also increased.

In 1877, before the Illinois Central had control of the railroad from Cairo to New Orleans, the fastest passenger trains consumed 47 hours and 45 minutes in going from Chicago to New Orleans (912 miles), and 47 hours in returning northward.

The time consumed has been reduced:

Chicago to New Orleans, from 35 hours 50 minutes to 26 hours, thus avoiding a second night in the cars.
Chicago to Sioux City, from 22 hours to 15 hours 30 minutes.
Chicago to St. Louis, from 10 hours 50 minutes to 8 hours.

In 1886 the number of passengers carried one mile per
  mile of railroad operated was---------------------54,840
In 1896 it was --72,381
                                                        _____
    Increase ----------------------------------17,541 · r 31.99%

Showing that, although so many miles of railroad have been added, the intensity of the service in the carriage of passengers has increased.

As a result of consolidation employees are privileged to work for standard wages under standard rules, with the assurance of continued employment and a chance to rise to the highest places in the service. Every one of the superior officers of the Illinois Central Railroad, excepting those in the legal department, has risen from the ranks in the service of that or some other railroad company.

The earnings, which have sustained a uniform rate of dividend since the close of 1890, have also enabled the company to, thus far, go on paying the standard scale of wages in all branches, without even a temporary reduction. It is to be hoped that with a return of prosperous times the men will be mindful of how far the enhanced purchasing power of the money given them has operated to increase their pay during all these hard times.

In 1877 reductions of from 10 to 25 per cent were made in a scale of compensation lower than the one now in force. The employees of the Illinois Central Railroad Company never have received higher pay than at present.

·In 1886 the company employed 8,516 persons, and paid them $4,937,955, being an average of $580 to each.

In 1896 it employed 19,647, and paid them $11,699,590, being an average of $595 to each.

The comparatively small increase in the yearly pay was due to lessened hours of work, and to the absence in recent years of any large payments to train crews for overtime.

On small, independent roads wages were often fixed by favor, and very generally limited to the utterly inadequate means of bankrupt concerns. Standard wages represent the maximum scale which has thus far been secured by thoroughly well organized combinations of labor from first one and then another of the railroad companies, which, through the personal vanity of their managers and the natural rivalry of the corporations, are, and have ever been, utterly unorganized for mutual protection.

I do not wish to be understood as opposing combinations of labor. On the contrary, I believe certain of them work for the general good, as do also certain combinations of capital. Moreover, the best paid men generally do the best work. But I am stating facts, and not writing an essay on what should be.

Except in the accounting offices and in the purely clerical branches of the service, I fail to see how consolidation can reduce the number of men employed. On the contrary, it generally leads to increased traffic and increased employment.

The number of miles operated and the number of men employed by the Illinois Central Railroad Company, and in and since 1892 by that company and the Yazoo & Mississippi Valley Railroad Company, taken together, have been as follows:

Years.	Miles Operated.	Men Employed June 30th.
1885	2,066	8,485
1886	2,066	8,576
1887	2,355	9,915
1888	2,355	11,316
1889	2,875	10,669
1890	2,875	13,823
1891	2,875	15,789
1892	3,695	20,314
1893	3,695	18,828
1894	3,695	16,095
1895	3,695	17,080
1896	3,934	20,581
1897	3,937	23,569
1898	4,615	25,212
1899	4,626	28,883

Increase in miles operated since 1885 ------------------- 2,560 or 123.91%
Increase in number of men employed------------------20,398 or 240.40%
Number of men employed per mile operated—
    In 1885 -- 4.11
    In 1899 -- 6.24
Increase slightly more than 2 men per mile, or over 50%,

Conditions of service on large railroads are controlled by standard rules, which clearly define each man's duties and powers and his relation to those around, above and below him. On small, independent railroads, the conditions were necessarily dependent almost solely on the temper, health and momentary engagements, in short, on the heredity and environment; of a local officer of limited experience. In this connection some valuable information might be gained by asking a great number of men now in the employ of several of the large railroad companies two questions, viz:

First—Have you ever worked on a small, independent railroad in your present capacity?

Second—If so, which service do you prefer?

Had I the time to do so, it would be an easy matter to take from the files of such a paper as the *Financial Chronicle* both the dividends and interest paid, and the prices of stocks and bonds. I cannot recall, in the last ten years, a single consolidation which has resulted in a higher rate of dividend or of interest being paid, and it is notorious that all the reorganizations made in recent years have been based on a very material reduction in interest.

Competition, adverse legislation, increased taxes, enhanced wages, and the better service required by the public, long since made it impossible for railroads in the West to sustain the 10 per cent rate of distribution which prevailed thirty years ago.

More than twelve years ago the rate on the Illinois Central had fallen to 7 per cent on the then capital of $29,000,000, the amount distributed in 1886 being $2,030,000.

The increase in the capital in 1887 to $40,000,000, the bad effects of legislation at that time, especially in Iowa, and of the interstate commerce law, forced a reduction, in 1888, to 6 per cent, which rate was maintained until 1890, when, on the increase of the capital to $45,000,000, a further reduction in the rate to 5 per cent was made necessary by a very material increase in the pay of employees, especially in the train service, and by the determination reached by the board of directors to bring the property, as rapidly as possible, up to higher standards of maintenance and of service.

During the long depression in railroad and general business, which has been almost continuous since the failure of Messrs. Baring Bros & Co. in November, 1890, the share capital of the company has again been increased from $45,000,000 to $52,500,-000. Through this period of 6½ years, dividends at the uniform rate of 5 per cent per annum have been earned and regularly paid. Investigation will show that no other large railroad company has, throughout this period, uniformly maintained its rate of dividend.

Not only is there no water in the stock of the Illinois Central, but the aggregate capitalization of the company, including all of the bonds and all of the stock, does not represent, by many millions of dollars, the money which has actually been put into the property.

Attention is invited to the following tables, which compare the capitalization of the railways of Great Britain with those of the United States in 1890 (which was the first year for which the Interstate Commerce Commission published statistical reports) and in 1898:

RAILWAYS IN THE UNITED KINGDOM.
STATED IN DOLLARS, £1 BEING TAKEN AS WORTH $5.

| | YEAR ENDED DEC. 31ST, 1890 | YEAR ENDED DEC. 31ST, 1898 | INCREASE IN NINE YEARS | |
			AMOUNT	PER CENT.
Miles operated ____	20,073	21,659	1,586	7.90
Capital paid up ___	$4,487,360,130	$5,672,342,310	$1,184,982,180	26.41
Capital paid up per Mile operated___	223,550	261,895	38,345	17.15
Gross Receipts____	399,743,510	481,262,505	81,518,995	20.39
Gross Receipts per Mile _____	19,915	22,220	2,305	11.57

RAILWAYS IN THE UNITED STATES.

| | YEAR ENDED JUNE 30TH, 1890 | YEAR ENDED JUNE 30TH, 1898 | INCREASE IN NINE YEARS | |
			AMOUNT	PER CENT.
Miles operated ____	156,404	184,648	28,244	18.06
Capitalization_____	$9,437,343,420	$10,818,554,031	$1,381,210,611	14.64
Capitalization per Mile _____	60,340	60,343	3	*0.00
Gross Receipts____	1,051,877,632	1,247,325,621	195,447,989	18.58
Gross Receipts per Mile _____	6,725	6,755	30	0.45

*Less than one-half of one-hundredth of one per cent.

The figures for the United Kingdom of Great Britain and Ireland are taken from the returns to the British Board of Trade, and those for the United States from the reports of the Interstate Commerce Commission on "Statistics of Railways in the United States."

It will be seen therefrom that, while the number of miles of railroad in the United States has increased 18.06 per cent, their capitalization, including both bonds and stock, has increased only 14.64 per cent; and that the increase in the capitalization per mile of railroad is $3, a sum too small to be expressed in percentages; less than one-half of one-hundredth of one per cent.

Also, that the gross receipts of the railroads in the United States have increased in almost exactly the same ratio as the miles operated, viz., 18.58 per cent, while their gross receipts per mile have increased $30, or less than one-half (45-100) of one per cent. This in a country which has developed enormously in the meanwhile, and whose population is estimated by the Interstate Commerce Commission to be increasing at the rate of 1,250,-000 per annum.

On the other hand, in the same time, in the United Kingdom:

The number of miles operated increased 7.9 per cent.
The capital increased 26.41 per cent.
The capital per mile operated increased 17.15 per cent.
Gross receipts increased in amount 20 39 per cent.
Gross receipts per mile operated, 11.57 per cent.

While it is true that, as a whole, the English railways are better built than ours, there are many points in which ours excel them, and there are also thousands of miles of railroad in the United States which are well and permanently constructed.

The capitalization, including bonds and stocks, of the railroads in the United States, is $60,343 per mile. That of the railways in Great Britain £53,379 per mile, which, at $5 to the pound, equals $261,895.

The increase in the capitalization of the railroads of the United States, per mile, in nine years, has been, as above stated, three dollars.

The increase in the capitalization of the British railways per mile, during the same nine years, has been £7,669, or, at $5 to the pound, $38,345.

The figures are given as reported, without accepting responsibility for their accuracy. Those for the railroads in the United States include the many millions of dollars of bonds and stocks of railroad companies which are owned by other railroad companies, and, to that extent, they greatly overstate the capital of the railroads in the United States actually held by the public. A candid consideration of these figures shows that the ancient myth about railways in the United States being over-capitalized has no basis in fact.

The only gauge of the value of railroad property is its returns in dividends, or the market price of its securities.

In January, 1877, of the $29,000,000 of Illinois Central capital stock outstanding, about $15,700,000 (or 54.14 per cent) was held in Great Britain, $7,700,000 (or 26.55 per cent) in Holland, and only $5,600,000 (or 19.31 per cent) in America.

At present 705 officers and employees, other than directors of the corporation, are registered on the books of the company as holding 2,554 shares.

The number of stockholders in each of the eleven states in which the company is now operating railways varies from seven in Indiana to 767 in Illinois. The total number of stockholders in those states is 1,126, and they hold 33,995 shares.

There are resident in the United States 3,868 stockholders, owning 346,207 shares, or over 57 per cent of the total capital stock of $60,000,000; in Great Britain 2,543, owning 198,616 shares; elsewhere 115, owning 55,125 shares.

All told, the books show 5 holdings of 5,000 shares or over; 85 of 1,000 shares or over; 93 of 500 shares or over; 694 of less than 500 but more than 100 shares; 455 of exactly 100 shares each, and 5,194 of less than 100 shares. The number of stockholders registered on the books is 6,526. Barely one-seventh of them own over 100 shares apiece.

By way of contrast, it should be remembered that in 1873 the capital consisted of 254,794 shares, or $25,479,000, of which 130,-438 shares, or 51.19 per cent, was owned in Great Britain; 79,863 shares, or 31.34 per cent, in Holland; 9,978 shares, or 3.92 per cent, elsewhere out of the United States, leaving as owned in the United States only 34,515 shares, or 13.55 per cent.

The number of stockholders in the United States then was 338, and they owned less than one-seventh of the capital and scarcely more than the number of shares which are now owned by residents of the eleven states served by the railroad. There was, at that time, practically no ownership of shares in any of those states.

The number of individual proprietors is, however, much larger than that of the registered stockholders, and the average interest of each much smaller than as shown above, owing to trusts in the settlement of estates, partnerships, joint ownerships, and the custom, so common, especially in England, of passing certificates registered in the names of bankers from hand to hand in settlement of transactions at the Stock Exchange.

Whether the inclusion of other railroads in the Illinois Central system has lessened purely local competition, is somewhat questionable. While I incline to think it has, the far more destructive general competition of rival markets and of rival railroads has gone on without let or hindrance. In the Western states there is no check on the building of new railroads, such as there is in New York, Massachusetts and elsewhere. Hence any Western company can at any time build into a territory already well served by existing railroads. There is nothing in the leasing or the acquiring of rival lines which amounts to a guarantee against future and new competition of the most destructive kind. Our leasing of other railroads has not intensified competitive conditions.

Of late I should say that the formation of so-called trusts and combinations has had no effect whatever upon rates. The present managers of industrial trusts are too broad-minded, and know the law too well, to hope to build themselves up in that way. The very fact of their enjoying a practical monopoly in their own line precludes the possibility of their profiting thereby.

So far as I know or have heard for a long time, there has been no discrimination in favor of such combinations. It is true that I was asked for something of the kind within a year, and promptly refused to grant it. If such discrimination exists, it is due to some radical difference in the circumstances, such as the large merchant owning his cars or giving prompt dispatch to those of the carrier, which the small merchant does not and cannot do, or to his shipping by the trainload as against a carload. This difference between wholesale and retail trade is recognized the world over and is unavoidable. It seems to be inherent in nature. Napoleon is credited with having said, "God fights on the side of the heavy battalions," and, what is more to the purpose, the planets revolve in their orbits in obedience to the attraction of the greater mass of the sun. Struggle against it as we may, this condition will continue to prevail in spite of "Bulls against the Comet." The thing is simply beyond human control. The federal government recognizes it in the sale of stamps, and, to the newspapers, in greatly lessened charges for postage.

Except in increasing the difference between the largest wholesale shipments and the smallest retail shipments of the same commodity, I think railroad consolidation exercises no influence for or against the trust idea. There was a time when the trusts, or certain of them, were believed to control certain railroads. Given unlimited consolidation of railroads—as their capital must exceed that of the industrial trusts—there seems little to be feared.

On the contrary, as the rate making power becomes centered in fewer hands, the men wielding it necessarily become more conservative and realize that the vastness of the interests committed to their care requires them to stand for law and equal justice to all. Railroad property is in its nature so scattered as to require the constant protection of the law, day and night, to such an extent as to make its managers and owners more dependent on just government than are any others. This fact is now very generally appreciated.

In thus considering certain questions which have come within the administration of the Illinois Central Railroad Company I express my personal views solely, and my statements are not intended, and must not be taken, as binding the corporation which I serve. All the powers of that corporation are, by law, vested in its board of directors, and they have not been consulted in respect to these statements, much less have they authorized me to make them.

A recess was taken at 1 o'clock until 3 o'clock.

AFTERNOON SESSION, SEPTEMBER 16.

MEETING OF COMMITTEE ON RESOLUTIONS.

When it became known that it was the desire of William Jennings Bryan to present resolutions to the committee, and had requested that no report be made until he was given a hearing, quite a change was wrought in the situation. Many who had opposed reporting resolutions promptly advocated their introduction, and it looked at one time, Friday afternoon, as though the New York and Nebraska delegations would be able to agree on the substance of resolutions. Saturday morning Chairman Luce assembled the committee, at the conclusion of Mr. Bryan's address; but, by this time, the idea spread that resolutions could not be passed without party politics getting into the question and marring the good effects of the conference. Furthermore it was felt that the adoption of resolutions would not enhance the influence of the conference upon the public mind.

The members at noon, and after long debate, reaffirmed its decision of the preceding day, recommending that no resolution expressing the views of the convention on the trust question be adopted. This conclusion was reached with a view of keeping politics out of the conference, and in the interests of harmony. After Chairman Luce had rapped for order Attorney-General Gaither, of Maryland, presented an order giving all delegates the privilege of submitting resolutions to the committee without being read or debated in the convention, with the understanding that all such documents were to be printed in the official proceedings. J. C. Hanley spoke in support of the suggestion. Delegate Dowe, of New York, expressed the opinion that no resolution should be passed at the conference. S. H. Greeley, of Chicago, followed and asserted it would be impossible to frame a resolution that would meet the approval of the entire body. He thought the committee should abide by its original decision. Edward Rosewater, of Nebraska, said that if a resolution were to be passed it should be intelligent and tangible. He did not want the conference to make itself ridiculous by trying to express its views in generalities. E. C. Crowe, of Missouri, objected to the Gaither order. He thought it would serve no good purpose and certainly would not accurately reflect the sentiments of the gathering, for the reason that many delegates would not avail themselves of the opportunity to have resolutions published in the proceedings. Edward Keasbey, chairman of the sub-committee of five. said he had talked with Mr. Bryan on the subject, and that Mr. Bryan, after reflection, had withdrawn the resolution he had prepared, and had advised that the conference take no action along that line.

It was noticeable all through the contest over resolutions that neither political nor trust lines were drawn. This is evident by a glance over the following names of some of the delegates who took pronounced positions.

FOR RESOLUTIONS.	AGAINST RESOLUTIONS.
Bryan, Neb.	Blair, N. H.
Cockran, N. Y.	Smith, Tex.
Shaw, N. Y.	Dill, N. J.
Rosewater, Neb.	Weil, Pa.
Gaines, Tenn.	Dowe, N. Y.
Jones, Ind.	Lockwood, Pa.
Atkinson, W. Va.	Clarke, Iowa.
Pingree, Mich.	Luce, Mich.
Thurber, N. Y.	Collins, Ill.
Potter, Pa. .	Jones, Wis.
Keasbey, N. J.	Search, Pa.
	Brown, Ark.
	Crow, Mo.
	Foster, Ohio.

Chairman Howe called the conference to order at 3 o'clock and appointed the following committee on finance and publication:

A. C. Bartlett, Ill.	EX-OFFICIO:
R. D. Sutherland, Neb.	Franklin H. Head, Ill.
Thomas M. Osborne, N. Y.	Ralph M. Easley, Ill.
William Dudley Foulke, Ind.	
T. B. Walker, Minn.	

George E. Clark, of Iowa, submitted the following:

Resolved, That all addresses prepared for delivery at this meeting and crowded out for lack of opportunity may be filed with the secretary, and thereby become a part of the official records of the proceedings, and as such entitled to publication, subject only to the same revision as addresses actually delivered. The resolution was adopted by unanimous vote.

The chair then announced that the final session would be devoted to an open debate consisting of five-minute talks. He called upon Gen. T. S. Smith, of Texas, who explained the workings of the anti-trust law in his state.

T. S. SMITH.

Attorney-General of Texas.

Before I came to this conference I arrived at the conclusion that in order to remedy the wrong and protect the right of the people and the corporations, it was necessary to have not only state legislation, but also national legislation along these lines.

I take the position that no corporation can do business in another state without the consent of that state. The Federal government cannot give a corporation the right to do business in a sovereign state without the consent of that state. It is only by comity between states that a corporation chartered in one state can do business in another.

The courts have decided that in forming corporations, they can only be formed by the association of individuals, and that one corporation cannot be formed by another corporation. So far as the Texas anti-trust law is concerned, we do not expect to confiscate anybody's property. We say to you: "You may come to Texas and transact any business, but it must be a legal business and open to competition, and that restriction bears alike upon individuals, partnership and corporations."

JAMES B. DILL.

North American Trust Company.

James B. Dill, of New York, an authority on the New Jersey law and one of its framers, said in part:

In the major part of the sentiment expressed here, I, as a corporation lawyer, agree with the speakers. I agree with what has been said by the labor organizations, that that corporation which fails to devote its earnings, first to the increase of wages, will eventually go to pieces. I cannot agree with Mr. Cockran that it makes not much difference how much you capitalize a corporation, provided you make it public. A corporation that issues a certificate of stock which says on the face of it that it represents $100, when these men know it does not represent $100, misrepresents the facts and should not and will not succeed. It makes a difference to the man who gets stock on that certificate, believing he is getting $100 worth. One of the greatest evils of the day is overcapitalization.

I agree with the proposition laid down by the honorable attorney-general of the state of Texas, and I say to you that New Jersey has been as much misunderstood in Texas, as Texas has been misunderstood in New Jersey. The secretary of state of New Jersey is obliged to take and place on file any charter which is properly presented, and it has been the abuse of the New Jersey law, and not the use of it, which has brought New Jersey into disrepute.

In speaking of honest combinations for business, I want to point out two dangers which are likely to arise: the first is over-

capitalization, and in the second place concealment. If, instead
of providing for the punishment of trusts, after being organized,
you will provide for the punishment of the man that promotes
them, you will kill the eggs in the nest before they are hatched.

I would simply provide for the English statute in this country
—that any article advertising the stock of a corporation, or any
prospectus issued in regard to the stock of a corporation, wherein
a sum of money is mentioned as the subscribed capital, shall truly
state the amount of money actually paid and subscribed as capital
of the corporation. I would pass the English law, which is that
every holder of stock, and every person through whose hands it
may have passed, shall be deemed to hold that stock, subject to
the payment in full in cash, unless the stock is issued, together
with a contract showing all the conditions of the issue of that
stock, which shall be filed in every state where the company does
business. Then everybody would find out in regard to it.

The effect of these meetings here, whatever resolutions are
passed to-day, I believe will check these dishonest combinations,
because it will show that men are still living who go about ready
to prick the bubbles of sham and fraud wherever they are found.

LAURENCE GRONLUND.

Socialist, Editorial Staff New York *Journal*. (Since deceased.)

We mean legitimate, sound trusts, not fraudulent concerns, such, for instance, where smooth scoundrels sell to gullible
people millions worth of worthless common stock, which they
know will never produce a dividend. There are plenty of means
and of laws to take care of this class. The legitimate trusts are
either associations of capital—and to these, department stores
belong—or unions of labor. We shall deal with both, though
it is the former alone that creates difficulties for us.

Let us at the start understand that it is impossible to crush
out either kind of trusts. The politicians who propose that
remedy are either supremely ignorant or downright demagogues.
In order to find out how to deal with trusts of capital, we must
understand their origin.

They are not the outcome of "prohibitive" or other tariffs;
neither are they the products of railroad discriminations, though
they often are considerably assisted thereby. They are economic
necessities, due to our complex civilization. Our commercial and
industrial affairs have shown during the last hundred years an
ever accelerating tendency to larger schemes, more elaborate or-

ganization, more intricate machinery. Our vast iron and steel industry comes down from the village blacksmith, our huge shoe factories from the village cobbler, our textile industry from the village hand-loom. At one time everyone worked for himself. Then came small, then large firms, followed by joint-stock companies and corporations. Finally, during the last generation, trusts, more and more extensive and intricate organizations, having for purpose to limit or abolish competition, since it was found to have become highly injurious and unprofitable.

Thus it cannot be too much emphasized that trusts are not due to any casual cause, not to wrong-headedness, not to vicious business principles, often even not to voluntary choice. A brewer in England declared, "We are compelled to take over the other breweries; we don't want to, but we are obliged to." It is an irresistible tendency, of late appalling in its rapidity, to be ascribed to increase of population, scientific discoveries and mechanical inventions.

Of course, it cannot be stopped. To try to crush the trusts would be like the attempt by a dam to stop the mighty Mississippi. The trusts will go on; the various industries in each line will come under a central management. They will in our country develop in all directions, till finally—some time during the Twentieth Century—all considerable industries will be under the control of trusts, extending from the Atlantic to the Pacific. There is absolutely no help for it.

Still we say, the trust is not at all a monster; it is a phenomenon at which to look fearlessly, and to utilize for the public welfare. For this purpose we must fully understand wherein the dangers of the trust consist. It is generally supposed that the only interest the public has is how the trust affects wages and prices. We think this is a great error. We do not believe that trusts as yet have seriously lowered wages or raised prices. They surely need not do it. And we know that in many cases they have lowered prices and raised wages.

But there are two very serious dangers that threaten in the future. Let us assume that the time has come when every considerable industry has come under one head, one manager, whose sway will extend from ocean to ocean. What powers will such a chief not have, what power especially for mischief! Then the trust, indeed, will be capable of seriously affecting the public welfare; then indeed it may lower wages and raise prices, if it has a mind to. Can a democracy like ours stand such a state of things? Can it tolerate in its midst a handful of such autocrats, whose aim is simply private greed, and who do not need to care a particle for social need? Already we are now living under an absolutism of capital to which other nations are strangers—but what will it be then?

Again, in every trust, the owners virtually abdicate all their powers in favor of the manager. Hence, when all our industries have become trusts, capital will have had its character completely changed. Formerly capitalists performed a highly important function, that of directing production; capital had a social character, and was subject to noteworthy social obligations, which sometimes were splendidly discharged. But in the future our capital-holders will become industrially and economically useless, first superfluous, then harmful; they actually will become rudimentary organs in the social organism, and capital-holding will become a pure personal privilege, subject to no social obligation whatever. Can a democracy like ours stand this; will a democracy stand it? No. Such a state of affairs will be simply the last step but one.

Even before trusts arose, when we only had large enterprises that controlled matters of vital interest to the people, the public was forced to step in, in order merely to secure the rights of consumers. Public control has again and again been asserted. Grandmother always has had her way. So with still greater force it will be in the future. The organization of trusts is admirable; it knocks into the heads of all with sledge-hammer blows the patent truth that system is better than planlessness. The machinery of the trust is all ready to the hands of democracy—to public control. No one would think of socializing an industry that was divided into a hundred thousand businesses. But this is a national monopoly. That is why the trust movement is an irreversible step along the path to universal co-operation.

This, we say, is the first answer to the question, what to do with the trusts: Look forward to the future public ownership and management of their enterprises, but let this change proceed slowly. However, prepare for it, make it the ideal of the coming century, and treat the trusts accordingly.

The second thing to do, meanwhile, is to protect labor against the trusts. That they in the future may raise prices arbitrarily is bad enough, but that they arbitrarily may reduce wages is much worse. Oh, if the trusts would believe that it is to their advantage to include their employes in the benefits which they achieve, if they would conclude to revive the ancient guilds on a higher plane, then the future might be quite bright—but they are too selfish for that!

How, then, protect labor? For our laboring people to help

our demagogues in attempting to crush the trust would be suicidal. They would be the first and only ones to feel the blows of such an enterprise. Undoubtedly our trades unions are trusts. Our work people generally do not know what they owe to trades unions, especially what they owe to the old English trades unionists, who kept up their unions in spite of parliamentary terrors. That they now enjoy higher wages and shorter hours is due to the unions. Though strikes often are disastrous to the participants, there never was one, either won or lost, that did not benefit the working people as a class.

It is well that work people are fast coming to look upon the workman as positively immoral who holds aloof from his fellows and refuses to enter the union of his trade. With the arrival of the trust, their ideal has become an organization, controlling the entire labor-force of the country, nothing less than a National Syndicate of Labor. They are right. Unless the labor trusts develop equally with trusts of capital, our civilization will soon come to a halt.

But the work people cannot achieve this ideal now with their own unaided efforts—still less when the trusts have gained their giant strength. The State must help them, and a demand is soon to be made on our politicians which they cannot resist. Such a demand has in fact been made by the well-known anti-socialist writer, William H. Mallock, to-wit: That the trades unions be made an "estate of the realm" by being granted "a privileged status-law." Our legislators must persuade every workman, induce him by every practicable motive, to join his union, even to the extent of granting to the unions the privilege of, in last resort, determining all labor questions—thus making the union the representatives of the men on an equal footing with the haughtiest employer. To those who will be horrified at this suggestion, we recommend the words of Thorold Rogers: "I would limit the franchise, parliamentary and local, to those and those only who enter into the guild of labor."

These unions, of course, must be organized in a thorough democratic fashion, so that every workman will have a vote that counts as much as that of everyone else. Moreover, the State, as the representative of the whole community, will rectify the many serious blunders that trades unions in the past have committed, and which sometimes have made them absolutely anti-social institutions, such as the limitation of apprentices and forbidding able workmen to do the best they can.

This is the way to protect adult labor. But we must also protect our growing-up youths against the trusts—both of capital and labor. We must have a new education for our boys—a truly democratic education. Every phase of civilization has had its appropriate education. A good education under the ancient régime was different from a good education during the Middle Ages, and that again very different from a good education for the Twentieth Century. Our boys must be trained into being all-round men, fit to take their places in a perfect democracy. Next, our people now are being forced—especially by the trusts—to take their places according to their capacity, as portions of a great machinery. That is, we are fast becoming a nation of specialists. Specialization evidently is the law that will govern our future. No man will amount to anything unless he becomes a specialist in something useful, and just by becoming such a specialist will he become a valuable member of a perfect democracy.

We must have such an education. Indeed, it has already been started under the name of "The New Education." It will make our boys into capable specialists and all-round men. For that purpose the State must have control of ten years of the lives of our boys, during which first the principles of the kindergarten and then the principles of manual training should govern. Thus the boys will be trained to take their places in the ranks of the producers, and both the trusts of capital and of labor must be made to submit.

Lastly, we come to the third thing we can do about the trusts. While public control of what is now strictly private business should be merely the ideal for the next century, and not be attempted until its close, there is some business that should immediately be entered upon. That is the so-called public utilities, such as municipal ownership and management of waterworks, of course, of street transportation in every form, of gas works, and electric power works. These may not yet be trusts—only large enterprises. But in Brooklyn we find surface and elevated roads already a trust, and in Manhattan they will soon be that. It would be highly desirable, and the best thing for itself, if the new democracy would in its next national platform incorporate a plank demanding municipal control. Nothing would so much convince our people of the blessings of public control, and prove to them that government can do business as well, and even better, than private parties, as such an object lesson.

But here we have still a suggestion to make. It is that the State should have more to say than now it has in municipal enterprises. For them to succeed, they must be undertaken, not with a view of giving labor employment, but with the object of furnishing the best and cheapest water, light, and transportation. This the State can effect better than the city. Hence the cry of "local self-government" is wrong. Capitalists might just as properly demand that the legislature shall grant the stockholders of a railroad "self-government free from State interference." The city is a creation of the sovereign State, and when a charter is granted it should safeguard State interests to the same extent that is supposed to be done in granting a charter for a railroad. We say that the State should exercise oversight and have final control, simply because it at least is one step further removed from local pressure, and hence will dare and be able to do things that the local authorities will not dare even attempt.

Then there are public utilities that come under the jurisdiction of the Nation which will furnish splendid opportunities for curbing the trusts. We should have a National express system, to which the late convention with Germany ought to give a great impulse, a National telegraph, National banks of deposit (postal savings banks) and National banks of loans from the funds thus accumulated, and finally National control of railroads. We do at present advocate National ownership and management of these latter; this might as yet be too big a mouthful to digest, but National control of railroad fares and freight-rates—this is perfectly practicable, and has been several times recommended to Congress. It would with one stroke abolish the unjust discrimination, both between localities and between shippers, which the interstate commission has been unable to effect. If trusts should ever dare to raise prices, such a National control of freight rates will immediately bring them to their senses. It is perfectly practicable, we contend. Through a committee of Congress it is just as easy to establish schedules of fares and freight rates on all our railroads, and to enforce them, as through the committee on ways and means to establish schedules of duties on imports and to enforce them, as is now done.

This is a practical way, and, we think, a far-seeing way to utilize the trusts for the public welfare, while to attempt to crush the trusts, we repeat, is simply the notion of the demagogues.

In conclusion, we beg those who want more information in this direction to read an English anonymous book entitled, "The Social Horizon," and this writer's last publication, "The New Economy."

CLEM STUDEBAKER.

Manufacturer, South Bend, Ind.

Within certain reasonable limits the combination of agencies for the production of a given article decreases the cost of production. Such combinations enable the use of the latest improved machinery, and the adoption of general facilities to expedite the progress of work usually impossible if the manufacture is carried on with limited capital, or with small productive capacity. Further, it is well known that managerial assistance usually costs little more for a business of great magnitude than for one the output of which is small. On the other hand, however, whenever a business becomes so large that its oversight is impossible by one executive head, then it is often the case that economies are less likely to be successfully practiced. Such I imagine would be the case if it were undertaken to operate plants widely separated throughout the country. As to whether the decrease of cost of production ought to be beneficial to society, or the reverse, I think this answers itself in the asking. Morally considered, society ought to be benefited by every honest and proper improvement of conditions in the material world.

To what extent a decrease of the cost of production will profit the consumer will depend largely on the necessity which constrains the purchaser to share with him his saving. If the combination in question were such as to utterly preclude competition, the benefit which would accrue to the consumer by a saving effected by the producer would quite possibly be inappreciable. Most producers under such circumstances would be quite likely to arrogate to themselves credit for the saving effected, and would consider that a division of the benefits under such circumstances would come under the head of philanthropy or benevolences rather than matter of fact business.

I would regard a general combination of all of the manufacturing plants for the production of any given article of manufacture as likely to be to some extent disadvantageous to the wage earner. The operation of some factories would perhaps be discontinued in favor of others more eligibly situated, and to the degree that concentration of forces would increase productiveness, there would be a correspondingly diminished demand for laborers. But this, of course, happens whenever improved machinery is introduced, or whenever there is a readjustment of production occasioned by a change in conditions affecting such production.

I do not imagine that combination among industrial enter-

575

prises will very seriously affect middlemen. In some cases commercial traveling men could be dispensed with, but the day when the public can be conveniently supplied without the intervention of the merchant, is a long ways off.

No true monopoly is possible in this country except that enjoyed by virtue of a patent granted by the United States. If those who undertake to inaugurate trusts had a monopoly of the trust business there would be cause for alarm. But any one can go into the trust or combination business who is able to find others who will join him. Herein is the safety of society. Combinations of capital build railroads and decrease the cost of travel and transportation. Some part of that saving they keep as profit, but whenever they undertake to keep so much of it from the public as to give them unusually large returns on their capital, a rival road springs up, and down goes the cost to the consumer. Trusts have undertaken to enfold producers so as to limit competition, but in vain. No sooner have they gathered into the fold all in sight than up springs another. And this will continue to be the case so long as there are profits made which allure outside capital, and outside capital is left free to take a hand in. Sugar refining, the manufacture of tobacco, etc., are cases in point. Whenever these great companies give evidence of making large profits, some powerful rival comes into the field, and competition proceeds to regulate prices on a lower plane.

Combination within reasonable lines is likely to be of benefit. This is already evident in the fact that our products in iron and steel are coming into large demand throughout the world, even in England herself.

The best service which our legislators can render the country, when considering the subject of our productive agencies, is to insure enterprise and home capital a fair field and no favor. It is folly to talk of restraining legitimate combinations. There is scarce a corner grocery in the land that is not witness to a combination of money and brains, a combination for the mutual benefit of the combined. The whole country is built up of combinations. They exist alike in society, in government and in business, and it is as futile and senseless to talk about restrictions in this particular as it would be to undertake to make Niagara flow up stream into Lake Erie.

As manufacturers we feel no concern about combinations of capital in our line of business. It is the brain power of a competitor, rather than his capital in money, which makes him formidable in the struggle.

S. A. MARTIN.

President Wilson College.

The determining question in all of life's activities is, will it pay? Will the outcome of the proposed enterprise compensate for the capital, the time and labor and whatever else must be invested, risked, or used in the work? Is there the prospect of a satisfactory *quid pro quo?* By this the enterprises of the business world are judged.

I am not here to criticise this rule of business. I do not question its validity if properly applied. But I venture to suggest that commercial and industrial methods cannot be wisely judged by the results which may appear only on the ledger. Still less can they be judged by such reports as cover only a year, or even twenty years.

Many of the forces which make for public weal or public woe require generations to effect their purposes. Some influences of sturdiest growth and richest fruitage ripen only after centuries of silent growth. The development of national character, the formation of those attributes which make a people great, is not the work of years or decades, but of generations.

In estimating the effects of such a movement as this which we are now discussing we do but belittle and obscure the subject when we speak of it as though it could be stated in terms of dollars and cents, or in any results of mere material prosperity. The prevalence of an industrial system dominated by great aggregations of capital and great federations of labor might result in such prosperity of business as the world has never seen, and yet prove an unmeasurable curse. It certainly will do so, if it in any considerable degree debauch the conscience or degrade our manhood.

> "Ill fares the state, to hastening ills a prey,
> Where wealth accumulates and men decay. '

Now it is not fair to presume that such will be the tendency of such a system; but it is important to inquire with great care what effect it will have on the average manhood of our people.

It is strongly urged that on the whole the influence of such combinations, such fuller organization of our industries, will be favorable to the development of a higher, stronger, purer type of character—that the average manhood will be elevated. In support of this we have been offered some considerations of importance, and we would gladly be convinced. But for myself I cannot without most serious apprehension see the small proprietor eliminated, the freedom of his will abridged, his conscience handicapped, and the sphere of his thought and actions circumscribed to very narrow limits. I cannot see in all that has been offered, nor does the range of my imagination find any compensation adequate for the surrender of so large a portion of the exercises which in all the ages we have depended on to make men manly.

We cannot forget that in all our history, the small proprietor, the independent workman, toiling with his own tools in his own shop, or driving his own team to till the farm he owns—that these men have been and are to-day the ultimate dependence of our civilization. In every social revolution in historic times this class has been the bulwark of the state, the conservator of justice. the savior of social order. Can we with safety eliminate this class, or even diminish its number or its power?

It is urged by some that trusts will not drive out the small proprietor, that there will always be a field for competition, but we doubt it. Even though our laws be strictly just, and our courts maintain their ermine spotless, which I trust they will do, though it must be in face of greater temptation than ever before. Still, the natural advantage of great combinations of wealth and influence is too great to be rivaled in an open field. The earthen pot may sail with the brazen pot on an open sea and with equal winds, but when the storm dashes them together, it is easy to predict which will go to the bottom.

But my chief concern is not for his business, but his character. Can the small proprietor lose his independence in business and not lose his integrity of character? It certainly is not impossible, but it certainly is extremely difficult.

Few men, if any, feel the same sense of responsibility for acts committed as an agent of a corporation as they feel for acts which they alone direct. Clerks and officers will share in fraud and rank injustice which they would not stand sponsor for before the world, and little at a time men are seduced from their high sense of honor and integrity because each small increment in the downward course is laid in the balance against the loss of their position.

Each point seems too small to fight for, but as one after another is given up, the conscience is corrupted and the manhood of the man enslaved.

What I have said is but an illustration of the evils which I fear from this intense and universal tendency to greater and still greater aggregation, combination and insatiate eagerness for organization. Yet I do not stand here to oppose it. I do not think it any more worth while to oppose the evolution of our business life by argument than it would be to rail at the precession of the equinoxes, or quarrel with the seasons of the year. The harm, if harm it be, is done; charters of the most liberal nature have been granted by the score, and we must face conditions which exist. I know of no power on earth that can prevent men from openly or secretly combining to get the best prices that the market will afford for what they have to sell, whether that be labor or the product of labor.

The state can withdraw the protection of the tariff, and the state will no doubt do so. The state can readjust taxation, so that great corporations shall have their fair share of the public burdens, which I think they do not now. But trusts are here and here to stay as the result of the inevitable laws of industrial development.

For us the duty is to recognize the facts, face the conditions of the age we live in; meet the evils of the present hour as they rise, protect the individual from the greed of wealth and the selfishness of labor, to educate the conscience, and devise new channels for individual enterprise. Thus with the unfaltering faith in the fair-minded honesty of the American people go on to occupy the fields of opportunity which open so abundantly before us in this age and country.

WILLIAM DUDLEY FOULKE.

William Dudley Foulke took issue with some of the remarks made by Col. Bryan, saying in part:

It seems to me that the plan suggested by Mr. Bryan for the annihilation of trusts will be found entirely inadequate for that purpose. He proposes that no corporation organized in one state shall be allowed to do business in any other state until a license shall be first secured, and that this license shall only be given upon proof that the corporation is not a monopoly, and is not attempting to become a monopoly.

Very few corporations will be prevented from doing business by such a provision. Every company which now exists can point to some competitor. Even the Sugar Trust, which once controlled 98 per cent of the business in that line of industry had 2 per cent of competition. The other trusts have a far greater proportion. Mr. Bryan himself said that we had at present no illustration of a complete monopoly. The corporations then can easily make the proof that they have no monopoly, and it certainly will not be hard for their officers to swear that they are

579

not attempting to establish monopolies. It will be very difficult, on the other hand, to show that these statements are untrue.

But even if a license should be refused, even if all the states should prohibit foreign corporations from doing business within their borders, this would not "annihilate" the trusts. They might sell their goods to a middle-man, who, if he should become the owner of property lawfully manufactured in his own state, could not under our federal constitution be excluded from selling it in other states. Even if you were to provide that a monopoly should not recover the price of its goods, still you could not annihilate the trusts. It would be important for buyers to preserve their credit, and they would hardly dare to take advantage of such a law. Or if it were found necessary, the trusts would sell for cash. So long as they could sell lower than any one else, they could still keep their present advantages.

The states have been passing laws for the abolition of trusts for more than ten years. As early as 1894 twenty-two states had enacted statutes for this purpose, yet all these laws as well as the federal act were found to be totally ineffective. The Supreme Court of the United States in the Knight case—the case of the Sugar Trust—decided in regard to the Sherman anti-trust law that it applied only to the agencies controlling transportation, and not to manufacturing industries at all, even though the products of these industries were sold in many states. The Court said that commerce merely "served manufacture to fulfill its functions," and indicated that the Constitution had given Congress no power over manufacturing trusts, and that the Sherman act had not prohibited them. To do this, therefore, an amendment to the Constitution will be required.

Now an amendment to the Constitution has to be adopted by two-thirds of both houses of Congress and ratified by three-fourths of all the states. It would be very hard to secure such an amendment. And if we are to have federal legislation and federal courts controlling our manufacturing industries, industries which now affect nearly all the agencies by which we live and move and have our being, it is evident that state lines will become very shadowy in the presence of these great industrial forces of a consolidated republic.

My friends, are we ready for that change?

Judge Harlan pointed out in his dissenting opinion in the Knight case the necessity for federal control if the trusts were to be overthrown. "If one great combination," he asked, "should control the sugar industry, another the flour mills, another the elevator business, another the cotton business, and so on, what power would be adequate to deal with such organizations except the federal power?"

But it seems to me that even if all corporations could be destroyed (which I think is impossible) we could not even then abolish the trusts. If the Standard Oil Company were dissolved the men who control it might with their vast capital organize a partnership to carry on the same business in the same way, or if that would involve too great a risk, or, if partnerships, too, should be made illegal, what is there to prevent the stockholders of the great companies from loaning the value of their stock to some manager, agreeing to receive in lieu of interest a proportionate part of the profits of the joint adventure? If you abolish one form of combination another will take its place. When you propose to annihilate trusts you are proposing to destroy the tendency of men to unite and organize their business, and it is just as impossible to destroy that as it is to annihilate the law of gravitation.

Mr. Gaines: Does the speaker desire to amend the Constitution and give the federal government exclusive power? Or does he want the states to have the power?

Mr. Foulke: I believe the power to annihilate the trusts cannot be given at all. When it comes to regulation, let the federal government exercise the powers it has and let the state governments exercise the powers they have to-day. Although we cannot annihilate the trusts, we may regulate and restrain their injurious influence. You cannot stop the Mississippi by a dam, but you may conduct it into safer and more convenient channels.

Something may be done by tariff legislation, and I believe that many even of those who are in favor of the protective system would be willing to see our tariff laws modified so as to prevent any industry which has thereby acquired a monopoly from using that monopoly for the purpose of exacting exorbitant prices.

But the greater part of the trusts do not owe their existence to the tariff. The Standard Oil Company did not acquire its power through legislation of this kind. Trusts exist even in free trade England, and if you change the tariff laws you will hardly do more than scratch the surface of the great question involved in these vast combinations.

The law may do something also to prevent unjust discriminations. I think that would be wise not only in respect to railroad companies, but in respect to all corporations.

Mr. Bryan spoke of the evils of over-capitalization. I agree that that ought to be prevented if possible, but even here we shall find difficulties. A government expert might be required to make the valuations, not only of the actual property of each company, but also of its good will. Often the good will of a business costs a great deal, and has a substantial value apart from tangible property. For instance, the circulation of a newspaper is perhaps the greater part of its capital. Mr. Bryan said that a dry goods merchant could not inflate the value of his goods. Yet there are many dry goods merchants who would not sell their business for a good deal more than their stock is worth. If you want to prevent over-capitalization you must have all these things estimated periodically by some competent and disinterested authority. That will be no easy task.

The requirement of publicity will do a great deal. In this respect the provisions of the national banking act point out the way for us to follow. But the information called for ought to be a great deal fuller than that now required of national banks. Periodical statements and examinations should be made not only of stock, salaries, property, dividends, wages, prices of materials bought and goods sold, but of all other matters which tend to throw light upon the condition of the corporation and its management of the particular industry involved. This publicity will restrain many abuses, and it will throw light upon the question as to what further legislation is needed.

The trusts cannot be annihilated, but as to their regulation, I have no doubt that our people will at last find remedies which shall be sufficient to counteract many of the injurious consequences of monopoly.

WILLIAM JENNINGS BRYAN.

There were loud calls upon Col. Bryan to respond to Mr. Foulke, and he did so, saying:

I would not occupy the time again but for the fact that the gentleman from Indiana (Mr. Foulke) has referred to a plan which I suggested, and I am afraid that he does not fully understand it.

Just a word in regard to the plan. I want to repeat that it was not presented as the only plan, nor is it necessarily the best plan. It is simply a plan. I was sorry that, when the gentleman got through destroying this plan, he did not suggest a better one. Political agnosticism is of no great benefit to the public. Not to know what to do is often a convenient position to occupy, but it contributes very little to the settlement of a question.

My plan is this: First, that the state has, or should have, the right to create whatever private corporations the people of the state desire.

Second, that the state has, or should have, the right to impose such limitations upon an outside corporation as the people of the state may think necessary for their own protection. That protects the right of the people of the state to say, first, what corporations they shall organize in their state, and second, what corporations they shall permit to come from other states to do business in their state.

Third, that the federal government has, or should have, the right to impose such restrictions as Congress may think necessary upon any corporation which does business outside of the state in which it is organized.

In other words, I would preserve to the people of the state all the rights that they now have, and at the same time have Congress exercise a concurrent remedy to supplement the state remedy. When the federal government licenses a corporation to do business outside of the state in which it was organized, it merely permits it to do business in any state, under the conditions imposed by that state, in addition to the conditions imposed by the federal government. I would not take away from the people of the state, any right now existing, but I would have the federal government and the state government exercise the powers that may be necessary to annihilate every monopoly.

I do not agree with the gentleman that you cannot annihilate a monopoly. I believe it is possible to do so. While the gentleman was speaking I could not help thinking of the lines of a song. While he was destroying every remedy suggested, and yet presenting no other, I thought of the lines:

"Plunged in a gulf of deep despair,
Ye wretched sinners lie."

Now, it is a great deal easier to find fault with a remedy proposed than to propose a remedy which is faultless. Macaulay— I think he is the author of the remark—has said that if any money was to be made by disputing the law of gravitation, able men could be found to write articles against the truth of that law. I have no doubt that any remedy that is proposed will be assaulted. But those who believe that the trusts must go will accept the best remedy they can find, try it and then accept a better one, if a better one is proposed, and keep on trying until the people are protected.

Now, this is a conference. We have not met here to destroy the trusts. Every law for the annihilation of the trusts must be secured through political action. We are here to discuss these questions. We are here to contribute what we can and to hear what others have to say. We are here to consider the various remedies proposed. I am not sure the remedy which I propose is unconstitutional. I am not sure that the Constitution would prohibit such an act of Congress as I suggest. Suppose that Congress should say that whenever a corporation wants to do business outside of the state it must apply to and receive from some body, created by Congress for the purpose, a license to do business. Suppose the law should provide three conditions upon which the license could be issued,

1. That the evidence should show that there is no water in the stock.

2. That the evidence should show that the corporation has not attempted in the past, and is not now attempting, to monopolize any branch of industry or any article of merchandise; and

3. Providing for that publicity which everybody has spoken of and about which everybody agrees.

Suppose that is done. Who is here to say that such a law would be unconstitutional? The Supreme Court in deciding the Knight case, did not say that a broader law than the present one would be unconstitutional. It is true there are things in the decision which suggest that, but until that question is presented to the court, you cannot say that the court has passed upon it. It is also true that Justice Harlan, in his dissenting opinion, assumed that a broader law would be held unconstitutional, but no one has a right to say that if such a law as I suggest were passed and reviewed by the Supreme Court, it would be held unconstitutional. But, suppose the law is passed and held unconstitutional; then we can amend the Constitution.

The gentleman suggests that it is a difficult thing to get two-thirds of both houses and three-fourths of the states to favor such an amendment. That is true; it is a difficult thing, but if the people want to destroy the trusts they can control two-thirds of both houses and three-fourths of the states. But what is the alternative? Sit down and do nothing? Allow them to trample upon you, ride rough-shod over you, and then thank God that you still have some life left? The people are told to be contented, but I think contentment may be carried too far.

I heard of a man once who had been taught to be contented

with his lot, and finally became very poor and traded off his coat for a loaf of bread. Before he had a chance to eat the bread a dog came along and snatched it away from him. He felt a little indignant at first, but finally that feeling of contentment came back to him, and as he watched the dog turn around a corner in the road carrying the bread away, he said: "Well, thank God, I still have my appetite left."

Now, there are some people who seem to think we ought to be satisfied with anything. My friends, the American people are entitled to the best that there is. The American people are entitled to the best system on every subject. I believe when these questions are presented to the American people they will select and secure the best system. I do not believe it necessary for us to sit down quietly and permit a great aggregation of wealth to strangle every competitor. I do not believe that it is in accordance with our dignity as a people, or in accordance with the rights of the people to say, that because a great corporation is organized, therefore, it should be permitted to go into the field of a rival, undersell it until it bankrupts it, raising the money by higher prices somewhere else. I don't think it necessary for us to do that.

I have only suggested a plan. It may not be the best plan. If you have anything better, propose it. If there is any amendment that you can think of that will improve it, suggest it. I am anxious to apply a remedy.

Let me suggest one other thing that I believe will be a step in the right direction. The great trouble has been that, while our platforms denounce corporations, corporations control the elections and place the men who are elected to enforce the law under obligations to them.

Let me propose a remedy—not a remedy, but a step in the right direction. Let the laws, state and national, make it a penal offense for any corporation to contribute to the campaign fund of any political party. Nebraska has such a law, passed two years ago. Tennessee has such a law, passed two years ago. Such a measure was introduced in the state of New York, but so far it has not become a law.

You remember the testimony taken before a senate committee a few years ago, when the head of the sugar trust testified that the sugar trust made it its business to contribute to campaign funds, and when asked to which one it contributed, replied that it depended upon circumstances.

"To which fund do you contribute in Massachusetts?" was asked. "To the Republican fund." "To which fund in New

York?" "To the Democratic fund." "To which fund in New Jersey?" and the man replied, "Well, I will have to look at the books, that is a doubtful state."

Now, that is almost a literal reproduction of the testimony of one great corporation on the subject of campaign contribution. I don't mean to say that that remedy will be a complete one, but I believe that when you prevent a corporation from contributing to campaign funds you will make it easier to secure remedial legislation, because some corporations are compelled to contribute; they are blackmailed into contributions, and such a law would protect a corporation that did not want to contribute, and also prevent a corporation from contributing that did want to contribute.

If the people are in earnest they can destroy monopoly, and you never can do anything in this country until the people are in earnest. When the American people understand what the monopoly question means, I believe there will be no power, political, financial or otherwise, to prevent the people from taking possession of every branch of government, from president to the supreme court, and making the government responsive to the people's will.

As Col. Bryan finished Mr. Cockran was called for.

W. BOURKE COCKRAN.

Just one moment while I express my complete concurrence in much that Mr. Bryan has said, and my great satisfaction that by taking the platform he has largely helped restore this debate to its natural limits.

I agree with Mr. Bryan that if there be an oppresssive monopoly in existence it should be suppressed, whatever may be the measures necessary to overthrow it. No constitutional limitation, no abstract theory of government, no mere human device, can deprive this people of the power to redress a wrong, when the existence of that wrong is clearly established.

The first question to which I think the attention of this conference should be directed is whether an oppressive monopoly exists, and if so, where it is. Before undertaking to discuss remedies we should make sure that evils exist. If their existence be established, the first step toward their redress is to define them in terms which everybody can understand. To call an industrial organization—a combine—a hydra-headed monster—or even an octopus—does not cast any light upon what it is, or illumine my pathway in attempting to deal with it.

I said yesterday that I have been suffering through every portion of this discussion from that dangerous intoxication of phrases which seems sufficient to maintain magnificent periods, but leaves us when all is over in such a state of mental bewilderment that we don't quite know what we have been talking about. I can understand how these phrases often produce great effect. Nothing frightens people so much as incomprehensible noises. Let an unaccountable noise be heard here now, and in a second we would all be trying to escape by the windows. Men may be put to intellectual as well as physical flight by the terrifying influences of sound. If, however, we are to succeed in making any recommendation of the slightest value to our fellow citizens we must at the outset compose our nerves and endeavor by the use of plain language to ascertain the precise nature of our industrial condition. Are we prosperous, or are we suffering? Is anybody injured, and by whom? Has this octopus of which we hear so much taken possession of anybody or anything? On whom or on what is it preying? Where is its lair?

To a very great extent these questions have been answered in the course of these proceedings. Representatives of labor organizations have told us from this platform that wages are higher than ever before. Certainly, these laborers do not appear to suffer from any form of oppression. But when we are about to express gratification at these comforting tidings, we are warned in solemn but mystical language that we are seeking to "place the dollar above the man." Now, what in the name of common sense can be the function of the dollar except to improve the condition of the man? Again, when we seek to ascertain the effect of corporate organizations on production, that is to say, on prosperity, we are told that a "God-made man" is one thing, and a "man-made man" is another; that the "God-made man" possesses in large degree the attributes of divinity, while the "man-made man" seems to have escaped from his creator, and to have developed habits of depravity during the separation. If this statement embodied a profound truth I am at a loss to understand what light it could throw on the question before us. We are discussing the effects, not the sources of corporate existence. But as matter of fact, is there such a thing as a "God-made man" in the world? There is, but he is scarce and rapidly growing scarcer. Why, the "God-made man" is the original savage.

Do you suppose that the oration delivered by Mr. Bryan this morning, or the rhetoric with which he moves multitudes to wild enthusiasm in every part of this country, could be evolved from the natural resources of man? The education which fits him for the platform, the books which he has read, the very clothes that he wears, have all been contributed to him by other men. He is, himself, at once a divine creation and a human development. In his natural abilities and disposition he is a "God-made man" and a credit to his creator; in his acquirements and in his extraordinary influence he is, thank heaven, a splendid type of the "man-made man."

I listened to my friend from Indiana with great interest while he advanced constitutional objections to remedies suggested by Mr. Bryan for what both appeared to regard as some evil or other in our industrial system. I wondered what the evil was of which they complained, and I had hoped that he would make it clear, but I am wondering yet. If there be an evil, Mr. Bryan's proposition that it must be suppressed through the Constitution, or in spite of it, is unanswerable. But, I repeat, what is the evil of which gentlemen here complain? The chief cause of alarm seems to be fear that competition will be stifled, yet the natural, nay, the inevitable result of competition, is the object of their most vehement denunciations. I confess I am at a loss to understand the mental processes which lead men to laud competition and yet to condemn the fruit which competition must always bear. Do you want competition, or do you not?

A Voice: Yes, we want competition.

Yes, you want competition. There is a very frank man, who, I believe, agrees in the main with the proposition of Mr. Bryan. He wants competition. Can you have competition without competitors? If there be competition must not somebody succeed in it? If one competitor far excells all others, will not that excellence constitute a monopoly? Will you suppress competition when it develops unapproachable merit? Will you place limits upon excellency?

A Voice: We object to the railroads being used for the benefit of one set of fellows to the detriment of another. That is a monopoly.

Mr. Cockran: I agree with you there. I would invoke all the power of government to prevent that abuse and to suppress any monopoly built on it or on any form of government favor. But for the same reason that I would suppress the monopoly built on favor, I would protect the monopoly created by excellence. There is no way to suppress a monopoly arising from conspicuous merit except by the suppression of merit. If the producer of the best commodity may not dominate the market for that particular article, neither should the possessor of particular ability in any other department of human endeavor. Must we place restrictions on capacity in law and medicine, so as to place the capable and the incapable on a common level? Must we prohibit the competent lawyer from being more successful in his advocacy than his incompetent brother? Must we prevent the experienced physician from being more efficient in checking disease and relieving pain than the beginner who has just hung out his shingle?

Mr. Bryan's position, as he states it, is that monopoly in private hands is always oppressive. Instead of distinguishing between corporations which dominate the market by excellence and those dominating it by favor, he appears to distinguish between those which are successful and those which are not.

The concern which has never been able to extend its trade beyond the limits of one locality he would not molest, while, as I understand it, his plan would practically exclude by a system of federal licenses the most prosperous industries from inter-state commerce, merely because they have succeeded in the field of competition—whether that success was due to merit or favor. This would be ruinous to them, but it would also prevent the vast body of consumers from enjoying the most efficient service and the cheapest goods. But if those who succeed in the field of industrial competition are to be punished by the exclusion of their products from other states, similar restrictions should be imposed on those who succeed in the field of intellectual competition. The most successful lawyer, physician or orator, should, so to speak, be localized—prevented from invading other states with his superior abilities, except under oppressive conditions. If successful lawyers are to be penalized, I know of one or two myself, whom I would be glad to see excluded from Washington and the Supreme Court of the United States. But it is hardly possible that Congress could be induced to pass a general law prohibiting excellence in all departments of human endeavor. Mr. Bryan's suggestion, like all other radical propositions, if it were ever brought within the domain of practical politics, would most likely result in a compromise. Congress might decide to discriminate against the successful in some one competition, but not in all. Its selection for repressive discrimination would very probably be the most successful orator, for the majority of the members would like to be his competitors, and they might be glad to embrace an effective plan for excluding from their districts whomsoever had proved himself a superior in the art.

A Voice: Do you contend that all the dominating industrial

forces of to-day have secured that superiority from fair competition?

Mr. Cockran: No, sir. As I said last night at some length,—perhaps at such length as to make it obscure,—some industries dominate the market through the merit of their products established by free competition, while others control it with products of inferior merit through government favor. Any industry maintaining a domination or monopoly of the market by the aid of government, direct or indirect, whether extended through favors granted by corporations exercising public franchises or through tariff laws, is necessarily an oppressive monopoly, because if it could flourish beyond all others through the excellency of its service, it would not need government favor and would not accept it.

For the same reason that free competition leads to the domination of the best, restricted competition leads to the domination of the baser, if not of the basest.

A Voice: Do you carry your principles of competition to the competition of workingmen for a job? Do you carry that competition—that principle—right down to that basis?

Mr. Cockran: Yes, sir. The effect of free competition among laborers is to secure highest wages and steadiest employment for the best. You surely would not prefer to see the inferior workman preferred to the superior—and one or the other must have the preference.

A Voice: I would like to ask you also, will you kindly repeat while you have the platform what you said last night in regard to the relationship of the employer and employee?

Mr. Cockran: If you can stand it, I might try. But if the statement was not clear last night to repeat it now would hardly be profitable. I will, however, refer to it before I leave the platform.

We seem to have drifted into an atmosphere of bewildering vagueness concerning what is called the evil of monopoly. I repeat if there be an evil pressing on the necks of people, whatever its source, I am ready to enlist under any banner to suppress it. If the Constitution stand in the way of redressing it, then I say let us smash the Constitution and from its fragments let us fashion weapons for the overthrow of the oppressor. If corporate organization be an evil thing, if you can show me an evil flowing out of it and inseparable from it, I would not hesitate a moment to adopt Mr. Bryan's remedy. But when it is admitted, as Mr. Bryan admitted this morning, that these evils of monopoly have not yet become apparent,—that they are evils anticipated, not suffered,—why, then, I say to him or to anybody who agrees with him, you are simply exciting yourself over a fanciful picture of your own creation. Your excessive affection for your fellows has conjured up a host of evils existing only in your own brain. You are constituting yourself a knight errant of political economy,— endangering the peace and prosperity of men by well-meant but foolish attempts to redress imaginary wrongs,—not,—it is true,— like Don Quixote tilting against windmills, but attempting to enlist the windmills on your side.

The change which has come over this world within the last ten years is the great phenomenon of civilization. A dozen years ago none but the largest cities contained public parks. The pleasure grounds laid out at the public expense, and the drives which led to them, were fully available only to those who owned their own carriages. To-day every town of considerable size possesses its place of recreation, while every mechanic and laborer can use the driveways on a bicycle of his own. The journey to and from the place of labor which formerly the laborer made every day at a snail's pace in wretched street cars, with spluttering oil lamps, drawn by miserable horses or mules, is made to-day in rapid comfortable vehicles, lighted and moved by electricity. Every workman is better housed, earns higher wages, eats more abundant and more wholesome food, reads more books and better books than ever before in the history of the race. Everywhere we find the masses of the people entering into the possession of their own, showing by the ruddier flush of health on their cheeks and the increased efficiency of their arms that God Almighty is guiding the race forward and upward,—that the height which man has reached is not a dizzy eminence from which he will fall back to disaster, but solid ground from which he will rise to still wider prosperity.

When we realize that this is an age of marvelous improvement, that the conditions of men are growing better and better every day, we ought to hesitate a while before we change the industrial system evolved from experience, for fanciful experiments suggested by exuberant rhetoric.

Mr. Morgan has called my attention to the relationship between employer and employee, and I will say one word about it before I leave the platform. It is a grievous disappointment to me that this conference which has wasted much time over what I cannot help calling fanciful conditions—conditions about which we are not agreed—has almost completely ignored the gravest peril to civilization, the most difficult question which civilized man must solve.

While we have been discussing shadowy evils and impalpable dangers, denouncing "corporate greed" and hurling defiance at the "octopus," we have paid little or no attention to these industrial disturbances which at recurring intervals threaten to arrest and paralyze industry. We may differ about the operations of trusts, we may deny their existence, but no man can be indifferent to the strike by which the convenience of thousands is invaded, the welfare of hundreds of thousands imperiled, the peace of whole communities disturbed, citizens ridden down and beaten in the streets who are at least the equals in civic virtue of the officers who club them.

A Voice: Is it not possible for the community as a whole to take possession of the machinery of government, and through that, the machinery of production and distribution, and taking possession of that machinery of production and distribution, use it to distribute the product among the men who produce, and them alone?

Mr. Cockran: My answer to that is this: it might be possible, but it would be highly imprudent. It may be that we are approaching a condition of socialism, but I don't think we are ready for it yet. As I said yesterday, I am never frightened by a word. If socialism meant a greater abundance of commodities I would be the first to welcome it. I believe, however, it would neither swell the total volume of production nor increase the laborer's share of it. If the state took into its own control the whole business of production and distribution, I do not believe that the laborer would get a larger share of the product than he enjoys to-day, or, in other words, that his wages would be higher. Under our existing industrial system nearly the whole value of every commodity is distributed among the laborers who produce it. The gentleman who has interrupted me evidently assumes that the difference between the value of the wages paid to the laborer who finishes an article and the whole value of that article represents the profit of his employer, but this is a grievous error. When an article is finally placed on the market for consumption, the price which it brings must repay not merely the laborer who finished it, but every person who contributed to its production. If this chair be worth five dollars and the wages of the laborer who finished it be one dollar, the difference does not go to the employer. From that fund of four dollars must be paid every man who has contributed to the chair, at any stage of its manufacture, from the moment when the axe was first swung against the root of the tree to the moment when the finished article was delivered to the purchaser. In fact, the proceeds of that chair is divided among laborers all over the world, the share of each being fixed by the proportion which his labor bears to the total labor bestowed upon it.

If the state replaced the private capitalist in the task of organizing or employing labor, the cost of discharging that duty would be deducted, as it is now, from the total value of the products, and I venture to say that the sum charged for that purpose would be more than the present profit of capital. Indeed, the distinction between capital and labor in my judgment is largely fanciful. Capital is but stored up labor. A man with his naked hands can labor, but not effectively. With his fingers he could turn over a few square feet of earth in a day; with a plow he could turn over several acres in the same period. A plow is capital. The tools by which the making of that chair was facilitated, the warehouse in which it was offered for sale, and the wagon in which it was delivered, are all capital. They are the products of labor expended in other days. The function of capital in production is to reinforce the efficiency of this day's labor by the labor of other days,—another instance of the close interdependence of men.

You ask me what are the functions of labor unions if the rate of wages be fixed by immutable laws. I answer that if they cannot change the relations between employer and employee, they can perform a better function. They can promote an enlightened conception of what these relations are. When employers and employees both realize that the rate of wages is regulated by fixed laws, that it cannot be more and it cannot be less than the value of the product, there will be no room for disputes, misunderstandings, or disturbances. That there is no inherent or insuperable difficulty in distributing the fruits of production is shown by the fact that strikes are not universal in the same fields of labor. It is no uncommon spectacle to see one great railway system paralyzed in the throes of a deadly conflict,—its service suspended,—its property deteriorating,—its very existence imperiled,— while in the same city another railway system, where no higher wages are paid and no longer hours of labor exacted, is in the enjoyment of industrial peace and in the full tide of prosperity. The laws governing both systems being the same, the difference in their conditions must spring from a radical difference in the characters of those charged with their administration.

I believe that as employers realize they are but captains of industry directing the labor of others, so as to make it more fruitful, they will encourage the formation of trades unions among their employees as a means of simplifying intercourse between them.

Employers and employees together cannot change the laws that govern their relationship, but they can aid each other to discover what these laws are. They can save time in the discovery, and the time saved from wrangling, disorder, riot and confusion, will be expended in profitable production, and in improving the condition of every human being throughout the country. Indeed, it is not a Utopian dream that before another conference of this character assembles, the great corporations which are the largest employers of labor, will not merely insist upon the formation of trades unions among their employees, to economize time in discussing the conditions of labor, but will require them to elect representatives to sit in the boards of direction, thus imposing on them some responsibility for the management of the joint industry—the partnership—in the prosperity of which all must share—in the decay of which all must suffer.

A Delegate: You have said we have been declaiming against the trust, and that in the entire conference nothing has been shown as to any evil committed by them.

Mr. Cockran: I spoke of those that don't enjoy any aid from government.

Same Delegate: Take the Federal Steel Trust. It was organized with a capital of $200,000,000. In less than six months' time every product of that trust, steel, iron, iron nails, barbed wire, and all necessities of the farmers, and everything that enters into the construction of buildings in every city in this country, and in the construction of every farmhouse in the United States, has been increased from 100 to 126 per cent, whereas, labor in those mills, as shown by the Amalgamated Steel Union, has only risen about 10 to 25 per cent. Now, I wish to know if the consumers of this country have not been robbed of that 90 and 100 per cent difference between the price of labor and the price of the finished product furnished to the 50,000,000 farmers in this country?

Mr. Cockran: One moment; you have asked me a question. I will answer it. (Mr. Garland rises.) I yield, however, to a gentleman who represents an organization of workingmen.

Delegate Garland: They increased the wages from 10 to 15 per cent.

Another Delegate: Now, I wish to say, with due regard to all the trades unions of this country, because I advocate their existence and I believe they are a public blessing, that any arrangements between the trades unions and the capitalized trusts which enforce from the consumers of this country more than an equitable wage, as compared with the product of the other producing factors, would be unjust.

Several delegates here arose and piled questions upon Mr. Cockran.

Mr. Cockran: It is quite useless to repeat constantly the same statements. I have said again and again on this platform that if a corporation or an industry dominates the market by any other means than the cheapness of its product, it is a public injury. Now, I say that an industrial organization which dominates the market by furnishing the best service, that is to say, the best commodities, can maintain its pre-eminence only by the same means. If it undertake to exact undue profits, if it abuse the advantage derived from excellence displayed in competition, and the government remains impartial, competition would arise in an instant.

A Delegate: Your position is, then, that monopoly is impossible?

Mr. Cockran: It depends again on what you mean by monopoly.

Same Delegate: What I mean by monopoly is the privileges and business enjoyed by one institution.

Mr. Cockran: I don't think any further discussion between you and me can be very useful (addressing delegate), as I can answer your questions only by repeating what I have said many times already. There is no way by which you can establish a monopoly without government favor, except by excellence in serving the public. While that excellence lasts I don't object to it, even though you call it a monopoly. The industrial history of this country proves that in the absence of government interference no monopoly ever advanced prices to exact undue profits without by that fact provoking opposition, and effective opposition.

Delegate Lockwood: Do you mean by government favor, railroad favor?

Mr. Cockran: Any kind of favor. Favor by tariffs, favor by railroads, favor by gas companies, favor by express companies, favor by any agency chartered by government to perform a public service. I say government should always be impartial between citizens. It should not merely be impartial itself, but every agency through which it performs any function should be impartial.

Let me revert once more to the question which I consider of vital importance. I hope these gentlemen who by their questions show they entertain socialistic opinions will come on this platform and expound them. I think, however, we will all admit that socialism, conceding it to be a remedy, is at least a distant one. I am not here to indulge in abstractions or speculations about remedies which are necessarily remote. I came to this conference in the hope that we could make some practical suggestions which might be immediately adopted. Everybody concedes that discrimination by corporations between citizens is an offence against economic laws, and should be made a serious offence against statutory laws. I believe we all concede that publicity if not a complete, is at least a partial remedy for this form of offence. Surely we may hope that our concurrence on this subject will take the form of recommendations which will soon be engrafted on the laws of every state. For my own part, I had hoped that we would go a step further and agree on some measure which might prove effective in preventing the recurrence of strikes. While we are some distance from socialism, there are insuperable objections to interference by government in the industry of private citizens, but it is entirely within the power of the state to provide that corporations exercising public franchises should be held to some accountability when the convenience of the public is disturbed by the suspension of their service. It seems to me this power could be exercised so as to maintain industrial peace.

When a railroad company fails to furnish transportation, when a gas company fails to furnish light to highways or to individuals, when any enterprise chartered by the state for public purposes fails to exercise its function, it is the business of the state to ask the reason why; in the absence of a proper explanation, its charter should be revoked, while every citizen inconvenienced by its collapse should have a right to substantial damages. I don't believe the state could settle industrial disputes as equitably or as effectually as employers and employees themselves would settle them, if they could be forced or induced to discuss them together. When, therefore, a railroad or other public corporation which has been prevented by a strike from exercising its functions can say we have met our employees by agencies of their own selection, and we are ready at any time to meet them again for full and free discussion of all questions between us, proof of that statement should be accepted as a complete defense to any action either by the state or by individuals. I had hoped that such a law might be recommended with the concurrence of every person in this conference, and I cherish that hope still. It would not be prescribing a new system of corporate management, it would be merely compelling a few concerns, —a minority whose management is ignorant and benighted,—to adopt the methods pursued to-day by the enlightened, well managed corporations which constitute a majority of all our industrial organizations.

The employer need not fear that this would reduce him to helplessness against unjust demands. There is no better method of meeting an unjust demand than by insisting that it be made public, and thus invoking against the laborer who advances it that public opinion, which is his sole support, and which furnishes him the formidable weapon of the boycott.

While the state, as I have said, would have no right to interfere in the management of a private business or manufacturing corporation to adjust disputes with its employees, it has a right to exercise its undoubted control of corporations discharging public functions in such a manner as to compel full and free discussion between these corporations and their employees of every question that threatens to interrupt their peaceful and efficient coöperation. The result of such a system would be so beneficial to the public corporations on which it had been imposed that private employers would be quick to adopt it and industrial peace would be established on the sure foundation of justice and mutual interest.

This is a suggestion of peace, of progress and prosperity,—not a suggestion to enact any new statute law, but to obey an immutable economic law, to acknowledge that partnership of all men in industry which has existed ever since free labor was established by the spread of Christianity throughout the world.

Mr. Bryan appears to think that the prosperity of the people, or, in other words, the amount of wealth which they can create is a sordid question. A sordid question! Why, upon the volume of production every form of prosperity, industrial or material, depends. Could the poet spend his days musing on the sublime and beautiful, if the necessaries of life were not supplied to him from the commodities produced by others? Must not the philosopher, surveying the wide expanse of the heavens, depend for his telescopes and mathematical instruments upon other hands whose labor he reinforces by his discoveries? Could the physician spend days and nights at the bedside of suffering, relieving pain and fighting death, if the food that supports him, the house that shelters him, the clothes that promote his comfort, and the medicines that reinforce his skill, were not produced by the industry of other men whom he has never seen? Does not the painter use the labor and ingenuity of a thousand persons in the pigments and paints with which he reproduces upon canvas the conceptions of his dreams? Is not the marble which the sculptor fashions into the semblance of life, the product of a ruder toil? Which of us can live independently of his fellows? Who can labor intelligently for his own benefit without contributing to the prosperity of this industrial partnership binding us all together in the great scheme of coöperation which is at once the object and the vital principle of civilized life?

Throughout Mr. Cockran's remarks there was a running fire of questions and comments from the delegates. This broke into his train of thought, but the speaker courteously replied to those on the floor, and after some time the interruptions ceased and the delegates only broke the silence with which they listened, to applaud the points made by the orator.

HAZEN S. PINGREE.

Governor Hazen S. Pingree, to whom Prof. George Gunton addressed some of his remarks Thursday night, replied in a letter as follows:

Prof. George Gunton,
Dear Sir: I listened with great interest to your address last evening before the trust conference, in defense of the trust. The mental equipment and training of your profession are supposed to enable you to comprehend a subject readily, correctly and thoroughly.

When, therefore, you skimmed across the surface, and trimmed around the edges, of the thought expressed in my address, criticising things which I did not emphasize, and ignoring the real truths which I sought to illustrate, perhaps I may be permitted to register an objection, or at least to set you aright in the matter.

You commenced by saying that the burden of my discourse was that the trust leads to industrial slavery, that industrial slavery destroys independence, and that without independence, American manhood is destroyed. You then proceeded to demonstrate, in the manner natural to professors, i. e., with a regard only to theoretical conditions, that where there is great wealth there is ample freedom.

Then, with an impressive tone, you asked me if I wanted the slavery that came with the poverty which would result if we check the development of trusts. I can only reply that the deduction which you make, from the statements in my paper, is unfair, but that, granting your logic, I am and would be entirely satisfied with the prosperity of this country before the trust reared its head.

Now I have no especial quarrel with professors, nor with their theoretical methods of dealing with things. But I do insist that if they are to deal with practical questions, they should not wander off into the realms of the speculative or the ideal by discussing things as they ought to be, and not as they actually are. I find no fault with your generalizations respecting poverty and wealth and slavery. I presume they are correct according to the text books.

But you entirely ignored the thought it was my purpose to express. I said that the actual, existing, present day trust, by its unlawful, indefensible methods, deprives the very best element of our people of that equality of opportunity which has been the foundation, the rock-bottom, of our greatness as a nation.

The monstrous commercial deformity, which you defend by the application of text book principles, by the crushing, conscienceless force of immense wealth and resources, inhumanly used, denies the independent business man the right to earn a living. Under trust domination, there will be no equality of opportunity. That is the point I made in my address, and you ignored it.

I think you will modify your opinions somewhat, if you will burn your text books, lock the door to your study, and come down into the market place and see the real thing at work. If you do I think you will no longer defend, or apologize for the trust. You will be glad, then, to leave that work to the newspapers, magazines, public men and orators—who are paid for it, and paid liberally, too.

When you enter into the market place, and perhaps enter some of the secret chambers, called directors' rooms, it will not take you long to find out that human selfishness and greed set at naught all the beautiful rules and axioms of political and social economy. You will then no longer be guilty of saying (as you did yesterday in answer to my paper) that because of the trust the purchasing power of the dollar is increasing every day, that with such increase comes individual wealth, that individual wealth gives independence, that independence means freedom, and that therefore my contention, that the effect of the trust (the concentration of wealth and business into the hands of a few) to separate our people into two classes—industrial masters and slaves—is all bosh.

I think that when you come face to face with actual conditions, in the market place, when you see the animals feeding and see upon what they are feeding, you will not deceive yourself longer into believing that any increase in purchasing power of the dollar necessarily means that those dollars are being distributed by the trust in larger quantities than ever before among all classes of our people. You are asking the people, the independent business men, whom the trust has forced out of business, to believe that because a dollar will buy more, therefore they have more dollars, than ever before. If this is not true, and it certainly is not, the beautiful fabric of logic which you have fashioned, as outlined in the preceding paragraph, falls to pieces. The trouble with it is that the owners of trusts are not philanthropists, and they keep the dollars themselves.

And that is the meat of this question. The trust tends to concentration of wealth into the hands of a very few, and because those few are nothing but men, they are ruled by the human motives of selfishness and greed, and not by the text book rules of social economy. When you are dealing with the trust, therefore, pardon me for suggesting that you recognize real conditions, face the real thing, and not generalize about some industrial organization that is entirely ideal.

I think you should also recognize that the trust is a human contrivance when you are discussing the matter of prices as affected by the trust. In the first place, it is your duty, as a defender, or advocate, or apologist of the trust, to point out a single instance in which a trust has voluntarily reduced prices. In the second place, I ask you if you sincerely believe that any trust, conducted by a human being, will ever reduce prices any lower than is absolutely necessary to preserve the monopoly?

Your associate on the platform yesterday, the attorney-general from Maryland, offered a panacea in the shape of government regulation through a commission. Government regulation is the remedy which the trusts themselves suggest. They would like nothing better. Their newspapers and orators are already advising such a course. They say it is conservative treatment, and that is catching. There are plenty of people who are eager to be looked upon as conservative. They want to be patted on the back by the "conservative press."

Why are the trusts satisfied with government regulation through a commission? The reason is plain enough. They recognize that a growing hostile public sentiment endangers their life. Therefore, it is important to them to pick out the remedy which will interfere the least with their operations. Hence the cry, quietly suggested by them, that government regulation through a commission is the proper thing. What has been our experience already with government commissions? I need refer only to the poor, weak, crippled interstate commerce commission. Everyone knows that the railroads look upon it as one of their best friends, and will continue to regard it as such as long as the people believe that the commission is a protection to them against rate discrimination and railroad oppression. Its uselessness is chiefly due to the fact that it is absolutely shorn of its power to do good work by lack of machinery and resources to make it effective. A commission to regulate trusts would be a similarly ineffective body. The power of money and organization would see to it that such a commission, while it might have ample powers, would have meager resources to execute them. We are facing a similar condition in my own state, where a commission whose duty it is to bring the tax dodger to justice, is being crippled and hindered by the state authorities, whose duty it is to furnish the funds necessary for the proper prosecution of the work of the commission.

I am of the opinion that the only way to treat an ulcer is with the surgeon's knife. Trusts should be cut entirely out of our industrial body. I am bold enough to predict that this will be the judgment of the people, and if it is, the method of doing it, the form which the legislation will take, is a matter of minor consideration.

The temper of last night's audience is strong evidence that the sovereigns of this country will not tolerate a temporizing or compromising treatment of this great problem. It was a representative audience. It plainly showed that it had opinions, and positive ones too. Perhaps some of them were born of a bitter experience. It is certainly true that this question comes home to everyone closer than the tariff question ever did. The attitude of that audience demonstrates that the political party or leader who remains silent on this question, or who temporizes with it (another name for conservatism) will dash itself to pieces against the rocks of a hostile public opinion that is crystallizing and growing with a rapidity that will unquestionably make the trust question greatly overshadow the artificial issues of imperialism, war, conquest, new possessions, the glory of the flag, etc.

H. S. PINGREE.

SAMUEL M. JONES.

Mayor of Toledo, Ohio.

I am inclined to regard the great growth of these organizations within the last few months rather complacently.

I believe in a large programme for society. I believe it to be our duty and privilege in this republic to find a plan big enough to provide for all of the people and I see in the growth of the trust an indication of the growing social movement toward collectivism. I believe in brotherhood; so do the makers of the trust. They believe in brotherhood for the fellows that are in the trust; I believe in the brotherhood of all men. The trust is the Great American Brotherhood (limited). We will yet learn to utilize the trust by amending the title, leaving off the last word.

The trust is preparing the way, showing society the great benefits that may be derived through association in industry and the great economic value of association, both in production and distribution. An invention that lightens the burden of the world's toilers and makes it possible for one man to do the work of twelve is called a "labor-saving machine." Does it matter whether the machine is made of wood and iron or composed of organizations and associations of men? If the result is the same it is a labor-saving machine. In this sense the trust is a labor-saving machine. The fact that the owners of the trust capture all the profit produced by the labor-saving machine does not affect the truth of this statement. That is the peculiar tendency of the modern "captain of industry." Labor-saving machinery made of wood and iron has done very little to lighten the toil of the workers. It has usually resulted in saving labor for those who do not work. Take the case of the sewing machine, one of the greatest of the labor-saving inventions. It ought to bless the world to a far greater extent than it does. All such inventions and combinations should lighten the labor of all, but within two years a committee of investigation of the Massachusetts legislature found women operating sewing machines in Boston sweat-shops twelve hours a day making boys' pants at 19 cents a dozen pairs. Because these women work in this slavish and dehumanizing way their employer, the "captain of industry," and his family were enabled to pass their summers at Nahant and their winters in a big house in the Back Bay.

According to the prevailing conception people who are thus able to live an idle, useless life at the expense of other people's toil are considered the fortunate members of society. I do not think this view, however, is the correct one. An idle life is a useless life, whether rich or poor. Indeed, there is reason to believe that if one is idle because of riches there must of necessity be guilt approaching crime in such possession and resultant idleness.

The triumph of the trust is one of the marvels of the closing years of the nineteenth century; but they are an economic development, strictly in the line of progress and our problem is not how to destroy them, but how to use them for the good of all. Like their prototype, the labor-saving machinery constructed of wood and iron, they have come to stay. A labor-saving machine might have great value on account of its producing capacity, but might be so destructive of human life as to make it imperative that it should be so improved that its "saving" power might be utilized without injury to the operative.

Thirty-five years ago I saw a mob of teamsters trying to destroy the first pipe line ever built for the transportation of oil. They feared that the pipe line was an "attack upon their craft." The movement against the trust rests identically on the same moral basis as the rage of a mob against the pipe line, elevators and labor-saving machinery generally, and I predict that it will have the same result in the end. All the legislation thus far against the trust has been almost as futile as a law against the change in the moon's phases or the ebb and flow of the tides.

We are not going back to the individualistic method of production. We are not going to pull down the department store in order that the people shall sustain fifty small stores in place of the one department store. If that is what we propose, let us continue the principle: destroy the small stores and turn the business over to peddlers. This will be carrying to logical conclusion the senseless objection to the department store and the trust.

What, then, shall we do with the trust, with the continually increasing army of unemployed thrown out by these organizations? I reply, we must organize government (society) in the interest of all, for the good of all, so that we may utilize the economic side of the trust.

We must leave off the word (limited) from the Great American Brotherhood that I have referred to and own and operate the trust for the benefit of the people, as we now own and operate the post-office trust. The profit that accrues to the organizations known as trusts, by reason of the economic production that arises from associating ten or more companies together, does not belong to those who compose the trust in any ethical sense. The profit is only made possible because the people are here, the cities are here and the means of transportation and communication are here and available, and this profit that arises from amending the ways of competition is in no just sense the property of those composing the trust.

It belongs to society, and may be properly called the "increment of associated organization." Neither the cities nor the earth have been created for the benefit of the trusts. It is clear that the earth and the "natural opportunities" that have resulted in building cities, highways, railways and commerce were created for the benefit of all alike. Equality of opportunity or brotherhood is the goal toward which the race is struggling, and the trust, while thoroughly selfish in its inspiration, is the expression of the great social spirit now stirring the hearts of the people.

I can see neither sense nor reason in the attempts to destroy the labor-saving machines by legislation, but I see both reason and hope for the American people in the movement that will utilize all kinds of labor-saving machines, including the trusts, for the benefit of the whole people. This can only come about by the process of general education that will bring the classes to understand and practice what the masses now believe in—that is, the brotherhood of industry.

The movement toward municipal ownership, toward public ownership, toward co-operation of every sort, indicates the channel through which the people are to come into possession of their own. When they are thoroughly enlightened they will simply retake in a perfectly orderly way the properties that have passed out of their hands and become private possessions, usually through the practice of deception and fraud. The people will own and operate their own trust; its name will be the Co-Operative Commonwealth.

HENRY W. BLAIR.

Ex-Senator New Hampshire.

Senator Blair, of New Hampshire, was called upon. He said in part:

I would, for a moment, call attention to one aspect of this discussion, and that is the frequent assertion which we have heard made during its continuance, that the tariff is the mother of trusts.

If you remove the tariff from the productions of our great industrial enterprises, trusts, already international, and other employers will put their capital where they can produce goods the cheapest. Their plants, machinery and money investments will be removed to other countries, where goods can be manufactured by cheaper labor and poured into our markets, thus destroying the home market for our home people.

Several delegates here propounded questions to Mr. Blair which led to a further statement of his views at some length, of which no stenographic report was made. At the suggestion of the committee Mr. Blair has reproduced the substance of what he said, as follows:

Speaking of the competition between home and foreign labor, under free trade, it must be remembered that while American labor is more intelligent and therefore more productive, yet nine-tenths of the work of the world is done by machinery, and that the European, the Asiatic, and later on, and not much later on either, the African and the islanders of the Oceanic world, can easily be taught to handle and manipulate the machine even if he cannot invent it; that capital and machinery are easily portable everywhere, while labor is not, and the more labor is civilized and enlightened, the more it is confined where it is, that is, to the locality of high conditions. Therefore the trust or any large employer of labor will go with capital and machinery wherever labor is cheapest and most subservient, *provided that by free trade he can still retain the American market.*

Any man can take a million dollar plant of cotton, woolen, sugar, or any product of manufacture to England, Russia, China, Japan, Africa or the Philippine Islands, in his pocket or in his check book, while the thousand laborers who have lived by working that plant for half their lives, in this country, are obliged to remain and starve, unless they choose to work for foreign pay.

He strongly emphasized the fact that foreign labor would soon learn how to run the machines as well, or nearly as well, as our own people. True they would not invent them or improve them at first.

We should still invent and construct machinery, but it would be for exportation to foreign lands, not for home use. In time foreign labor would become intelligent and so inventive, under the same conditions which have made us intelligent and inventive.

The truth is simply this: Free trade is the highest form of protection to labor and capital in all the rest of the world, while it ruins us. The highest civilization always costs the most, and the people of every country have just what their wages, or the income of their labor, will buy for them, measured in the standard purchasing power of the world. Commercially mankind are a unit and nothing on earth can prevent it and such they will remain. There is no escape from the laws of trade. The man who gets five cents a day lives like a dog, or worse, because he has nothing to buy a better life with, and if he gets no work at all, he dies. There are gradations in the condition of mankind just because there is more work to be done in some countries than in others. The plant, working capital, machinery, etc., and living labor must combine in order that there may be work in a producing sense, and a farm manufactures food just as much as a cotton mill manufactures cloth. The cheapest production will command the market provided that it can get there, and nothing but protection can keep foreign products from ours.

The American market is the best in the world, and under free trade (which is what this whole howl that the "tariff is the mother of trusts" is after) the world will take it from the American producer unless he works and sells just as cheaply as the Germans and the Japanese.

If American laborers, farmers and other producers want the American market, they have got to protect it, that is keep it to themselves by a tariff so high that the foreigner can not get into it. But it is said that we must have free trade in raw materials, in order that we may meet foreign competitors in foreign markets, and thus build up our foreign commerce. We already have free trade in foreign raw material for the manufacture of all such materials into articles for exportation to any foreign market.

The rebate clause in the tariff law returns from the treasury the duty paid upon the foreign raw material when the article is exported. That keeps our capital and labor employed at home, while we meet our foreign competitior on equal terms in every market of the world.

Where now is your argument for free foreign raw materials? And protection still takes care of the producer of American raw materials and of everything else American, by preserving to him intact the home market of seventy-five millions of the most highly civilized people, and therefore the greatest consumers on earth.

In fact our home market alone is worth that of any other three hundred millions of mankind.

So much for the rebate provisions of the protective tariff, in which I feel some pride, as, so far as I know, I had the honor first to urge their adoption as a general law. These provisions are the only secure foundation of a colossal and perpetual foreign trade.

Under them we manufacture the wheat of Canada at Minneapolis, and sell the flour in Canada, England, or anywhere else in the world. If we can keep our laws as they are and their administration in the hands of those who believe in them, and who are not, either openly or secretly, working to destroy, then the future of the country is stable and full of hope. If we cannot do this the future is full of despair. We must not, we cannot trust any man or party that is doubtful or shaky in the support of a protective tariff, or of our existing gold standard of value. The contracts and wages of the world have long been made and are now measured in gold. It is impossible now, or for years, to abandon the protective tariff or adopt a new standard of values, without once more destroying business and dislocating society. Agitation, or the suspicion that there may be agitation, upon these points by men or parties in power destroys confidence, and loss of confidence is calamity.

In this connection Mr. Blair filed two short papers previously prepared by him further elucidating the relation between the tariff and trusts, as follows:

I.

It is frequently observed that the trusts are a natural development of the protective tariff, and the strong prejudice against the evils which appear to be flowing from them is used as an argument against the protective system. That is to say, the existence of the trust is an argument for free trade. The ordinary and perhaps sufficient reply to this assertion is the fact that the trust exists in free trade countries as well as in our own. This fact is in itself conclusive that the trust does not originate in protection. It must be remembered that trusts are international already, and if unrestrained the tendency of capital to combine will become worldwide. Capital will combine and locate industries wherever in the world conditions are most favorable to cheap production, and naturally will go, in the long run, to those points where labor, the other great factor in production, is cheapest, the result of which will be that the laborer must follow the location of capital all over the world, in order to find employment at all. The existence of the people depends upon the work they have to do, and if the work of the American people is not done by them, they will have no purchasing power, and must starve. If the protective tariff be removed, trusts will locate American capital in Canada, in European countries, in Asiatic countries, and wherever labor can be employed at the lowest prices.

Perhaps nine-tenths of the productive power of the world is in machinery and improved tools, all of which is owned by capital, that is to say, by trusts, or will be if these great combinations continue and enlarge. So that without the protective system to interpose as an obstacle to the bringing of outside productions to the markets of the United States, it will be impossible for American laborers to obtain employment at all, unless their wages be reduced to the level of the cheap labor of other countries. So far, then, from the existence of trusts being an argument for the abolition of the protective tariff, the protective tariff is the only thing that can save to the American people their work, which is only another name for their life, and their status of civilization.

Various remedies are being proposed to cure the evils of the trust system, and the wisdom of the country is likely to be concentrated upon them.

I do not feel that I can add any particular light to the subject. I have sometimes thought that provisions by law nullifying conveyances to trusts, made with the understanding that while they are not to be employed in production, dividends are nevertheless to be paid upon the consideration given for them; that, if such conveyances were declared by law to be illegal and void, it would do more to end these combinations than anything else. Such conveyances ought certainly to be deemed against public policy because there is little difference between such transfers of property, with an understanding that the property is to become useless or partially useless, and the transfer of the property with the understanding that it is to be destroyed by fire; and when to this is added another understanding that the community is to be taxed in the form of increased prices for commodities to pay income upon this useless property, there can be no doubt that the transaction is injurious to the public, and should be made void and criminal by the general laws of the land.

I am inclined to think that the application of this principle would end the whole difficulty. It would seem to be easy of application, for every member of the body politic would be injured by the increased price of consumption, and would have the right to attack such a conveyance in the courts, and if the transaction were made a criminal offense the entire force of the community could be brought to bear, as in the case of other crimes. There are many establishments in various parts of the country which have been conveyed to trusts, with the understanding that they should not be used, and which have not been used as plants for production since they went into the possession of the trusts, and yet this idle capital receives dividends drawn from the public at large.

I do not much fear the prolonged continuance of these abusive trusts, for I believe that great financial disasters will follow their general introduction, within the next few years, which will be such a lesson to foolish and hasty investors that the system will disappear in its own ruins. The best way to cure trusts of the evils is to let them alone, to keep out of them. There are some good things about them. They are labor-saving machines in a good many respects, but what good there is in them can be applied under our old system of competitive production.

II.

The most objectionable trusts originate in the efforts of the owners of unprofitable plants to save themselves by combination with others. It would seem to be a complete answer to the proposition that protection is the mother of trusts, that trusts exist in free trade countries as well as in this, where protection prevails, and that the principal trusts of our own country are not dependent on protection for their existence or for their growth. The product of the Standard Oil Company nor the sugar trust itself are dependent either for their creation or for their growth upon the tariff. The attack of Mr. Havemeyer upon the tariff is easily explainable upon the ground that the interests of his trust would be promoted by a diminution of protection, and probably still more promoted by absolute free trade in sugar; and in the long run still more promoted by absolute free trade.

You may be sure that if the tariff was the mother of trusts, that trusts would not be attacking the tariff, but this is not in my mind the real argument of the case.

The leading trusts are already international. Their capital is invested everywhere. Naturally, they will seek the other great element of production, that is to say, labor, where it is cheapest. If the protective tariff is removed so that production outside the limits of our country can reach our markets, capital will inevitably be invested where that cheaper labor is to be found, and the work of the American people would come to be done by the laborers of foreign lands unless the American people are contented with a wage such as that of England, the continent, or of Asiatic laborers, that is to say, the cheapest labor in the world wherever it may be found.

Nothing can protect the American people in their work but the tariff. Remove it, and the destruction of our industries would be sure. The trusts, so far as they merely employ great masses of capital in legitimate competitive production cannot be objected to. The great abuse connected with them seems to me to be the fact that they seek to destroy competition by combination of unprofitable plants, which they design to close up, and substantially destroy, with those which are retained for active production, and guarantee returns upon this idle capital, to obtain the money to pay which they must unduly tax the community in prices unnaturally high. Having destroyed competition, the trust is enabled to fix the prices of commodities so as to yield returns upon this idle capital. Idle property is no longer property, and to pay an income upon it somebody must be robbed. If non-productive it should be sold for what it will bring and put into some new and active form.

Combinations of this description must be against public policy. If conveyances which have been made in the past are valid because there is no public law against them, certainly new laws could now be enacted which would declare such future conveyances illegal and void, and if in the future such conveyances were declared illegal and void *ab initio*, I believe that evil would cease. Such conveyances and guarantees of returns upon idle capital could be prohibited by suitable penalties, and as the offense is in its nature public, every individual in the community would have the right to set in motion the remedy.

It would be found impossible perhaps without new legislation to prevent the conveyances which until now have constituted the initiation of trusts and are the very basis of the whole system. Such legislation would not interfere with legitimate investment and the employment of great masses of capital in productive enterprises. Thus we should get the benefit of gigantic combinations of labor and capital without destroying naturally healthy competition. The so-called trust, when organized and managed in accordance with just business principles, is simply the idea of the labor-saving machine carried into business methods and affairs, and I believe that the objection to the trust system as an improvement in business methods, thus saving time and expense in production, can be just as legitimately urged against new improvements in labor-saving machinery. The thing is to find a true line of action, which will save to us all the benefits of the trusts in business methods and management, without yielding to the tendency to abuse the law and the interests of society by ripening the system into gigantic monopolies. Like every other improvement and good thing the trust is liable to abuses, and without proper restraint and wise legislation, and the continual vigilance of society it is sure to develop them. But to refer again to the main point, as I said in the beginning, trusts are already international. More and more they will own the capital which does the business of the world, and all the machinery, which is but another form of capital.

Inevitably, then, they will seek the cheapest labor, for capital and machinery are in their nature portable, and will go where the cheapest labor is to be found. It is clear that the tariff, instead of being the occasion of trusts, is our only protection against them. One thing is very sure—the trusts would never assail their own mother.

In conclusion Mr. Blair presented the following resolutions which he had proposed to offer for the consideration of the conference had it been decided to formulate resolutions expressing its sentiments. As it had been decided not to do this, he desired that they be printed simply as a part of his remarks, and mere personal suggestions.

Resolved, That all artificial persons known as partnerships, corporations, trusts, and all combinations of like nature, which may compete in business with individual men, should be created and should be permitted to exist only by the supreme power of the state, or nation, within whose jurisdiction they may operate, and with care to so limit and control the same in duration, capital, sphere and methods of action, and in all other respects, as not to injure but rather to promote the general welfare.

Resolved, Whenever such artificial person is created which is to operate outside the limits of the state of its origin, it should be made subject to supervision and control by the sovereignty of the nation and of any state in which it shall transact business, and to this end, and that there may be no longer any doubt of its jurisdiction, we hold that the national constitution should be amended so as expressly to confer such jurisdiction.

Resolved, Whenever such artificial person shall have violated any of the conditions upon which life was given to it, that life should be taken away by the power which gave or controls it, and its property and franchises disposed of by law; while the individuals composing, controlling, or responsible for the control of such artificial person, should at all times be held to rigid accountability, both civilly and criminally, as private individuals in like cases are held by the laws of the land.

Resolved, We demand of the government, both in the nation and in the several states, the most rigid scrutiny and control of all artificial persons, the function of which is to develop and handle the primal resources of the earth, and of those great lines of transportation which distribute to the consumer the tremendous productions of American agriculture and the commodities of our marvelous manufacturing skill, to the end that everywhere the evils of monopolistic combinations may be rooted out, exposed and destroyed.

Resolved, We recognize in full the rights of organized labor, and would still further increase them and their sphere of peaceful operation. We have no sympathy with' that theory which classifies and confounds these organizations, existing only to enable the individual man to preserve his power, capacity and opportunity to labor, with his hands, in order that himself and family may at least exist, and if possible, better their condition, as being the same in nature with those gigantic artificial combinations which operate inanimate machines, dispensing with the living labor as much as possible, by means of the wealth which the laborer has already created by the sweat of his brow, and continues to pour out that he may barely live, while the combination thrives. But in co-operation, arbitration, and the free adjustments growing out of increasing mutual respect and good will, we hail the glad assurance, for both the laborer and the employer, of a happier day.

Resolved, That the protective tariff is not the mother of trusts, but the protective tariff is the mother of American wealth and power.

Resolved further, That the protective tariff is the only means by which the American people can protect themselves against the most dangerous of all trusts, which is the international trust, and can also preserve to themselves, against all competition, their own market for the results and rewards of their own work, thus avoiding the destruction of their prosperity, independence, manhood, and civilization.

GEORGE A. SCHILLING.

Ex-Secretary Bureau of Labor Statistics of Illinois.

It has been remarked by Mr. Cockran that in his judgment before another conference of this character shall take place, that a majority of the trust employers of the United States will have associated with them their wageworkers as official partners in their business; that is to say, they will be admitted to representation upon their boards of directors. This, according to Mr. Cockran, would be simply giving an official recognition of the partnership which already exists in fact between the employer and the employee.

I am myself a member of a labor union, though not officially representing one here, but in my judgment, if this consolidation between the labor unions and the trusts is ever consummated, it will be for one of two reasons: First, either because organized labor will demand recognition and organized capital will be too weak to resist the demand, or secondly, because the trusts fear that they cannot continue to perpetrate grand larceny upon the public unless they take the labor organizations in with them.. There will be no humanity about it; no sentiment nor brotherly love whatever. It will be a cold matter of business.

But I did not rise for the purpose of further inflaming you, but rather to make clear the problem and to see to what extent some of the fog which has been diffused on all sides may be dispelled. Generally speaking, there are two divisions in this convention; closer sifting would classify them into four or five, but there are primarily two. One division consists of those that do not want the trusts to be interfered with at all, while the other wishes to deal with the problem through restrictive legislation. Now, in order to determine whether the trust shall be interfered with at all, and how, we ought first to find out the difference between the capitalistic trust and the trust known as the labor union, and I think if we can clearly determine the difference between the two we will have some light to guide us on our way.

Now, the workingman in any craft realizes that standing alone in the presence of modern economic forces, he would be annihilated and would stand no show to make any agreement satisfactory to himself, therefore he joins himself unto his fellow-workmen and multiplies his power through the law of association, and in the character of this composite man he stands in the labor world with sufficient influence to, at least in a degree, determine the conditions under which he shall be employed.

The capitalistic corporations contending against unfavorable conditions, likewise look about 'and ask what can be done to get rid of the wasteful and injurious methods of business, and they, too, invoke the law of association, and begin to consolidate all the allied interests in their line.

Now, up to this point, there is absolutely no difference in the character of the organization of labor and the organization of capital. Both are utilizing their power to associate—an attribute that God has given to man to a greater degree than to any other thing that walks or creeps on this earth. But right here the similarity ends, and the paths diverge. It is this difference in character which these two organizations at this point assume that exposes "the negro in the woodpile" and justifies public interference with the capitalistic trust, but does not justify similar interference with the labor organization.

I have said that up to this point both capital and labor augment and multiply their power many fold solely through the law of association; but the workingman has nothing but this law to aid him, whereas capital has all of its advantages plus all of the monopolies which are conferred through special privileges that give additional power and strength to the trust. And it is because of this that Mr. Cockran in his otherwise very able speech, was, in my judgment, so fallacious, when illustrating in the manufacture of his chair his self-acting, unvarying law by which wages were distributed regardless of the power or influence of the trades union. Had Mr. Cockran taken an industrial society entirely devoid of special privileges, then he would have proven his case. But he assumed that the law by which wages are distributed operated now in that unvarying and equitable way.

Let us suppose that there is a train of cars loaded with grain to be dumped through a chute into this building and that this chute is made so tight that every particle of grain that goes in at one end will surely be deposited at the other, there is then no flaw from the point where the grain is received to the point where it is deposited. But suppose instead of being perfectly tight this chute had several holes in it known as special privileges through which from 25 to 50 per cent of the grain would leak while in transit. Now, anyone can see that under such circumstances you cannot divide any more grain at the final point of deposit than reaches it. That there are such holes through which industry is despoiled no thoughtful person will deny. They are the monopolies of tariffs, franchises of public utilities, money, patents and land—and it is the possession of these special privileges by the capitalistic trust that justifies public interference.

But I am not in favor of restrictive legislation. Instead of "Be it enacted," I would prefer to solve the problem by "Be it repealed." The restrictive legislation enacted within the past thirty years against corporate wealth has not brought the results intended. Contrariwise, in many instances these enactments have been employed for the suppression of the masses. The belief that our industrial ills can be cured by filling our statute books with restrictive legislation, is delusive, yet everywhere this tendency is taking shape, and everywhere it fails to remove the evils complained of. Instead of cutting the Gordian knot of monopoly and allowing the full play of industrial forces to liberate man from his thralldom, prohibitory legislation is relied upon as the panacea. Instead of crushing the head of the serpent—monopoly—that poisons all the streams of our industrial and political life, we give it full sway and then consume large quantities of restrictive legislation as a means of neutralizing the poison. The result is that society and industry are being tied up in an inextricable tangle. Rather than to continue thus I should prefer to take out from under these trusts the props of special privileges that give them this undue power to fleece the public.

First of all, I would repeal the entire tariff laws and place the United States upon an absolutely free trade basis with all the world. This would compel us to revise our entire fiscal system, in the remodeling of which we might place many of the burdens where they properly belong. It would even give the Single Taxers an opportunity to present their views, and if enacted into law would rob landlordism of its power.

I would repeal the 10 per cent tax on banks of issue, and the national banking laws, and would make the issuing of money as free as the air.

While I am not clear as to the utility of repealing all of the patent laws, I believe that the time permitted under the present laws could be reduced one-half to the general benefit of the public.

F. E. HALEY.

Secretary Iowa State Traveling Men's Association.

The commercial travelers of the United States almost to a man are decidedly against trusts and trade combines. In fact, I might state with accuracy, the people in general are opposed to the combinations that have been capitalizing themselves with the sole view of enriching the few at the expense of the masses. Trusts are, in my opinion, a menace to the people. Their principal object is that the army of consumers should pay tribute to the few. They should be placed under federal control, but the law enacted to bring about this state of affairs should be straightforward and not evasive, as it seems to be at the present time. A constitutional amendment, clearly defining the rights of the capitalists as well as to protect the purchasers or consumers, would be productive of the most good to the greatest number. It is self-evident that trusts are looked upon with mistrust by the wage-earner and common people. If such is the case, just to such an extent are trusts a menace to the interest of the country. The question of trusts and trade combines, by concentrating the wealth of the country into the hands of the few, is and has been producing discontent for the past year. Hence, a readjustment of affairs in the near future is absolutely necessary in order that the business interests of the country may be put upon a calm and businesslike basis.

HENRY W. PEABODY.

Merchant, Boston.

Combinations bear most heavily upon the individual producer, or the middleman, who before constituted the machinery of business. Large numbers of heretofore active and successful producers, tradesmen and agents are being frozen out of business by the combinations, and opportunities to build up anew with small capital are very hard to find in any department.

I regard very seriously the advancing strides of combinations, especially the joining of already colossal capital with other multimillions, and in one interest producing the raw material, and its manufacturers and also utilizing it in structural work. Such monopolies by the already rich tend to make the very rich richer, and those before well off, poorer, as their opportunities are shattered.

A monopoly which appropriates to itself all the benefits of its economies and capital, and establishes high prices unduly, will make no friends in the community.

So far only as combination can produce, and so can sell more cheaply than an individual manufacturer, it may be able to better compete with other countries for the world's trade, but the competition would be more national, and in accord with trade customs, in the hands of the larger number of producers, bidding against each other.

There is a tendency in foreign as well as domestic trade for combination to dispense with the middlemen, the jobber, the merchant.

Labor organizations can only be regarded as the counterpart of the combinations of capital, when their power is violently applied in strikes to compelling or demanding better wages, when they are a menace to society. At other times they are useful to protect the rights of wage earners who as individuals are not influential. Labor organizations will naturally be opposed to trusts, as employers having increased power, and including the element of large capital. The labor organizations are often useful to all employers, in so far as they establish uniformity of wages and hours of labor.

There is a tendency of the rapid growth of trusts and combinations to create new allies to the organized labor, in the thousands of men of business who are being thrown out of all business by the absorption of their establishment or inability to profitably continue or to apply moderate capital in a new enterprise. The large numbers of these joined classes will constitute a powerful agency in opposition to the trusts, for the shaping of legislation, or in the exercise of the franchise.

The contention of labor and the unemployed with great wealth and combined production ought not to be a political issue, but there is danger that it will assume that form.

EMERSON McMILLIN.

Banker, New York.

Emerson McMillin said in part:

Combination will decrease cost of production. It will benefit society in this, that it will tend to do away with spasmodic and extreme advances in prices, followed by long periods of depression and the discontent of the masses incident thereto.

The consumer and the laborer should be the chief beneficiaries. By combination a solidity is given to investments that makes the investor content with smaller net returns.

In many instances the share capital issued is ridiculously large. The excess of engraved sheets of paper can profit no one, and it may be a source of danger to uninformed investors, and in times of depression the collapse of these excessively capitalized companies will tend to create alarm and distrust in the financial system of the country.

Wages ought to be higher, owing to absence of ruinous competition and consequent disposition of employer to reduce expenses. The condition of the wage-earner should be improved. Regular employment at fair wages is what the wage-earner desires, and is essential to his contentment.

I am not clear in my own mind as to result with middlemen. But even if disastrous, that fact should not condemn combinations if the general result is "the greatest good to the greatest number." The change must come slowly, if at all, and middlemen will adjust their affairs to changed conditions. This has always occurred, and will continue to occur so long as civilization progresses.

I do not regard the tendency to combination with any apprehension on the ground that it does or may create monopolies contrary to the general welfare. But to quiet any apprehension in that direction there ought to be national legislation. If the general government can assume control of a bankrupt's affairs and discharge his debts, it can protect him from being driven to bankruptcy by the strong.

Patents are monopolies; much of the prosperity of our country is due to our patent laws. Gas, electric light and street railways are practically monopolies in most cities. The public would profit by making them absolute monopolies as they are in a large measure in England. The strongest argument in favor of "municipal ownership" is the fact that all possible competition is destroyed and duplication of capital prevented.

Combination will benefit this country in competition with other nations for the world's trade. Goods can be produced cheaper and excess unloaded on foreign markets at cost, if necessary, to prevent shutting down works in America.

Ways in which combinations may and will injure the public will doubtless develop during the next few years. None occur to me now.

It will be a serious mistake to recognize "class" in any form. Labor organizations or combinations should be, in the eyes of the law, the same as combinations of capitalists. Labor organizations are right and absolutely essential to the preservation of the rights of labor. This, of course, in general and not applying to particular cases. These unions should have the same lawful protection as is given to incorporated capital. Their efficiency would be greatly augmented if they were managed in about the same way.

Quite positive legislation must be had by Congress. Utter confusion will result if states are depended on for protective legislation. Again, state legislatures are governed by local prejudices. In one state, at least, it is now lawful for the farmer and the stock raiser to form combinations, but illegal for the merchant, the miner or the manufacturer to do so.

JAMES W. ELLSWORTH.

Merchant, New York.

The combining of producing agencies will decrease cost of production and therefore be beneficial.

The amount of decrease in cost of production should increase as progression is made under the proposed changed conditions, the combining of producing agencies resulting in lessening the cost, the same as labor-saving machinery has accomplished.

Regarding combinations as employers of labor, and what should be the effect on wages or the condition of the wage earner, I think the result should be beneficial. The proposition is similar to the question that was raised when labor-saving machinery was first introduced, and the protest of labor still comes to the surface as advancement in this direction is made—that labor will be crowded out of employment. The opposite has been the result. On account of labor-saving machinery the cost of production has been reduced, thereby multiplying the demand, and in place of lessening the demand for labor, the effect is to increase.

Combination of similar interests will cheapen the cost of the commodity, and, as in all cases where radical change is made, the individual must give way to the principle. Many employees will be thrown out of work, but it will be for the reason that their labor is not required and therefore wasted, or a tax on the public. New fields will be created, on account of the changed conditions, which will give adequate employment at remunerative wages; believing as I do that on account of the changes that are now working out in this connection, products will be so cheapened that it will open up new markets at home and abroad, resulting in a prosperity to this country that has never been equaled before in the world.

In individual cases monopoly may result, but it will be at the expense of success to the interest so managed, and which will be readily demonstrated, as the greatest gain accruing to both employer and employee comes by cheapening the cost of production, thereby multiplying the output.

I do not regard labor organizations as being in the same category with other forms of combination. Labor, as at present organized, destroys, while capital is creative. When labor organizes with the same idea that actuates capital—for the purpose of obtaining solely better results, discarding all thought of coercion and taking into consideration simply supply and demand, both labor and the product created by capital and labor (when production is oversupplied curtail in every way possible, husbanding the resources, and when changed conditions come, expand), then the laborer will own his own home and peace and happiness will surround his fireside.

Legislative action is desirable for the purpose of preventing extortion and coercion. Rightful combination of interests will cheapen production to that extent that there should be no fear of non-competition, and such laws should be enacted as will protect any individual or combination of individuals from persecution; it being my belief that if the latter protection is given there will be no danger of extortion, except in rare cases where there is an absolute monopoly, and then legislative protection should also be given.

CHARLES J. BONAPARTE.

Attorney, Baltimore, Md.

I regard the tendency of combination as an inevitable feature of modern civilization from which no free and enlightened country can escape, and which has force in proportion to each country's freedom and enlightenment. It does not follow from this that I regard it as a good thing, for I consider it a complete fallacy that all the changes brought about by modern civilization have been for the better; not a few of them are, to my mind, distinctly harmful. I am not, however, prepared to say that this tendency is harmful; it has a good side and a bad side, and there is the less reason to make up our minds as to its merits, because, whatever we may think, we cannot prevent it, except at the price of liberty and civilization. There is an antidote to its excess in the fact that, as a business enterprise may be on too small, so this may be on too large a scale to be profitable; the difficulty and consequent cost of effective supervision become, when a certain stage of growth has been reached, too great for the attendant profits, and, usually, although not, perhaps, always, this point will be reached before a seriously injurious monopoly can be created. As the tendency is in no wise confined or peculiar to this country, but exists in all the more advanced foreign nations, it does not seem to me likely to injuriously affect our comparative commercial standing, although it can hardly benefit this. In this connection it must be remembered that there are already international combinations of capitalists, as well as of laborers, and that the former, at all events, seem likely to greatly increase in number. There are, however, two points at which the formation of combinations affects the public interest injuriously, in my opinion. As a matter of convenience, although not of necessity, it often involves the aid of the legislative power, national, state or municipal, and thus debauches our public men and introduces a deplorable element of venality and corruption into our politics. Moreover, through the natural jealousy with which such "combinations" are regarded by the laborers whose interests they affect, their formation furnishes a theme for declamation and consequent profit to a class of insincere, unscrupulous and generally ignorant demagogues, inflames class prejudices and favors the spread of socialistic and other false and mischievous doctrines.

Labor organizations resemble what are commonly known as trusts (a very inaccurate and misleading name, by the way) in that they constitute organizations designed to advance the price of the stock-in-trade of their members by shutting out competitors from the market; but their advantages and disadvantages to the community are both altogether different from those of the trusts, and, while I am neither a blind admirer nor a fanatical enemy of either, I do not think they can be satisfactorily thought of or dealt with under the same category.

I think the consolidation or combination of railway companies into large systems has been shown by experience to be desirable.

If concentration is carried so far as to create a practical monopoly of the product, the cost of production may be further decreased from the facts that the combination will become the only purchaser of the raw material and the only employer of the specially skilled labor needed to produce this, and can therefore bring down the price of the former, and the wages of the latter, indefinitely, provided it stops short of the points where the production of the raw material ceases to be profitable and where the labor is driven into other forms of employment. If a combination of producing agencies means, or includes, a combination of laborers, as in a trade union or a federation of such unions, the result of such a combination, in so far as it affects the cost of production, must be to increase this, since its purpose and tendency is to raise the wages of the labor employed.

The consumer will, other things being equal, profit by a decrease in the cost of production, whenever there is free competition among producers in the market. If, therefore, the combination of producing agencies does not affect the freedom of competition, the consumer will benefit by the reduction in the cost of production thereby caused; if the combination creates a virtual monopoly, the consumers will not ordinarily benefit by the decrease of cost; on the contrary, the tendency of such a combination is to increase the price, whilst reducing the cost, of the product; although it must be remembered that this tendency may be, in a greater or less measure, counteracted by fear lest increase in price may lead to a decrease in consumption, or call into existence rival producing agencies or, under certain circumstances, lead to interference by the state.

The productive wealth of the country consists of the material products of past labor which have not been consumed, but economized, and which are now employed as agencies to produce further wealth, and of nothing else; the country is therefore rendered neither richer nor poorer by the placing on the market of large amounts of share capital in such combinations as those under consideration, unless possibly this may, to some extent, cause foreign capital to seek investment here; I do not feel competent to say whether it could have this effect to an appreciable extent; if it could, *pro tanto* it would be desirable; otherwise I see nothing desirable in it, for it simply changes the form of ownership of the things which alone have real value. On the other hand, I see no peculiar dangers which it involves either to the individual investor or the financial system of the country. The former may often lose his money through injudicious investments in such share capital, for it is an old maxim that "a fool and his money are soon parted," and a large proportion of individual investors are too greedy and conceited to show common sense in their investments; but their money, although lost to them, is not lost to the community; it goes into the pockets of others who are, on the whole, at least, equally deserving and more shrewd and judicious, and therefore more likely to make a beneficial use of it.

The tendency of the combinations must be to decrease the demand for the kinds of labor employed in their work, and consequently to reduce, at least temporarily, the compensation received by wage-earners generally throughout the country. The natural effects of this on the condition of the latter, speaking very broadly, would be, first, more or less individual hardship and suffering, and, afterwards, in the United States, the conversion of some among them into agriculturalists through the cultivation of a larger area of our land.

Emphatically no legislative action in regulation or restraint of combinations, whether by Congress or State legislature, is desirable. Our public men (with, I need not say, some honorable exceptions) are wholly unfit to deal with any such matters. The attempt will be highly demoralizing to all concerned, the practical results (except in the levy of blackmail) altogether nugatory.

CHARLES A. SCHIEREN.

Ex-Mayor, Brooklyn.

I am deeply interested in the subject. It is one of the leading questions of the hour. Evidently trusts have come to stay. They are formed in almost every commodity manufactured in this country.

I have watched with special interest the progress made by the United States Leather Company—so-called Leather Trust—it being in my line of business. This trust was formed about six years ago. It has only been partially successful. It has not checked competition; on the contrary, those tanners outside of the trust seemed to have profited by the formation of the big company. While the trust, by operating all their tanneries upon a uniform plan, may have reduced the cost cf tanning leather, still their fixed charges on their enormous capital are so large that they cannot reduce prices if they wish to earn a small dividend on only their preferred stock. This enables their competitors not only to meet prices, but in some instances make the market price of leather.

The principal cause is overcapitalization and buying old and unproductive properties, thinking thereby to stop competition. The result has been that active, enterprising men with sufficient capital for their business have erected modern factories with up-to-date improvements, and successfully compete with some of these trusts.

There may be exceptions, but the average combination or trust is built upon these lines, and with their antiquated facilities and watered stock they expect to compete with wideawake business men. While trusts may be a menace to business for a while, on the whole they are not as dangerous as generally believed to be.

Overcapitalized trusts must either reorganize on a proper basis, or reduce their capital to real value, else fall to pieces of their own weight. When reorganized with actual capital, they will come into line with business concerns having actual capital invested. No special legislation is necessary nor desired. Such laws hardly mitigate the evil. Business laws are based upon competition, and that will suffice to bring even our immense trusts to terms.

WILLIAM WIRT HOWE.

New Orleans Board of Trade.

When I came to this meeting as a delegate from the New Orleans Board of Trade, I prepared, at the request of the Civic Federation, a paper on some of the questions here in debate; but when by your kindness I was called to preside over your deliberations, it was deemed more becoming that your chairman should not undertake to express any views on these questions, or undertake, even if I could, to influence any opinion. And so, with a little of that paternal anguish which may have visited the soul of Abraham when he thought himself in conscience bound to sacrifice his son, I suppressed the little paper. The suppression was fortunate, because if the paper were to be written this evening it would be a better one, for the reason that its author has learned a good deal in the last four days.

In what are called courts of conciliation, in some jurisdictions, the constant aim of the presiding magistrate is to note those admissions and concessions of the contending parties themselves which may be found even in apparently hopeless disputes, and to make those admissions and concessions a basis for a judgment substantially just.

Now, following this sensible idea, where do we stand after four days of discussion, always interesting, often profoundly scientific, and sometimes passing into the brilliant sphere of oratory? It seems to me—simply as an individual, of course—that almost every paper or address we have heard has made some admissions or concessions which may form a basis for some conclusions, and if you will allow me I will formulate some of them only, as follows:

1. Combinations and conspiracies in the form of trusts or otherwise in restraint of trade or manufacture, which by the consensus of judicial opinion are unlawful, should so be declared by legislation, with suitable sanctions, and, if possible, by a statute uniform in all jurisdictions, and also uniform as to all persons, and such a statute should be thoroughly enforced, so that those who respect it shall not be at a disadvantage as compared with those who disregard it.

2. That the organization of trading and industrial corporations, whether under general or special laws, be permitted only under a system of careful governmental control, also uniform, if possible, in all jurisdictions, whereby many of the evils of which complaint is now made may be avoided.

3. The objects of the corporation should be confined within limits definite and certain. The issue of stock and bonds, which has been a matter of so much just criticism and complaint, should be guarded with great strictness. If mortgage bonds seem to be required, they should be allowed only for a moderate fraction of the true cash value of the property that secures them. As .for issues of stock, they should be safeguarded in every possible way. They should only be allowed either for the money or for property actually received by the company, and dollar for dollar, and when the property is so conveyed it should be on an honest appraisement of actual value, so that there may be no watering of stock.

4. And finally, there should be a thorough system of reports and governmental inspection, especially as to issues of bonds and stock and the status and value of property, whether corporeal or incorporeal. Yet, at the same time, in the matter of trading and industrial companies, there are legitimate business

secrets which must be respected by the general public. In short, we need to frankly recognize the fact that trading and industrial corporations are needed to organize the activities of our country, and that they are not to be scolded or belied, but controlled, as we control steam and electricity, which are also dangerous if not carefully managed, but of wonderful usefulness if rightly harnessed to the car of progress.

5. We agree without dissenting voice in thanking the Civic Federation of Chicago for furnishing this opportunity for education, and the people of Chicago not only for a hospitality as large as its limits, but for the object-lesson their city affords to teach us what can be done in America by enlightened public spirit in associated effort.

Gaines, of Tennessee, introduced the following:

"We have met here in convention through the courtesy of the Civic Federation and the city of Chicago. We have been royally entertained, not only by the convention itself, but by the citizens of Chicago. A vote of thanks is extended to the Civic Federation and to Chicago; to our distinguished chairman, who has proved himself peculiarly efficient and manifestly fair; to the conference secretary, and to those who by their participation have made the conference a success."

The resolution was unanimously adopted.

The report of the committee on resolutions was presented by Chairman Luce as follows:

"Your committee begs leave to report that after discussion and careful deliberation it has adopted the following resolutions:

"Whereas, The call of the Civic Federation, under which this conference is gathered, inviting us to consider the subject of trusts, contains the following language:

" 'While it is not expected that a thorough investigation of even any branch of this great question can be made in so short a time, it is hoped that a beginning may be made and a plan adopted for following up the work along practical lines. The local committee in charge of the arrangements is composed of representatives of all political parties and, as indicated on this letterhead, is chosen from the various walks of life. The committee has no ideas or schemes of any kind to place before the conference. Its members have different views on the problems to be discussed, but

625

are agreed on the proposition that a fair hearing should be given at the conference to all sides, and that everything should be done to make it of value to the public from an educational rather than a political standpoint.'

"Therefore be it resolved, That in the opinion of the committee on resolutions, this conference is without authority, and it would be inexpedient for it to adopt resolutions purporting to declare the sense of the conference upon any aspect of the subject of discussion."

The report was adopted without debate.

On motion of Louis F. Post the convention, at 5:50 o'clock, adjourned sine die.

Big Business

Economic Power in a Free Society

An Arno Press Collection

Alsberg, Carl L. **Combination in the American Bread-Baking Industry:** With Some Observations on the Mergers of 1924-25. 1926

Armes, Ethel. **The Story of Coal and Iron in Alabama.** 1910

Atkinson, Edward. **The Industrial Progress of the Nation:** Consumption Limited, Production Unlimited. 1889

Baker, John Calhoun. **Directors and Their Functions:** A Preliminary Study. 1945

Barron, Clarence W. **More They Told Barron:** Conversations and Revelations of an American Pepys in Wall Street. 1931

Bossard, James H. S. and J. Frederic Dewhurst. **University Education For Business:** A Study of Existing Needs and Practices. 1931

Bridge, James H., editor. **The Trust:** Its Book. Being a Presentation of the Several Aspects of the Latest Form of Industrial Evolution. 1902

Civic Federation of Chicago. **Chicago Conference on Trusts.** 1900

Clews, Henry. **Fifty Years in Wall Street.** 1908

Coman, Katharine. **The Industrial History of the United States.** 1910

Crafts, Wilbur F. **Successful Men of To-Day:** And What They Say of Success. 1883

Davis, John P. **The Union Pacific Railway:** A Study in Railway Politics, History, and Economics. 1894

Economics and Social Justice. 1973

Edie, Lionel D., editor. **The Stabilization of Business.** 1923

Edwards, Richard, editor. **New York's Great Industries.** 1884

Ely, Richard T. **Monopolies and Trusts.** 1912

Ford, Henry. **My Life and Work.** 1922

Freedley, Edwin T. **A Practical Treatise on Business.** 1853

Hadley, Arthur Twining. **Standards of Public Morality.** 1907

Hamilton, Walton, et al. **Price and Price Policies.** 1938

Haney, Lewis H. **Business Organization and Combination.** 1914

Hill, James J. **Highways of Progress.** 1910

Jenks, Jeremiah Whipple and Walter E. Clark. **The Trust Problem.** Fifth Edition. 1929

Keezer, Dexter Merriam and Stacy May. **The Public Control of Business.** 1930

La Follette, Robert Marion, editor. **The Making of America:** Industry and Finance. 1905

Lilienthal, David E. **Big Business:** A New Era. 1952

Lippincott, Isaac. **A History of Manufactures in the Ohio Valley to the Year 1860.** 1914

Lloyd, Henry Demarest. **Lords of Industry.** 1910

McConnell, Donald. **Economic Virtues in the United States.** 1930

Mellon, Andrew W. **Taxation:** The People's Business. 1924

Meyer, Balthasar Henry. **Railway Legislation in the United States.** 1909

Mills, James D. **The Art of Money Making.** 1872

Montague, Gilbert Holland. **The Rise and Progress of the Standard Oil Company.** 1904

Mosely Industrial Commission. **Reports of the Delegates of the Mosely Industrial Commission to the United States of America, Oct.-Dec., 1902.** 1903

Orth, Samuel P., compiler. **Readings on the Relation of Government to Property and Industry.** 1915

Patten, Simon N[elson]. **The Economic Basis of Protection.** 1890

Peto, Sir S[amuel] Morton. **Resources and Prospects of America.** 1866

Ripley, William Z[ebina]. **Main Street and Wall Street.** 1929

Ripley, William Z[ebina]. **Railroads:** Rates and Regulation. 1912

Rockefeller, John D. **Random Reminiscences of Men and Events.** 1909

Seager, Henry R. and Charles A. Gulick, Jr. **Trust and Corporation Problems.** 1929

Taeusch, Carl F. **Policy and Ethics in Business.** 1931

Taylor, Albion Guilford. **Labor Policies of the National Association of Manufacturers.** 1928

Vanderlip, Frank A. **Business and Education.** 1907

Van Hise, Charles R. **Concentration and Control:** A Solution of the Trust Problem in the United States. 1912

The Wealthy Citizens of New York. 1973

White, Bouck. **The Book of Daniel Drew.** 1910

Wile, Frederic William, editor. **A Century of Industrial Progress.** 1928

Wilgus, Horace L. **A Study of the United States Steel Corporation in Its Industrial and Legal Aspects.** 1901

[Youmans, Edward L., compiler] **Herbert Spencer on the Americans.** 1883

Youngman, Anna. **The Economic Causes of Great Fortunes.** 1909